First County Court Minutes
of
Lincoln County, Tennessee

VOLUME TWO

I0028340

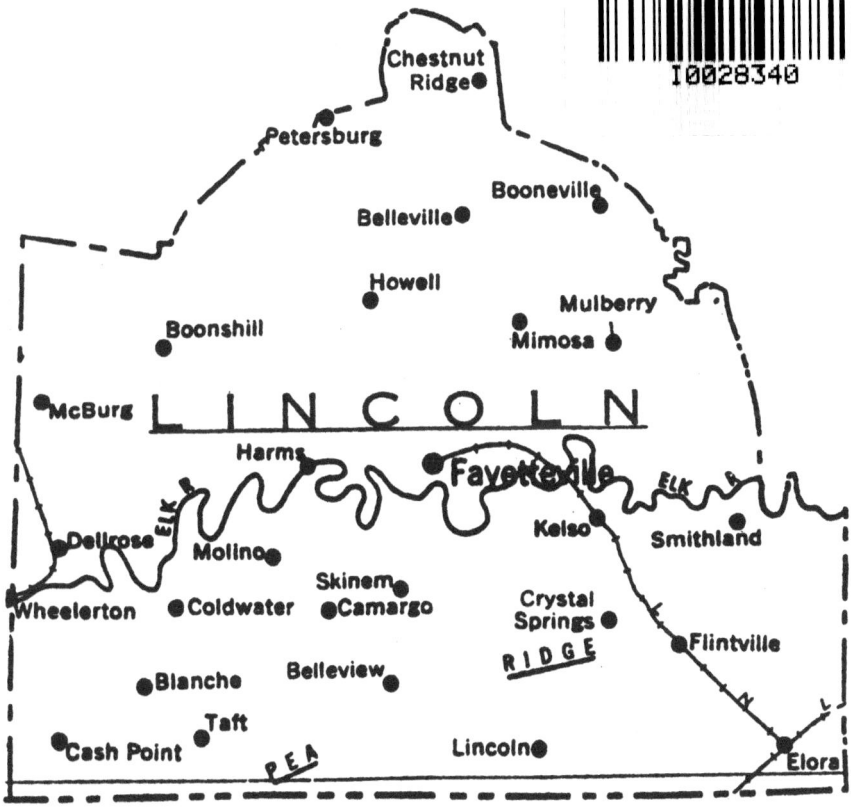

By
HELEN C. AND TIMOTHY R. MARSH
Shelbyville, Tennessee
1990

Please direct all correspondence and orders to:

www.southernhistoricalpress.com
or
SOUTHERN HISTORICAL PRESS, Inc.
PO BOX 1267
375 West Broad Street
Greenville, SC   29601
southernhistoricalpress@gmail.com

ISBN #0-89308-453-0

Printed in the United States of America

PREFACE

This second volume of abstracts of early minutes of the Court of Pleas and Quarter Sessions of Lincoln County, Tennessee, combined with volume one published by us in 1988 should give the researcher a clear view of the formative years of Lincoln County and its pioneer settlers, including a written record of many of them.

We regret that a few of the records did not survive the ravages of war and time and no record of them exist today in the Lincoln County courthouse to the State Archives. The early minutes contained in this publication were abstracted by us in the clerks office in Fayetteville, Tennessee, between 1968 and 1972. All of the records contained in this publication are recorded on microfilm and may be found in the Tennessee State Archives and Library in Nashville, Tennessee.

A brief history of the formative years of Lincoln County written by us and including original maps researched and drawn by us may be found in volume one.

Helen C. Marsh
Timothy R. Marsh
Shelbyville, Tennessee

1990

FIRST COUNTY COURT MINUTES OF LINCOLN COUNTY, TENNESSEE

VOL II

MONDAY JANUARY 17, 1820

Ordered by the Court that the Sheriff let out ELIJAH CONWAY, one of the poor of the county, to the lowest bidder, this dat at the Court House door.

AMBROSE, BARKER, JOHN PINKERTON, RICHARD FLYNT, ANDREW W. WALKER, JOHN PORTER, WM. BEAVERS, THOMAS GAITHER, CORNELIUS DARNOLD, JOHN MARR, GEORGE BLAKEMORE, ELISHA BAGLEY, JESSE JONES, JOEL PINSON, and WM. GIVENS appear in Court and was sworn as Justices of the Peace for Lincoln County.

Pursuant to an Act of Assembly, the Justices proceed to elect from their own body five persons to hold the Court of Pleas and Quarter Sessions in the county for the trials of issue causes and upon counting the ballots, it appeared that CHARLES BOYLES, PHILLIP KOONCE, JAMES HOLEMAN, WM. KINNON, and SAMUEL BUCHANAN were elected to hold said courts for one year.

Ordered by the Court that DANIEL BACHMAN be overseer of the road in the room of WM. DAVIS resigned and call on the usual hands.

Ordered by the Court that JAMES LEDBETTER be overseer of the road in the room of DANIEL COBLE resigned and call on the usual hands.

Ordered by the Court that THOMAS CLARK be overseer of the Pulaski road from the top of the ridge dividing Cain Creek and Swan Creek in the room of JOHN FULLERTON and call on the hands in the following bound beginning where the Pulaski (road) crosses the main East Fork of Swan Creek running south so as to include the plantation of DAVID SAWYERS and MARTHA ADAMS then northwardly so as to include the plantation of JAMES BLAIR, ALEXANDER EDMISTON and GEORGE TITUS then westwardly so as to include the plantation of JOHN DAVIS and THOMAS CLARK.

A Deed of Conveyance from HUGH M. BLAKE to ROBERT WILSON for 100 acres of land and ordered to be certified.

A Deed of Conveyance from WM. HAMMOCK to NOAH WARD for 50 acres of land, proven by COLESBY GRAY and CLIFFORD GRAY and ordered to be certified.

A Bill of Sale from JOHN TURNER to JOHN CONE and was ordered to be certified.

A Deed of Conveyance from RANDOLPH QUARLES to JOHN W. SMITH for 111 acres of land and ordered to be certified.

A Deed of Conveyance from BENJAMIN HARRIS to JOSHUA SEAMONS for 173 acres of land, proven by WILLIAM STEVENSON and JACOB VANHOOZER and ordered to be certified.

A Deed of Conveyance from JOSHUA SEAMONS to ELIZABETH STEVENSON for 173 acres of land, proven by WILLIAM STEVENSON and JOHN DICKEY and ordered to be certified.

A Deed of Conveyance from CHARLES BRIGHT to WILLIAM McELROY for 55 acres of land and ordered to be certified.

A Deed of Conveyance from ADAM HOUSE to HUGH M. BLAKE for 142½ acres of land, proven by JOHN W. BLAKE and JOHN S. PRICE and ordered to be certified.

A Deed of Conveyance from JOSHUA INMAN to JOHN COOPER for 8 acres of

1

land, proven by JOHN CRINER and JOSEPH CLARK and ordered to be certified.

A Deed of Conveyance from JOSHUA INMAN to JOHN COOPER for 20 acres of land, proven by JOHN COOPER and JOSEPH CLARK and ordered to be certified.

A Deed of Conveyance from JOHN WILSON to the heirs of ROBERT GRAY for 600 acres of land and ordered to be certified.

A Deed of Conveyance from THOMAS DOAK to FRANCIS WYATT for 160 acres of land and ordered to be certified.

A Deed of Conveyance from SAMUEL NISBET to ELIJAH HURLEY for 5 acres of land, proven by JOHN McMILLEN and AMOS HURLEY and ordered to be certified.

A Deed of Conveyance from THOMAS MATHEWS to JAMES MILLER for 52 acres of land, proven by NATHANIEL MILLER and JAMES MILLER and ordered to be certified.

A Deed of Conveyance from THOMAS ROUNTREE to McQUINCY & AKEN for one town lot in Town Linchburgh No. 1, proven by J. FLOYD and JOHN ENOCHS and ordered to be certified.

A transfer of a plat and certificate of survey from WALTER HARKINS to MOSES SANDERS and ordered to be certified.

The Last and Testament of ROBERT ADAMS, deceased, was exhibited in court for probate whereupon came THOMAS McGAUGH and JAMES KENNEDY, witnesses, said that ROBERT ADAMS was at time of signing was of sound mind and memory. Whereupon came JAMES McCOOKE and GILBERT KENNEDY, executors named in said will and gave bond.

WILLIAM HUSBANDS made return that he let out ELIJAH CONWAY, one of the poor of this county to JOHN DOBBINS for $69.75 who gave bond with security. Issued 20 April 1820.

Ordered that ROBERT PARKS be overseer of the road in the room of WILLIAM PARKS resigned.

Ordered by the court that MARTIN L. PARKS be overseer of the road in the room of ENOCH DOWTHET resigned.

Ordered by the court that ISHAM PARR be overseer of the road from the corner of JOHN REEVES' lot to MALLARD'S and call on the usual hands.

Ordered by the court that JAMES COLE be appointed overseer of the road in the room of JEREMIAH DENNIS resigned and call on the usual hands.

NANCY McCOWEN and JOHN McCOWEN obtained letters of administration of the estate of FRANCIS McCOWEN, deceased, and intered into (bond) with security.

SARAH LOYD obtained letters of administration of the estate of EPHRAIM LOYD, deceased, and bond and security in the sum of $800.00.

THOMAS BOWEN is appointed overseer of the road in the room of JOHN MILSTEAD resigned and call on the usual hands.

Ordered by the court that the County Trustee of Lincoln County pay to WILLIAM R. DAVIS the sum of $49.75 for keeping of HENRY DICKSON, THOMAS FRANKS and WYATT ATKINS in Giles County jail out of any county monies in his hands not otherwise appropriated.

Ordered by the court that the County Trustee of Lincoln County pay to JAMES PERRY, Sheriff of Giles County for $22.00 for removing FRANK L. DICKSON from Giles County jail to Lincoln County jail out of the county monies not otherwise appropriated. Issued to B.M.E.

An Inventory of the property of SAMUEL W. GLATHERY, deceased, was returned to court by his administrator which was ordered to be certified.

The Amount of Sale of THOMAS JOYCE, deceased, was returned to court by his administrator which was ordered to be certified.

An Inventory of the property of EPHRAIM LOYD, deceased, was returned to court

2

which was ordered to be certified.

Ordered by the court that SAMUEL THOMPSON be overseer of the road beginning at the Winchester Road near TUNSTALL GREGORY's to the road that leads from Hickory Flat to Shelbyville and call on the usual hands.

Ordered by the court that DAVID P. MUNROE, JAMES BLAKEMORE and JACOB WRIGHT be appointed commissioners to settle with POLLY CONWELL, admrx of WILLIAM CONWELL, deceased, and return to next court.

Ordered by the court that JESSE JONES, DAVID JONES, GEORGE McCOWEN, JAMES SWINEA and JOHN COOPER be appointed to lay off one years support for the widow of FRANCIS McCOWEN, deceased, and make return to next court.

NATHANIEL MILLER produced one wolf scalp in open court over two years old and made oath that he killed the same in Lincoln County.

JAMES GIBSON, SR., appeared in court and was appointed by the court, guardian for JOHN, MARGARET, ELIZABETH, THOMAS, and JOSEPH LONGMIRE, minor heirs of WILLIAM LONGMIRE, deceased, under 16 years of age for the purpose of receiving from government the balance of the pension due to said heirs by virtue of the widow of the said WILLIAM LONGMIRE intermarrying on the 6 day of March 1819 who gave bond and security as guardian as aforesaid.

TUESDAY JANUARY 18, 1820

Justices present were JAMES HOLEMAN, CHARLES BOYLES and GEORGE BLAKEMORE.

The Sheriff made return of the following to serve as Grand Jurors and Petit Jurors to this term, to wit, JAMES ESHMAN, DANIEL JONES, ERWIN McADAMS, JAMES BROWN, JAMES TOOL, JOEL DOLLINS, JOHN KING, HENRY WARREN, HENRY CLIFT, ROBERT BROOKS, HERBERT GRIFFIS, PEYTON WELLS, JAMES GREER, HENRY BAGLEY, JAMES RANDOLPH, ELIJAH DAVIS and JOHN GRIFFIS of whom being elected as Grand Jurors, to wit, JAMES GREER, JAMES ESLEMON, DANIEL JONES, JOEL DOLLINS, JOHN KING, HENRY WARREN, HENRY CLIFT, ROBERT BROOKS, HERBERT GRIFFIS, HENRY BAGLEY, PEYTON WELLS, JAMES RANDOLPH, and ELIJAH DAVIS who after receiving a charge from the returned to consider of their presentments.

ARON PARKS constable sworn to wait on the Grand Jury.

JAMES ROTSON is released from his guardianship of ELINOR BIGAR.

On motion and it appearing to the satisfaction of the court that CHARLES SPRINKLE to whom PETER ROSS an orphan was bound by an order of the court has been harshly and improperly and inhumanly treated by said SPRINKLE and that said PETER ROSS is not likely to be properly treated by said SPRINKLE, it is ordered by the court that the said CHARLES SPRINKLE be and appear before this court on 4th Monday of this month the next day for doing county business and show cause why PETER ROSS shall not be taken from said CHARLES and be bound out to some other person.

Ordered by the court that ELI GARRETT, JOHN CRITHERS and MICHAEL ROBERTSON be commissioners to settle with JANE BRADLY, guardian   for   the children of ARON BRADLY, deceased, and make return to next court.

Proclamation being made for the election of Coroner whereupon came BENJAMIN W. SHIRLY and offered himself as a candidate and was duly elected Coroner for Lincoln County.

Proclamation being also made for the election of Sheriff whereupon came JOHN GREER and WILLIAM MOORE and offered themselves as candidates for said appointment, a balloting took place and an accounting the ballots, JOHN GREER was declared to be duly elected Sheriff of Lincoln County for two years who took oath and entered into bond.

Proclamation being also made for the election of County Trustee whereupon came EBENEZER McEWEN, VANCE GREER and WILSON FROST and declared themselves as candidates for said appointment and after counting the ballots, EBENEZER McEWEN was declared duly elected Trustee for Lincoln County for two years and gave bond and security.

A Deed of Conveyance from THOMAS EASTLAND to JOHN WHITAKER for 59 acres of land, proven by HARDY HOLEMAN, Attorney in Fact for THOMAS EASTLAND which was

3

ordered to be certified.

A Deed of Conveyance from JAMES CHAPMAN to HARBERT GRIFFIS for 40 acres of land and ordered to be certified.

A Deed of Conveyance from JOB PULLECT(?) to JOSEPH GIBSON for 58 acres of land and ordered to be certified.

A Deed of Conveyance from WALTER HARKINS to ANDREW McCARTNEY for 39 acres of land and ordered to be certified.

Ordered by the court JOHN GREER, Sheriff, be released from the payment of $94.83¼ the amount of taxes returned by said Sheriff that cannot be collected for the year 1819.

THOMAS HAMBLETON was appointed Constable who gave bond and security.

THOMAS H. SHAW was appointed a Constable who gave bond and security.

REUBEN H. ROAN was appointed a Constable, took oath and gave bond and security.

Ordered by the court that JOHN CLARK overseer of the road leading from Fayetteville to Columbia be allowed all the hands on the west side of said road within the following bounds, to wit, beginning where said road crosses Morton Creek and run westwardly so as to include JOHN HARDING then with the dividing ridge between Swan and Bradshaw to where said road crosses the said ridge and the hands on the east side of said road as agreed on between the commissioners appointed by the court and the overseer of the Nashville Road.

Ordered by the court that JOHN CURRY be overseer of the road from THOMAS WARREN's to Fayetteville Road at JOHN CURRY's.

JOSEPH CAMPBELL was appointed a Constable who took the oath and gave bond and security.

Ordered by the court that WILLIAM SMITH (of Coffee Creek) be overseer of a part of a road that THOMAS MELTON is overseer of beginning at WILLIAMS'cabin on the road and continued to Coffey's Creek and call on the hands on said creek to work on that part of the road.

A Bill of Sale from BENJAMIN WOODRUFF to WYATT WOODRUFF for three negroes was acknowledged and ordered to be certified.

ABRAHAM ISAACKS appeared in court and was sworn in as a Justice of the Peace for Lincoln County.

WEDNESDAY JANUARY 19, 1820

Justices present were SAMUEL BUCHANAN, JAMES HOLEMAN and WILLIAM KENNON, Esquires.

Ordered by the court that JAMES RALSTON guardian for ELINOR BIGGAR, $14.37½ out of the estate of ELINOR BIGGAR for services rendered as guardian as aforesaid.

WILLIAM W. THOMPSON vs THOMAS EAST - Defendant appeared in court and surrenders himself in discharge of appearance bail and the plaintiff in his own person and release the defendant from being in custody of the Sheriff.

The Grand Jurors again returned into court with a Bill of Indictment, The State against ARCHELUS WILSON, JAMES WILSON and GEORGE WILSON, a true bill as to JAMES WILSON and not a true bill against ARCHELUS WILSON and GEORGE WILSON and again returned to consider for further presentments.

GEORGE GOFORTH vs SAMUEL TOOD - This day came the plaintiff in person and said that he wishes no further to prosecute this suit and the defendant in his proper person and assumes the payment of all costs. It is considered by the court that this suit be dismissed and the plaintiff recover against defendant his costs.

CHARLES BOYLES vs EARON LOYD - This day came the defendant in person and said that he does owes the plaintiff $106.56¼ and the plaintiff hath sustained damages of 43 3/4 cents. It is considered by the court that the plaintiff recover against the defendant cost and damages.

4

WILLIAM HUSBANDS appeared in court and was sworn in as Deputy Sheriff for Lincoln County.

ABEL BIVENS vs NATHANIEL BIVENS - This day the plaintiff appeared in court and said he intends no further prosecution this suit and assumes the payment of all costs. It is considered by the court that this bill be dismissed and the defendant recover against the plaintiff his costs and damage.

SAMUEL PAINTER vs WILLIAM D. FERGUSON and THOMAS PARHAM - This cause is continued until next term of this court and the plaintiff to pay the cost.

CHARLES BOYLES &c vs JOHN HANBY - Debt - This day the defendant appeared in court and confessed that he owes the plaintiff the sum of $91.81¼ and damages of $10.55. It is considered by the court that the plaintiff recover against the defendant his cost and damages.

CHARLES BOYLES vs NATHANIEL O. KENDRICK - Debt - This day the defendant appeared in court and confessed that he owes the plaintiff $121.85 3/4 and ordered the plaintiff recover against the defendant his costs.

WILLIAM W. THOMSON vs THOMAS EAST - This cause by the consent of the parties is referred to the arbitrament of ASA STREET, JAMES MARTIN, HENRY KELSO, Esquire, ALEXANDER SIMMONS, WILLIAM WILSON, and AMBROSE BARKER, Esq., Artibrators mutually by said parties whose award is to be returned to the next term of this court, and made the judgement of said court, except as to the costs which are not referred to said arbitrators. But in case said arbitrators agreed upon the other point of controversy each party agrees to pay his own costs.

THURSDAY JANUARY 20, 1820

Justices present were CHARLES BOYLES, JAMES HOLEMAN and SAMUEL BUCHANAN, Esquire.

CHARLES BOYLES vs ALLEN MOBLEY - This day came the defendant in court and confessed that he does owe the plaintiff $86.31¼. It is considered by the court that the plaintiff recover against the defendant his costs.

ROBERT & W. DICKSON vs VANCE GREER - This day the defendant in court and confessed that he owes the plaintiff $1128.93 1/3 and $2.82½ damages. It is considered by the court that the plaintiff recover against the defendant his cost and damages.

The Grand Jurors again returned into court with a Bill of Indictment, the State vs ARCHELUS WILSON, JAMES WILSON and GEORGE WILSON a true bill and again returned to consider for further presentments.

The Grand Jurors again returned into court with a Bill of Indictment, the State vs BENJAMIN BROWN, a true bill and again returned to consider for further presentments.

State vs BENJAMIN BROWN - JACK H. LEFTWICH and JESSE BROWN who was bound for the appearance of the defendant this day surrenders the defendant in court in discharge of themselves and it is ordered that the defendant be in custody of the Sheriff.

JOHN HAWKINS vs WILLIAM SHAW - This cause by consent of the parties is referred to the arbitrament of WILLIAM DOAK, JOHN RHEA, WILLIAM WALLIS, ELISHA THOMISON and JESSE WOODROOF, arbitrators, chosen by said parties whose award is to be returned to this court and made the judgement of said court.

HENRY ALLEN appeared in court and was sworn as Deputy Sheriff of Lincoln County.

STATE vs WILLIAM KYMES - Indictment - This day came the defendant in court and being charged on the indictment pleaded not guilty and for his trial puts himself upon the county and WILLIAM B. MARTIN who prosecutes on behalf of the State and a jury of men, JACKSON BLAKEMORE, JOSEPH HENDERSON, MICAJAH McELROY, JAMES BROADWAY, JOHN BROADWAY, AMOS DAVIS, ARCHABALD ESLEMAN, PETER KENT, DAVID SMITH, ANGUISH JOHNSON, WILLIAM STUART and JAMES COALTER being elected and sworn and said that the defendant is guilty as charged in the indictment. Court orders that the defendant be fined $100.00 and pay cost of indictment. HENRY KYMES security for defendant.

On motion, it is considered by the court that the order made at last term of court for making division of the real estate of JOHN MORGAN, deceased, be extended until next court.

The Grand Jurors again returned into court with a Bill of Indictment, the State vs ARCHELUS WILSON, JAMES WILSON and GEORGE WILSON, a true bill and again returned to consider for presentment.

State vs JOSEPH HENDERSON - Indictment - This day the defendant came into court and being charged on the indictment pleads not guilty and for his trial puts himself upon the county and WILLIAM B. MARTIN, Solicitor General who prosecutes in behalf of the State and a jury of men, to wit, JACKSON BLAKEMORE, MICAJAH McELROY, JAMES BROADWAY, JOHN BROADWAY, AMOS DAVIS, ARCHABALD ESLEMAN, PETER KENT, DAVID SMITH, ANGUISH JOHNSON, WILLIAM STUART, JAMES COALTER and JOHN HAWKINS being elected and sworn and said the defendant is guilty as charged and be fined $5.00 and costs.

State vs BENJAMIN BROWN - Indictment - This day the defendant came into court and pleads guilty and it is considered by the court that the defendant be fined $5.00 and costs. JESSE BROWN and JACK H. LEFTWICH, securities.

SAMUEL PAINTER vs ROBERT DICKSON - This day came by their attorneys and a jury of men, to wit, JAMES TOOL, JAMES BROWN, JOHN GRIFFIS, ERWIN McADAMS, ARCHABALD CAMPBELL, ROBERT FROST, ABSALOM BEARD, JONATHAN BARKLY, WILLIAM C. SMITH, ARCHELUS WILSON, PRESLY GEORGE and JAMES SWEET being elected and sworn and said that they cannot agree and by consent of the parties and jury was permitted to resume next day.

FRIDAY JANUARY 21, 1820

Justices present were CHARLES BOYLES, JAMES HOLEMAN and SAMUEL BUCHANAN, Esquires.

State vs SAMUEL LYNCH - Indictment - This day the defendant appeared in court and being charged on the Bill of Indictment pleads not guilty. This case is continued until next term of court.

ABRAHAM LUMBRICK who prosecuted in behalf of the State against SAMUEL LYNCH appeared in court and said that he is indebted to the State of Tennessee for $200.00 to be levied on his goods and chattles &c and to the use of the State rendered but to be void on conditions that he and ELIZABETH LUMBRICK his wife appear in court in April to prosecute and give evidence in behalf of the State against SAMUEL LYNCH and not depart without leave first had and obtained by the court.

A Bill of Sale from JOHN J. WHITAKER to JAMES HOLEMAN for a negro man named JAMES, acknowledged in court and ordered to be certified.

State vs ARCHELUS WILSON - Indictment - The defendant appeared in court and being charged, pleads not guilty and WILLIAM B. MARTIN, who prosecutes for the State, whereupon this cause was continued on affidavit of the defendant.

The Grand Jurors again return to court with a Bill of Indictment, the State against HENRY MOORES, a true bill again returned to consider for further presentments.

State vs ARCHELUS WILSON - Indictment - The defendant being charged and pleaded not guilty and the prosecutor in this cause is continued on affidavit of the defendant.

JEREMIAH & MOSES BROWN vs VANCE GREER - Defendant came into court and confessed that he owes the plaintiff $377.44 and $7.54 damages. It is considered by the court that the plaintiff recover against the defendant his costs.

A Grand Jurors again returned into court with a Bill of Indictment, the State against ARCHELUS WILSON and GEORGE WILSON, a true bill and again returned to consider for further presentments.

REPS O. CHILDRESS vs CORNELIUS SLATER - The defendant appeared in court and confessed that he owes the plaintiff $241.32 and $22.31¼ damages. It is considered by the court that the plaintiff recover against the defendant his costs.

PETER VAUGHN vs MAY BUCHANAN & JAMES CHAPMAN - This day the plaintiff appeared in court and says he wishes no further to prosecute this suit and the defendant assumed the payment of all costs. Court ordered that the plaintiff recover against the defendant and his costs.

State vs SAMUEL LYNCH - This day the defendant appeared in court and acknowledged himself indebted to the State of Tennessee for $250.00 and MARGARET ADAMS in the sum of $250.00 to be paid of their goods and chattels &c but to be void on condition the said SAMUEL LYNCH appear in April Term next and answer the charge of malicious mischief and not depart without leave first had and obtained of the court.

State vs JAMES WILSON - JAMES WILSON who was bound in recognizance to appear at the Court House on the town of Fayetteville on the 3rd Monday of this month to answer a charge of committing and assault and battery and not depart the same without leave, was called and came not but made default. Court said that he forfeited and that judgement be entered against JAMES WILSON in favor the State of Tennessee for $500.00.

GEORGE W. DENNIS who was bound in recognizance for the appearance of JAMES WILSON at this term of court, was called to bring with him into court the body of JAMES WILSON as he was bound to failed so to do. Court said recognizance is forfeited and that judgement be entered against GEORGE W. DENNIS for sum of $200.00.

State vs GEORGE WILSON - Indictment - GEORGE WILSON who was bound in a recognizance to appear to answer a charge of committing an assault and battery and came not but made default. Court the recognizance is forfeited and a judgement be entered against GEORGE WILSON in favor of the State for $500.00.

GEORGE W. DENNIS who was bound in a recognizance for the appearance of GEORGE WILSON was called to being with him the said GEORGE WILSON as he wasbound failed to do so. Court ordered that said recognizance is forfeited and judgement be entered against GEORGE W. DENNIS in favor of the State for $250.00.

On motion of JOHN MURPHY by his attorney, it is ordered by the court that writs &c bring into court the papers relative to a cause true before ABRAHAM SUMMERS, Esquire, in which MARGARET ADAMS was plaintiff and JOHN MURPHY defendant.

State vs JAMES WILSON - Indictment - This instrument is same as suit above.

GEORGE W. DENNIS (Same as suit above).

State vs GEORGE WILSON (same as above instrument).

GEORGE W. DENNIS (Same as above).

FLETCHER & McCLELLAN vs JONATHAN ESTILL - This cause is continued on the affidavit of the defendant by his paying the costs of this term and a commission is awarded him to take the deposition of WILLIAM McNEAL anywhere in the United States to be read as evidence in the trial of the above cause and to give the plaintiff's attorney 30 days notice of time and place.

JOSEPH SPENCE & CO. vs WILLIAM B. & WILLIAM Y. HIGGINS - JAMES HIGGINS the appearance bail of the defendants surrenders WILLIAM Y. HIGGINS one of the defendants in court in discharge of himself whereupon WILLIAM Y. HIGGINS was ordered in custody of the Sheriff.

On motion it is ordered by the court DAVID COWEN, Commissioner, to settle with NANCY KELLY, admrx of JOSEPH KELLY, deceased, in room of ROBERT HODGES who was appointed and that return the settlement to this court.

SATURDAY JANUARY 22, 1820

Justices present were SAMUEL BUCHANAN, WILLIAM KENNON, JAMES HOLEMAN and PHILIP KOONCE, Esquires.

On motion of JOHN J. HENRY by his attorney, it is ordered by the court thatWrits of Certiorari &c issue to bring to court the papers relative to be tried before WILLIAM DICKSON, Esquire, wherein DOCTOR CLARK was plaintiff and JOHN J. HENRY defendant.

Ordered by the court that JOHN PORTER, Esquire, take in lists of Taxable property in CAPTAIN WILSON Company for the 1820 and take return to next court.

ALLEN WARD vs JOHN B. HOLLOWAY - This day came the parties by their

7

attorneys appeared in court on a motion of the plaintiff. It is considered by the court that the plaintiff be non suited and the defendant go hence without day and recover against the plaintiff his costs.

State vs HENRY MOORE - Indictment - The defendant appeared in court and being charged, pleaded guilty. It is considered by the court that HENRY MOORE be fined $100.00 to the State.

SAMUEL BUCHANAN and STEPHEN MARLOW appeared in court and acknowledged himself indebted to the State of Tennessee for $100.00 each, and appear in court and give evidence in behalf of the State against JAMES WILSON.

On motion, it is ordered by the court that the plaintiff or County Trustee pay to ARGYLE CAMPBELL the sum of $8.70 paid by him for GEORGE W. CAMPBELL, tax for the year 1819 more than was actually due for said tax.

State vs ARCHELUS WILSON - Indictment - The defendant appeared in court and being charged on this Bill of Indictment and pleaded not guilty and this cause is continued until next term of court.

JOHN P. McCONNELL, JESSE DAVIS and STEPHEN MARLOW appeared in court and acknowledged himself indebted to the State of Tennessee for $100.00 each and on condition that they appear next court and give evidence against ARCHELUS WILSON, JAMES WILSON and GEORGE WILSON on a Bill of Indictment for committing an assault and battery.

GILLIAM BARKER, JESSE DAVIS and STEPHEN MARLOW appeared in court and acknowledged themselves indebted to the State of Tennessee for $100.00 each and that they appear at next court and give evidence in behalf of the State against ARCHELUS WILSON, JAMES WILSON and GEORGE WILSON.

HENRY MOORE and JORDAN REECE appeared in court and acknowledged themselves indebted to the State of Tennessee for $100.00 each and they are to appear in next court and give evidence in behalf of the State against ARCHELUS WILSON and GEORGE WILSON.

State vs ARCHELUS WILSON - Indictment - The defendant appeared in court and acknowledged himself indebted to the State of Tennessee for $200.00 and JEREMIAH DENNIS in the sum of $200.00 and that he appear at next court and answer a charge of committing an assault and battery.

State vs ARCHELUS WILSON - Indictment - (same as above).

State vs ARCHELUS WILSON - Indictment - (same as above).

The Grand Jurors again returned to court with a Bill of Indictment, the State vs ARCHELUS WILSON and GEORGE WILSON, a true bill, and again returned to consider further presentments.

The Last Will and Testament of ARTHUR BROOKS, deceased, was exhibited in court for probate whereupon came JAMES BROOKS and HENRY TALLY and acknowledged the same to be his Last Will and Testament and he was at the time of sound mind and memory.

A Deed of Conveyance from HENRY TALLY to JAMES BROOKS for 360 acres of land and ordered to be certified.

A Bill of Sale from MAY BUCHANAN to PETER VAUGHN for two negro girls named SELL and PHILLIS and ordered to be certified.

State vs ARCHELUS & GEORGE WILSON - Indictment - REUBEN H. BOON, JAMES FORRESTER and WALKER JONES appeared in court and acknowledged themselves indebted to the State of Tennessee for $100.00 each to be levied upon their goods and chattels &c but to be void on condition that they appear to prosecute and give evidence in behalf of the State against ARCHELUS WILSON and GEORGE WILSON.

State vs JOHN PYBUS - Indictment - REUBEN H. BOON, JAMES FORRESTER and WALKER JONES appeared in court and acknowledged themselves indebted to the State of Tennessee for $100.00 each to be levied upon their goods and chattels &c but to be void on condition that they appear to prosecute and give evidence in behalf of the State against JOHN PYBUS.

8

State of Tennessee & WILLIAM D. FERGUSON vs LEVI BRADLEY - This day came the parties by their attorneys and a jury of men, to wit, ALEXANDER ESLEMAN, ESASU COALTER, FRANCIS FINCHER, JOHN A. CHAPMAN, PETER MOYER, JOHN MARSHALL, GRIFFIN CHESLY, NOAH WARD, ANDREW McCARTNEY, WARREN CALHOUN, WILLIAM C. JACKSON, and JAMES BOON being elected and sworn and said that the defendant does owe the plaintiffs. WILLIAM D. FERGUSON who sues for himself as well as the State of Tennessee for $100.00 the debt in the plaintiffs declaration mentioned that he did sell and retail goods as a pedler before first having obtained licences to do so.

SAMUEL PAINTER vs ROBERT DICKSON - The jury elected and sworn and charged in this case returned into court and say that they cannot agree upon their verdict in this cause and court ordered the jury be discharged.

MONDAY JANUARY 24, 1820

Justices present were WILLIAM KENNON, WILLIAM EDMISTON, PHILLIP KOONCE, SAMUEL BUCHANAN and JAMES HOLEMAN, Esquires.

A Deed of Conveyance from BRICE M. GARNER to JAMES STRINGER for 90 acres of land and ordered to be certified.

A Bill of Sale from WILLIAM SMITH to WILLIAM S. SMITH for a negro boy named HANY and a negro girl named NANNY and ordered to be certified.

A Bill of Sale from WILLIAM SMITH to JOHN T. SMITH for a negro boy named JOHN and a negro girl named PHILADELPHIA and ordered to be certified.

The due execution of a Bill of Sale from WILLIAM SMITH to JOANNA HUNTER for a negro named ELIZA and a girl named MILLY and ordered to be certified.

A Bill of Sale from WILLIAM SMITH to FANNY ESKRIDGE for a negro woman named CREANER and a boy named WASHINGTON and ordered to be certified.

A Deed of Conveyance from JOHN YOUNT to MORGAN CLAYTON for 252 acres of land, proven by JOHN R. MOORES and ARCHABALD ESLEMAN and ordered to be certified.

A Deed of Conveyance from BRICE M. GARNER to NATHAN WARREN for 100 acres of land, proven by CORNELIUS DARNELL and DANIEL WARREN and ordered to be certified.

A Bill of Sale from BAZEL HARRIS to JESSE JONES, proven by JOHN CORN and WILLIAM STEPHENS and ordered to be certified.

A Deed of Conveyance from HENRY BUNN to TUNSTAL GREGORY for 50 acres of land, proven by JOHN DYER and THOMAS JOYNER and ordered to be certified.

It is ordered by the court that WILLIAM HOWARD be overseer of the road in the room of JOHN R. ENOCHS and call on the usual hands.

Ordered by the court that ROBERT BRADEN be overseer of a road from WILLIAM SMITH to THOMAS JOYCE spring branch and call on the usual hands.

Ordered by the court that JAMES CRAWFORD be overseer of the road in the room of RANDOLPH QUARLES resigned and call on the usual hands.

Ordered by the court that EASTHER KENNEDY, guardian of MIRIAM L. KENNEDY have leave to sale all that part of the land of SARAH B. KENNEDY, deceased, which descended to said MIRIAM L. upon the death of said SARAH B. and that she convey the same by deed to pay the necessary expenses of MIRIAM L. and it appears to the court that there is not suitable perishable property of MIRIAM L. sufficient to pay her expenses.

Ordered by the court that RICHARD WELCH be overseer of the road leading from PETER LUNA's to Elk Ridge and call on the usual hands.

Ordered by the court that the Sheriff let out JOHN PARKER to the lowest bidder to maintain three months from this time.

Ordered by the court that the taxes for the year 1820 be as high as the law will allow it.

Ordered by the court that THOMAS ORRICK, THOMAS TEDFORD and HOWELL

9

JOHNSON be overseers of the road from near JOHN McMILLIN's to near DAVID LEVINGS and ISAAC CONGER and JAMES HOLEMAN appointed to lay off and designate the hands to work on said road.

WILLIAM P. ANDERSON is authorized to establish a ferry across Elk River at the mouth of Farris Creek.

Ordered by the court that JOHN DAMEROLL be overseer of the road leading from Winchester to Huntsville on that part of the road that lies between DAMEROLL house and the State Line, and call on all the hands on the south side of said road and all on the west side that lives within the distance of two miles from the road within the county.

Ordered by the court that WILLIAM DOAK, JESSE BROADWAY, THOMAS DOAK, FRANCIS WYATT, ANGUISH JOHNSON, and DAVID JONES be a Jury of View to view and turn the road leading from this place to Norris Creek to begin at the house of JOHN H. RODGERS and to run with the line that divides the lands of RODGERS and EZEKIEL NORRIS' and make return to next court.

JOHN PARKER, Sheriff, made return to court that he had let out JOHN PARKER to WILLIAM C. JACKS for $34.50.

AMOS HURLEY & JEREMIAH BRYANT appeared in court and was appointed admrs of the estate of ELIJAH HURLEY, deceased, who gave bond with ELI GARRETT and JOHN PORTER securities for $5000.00.

WILLIAM HODGES, JOHN R. MOORE and MORGAN CLAYTON is appointed commissioners to lay off one years provision for the support of the widow of ROBERT ADAMS, deceased, and make return to next court.

ABSALUM BOSTICK, JONAS LEATHERMAN, JOSEPH JONES, HENRY HUGHEY, Sr., and JOBE H. BELL is appointed commissioners to lay off one years support for the widow of ELIJAH HURLEY, deceased, out of the said estate and make return to next court.

A Deed of Conveyance from WILLIAM BLEDSOE to WILLIAM THOMAS for 50 acres of land and ordered to be certified.

A Deed of Conveyance from LAWSON H. ALEXANDER & SARAH C. ALEXANDER, heirs of WILLIAM ALEXANDER, deceased, to WILLIAM P. ANDERSON for 1000 acres of land and ordered to be certified.

A Deed of Conveyance from JAMES BRIGHT to REUBEN GRAY for 85 acres of land and ordered to be certified.

An inventory of the property of ELIJAH HURLEY, deceased, was exhibited in court by his admrs and ordered to be recorded.

On motion, it is ordered by the court that WILLIAM EDMISTON & ALEXANDER MORTON be (blank) from being security to the Last Will and Testament of HENRY FEATHERSTON, deceased, because the court not examining the will and it appearing that no security was required in said will. Therefore they are hereby released from the same and that said bond be given up and cancelled.

State vs JOHN PYBUS - Indictment - The defendant appeared in court and is charged and pleaded guilty and put himself upon the clemency and mercy of the court. The court considered that the defendant be fined $1.00 and pay costs. REUBEN H. BOON was security.

State vs ARCHELUS WILSON - Indictment - The defendant appeared in court and being charged, pleads guilty and court fined him $1.00 and pay costs. Whereupon came ELLIS MILLS as security.

It is ordered by the court that PRESLY DOLLINS be allowed $30.00 for keeping of MALIND JORDAN an infant one year from this time. Issued 11 Sept 1821.

HENRY CARTER is allowed $10.00 for keeping his son who is an idiot one year from this time.

It is ordered by the court that WILLIAM B. MARTIN, the Solicitor General, be allowed $50.00 for year 1819.

Ordered by the court that BRICE M. GARNER, Clerk, be allowed $50.00 for year of

1819 also $25.00 for making out the tax list for year 1819.

State vs JAMES WILSON - Indictment - GEORGE W. DENNIS who was bound in a recognizance for the appearance of JAMES WILSON surrenders him in court is discharged of his recognizance. Court ordered that the judgement entered against him and to be set aside by his paying the cost of judgement.

State vs JAMES WILSON - (same as above)

State vs JAMES WILSON - Indictment - (same as above)

State vs JAMES WILSON - Indictment - Defendant appeared in court and acknowledged himself indebted to the State of tennessee for $200.00 and GEORGE W. DENNIS for $200.00. They are to appear in April Term next to answer a charge of committing an assault and battery.

State vs JAMES WILSON - Indictment - (same as above)

State vs JAMES WILSON - Indictment - (same as above)

The Chairman of the County Court vs CHARLES SPRINKLE - Motion to take PETER ROSS away from CHARLES SPRINKLE. PETER ROSS was offered as a witness to prove the abuse he had received to which witness the defendant by his attorney objected and the court refused to hear the testimony. Court said the plaintiff by his attorney excepts and tendered his bill of exceptions which was signed, sealed and made apart of the record. Court said that PETER ROSS remain with CHARLES SPRINKLE to whom he was bound. Defendant prays for an appeal.

TUESDAY JANUARY 25, 1820

Justices present were SAMUEL BUCHANAN, WILLIAM KENNON and JAMES HOLEMAN, Esquires.

The due execution of an indenture and bargain and sale from JAMES A. CROWDER to WILLIAM P. ANDERSON for 160 acres of land, proven by oaths of BRICE M. GARNER and THOMAS L. TROTTER and ordered to be certified.

The due execution of a Bill of Sale from NATHANIEL B. BUCKINGHAM to WILLIAM P. ANDERSON for a negro boy named MOSES and ordered to be certified.

THOMAS M. HARPER vs GEORGE C. BOGGS - The defendant surrenders himself in court in discharge of WASHINGTON McGOURMY is appearance bail whereupon said WASHINGTON McGOURMY is released from any further liability as appearance bail for said defendant. The defendant is ordered in custody of the Sheriff.

JOHN GEORGE vs JAMES L. BEARD - Motion to dismiss certiorari - This day came the parties by their attorneys and an argument of the motion to divide the certiorari being heard and fully understood by the court. It is considered by the court that the certiorari be dismissed and the plaintiff recover against the defendant constant scales his security the sum of $67.83¼ and damages of 70¢.

NIMROD BAILY vs THOMAS BAILY - Motion - On motion of the plaintiff by his attorney against THOMAS BAILY to recover the amount of a judement which said NIMROD BAILY had paid for THOMAS BAILY as his security and it appearing that NIMROD BAILY was security for THOMAS BAILY the following persons, to wit, JAMES TOOL, JAMES BROWN, JOHN GRIFFIS, ERWIN McADAMS, FRANCIS FINCHER, WILLIAM PATERSON, WILLIAM STEWART, GEORGE CUNNINGHAM, AMOS SMALL, WILLIAM C. JACKSON, ABNER DYER, and JEREMIAH DENNIS were impaneled to assertain the fact who upon their oaths do say that NIMROD BAILY was only bound as security for THOMAS BAILY. NIMROD to recover against THOMAS for $71.59.

BAILY & SHIRLY vs FRANCIS FINCHER - The defendant appeared in court and confessed that he owes the plaintiff for $203.20 and damages of $6.10. It is considered by the court that the plaintiff recover against the defendant his costs.

BENJAMIN DUNCAN vs BRICE M. GARNER - This day came the parties by their attorneys and a jury of men, to wit, JAMES TOOL, JAMES BROWN, JOHN GRIFFIS, ERWIN McADAMS, FRANCIS FINCHER, WILLIAM PATTERSON, WILLIAM STEWART, GEORGE CUNNINGHAM, AMOS SMALL, WILLIAM C. JACKSON, ABNER DYER, and JEREMIAH DENNIS being elected and sworn and said that the defendant has not paid all the debt of

11

$1879.00 and does owe $389.00 and damages of $26.91. It is ordered by the court that the plaintiff recover against the defendant his costs.

THOMAS STEEL vs BRICE M. GARNER - This day came the parties by their attorneys and a jury of men, to wit, JAMES TOOL, JAMES BROWN, JOHN GRIFFIS, ERWIN McADAMS, FRANCIS FINCHER, WILLIAM PATTERSON, WILLIAM STEWART, GEORGE CUNNINGHAM, AMOS SMALL, WILLIAM C. JACKSON, ABNER DYER, and JEREMIAH DENNIS being elected and sworn and said that the defendant has not paid all the debt to the plaintiff but does owe $451.50 and damages of $41.25. Cort ordered that the plaintiff recover against the defendant his costs.

ALEXANDER McLIN vs THOMAS L. TROTTER - The plaintiff appeared in court to say he intends no further to prosecute this suit and assume the payment of all costs. It is considered by the court that this suit be dismissed and the defendant recover against the plaintiff his costs.

WILLIAM McELROY vs JOHN & JACOB ALLBRIGHT - Plaintiff appeared in court and says he intends no further to prosecute this suit and assumes the payment of all costs. It is considered by the court that this suit be dismissed and the defendant recover against the plaintiff his costs.

LINDENBERGER & HEBB vs BRICE M. GARNER - This day came the parties by their attorneys and a jury of men, to wit, JAMES TOOL, JAMES BROWN, JOHN GRIFFIS, ERWIN McADAMS, FRANCIS FINCHER, WILLIAM PATTERSON, WILLIAM STEWART, GEORGE CUNNINGHAM, AMOS SMALL, WILLIAM C. JACKSON, ABNER DYER, and JEREMIAH DENNIS being elected and sworn and said that the defendant has paid the debt to the plaintiff of $1605.04 and $272.85. Court orders that the plaintiff recover against the defendant his costs.

PHILIP (illegible) vs BRICE M. GARNER - This day came the parties by their attorneys and a jury of men, to wit, JAMES TOOL, JAMES BROWN, JOHN GRIFFIS, ERWIN McADAMS, FRANCIS FINCHER, WILLIAM PATTERSON, WILLIAM STEWART, GEORGE CUNNINGHAM, AMOS SMALL, WILLIAM C. JACKSON, ABNER DYER, and JEREMIAH DENNIS being elected and sworn and said that the defendant has not paid the debt of $844.35 and damages of $62.24. Court orders the plaintiff to recover against the defendant his costs.

CARROLL & WHIGHTING vs JONATHAN ESTILL - This day came the parties by their attorneys and a jury of men, to wit, JAMES TOOL, JAMES BROWN, JOHN GRIFFIS, ERWIN McADAMS, FRANCIS FINCHER, WILLIAM PATTERSON, WILLIAM STEWART, GEORGE CUNNINGHAM, AMOS SMALL, WILLIAM C. JACKSON, ABNER DYER, and JEREMIAH DENNIS being elected and sworn and said that the defendant has not paid the debt of $101.00 and damages of $5.50. It is ordered by the court that the plaintiff recover against the defendant his costs.

THOMAS M. HARPER vs GEORGE C. BOGGS - This day came the parties by their attorneys and a jury of men, to wit, JAMES TOOL, JAMES BROWN, JOHN GRIFFIS, ERWIN McADAMS, FRANCIS FINCHER, WILLIAM PATTERSON, WILLIAM STEWART, GEORGE CUNNINGHAM, AMOS SMALL, WILLIAM C. JACKSON, ABNER DYER, and JEREMIAH DENNIS being elected and sworn and said that the defendant has not paid the debt of $135.00 and damages of $17.85. It is ordered by the court that the plaintiff recover against the defendant his costs.

ROBERT CHAPMAN vs JAMES MARTIN - This day came the parties by their attorneys and a jusy of men, to wit, JAMES TOOL, JAMES BROWN, JOHN GRIFFIS, ERWIN McADAMS, FRANCIS FINCHER, WILLIAM PATTERSON, WILLIAM STEWART, GEORGE CUNNINGHAM, AMOS SMALL, WILLIAM C. JACKSON, ABNER DYER, and JEREMIAH DENNIS being elected and sworn and said that the defendant has not paid the debt of $85.00 and damages of $2.50. It is ordered by the court that the plaintiff recover against the defendant his costs.

JOSEPH HINKLE vs RICHMOND HUGHES - The plaintiff by his attorney appeared in court and says he intends no further to prosecute this suit and assumes the payment of all costs. The court ordered that this suit be dismissed and the defendant recover of the plaintiff his costs.

THOMAS M. HARPER vs GEORGE C. BOGGS - The plaintiff appeared in court and says he wishes the defendant to be released from being in custody of the Sheriff. The court ordered the defendant be released.

˙ SHELTON & LUSK vs FRANCIS FINCHER - By consent of the parties, this cause is referred to the arbitration of two Justices of the Peace, one to be chosen by each party and if they cannot agree, they are to choose a third one to be a Justice of the Peace and their award to be the judgement of the court at next term of court.

JOHN HAWKINS vs WILLIAM SHAW - It is ordered that the plaintiff recover no damages of the defendant and the defendant pay the cost of this suit.

JAMES BROWN vs CARTER WALKER - The plaintiff by his attorney appeared in court and the defendant being called but came not but made default. The court being uncertain what the damages the plaintiff had sustained, it is considered that a report be brought to next term of court.

AUGUSTINE YEARGER vs JONATHAN BOX - The plaintiff by his attorney came into court and says he intends no further to prosecute this suit and assumes the payment of all costs. Court ordered this suit be dismissed and the defendant recover against the plaintiff his costs.

JOHN BLACKWELL vs JOHN J. HENRY - The plaintiff by his attorney appeared in court and says he wishes to dismiss this suit and assumes the payment of all costs. Court dismisses this suit and the defendant to recover against the plaintiff his costs.

EDMOND B. PEARSON vs JONATHAN ESTILL - In Debt - This day came the parties by their attorneys and a jury of men, to wit, JAMES TOOL, JAMES BROWN, JOHN GRIFFIS, ERWIN McADAMS, FRANCIS FINCHER, WILLIAM PATTERSON, WILLIAM STEWART, GEORGE CUNNINGHAM, AMOS SMALL, WILLIAM C. JACKSON, ABNER DYER, and JEREMIAH DENNIS being elected and sworn and said that the defendant had not paid to the plaintiff his debt of $163.86 and damages of $11.47. Court ordered that the plaintiff recover against the defendant his costs.

WEDNESDAY JANUARY 26, 1820

Justices present were WILLIAM KENNON, JAMES HOLEMAN, SAMUEL BUCHANAN and CHARLES BOYLES.

The due execution of an Indenture of Bargain and Sale between BRICE M. GARNER of one part and WILLIAM P. ANDERSON of other part for 160 acres of land in the Territory of Missouri, north being the north east quarter of Section 22 of Township 53 north in Range 21 west in the tract appropriated for the Military Counties, proven by oaths of JAMES BRIGHT and WILLIAM E. KENNEDY and ordered to be certified.

State vs GEORGE WILSON - Indictment - GEORGE WILSON who was found in a recognizance to appear and to answer charge of committing an assault and battery was called and came not but made default. The recognizatance id forfeited and that judgement be entered against GEORGE WILSON in favor of the State for $500.00. JAMES BROOK who was bound in a recognizance for the appearance of GEORGE WILSON was called to bring with him GEORGE WILSON failed to do so. Court said that judgement be entered against him for sum of $250.00.

JAMES BLAKEMORE, Esquire, is appointed by the court to take in lists of taxable property in CAPTAIN MAULDEN's Company for the year 1821 and make return to next court.

GRISSOM MORRIS vs GEORGE AWALT - Appeal - The defendant by his attorney appeared in court and the plaintiff being called to come and prosecute this appeal failed to do so. Court ordered the plaintiff be no proper and the defendant go hence without day and recover against the plaintiff his costs.

GEORGE COALTER vs JOHN HENDERSON - Debt Appeal - This day came the parties by their attorneys and a jury of men, to wit, JAMES TOOL. JAMES GREER, DANIEL JONES, JOEL DOLLINS, HENRY WARREN, ROBERT BROOKS, HENRY CLIFT, HARBERT GRIFFIS, HENRY BAGLEY, PAYTON WELLS, JAMES RANDOLPH, and ELIJAH DAVIS being elected and sworn and said that the defendant does owe the plaintiff the sum of $50.00. It is considered by the court that the plaintiff recover against the defendant his costs.

JOHN C. McADA vs ABSOLUM BEARD - On motion of the defendant by his attorney, it is ordered by the court that the plaintiff appear here on the first Tuesday of next court to give other or better security for this suit or the suit will be dismissed.

ALEXANDER NEIL vs JOHN MURPHY - This cause is continued by consent until next term of court.

13

Justices present were WILLIAM KENNON, JAMES HOLEMAN and SAMUEL BUCHANAN, Esquires.

EZEKIEL GILLUM vs JOHN MURPHY - Appeal - The parties came by their attorneys and a jury of men, to wit, JAMES ESLEMAN, DANIEL JONES, JOHN KING, HENRY WARREN, HENRY CLIFT, ROBERT BROOKS, HENRY BAGLEY, PAYTON WELLS, ELIJAH DAVIS, JAMES GREER, JAMES BROWN, and ERWIN McADAMS being elected and sworn and said that the defendant is not indebted to the plaintiff anything. Court orders the defendant recover against the plaintiff his costs.

FRANCIS PATTON appeared in court and resigned his appointment as a Justice of the Peace for Lincoln County.

DANIEL YOUNG vs GEORGE ST. J. BASKINS - Appeal - The parties came by their attorneys and a jury of men, to wit, JAMES TOOL, JOHN GRIFFIS, HARBERT GRIFFIS, JOEL DOLLINS, JAMES RANDOLPH, JOSEPH MOONEY, SPENCER A. PUGH, WILLIAM WILLINGHAM, JESSE LAMB, THOMAS KERCHEVAL, GEORGE TITUS, and JOHN W. SMITH being elected and sworn and said that the defendant does owe the plaintiff the sum of $3.75. The plaintiff to recover against the defendant his costs. Defendant prays for an appeal to next court.

It is ordered by the court that WILLIAM STEVENSON, JOHN COX, JESSE GEORGE, RICHARD STUARD, JESSE PUGH, JAMES SANDERS, JOHN SANDERS, JOSEPH DEAN, and JOHN PINKERTON be a Jury of View to lay off and mark a road, beginning at or near the south east corner of Lincoln County to run in the direction of the State Line Road to JESSE GEORGE's cotton gin from thence the nearest and best way to Florence and make return at next court.

JOSEPH SPENCE vs JAMES HIGGINS - The parties came by their attorneys and a jury of men, to wit, JAMES TOOL. JOHN GRIFFIS, HARBERT GRIFFIS, JOEL DOLLINS, JAMES RANDOLPH, JOSEPH MOONEY, SPENCER A. PUGH, WILLIAM WILLINGHAM, JESSE LAMB, THOMAS KERCHEVAL, and JOHN W. SMITH being elected and sworn and said that the defendant did not surrender WILLIAM B. HIGGINS.

FRIDAY JANUARY 28, 1820

Justices present were CHARLES BOYLES, JAMES HOLEMAN and SAMUEL BUCHANAN, Esquires.

WILLIAM WILLINGHAM vs JOHN C. McADA - Motion to dismiss certiorari - The parties came by their attorneys and a motion to dismiss certiorari being heard and it is considered by the court that the plaintiff recover against the defendant and WILLIAM MOORE his security the sum of $61.10 and interests from 15 Oct 1819.

ROBERT & W. DICKSON vs JOHN GEORGE - The plaintiff by his attorney appeared in court and says he intends no further to prosecute this suit and assumes the payment of all costs. Court ordered cause be dismissed.

PHILLIP KOONCE, Ranger vs EZEKIEL ABELS - The plaintiff by his attorney appeared in court and the defendant being called to come and plead to the plaintiff suit brought against him, failed to do so. Court considered that the plaintiff recover against the defendant his costs.

SATURDAY JANUARY 29, 1820

Justices present were JAMES HOLEMAN, CHARLES BOYLES and WILLIAM KENNON, Esquires.

WILLIAM C. COLLINS vs BENJAMIN B. RODGERS - Motion to dismiss certiorari - This day came the parties by their attorneys and an argument to dismiss this cause the court considered that the certiorari be dismissed and the plaintiff recover against the defendant and JORDAN SOLOMON his security sum of $20.00.

The due execution of an Indenture of Bargain and Sale from CHARLES BOYLES to WILSON FROST for 50 acres of land and ordered to be certified.

ISHAM HARRIS vs WILLIAM GEORGE - The defendant by his attorney appeared in court and the plaintiff being called to come and prosecute his suit failed to do so. It is considered by the court that the defendant recover against the plaintiff his costs.

ARCHELUS WILSON vs HENRY MOORE - The defendant by his attorney appeared in court and the plaintiff being called to come and prosecute his suit failed to do so. It is considered by the court that the defendant recover against the plaintiff his costs.

JOSEPH SPENCE vs JAMES HIGGINS - This day came the parties by their attorneys and on argument of the first plea of the defendant being heard and understood, the court considered that there is no such record as the plaitiff alledged and on argument of the second plea in behalf of him pleaded, the court considered the plaintiff take nothing by his suit and the defendant go hence without day and recover against plaintiff his costs.

JOHN BLACKWELL vs JOHN J. HENRY - Motion to dismiss certiorari - This day came the parties by their attorneys and on argument of the motion of, to dismiss the certiorari. Court ordered the motion overruled and this cause set for trial at the next term of court.

JAMES BROADWAY vs McELROY & McCLELLAN - The plaintiff by his attorney appeared in court and the defendant being called to come and defend the suit failed to do so. Court ordered the plaintiff to recover against the defendant $307.05 and damages of $10.74.

JOHN W. CRUNK vs AMBROSE PEARCE - Motion to Dismiss - The parties by their attorneys came into court to dismiss the certiorari. Court considered that this motion be overruled and set for trial at next term of court.

It is ordered by the court that the commissioners, to wit, ELI GARRETT and DAVID COWEN was appointed to settle with admrs of the estate of JOHN KELLY, deceased, and make return at this term, have the further time until next term to make a report and commissioners are authorized to go out of the bounds of the county to comply with the request of the order. Court further ordered that all papers relative to or all demands to or all demands to the estate be immediately deliver and surrendered to ELI GARRETT to be by him collected, liquidated and administered according to law.

State of Tennessee & WILLIAM D. FERGUSON vs LEVI BRADLY - This day the parties by their attorneys came into court and on argument of the plaintiff's demurer. It is considered by the court that the demurer be sustained and other issues found in favor of the plaintiffs. The defendant by his attorney filed the following reasons in arrest of the judgement, to wit, (1) that the deal does not include the wards expanding the act was done in a contempt of the law. (2) that it is not alledged in the (blank) to be an unlawful selling. (3) that a plea in abatement was filed which is not true, was not replied to nor was it stricken out by order of the court. (4) that it is not alledged in the (blank) that he sold such goods as was lawful to sell without causes. (5) he has not stated that goods sold were prohibited by the act. (6) it is not stated that the Act of Assembly prohibited the selling of goods of this kind which motions being heard and understood by the court. It is considered by the court that said reasons is arrest of judgement be overruled and the plaintiff recover against the defendant $100.00 debt.

WILLIAM HODGE vs VANCE GREER - On argument of the plaintiff for leave to strike out the defendant plea in abatement filed. It is considered by the court that the plea be stricken out and the plaintiff recover against the defendant $119.95 balance of debt and 75¢ damages. Dependant by his attorney desired to file for leave but the court considered that the defendant shall not be permitted to file such plea unless first making affidavit that he has merits in such defence.

A Deed of Conveyance from JOHN GREER, Sheriff, to CHARLES BOYLES for 30 acres of land and ordered to be certified.

WILLIAM WOOSLY vs REECE GULLETT - Motion - On motion, it is ordered by the court that the Sheriff to expose to sale 20 acres of land as the property of said GULLETT on the headwaters of McCullough Creek adjoining the lands of FULLER, the place whereon ANTHONY DELANY now lives also 19 acres of land levied on as the property of said GULLETT being the head of Flint, the place whereon REECE GULLETT and JOHN HIND now lives, a judgement that WILLIAM WOOSLY recovered against said GULLETT before ELI GARRETT, Esquire, on 8 January 1820 for sum of $50.12½ and all legal costs.

Ordered by the court that JAMES SCOTT, DANIEL WAGGONER, JOHN WATKINS, MOSES CHAMBERS, LEMUEL BRANDON, PETER SHELTON, JAMES SMITH, JOEL JOHNSON, JOHN DAVIS, GEORGE W. HUNT, DOILY GRIFFIS, JOHN BOYLES, LEWIS SHIP, BENJAMIN PORTER, JOHN NORTON, JESSE BONNER, WILLIAM FARRAR, TRYON GIBSON, JOHN MOORE, BENJAMIN JOHNSON, REUBEN HUNTER, MOSES STONE, WILLIAM TOWNSEND,

DAVID JONES, JOHN PARK, DAVID LAURANCE, and DANIEL BACHMAN be summoned as Jurors to the next County Court held in April next. STERLING McLEMORE and WILLIAM P. PULLUM, Constables, to wait on said court and jury.

NIMROD BAILEY vs THOMAS ALLEY - The plaintiff by his attorney came into court and the defendant being called to come and defend the suit, failed to do so but made default. It is considered by the court that the plaintiff recover against the defendant the sum of $100.25 debt and $3.26 damages.

MONDAY APRIL 17, 1820

It is ordered by the court that JOHN BEATY, WILLIAM SMITH, WILLIAM HARRIS, JAMES TOOL, GENERAL W.C. EDMISTON and STEPHEN CLAYTON be a Jury of View and turn the road around SAMUEL S. BUCHANAN's field and make return to next court.

Ordered by the court that BENJAMIN RUDD be overseer of the road in the room of ALEXANDER DACUS resigned and call on the usual hands.

Ordered by the court that ELIJAH DAVIS be overseer of the road in the room of GEORGE CUNNINGHAM resigned.

It is ordered by the court that PHILLIP KOONCE, WILLIAM PATTERSON, ELISHA THOMASON, ABNER DYER, ABSOLUM BEARD, ALEXANDER BEARD, GEORGE W. DENNIS and ANDREW McCARTNEY be a Jury of View to change the road to Winchester from the far corner of JOHN R. JOHNSON's field to Clements Ford on Elk River so as to run in a direct course from said field to said Ford also on to WILLIAM PATTERSON's on the ridge and make return to next court.

Ordered by the court that JAMES McGEHEE be overseer of the Winchester Road from the Crossroads to the County Line and call on all the hands belonging to said road.

Ordered by the court that JOHN CAMPBELL be allowed the sum of $4.50 for apprehending and bringing to justice JAMES MOORE and WILLIAM MOORE and that the County Trustee of Lincoln County pay the same out of the county money in his hands not otherwise appropriated.

JOHN B. BUCHANAN is appointed overseer of the road in the room of JAMES W. BURNES resigned and call on the usual hands.

JAMES McCARMACK is appointed overseer of the road in the room of EZEKIEL GILLUM resigned.

JESSE BROWN is released from the payment of the appraised value of a stray heifer that he posted and was proven away.

ISOM BURNETT is released from the payment of the appraised value of a stray hog which he posted and was proven away.

WILLIAM VANCE is appointed overseer of the road in the room of ISSAC JAMES resigned.

WILLIAM JACKSON is released from the payment of the appraised value of three stray horses which he posted and was proven away.

DANIEL W. HARRISON is appointed overseer of the road in the room of HENRY MOORE resigned and call on the usual hands.

Ordered by the court that GEORGE KOONCE be overseer of that part of the new road from the south east corner of this county to JESSE GEORGE's cotton gin to begin at the Franklin County Line to COCK's old place.

Ordered by the court that JAMES SANDERS be overseer of the new road from COCK's to his house and call on the usual hands.

Ordered by the court that JOHN CAMPER be overseer of the road from SANDER's to JOSEPH DEAN's and call on the usual hands.

Ordered that JESSE PUGH be overseer of that part of the new road from DEAN's to the FRAZER Grove and call on the usual hands.

16

Ordered that JOHN COCKS be overseer of the road from the grove to JESSE GEORGE's cotton gin and call on the usual hands.

Ordered that RICHARD STUART be overseer of the road from the JESSE GEORGE's cotton gin to the county line and call on the usual hands.

WILLIAM FARRAR is released from serving as a Juror to this term.

Ordered by the court that DAVID READ be overseer of the road from the fork of the road near Cain (Cane) Creek to DANIEL TOUCHSTONE's and call on the usual hands.

Ordered by the court that JOHN GAVIN, WILLIAM HOWARD, JOHN F. COUSETT, JAMES CURRY, HOWELL DAWDY, JAMES McCULLERS and MARK LANGSTON be a jury to view and mark out a road beginning at or near the south east corner of JOHN PRICE's land and to intersect the Fayetteville Road south of SQUIRE FLOYD's house and make a return to next court.

Ordered by the court that THOMAS GIBSON, JAMES RALSTON, DAVID L. HAWKINS, JESSE FARRAR and HARDY BROWN be a Jury of View to turn the Columbia Road around ALLEN ELSTON's plantation and make return to this court.

JOHN DILLEN is appointed overseer of the road in the room of JAMES RODGERS resigned.

Ordered by the court that PHILIP KOONCE, ROBERT DICKSON and WILLIAM DICKSON be commissioners to settle with EDWARD TATUM, admr of the estate of WILLIAM TATUM, deceased, and make return to this court.

WILLIAM MILNER was qualified as a Justice of the Peace for Lincoln County.

Ordered by the court that SOLOMON BURFORD, JOSHUA EWING, SAMUEL ASTON, JESSE BONNER and ISAAC SMITH be a Jury of View to view and mark out a road the nearest and best way leading from Click Ford on Elk River running past CAPTAIN JOHN DICKEY's on the nearest and best way to intersect the road lately laid off leading to Florence below ISAAC's then the nearest and best way to the county line in a direction to Athens and make return to next court.

JOHN C. SAWYERS appeared in court and was appointed admr of the estate of DAVID SAWYERS, deceased, entered into bond with JOHN CRAWFORD and WILLIAM CRAWFORD in sum of $3000.00.

DANIEL HARKINS, JR. is appointed guardian for HIRAM HARKINS, DANIEL HARKINS, JINCY HARKINS, infant heirs of CHARLES HARKINS, deceased, entered into bond with JAMES MAXWELL and DANIEL HARKINS, SR., his securities in sum of $1500.00.

An inventory of the property of ELIJAH LOYD, deceased, was returned into court by his admr and ordered to be recorded.

A Deed from JOHN GREER, Sheriff, to ROBERT DICKSON for one Town Lot and ordered to be certified.

JOHN PARK records his stock mark, a crop and a slit in the right and under bit in the left.

JOEL HARRIS is appointed a Constable who gave bond and security and qualified.

GEORGE WILKINS is released from the payment of the appraised value of two stray horses by him posted and was proven away.

An inventory of the property of DAVID SAWYERS, deceased, was returned to court by his admr which was ordered to be recorded.

PRESLEY S. GEORGE was appointed a Constable and gave bond and security and qualified.

AMOS SMALL was appointed a Constable, gave bond and security and qualified.

A Bill of Sale from MARK PITTS to JOSEPH PITTS and ordered to be certified.

A Deed from ZACHARIAH ARNOLD to JOHN STILES for 58½ acres of land was

17

acknowledged and ordered to be registered.

A Deed of Conveyance from WILEY GARRETT to WILLIAM THOMISON for 10 acres of land and ordered to be certified.

A Deed from WILEY GARRETT to WILLIAM THOMISON for 15 acres of land and ordered to be certified.

A Deed of Conveyance from BRICE M. GARNER to JAMES CUNNINGHAM for 65 acres of land, proven by WILLIAM C. KENNEDY and ROBERT EDMISTON and ordered to be certified.

A Deed from OLIVER WILLIAMS, attorney in fact for WILLIAM H. MURPHREY to JESSE LAURANCE for 444 acres of land, proven by WILLIAM LEE and JOHN PARK and ordered to be certified.

A Deed of Conveyance from MOSES CHAMBERS to DANIEL COOK for 90 acers of land and ordered to be certified.

A Deed of Conveyance from WILLIAM P. McGEHEE to WILLIAM STOGSDILLE for 15 acres of land, proven by WILLIAM McGEHEE and ROBERT DUNCAN and ordered to be certified.

A Deed of Conveyance from OLIVER WILLIAMS, attorney in fact for WILLIAM H. MURPHREE to JOHN DAVIS for 549 acres of land, proven by J. LAURANCE and WILLIAM LEE and ordered to be certified.

A Deed of Conveyance from OLIVER WILLIAMS, attorney in fact, for WILLIAM H. MURPHREE to WILLIAM LEE for 279 acres of land, proven by J. LAURANCE and JOHN PARK and ordered to be certified.

A Deed of Conveyance from STEPHEN BEAVERS to JOHN WATKINS and JOSEPH HUGSTON for 215½ acres of land and ordered to be certified.

A Deed of Conveyance from WILLIAM P. McGEHEE to WILLIAM STOGSDILLE for 40 acres of land, proven by WILLIAM McGEHEE and ROBERT DUNCAN and ordered to be certified.

A Deed of Conveyance from CONSTANT SCALES to JOSEPH VINES for 15 acres of land and ordered to be certified.

A Bill of Sale from DANIEL R. SUMNER to ROBERT & WILLIAM DICKSON for a negro boy named NOAH and ordered to be certified.

A Deed of Conveyance from JAMES BOWEN to THOMAS GEORGE for 20 acres of land and ordered to be certified.

A Deed of Conveyance from WILLIAM P. ANDERSON to JOHN SIVILY for 100 acres of land, proven by DANIEL SIVILY and JOHN SIVILY and ordered to be certified.

A Deed of Conveyance from JOHN HENSON to JAMES BOWEN for 58 acres of land, proven by JOHN GEORGE and ordered to be certified.

It is irdered by the court that a commission issue to the Sheriff to summon twelve freeholders whereupon their oaths will try to examine a certain JOHN PARKER and say whether he is of sound mind or a lunatic and report before court.

A Deed of Conveyance from WILLIAM ANDERSON to SOLOMON BURFORD for 44¼ acres of land, proven by A. ISAACS and JOHN NORTON and ordered to be certified.

The transfer of a plat and certificate of survey from JAMES NELSON to DANIEL COOK, proven by MOSES CHAMBERS and ordered to be certified.

A Deed of Conveyance from EDWARD POWER to MOSES CHAMBERS for 15 acres of land, proven by DANIEL COOK and ELI EVANS and ordered to be certified.

TUESDAY APRIL 18, 1820

Justices present were JAMES HOLEMAN, WILLIAM KENNON, SAMUEL BUCHANAN and PHILIP KOONCE, Gentlemen.

18

The Sheriff made return of the following to serve as Grand Jurors and Petit Jurors, to wit, JAMES SCOTT, DANIEL WAGGONER, JOHN WATKINS, MOSES CHAMBERS, LEMUEL BRANDON, JAMES SMITH, JOEL JOHNSON, JOHN DAVIS, GEORGE W. HUNT, DOILY GRIFFIS, JOHN BOYLES, LEWIS SHIPP, BENJAMIN PORTER, JOHN NORTON, JESSE BONNER, WILLIAM FARRAR, BENJAMIN JOHNSON, TRYON GIBSON, ROBERT MOORE, REUBEN HUNTER, MOSES STONE, WILLIAM TOWNSEND, DANIEL JONES, and JOHN PARK being elected. Those elected to serve as Grand Jurors are BENJAMIN JOHNSON, JOHN DAVIS, JOHN PARK, REUBEN HUNTER, DOILY GRIFFIS, JOHN NORTON, JOEL JOHNSON, BENJAMIN PORTER, LEMUEL BRANDON, LEWIS SHIPP, TRYON GIBSON, ROBERT MOORE, and JAMES SCOTT.

STERLING McLEMORE, Constable sworn to wait on the Grand Jury.

DANIEL JONES released from serving as a juror this term.

MOSES CHAMBERS released from serving as juror this term.

JOHN DAVIS is released from the payment of the appraised value of a stray nag which he posted and proven from him.

A Deed of COnveyance from JOSEPH HOUGHSTON to JOHN WATKINS for (blank) acres of land and ordered to be certified.

A Deed of Conveyance from OLIVER WILLIAMS, attorney in fact, for WILLIAM H. MURPHREE to JOSEPH McALISTER for 620 acres of land and ordered to be certified.

The Commissioners appointed to settle with EDWARD TATUM, admr of WILLIAM TATUM, deceased, made return of the settlement by them.

The due execution of an Indenture of Bargain and Sale from REECE HOWELL to JOHN WATKINS for 108 acres of land and ordered to be certified.

JOHN W. CRUNK vs AMBROSE PEARCE - The plaintiff says that he intends no further to prosecute this his suit and the defendant in person assumes the payment of all costs. It is considered by the court that this suit be dismissed. Plaintiff go without day and recover against the defendant his costs.

The Grand Jurors again returned into court with a Bill of Indictment, the State against JOHN PARKINSON, a true bill and again return to consider for further presentments.

MALCOMB GILCHRIST vs THOMAS HARPER - In Debt - The defendant appeared in court and says that he does owe the plaintiff $163.00. It is considered by the court that the plaintiff recover against the defendant his costs.

The Grand Jurors again returned into court with a Bill of Indictment, the State against VINCENT ADAMS and again return to consider for further presentments.

The transfer of a plat and certificate of survey from GEORGE THOMAS to PRYOR STONE, acknowledged and ordered to be certified.

The due execution of an Indenture of Bargain and Sale from ADLAI SHARP to JOHN DAVIS for two town lots, proven by SAMUEL BUCHANAN and CONSTANT SCALES and ordered to be certified.

The Commissioners appointed to settle with admrs of the estate of JOHN KELLY, deceased, made return of the settlement and ordered to be certified.

A Deed of Conveyance from ROBERT BRADEN to JOHN BEATIE for 8 acres of land and ordered to be certified.

A Bill of Sale from JOHN HENDERSON to WILLIAM HUSBANDS for a negro girl named PATSEY and ordered to be certified.

JOHN DYER is appointed overseer of the road in the room of WILLIAM PATTERSON resigned and call on the usual hands.

ROBERT MOORE vs JAMES EVENELL - The defendant by his attorney says he wishes to dismiss his appeal in this cause and assumes the payment of all costs. It is considered by the court that this appeal be dismissed and the plaintiff recover his costs.

JACOB WAGGONER vs JOHN HANBY - This day the defendant appeared in court and confessed that he owes the plaintiff $227.00. It is considered by the court that the plaintiff recover against the defendant his costs.

The Commissioners appointed to make a division of the real estate of JOHN MORGAN, deceased, made return and was ordered to be certified.

The amount of sale of property of ROBERT ADAMS, deceased, was returned to court by his admr and ordered to be certified.

A Deed of Trust from JOHN McADA & JOHN S. McADA to JOHN BEARD, proven by ARGYLE CAMPBELL and ordered to be certified.

On motion, it is ordered by the court that ALEXANDER FULTON be released from paying double tax for the year 1819 that he pay a single tax only.

SAMUEL PAINTER vs WILLIAM D. FERGUSON & THOMAS PARHAM - This day the parties by their attorneys and a jury of men, to wit, GEORGE W. HUNT, DANIEL WAGGONER, JONATHAN FROST, ADAM MEEK, ASA STREET, JACOB SILVERTOOTH, WILLIAM PATTERSON, WILLIAM BOON, DANIEL WARREN, THOMAS DOAK, JOHN BUCHANAN and SAMUEL MINOR being elected and sworn and says that the defendants is not guilty as charged. It is considered by the court that the defendant go hence without day and recover against the plaintiff their costs.

This day came SALLY DOWNING into court and it appearing to the court that the testimony that SALLY DOWNING and JOHN M. DOWNING, deceased, were lawfully married and that she is now the widow of him the said JOHN M. DOWNING, deceased, and is only heir at law. On motion of her the said SALLY DOWNING is certified as being the widow and the only heir agreeable to the rule of descents of real estate in State of Tennessee. It is ordered that the clerk of this court deliver properly certified copy of this their certificate, for the purpose of SALLY DOWNING obtaining a warrant for Military Bounty Lands in right of the said JOHN M. DOWNING, deceased, agreeable to the laws of the United States in such cases made and provided.

WEDNESDAY APRIL 19, 1820

Justices present were SAMUEL BUCHANAN, CHARLES BOYLES and JAMES HOLEMAN, Esquires.

DAVID HARRIS vs JOHN P. McCONNELL - This day the defendant appeared in court and confessed that he owes the plaintiff $131.06¼. It is considered by the court that the plaintiff recover against the defendant his costs.

MARY INGLE vs JOHN MARR - This day the defendant by his attorney and on motion, it is ordered by the court that the plaintiff appear at next term of this court to give other or better security for the prosecution of this suit or it will be dismissed.

MARY INGLE vs WILLIAM HUSBANDS - On motion of the defendant by his attorney. It is ordered by the court that the plaintiff appear here at next court to give other or better security for the prosecution of this suit or this suit will be dismissed.

The due execution of an Indenture of Bargain and Sale from HENRY RUTHERFORD to WILLIAM BEATIE for 209 acres of land, proven by DAVID P. MUNROE & STEPHEN C. CHITWOOD and ordered to be certified.

The due execution of an Indenture of Bargain and Sale from JOHN WILSON & JOHN PORTER, attorney in fact, for JAMES DAVIS to REPS O. CHILDRESS, JR. for 350 acres of land and ordered to be certified.

GEORGE HARDING vs FRANCIS WYATT - The plaintiff by his attorney said he wishes no further to prosecute his suit and the defendant assumes the payment of one half of the costs. The court ordered this suit be dismissed and the plaintiff recover against the defendant one half of the costs.

JAMES WALKER vs DANIEL COOK - The plaintiff appeared in court and says that he wishes no further to prosecute his suit and the defendant assumes the payment of all costs. It is considered by the court that this suit be dismissed and the plaintiff recover against the defendant his costs.

JOHN LANGISTEN is appointed overseer of the road from JOHN KING's lane to

JOSHUA SMITH's plantation and call on the usual hands.

It is ordered by the court that the County Trustee of Lincoln County pay to the Sheriff of the county the sum of $15.85 out of any monies in his hands not appropriated.

A Bill of Sale from JOHN J. HENRY to JOHN BLACKWELL for a negro man names MOSES and ordered to be certified.

A Deed of Conveyance from PETER ROZEL to STEPHEN C. CHITWOOD for 118 acres of land, proven by ALEXANDER MORTON and JOSEPH PENN and ordered to be certified.

The Grand Jury again returned into court with a Bill of Indictment, the State against BENJAMIN GEORGE, ALDEN TUCKER, WILLIAM A. TUCKER, and ALLEN TUCKER a true bill against ALDEN TUCKER, ALLEN TUCKER and WILLIAM A. TUCKER and not a true bill against BENJAMIN GEORGE and again returned to consider for further presentments.

The Grand Jury again returned into court with a Bill of Indictment, the State against SAMUEL CARMACK a true bill and again return to consider for further presentments.

The Grand Jury again returned into court with a Bill of Indictment, the State against JAMES GEORGE & WILLIAM PHILLIPS, a true bill and again returned to consider for further presentments.

BENJAMIN THOMAS vs JOHN J. HENRY - JOHN BARNETT & PETER HOLLAND the appearance bail of JOHN J. HENRY, surrenders him in court in discharge of themselves whereupon JOHN BARNETT & PETER HOLLAND is released and JOHN J. HENRY is ordered in custody of the Sheriff.

A Deed of Conveyance from BRICE M. GARNER to JACOB VINZANT for 208 acres of land was proven by GEORGE ST. JOHN BASKINS, as witness, that THOMAS A. YOUNG attested as a witness also WILLIAM HUSBANDS proved that said THOMAS A. YOUNG lives out of the State of Tennessee and ordered to be certified.

A Deed of Conveyance from JOHN DAVIS to JOSEPH PENN for 40 acres of land and ordered to be certified.

A Deed of Conveyance from JOHN DAVIS to SAMUEL BUCHANAN for 98 acres of land and ordered to be certified.

A Deed of Conveyance from JOHN DAVIS to THOMAS BUCHANAN for 235 acres of land and ordered to be certified.

A Bill of Sale from CROFT & HOLLY to ROBERT & WILLIAM DICKSON for three negroes, proven by BRICE M. GARNER and ordered to be certified.

State vs ALDEN TUCKER, WILLIAM A. TUCKER & ALLEN TUCKER - THOMAS W. HAMILTON appeared in court and acknowledged himself indebted to the State of Tennessee for $150.00 to be levied on his goods and chattels &c to the use of the State rendered but to be void on condition that he appear in July next to prosecute and give evidence in behalf of the State against ALDEN TUCKER, WILLIAM A. TUCKER and ALLEN TUCKER and not depart the same without have first had and obtained of the court.

THOMAS W. HAMILTON appeared in court and acknowledged himself indebted to the State of Tennessee for $100.00 to be levied on his goods and chattels &c and to the use of the State but to be void on condition that he appear in July court to prosecute and give evidence in behalf of the State against JAMES GEORGE & WILLIAM PHILLIPS and not depart without have first had and obtained of the court.

It is ordered by the court that PETER SHELTON be fined $5.00 for not attending as a juror this term.

FLETCHER & McCLELLAN vs JONATHAN ESTILL - This day came the parties by their attorneys and a jury of men, to wit, GEORGE W. HUNT, DANIEL WAGGONER, THOMAS ALLY, THOMAS BUCHANAN, OLIVER WILLIAMS, VANCE GREER, JOHN R. JOHNSON, ABNER DYER, ABSALOM BEARD, CLABORN WHITWORTH, PETER MOYERS, and DANIEL B. SUMNER being elected and sworn and said that they cannot agree whereupon by consent of the parties by their attorneys the jury was permitted to disperse until next day.

Justices present were JAMES HOLEMAN, CHARLES BOYLES and SAMUEL BUCHANAN.

State vs JAMES WILSON - Assault and Battery - The defendant appeared in court and being charged, pleads guilty. It is considered by the court that the defendant be fined 25¢ and be imprisoned six days and pay the costs of this indictment.

The Grand Jury again returned into court with a Bill of Indictment, the State vs JAMES MOORE and WILLIAM MOORE, a true bill and again returned to consider for further presentments.

A Deed of Conveyance from DANIEL MALLOY to JAMES BAUGH for 151 3/4 acres of land and ordered to be certified.

FLETCHER & McCLELLAN vs JONATHAN ESTILL - The jury elected impaneled and sworn in this cause yesterday, appeared in court and said that the defendant did assume upon himself in manner and form as the plaintiff in declaring against him had alledged and they assess the plaintiff's damages to $2842.00. It is considered by the court that the plaintiff recover against the defendant his costs.

State vs JAMES LYNCH - WILLIAM B. MARTIN, the solister, and the defendant appeared in court and a jury of men, to wit, CORNELIUS WEBB, FRANCIS PORTERFIELD, JAMES BROOKS, RICHARD AUTIN (AUSTIN), WILLIAM SMITH, DRURY K. SMITH, ALEXANDER McCULLOUGH, JESSE LAMB, REECE HOWELL, JOHN SANDERS, JOHN PYBUS, and SPENCER A. PUGH being elected and sworn and said that the defendant is guilty in manner as charged.

FRIDAY APRIL 21, 1820

Justices present were CHARLES BOYLES, SAMUEL BUCHANAN and JAMES HOLEMAN, Esquires.

The State vs VINCENT ADAMS - The defendant appeared in court and being on this Bill of Indictment, pleades guilty. It is considered by the court that the defendant be fined to the State for $10.00 and pay the costs of this indictment whereupon came JOHN CURRY and JAMES A. HUGHES, securities for the above fine and costs.

A Deed of Conveyance from GEORGE COALTER to JOHN GREER for one town lot No. 18, was proven by WILLIAM DICKSON and CONSTANT SCALES and ordered to be certified.

It is ordered by the court that JOHN WILSON be released from the appraised value of a stray hog which he posted.

The State vs SAMUEL CARMACK - Assault and Battery - The defendant appeared into court and pleads guilty. It is considered by the court that the defendant be fined $1.00 and pay cost of indictment. OLIVER WILLIAMS, security. Cost of case is $5.00.

The State vs ARCHELUS WILSON - Assault and Battery - This day came WILLIAM B. MARTIN, the solicitor, and a jury of men, to wit, GEORGE W. HUNT, DANIEL WAGGONER, THOMAS KERCHEVAL, WILLIAM CROCKETT, JOHN JACKSON, WILLIAM C. JACKSON, JAMES SWEET, SAMUEL S. HOLDING, FRANCIS SMITH, TRAVIS ASHBY and JOHN CURRY being elected and sworn and said that the defendant is not guilty. On motion that there was strong probability of his guilt. Court said that the defendant pay the costs of this indictment.

State vs SAMUEL LYNCH - Motion in arrest of Judgement - The motion of the defendant in arrest of judgement is withdrawn. Court considered that the defendant be fined $10.00 and whereupon came MARGARET ADAMS as security for said defendant confess judgement jointly with defendant.

State vs GEORGE WILSON - JAMES BROOKS who was bound in a recognizance for the appearance of GEORGE WILSON. JAMES BROOKS is discharged from his recognizance and the said GEORGE WILSON ordered in custody of the Sheriff.

The State vs JAMES WILSON - GEORGE W. DENNIS who was bound in a recognizance for the appearance of JAMES WILSON. GEORGE W. DENNIS is discharged from his recognizance and JAMES WILSON ordered in custody of the Sheriff.

The State vs GEORGE WILSON - GEORGE W. DENNIS who has bound in a recognizance for the appearance of GEORGE WILSON. GEORGE W. DENNIS is released and GEORGE WILSON ordered in custody of the Sheriff.

The State vs JOHN PARKERSON - Petit Larceny - The defendant appeared in court and being charged and pleads not guilty. A jury of men, to wit, GEORGW W. HUNT, DANIEL WAGGONER, JORDAN REESE, ALEXANDER McCULLOUGH, HENRY MOORE, THOMAS WITT, HAMBLETON MOFFIT, STEPHEN BEAVERS, WALTER KINNARD, JESSE DAVIS, GEORGE W. DENNIS, and JOHN CAMPBELL being elected and sworn and said that the defendant is guilty as charged and be fined 6½¢ and pay the costs and receive twenty lashes at the public whipping post between the hours of six and seven o'clock this evening, well laid on his back by the Sheriff.

SATURDAY APRIL 22, 1820

Justices present were JAMES HOLEMAN, SAMUEL BUCHANAN and CHARLES BOYLES, Esquires.

State vs JAMES WILSON - Indictment of Assault and Battery - The defendant appeared in court and pleaded guilty. It is considered by the court that the defendant be fined $5.00 and pay costs.

The State vs GEORGE WILSON - The defendant appeared in court and pleaded guilty. It is considered by the court that the defendant be fines $5.00 and remain in custody of the Sheriff until the fine and costs are paid.

State vs JAMES WILSON - Assault and Battery - The defendant pleaded guilty and the court fined him $1.00 and pay costs and to remain in custody of the Sheriff until the costs and fine are paid.

The State vs GEORGE WILSON - Assault and Battery - The defendant pleaded guilty and the court fined him $1.00 and pay costs and be imprisoned four days and remain in custody of the Sheriff until the fine and costs are paid.

The State vs GEORGE WILSON - Indictment of Assault and Battery - The defendant came into court as did WILLIAM B. MARTIN, the solicitor, and a jury of men, to wit, GEORGE W. HUNT, DANIEL WAGGONER, JAMES SWEET, JAMES GILFRY, VANCE GREER, ASA STREET, ABSALUM BEARD, ALEXANDER McCULLOUGH, WILLIAM C. SMITH, ABNER DYER, JOHN SANDERS, and JOHN DYER being elected and sworn and said that the defendant is guilty as charged and fined 25¢ and the costs and remain in custody of the Sheriff until the costs and fine are paid or give security.

This day ELIZABETH BUNN, widow and relict of HENRY BUNN, deceased, came into court and prayed to be appointed admrx of all and singular the goods and chattels and of said deceased. It appearing to the court that HENRY BUNN of our county of Lincoln has died intestate and that ELIZABETH BUNN is his widow. It is ordered by the court that ELIZABETH BUNN be appointed admrx and entered into bond with ASA STREET and BRICE M. GARNER as securities.

A Power of Attorney from BRICE M. GARNER to BENJAMIN PATTERSON was acknowledged in court and ordered to be recorded.

A Bill of Sale from NANCY FEATHERSTON to HARRIS MAULDIN for a negro girl named MARIAH, proven by HIRAM MAULDIN and ordered to be certified.

The State vs GEORGE WILSON - Indictment of Assault and Battery - The defendant and WILLIAM B. MARTIN, the solicitor, appeared in court and a jury of men, to wit, GEORGE W. HUNT, DANIEL WAGGONER, JESSE CLEMENTS, WILLIAM STEWART, SAMUEL BUCHANAN, THOMAS McGAUGH, DRURY K. SMITH, LARKIN SMITH, FRANCIS ROSS, JOHN JACKSON, JEREMIAH STUBBLEFIELD, and JESSE CONWELL being elected and sworn and said that the defendant is guilty as charged. Court ordered the defendant be fined 6½¢ and pay costs.

The State vs ARCHELUS WILSON - JEREMIAH DENNIS who was bound in recognizance for the appearance of ARCHELUS WILSON surrenders him into court. JEREMIAH DENNIS is released from his recognizance and ARCHELUS WILSON ordered in custody of the Sheriff.

The State vs JAS. & WILLIAM MOORE - On motion of WILLIAM B. MARTIN, the solicitor, and by permission of the court, a nolleprosequi (unwilling to pursue) is entered as to

23

the third court in the Bill of Indictment in this cause.

The State vs WILLIAM MOORE - The defendant appeared in court and pleads (guilty) and is fined $1.00 and pay the cost of this indictment.

The State vs WILLIAM MOORE - On motion of WILLIAM B. MARTIN, the solicitor, and by permission of the court, the nolleproswqui (unwilling to pursue) is entered in this cause and the defendant came and confessed judgement for the costs.

The State vs ARCHELUS WILSON - Assault and Battery - This day came WILLIAM B. MARTIN, the solicitor, as well as the defendant and a jury of men, to wit, JOSEPH COMMONS, CLABORN WHITWORTH, PETER MOYERS, JAMES STEPHENS, KENNETH McKINSEY, WILLIAM B. L(S)EWELL, EARMINE CHITWORTH, PETER BURROW, ALEXANDER ESLEMAN, JOHN JACKSŌN, JAMES SWEET, and WILLIAM STEWART being elected and sworn and said that the defendant is guilty and be fined 25¢ and remain in custody of the Sheriff until the cost and fine are paid or give security.

A Deed of Trust from JONATHAN ESTILL to WILLIAM WELLS for one town lot, proven by WILLIAM E. KENNEDY and ordered to be certified.

A Deed of Trust from JONATHAN ESTILL to ISAAC ESTILL, JAMES ESTILL and GARLAND B. MILLEN for six negroes together with his household and kitchen furniture, proven by JOHN W. ESTILL and ordered to be certified.

NATHANIEL B. BUCKINGHAM vs WILLIAM D. FERGUSON - Motion to dismiss Certiorari - This day came the parties by their attorneys and on argument of the motion to dismiss the certiorari and the court dismissed and ordered the plaintiff recover against the defendant and ALEXANDER FERGUSON and NATHANIEL BLACKMORE his securities, sum of $65.33 with interest his costs.

SHELTON & LUSK vs FRANCIS FINCHER - The defendant appeared in court and says he owes the plaintiff $7.50. Court ordered the plaintiff to recover against the defendant his costs.

MONDAY APRIL 24, 1820

A Deed of Conveyance from HOWELL HARRIS to JESSE ROBERTSON for 23 acres of land and ordered to be certified.

A Deed of Conveyance from WILLIAM B. WOODY & JANE WOODY to JAMES BROADWAY for 70 acres of land, proven by LEMUEL BROADWAY and JOEL ORRICK and ordered to be certified.

A Deed of Conveyance from JAMES McADAMS to JAMES RALSTON for 50 acres of land, proven by WILLIAM WELCH and JOHN DOCKERY and ordered to be certified.

A Deed of Conveyance from JOHN GREER, Sheriff, to SAMUEL DOBBINS for 30 acres and ordered to be certified.

A Deed of Conveyance from JOHN ASHER to SAMUEL S. HOLDINGS & GEORGE HARDING for one town lot, proven by ARGYLE CAMPBELL and ordered to be certified.

A Deed of Conveyance from GEORGE W. DENNIS to SAMUEL S. HOLDING & GEORGE HARDING for one town lot and ordered to be certified.

A Deed of Conveyance from SAMUEL S. HOLDING to GEORGE HARDING for one town lot and ordered to be certified.

A Deed of Conveyance from JAMES BUCHANAN to JOSEPH PENN for 25 acres of land, proven by HOWELL HARRIS & ALEXANDER MORTON and ordered to be certified.

The transfer of a plat and certificate from SAMUEL DAVIS to JAMES BLACK, proven by JAMES RALSTON & WILLIAM WELCH and ordered to be certified.

The transfer of a plat and certificate from JAMES BLACK to JOHN McADAMS, proven by JAMES RALSTON & WILLIAM WELCH and ordered to be certified.

A Deed of Conveyance from WILLIAM KENNON to WILLIAM MILNER for 100 acres of land and ordered to be certified.

Ordered by the court that THOMAS SIMMONS be overseer of the road in the room of JAMES ALEXANDER resigned and call on the usual hands.

DAVID BOYERS is appointed overseer of the road in the room of SAMUEL BOYERS and call on the usual hands.

It appearing to the court that the Will of NATHANIEL TATUM, deceased, had been proven by witnesses at Oct Term 1819 and no letters Testamentary had issue to EDWARD TATUM, the executor of said Will and he giving bond and security with BRICE M. GARNER and WILLIAM HUSBANDS, his securities for $2000.00. Letters Testamentary issue EDWARD TATUM to execute the Will.

WILLIAM PARKS & THOMAS PARKS appeared in court and was appointed admrs of the estate of ARON PARK, deceased, who gave bond with WILLIAM HUSBAND & PHILIP KOONCE, their securities for $10,000.00.

WILLIAM PARKES is appointed guardian for JOEL PARKES, FIELDING PARKS and PARTHENA PARKS, infants heirs of ARON PARKS, deceased, gave bond with THOMAS PARKS & CHARLES BOYLES, his securities for $3000.00.

An inventory of the estate of NATHANIEL TATUM, deceased, was returned to court by EDWARD TATUM, his executor and ordered to be recorded.

An inventory of the estate of ARON PARKS, deceased, was returned to court by his admr and ordered to be recorded.

On petition of NATHANIEL B. BUCKINGHAM leave is given him to build a mill on Swan Creek on a tract of School Land where he now lives.

Ordered by the court that FRANCIS WYATT, WILLIAM CUNNINGHAM, WILLIAM SOLOMON, JOHN McCLARY and WILLIAM SHAW be a Jury of View to turn the road through JOHN RHEA's field and make return to next court.

JAMES CURRY is appointed a Constable, gave bond and security.

Ordered by the court that JAMES F. DRIVER be overseer of a new road from where it intersects the Columbia Road to WILLIAM CRUNK's and call on the hands in a proper distance.

JACOB WRIGHT is appointed overseer of a new road from WILLIAM CRUNK's to the top of the ridge between the Wolf Pen Fork of Cain Creek and JOHN H. MOORE's.

DAVID ARMSTRONG is appointed overseer of the road from the top of the ridge between Wolf Pen Fork of Cane Creek and JOHN H. MOORE's to WILLIAM HAYS on the Shelbyville Road.

WILLIAM HAYS is appointed overseer of the road from his house on by SQUIRE GARLAND to the Bedford County Line.

JOHN PRICE is appointed overseer of the road from Bedford County Line to where it intersects the Shelbyville Road at GEORGE PRICE's.

JOHN J. WHITAKER, JAMES HOLEMAN and EBENEZER McEWEN is appointed Commissioners to lay off one years support for the widen and children of ARON PARKS, deceased, and make return to next court.

JAMES McCARMACK, WILLIAM CRAWFORD and JOHN CRAWFORD is appointed to lay off one year support for the widow and children of DAVID SAWYERS, deceased, out of said estate and make return to next court.

It appearing to the court that WILLIAM McCALL heretofore appointed guardian for ELIAS ONEAL and CHARLES ONEAL, orphan children of JAMES ONEAL, deceased, hath removed out of this State, it is ordered by the court that the bond given by said McCALL and his securities and discharged from all liability on account of said security.

ABSALUM BOSTICK & NATHANIEL B. BUCKINGHAM is appointed to settle with ELIZABETH LYNCH & JAMES LYNCH, admrs of HENRY PORCH, deceased, and make return to next court.

ABRAHAM SUMNERS & JOHN DOBBINS is appointed to settle with JAMES

DOWNING, admr of JOHN DOWNING, deceased, and make return to next court.

WILLIAM WILLBORN is permitted to keep a tavern at his house in Fayetteville one year from this time.

THOMAS PARKER came into court and acknowledged himself indebted to the chairman of the County Court for $100.00 to be levied of his goods and chattels &c but to be void on condition that he take due care of JOHN PARKER, his son, who appears to be an idiot and that he prevent JOHN from doing any injury to this court on the first day of next court. It is ordered by the court that THOMAS PARKER be allowed $35.00 for the above services.

It appearing to the court from information to them that JOHN PARKER is an idiot. It is ordered that the Sheriff summons twelve freeholders to assertain by inquisition whether JOHN be an idiot or lunatic or otherwise a non-sane memory and make return on first day of next term of court.

JOHN GIBSON, JAMES TOOL and WILLIAM HARRIS appointed to lay off one years support for the widow and children of ROBERT EDMISTON, deceased, and make return to next court.

TUESDAY APRIL 25, 1820

Justices present were CHARLES BOYLES, JAMES HOLEMAN, PHILIP KOONCE and SAMUEL BUCHANAN.

State vs JAMES MOORE - JAMES McDAVID, PATRICK and JOHN CAMPBELL appeared in court and acknowledged themselves indebted to the State of Tennessee for $150.00 each, to be levied on them respective goods and chattels &c but to be void on condition that they appear here on first Thursday after third Monday in July next to present and give evidence in behalf of the State against JAMES MOORE and not depart the same without leave first had and obtained of the court.

JOHN H. WOODCOCK vs JOHN J. HENRY - Debt Appeal - This day came the parties by their attorneys and a jury of men, to wit, GEORGE W. HUNT, DANIEL WAGGONER, THOMAS KERCHEVAL, THOMAS ALLY, CLABORN WHITWORTH, JOHN CAMPBELL, GEORGE W. DENNIS, SPENCER A. PUGH, JOHN BOSTICK, EDWARD MOSS, VANCE GREER, and GEORGE MOSS being elected and sworn and said that the defendant does owe the plaintiff $40.00 and damages of $7.37½. It is ordered that the plaintiff recover against the defendant his costs. JOHN BARNARD his security.

The Grand Jury again returned into court with a Bill of Indictment, the State against JAMES C. CAMPBELL a true bill and again returned to consider for further presentments.

The State vs JAMES C. CAMPBELL - Assault and Battery - The defendant appeared in court and pleads guilty as charged and is fined $20.00 and pay cost of this indictment and remain in custody of the Sheriff until the fine and cost are paid. WILLIAM NEELD as security.

JOHN C. McADA vs WILLIAM YOUNG - Appeal - This day came the parties of their attorneys and a jury of men, to wit, GEORGE W. HUNT, DANIEL WAGGONER, THOMAS KERCHEVAL, THOMAS ALLY, CLABORN WHITWORTH, JOHN CAMPBELL, GEORGE W. DENNIS, SPENCER A. PUGH, JOHN BOSTICK, EDWARD MOSS, VANCE GREER, and GEORGE MOSS being elected and sworn and said that the defendant is indebted to the plaintiff for $10.00. It is considered by the court that the plaintiff recover against the defendant his costs.

JOHN TURNER vs JOHNSON WELLBORN - Debt Appeal - This day came the parties by their attorneys and a jury of men, to wit, ROBERT H. McEWEN, PETER MOYERS, WILLIAM C. SMITH, WILLIAM NORRIS, THOMAS FLACK, ABNER DYER, ALEXANDER McCULLOUGH, JOHN DYER, DRURY K. SMITH, JOHN WILSON, ABSALOM BEARD, and JOHN R. JOHNSON being elected and sworn and said that the defendant is indebted to the plaintiff for $24.62½ and damages of 61¢. It is considered by the court that the plaintiff recover against the defendant and THOMAS H. MAY his security, his costs.

EZEKIEL GILLUM vs JOHN MURPHY - This day came the parties by their attorneys and a jury of men, to wit, GEORGE W. HUNT, DANIEL WAGGONER, THOMAS KERCHEVAL, THOMAS ALLY, CLABORN WHITWORTH, JOHN CAMPBELL, FRANCIS ROSS, SPENCER A. PUGH, JOHN BOSTICK, JOHN BLAND, VANCE GREER, and EDWARD McBRIDE being elected and sworn and said that the defendant is indebted to the plaintiff for $20.00 and damages of 56¢. It is considered by the court that the plaintiff recover his costs.

THOMAS L. TROTTER vs SAMUEL MIXON - This day came the parties into court and the plaintiff says he wishes to dismiss his suit and each party agrees to their own costs. Court dismisses this suit.

CHARLES BOYLES &c vs NANCY FEATHERSTON - Debt - This day came the parties by their attorneys and a jury of men, to wit, GEORGE W. HUNT, DANIEL WAGGONER, THOMAS KERCHEVAL, THOMAS ALLEY, CLABORN WHITWORTH, JOHN CAMPBELL, FRANCIS ROSS, SPENCER A. PUGH, JOHN BOSTICK, JOHN BLAND, VANCE GREER, and EDWARD McBRIDE being elected and sworn and said that the defendant had not paid the debt to the plaintiff of $102.12½ and $13.26½ damages and that the plaintiff recover his costs.

ALFRED BALCH vs VANCE GREER - The defendant appeared in court and withdraws his pleas and says that he owes the plaintiff $200.00 and $5.00 damages. Ordered by the court that the plaintiff recover his costs.

ALEXANDER BOTELER vs JOEL JOHNSON - Debt - This day came the parties by their attorneys and a jury of men, to wit, GEORGE W. HUNT, DANIEL WAGGONER, THOMAS KERCHEVAL, THOMAS ALLY, CLABORN WHITWORTH, JOHN CAMPBELL, FRANCIS ROSS, SPENCER A. PUGH, JOHN BOSTICK, JOHN BLAN(D), VANCE GREER, and EDWARD McBRIDE being elected and sworn and said that the defendant had not paid the debt of $108.50 to the plaintiff and $4.32 in damages. It is considered by the court that the plaintiff recover his costs.

MALCOM GILCHRIST vs JOSEPH HINKLE - Debt - This day came the parties by their attorneys and a jury of men, to wit, GEORGE W. HUNT, DANIEL WAGGONER, THOMAS KERCHEVAL, THOMAS ALLY, CLABORN WHITWORTH, JOHN CAMPBELL, FRANCIS ROSS, SPENCER A. PUGH, JOHN BOSTICK, JOHN BLAN(D), VANCE GREER, and EDWARD McBRIDE being elected and sworn and said that the defendant has not paid the debt to the plaintiff of $700.00 and damages of $19.75. Plaintiff is to recover against the defendant his costs.

CHARLES BOYLES vs THOMAS HARPER - This day came the parties by their attorneys and a jury of men, to wit, GEORGE W. HUNT, DANIEL WAGGONER, THOMAS KERCHEVAL, THOMAS ALLY, CLABORN WHITWORTH, JOHN CAMPBELL, FRANCIS ROSS, SPENCER A. PUGH, JOHN BOSTICK, JOHN BLAN(D), VANCE GREER, and EDWARD McBRIDE being elected and sworn and said that the defendant has not paid the debt to the plaintiff of $86.23 3/4 and damages of $1.75. Plaintiff to recover against the defendant his costs.

CHARLES BOYLES, surviving partner &c vs THOMAS HARPER - Debt - This day came the parties by their attorneys and a jury of men, to wit, GEORGE W. HUNT, DANIEL WAGGONER, THOMAS KERCHEVAL, THOMAS ALLY, CLABORN WHITWORTH, JOHN CAMPBELL, FRANCIS ROSS, SPENCER A. PUGH, JOHN BOSTICK, JOHN BLAN(D), VANCE GREER, and EDWARD McBRIDE being elected and sworn and said that the defendant has not paid the debt of $86.63 3/4 and damages of $1.75. Plaintiff to recover against the defendant his costs. (two accounts being the same)

The Grand Jurors again returned into court with a Bill of Indictment, the State against THOMAS GROOMES, a true bill and again returned to consider for further presentments.

ROBERT & WILLIAM DICKSON vs EDWARD McBRIDE - Debt - This day came the parties by their attorneys and a jury of men, to wit, GEORGE W. HUNT, DANIEL WAGGONER, THOMAS KERCHEVAL, THOMAS ALLY, CLABORN WHITWORTH, JOHN CAMPBELL, FRANCIS ROSS, SPENCER A. PUGH, JOHN BOSTICK, JOHN BLAN(D), VANCE GREER, and JOHN B. JOHNSON being elected and sworn and said that the defendant has not paid the debt to the plaintiff $165.46 and damages of $7.00. Plaintiff to recover against the defendant his costs.

CARLTON WELLBORN vs JAMES ZIVELEY - Debt - This day came the parties by their attorneys and a jury of men, to wit, GEORGE W. HUNT, DANIEL WAGGONER, THOMAS KERCHEVAL, THOMAS ALLY, CLABORN WHITWORTH, JOHN CAMPBELL, FRANCIS ROSS, SPENCER A. PUGH, JOHN BOSTICK, JOHN BLAN(D), VANCE GREER, and JOHN R. JOHNSON being elected and sworn and said that the defendant has not paid the debt to the plaintiff of $80.00 and damages of $11.20. Plaintiff to recover against the defendant his costs.

The State vs THOMAS GROOMES - Petit Larceny - The defendant came into court and being charged on Bill of Indictment, pleads not guilty and a jury of men, to wit, GEORGE

W. HUNT, DANIEL WAGGONER, THOMAS KERCHEVAL, THOMAS ALLY, CLABORN WHITWORTH, JOHN BOSTICK, FRANCIS ROSS, SPENCER A. PUGH, VANCE GREER, PETER MOYERS, ROBERT H. McEWEN, and WILLIAM C. SMITH elected and sworn and said that the defendant is guilty and fined $1.00 and receive ten lashes at the Public Whipping Post on his bare back well laid on between now and six o'clock this ecening.

The Grand Jury again returned into court with a Bill of Indictment, the State against GEORGE CUNNINGHAM, a true bill and again returned to consider for further presentments.

REUBEN WASHBURN & REBIN H. BON appeared in court and acknowledged themselves indebted to the State of Tennessee for $50.00 each to be levied of their goods and chattels &c to the use of the State rendered, but to be void on condition that they appear here from day to day to prosecute and give evidence in behalf of the State against GEORGE CUNNINGHAM and not depart without leave first had obtained by the court.

The Grand Jury again returned into court with a Bill of Indictment, the State against CHRISTOPHER E. LOVE, ABSOLUM COLLINS and DANIEL YOUNG, a true bill and again returned to consider for further presentments.

JAMES HOLLAND appeared in court and acknowledged himself indebted to the State of Tennessee for $300.00 to be levied of his goods and chattels &c to the use of the State rendered, but to be void on conditions that he and his wife CREACY HOLLAND and his daughter WINNY HOLLAND appear here in July next to prosecute and give evidence in behalf of the State against CHRISTOPHER E. LOVE, ABSOLUM COLLINS and DANIEL YOUNG and not depart without leave first had and obtained by the court.

A Mortgage from JONATHAN ESTILL to ISAAC ESTILL, JAMES ESTILL and GARLAND B. MILLER was proven in court by oaths of JOHN W. ESTILL.

The Grand Jury again returned into court with a Bill of Indictment, the State against CHRISTOPHER E. LOVE, DANIEL YOUNG, FRANCIS BEARD, ABSOLUM COLLINS, and THOMAS BEARD, a true bill against above named, but not a true bill against FRANCIS BEARD and again returned to consider for further presentments.

JAMES HOLLAND appeared in court and said he was indebted to the State of Tennessee for $300.00 to be levied of his goods and chattels &c to the use of the State rendered but to be void on conditions that he and his wife CREACY HOLLAND and his daughter SALLY HOLLAND appear here in July next to prosecute and give evidence in behalf of the State against CHRISTOPHER E. LOVE, DANIEL YOUNG, ABSOLUM COLLINS, and THOMAS BEARD and not depart without have first had and obtained of the court.

WEDNESDAY APRIL 26, 1820

Justices present were PHILIP KOONCE, JAMES HOLEMAN and SAMUEL BUCHANAN, Esquires.

JOHN SHAW vs WILLIAM SHAW - Debt - This day came the parties by their attorneys and a jury of men, to wit, JOHN DAVIS, JOHN PARK, REUBEN HUNTER, DOILY GRIFFIS, JOHN NORTON, JOEL JOHNSON, BENJAMIN PORTER, LEMUEL BRANDON, LEWIS SHIP, ROBERT MOORE, and JAMES SCOTT being elected and sworn and said that the defendant has not paid the debt to plaintiff of $500.00 and damages of $34.16. Plaintiff to recover against the defendant his costs.

WILLIAM PITTMAN vs HENRY RULEMAN - Debt - This day came the parties by their attorneys and a jury of men, to wit, JOHN DAVIS, JOHN PARKS, REUBEN HUNTER, DOILY GRIFFIS, JOHN NORTON, JOEL JOHNSON, BENJAMIN PORTER, LEMUEL BRANDON, LEWIS SHIP, TRYON GIBSON, ROBERT MOORE, and JAMES SCOTT being elected and sworn and said that the defendant has not paid the debt to plaintiff of $54.00 and damages and the plaintiff to recover against the defendant his costs.

SCHELY & SCHROEDER vs JAMES COALTER - Debt - This day came the parties by their attorneys and a jury of men, to wit, JOHN DAVIS, JOHN PARK, REUBEN HUNTER, DOILY GRIFFIS, JOHN NORTON, JOEL JOHNSON, BENJAMIN PORTER, LEMUEL BRANDON, LEWIS SHIP, TRYON GIBSON, ROBERT MOORE, and JAMES SCOTT being elected and sworn and said that the defendant had not paid the debt to the plaintiff of $815.41 and damages of $14.25. Plaintiff to recover against the defendant his costs.

CHARLES BOYLES, assignee &c vs RICHARD AUTIN (AUSTIN) - Debt - This day came the parties by their attorneys and a jury of men, to wit, JOHN DAVIS, JOHN PARK, REUBEN HUNTER, DOILY GRIFFIS, JOHN NORTON, JOEL JOHNSON, BENJAMIN PORTER,

LEMUEL BRANDON, LEWIS SHIPP, TRYON GIBSON, ROBERT MOORE, and JAMES SCOTT being elected and sworn and said that the defendant has not paid the debt to the plaintiff of $109.25 and damages of $2.54. Plaintiff to recover against the defendant his costs.

HENRY ALLEN vs CHARLES SPRINKLE - Debt - This day came the parties by their attorneys and a jury of men, to wit, JOHN DAVIS, JOHN PARK, REUBEN HUNTER, DOILY GRIFFIS, JOHN NORTON, JOEL JOHNSON, BENJAMIN PORTER, LEMUEL BRANDON, LEWIS SHIPP, TRYON GIBSON, ROBERT MOORE and JAMES SCOTT being elected and sworn and said that the defendant has not paid his debt to the plaintiff of $86.51 and damages of $3.24. Plaintiff to recover against said defendant his costs.

JOHN WHITE vs WILLIS L. CALVERT - Debt - This day came the parties by their attorneys and a jury of men, to wit, JOHN DAVIS, JOHN PARK, REUBEN HUNTER, DOILY GRIFFIS, JOHN NORTON, JOEL JOHNSON, BENJAMIN PORTER, LEMUEL BRANDON, LEWIS SHIPP, TRYON GIBSON, ROBERT MOORE, and JAMES SCOTT being elected and sworn and said that the defendant has not paid the debt to the plaintiff of $200.00 and damages of $4.00. Plaintiff to recover against the defendant his costs.

ROBERT BRADEN vs WILLIAM PUGH - The defendant appeared in court and confessed that he owes the plaintiff $337.30. Plaintiff to recover against the defendant his costs.

JOHN McNARY, assignee vs JOSEPH BRADLEY - The defendant came into court and says he owes the plaintiff $180.92. Plaintiff to recover against the defendant his costs.

ROBERT & WILLIAM DICKSON vs GEORGE W. DENNIS - Debt - This day came the parties by their attorneys and a jury of men, to wit, JOHN DAVIS, JOHN PARK, REUBEN HUNTER, DOILY GRIFFIS, JOHN NORTON, JOEL JOHNSON, BENJAMIN PORTER, LEMUEL BRANDON, LEWIS SHIPP, TRYON GIBSON, ROBERT MOORE, and JAMES SCOTT being elected and sworn and said that the defendant has not paid the debt to the plaintiff of $76.22 and damages of $1.50. Plaintiff to recover against the defendant his costs.

BENJAMIN THOMAS vs JOHN J. HENRY - This day came the parties by their attorneys and a jury of men, to wit, JOHN DAVID, JOHN PARK, REUBEN HUNTER, DOILY GRIFFIS, JOHN NORTON, JOEL JOHNSON, BENJAMIN PORTER, LEMUEL BRANDON, LEWIS SHIPP, ROBERT MOORE, TRYON GIBSON, and JAMES SCOTT being elected and sworn and said that the defendant has not paid the debt to the plaintiff for $90.46¼ and damages of $11.30½. Plaintiff to recover against the defendant his costs.

SPENCER REYNOLDS, assignee vs NATHAN WARREN - This day came the parties by their attorneys and a jury of men, to wit, JOHN DAVIS, JOHN PARK, REUBEN HUNTER, DOILY GRIFFIS, JOHN NORTON, LEWIS SHIPP, JOEL JOHNSON, BENJAMIN PORTER, LEMUEL BRANDON, TRYON GIBSON, ROBERT MOORE, and JAMES SCOTT being elected and sworn and said that the defendant has not paid the debt of the plaintiff of $440.40 and damages of $8.80. Plaintiff to recover against the defendant his costs.

JAMES COALTER vs ABSALUM BEARD - Debt - This day came the parties by their attorneys and a jury of men, to wit, JOHN DAVIS, JOHN PARK, REUBEN HUNTER, DOILY GRIFFIS, JOHN NORTON, JOEL JOHNSON, BENJAMIN PORTER, LEMUEL BRANDON, LEWIS SHIPP, TRYON GIBSON, ROBERT MOORE, and JAMES SCOTT being elected and sworn and said that the defendant has not paid the debt of the plaintiff of $199.75 and damages of $3.00. Plaintiff to recover against the defendant his costs.

NATHAN G. PINSON vs JOHN NORTON - Debt - This day came the parties by their attorneys and a jury of men, to wit, JOHN DAVIS, JOHN PARK, REUBEN HUNTER, DOILY GRIFFIS, BENJAMIN JOHNSON, JOEL JOHNSON, BENJAMIN PPORTER, LEMUEL BRANDON, LEWIS SHIPP, TRYON GIBSON, ROBERT MOORE, and JAMES SCOTT being elected and sworn and said that the defendant has not paid the debt of the plaintiff of $100.00 and damages of $6.90. Plaintiff to recover against the defendant his costs.

JOHN C. McADA vs ABSOLUM BEARD - This day came the parties by their attorneys and a jury of men, to wit, JOHN DAVIS, JOHN PARK, REUBEN HUNTER, DOILY GRIFFIS, JOHN NORTON, JOEL JOHNSON, BENJAMIN PORTER, LEMUEL BRANDON, LEWIS SHIPP, TRYON GIBSON, ROBERT MOORE, and JAMES SCOTT being elected and sworn and said that the defendant did assume upon himself the plaintiff's damages of $41.25 and they came to argue the amount. This cause to return to next court. Plaintiff to recover against the defendant his costs.

The State vs GEORGE CUNNINGHAM - The defendant appeared in court and pleaded not guilty and a jury of men, to wit, GEORGE W. HUNT, DANIEL WAGGONER, WILLIAM

LEDFORD, PETER MOYERS, JOHN BOSTICK, EDWARD McBRIDE, JESSE LAMB, JOSEPH COMMONS, ALEXANDER McLIN, REECE HOWELL, JOHN JACKSON, and ABNER DYER being elected and sworn and said that the defendant is guilty and fined $1.00.

THURSDAY APRIL 27, 1820

Justices present were CHARLES BOYLES, PHILLIP KOONCE and SAMUEL BUCHANAN, Esquires.

HENRY W. NALL vs NIMROD BAILY - The plaintiff by his attorney appeared in court and says he intends no further to prosecute his suit and assume the payment of all costs. The suit is dismissed and the defendant recover against the plaintiff his costs.

THOMAS HILL vs JONATHAN ESTILL - This day came the parties by their attorneys and a jury of men, to wit, BENJAMIN JOHNSON, JOHN DAVIS, JOHN PARK, REUBEN HUNTER, DOILY GRIFFIS, JOHN NORTON, JOEL JOHNSON, LEMUEL BRANDON, LEWIS SHIPP, TRYON GIBSON, ROBERT MOORE, and JAMES SCOTT beint elected and sworn and said that the defendant has not paid the debt of the plaintiff of $300.00 and damages of $13.50. Plaintiff to recover against the defendant his costs.

CHARLES BOYLES vs CHARLES TULY - This day came the parties by their attorneys and a jury of men, to wit, BENJAMIN JOHNSON, JOHN DAVIS, JOHN PARK, REUBEN HUNTER, DOILY GRIFFIS, JOHN NORTON, JOEL JOHNSON, LEMUEL BRANDON, LEWIS SHIPP, TRYON GIBSON, ROBERT MOORE and JAMES SCOTT being elected and sworn and said that the defendant has not paid the debt of $224.18 and damages of $7.35. Plaintiff to recover against the defendant his costs. Report to next court.

JOSEPH GARNER vs WALTER KINNARD - This day came the parties by their attorneys and a jury of men, to wit, BENJAMIN JOHNSON, JOHN DAVIS, JOHN PARK, REUBEN HUNTER, DOILY GRIFFIS, JOHN NORTON, JOEL JOHNSON, LEMUEL BRANDON, LEWIS SHIPP, TRYON GIBSON, ROBERT MOORE, and JAMES SCOTT being elected and sworn and said that the defendant has not paid the debt of $120.84 and damages of $3.45. Plaintiff to recover against the defendant his costs.

GEORGE W. DENNIS vs ROBERT TINKLE - This day came the parties by their attorneys and a jury of men, to wit, BENJAMIN JOHNSON, JOHN DAVIS, JOHN PARK, REUBEN HUNTER, DOILY GRIFFIS, JOHN NORTON, JOEL JOHNSON, LEMUEL BRANDON, LEWIS SHIPP, TRYON GIBSON, ROBERT MOORE, and JAMES SCOTT being elected and sworn and said that the defendant has not paid the debt of $100.00 and damages of $5.00. Plaintiff to recover against the defendant his costs.

ROBERT DICKSON vs ROBERT HODGE - This day came the parties by their attorneys and a jury of men, to wit, BENJAMIN JOHNSON, JOHN DAVIS, JOHN PARK, REUBEN HUNTER, DOILY GRIFFIS, JOHN NORTON, JOEL JOHNSON, LEMUEL BRANDON, LEWIS SHIPP, TRYON GIBSON, ROBERT MOORE, and JAMES SCOTT being elected and sworn and said that the defendant has not paid the debt of $226.00 and damages of $7.91. Plaintiff to recover against the defendant his costs.

ROBERT DICKSON vs ROBERT HODGE - This day came the parties by their attorneys and a jury of men, to wit, BENJAMIN JOHNSON, JOHN DAVIS, JOHN PARK, REUBEN HUNTER, DOILY GRIFFIS, JOHN NORTON, JOEL JOHNSON, LEMUEL BRANDON, LEWIS SHIPP, TRYON GIBSON, ROBERT MOORE and JAMES SCOTT being elected and sworn and said that the defendant has not paid the debt of $305.22½ and damages of $47.32. Plaintiff to recover against the defendant his costs.

GEORGE W. DENNIS vs ROBERT TINKLE - This day came the parties by their attorneys and a jury of men, to wit, BENJAMIN JOHNSON, JOHN DAVIS, JOHN PARK, REUBEN HUNTER, DOILY GRIFFIS, JOHN NORTON, JOEL JOHNSON, LEMUEL BRANDON, LEWIS SHIPP, TRYON GIBSON, ROBERT MOORE, and JAMES SCOTT being elected and sworn and said that the defendant did assume upon himself the debt and damages of $72.60. Plaintiff to recover against the defendant his costs.

CHARLES BOYLES vs JAMES D. EASTIS - Debt - This day came the parties by their attorneys and a jury of men, to wit, BENJAMIN JOHNSON, JOHN DAVIS, JOHN PARK, REUBEN HUNTER, DOILY GRIFFIS, JOHN NORTON, JOEL JOHNSON, LEMUEL BRANDON, LEWIS SHIPP, TRYON GIBSON, ROBERT MOORE and JAMES SCOTT being elected and sworn and said that the defendant has not paid the debt of $111.00 and damages of $2.12½. Plaintiff to recover against the defendant his costs.

JAMES COALTER & CO. vs NATHANIEL B. BUCKINGHAM - This day came the

30

parties by their attorneys and a jury of men, to wit, BENJAMIN JOHNSON, JOHN DAVIS, JOHN PARK, REUBIN HUNTER, DOILY GRIFFIS, JOHN NORTON, JOEL JOHNSON, LEMUEL BRANDON, LEWIS SHIPP, TRYON GIBSON, ROBERT MOORE and JAMES SCOTT being elected and sworn and said that the defendant has not paid the debt of $155.96½and damages of $7.00. Plaintiff to recover against the defendant his costs.

ENOS LACKY vs JOHN & THOMAS HARRISON - Plaintiff appeared in court and says he intends no further to prosecute this suit and assumes the payment of all costs. The suit is dismissed and the defendant recover against the plaintiff his costs.

EDWARD McBRIDE vs JONATHAN FROST - This day came the parties by their attorneys and a jury of men, to wit, BENJAMIN, JOHN DAVIS, JOHN PARK, REUBEN HUNTER, DOILY GRIFFIS, JOHN NORTON, JOEL JOHNSON, LEMUEL BRANDON, LEWIS SHIPP, TRYON GIBSON, ROBERT MOORE and JAMES SCOTT being elected and sworn and said that the defendant is indebted to the plaintiff the sum of $13.06¼. Plaintiff to recover against the defendant his costs.

JOHN BLACKWELL vs MARTIN GRAY - The plaintiff appeared in court and says he wishes no further to prosecute his suit and assumes the payment of all costs. Case dismissed and defendant recover against the plaintiff his costs.

W.H. & D.W. RAGSDALE vs JAMES LAWSON - This day came the parties by their attorneys and a jury of men, to wit, BENJAMIN JOHNSON, JOHN DAVIS, JOHN PARK, REUBEN HUNTER, DOILY GRIFFIS, JOHN NORTON, JOEL JOHNSON, LEMUEL BRANDON, LEWIS SHIPP, TRYON GIBSON, ROBERT MOORE and JAMES SCOTT being elected and sworn and said that the defendant is indebted to the plaintiff the sum of $20.07½ and damages of $2.12½. Plaintiff to recover against the defendant and JOHN MURPHY and SAMUEL BUCHANAN his securities.

CHARLES BEDWELL vs THOMAS ALLY - This cause is continued as an affidavit of the plaintiff. A Commission is awarded to examine and take the deposition of WASHINGTON LOWE to be read at the trial of this cause by giving the defendant ten days notice of time and place of taking the same.

JOSEPH BRADLY vs JOHN KELLY, admr - Plaintiff appeared in court by his attorney and says he intends no further to prosecute this suit and assume the payment of all costs. The case is dismissed and the defendant recover against the plaintiff his costs.

JAMES RODGERS vs JAMES SWEET - Motion to dismiss Certiorari - This day came the parties by their attorneys and an argument to dismiss the certiorari in this case. Court overruled and this cause set for trial at the next term of court.

STEPHEN BEAVERS vs JESSE CONWELL - Motion to dismiss Certiorari - The parties came by their attorneys and on motion to dismiss the certiorari in this cause. Court overruled and this cause set for trial at next court.

SAMUEL RAMSEY vs JESSE CONWELL - Motion to dismiss Certiorari - The parties cane by their attorneys and a motion to dismiss the certiorari in this cause. Motion was overruled and this cause set for hearing at next court.

FRIDAY APRIL 28, 1820

Justices present were CHARLES BOYLES, PHILIP KOONCE, JAMES HOLEMAN, SAMUEL BUCHANAN and WILLIAM KENNON, Esquires.

FLETCHER & McCLELLAN vs JONATHAN ESTILL - Motion for a new trial - This day came the parties by their attorneys on motion for a new trial. Court ordered that the defendant have a new trial at next court.

HIRAM BURKES by his next friend JOHN BURK vs JOSEPH HENDERSON - On motion of the defendant, Commission is awarded him to take the deposition of DRURY ABBOTT and SUSANNAH ABBOTT to be read as evidence in the trial of this cause by giving the plaintiff twenty days notice of time and place of taking the same.

It is ordered by the court that ABRAHAM SUMMERS, WILLIAM MILNER, HENRY KELSO, JOHN MARRS, JOHN GIBSON, JOHN CRAWFORD, ISAAC BROYLES, BENJAMIN WHITAKER, JAMES HOLEMAN, CORNELIUS DARNALL, WILLIAM BEAVERS, GEORGE BLAKEMORE, ELISHA BAGLEY, JOHN PINKERTON, RICHARD FLYNT, JOHN PORTER, JESSE JONES, ABRAHAM ISAACS, ANDREW W. WALKER, JOEL PINSON, FRANCIS PORTERFIELD, WILLIAM GIVINS, JOHN J. WHITAKER, ALLEN MOBLY, GEORGE

CUNNINGHAM, ISAAC HOLEMAN, and ISAAC SEBASTIAN be summoned as Jurors to the next Circuit of the County held on the 3rd Monday in September next and that STERLING C. McLEMORE and JOHN C. TAYLOR Constables to wait on said court and jury.

It is ordered by the court JAMES CLARK, CORDIAL SHUFFIELD, JOHN DAVIS, JOHN PRYOR, GEORGE RENEGAR, WILLIAM RODGERS, REECE HOWELL, JOSHUA DOTSON, ENOCH K. WEATHERS, JESSE DANIEL, TUNSTILL GREGORY, DAVID TWING, WILLIAM BOON, MOSES HARBEN, JOHN GRIDER, JAMES HIGGINS, JAMES GEORGE, WILLIS WARREN, JOSHUA CLARK, JAMES GANT, JOHN PRICE, CHAMPION BLYTHE, KEYS MEEKS, WILLIAM CRAWFORD, JOHN BEATY, and ALEXANDER MEEK be summoned as jurors to the next County Court of this county on the first Tuesday after the third Monday in July next and that REUBEN H. BOON and WILLIAM P. PULLIAM be summoned to wait on said court and jury.

JOHN McNARY vs WILLIAM BLEDSOE - The defendant appeared in court and withdraws his plea of payment and says he owes the plaintiff $200.00 and that the plaintiff has sustained damages of $62.50. Plaintiff to recover against the defendant his costs.

JOHN P. McCONNELL vs THOMAS H. MAY - Motion - On motion of JOHN P. McCONNELL by his attorney against THOMAS H. MAY, the defendant. Court ordered that judgement was rendered against JOHN P. McCONNELL on a note executed by him and THOMAS H. to DAVID HARRIS for $130.06¼ debt and $8.74 costs. On execution has issued against JOHN P. for the amount of judgement and that he has paid the same upon the judgement. GEORGE W. HUNT, DANIEL WAGGONER, THOMAS KERCHEVAL, THOMAS ALLY, CLABORN WHITWORTH, JOHN CAMPBELL, GEORGE W, DENNIS, SPENCER A. PUGH, JOHN BOSTICK, EDWARD MOSS, VANCE GREER, and GEORGE MOSS were impaneled to assertain the fact that said JOHN P. was duly bound as security in said note for THOMAS H. JOHN P. recover against the said THOMAS H. for $139.80¼.

CHARLES BOYLES vs JOHN HANBY - This day came the parties by their attorneys and a jury of men, to wit, GEORGE W. HUNT, DANIEL WAGGONER, THOMAS KERCHEVAL, THOMAS ALLY, CLABORN WHITWORTH, JOHN CAMPBELL, GEORGE W. DENNIS, SPENCER A. PUGH, JOHN BOSTICK, EDWARD MOSS, VANCE GREER, and GEORGE MOSS being elected and sworn and said that the defendant did assume as the plaintiff hath alledged and they assess the plaintiff's damages $136.08. Plaintiff to recover against the defendant his costs.

CHARLES BOYLES vs WILLIAM SNODY - Judicial Attachment - The plaintiff by his attorney appeared in court and the defendant was called to come and replevy (return goods that were unlawfully taken) the property levied on by attachment and plead to the suit failed to do so. Plaintiff recover against the defendant $270.00, the debt and $7.10 damages.

JULY 17, 1820

ISAAC HOLEMAN is appointed overseer of the road in the room of JOHN T. KING resigned and call on the usual hands.

HUGH McCLAIN is appointed overseer of the road from the Cross Roads to the Gum Spring and call on all the hands within two miles of said road.

JOSIAH SMITH is appointed overseer of the road in the room of JOHN R. JOHNSON resigned and call on the usual hands.

DAVID RORAX is appointed overseer of the road in the room of THOMAS ALLY resigned and to call on the usual hands.

JOHN NICHOLS is appointed overseer of the road in the room of ALLEN ELSTON resigned and to call on the usual hands.

It is ordered by the court that RICHARD WELCH be allowed a crowbar and sledge to keep that part of the road in repair that he overseer of.

HOWELL HARRIS is appointed overseer of the road in the room of DAVID P. MUNROE resigned and call on the usual hands.

JAMES RUTHERFORD is released from the payment of the appraised value of a stray horse which he had posted.

WILLIAM LINDSEY is released from the payment of the appraised value of a stray steer which he had posted.

ALEXANDER GRAY, JOEL DODD, JAMES POOL, JESSE DODD, JAMES MULLINS, MALCOM McCOWEN and JAMES STEPHENS are appointed a Jury of View to view the road leading to Athens at JESSE DODD's to go the nearest and best way so as to intersect old road at the State Line and make return to next court.

The Commisioners appointed at last term to lay off years support for the widow and children of ARON PARKS, deceased, made return of the allowance by them made.

JAMES STEPHENS is appointed overseer of the road in the room of JOHN WARREN and call on the usual hands.

Ordered by the court that the Sheriff let out NANCY JOHNSON, one of the poor of this county to the lowest bidder at the Courthouse door.

It is ordered by the court that POLLY INGLE be allowed $28.00 for keeping of LUSINDA GUTHERY, an infant, one year from this time.

On Motion, THOMAS H. BELL is appointed guardian of JOHN BELL, an infant of MATHEW BELL, deceased, who gave bond with DANIEL YOUNG and ROBERT M. WHITE securities for sum of $2000.00.

ABRAHAM SUMMERS is released from the payment of the appraised value of a stray mare which he posted and valued to $70.00.

Ordered by the court that STERLING PARKER be allowed $12.00 for keeping of JOHN PARKER, three months.

Ordered by the court that WILLIAM MILNER and ABRAHAM BARKER, Esquires, be Commissioners to appoint hands to work under JOSHUA WILLIAMS as overseer of the road from the mouth of Mulberry Creek to the Cross Roads.

Ordered by the court that JAMES HOLEMAN, JACOB WAGGONER, Esquires, and JASPER SMITH be appointed Commissioners to settle with SALLY WATS (WATTS), admrx of ROBERT WATS (WATTS), deceased and make return to next court.

Ordered by the court that HENRY HOLEMAN, BRITON PHELPS and JAMES GRANT be appointed to assign to EDWARD BASINGER his distributive estate of GEORGE WAGGONER, deceased, as heir of said intestate and make return to next court.

Ordered by the court that BARBARY OWNEY (ONY) be allowed $28.00 for keeping BENJAMIN GUTHREY, an infant, one year from this time.

WILLIAM LINDSEY is released from the payment of the appraised value of a stray steer which he had posted.

Ordered by the court that JOHN ENOCH and JONATHAN FLOYD, Esquires, be appointed to settle with DANIEL ARCHER, executor of GEORGE ARCHER, deceased, and make return to next court.

On motion, it is ordered by the court that the County Trustee of Lincoln County pay the costs in the suit, the State against FRANCIS TROOP.

WILLIAM HUSBANDS, Deputy Sheriff, made return to court that he had let out NANCY JOHNSON, of the poor of this county, to THOMAS CHAPMAN for $30.00.

It is ordered by the court that CALEB TROOP be allowed $100.00 for keeping of ANN FARMER one year from this time.

The Last Will and Testament of WILLIAM HARRIS, deceased, was exhibited in court to probate whereupon came JAMES TOOL and WILLIAM MIDDLETON, witnesses, and said that he was at the time of sound mind and memory whereupon came HOWELL HARRIS, one of the executors named in said will and gave bond and security. Letters issued accordingly.

An Account of Sale of the estate of DAVID SAWYERS, deceased, was returned into which was ordered to be recorded.

Amount of the sale of the estate of NATHANIEL TATUM and was returned into which was ordered to be recorded.

The Last Will and Testament of JOHN WARREN, deceased, was exhibited in court to

33

probate whereupon came STEPHEN ALEXANDER and JOHN DUKE, witnesses and made oath that heard the said JOHN WARREN and acknowledged the same to be his Last Will and Testament and that he was at the time of sound mind and memory.   HENRY WARREN and WILLIS WARREN, the executors, gave bond and security and letter were issued.

The Commissioners appointed to lay off a support for the widow and children of DAVID SAWYERS, deceased, made return of the allowance by them made.

An inventory of the property of JOHN WARREN, deceased, was returned into court which was ordered to be recorded.

An Indenture of Bargain and Sale from JOHN A. CHAPMAN to BRICE M. GARNER for 126¼ acres of land and ordered to be certified.

An Indenture of Bargain and Sale from GEORGE W. DENNIS to JOHN BOOTH for one town lot and ordered to be certified.

A Deed of Conveyance from JOHN GREER, Sheriff &c to ROBERT H. McEWEN for one town lot was proven by WILLIAM F. MASON and SAMUEL E. GILLILAND and ordered to be certified.

A Bill of Sale from FRANCIS WYATT to WILLIAM DOAK for a negro boy ELIJAH and ordered to be certified.

An Indenture of Bargain and Sale from THOMAS BUCHANAN to JAMES BUCHANAN for 95 acres of land and ordered to be certified.

An Indenture of Bargain and Sale from JAMES A. WHITE to JEREMIAH WALKER for 30 acres of land, proven by JOSEPH CAMPBELL and A. ISAACS and ordered to be certified.

An Indenture of Bargain and Sale from JAMES A. WHITE to JEREMIAH WALKER for 10 acres of land, proven by JOSEPH CAMPBELL and A. ISAACS and ordered to be certified.

An Indenture of Bargain and Sale from WILLIAM PUGH to JOHN PINKERTON for 100 acres of land and ordered to be certified.

An Indenture of Bargain and Sale from JOHN CAMPBELL to REUBEN WASHBURN for 40 acres of land and ordered to be certified.

An Indenture of Bargain and Sale from JAMES BOYD to JACOB V. HOOSER for 40 acres of land and ordered to be certified.

An Indenture of Bargain and Sale from ASA PENNINGTON to JAMES ISBEL for 37½ acres of land, proven by E. BURCHFIELD and JONATHAN KING and ordered to be certified.

An Indenture of Bargain and Sale from WILLIAM POLK by his attorney in fact SAMUEL POLK to POLLY ROBINSON for 70½ acres of land, proven by MICHAEL ROBINSON and JOSEPH CAMPBELL and ordered to be certified.

An Indenture of Bargain and Sale from BRICE M. GARNER and JAMES MARTIN to DRURY BASSHAM for 150 acres of land, proven by GARNER & MARTIN and ordered to be certified.

A mortgage from SAMUEL PORTER to EDWARD TEEL for 480 acres of land in Bedford County, proven by JOSEPH GREER and RICHARD PORTER and ordered to be certified.

An Indenture of Bargain and Sale from HENRY RUTHERFORD to THOMAS BELL for 640 acres of land, proven by JOHN DONALDSON and JAMES BOON and ordered to be certified.

An Indenture of Bargain and Sale from DRURY SMITH to JAMES ALSUP for 10 acres of land, proven by ARON V. BROWN and WILLIAM H. FIELDS and ordered to be certified.

A Deed of Conveyance from POLLARD D. GRAY to JAMES ALSUP for 30 acres of land, proven by RANDOLPH ALSUP and DANIEL ALLSUP and ordered to be certified.

An Indenture of Bargain and Sale from WILLIAM H. MURPHREY by his attorney in fact OLIVER WILLIAMS and JESSE LEDBETTER for 200 acres of land and ordered to be certified.

An Indenture of Bargain and Sale from JOHN A. CHAPMAN to STEPHEN ALEXANDER and JOHN DUKE for 126 acres of land, proven by NATHAN WARREN and DANIEL WARREN and ordered to be certified.

An Indenture of Bargain and Sale from JOSHUA INMAN to JOHN COOPER for 30 acres of land, proven by GEORGE McCOWN and ELIZABETH McCOWN and ordered to be certified.

An Indenture of Bargain and Sale from ROBERT HENRY to HENRY KELSO for 300 acres of land, proven by JAMES BRIGHT and JOHN R. JOHNSON and ordered to be certified.

An Indenture of Bargain and Sale from HENRY KELSO to ROBERT HENRY for 15 acres of land and ordered to be certified.

An Indenture of Bargain and Sale from ALEXANDER BEARD to ROBERT HENRY for 143 acres of land, proven by JOHN R. JOHNSON and ABSOLUM BEARD and ordered to be certified.

An Indenture of Bargain and Sale from JOHN SILVERTOOTH to JOHN DAWDY for 100 acres of land and ordered to be certified.

A transfer of a plat and certificate from ISAIAH HEWETT to GRIFFITH LENARD, proven by THOMAS GIBSON and GEORGE L. LENARD and ordered to be certified.

An Indenture of Bargain and Sale from JAMES STALLARD to ALEXANDER DUKE for 70 acres of land, proven by DAVID McCARMACK and WILLIAM ROGERS and ordered to be certified.

An Indenture of Bargain and Sale from WILLIAM H. MURFREE by his attorney in fact OLIVER WILLIAMS to JAMES LEDBETTER for 640 acres of land and ordered to be certified.

An Indenture of Bargain and Sale from CHARLES WAKEFIELD to JOHN DOBBINS for 50 acres of land, proven by ALEXANDER DOBBINS and JOHN HARDING and ordered to be certified.

An Indenture of Bargain and Sale from SAMUEL DOBBINS to JOHN DOBBINS for 385 acres of land and ordered to be certified.

An Indenture of Bargain and Sale from SAMUEL DOBBINS to SAMUEL HALL for 320 acres of land and ordered to be certified.

An Indenture of Bargain and Sale from MOSES FERGUSON to JOHN TODD for 142½ acres of land, proven by JOSEPH DEAN and WILLIAM T. TODD and ordered to be certified.

A Bill of Sale from GEORGE TITUS to AARON WELLS for a negro boy ISHAM and ordered to be certified.

An Indenture of Bargain and Sale from MALCUM McCOWN to MICHAEL ROBINSON for 15 acres of land and ordered to be certified.

TUESDAY JULY 18, 1820

Justices present were JAMES HOLEMAN, SAMUEL BUCHANAN and WILLIAM KENNON, Esquires.

ROBERT DICKSON vs ROBERT HODGE - This day came the parties by their attorneys and a jury of men, to wit, BENJAMIN JOHNSON, JOHN DAVIS, JOHN PARKS, REUBEN HUNTER, DOILY GRIFFIS, JOHN NORTON, JOEL JOHNSON, LEMUEL BRANDON, LEWIS SHIPP, TRYON GIBSON, ROBERT MOORE and JAMES SCOTT being elected and sworn and said that the defendant has not paid the debt of $226.00 and damages of $7.91. Plaintiff to recover against the defendant his costs.

ROBERT DICKSON vs ROBERT HODGE - This day came the parties by their attorneys and a jury of men, to wit, BENJAMIN JOHNSON, JOHN DAVIS, JOHN PARKS, REUBEN HUNTER, DOILY GRIFFIS, JOHN NORTON, JOEL JOHNSON, LEMUEL BRANDON, LEWIS SHIPP, TRYON GIBSON, ROBERT MOORE and JAMES SCOTT being elected and sworn and said that the defendant has not paid the debt of $305.22½ and damages of $47.32. Plaintiff to recover against the defendant his costs.

GEORGE W. DENNIS vs ROBERT TINKLE - This day came the parties by their attorneys and a jury of men, to wit, BENJAMIN JOHNSON, JOHN DAVIS, JOHN PARK, REUBEN HUNTER, DOILY GRIFFIS, JOHN NORTON, JOEL JOHNSON, LEMUEL BRANDON, LEWIS SHIPP, TRYON GIBSON, ROBERT MOORE, and JAMES SCOTT being elected and sworn and said that the defendant has not paid the debt of $226.00 and damages of $7.91. Plaintiff to recover against the defendant his costs.

GEORGE W. DENNIS vs ROBERT TINKLE - This day came the parties by their attorneys and a jury of men, to wit, BENJAMIN JOHNSON, JOHN DAVIS, JOHN PARK, REUBEN HUNTER, DOILY GRIFFIS, JOHN NORTON, JOEL JOHNSON, LEMUEL BRANDON, LEWIS SHIPP, TRYON GIBSON, ROBERT MOORE, and JAMES SCOTT being elected and sworn and said that the defendant did assume upon himself as charged and the damages of the plaintiff amounted to $72.60. Plaintiff to recover against the defendant his costs.

CHARLES BOYLES vs JAMES D. EASTIS - Debt - This day came the parties by their attorneys and a jury of men, to wit, BENJAMIN JOHNSON, JOHN DAVIS, JOHN PARK, REUBEN HUNTER, DOILY GRIFFIS, JOHN NORTON, JOEL JOHNSON, LEMUEL BRANDON, LEWIS SHIPP, TRYON GIBSON, ROBERT MOORE, and JAMES SCOTT being elected and sworn and said that the defendant has not paid his debt of $111.00 and damages of $2.12½. Plaintiff to recover against the defendant his costs.

JAMES COALTER & Co. vs NATHANIEL B. BUCKINGHAM - This day came the parties and a jury of men, to wit, BENJAMIN JOHNSON, JOHN DAVIS, JOHN PARK, REUBEN HUNTER, DOILY GRIFFIS, JOHN NORTON, JOEL JOHNSON, LEMUEL BRANDON, LEWIS SHIPP, TRYON GIBSON, ROBERT MOORE, and JAMES SCOTT being elected and sworn and said that the defendant has not paid his debt of $155.96½ and damages of $7.00. Plaintiff to recover against the defendant his costs. Appeal made to return to next court.

ENOS LACKY vs JOHN & THOMAS HARRISON - The plaintiff appeared in court and says he intends no further to prosecute this case and assumes the payment of all costs. Suit to be dismissed and the defendant recover against the plaintiff his costs.

EDWARD McBRIDE vs JONATHAN FROST - This day came the parties by their attorneys and a jury of men, to wit, BENJAMIN JOHNSON, JOHN DAVIS, JOHN PARK, REUBEN HUNTER, DOILY GRIFFIS, JOHN NORTON, JOEL JOHNSON, LEMUEL BRANDON, LEWIS SHIPP, TRYON GIBSON, ROBERT MOORE, and JAMES SCOTT being elected and sworn and said that the defendant is indebted to the plaintiff $13.06¼. Plaintiff to recover against the defendant his costs.

JOHN BLACKWELL vs MARTIN GRAY - The plaintiff appeared in court and says he wishes no further to prosecute his suit and assumes the payment of all costs. This suit is dismissed and the defendant recover against the plaintiff his costs.

W.H & D.W. RAGSDALE vs JAMES LAWSON - This day came the parties by their attorneys and a jury of men, to wit, BENJAMIN JOHNSON, JOHN DAVIS, JOHN PARK, REUBEN HUNTER, DOILY GRIFFIS, JOHN NORTON, JOEL JOHNSON, LEMUEL BRANDON, LEWIS SHIPP, TRYON GIBSON, ROBERT MOORE, and JAMES SCOTT being elected and sworn and said that the defendant is indebted to the plaintiff for $20.07½ and damages of $2.12¼. Plaintiff to recover against the defendant his costs. JOHN MURPHY and SAMUEL BUCHANAN, securities.

CHARLES BEDWELL vs THOMAS ALLY - This cause is continued on an affidavit of the plaintiff and by consent of the parties by their attorneys, a Commission is awarded the plaintiff to examine and take the deposition of WASHINGTON LOWE to be read at the trial of this cause by giving the defendant ten days notice of time and place of taking the same.

JOSEPH BRADLY vs JOHN KELLY - This day the (plaintiff) by his attorney appeared in court and says he intends no further to prosecute his suit and assumes the payment of all costs. Defendant to recover against the plaintiff his costs.

JAMES RODGERS vs JAMES SWEETE - Motion - The parties by their attorneys and on motion to dismiss this cause, the court overruled and this cause set for trial at next term of court.

STEPHEN BEAVERS vs JESSE CONWELL - Motion to Dismiss - This day came the partied by their attorneys and on motion to dismiss this cause and the court overruled and this cause set for trial at next court.

SAMUEL RAMSEY vs JESSE CONWELL - Motion to Dismiss - This day came the parties by their attorneys and on motion to dismiss this cause and the court overruled and this cause set for hearing at next term of court.

36

Justices present were CHARLES BOYLES, PHILIP KOONCE, JAMES HOLEMAN, SAMUEL BUCHANAN and WILLIAM KENNON, Esquires.

FLETCHER & McCLELLAN vs JONATHAN ESTILL - Motion for a New Trial - This day came the parties by their attorneys and on motion for a new trial and court ordered that a new trial in this cause at the next term of this court.

HIRAM BURKES by his next friend JOHN BURK vs JOSEPH HENDERSON. On motion of the defendant, Commission is awarede him to take the deposition of DRURY ABBOTT and SUSANNAH ABBOTT to be read as evidence in the trial of this cause by giving the plaintiff twenty days notice of time and place of taking the same.

It is ordered by the court that ABRAHAM SUMMERS, WILLIAM MILNER, HENRY KELSO, JOHN MARRS, JOHN GIBSON, JOHN CRAWFORD, ISAAC BROYLES, BENJAMIN WHITAKER, JAMES HOLEMAN, CORNELIUS DARNOLD, WILLIAM BEAVERS, GEORGE BLAKEMORE, ELISHA BAGLEY, JOHN PINKERTON, RICHARD FLYNT, JOHN PORTER, JESSE JONES, ABRAHAM ISAACS, ANDREW W. WALKER, JOEL PINSON, FRANCIS PORTERFIELD, WILLIAM GIVENS, JOHN J. WHITAKER, ALLEN MOBLY, GEORGE CUNNINGHAM, ISAAC HOLEMAN and ISAAC SEBASTIAN be summoned as jurors to the next circuit of the county held the 3rd Monday in September next and that STERLING C. McLEMORE and JOHN C. TAYLOR, Constables to wait on said Court and Jury.

It is ordered by the court that JAMES CLARK, CORDIAL SHUFFIELD, JOHN DAVIS, JOHN PRYOR, GEORGE RENEGER, WILLIAM RODGERS, REECE HOWELL, JOSHUA DOTSON, ENOCK K. WEATHERS, JESSE DANIEL, TUNSTAL GREGORY, DAVID TWING, WILLIAM BOON, MOSES HARDIN, JOHN GUIDEN, JAMES HIGGINS, JAMES GEORGE, WILLIS WARREN, JOSHUA CLARK, JAMES GANT, JOHN PRICE, CHAMPION BLYTH, KEYS MEEK, WILLIAM CRAWFORD, JOHN BEATY, and ALEXANDER MEEK be summoned as jurors to the next County Court of this county on the first Tuesday after the third Monday in July next and that REUBEN H. BOON and WILLIAM P. PULLIAM be summoned to wait on said Court and Jury.

JOHN McNARY vs WILLIAM BLEDSOE - The defendant appeared in court and withdraws his plea of payment and confesses that he owes the plaintiff $200.00 and damages of $62.50. Plaintiff to recover against the defendant his costs.

JOHN P. McCONNELL vs THOMAS H. MAY - On motion of JOHN P. McCONNELL by his attorney against THOMAS H. MAY the defendant and it appearing to the court that judgement was rendered against the said JOHN P. on a note executed by him and the said THOMAS H. to DAVID HARRIS for $131.06¼ debt and $8.74 costs. It appearing to the court that execution has issued againsy JOHN P. for the amount of said judgement and that he has paid and satisfied the same and it not appearing from the face of said note nor upon the said judgement that the said JOHN P. executed said note as security only for the said THOMAS H. the following persons, to wit, GEORGE W. HUNT, DANIEL WAGGONER, THOMAS KERCHEVAL, THOMAS ALLY, CLABORN WHITWORTH, JOHN CAMPBELL, GEORGE W. DENNIS, SPENCER A. PUGH, JOHN BOSTICK, EDWARD MOSS, VANCE GREER, and GEORGE MOSS are impaneled to assertain the fact who upon their oaths do say that JOHN P. was only bound as security in said note for THOMAS H. It is considered by the court that JOHN P. recover against THOMAS H. the sum of $139.80¼.

CHARLES BOYLES vs JOHN HANBY - This day came the parties by their attorneys and a jury of men, to wit, GEORGW W. HUNT, DANIEL WAGGONER, THOMAS KERCHEVAL, THOMAS ALLY, CLABORN WHITWORTH, JOHN CAMPBELL, GEORGE W. DENNIS, SPENCER A. PUGH, JOHN BOSTICK, EDWARD MOSS, VANCE GREER, and GEORGE MOSS being elected and sworn and said that the defendant did assume upon himself in manner and form as the plaintiff hath alledged and they assess the plaintiff's damages as $136.08. Plaintiff to recover against the defendant his costs.

CHARLES BOYLES vs WILLIAM SNODY - Judicial Attachment - The plaintiff by his attorney came into court and the defendant being called to come and replevy the property levied on by attachment and plead to the suit, failed to do so. It is considered by the court that the plaintiff recover against the defendant $270.00 debt and $7.10 damages, his costs.

JULY 18, 1820

ISAAC HOLEMAN is appointed overseer of the road in the room of JOHN T. KING resigned and call on the usual hands.

HUGH McCLAIN is appointed overseer of the rood from the Cross Roads to the Gum Spring and call on all the hands within two miles of said road.

JOSIAH SMITH is appointed overseer of the road in the room of JOHN R. JOHNSON resigned and to call on the usual hands.

DAVID RORAX is appointed overseer of the road in the room of THOMAS ALLY resigned and to call on the usual hands.

JOHN NICHOLS is appointed overseer of the road in the room of ALLEN ELSTON resigned and to call on the usual hands.

It is ordered by the court that RICHARD WELCH be allowed a crowbar and sledge to keep that part of the road in repair that he is overseer of.

HOWELL HARRIS is appointed overseer of the road in the room of DANIEL P. MUNROE resigned and call on the usual hands.

JAMES RUTHERFORD is released from the payment of the appraised value of a stray horse which he had posted.

WILLIAM LINDSEY is released from the payment of the appraised value of a stray steer which he had posted.

ALEXANDER GRAY, JOEL DODD, JAMES POOL, JESSE DODD, JAMES MULLINS, MALCOM McCOWEN, and JAMES STEPHENS are appointed a Jury of View to view the road leading to Athens at JESSE DODDS to go the nearest and best way so as to interest old road at the State Line and make return to next court.

The Commissioners appointed at last term to lay off one years support for the widow and children of ARON PARKS, deceased, made return of the allowance by them made.

JAMES STEPHENS is appointed overseer of the road in the room of JOHN WARREN and to call on the usual hands.

Ordered by the court that the Sheriff let out NANCY JOHNSON, one of the poor of this county, to the lowest bidder at the Courthouse door.

It is ordered by the court that POLLY INGLE be allowed $28.00 for keeping of LUCINDA GUTHERY, an infant, one year from this time.

On motion, THOMAS H. BELL is appointed guardian of JOHN BELL, and infant of MATHEW BELL, deceased, who gave bond with DANIEL YOUNG and ROBERT M. WHITE, securities, in sum of $2000.00.

ABRAHAM SUMMERS is released from the payment of the appraised value of a stray mare which he posted and valued to $70.00.

Ordered by the court that STERLING PARKER be allowed $12.00 for keeping of JOHN PARKER three months.

Ordered by the court that WILLIAM MILNER and ABRAHAM BARKER be Commissioners to appoint the hands to work under JOSHUA WILLIAMS as overseer of the road from the mouth of Mulberry Creek to the Cross Roads.

Ordered by the court that JAMES HOLEMAN, JACOB WAGGONER, Esquires, and JASPER SMITH be appointed Commissioners to settle with SALLY WATS (WATTS) admrx of ROBERT WATS (WATTS) and make return to next court.

Ordered by the court that HARDY HOLEMAN, BRETON PHELPS and JAMES GRANT be appointed to assign to EDW. BASINGER his distributive estate of GEORGE WAGGONER, deceased, as heir of said intestate and make return to next court.

Ordered by the court that BARBARY OWNEY be allowed $28.00 for keeping of BENJAMIN GUTHERY, an infant, one year from this time.

WILLIAM LINDSEY is released from the payment of the appraised value of a stray steer which he had posted.

Ordered by the court that ENOCK & JONATHAN FLOYD, Esquires, be appointed to

Ordered by the court that ENOCK & JONATHAN FLOYD, Esquires, be appointed to settle with DANIEL ARCHER, executor of GEORGE ARCHER, deceased, and make return to next court.

On motion, it is considered by the court that the County Trustee of Lincoln County pay the costs in the suit, the State against FRANCIS TROOP.

WILLIAM HUSBANDS, Deputy Sheriff, made return to court that he had let out NANCY JOHNSON, one of the poor of this county, to THOMAS CHAPMAN for $30.00.

It is ordered by the court that CALEB TROOP be allowed $100.00 for keeping of ANN FARMER one year from this time.

The Last Will and Testament of WILLIAM HARRIS, deceased, was exhibited in court to probate whereupon came JAMES TOOL and WILLIAM MIDDLETON, witnesses, to make oath that they acknowledged the same to be his Last Will and Testament and that he was of sound mind and memory whereupon came HOWELL HARRIS one of the executors named and gave bond and security. Letters issued accordingly.

An account of the sale of the estate of DAVID SAWYERS, deceased, was returned into court and ordered to be recorded.

An amount of the sale of the estate of NATHANIEL TATUM was returned into court and ordered to be recorded.

The Last Will and Testament of JOHN WARREN, deceased, was exhibited in court to probate whereupon came STEPHEN ALEXANDER and JOHN DUKE, witnesses, and made oath that JOHN WARREN was at the time of sound mind and memory. HENRY WARREN and WILLIS WARREN, executors named in said will and letters issued accordingly.

The Commissioners appointed to lay off a support for the widow and children of DAVID SAWYERS, deceased, made return of the allowance by them made.

An inventory of the property of JOHN WARREN, deceased, was returned into court and ordered to be recorded.

An Indenture of Bargain and Sale from JOHN A. CHAPMAN to BRICE M. GARNER for 126¼ acres of land and ordered to be certified.

An Indenture of Bargain and Sale from GEORGE W. DENNIS to JOHN BOOTH for one town lot and ordered to be certified.

A Deed of Conveyance from JOHN GREER, Sheriff &c to ROBERT H. McEWEN for one town lot, proven by WILLIAM F. MASON and SAMUEL E. GILLILAND and ordered to be certified.

A Bill of Sale from FRANCIS WYATT to WILLIAM DOAK for a negro boy ELIJAH and ordered to be certified.

An Indenture of Bargain and Sale from THOMAS BUCHANAN to JAMES BUCHANAN for 95 acres of land and ordered to be certified.

An Indenture of Bargain and Sale from JAMES A. WHITE to JEREMIAH WALKER for 30 acres of land, proven by JOSEPH CAMPBELL and A. ISAACS and ordered to be certified.

An Indenture of Bargain and Sale from JAMES A. WHITE to JEREMIAH WALKER for 10 acres of land, proven by JOSEPH CAMPBELL and A. ISAACS and ordered to be certified.

An Indenture of Bargain and Sale from WILLIAM PUGH to JOHN PINKERTON for 100 acres of land and ordered to be certified.

An Indenture of Bargain and Sale from JOHN CAMPBELL to REUBEN WASHBURN for 40 acres of land and ordered to be certified.

An Indenture of Bargain and Sale from JAMES BOYD to JACOB V. HOOSER for 40 acres of land and ordered to be certified.

An Indenture of Bargain and Sale from ASA PENNINGTON to JAMES ISBEL for 37½ acres of land, proven by E. BURCHFIELD and JONATHAN KING and ordered to be certified.

An Indenture of Bargain and Sale from WILLIAM POLK by his attorney in fact SAMUEL POLK to POLLY ROBINSON for 70½ acres of land, proven by MICHAEL ROBINSON and JOS. CAMPBELL and ordered to be certified.

An Indenture of Bargain and Sale from BRICE M. GARNER & JAMES MARTIN to DRURY BASSHAM for 150 acres of land and ordered to be certified.

A Mortgage from SAMUEL PORTER to EDWARD TEEL for 480 acres of land in Bedford County, proven by JOSEPH GREER and RICHARD PORTER and ordered to be certified.

An Indenture of Bargain and Sale from HENRY RUTHERFORD to THOMAS BELL for 640 acres of land, proven by JOHN DONALDSON and JAMES BOON and ordered to be certified.

An Indenture of Bargain and Sale from DRURY SMITH to JAMES ALSUP for 10 acres of land, proven by ARON V. BROWN and WILLIAM H. FIELDS and ordered to be certified.

A Deed of Conveyance from POLLARD GRAY to JAMES ALSUP for 30 acres of land, proven by RANDOLPH ALSUP and DANIEL ALLSUP and ordered to be certified.

An Indenture of Bargain and Sale from WILLIAM H. MURPHREY by his attorney in fact OLIVER WILLIAMS to JESSE LEDBETTER for 200 acres of land and ordered to be certified.

An Indenture of Bargain and Sale from WILLIAM H. MURPHREY by his attorney in fact OLIVER WILLIAMS to THOMAS MIERS for 440 acres of land and ordered to be certified.

An Indenture of Bargain and Sale from JOHN A. CHAPMAN to STEPHEN ALEXANDER and JOHN DUKE for 126 acres of land, proven by NATHAN WARREN and DANIEL WARREN and ordered to be certified.

An Indenture of Bargain and Sale from ROBERT HENRY to HENRY KELSO for 300 acres of land, proven by JAMES BRIGHT and JOHN R. JOHNSON and ordered to be certified.

An Indenture of Bargain and Sale from HENRY KELSO to ROBERT HENRY for 15 acres of land and ordered to be certified.

An Indenture of Bargain and Sale from ALEXANDER BEARD to ROBERT HENRY for 143 acres of land, proven by JOHN R. JOHNSON and ABSALUM BEARD and ordered to be certified.

The transfer of a plat and certificate from ISAIAH HUNT to GRIFFITH LENARD, proven by THOMAS GIBSON and GEORGE L. LENARD and ordered to be certified.

An Indenture of Bargain and Sale from JAMES STALLARD to ALEXANDER DUKE for 70 acres of land, proven by DAVID McCARMACK and WILLIAM ROGERS and ordered to be certified.

An Indenture of Bargain and Sale from WILLIAM H. MURPHREE by his attorney in fact OLIVER WILLIAMS to JAMES LEDBETTER for 640 acres of land and ordered to be certified.

An Indenture of Bargain and Sale from CHARLES WAKEFIELD to JOHN DOBBINS for 50 acres of land, proven by ALEXANDER DOBBINS and JOHN HARDING and ordered to be certified.

An Indenture of Bargain and Sale from SAMUEL DOBBINS to JOHN DOBBINS for 385 acres and ordered to be certified.

An Indenture of Bargain and Sale from SAMUEL DOBBINS to SAMUEL HALL for 320 acres of land and ordered to be certified.

An Indenture of Bargain and Sale from MOSES FERGUSON to JOHN TODD for 142½ acres of land, proven by JOSEPH DEAN and WILLIAM T. TODD and ordered to be certified.

A Bill of Sale from GEORGE TITUS to AARON WELLS for a negro boy ISHAM and ordered to be certified.

An Indenture of Bargain and Sale from MALCOM McCOWEN to MICHAEL ROBINSON for 15 acres of land and ordered to be certified.

TUESDAY JULY 18, 1820

Justices present were JAMES HOLEMAN, SAMUEL BUCHANAN and WILLIAM KENNON, Esquires.

The Sheriff made return to court the following venire to serve as Grand Jurors and Petit Jurors to this term, to wit, JAMES CLARK, CORDIAL SHUFFIELD, JOHN DAVIS, JOHN PRIOR, GEORGE RENEGER, WILLIAM ROGERS, REECE HOWELL, JOSHUA DODSON, ENOCK K. WEATHERS, JESSE DANIEL, TUNSTAL GREGORY, DAVID THWING, WILLIAM BOON, MOSES HARDING, JOHN GUIDER, JAMES HIGGINS, JAMES GEORGE, WILLIS WARREN, JOSHUA CHURCH, JAMES GANT, JOHN PRICE, CHAMPION BLYTHE, KEYS MEEK, WILLIAM CRAWFORD, JOHN BEATY and ALEXANDER MEEK of whom were elected to serve as Grand Jurors, to wit, JAMES HIGGINS, JOSHUA CHURCH, WILLIAM BOON, JOSHUA DODSON, ENOCK K. WITHERS, JOHN BEATY, JOHN DAVIS, CHAMPION BLYTH, ALEXANDER MEEK, JAMES GEORGE, WILLIAM ROGERS, GEORGE RENEGER and JOHN PRIOR being elected impaneled and sworn and often receiving the charge from the solicitor return to consider of their presentments.

WILLIAM P. PULLIAM a Constable sworn to wait on the Grand Jurors.

REECE HOWELL vs JACOB GROSS - The plaintiff appeared in court and said he intends no further to prosecute this suit and the defendant assumed the payment of all costs. Suit be dismissed and the plaintiff recover against the defendant his costs.

EDWARD TEAL vs WILLIAM SNODDY - The plaintiff appeared in court and says he intends no further to prosecute this suit and assumes the payment of all costs. Suit be dismissed and the defendant recover against the plaintiff his costs.

EDWARD TEAL vs WILLIAM SNODDY - The plaintiff appeared in court and says he wishes no further to prosecute this suit and assumes the payment of all costs. The suit to be dismissed and the defendant recover against the plaintiff his costs.

MARTIN PUGH vs SAMUEL PENNINGTON - The plaintiff appeared in court and says he intends no further to prosecute this suit and assumes the payment of all costs. This suit to be dismissed.

The Grand Jury returned to court and brought a Bill of Indictment, the State against EZEKIEL VICKERS and WILLIAM VICKERS a true bill and again return to consider further presentments.

The Grand Jury again returned to court and brought a Bill of Indictment, the State against JOHN VICKERS a true bill and again returned to consider for further presentments.

The Grand Jury again returned to court with a Bill of Indictment, the State against WILICE(?) GARRETT a true bill and again returned to consider for further presentments.

The Grand Jury again returned to court with a Bill of Indictment, the State against WILLIAM PORCH a true bill and again returned to consider for further presentments.

The Grand Jury again returned to court with a Bill of Indictment, the State against AUGUSTINE YEAGER a true bill and again returned to consider for further presentments.

It is ordered by the court that NELSON YARBOROUGH be released from the payment of the appraised value of a stray mare which he posted and appraised to $45.00.

An Indenture of Bargain and Sale from CHARLES FITZHUGH to WILSON C. SELMAN(?) for one lot in Alexandria and ordered to be certified.

The Grand Jury again returned to court and brought with them a Bill of Indictment, the State against BENJAMIN MERRELL a true bill and again returned to consider for further presentments.

JAMES F. JOHNSON vs PRESLEY DOLLINS - The plaintiff by his attorney and says he wishes no further to prosecute this suit and the defendant assumes the payment of all costs. This case to be dismissed and the plaintiff recover against the defendant his costs.

JOHN BRYANT vs AMBROSE PEARCE - On motion of the defendant by his attorney, it is ordered that the plaintiff appear on 2nd day of next court and give other and better

41

security for prosecution of this cause or it will be dismissed.

The transfer of a plat and certificate of survey from WILLIAM OGILVIE to WILLIAM FARRAR and ordered to be certified.

An Indenture of Bargain and Sale from THOMAS HOPKINS to POLLY GRAY for 100 acres of land, proven by ELI GARRETT and JAMES BRIGHT and ordered to be certified.

An Indenture of Bargain and Sale from BRICE M. GARNER and JAMES MARTIN to ANDREW CLARK for 150 acres of land and ordered to be certified.

An Indenture of Bargain and Sale from BRICE M. GARNER, JAMES MARTIN and JACOB SCOTT to JOHN COWAN and SILAS McCLELLAND for 526 acres of land and ordered to be certified.

An Indenture of Bargain and Sale from BRICE M. GARNER and JAMES MARTIN to SAMUEL DAVIS for 7 acres of land and ordered to be certified.

An Indenture of Bargain and Sale from JOHN M. ROBINSON to PARK GIBSON for 94 acres of land, proven by OLIVER WILLIAMS and JOHN GIBSON and ordered to be certified.

An Indenture of Bargain and Sale from TRAVIS CARTER to JOHN DURLEY for 150 acres of land and ordered to be certified.

An Indenture of Bargain and Sale from TRAVIS CARTER to JOHN DURLEY for 25 acres of land and ordered to be certified.

An Indenture of Bargain and Sale from WILLIAM BROWN to WILLIAM HAMBLETON for 100 acres of land and ordered to be certified.

An Indenture of Bargain and Sale from JAMES HARPER to ABSALUM DAVIS for 14 3/4 acres of land and ordered to be certified.

A Bill of Sale from STEPHEN CHITWOOD to THOMAS GIBSON for a negro boy named NELSON and ordered to be certified.

An Indenture of Bargain and Sale from CHRISTINA MATTS to WILLIAM REECE for 11 acres of land, proven by JACK H. LEFTWICH and HENRY MORGAN and ordered to be certified.

MATHEW McGEHEE is appointed overseer of the road in the room of DANIEL BENSON resigned.

JOSHUA GUNTER is appointed ovewrseer of the road in the room of REPS O. CHILDRESS resigned.

BENJAMIN ARRINGTON is appointed overseer of the road in the room of JAMES McGEHEE and call on the usual hands.

PHILIP KOONCE, JUNIOR, is appointed overseer of the road in the room of MICAJAH STONE resigned.

ALLEN SCRUGGS vs JOHN TOMERSON - This cause by the consent of the parties is referred to the arbitrament of THOMAS McGEHEE, DRURY M. ALLEN, ROBERT BRANDESFORD, JAMES MOOR, ROBERT FLETCHER, and JOHN PRIOR, arbitrators, chosen by said parties who is a ward is to be returned to the next term of this court and made the judgement of said court.

ANDREW DYSET (DYSART) vs RICHARD HOOPER - BENJAMIN SIMMONS a garnishee being sworn: First question - Are you indebted to RICHARD HOOPER, anything. Answer - I did at the time of serving this garnishee and do yet owe the firm of HOOPER & FARRAR to the amount of $8.00 or $10.00, it was on an open account of the debt is but am certain it is not more than $12.50. 2nd question - Do you know what effects or debts of the defendant or in the hands of any and what person. Answer - I do not know of any.

THOMAS HOLLAND, a garnishee, in the above cause sworn. Question first - Are you indebted to RICHARD HOOPER and what effects of his are in your hands or was at the time of serving the garnishee. Answer - I am indebted to said HOOPER for a note given to him for $19.13 3/4 which is due and I have been sued on said note and took the stay which stay is not yet expired.

42

JAMES LAND, a garnishee in the above cayse, sworn. First question - Are you indebted to RICHARD HOOPER and what effects of the defendant have you in your hands and had at the time of serving the garnishee. Answer - I am indebted to said HOOPER in sum of $13.06¼ it being a balance hue him on note executed to said defendant by me, due about 1st January 1820. I am also indebted to a WILLIAM FARRAR or HOOPER & FARRAR which I do not know the amount of $25.00 balance of a note I executed to him or them for goods due in January 1820 sometime, which note I understand has been transferred to DOCTOR WEBB but do not know whether or not.

ROBERT BROOKS, a garnishee in the above cause, being sworn. First question - Are you indebted to RICHARD HOOPER and what effects of his are in your hands and was at the time of serving the garnishee. Answer - I think I owe the firm of FARRAR & HOOPER about $16.94½ in open account, the goods when purchased between August 1819 and May or June 1820.

JAMES CLARK vs ABEL BE--- - The plaintiff by his attorney appeared in court and says he wishes no further to prosecute this (suit). The defendant assumes the payment of all costs. It is ordered by the court that this suit be dismissed and the plaintiff recover against the defendant his costs.

WEDNESDAY JULY 19, 1820

Justices present were SAMUEL BUCHANAN, JAMES HOLEMAN and PHILLIP KOONCE, Esquires.

An Indenture of Bargain and Sale from JAMES BRIGHT to WILLIAM PURNELL for one town lot No. 50 in upper Elkton and ordered to be certified.

An Indenture of Bargain and Sale from JAMES BRIGHT to NICHOLAS FAIN, SAMUEL FAIN and ROBERT LOCKHART for part of Lot No. 34 in upper Elkton and ordered to be certified.

An Indenture of Bargain and Sale from JAMES BRIGHT to JOHN H. KEMP, JOHN BASS and BENJAMIN CARTER for part of Lot No. 34 in upper Elkton and ordered to be certified.

An Indenture of bargain and Sale from JAMES BRIGHT to JOHN MENEFEE for 112 acres of land in Giles County and ordered to be certified.

The transfer of a plat and certificate for 6 3/4 acres of land in this county from THOMAS BRIGHT to WILLIAM S. MOFFET, proven by JAMES BRIGHT, attorney in fact for said THOMAS BRIGHT, and was ordered to be certified.

JOHN BUCHANAN vs CORNELIUS DARNOLD - Debt - The defendant appeared in court and confessed that he owes the plaintiff $472.00 and damages of $26.94. Court ordered the plaintiff recover against the defendant his costs.

State of Tennessee & HIRAM WHITE vs NOBLE PENLAND - The plaintiff, HIRAM WHITE, appeared in court and says he wishes no further to prosecute this suit and the defendant assumes the payment of the costs. Court ordered that the suit be dismissed and the plaintiff recover against the defendant his costs.

An Indenture of Bargain and Sale from KELLY STEGALL to CHARLES BOYLES for 90 acres of land and ordered to be certified.

An Indenture of Bargain and Sale from MARTIN HOLBERT to JOHN PRYOR for 105 acres and ordered to be certified.

A Bill of Sale from EBENEZER McEWEN to SAMUEL E. GILLILAND for a negro boy named JACK and ordered to be certified.

S. & J.N. PORTER vs T. & GRIFFITH LENARD - The defendants appeared in court and withdraws their plea and confessed that they owe the plaintiff $154.00 and damages of $3.53. The plaintiff to recover against the defendant his costs.

On petition of JOEL PINSON, one of the securities of JESSE HOLBERT and JOHN W. SMITH, admrs of JOEL (HALBERT), deceased. Court ordered JESSE HOLBERT appear at next court and give security or surrender according to Act of Assembly.

An Indenture of Bargain and Sale from JOSEPH DEAN to JOHN B. TODD for 40 acres of land and ordered to be certified.

An Indenture of Bargain and Sale from ROBERT KERR to JOHN PUTMAN for 16 acres of land, proven by JOHN GRAY and ALEXANDER GRAY and ordered to be certified.

An Indenture of Bargain and Sale from STEPHEN LOYD to THOMAS PULLY for 8 acres of land and ordered to be certified.

SAMUEL PAINTER vs ROBERT DICKSON - This day came the parties by their attorneys and a jury of men, to wit, DAVID THWING, WILLIS WARREN, REECE HOWELL, KEYS MEEK, JESSE DANIEL, JOHN GUYDER, CORDIAL SHUFFIELD, JAMES GANT, JOHN PRICE, WILLIAM CRAWFORD, TUNSTAL GREGORY, and WILLIAM LEDFORD being elected and sworn and said that the defendant is guilty as charged and they assess the plaintiff's damages to $118.55. Court orders that the plaintiff recover against the defendant his costs. Defendant prays an appeal to the next Circuit Court and having given bond and security and filed his reason according to law.

JOHNSON WELLBORN vs KELLY STEGALL - Attachment - The defendant moved the court that the Judgement by Default at last court may be set aside and he be permitted to replevy the proper and give security. It is ordered by the court that the defendant be permitted to do so whereupon the defendant gave CHARLES BOYLES for security.

THURSDAY JULY 20, 1820

Justices present were JAMES HOLEMAN, CHARLES BOYLES and SAMUEL BUCHANAN, Esquires.

WILLIAM W. THOMPSON vs THOMAS EAST - The plaintiff by his attorney came into court and says he intends no further to prosecute this suit and assume the payment of all costs. Court ordered that this suit be dismissed and the defendant recover against the plaintiff his costs.

THOMAS DOAK vs ELIJAH & ARCHABALD MAYFIELD - The plaintiff came into court and says he wishes to dismiss this suit and the defendant assumes the payment of all costs. It is ordered by the court that this suit be dismissed and the plaintiff recover against the defendant his costs.

The Grand Jury again returned into court with a Bill if Indictment, the State against HUGH MONTGOMERY, a true bill and again return to consider for further presentments.

The Grand Jury again returned into court with a Bill of Indictment, the STATE against HIRAM S. MORGAN, a true bill and again return to consider for further presentments.

ANDREW DYSART vs RICHARD HOOPER - WILLIAM HUDSON, a garnishee in this cause, being swoen. Question 1 - Are you indebted to RICHARD HOOPER and how much and what effects have you of his in your hands, and what in the hands of others to your knowledge. Answer - I owe HOOPER nothing nor do I know of any of his effects in the hands of any other person there are now in my possession.

JOHN C. LUNA, a garnishee in said cause, being sworn. Question 1 - Are you indebted to RICHARD HOOPER and what effects of his are in your hands, and what in the hands of any other person to your knowledge. Answer - I owe the firm of REYNOLDS & HOOPER about $6.00 as well as I can recollect for goods purchased of them. I do not know of any of his effects in the hands of others their name in mind only the debts above mentioned.

ASA HOLLAND, a garnishee in the above cause being sworn. Question 1 - Are you indebted to RICHARD HOOPER. Answer - I executed to RICHARD HOOPER my note for about $6.50 on which I have been sued and execution stayed.

PETER HOLLAND, a garnishee in the above cause being sworn. Question 1 - Are you indebted to RICHARD HOOPER. Answer - I executed my note to HOOPER & REYNOLDS for $6.56¼ and about 1st January 1819. I also gave my note to RICHARD HOOPER for $29.74 and about 1 January 1820, been sued on both notes and stayed. Question 2 - Do you know of any of his effects in the hands of any other persons. Answer - I believe ISAAC HOBBS does owe HOOPER about $17.75.

ANDREW C. HOGAN, a garnishee in the above cause being sworn. Question 1 - Are you indebted to RICHARD HOOPER. Answer - I believe I executed to RICHARD HOOPER my note for $10.25 and about February or March last, I have been sued on said note. I took the stay according to law and gave my note I believe to FARRAR & HOOPER for about $9.00 or $10.00.

MATHIAS NICHOLS, a garnishee in the above cause being sworn. Question 1 - Are you indebted to RICHARD HOOPER. Answer - I do not know that I owe him one cent. I have the receipt of his agent in full until the 14th of June 1820.

JOHN N. PORTER vs SAMUEL PORTER - Attachment - JOSEPH GREER, a garnishee in this cause being sworn. Question 1 - Are you entitled to SAMUEL PORTER for any thing if any how much. Answer - I don't know that I owe him anything or not. Question 2 - Have you any of his effects in your hands or know of any in the hands of any other person. Answer - I know nothing about what any other person has or owes him, nor have I any of his effects in my hands that I know.

VANCE GREER, a garnishee in the above cause being sworn. Question 1 - Are you indebted to SAMUEL PORTER anything and if any how much. Answer - I do not know whether I am indebted to him any or not if any, very little. Question 2 - Do you know of any other persons owing him. Answer - I do not. Question 3 - Do you know of any of his effects in the hands of any other person. Answer - I do not.

The State vs AUGUSTINE YEAGER - Indictment - The defendant appeared in court and being charged on this Bill of Indictment, pleads guilty and was fined $2.50 and remain in custody of the Sheriff until the costs and fines are paid and give security. MARTIN PUGH as security.

The State vs WILICE (WILEA) GARRETT - Indictment - The defendant came into court and being charged on this indictment pleads guilty and was fined $5.00 and pay the costs of this indictment and remain in custody of the Sheriff or give security for the fine and cost. BENJAMIN MERRELL as security.

The State vs EZEKIEL VICKERS, JOHN VICKERS and WILLIAM VICKERS - SWAN THOMPSON, RICHARD STUART and SOWELL GEORGE who was bound in a recognizance for the appearance of the defendants in this cause surrenders the defendants in court in discharge of their recognizance. They were received by the court and ordered in custody of the Sheriff and SWAN THOMPSON, SOWELL GEORGE and RICHARD STUART are released for their recognizance.

The Grand Jury again returned into court with a Bill of Indictment, the State against DAVID LEMONS, MARTIN CLAYTON, ALFRED SMITH, DAVID SMITH, CONSTANT SMITH, JOHN DAVIS, DAVIS SMITH and JOSHUA SMITH, not a true bill and again returned to consider for further presentments.

The State vs JOHN VICKERS - Indictment - The defendant came into court and being charged on this indictment and pleads guilty and was fined $5.00 and pay costs and remain in custody of the Sheriff until the costs and fine are paid or give security. WILLIAM TOWNZEND as security.

The State vs WILLIAM VICKERS - Indictment - The defendant came into court and pleads guilty and is fined $5.00 and pay the cost and remain in custody of the Sheriff until the costs and fine are paid or give security. ELIJAH CAPEL (CASSEL?) as security.

The State vs EZEKIEL VICKERS - Indictment - The defendant came into court and pleads guilty ans is fined $5.00 and pay the cost and to remain in custody of the Sheriff until the costs and fine are paid or give security. WILLIAM TOWNZEND as security.

The State vs JOHN VICKERS - Indictment - The defendant came into court and pleads guilty and is fined $5.00 and pay the cost and remain in custody of the Sheriff until the costs and fine are paid or give security. WILLIAM TOWNZEND as security.

The State vs BENJAMIN MERRELL - Indictment - The defendant came into court and pleads guilty and fined $5.00 and pay the cost, whereupon came WILEA GARRETT as security for the defendant.

The State vs HUGH MONTGOMERY - Indictment - The defendant came into court and pleads guilty and is fined $5.00 and JOHN T. KING as security.

The State vs CHRISTOPHER E. LOVE - The defendant appeared in court and acknowledged himself indebted to the State of Tennessee $250.00 and DANIEL YOUNG and ABSALUM COLLINS for $125.00 each to be levied respectively upon their goods and chattels

&c but to be void on conditions that CHRISTOPHER E. LOVE will keep the peace towards the citizens of this State particular towards JAMES HOLLAND for six months and appear here on 1st Thursday after the 3rd Monday in January next.

JOHN N. PORTER vs SAMUEL PORTER - GEORGE D. CONWAY who was garnished, to appear here within four first days of this term, was this day called to answer to said garnishee, failed to do so but made default.

The State vs WILLIAM PORCH - Indictment - The defendant pleads not guilty and WILLIAM B. MARTIN, solicitor general who prosecutes in behalf of the State and a jury of men, to wit, DAVID THWING, WILLIS WARREN, KEYS MEEKS, JESSE DANIEL, JOHN GUYDER, CORDIAL SHUFFIELD, JAMES GANT, JOHN PRICE, MOSES HARDING, JOEL JOHNSON, JESSE LAMB and ALDEN TUCK (TUCKER) being elected and sworn and said that the defendant is not guilty. Court found this prosecution was frivolous and malicious. Court orders the solicitor, JOHN W. LESLIE pay the costs of this indictment.

FRIDAY JULY 21, 1820

Justices present were PHILIP KOONCE, JAMES HOLEMAN and WILLIAM KENNON, Esquires.

The State vs JAMES GEORGE - Indictment - The defendant came into court and pleads guilty and is fined $3.00 whereupon came CHAMPION BLYTH as security.

The Grand Jury again returned into court with a Bill of Indictment, the State against WILLIAM D. FERGUSON, a true bill and again returned to consider for further presentments.

The State vs WILLIAM PHILLIPS - Indictment - The defendant came into court and pleads not guilty and a jury of men, to wit, DAVID THWING, WILLIS WARREN, REECE HOWELL, JESSE DANIEL, JOHN GUYDER, CORDIAL SHUFFIELD, JAMES GARET (GARRETT), JOHN PRICE, MOSES HARDING, WILLIAM CRAWFORD, TUNSTAL GREGORY and KEYS MEEK being elected and sworn and said that the defendant is not guilty. Court ordered that the defendant be released and the County of Lincoln pay the costs.

An Indenture of Bargain and Sale from THOMAS HICKMAN to ISAAC CONGER for 75 acres of land, proven by A.A. KINCANNON and ISAAC BROILES (BROYLES) and ordered to be certified.

An Indenture of Bargain and Sale from THOMAS HICKMAN to ISAAC CONGER for 25 acres of land, proven by A.A. KINCANNON and ISAAC BROYLES and ordered to be certified.

BENJAMIN PROCTOR vs JOHN CAMPBELL - The plaintiff appeared in court and says he intends no further to prosecute this suit and assumes the payment of all costs. The defendant is to recover against the plaintiff his costs.

JOHN A. McKINNEY, for the use &c vs JOHN R. MOORE - Debt - The defendant came into court and confessed that he owes the plaintiff $454.25 and damages of $19.62. Plaintiff to recover against the defendant his costs.

The transfer of a plat and certificate from JOHN HANBY to ISAIAH ALLY for 15 acres of land and ordered to be certified.

An Indenture of Bargain and Sale from WILLIAM H. RAGSDALE, SAMUEL RAGSDALE, GABRIEL B. RAGSDALE, DANIEL W. RAGSDALE, JOHN O. DAVIDSON and RUTH R. DAVIDSON to WILLIAM PITTMAN for 500 acres of land in the County of Franklin, proven by KENCHEN HOLCOMB and TRAVIS CARTER and ordered to be certified.

A Bill of Sale from BRICE M. GARNER and ROBERT DICKSON to BENJAMIN CLEMENTS for 12 negroes, proven by JOSEPH HINKLE and CHARLES GILLILAND and ordered to be certified.

The State vs WILLIAM D. FERGUSON - Indictment - The defendant appeared in court and pleads guilty and is fined $10.00 and pay the costs and remain in custody of the Sheriff until the costs and fine are paid or give security.

An Indenture of Bargain and Sale from WILLIAM H. RAGSDALE and SAMUEL RAGSDALE and others to JOEL FOSTER for 300 acres of land and ordered to be certified.

SAMUEL PAINTER vs ROBERT DICKSON - On motion of the defendant by his council, leave is given him to show cause why a new trial should be granted.

Ths State vs ALDEN TUCKER - Indictment - The defendant came into court and pleads not guilty and a jury of men, to wit, DAVID THWING, WILLIS WARREN, REECE HOWELL, JESSE DANIEL, JOHN GUYDER, CORDIAL SHUFFIELD, JAMES GANT, JOHN PRICE, MOSES HARDING, TUNSTALL GREGORY, KEYS MEEKS, and ARCHABALD D. GARVEN being elected and sworn and said that the defendant is not guilty. Court orders the county to pay the costs.

The State vs ALDEN TUCKER - Indictment - The defendant appeared in court and pleads not guilty and this cayse was continued until next term on affidavit of THOMAS W. HAMILTON the prosecutor.

The State vs WILLIAM A TUCKER - The defendant appeared in court and pleads not guilty and this cause was continued until next term on affidavit of THOMAS W. HAMILTON the prosecutor.

ALLEN TUCKER appeared in court and acknowledged himself indebted fo the State of Tennessee for $200.00 and ALLEN TUCKER in the sum of $200.00 to be levied of their goods and chattels &c and to be void on condition that ALLEN TUCKER appear here on 1st Thursday after 3rd Monday in October next and not depart without leave first had and obtained of the court.

WILLIAM A. TUCKER appeared in court and acknowledged himself indebted to the State of Tennessee for $200.00 and ALDEN TUCKER for $200.00 to be levied upon their goods and chattels &c and to be void on condition that WILLIAM A. TUCKER appear here (same date as above) and not depart without leave first had and obtained by the court.

THOMAS W. HAMILTON appeared in court and acknowledged himself indebted to the State of Tennessee for $100.00 to be levied of his goods and chattels &c but to be void on condition that he appear here (same date as above) and give evidence in behalf of the State against ALLEN TUCKER and WILLIAM A. TUCKER and not depart without leave obtained of the court.

The State vs HIRAM S(L). MORGAN - Indictment - The defendant came into court and pleads not guilty and a jury of men, to wit, DAVID THWING, WILLIS WARREN, JESSE DANIEL, REECE HOWELL, JOHN GUYDER, JAMES GANT, CORDIAL SHUFFIELD, JOHN PRICE, MOSES HARDING, TUNSTALL GREGORY, KEYS MEEKS, and JOSEPH HENDERSON being elected and sworn and said that the defendant is guilty and is fined $5.00 and pay the costs.

On petition of ISAAC HOLEMAN, WILLIAM MOORE and JOSEPH HINKLE, securities for EDWARD TATUM, admr and PARTHENA TATUM, admrx of WILLIAM TATUM, deceased, appear here on next Tuesday of this term and give other security or surrenders according to assembly.

ROBERT DICKSON vs JONATHAN ESTILL - It is ordered by the court that WILLIAM WELLS, the landlord of the tenant in possession be allowed a defendant in this case upon the common rule to confess lease entry and ouster, pleads not guilty and for his defence to rely upon the title only.

SATURDAY JULY 22, 1820

Justices present were CHARLES BOYLES, WILLIAM KENNON and JAMES HOLEMAN, Esquires.

The transfer of a plat and certificate from HENDERSON TALLY for 10 acres of land to THOMAS BOAZ, proven by THOMAS PARKS and ELIPHAS BOAZ and ordered to be certified.

An Indenture of Bargain and Sale from BRICE M. GARNER to DAVID CANNON for 100 acres of land and ordered to be certified.

ONEY PARKS vs WILLIAM PARKS and others - Petition - The petition being heard and it appearing to the court that ten days notice had been served on the admrs of AARON PARKS, SR., deceased, and on his heirs and guardians of those who are minors and the facts stated in the petition of said ONEY being admitted to be true. It is considered by the court that the petition be granted and it is considered, ordered, and decreed that the Sheriff proceed to lay off and allot to ONEY her dower out of the estate of the said AARON PARKS, deceased, both real and personal and make return to next court.

47

WILLIAM PARKS and others - Petition for Distribution - This petition being heard and it appearing to the court that ten days notice had been given to said admrs of AARON PARKS, deceased, of the object of this petition. It is ordered that the petition be granted and it is decreed that JAMES HOLEMAN, EBENEZER McEWEN, JOHN J. WHITAKER, WILLIAM KENNON and ISAAC HOLEMAN be appointed Commissioners to lay off and divide the estate of AARON PARKS, deceased, and make return to next court.

An Indenture of Bargain and Sale from RANDOLPH QUARLES to HOWELL HARRIS for 6 acers of land and ordered to be certified.

An Indenture of Bargain and Sale from THOMAS HAYWOOD and SUSAN HAYWOOD to DAVID MOORE for 1653 acres, proven by BRICE M. GARNER and BENJAMIN HARRIS and ordered to be certified.

The State vs THOMAS BEARD - On motion of WILLIAM B. MARTIN, the solicitor general, and by permission of the court a Noli Proseque is entered in this cause.

The State vs ABSOLUM COLLINS - Indictment - The defendant came into court and pleads not guilty and the cause is continued as on affidavit of the defendant until the next term.

This day came ABSOLUM COLLINS into court and acknowledged himself indebted to the State of Tennessee for $200.00 and JAMES CARITHERS for $200.00 to be levied of their goods and chattels &c on conditions that ABSOLUM COLLINS appear here on first Thursday after third Monday in October next to answer charge and not depart the same without leave first had and obtained of the court.

JAMES HOLLAND appeared in court and acknowledged himself indebted to the State of Tennessee for $400.00 to be levied of his goods and chattels &c but to be void on conditions that he and his wife CRACY HOLLAND and his daughters, SALLY HOLLAND and WINNA HOLLAND appear here in October next to prosecute and give evidence in behalf of State of Tennessee against ABSOLUM COLLINS and not depart the same without leave first had and obtained of the court.

The State vs ABSOLUM COLLINS - Indictment - The defendant came into court and pleads not guilty and this cause is continued as on a affidavit of the defendant.

ABSOLUM COLLINS appeared in court and acknowledged himself indebted to the State of Tennessee for $200.00 and JAMES CARITHERS for $200.00 to be levied of their goods and chattels &c but to be void on conditions that ABSOLUM COLLINS appear here and answer the charge and not depart the same without leave first had and obtained of the court.

JAMES HOLLAND appeared in court and acknowledged himself indebted to the State of Tennessee for $400.00 to be levied of his goods and chattels &c but to be void on conditions that he and his wife CREACY HOLLAND and his daughters SALLY HOLLAND and WINNA HOLLAND appear in October court and give evidence in behalf of the State against ABSOLUM COLLINS and not depart the same without leave first had and obtained of the court.

MONDAY JULY 24, 1820

Present were twelve Justices.

Ordered by the court that LEMUEL BRANDON be overseer of the road from the top of the ridge to where JACOB WAGGONER works, to the county line on Coffey's Creek and call on the usual hands and the hands on Short Creek that don't work on any other road.

An Indenture of Bargain and Sale from ALEXANDER McLIN to CHARLES McKINNEY for two town lots No. 31 and No. 34 and ordered to be certified.

An Indenture of Bargain and Sale from THOMAS HAYWOOD to PRESTON HAMPTON for 50 acres of land, proven by WILLIAM HODGE and JAMES HOLBERT and ordered to be certified.

It is ordered by the court that THOMAS HALE be released from the payment of four sheep which he had posted and ran away from him.

JOHN MARSH is appointed overseer of the road in the room of SAMUEL ROE resigned and to call on the usual hands.

It is ordered by the court that JAMES McKREE be allotted $20.00 for keeping of POLLY FRAME three months from this time.

ESTHER KENNEDY is authorized to built and have a public Griss Mill on the West Fork of Norris Creek on the land whereon she now lives.

It is ordered by the court that HARDY HOLEMAN be allotted $12.00 for running the line between this county and Franklin County.

An Indenture of Bargain and Sale from ARCHELOUS WILSON to PHILIP KOONCE for 30 acres of land, proven by WILLIAM M. COLLINS and AMOS SMALL and ordered to be certified.

An Indenture of Bargain and Sale from FRANCIS FINCHER to ROBERT DICKSON for 176 acres of land and ordered to be certified.

A Bill of Sale from WILSON DAVIS to WILLIAM HUSBANDS for a negro woman named EADY, proven by FRANCIS PORTERFIELD and ordered to be certified.

An Inventory of the estate of HENRY BUNN, deceased, was exhibited in court which was ordered to be recorded.

An Indenture of Bargain and Sale from ANDREW E. BEATY to JOSEPH McMILLEN for 114 acres of land and ordered to be certified.

JOHN BASINGER and EADY, his wife, petition for distributive share - The petition being read and appearing to the court that ten days notice had been given to the administration of GEORGE WAGGONER, deceased. It is considered by the court that said petition be granted and it is ordered that HARDY HOLEMAN, BRITAIN PHELPS, JASPER SMITH, JAMES HOLEMAN and JAMES GRANT be appointed Commissioners to divide the said land and allott and lay off the distributive share of the landed estate of GEORGE WAGGONER, deceased, to JOHN BASINGER and EADY, his wife, and make return to next court.

Ordered by the court that ABSALUM BEARD, ELISHA TOWNSON, JOHN DYER, WILLIAM PATTERSON, DRURY K. SMITH, ALEXANDER McCULLOUGH, ABNER DYER, GEORGE W. DENNIS and HUGH McCLAIN be a Jury of View to turn the road from the Cross Roads to the Gum Spring and make return to next court.

An Indenture of Bargain and Sale from PARK GIBSON to MICHAEL BEAVERS for 94 acres of land and ordered to be certified.

A Bill of Sale from AUGUSTINE YEAGER to MARTIN PUGH for one wagon and team and ordered to be certified.

A Bill of Sale from AUGUSTINE YEAGER to MARTIN PUGH for one wagon and ordered to be certified.

An Indenture of Bargain and Sale from ROBERT KERR to JOHN PUTMAN, proven by JOHN GRAY and ALEXANDER GRAY and ordered to be certified.

TUESDAY JULY 25, 1820

Justices present were SAMUEL BUCHANAN, WILLIAM KENNON and JAMES HOLEMAN, Esquires.

REUBIN W. REYNOLDS vs THOMAS MILEHAM - The plaintiff came into court and says he wishes to dismiss his suit in this cause and assumes the payment of all costs. Court dismisses this cause and the plaintiff recover against the defendant his costs.

CHARLES BOYLES vs JOHN WASHBURN - Motion - On motion of the plaintiff, it is ordered by the court that the Sheriff expose to sale 40 acres of land levied on as the property of JOHN WASHBURN, lying on the waters of the Barren Fork of Flint, the place where JOHN WASHBURN now lives, to satisfy a judgement that CHARLES BOYLES recovered against JOHN WASHBURN is before WILLIAM MILNER, Esquire, on 10 June 1820 for $36.90½ and all legal costs.

CHARLES BOYLES vs JOHN WASHBURN - Motion - On motion of the plaintiff, it is ordered by the court that the Sheriff expose to sale JOHN WASHBURN's 40 acres of land, lying on the waters of the Barren Fork of Flint, it being the place whereon WASHBURN now lives, to satisfy a judgement that CHARLES BOYLES before WILLIAM MILNER, Esquire, on 10 June 1820 for $6.06¼ and all legal costs.

An Indenture of Bargain and Sale from WALTER KINNARD to MATHEW GIBSON for four town lots No. 95, 96, 100 and 102 in the town of Fayetteville and ordered to be certified.

DANIEL YOUNG appeared in court and acknowledged himself indebted to the State of Tennessee for $200.00 and JOSEPH JONES for $200.00 to be levied on their respectively goods and chattels &c·but to be void on condition that DANIEL YOUNG appear here in October next to answer charge and not depart the same without leave first had and obtained of the court.

DANIEL YOUNG appeared in court and acoknowledged himself indebted to the State of Tennessee for $200.00 and JOSEPH JONES for $200.00 to be levied on their respectively goods and chattels &c but to be void on condition that DANIEL YOUNG appear here in October next to answer charge and not depart the same without leave first had and obtained by the court.

ISAAC HOLEMAN and others vs EDWARD TATUM - Petition for Counter Security - EDWARD TATUM, admr. and PARTHENA TATUM, admrx of WILLIAM TATUM, deceased. This day the defendants came into court. and said that they are willing to surrender the effects of the estate of WILLIAM TATUM, deceased, and it is ordered by the court that FRANCIS PORTERFIELD, WILLIAM DICKSON and AMBROSE BARKER be appointed Commissioners to settle with EDWARD TATUM, admr and PARTHENA TATUM, admrx of WILLIAM TATUM, deceased, and make return instant.

A Deed of Trust from JONATHAN ESTILL to JOHN MILLER for one town lot No. 5 in the town of Fayetteville, proven by JOHN W. ESTILL and ordered to be certified.

ISAAC HOLEMAN and others vs EDWARD TATUM, admr and PARTHENA TATUM, admrx - The Commissioners heretofore appointed to settle with the defendants and made return and it is ordered by the court that ISAAC HOLEMAN be appointed admr of the goods and chattels &c which was of the estate of WILLIAM TATUM, deceased. HOLEMAN came into court and made bond and security.

It is ordered that ISAAC HOLEMAN be appointed guardian of POLLY TATUM, BETSEY TATUM and JOHN TATUM, infants, heirs of WILLIAM TATUM, deceased, who gave bond and security.

FLETCHER & McCLELLAN vs JONATHAN ESTILL - Case - This day came the parties by their attorneys and a jury of men, to wit, REECE HOWELL, JESSE DANIEL, JOHN GUYDER, JAMES GANT, CORDIAL SHUFFIELD, MOSES HARDING, WILLIS WARREN, WILLIAM CRAWFORD, TUNSTAL GREGORY, KEYS MEEK, ALEXANDER GREER and ANDREW McCARTNEY being elected and sworn and said that the defendant did assume upon himself in manner and form as the plaintiffs in declaring against him and the damages were assessed to $1452.00 with interest. It is ordered that the plaintiff recover against the defendant his costs.

WEDNESDAY JULY 26, 1820

Justices present were JAMES HOLEMAN, SAMUEL BUCHANAN, CHARLES BOYLES and PHILIP KOONCE, Esquires.

T. PATE vs LEVEL LORD & CHARLES McKELLEN - Motion - On motion of the plaintiff by his attorney, it is ordered by the court that the Sheriff expose to sale 20 acres of land levied on as the property of CHARLES McKELLEN lying on the West Fork of Cane Creek adjoining the lands of FRANCIS FINDLY to satisfy a judgement that T. PATE recovered against LEVEL LORD and CHARLES McKELLEN before JAMES BLAKEMORE, Esquire, on the 2nd day of November 1819 for $66.31¼ and all legal costs.

HIGGINBOTHAM & PERKINS vs THOMAS L. TROTTER - Debt - The defendant appeared in court and withdraws his plea and confesses that he owes the plaintiff $89.12¼ and damages of $6.20. The plaintiff to recover against the defendant his costs.

THOMAS FLACK vs HAYS BLAIR - This cause is continued as on affidavit of the plaintiff by his paying the costs of this term.

CHARLES BOYLES vs DANIEL WARREN - Debt - The defendant came into court and confessed that he owes the plaintiff $94.60 and the plaintiff agrees to stay execution until next court. The plaintiff to recover against the defendant his costs.

CHARLES BEDWELL vs THOMAS ALLEY - The parties by their attorneys appeared in court and it is ordered by the court that the plaintiff be nonsuited and the defendant recover against the plaintiff his costs.

JOHN DILLINGHAM vs JAMES BROWN - The defendant by their attorneys appeared in court and it is ordered by the court and the plaintiff being called to come and prosecute this suit, failed to do so. It is ordered by the court that the plaintiff be nonprocessed and the defendant go hence without day and recover against the plaintiff his costs.

A Grand Jury again returned with a Bill of Indictment, the State against JOHN DUKE, a true bill and again return to consider for further presentments.

The Grand Jury again returned into court with a Bill of Indictment, the State abainst JOHN WISEMAN, a true bill and again return to consider for further presentments.

The Grand Jury again returned to court with a Bill of Indictment, the State against AUGUSTINE YEAGER, a true bill, and again return to consider for further presentments.

JAMES ROGERS vs JAMES SWEET - Certiorari - This day came the parties by their attorneys into court and a jury of men, to wit, REECE HOWELL, JESSE DANIEL, JOHN GUYDER, JAMES GANT, CORDIAL SHUFFIELD, MOSES HARDING, WILLIS WARREN, WILLIAM CRAWFORD, TUNSTAL GREGORY, KEYS MEEKS, JOHN PRICE, and JOHN MARTIN being elected and sworn and said that the defendant is indebted to the plaintiff of $15.18 3/4 and on motion of the court that the plaintiff recover against the defendant and JAMES MOORE, his security, his costs.

E.B. CLARK vs JOHN J. HENRY - Certiorari - This day came the parties by their attorneys and a jury of men, to wit, JAMES HIGGINS, JOSHUA CHURCH, WILLIAM BOON, JOSHUA DODSON, ENOCK K. WEATHERS, JOHN BEATY, JOHN DAVIS, CHAMPION BLYTHE, ALEXANDER MEEK, JAMES GEORGE, WILLIAM ROGERS, and GEORGE RENEGER being elected and sworn and said that the defendant is indebted to the plaintiff for $17.00 and damages of $1.08. The plaintiff is to recover against the defendant and WILLIAM MUNROE his security his costs.

Ordered by the court that ROBERT HODGE, Esquire, be allowed $6.00 for his services as a Commissioner in settling with the admrs of JOHN KELLY, deceased.

MARGARET ADAMS vs JOHN MURPHEY - This day came the parties by their attorneys and a jury of men, to wit, JAMES HIGGINS, JOSHUA CHURCH, WILLIAM BOON, JOSHUA DODSON, ENOCH K. WEATHERS, JOHN BEATY, JOHN DAVIS, CHAMPION BLYTHE, ALEXANDER MEEK, JAMES GEORGE, WILLIAM ROGERS, and GEORGE RENEGER being elected and sworn and said that the defendant is indebted to the plaintiff for $30.00 and damages of $6.60.

STEPHEN BEAVERS vs JESSE CONWELL - Certiorari - This day the parties by their attorneys appeared in court and a jury of men, to wit, JAMES HIGGINS, JOSHUA CHURCH, WILLIAM BOON, JOSHUA DODSON, ENOCK K. WEATHERS, JOHN BEATY, JOHN DAVIS, CHAMPION BLYTH, ALEXANDER MEEK, JAMES GEORGE, WILLIAM ROGERS, and GEORGE RENEGER being elected and sworn and said that the defendant is indebted to the plaintiff for $55.75 and damages of $1.11½. Court ordered the plaintiff recover against the defendant and JEREMIAH STUBBLEFIELD his security, his costs.

SAMUEL RAMSEY vs JESSE CONWELL - Certiorari - This day came the parties by their attorneys and a jury of men, to wit, JAMES HIGGINS, JOSHUA CHURCH, WILLIAM BOON, JOSHUA DODSON, ENOCK K. WEATHERS, JOHN BEATY, JOHN DAVIS, CHAMPION BLYTH, ALEXANDER MEEK, JAMES GEORGE, WILLIAM ROGERS, and GEORGE RENEGER being elected and sworn and said that the defendant is indebted to the plaintiff for $47.75 and damages of $1.21. The plaintiff to recover against the defendant and JEREMIAH STUBBLEFIELD, his security, his costs.

It is ordered by the court that JOSEPH KELLY and NANCY KELLY heretofore admr of JOHN KELLY, deceased, be hereby revoked, they having surrendered the effects of the estate of the intestate to ELI GARRETT agreeable to an order of the court. ELI GARRETT be appointed admr of the estate and gave bond and security.

NATHANIEL B. BUCKINGHAM vs GEORGE TITUS - This day came the parties by their attorneys into court and a jury of men, to wit, JAMES HIGGINS, JOSHUA CHURCH, WILLIAM BOON, JOSHUA DODSON, ENOCK K. WEATHERS, JOHN BEATY, JOHN DAVIS,

CHAMPION BLYTH, ALEXANDER MEEK, JAMES GEORGE, WILLIAM ROGERS and GEORGE RENEGER being elected and sworn and said that the defendant has not paid the debt to the plaintiff of $164.03½ and damages of $5.25. The plaintiff to recover against the defendant his costs.

MARY INGLE vs JOHN MORE - This cause is continued on affidavit of the defendant until next term of court and a Commission is awarded him to take the deposition of JOHNSTON WELLBORN by giving the plaintiff thirty days notice if taken in Georgia and if taken in Alabama twenty days notice and if taken in this county five days notice to be used as evidence on this trial.

THURSDAY JULY 27, 1820

Justices present were CHARLES BOYLES, JAMES HOLEMAN and SAMUEL BUCHANAN, Esquires.

ARGYLE CAMPBELL vs THOMAS L.D. PARKS - The defendant came into court and confessed that he owes the plaintiff $93.00 and damages of 69¢. The plaintiff to recover against the defendant his costs.

It is ordered by the court that EZEKIEL NORRIS be released from paying a tax on two tracts of land in this county containing 2280 acres.

MARY HURLEY vs MAY BUCHANAN - Petition - The petition being read and heard and it appearing to the court that ten days notice had been served on the admrs of ELIJAH HURLEY, deceased, and his heirs and the guardian of those who are minors and the facts stated in the petition of the said MARY HURLEY being admitted to be true. Petition was granted and the Sheriff was ordered to lay off to MARY HURLEY her dower out of the estate of ELIJAH HURLEY, deceased, both real and personal and make return to next court.

HARDY HIGHTOWER vs BRICE M. GARNER - The plaintiff by his attorney came into court and says he wishes to dismiss his suit and the defendant assumes the payment of all costs. The suit was dismissed and the plaintiff recover against the defendant his costs.

It is ordered by the court that KEYS MEEK, ALEXANDER MEEK, WILLIAM C. ABEL, EDWARD TOWERY, ROBERT HAIRSTON, JOHN GRIFFIS, and WILLIAM P. PULLIAM be a Jury of View to view and lay off and mark out a road the nearest and best way from Fayetteville to cross Elk River at Sims Ford and to intersect the Fort Hampton Road eight or ten miles from Fayetteville or intersect the said Fort Hampton Road at such place as they may think best and make return to next court.

An Indenture of Bargain and Sale from JAMES BRIGHT to SAMUEL HOWELL for 30 acres of land and ordered to be certified.

An Indenture of Bargain and Sale from RANDOLPH QUARLES to CORNELIUS DARNELL for 182 3/4 acres of land and ordered to be certified.

A transfer of a plat and certificate from BRICE M. GARNER and BENJAMIN HARRIS to BENJAMIN HUDSON for 10 acres of land and ordered to be certified.

The transfer of a plat and certificate from BRICE M. GARNER and BENJAMIN HARRIS to BENJAMIN HUDSON and ordered to be certificate.

The transfer of a plat and certificate from BRICE M. GARNER and BENJAMIN HARRIS to ISAAC HENSON for 25 acres of land and ordered to be certified.

MICHAEL LUTTRELL vs WILSON FROST - This cause is referred to the arbitrament of ZACHARIAH ARNOLD and JOHN STILES and if they cannot agree they are to choose JAMES FORSYTH and their award to be the judgement of the court at next court.

CHARLES BOYLES vs DAVID THWING - Debt - The defendant confessed that he owes the plaintiff $75.00 and damages of $2.25. The plaintiff is to recover against the defendant his costs.

CHARLES BOYLES to WILSON FROST - The defendant confessed that he owes the plaintiff $383.37½ and the plaintiff agree to stay execution until 1st January next. The plaintiff to recover against the defendant his costs.

ANGEL & GILLASPIE vs WILLIAM D. FERGUSON - On motion for Judgement - This day came the parties by their attorneys and on motion of the plaintiff for judgement against

WILLIAM D. FERGUSON, as Constable, and HENRY ALLEN and ARGYLE CAMPBELL his securities for sum of $7.31¼ and interest and damages and the court considered that the motion be overruled and the defendant go hence without day and recover against the plaintiff their costs. Plaintiff appeals to next Circuit Court.

HIRAM BURKS by his next friend JOHN BURKS vs JOSEPH HENDERSON - This day came the parties by their attorneys and a jury of men, to wit, REECE HOWELL, JESSE DANIEL, JAMES HUNT, MOSES HARDING, TUNSTAL GREGORY, JOHN PRICE, WILLIS WARREN, JAMES HIGGINS, JOSHUA DODSON, WILLIAM BOON, JOHN DAVIS and WILLIAM ROGERS being elected and sworn and said that the defendant is guilty. Ordered by the court that the plaintiff recover against the defendant $82.00 damages.

FRIDAY JULY 28, 1820

Justices present were PHILLIP KOONCE, JAMES HOLEMAN and WILLIAM KENNON, Esquires.

It is ordered by the court that NICHOLAS CARRIGER, JOHN REECE, JOHN NEECE, DANIEL W. HARRISON, JOHN S. JOHNSON, REUBEN H. BOON and ZACHARIAH HARRISON be a Jury of View to view, lay and mark out a road, the neatest and best way to leave the road that runs up the West Fork of Norris Creek at or near the ten mile post and on by NICHOLAS CARRIGER and to intersect the road leading by HARDY HOLEMAN to Lynchburg at or near SAMUEL HARTS and make return to next court.

SPENCER A. PUGH vs GEORGE E. SANDERSON - This day came the parties by their attorneys and a jury of men, to wit, CORDIAL SHUFFIELD, JOHN GUYDER, JESSE DANIEL, JAMES GANT, MOSES HARDING, TUNSTAL GREGORY, WILLIS WARREN, JOHN PRICE, KEYS MEEK, ROBERT BRADON, JOHN MARTIN, and LEMUEL BROADWAY being elected and sworn and said that the defendant has not kept and performed the Covenant and the damages were $58.79 3/4. It is ordered that the plaintiff recover against the defendant his costs.

The State vs JOHN WISEMAN - Indictment - The defendant appeared in court and pleads guilty and is fined $1.00 and cost of indictment.

JOHN DOBBINS vs JAMES WYATT - The parties by their attorneys came into court and a jury of men, to wit, CORDIAL SHUFFIELD, JOHN GUYDER, JESSE DANIEL, JAMES GANT, MOSES HARDING, TUNSTAL GREGORY, WILLIS WARREN, JOHN PRICE, KEYS MEEK, ROBERT BRADEN, JOHN MARTIN and LEMUEL BRANDON being elected and sworn and said that the defendant did assume upon himself in manner and form as the plaintiff in declaring against him and assessed damages of $103.87½. It is ordered that the plaintiff recover against the defendant his costs.

BRICE M. GARNER vs JOHN A. CHAPMAN - Debt - This day came the parties by their attorneys and a jury of men, to wit, CORDIAL SHUFFIELD, JOHN GUYDER, JESSE WARREN, JOHN PRICE, KEYS MEEK, ROBERT BRADEN, JOHN MARTIN and LEMUEL BRANDON being elected and sworn and said that the defendant has not paid the debt of $313.00 and damages of $18.78. The plaintiff to recover against the defendant his costs.

JESSE RIGGS vs JOHN A. CHAPMAN - Debt - This day came the parties by their attorneys and a jury of men, to wit, CORDIAL SHUFFIELD, JOHN GUYDER, JESSE DANIEL, JAMES GANT, MOSES HARDING, TUNSTALL GREGORY, WILLIS WARREN, JOHN PRICE, KEYS MEEKS, ROBERT BRADEN, JOHN MARTIN, and LEMUEL BROADWAY (BRANDON) being elected and sworn and said that the defendant has not paid the debt of $150.00 and damages of $6.50. The plaintiff to recover against the defendant his costs.

WILLIAM DOBBS vs SAMUEL PORTER - Debt - This day came the parties by their attorneys and a jury of men, to wit, CORDIAL SHUFFIELD, JOHN GUYDER, JESSE DANIEL, JAMES GANT, KEYS MEEK, ROBERT BRADEN, JOHN MARTIN, and LEMUEL BROADWAY (BRANDON) being elected and sworn and said that the defendant has not paid the debt of $130.00 and damages of $6.50. The plaintiff to recover against the defendant his costs.

BUCHANAN & WILLIAM vs VANCE GREER - Debt - This day came the parties by their attorneys and a jury of men, to wit, CORDIAL SHUFFIELD, JOHN GUYDER, JESSE DANIEL, JAMES GANT, MOSES HARDING, TUNSTAL GREGORY, WILLIS WARREN, JOHN PRICE, KEYS MEEK, ROBERT BRADEN, JOHN MARTIN, and LEMUEL BROADWAY being elected and sworn and said that the defendant has not paid the debt of $310.00 and damages of $30.00. The plaintiff to recover against the defendant his costs.

BENJAMIN GEORGE vs ALLEN TUCKER - Debt - This day came the parties by their

53

attorneys and a jury of men, to wit, CORDIAL SHUFFIELD, JOHN GUYDER, JESSE DANIEL, JAMES GANT, MOSES HARDING, TUNSTAL GREGORY, WILLIS WARREN, JOHN PRICE, KEYS MEEK, ROBERT BRADON, JOHN MARTIN and LEMUEL BROADWAY being elected and sworn and said that the defendant has not paid the debt of $94.50 and damages of $1.89. The plaintiff to recover against the defendant his costs.

ALLEN ELSTON vs FRANCIS WYATT - Debt - This day came the parties by their attorneys and a jury of men, to wit, CORDIAL SHUFFIELD, JOHN GUYDER, JESSE DANIEL, JAMES GANT, MOSES HARDING, TUNSTAL GREGORY, WILLIS WARREN, JOHN PRICE, KEYS MEEK, ROBERT BRADON, JOHN MARTIN and LEMUEL BROADWAY being elected and sworn and said that the defendant has not paid the debt of $372.20 and damages of $9.66¼. Plaintiff to recover against the defendant his costs.

JAMES MARTIN vs GEORGE J. PREWIT - Debt - This day came the parties by their attorneys and a jury of men, to wit, CORDIAL SHUFFIELD, JOHN GUYDER, JESSE DANIEL, JAMES GANT, MOSES HARDING, TUNSTAL GREGORY, WILLIS WARREN, JOHN PRICE, KEYS MEEK, ROBERT BRADON, JOHN MARTIN and LEMUEL BROADWAY being elected and sworn and said that the defendant has not paid the debt of $302.00 and damages of $10.57. The plaintiff to recover against the defendant his costs. Defendant wants appeal to next Circuit Court.

WILLIAM BOON appeared in court and acknowledged himself indebted to the State of Tennessee for $100.00 to be levied upon his goods and chattels &c but to be void on condition that he appear in October court to prosecute and give evidence in behalf of the State against JOSEPH WHITAKER and JOHN HOLEMAN and not part without leave first had and obtained of the court.

WILLIAM BOON appeared in court and acknowledged himself indebted to the State of Tennessee for $100.00 to be levied upon his goods and chattels &c but to be void on condition that he appear in October court to prosecute and give evidence in behalf of the State against JOHN PARKS and not depart without leave first had and obtained by the court.

WILLIAM BOON vs FRANCIS MAY - Motion - On motion of the plaintiff by his attorney, it is ordered that the Sheriff expose to sale 5 acres of land levied on as the property of FRANCIS MAY before CHARLES BOYLES, Esquire, on 4th March 1820 for $6.17 and costs.

An Indenture of Bargain and Sale from ARTHENIEL RICE to GEORGE KOONCE for 10 acres of land, proven by PHILIP KOONCE and ELIJAH PHILLIPS and ordered to be certified.

An Indenture of Bargain and Sale from ARTHENIEL RICE to GEORGE KOONCE for 10 acres of land, proven by PHILIP KOONCE and ELIJAH PHILLIPS and ordered to be certified.

An Indenture of Bargain and Sale from EDWARD HARDING to ARCHER BEASLEY for 100 acres of land and ordered to be certified.

JOHN W. McGUINSEY vs JOHN DAVIS - Motion - On motion of the plaintiff by his attorney, it is ordered by the court that the Sheriff expose to sale 50 acres of land lying in Franklin County on Hurricane Creek adjoining DANIEL ARCHER on the north to satisfy a judgement that JOHN W. GUINSEY recovered against JOHN DAVIS before the Justices of the Court of Pleas and Quarter Sessions for Lincoln at January Term 1819.

McGUINSEY & AKIN vs MARTIN JONES - Motion - On motion of the plaintiff by his attorney that the Sheriff expose for sale 25 acres of land lying on East Fork of Mulberry and east of WILLIAM BROWN to satisfy a judgement that McGUINSEY & EAKIN recovered against him before JACOB WAGGONER, Esquire, on 3rd July 1819.

WHITNEY & HOOPER vs MARTIN JONES - Motion - On motion of the plaintiff by his attorney, it is ordered that the Sheriff expose for sale 25 acres of land lying on East Fork of Mulberry Creek and east of WILLIAM BROWN, levied on the property of said JONES to satisfy a judgement that WHITNEY & HOOPER recovered against him on 8th January 1820 before JONATHAN FLOYD, Esquire.

JAMES McDAVID and others vs WILLIAM PUGH - On motion of the defendant by his attorney, it is ordered by the court that a Writ of Certiorari issue to bring up to court the papers relative to a suit true before WILLIAM C. ABELS, Esquire, wherein JAMES McDAVID, admr and NANCY McDAVID, admrx of (WILLIAM) McDAVID, deceased, was plaintiff and WILLIAM PUGH defendant.

JOEL JOHNSON vs SAMUEL GARLAND - Motion to dismiss Certiorari - This day came the parties by their attorneys and on argument of the motion to dismiss the certiorari in this cause. Court considered that the plaintiff recover against the defendant and WILLIAM HUSBANDS his security sum of $1.00 with interest.

SATURDAY JULY 29, 1820

Justices present were SAMUEL BUCHANAN, CHARLES BOYLES, WILLIAM KENNON, PHILIP KOONCE and JAMES HOLEMAN, Esquires.

It is ordered by the court that JOHN DAVIS work under JAMES HIGGINS as overseer of a road and ADELAI SHARP work under ELIJAH DAVIS as overseer of a road.

HALLET PEARCE vs JAMES MEEK - Motion to dismiss Certiorari - This day came the parties by their attorneys and on argument of the motion to dismiss, it is considered by the court that the motion be overruled.

On motion, it is ordered by the court that the Clerk receive and place on the Tax List 141 acres of land on the West Fork of Norris Creek in the name of GEORGE MARTIN and that he pay a single tax for the same.

JOHN W. CRUNK vs ROBERT BRADON - Appeal - The defendant by his attorney came into court and the plaintiff being called to come and prosecute, failed to do so. The plaintiff be non-(illegible) and the defendant go hence without day and recover against the plaintiff.

JOHN ZIVELY vs CHAPMAN HANBY - Certiorari - The defendant and their attorneys came into court and the plaintiff being called and prosecute this certiorari failed to do so. The plaintiff be nonprossed and the defendant go hence without day and recover against the plaintiff their costs.

CHARLES BOYLES vs JOHN BROWN - Debt - The plaintiff by his attorney came into court and the defendant being called to come and defend this suit failed to do so but made default. The plaintiff to recover against the defendant $93.91 and damages of 46¢ his costs.

It is ordered by the court that JOHN D. SPAIN be released from payment of the appraised value of a stray sorrel mare and sorrel colt which he had posted and was proven away from him.

ROBERT H. McEWEN and others vs JOHN PARKS and others - The plaintiff by his attorney came into court and the defendants being called to come and defend this suit came not but made default. The plaintiff to recover against the defendant $1500.00 and $22.50 damages his costs.

ROBERT H. McEWEN and others vs JOHN PARKS and others - The plaintiff by his attorney came into court and the defendants being called to come and defend this suit failed to do so. The plaintiff to recover against the defendants $1200.00 and damages of $54.00.

WILLIAM BLEDSOE vs JOSEPH KELLY, admr - The plaintiff by his attorney came into court and says he wishes to dismiss this suit and assume the payment of all costs. Court dismisses the suit and the defendant recover against the plaintiff his costs.

A Power of Attorney from WILLIAM KELLY to BENJAMIN CLEMENTS and ANDREW SMITH was acknowledged by WILLIAM KELLY and ordered to be certified.

DAVID KELLER vs NATHANIEL B. BUCKINGHAM - This day came the plaintiff by his attorney and the defendant being called to come and defend this suit failed to do so but made default. The plaintiff to recover against the defendant $79.89 and $14.67 damages his costs.

JOHN N. PORTER vs SAMUEL PORTER - Attachment - The plaintiff by his attorney came into court and the defendant being called to defend this suit failed to do so. The plaintiff to recover against the defendant $2500.00 and $130.00 damages his costs.

BUCHANAN & PORTERFIELD vs NANCY FEATHERSTON - Attachment - The plaintiff by his attorney came into court and the defendant being called to come and reply and defend this suit failed to do so. The plaintiff to recover against the defendant $102.62½ and $3.99 damages his costs.

AMBROSE PEARCE vs FELIX CRUNK - Motion - On motion of AMBROSE PEARCE by his attorney against FELIX CRUNK and the judgement was rendered against AMBROSE PEARSON on a note executed by him and FELIX CRUNK for $21.65. AMBROSE PEARCE has paid and satisfied the same and the following persons, to wit, DAVID THWING, WILLIS WARREN, REECE HOWELL, KEYS MEEK, JESSE DANIEL, JOHN GUYDER, CORDIAL SHUFFIELD, JAMES GANT, JOHN PRICE, WILLIAM CRAWFORD, TUNSTALL GREGORY and WILLIAM LEDFORD were to ascertain the fact and they say that AMBROSE was only bound as security in said note. The plaintiff to recover against the defendant $21.65 his costs.

SAMUEL BUCHANAN vs JAMES LAWSON - Motion - SAMUEL BUCHANAN was security for JAMES LAWSON and has paid $34.28 as security. The plaintiff to recover against the defendant his costs.

JOHN MAZE vs WILLIAM K. PAULLING - Motion - JOHN MAZE was security for WILLIAM K. PAULLING in the suit JAMES STUART against WILLIAM K. PAULLING and that JOHN MAZE had paid $217.60 as security. The plaintiff to recover against the defendant his costs.

JOHN W. SMITH vs SAMUEL L. FINDLEY and ISHAM BURKS - Motion - JOHN W. SMITH was security for the defendant and that he has paid $149.16. The plaintiff to recover against the defendant his costs.

SAMUEL RAMSEY vs JESSE CONWELL - Certiorari - This day came the parties by their attorneys and a jury of men, to wit, JAMES HIGGINS, JOSHUA CHURCH, WILLIAM BOON, JOSHUA DODSON, ENOCK K. WEATHERS, JOHN BEATY, JOHN DAVIS, CHAMPION BLYTH, ALEXANDER MEEK, JAMES GEORGE, WILLIAM ROGERS and GEORGE RENEGER being elected and sworn and said that the defendant is indebted to the plaintiff for $47.75 and damages of $1.21. The plaintiff to recover against the defendant his costs.

It is ordered by the court that JOSEPH KELLY, NANCY KELLY appointed admrs of JOHN KELLY, deceased, be hereby revoked, they having surrendered the effects of the estate of the intestate to ELI GARRETT agreeably to an order of the court. ELI GARRETT was appointed and gave bond and security.

NATHANIEL B. BUCKINGHAM vs GEORGE TITUS - Both parties with their attorneys came into court and a jury of men, to wit, JAMES HIGGINS, JOSHUA CHURCH, WILLIAM BOON, JOSHUA DODSON, ENOCK K. WEATHERS, JOHN BEATY, JOHN DAVIS, CHAMPION BLYTH, ALEXANDER MEEK, JAMES GEORGE, WILLIAM ROGERS and GEORGE RENEGER being elected and sworn and said that the defendant has not paid the debt to the plaintiff for $164.03½ and $5.25. The plaintiff to recover against the defendant his costs.

MARY INGLE vs JOHN MARR - This cause is continued on affidavit of the defendant until next term of court and a Commission is awarded him to take the deposition of JOHNSTON WELLBORN by given the plaintiff thirty days notice if taken in Georgia and if taken in Alabama twenty days and if taken in this county five days notice.

THURSDAY JULY 27, 1820

Justices present were CHARLES BOYLES, JAMES HOLEMAN and SAMUEL BUCHANAN, Esquires.

ARGYLE CAMPBELL vs THOMAS L.D. PARKS - The defendant confessed that he owes the plaintiff $93.00 and damages of 69¢. The plaintiff to recover against the defendant his costs.

It is ordered by the court that TRYON GIBSON be released from the payment of two stray nags which he had posted and proven from him.

It is ordered by the court that EZEKIEL NORRIS be released from paying a tax on two tracts of land in this county containing 2280 acres.

MARY HURLEY vs MAY BUCHANAN and others - Petition - The court ordered that ten days notice had served on the admrs of ELIJAH HURLEY, deceased, and his heirs and the guardian of those who are minors. Court ordered that the petition be granted and ordered that the Sheriff proceed to lay off to MARY her dower out of the estate and make return to next court.

HARDY HIGHTOWER vs BRICE M. GARNER - The plaintiff wishes to dismiss his suit and the defendant assumes the payment of all costs. Suit to be dismissed and the plaintiff recover against the defendant his costs.

It is ordered by the court that KEYS MEEK, ALEXANDER MEEK, WILLIAM C. ABEL, EDWARD TOWERY, ROBERT HAIRSTON, JOHN GRIFFIS, and WILLIAM P. PULLIAM be a Jury of View to view and lay off and mark out a road the nearest and best way from Fayetteville to cross Elk River at Sims Ford and to intersect the Fort Hampton Road eight or ten miles from Fayetteville or intersect the Fort Hampton Road at such a place as they may think best and make return to next court.

An Indenture of Bargain and Sale from JAMES BRIGHT to SAMUEL HOWELL for 30 acres of land and ordered to be certified.

An Indenture of Bargain and Sale from RANDOLPH QUARLES to CORNELIUS DARNELL for 182 3/4 acres of land and ordered to be certified.

The transfer of a play and certificate from BRICE M. GARNER and BENJAMIN HARRIS to BENJAMIN HUDSON for 10 acres of land and ordered to be certified.

The transfer of a plat and certificate from BRICE M. GARNER and BENJAMIN HARRIS to BENJAMIN HUDSON for 10 acres of land and ordered to be certified.'

The transfer of a plat and certificate from BRICE M. GARNER and BENJAMIN HARRIS to ISAAC HENSON for 20 acres of land and ordered to be certified.

MICHAEL LUTTRELL vs WILSON FROST - This cause is referred to the arbitrament of ZACHARIAH ARNOLD to JOHN STILES and if they cannot agree, they are to chose JAMES FORSYTH and make return to next court.

CHARLES BOYLES vs DAVID THWING - Debt - The defendant confesses that he owes the plaintiff $75.00 and damages of $2.25. Plaintiff to recover against the defendant his costs.

CHARLES BOYLES vs WILSON FROST - The defendant confesses that he owes the plaintiff $383.37½ and agrees to stay execution until January Court. The plaintiff to recover against the defendant his costs.

ANGEL & GILLASPIE vs WILLIAM D. FERGUSON, HENRY ALLEN and ARGYLE CAMPBELL his securities - On Motion for Judgement - On motion for judgement against WILLIAM D. FERGUSON, a Constable and his securities (above named) for $11.31¼ with interest and damages. Court overruled the motion and the defendants recover against the plaintiff their costs. The plaintiff prays for an appeal to next Circuit Court and gave bond and security.

HIRAM BURKS by his next friend JOHN BURKS vs JOSEPH HENDERSON - Case - Both parties and their attorneys came into court and a jury of men, to wit, REECE HOWELL, JESSE DANIEL, JAMES GANT, MOSES HARDING, TUNSTAL GREGORY, JOHN PRICE, WILLIS WARREN, JAMES HIGGINS, JOSHUA DODSON, WILLIAM BOON, JOHN DAVIS, and WILLIAM ROGERS being elected and sworn and said that the defendant is guilty and the damages of $82.00. Plaintiff to recover his costs.

FRIDAY JULY 28, 1820

Justices present were PHILIP KOONCE, JAMES HOLEMAN and WILLIAM KENNON, Esquires.

It is ordered by the court that NICHOLAS CARRIGER, JOHN REECE, JOHN NEECE, DANIEL W. HARRISON, JOHN S. JOHNSON, REUBEN H. BOON, and ZACHARIAL HARRISON be a Jury of View to view, lay off and mark out a road the nearest and best way to have the road that runs up the West Fork of Norris Creek at or near the ten mile post and on by NICHOLAS CARRIGER and to intersect the road leading by HARDY HOLEMAN to Lynchburg at or near SAMUEL HART's and make return to next court.

SPENCER A. PUGH vs GEORGE E. SANDERSON - Covenant - Both parties by their attorneys came into court and a jury of men, to wit, CORDIAL SHUFFIELD, JOHN GUYDER, JESSE DANIEL, JAMES GANT, MOSES HARDING, TUNSTAL GREGORY, WILLIS WARREN, JOHN PRICE, KEYS MEEK, ROBERT BRADON, JOHN MARTIN, and LEMUEL BROADWAY being elected and sworn and said that the defendant has not kept and performed the covenant and they assess the damages to $58.79 3/4. Plaintiff to recover his costs.

The State vs JOHN WISEMAN - Indictment - The defendant pleads guilty and was fined $1.00 and pay the cost of this indictment.

JOHN DOBBINS vs JAMES WYATT - Both parties by their attorneys came into court and a jury of men, to wit, CORDIAL SHUFFIELD, JOHN GUYDER, JESSE DANIEL, JAMES GANT, MOSES HARDING, TUNSTAL GREGORY, WILLIS WARREN, JOHN PRICE, KEYS MEEK, ROBERT BRADON, JOHN MARTIN and LEMUEL BROADWAY being elected and sworn and said that the defendant did assume upon himself the damages of $103.87½. Plaintiff to recover his costs.

BRICE M. GARNER vs JOHN A. CHAPMAN - Debt - Both parties by their attorneys came into court and a jury of men, to wit, (same jurors as above) being elected and sworn and said that the defendant has not paid the debt of $313.00 and damages of $18.78. Plaintiff to recover his costs.

JESSE RIGGS vs JOHN A. CHAPMAN - (same as suit above) being elected and sworn and said that the defendant has not paid the debt of $150.00 and damages of $6.50. The plaintiff to recover his costs.

WILLIAM DOBBS vs SAMUEL PORTER - Debt - (same as suit above) being elected and sworn and said that the defendant has not paid the debt of $130.00 and damages of $6.50. The plaintiff recover his costs.

BUCHANAN & WILLIAMS vs VANCE GREER - Debt - (same as suit above) being elected and sworn and said that the defendant has not paid the debt of $310.00 and damages of $30.00. The plaintiff recover his costs.

BENJAMIN GEORGE vs ALLEN TUCKER - Debt - (same as suit above) being elected and sworn and said that the defendant has not paid the debt $94.50 and damages of $1.89. The plaintiff recover his costs.

ALLEN ALSTON vs FRANCIS WYATT - Debt - (same as suit above) being elected and sworn and said that the defendant has not paid the debt of $322.20 and damages of $9.66½. The plaintiff to recover his costs.

JAMES MARTIN vs GEORGE & PREWIT - Debt - (same as suit above) being elected and sworn and said that the defendant has not paid the debt of $302.00 and damages of $10.57. The plaintiff to recover his costs. Defendant prays for appeal to Circuit Court.

WILLIAM BOON appeared in court and acknowledged himself indebted to the State of Tennessee $100.00 to be levied upon his goods and chattels &c but to be void on condition that he appear here to prosecute and give evidence in behalf of the State against JOSEPH WHITAKER and JOHN HOLEMAN.

WILLIAM BOON (same as above) in behalf of the State against JOHN PARKS.

WILLIAM BOWEN vs FRANCIS MAY - Motion - Court ordered the Sheriff to expose for sale 5 acres of land levied on as property of FRANCIS MAY to satisfy a judgement.

An Indenture of Bargain and Sale from ARTHENIEL RICE to GEORGE KOONCE for 10 acres of land and proven by PHILIP KOONCE and ELIJAH PHILLIPS and ordered to be certified.

An Indenture of Bargain and Sale from ARTHENIEL RICE to GEORGE KOONCE for 10 acres of land and proven by PHILIP KOONCE and ELIJAH KOONCE and ordered to be certified.

An Indenture of Bargain and Sale from EDWARD HARDING to ARCHER BEASLEY for 100 acres of land and ordered to be certified.

JOHN W. McGIMSEY vs JOHN DAVIS - Motion - The Sheriff was ordered to expose for sale 50 acres of land lying in Franklin County on Hurricane Creek adjoining DANIEL ARCHER on the north to satisfy a judgement.

McGIMSEY & AKIN (EAKIN) vs MARTIN JONES - Motion - The Sheriff was ordered to expose to sale 25 acres of land lying on East Fork of Mulberry and east of WILLIAM BROWN's to satisfy a judgement.

WHITNEY & HOOPER vs MARTIN JONES - Motion - The Sheriff was ordered to expose to sale 25 acres of land lying on East Fork of Mulberry Creek and east of WILLIAM BROWN's levied on as property of said JONES to satisfy a judgement.

JAMES McDAVID vs WILLIAM PUGH - On motion of the defendant by his attorney, it is ordered by the court that a Writ of Certiorari issue to bring up to court the papers relative to a suit tried before WILLIAM C. ABELS, Esquire, wherein JAMES McDAVID, admr, and NANCY McDAVID, admrx, of WILLIAM McDAVID, deceased, was plaintiff and WILLIAM PUGH defendant.

JOEL JOHNSON vs SAMUEL GARLAND - Motion to Dismiss Certiorari - Both parties by their attorneys and on argument of the motion to dismiss the certiorari in this cause. Court dismissed cause and the plaintiff recover against the defendant and WILLIAM HUSBANDS his security of $21.00 and interest.

SATURDAY JULY 29, 1820

Justices present were SAMUEL BUCHANAN, CHARLES BOYLES, WILLIAM KENNON, PHILIP KOONCE and JAMES HOLEMAN.

It is ordered by the court that JOHN DAVIS work under JAMES HIGGINS as overseer of a road and ADELAI SHARP work under ELIJAH DAVIS as overseer of a work.

HALLET PEARCE vs JAMES MEEK - Motion to Dismiss Certiorari - Both parties by their attorneys and on argument of motion dismiss being heard and court overruled.

On motion, it is ordered by the court that the Clerk receive and place on the Tax List 141 acres of land on West Fork of Norris Creek in the name of GEORGE MARTIN and that he pay a single tax for the same.

JOHN W. CRUNK vs ROBERT BRADON - Appeal - The defendant by his attorney came into court and the plaintiff being called to come and prosecute this appeal failed to do so. The defendant recover against the plaintiff his costs.

JOHN ZIVELY vs CHAPMAN & HANBY - Certiorari - The defendants by their attorneys came into court and the plaintiff being called to come and prosecute this certiorari failed to do so. Defendant to recover against the plaintiff his costs.

CHARLES BOYLES vs JOHN BROWN - Debt - The plaintiff by his attorney came into court and the defendant being called to come and defend this suit failed to do so but made a default. The plaintiff to recover against the defendant his costs.

It is ordered by the court that JOHN D. SPAIN be released from payment of the appraised value of a stray sorrel mare and sorrel colt which he had posted and was proven away from him.

ROBERT H. McEWEN and others vs JOHN PARKS and others - The plaintiff by their attorney came into court and the defendant being called to come and defend this suit came not but made default. The plaintiff to recover against the defendant his cost of $1500.00 and $22.50 damages.

ROBERT H. McEWEN and others vs JOHN PARKS and others - The plaintiff by his attorney came into court all the defendant being called to come and defend this suit failed to do so but made default. The plaintiff to recover against the defendant with the further sum of $54.00 damages.

WILLIAM BLEDSOE vs JOSEPH KELLY, admr - The plaintiff came by his attorney and says he wishes to dismiss this suit and assumes the payment of all costs. This suit be dismissed and the defendant recover against the plaintiff his costs.

A Power of Attorney from WILLIAM KELLY to BENJAMIN CLEMENTS and ANDREW SMITH was acknowledged in court by said WILLIAM KELLY and ordered to be certified.

DAVID KELLER vs NATHANIEL B. BUCKINGHAM - The plaintiff by his attorney came into court and the defendant being called to come and defend this suit failed to do so but made default to recover against the defendant $79.89 and damages of $14.67.

JOHN N. PORTER vs SAMUEL PORTER - Attachment - The plaintiff by his attorney came into court and the defendant being called to come and defend this suit failed to do so but made default. The plaintiff to recover against the defendant $2500.00 and damages $130.00.

BUCHANAN & PORTERFIELD vs NANCY FEATHERSTON - Attachment - The plaintiff by his attorney came into court and the defendant being called to come and defend this suit failed to do so but made default. The plaintiff to recover against the defendant

$102.62½ and damages of $3.99.

AMBROSE PEARCE vs FELIX CRUNK - Motion - On motion of AMBROSE PEARCE by his attorney against FELIX CRUNK, judgement was rendered against PEARCE and the following persons were summoned to assertain the facts, to wit, DAVID THWING, REECE HOWELL, KEYS MEEK, JESSE DANIEL, JOHN GUYDER, CORDIAL SHUFFIELD, JAMES GANT, JOHN PRICE, WILLIAM CRAWFORD, TUNSTALL GREGORY, and WILLIAM LEDFORD and they do say that AMBROSE PEARCE was only bonded as security. Court ordered that the plaintiff recover against the defendant for $21.65.

SAMUEL BUCHANAN vs JAMES LAWSON - Motion - On motion of the plaintiff by his attorney for judgement the defendant in this cause and it appearing from the records of the office that SAMUEL BUCHANAN was security for JAMES LAWSON and has paid $34.28 as security for said LAWSON. The plaintiff to recover against the defendant his costs.

JOHN MAZE vs WILLIAM K. PAULLING - Motion - On motion of the plaintiff by his attorney for judgement against the defendant and it appearing that JOHN MAZE was security for WILLIAM K. PAULLING. JAMES STUART against WILLIAM K. and that JOHN MAZE had paid $217.60 as security for WILLIAM K. plaintiff to recover against defendant his costs.

JOHN W. SMITH vs ISHAM BURKS - Motion - On motion of the plaintiff by his attorney for judgement against the defendant and it appearing from the records that JOHN W. SMITH as security for the defendant and has paid $149.16. Plaintiff to recover against the defendant his costs.

On this 22nd day of July 1820, personally appeared in open court, being a Court of Record enacted by statue of unlimited civil jurisdiction on the law side of said court for the county aforesaid JOHN JACKSON about sixty nine years of age the 12th day of next November, residing in said county who being first solemnly sworn according to law doth on his oath declare that he served in the Revolutionary War as follows, to wit, that he enlisted on the tenth of June 1775 for eighteen months in a company of rangers commanded by CAPTAIN JOHN PURVIS and in the latter part of July or the first of August 1776 he enlisted again for three years in the Third Regiment of the South Carolina Line in the Continental Establishment commanded by COLONEL WILLIAM THOMPSON and that he was discharged in April 1778, he was in the Battle of Stones and Sullivans Island and I do solemnly swear that I have been placed on the Pension List Roll of West Tennessee Agency, by Pension Certificate No. 15.822 and that I made my original declaration for a pension on the 21st day of September 1818 and that I have no particular trade or profession and my family consists of my wife about sixty eight years old and my daughter nineteen years old who are very unhealthy and unable to support themselves and I do solemnly swear that I was a resident citizen of the United States on the 18th day of March 1818 and that I have not since that time by gift, sale, or in any way disposed of my property or any part thereof, with intent thereby so to diminish it as to bring myself within the provisions of An Act of Congress entitled "An Act to provide for certain persons in the Land and Naval Service of the United States in the Revolutionary War, passes the 18th day of March 1818 and that I have not nor has any person in trust for me any property or securities, contracts or debts due to me, nor have I any income other that what is cintained in the schedule here unto annexed".

Signed: JOHN JACKSON

7 head of cattle, two of which is grown cows, two young hogs
1 horse beast worth twenty dollars, strayed off the last of November 1819
2 ploughs, 1 hoe, 2 axes, 1 drawing knife, 2 augers, 2 or 3 pots and oven, and some table furniture not amounting to more than about $15.00
The above is a true schedule of all the property that I do in any wise own or possess except my wearing apparel and the wearing apparel of my wife and daughter and necessary beding. July 22, 1820.
The above property estimated by the court to be worth fifty dollars.

S. JOHNSON vs JAMES HOBBS - Motion to Dismiss Certiorari - Both parties by their attorneys came into court and on motion to dismiss the certiorari in this cause. Court to dismiss certiorari and the plaintiff recover against the defendant $70.70 his costs.

MONDAY OCTOBER 16, 1820

JOSHUA CHURCH is appointed by the court overseer of the road in the room of JOHN WISEMAN resigned and call on the usual hands.

An additional inventory of the estate of DAVID SAWYERS, deceased, was exhibited in court by his admr which was ordered to be recorded.

An amount of sales of the property of WILLIAM HARRIS, deceased, was exhibited in court by his executor which was ordered to be recorded.

The Commissioners appointed to settle with the admrs of WILLIAM CONWELL, deceased, made return of the settlement by them and ordered to be recorded.

THOMAS WASHBURN is appointed overseer of the road in the room of THOMAS BLYTH resigned and call on the usual hands.

ARCHABALD McELROY is appointed overseer of the road in the room of JOHN ALLBRIGHT resigned and call on the usual hands.

JAMES BROOK is appointed overseer of the road in the room of WILLIAM BEATY resigned and call on the usual hands.

ISAAC BRIDGEWATERS is appointed overseer of the road in the room of ELIJAH DILLINDER resigned and call on the usual hands.

RANDOL BRIANT is appointed overseer of the road in the room of BENJAMIN ARRINGTON resigned and the magistrates in his bounds are to appoint the hands to work on said road.

JOHN RHEA, WILLIAM SHAW, JOHN H. RODGERS, WILLIAM DOAK, WILLIAM SOLOMON, EPHRAIM PARHAM, and JESSE BROADWAY is appointed a Jury of View to turn the Mulberry Road leaving the present road on the top of the hill by WILLIAM DOAK and to intersect the old road again between FRANCIS WYATT and JOHN RHEA and make return to next court.

FRANCIS WYATT is appointed overseer of the road in the room of JOHN H. ROGERS resigned and call on the usual hands.

ISAAC BROILES is appointed overseer of the road in the room of JOSEPH WHITAKER resigned and to call on the usual hands.

PHILLIP FOX is appointed overseer of the road from the forks of the road near DAVID THWING to the top of the ridge west of WILLIAM DICKSON's farm and that ISAAC MARTIN, THOMAS GROSS, HOWELL JOHNSON, JAMES MILLS, the hands on JOSEPH MOONY's land, JOHN GOFORTH, THOMAS GLASSCOCK, WILLIAM ASHBY, WILLIAM DICKSON's hands, THOMAS LEDFORD hands and all the hands with that bounds worked on said road.

An amount of the sale of FRANCIS McCOWEN, deceased, was returned to court by his admrs and ordered to be recorded.

It is ordered by the court that THOMAS W. HAYS be allowed $6.50 for summoning a guard to bring DANIEL F. MOORE to kail and for other services.

AMOS DAVIS is released from paying a double tax for the year 1820 and authorized to pay a single tax only.

JOSEPH PATRICK is appointed admr of the estate of EZEKIEL NAILS, deceased, who gave bond with JOHN WISEMAN and ISAAC MORGAN his securities in the sum of $5000.00.

JANE WAKEFIELD is appointed admrx and JOHN W. McGIMSEY admr of the estate of JOHN WAKEFIELD, deceased, and gave bond with THOMAS CRAWFORD, JAMES CLARK, JONATHAN FLOYD and JOHN ENOCKS for security for $5000.00.

THOMAS WASHBOURN is released from paying a double tax for the year 1820 and authorized to pay a single tax only.

JOHN CLARK, WILLIAM CARITHERS and SAMUEL WAKEFIELD is appointed Commissioners to lay off one years support for the widow and children of JOHN WAKEFIELD, deceased, and make return to next court.

STEPHEN ALEXANDER, WILLIAM KENNON and ISAAC CONGER is appointed to settle with SAMUEL ROSEBOROUGH, admr of JOSEPH WHITENBURGH, deceased, and make return to next court.

JOHN WISEMAN appeared in court and was sworn in as a Justice of the Peace for Lincoln County.

The Last Will and Testament of RICHARD DOWNS, deceased, was exhibited in court for probate, WILLIAM ESLICK and ROBERT STORIES (STORY), witnesses, proved the same to be his Last Will and Testament whereupon came JOHN SMITH and was approved admr with the will annexed of all and singular the goods and chattels of RICHARD DOWNS, deceased, gave bond with JOHN WHITAKER his security for $1500.00.

A Bill of Sale from RICHARD DOWNS to JOHN SMITH for two negroes was proven in court by WILLIAM ESLICK and ROBERT STORIES (STORY), witnesses and ordered to be certified.

The transfer of a plat and certificate of survey from JOHN GREER, Sheriff, to HENRY OLD for 50 acres of land and ordered to be certified.

The transfer of a plat and certificate of survey from AMOS DAVIS to JESSE DAVIS for 20 acres of land and ordered to be certified.

The due execution of an Indenture of Bargain and Sale from MORDICAI PILLOW to ELISHA BAGLEY for 70 acres of land, proven by JESSE C. FARRAR and RICHARD WELCH and ordered to be certified.

A Deed of COnveyance from MORDICAI PILLOW to ROBERT PATTON for 50 acres of land, proven by JESSE C. FARRAR and ELISHA BAGLEY and ordered to be certified.

A Deed of Conveyance from ROBERT GEE to DANIEL WARREN for 50 acres of land, proven by NATHAN WARREN and SETH MEED (MEAD) and ordered to be certified.

A Deed of Conveyance from JOEL PAYNE to ROBERT GEE for 50 acres of land, proven by ROBERT DICKSON and B. CLEMENTS and ordered to be certified.

A Deed of Conveyance from ISAAC SEBASTIAN to GRIFFITH R. CUNNINGHAM for 125 acres of land and ordered to be certified.

A Deed of Conveyance from MICHAEL SPENCER to JAMES HALL for 40 acres of land and ordered to be certified.

A Deed of Conveyance from JOHN McNARY to WILLIAM BONER (BONNER) for 313 acres of land, proven by ELI GARRETT and JOSEPH BRADLY and ordered to be certified.

A Deed of Conveyance from JOHN GREER, Sheriff, to JOHN W. McGIMSEY and JOHN EAKIN for part of town lot No. 15 in the town of Lynchburgh and ordered to be certified.

A Deed of Conveyance from WILLIAM SMITH and SPENCER ROGERS to DANIEL BAKER for 67 3/4 acres of land and ordered to be certified.

A Deed of Conveyance from JESSE HADEN to MARNOCK GLAZIER for 100 acres of land, proven by JOHN H. ALLEN and ordered to be certified.

A Deed of Conveyance from JOSEPH GREER and JAMES TORRENTINE to DAVID ARMSTRONG for 216 acres of land, proven by JOHN H. MOORE and PETER J. COTTON and ordered to be certified.

A Deed of Conveyance from JOHN B. BUCHANAN to SAMUEL MIXON for 108 acres of land and ordered to be certified.

A Deed of Conveyance from ROBERT BUCHANAN to MOSES BUCHANAN for 100 acres of land and ordered to be certified.

A Deed of Conveyance from ALEXANDER STUART to WILLIAM PINSON for 50 acres of land, proven by DAVID BYERS and SAMUEL BYERS and ordered to be certified.

The transfer of a plat and certificate from EDWARD GORE to WILLIAM MUCKELROY for 5 acres of land, proven by JONATHAN FLOYD and JOHN ENOCKS and ordered to be certified.

The transfer of a plat and certificate from WILLIAM ALEXANDER to WILLIAM MUCKELROY for 7 acres of land, proven by JONATHAN FLOYD and JOHN ENOCKS and ordered to be certified.

The transfer of a plat and certificate from WILLIAM ALEXANDER to THOMPSON

ENOCKS for 3½ acres of land, proven by JONATHAN FLOYD and JOHN ENOCKS and ordered to be certified.

The transfer of a plat and certificate from HOWELL DAWDY to THOMPSON ENOCKS for 20 acres of land, proven by JONATHAN FLOYD and JOHN ENOCKS and ordered to be certified.

The transfer of a plat and certificate from THOMAS JONES to JAMES ELLIS for 6 acres of land, proven by JONATHAN FLOYD and JOHN ENOCKS and ordered to be certified.

A Deed of COnveyance from WILLIAM PINSON to SARAH FOWLER for 50 acres of land, proven by JOHN H. McCURRY and NANCY FOWLER and ordered to be certified.

A Deed of Conveyance from WILLIAM CROFT to YOUNG TAYLOR for 15 acres of land, proven by ALLEN TUCKER and R.C. PRUETT and ordered to be certified.

A Deed of Conveyance from JOHN HANBY to ISAIAH ALLEY for 156 acres of land and ordered to be certified.

A Deed of Conveyance from JAMES NELSON to SPENCER ROGERS for 73 acres of land, proven by WILLIAM SMITH and DANIEL BAKER and ordered to be certified.

A Deed of Conveyance from WILLIAM B. LEWIS to RALPH SMITH for 50 acres of land, proven by JOHN GREER and JOHN H. MOORE and ordered to be certified.

STEPHEN C. CHITWOOD was appointed a Constable, gave bond with EDMOND CHITWOOD and JOSEPH PEN (PENN) his securities.

ELIJAH McLAUGHLIN appointed a Constable, took the oath and gave bond with AMBROSE BARKER and C. DANIEL his securities.

DANIEL SIVELY was appointed a Constable, took the oath, gave bond with JOHN WISEMAN and LEMUEL BRANDON his securities.

Ordered by the court that DANIEL ARCHER securities notify him to attend here on next Monday next to give other security.

It is ordered by the court that next Monday be set apart for doing the county business.

It is ordered by the court that the tavern rates be as follows, to wit, for each diet 25¢, lodging 12½¢, whiskey per half pint 12½¢, for keeping a horse per night 37½¢, for a single feed for horse 12½¢. Total $1.00. Ferriages for man and horse 12½¢, for wagon and team 50¢.

TUESDAY OCTOBER 17, 1820

Justices present were PHILIP KOONCE, SAMUEL BUCHANAN, JAMES HOLEMAN and WILLIAM KENNON, Esquires.

The Sheriff made return to court that he had summoned the following venire, to wit, EPHRAIM M. BUGG, JOHN TOWERY, JOEL DODSON, PAYTON WELLS, DAVID BYERS, JOSEPH DEAN, JAMES ROGERS, BENJAMIN PROCTOR, SAMUEL BUTLER, JOHN MOREHEAD, JOHN D. SPAIN, JAMES RUTHERFORD, ALEXANDER COWEN, DAVID COOPER, SAMUEL RAMSEY, BRITON PHELPS, JOHN DUSENBERRY, RANDOLPH QUARLES, SAMUEL S. BUCHANAN, ASA STREET, HIRAM HOWELL, and WILLIAM HORTON, of whom were elected to serve a Grand Jurors, to wit, RANDOLPH QUARLES, Foreman, JAMES ROGERS, JOEL DODSON, BRITON PHELPS, ASA STREET, SAMUEL RAMSEY, DAVID COOPER, JOHN TOWERY, SAMUEL BUTLER, BENJAMIN PROCTOR, WILLIAM HORTON, JOSEPH DEAN and JOHN MOREHEAD who after receiving their charge from the solicitor returned to consider for further presentments.

STERLING C. McLEMORE, a Constable, sworn to wait on the Grand Jury this term.

SAMUEL S. BUCHANAN released from serving as a Juror this term.

JAMES FULTON, Esquire, produced into court a license and was permitted to qualify as a practicing attorney in this county.

THOMAS FLACK vs HAYS BLAIR - Appeal - This day came the parties by their attorneys and a jury of men, to wit, ALEXANDER COWEN, HIRAM HOWELL, DAVID BYERS, EPHRAIM M. BUGG, PAYTON WELLS, ABNER DYER, SAMUEL ROSEBOROUGH, WILLIAM BOON, JAMES BROADWAY, ISAAC MILLER, JOHN McCLARY, and JACOB WRIGHT who being elected and sworn and said that the defendant is not indebted and recover against the plaintiff his costs.

ALLEN SCRUGGS vs JOHN TOMERSON - The rule referring this cause to arbitrators by consent is rescinded had been made and is continued at next term of this court.

WILLIAM P. ANDERSON vs BRICE M. GARNER - The parties by their attorneys came into court and a jury of men, to wit, RANDOLPH QUARLES, JONES ROGERS, JOEL DODSON, BRITON PHELPS, ASA STREET, DAVID COOPER, JOHN TOWERY, SAMUEL BUTLER, BENJAMIN PROCTOR, WILLIAM HORTON, JOSEPH DEAN, and JOHN MOREHEAD being elected and sworn and said that the defendant did not assume upon himself as charged. Defendant recover against the plaintiff his costs. Plaintiff prays for an appeal.

SAMUEL H. SMITH vs THOMAS L. TROTTER - The plaintiff appeared in court and says he wishes no further to prosecute this his suit to be dismissed and the plaintiff recover against the defendant his costs.

CARROLL & WHITTING vs ROBERT DICKSON - The parties came by their attorneys and a jury of men, to wit, RANDOLPH QUARLES, JONES ROGERS, JOEL DODSON, BRITON PHELPS, ASA STREET, DAVID COOPER, JOHN TOWERY, SAMUEL BUTLER, BENJAMIN PROCTOR, WILLIAM HORTON, JOSEPH DEAN, and JOHN MOREHEAD being elected and sworn and said that the defendant did assume upon himself as charges against him. Plaintiff to recover against the defendant $746.70 his costs. Defendant prays for an appeal.

JANE B. CAMPBELL vs EDMOND CHITWOOD - Case - This day came the parties by their attorneys and a jury of men, to wit, RANDOLPH QUARLES, JONES ROGERS, JOEL DODSON, BRITON PHELPS, ASA STREET, DAVID COOPER, JOHN TOWERY, SAMUEL BUTLER, BENJAMIN PROCTOR, WILLIAM HORTON, JOSEPH DEAN and JOHN MOREHEAD being elected and sworn and said that the defendant did assume upon himself as charged in this suit. The plaintiff's damages are $104.56¼. Plaintiff to recover against the defendant his costs. Defendant prays for an appeal.

A Bill of Sale from JOHN GREER to ROBERT DICKSON for a negro girl JENNY and ordered to be certified.

JOHN MARTIN vs EPHRAIM M. BUGG - The plaintiff wishes to dismiss his suit and the defendant assumes the payment of one half of the costs. It is considered by the court that this suit be dismissed and the plaintiff recover against the defendant one half of the costs.

HALLET PEARCE vs JAMES MEEKS - The plaintiff says he wishes to dismiss this suit and assume the payment of all costs. Suit is dismissed and the defendant recover against the plaintiff his costs.

MARY INGLE vs JOHN MARR - Both parties came by their attorneys and a jury of men, to wit, ALEXANDER COWEN, HIRAM HOWELL, DAVID BYERS, EPHRAIM M. BUGG, PAYTON WELLS, ABNER DYER, JAMES BROADWAY, SAMUEL S. HOLDING, ABSOLOM BEARD, KEYS MEEKS, JOHN McCLARY, and JAMES ESLEMAN being elected and sworn and said that the consent of both parties that the jury is permitted to disperse until tomorrow nine o'clock.

WEDNESDAY OCTOBER 18, 1820

Justices present were SAMUEL BUCHANAN, JAMES HOLEMAN and PHILIP KOONCE, Esquires.

A Deed of COnveyance from WILLIAM COLLIE to ANDREW SEARIGHT for 40 acres of land and ordered to be certified.

A Bill of Sale from BRICE M. GARNER to ROBERT DICKSON for six negroes, to wit, GEORGE, PATTY, GEORGE, PATSEY, BETSEY, and NAT and ordered to be certified.

A Deed of Conveyance from EDWARD TEAL to BRICE M. GARNER for 702 acres of land and ordered to be certified.

The Grand Jury returned into court with a Bill of Indictment, the State against RICHARD PORTER, a true bill and again returned to consider for further presentments.

GEORGE KOONCE vs JOEL JOHNSON - Debt - This day came the parties by their attorneys and a jury of men, to wit, ALEXANDER COWEN, HIRAM HOWELL, DAVID BYERS, EPHRAIM M. BUGG, PAYTON WELLS, ABNER DYER, JAMES BROADWAY, SAMUEL S. HOLDING, ABSOLEM BEARD, KEYS MEEK, JOHN McCLARY, and JAMES ESLEMAN being elected and sworn and said that the defendant has not paid all the debt to the plaintiff of $200.00 but owes $180.00 and $9.37½. The plaintiff to recover against the defendant his costs.

WILLIAM MOREHEAD vs ROBERT LACKEY - Debt - This day came the parties by their attorneys and a jury of men, to wit, ALEXANDER COWEN, HIRAM HOWELL, DAVID BYERS, EPHRAIM M. BUGG, PAYTON WELLS, ABNER DYER, JAMES BROADWAY, SAMUEL S. HOLDING, ABSOLOM BEARD, KEYS MEEK, JOHN McCLARY, and JAMES ESLEMAN being elected and sworn and said that the defendant has not paid the debt of $100.00 and damages of $4.75. The plaintiff to recover against the defendant his costs.

ROBERT MALLOY vs JAMES Q. STRAIN - The plaintiff says he wisges to dismiss his suit and assumes the payment of one half of the costs and the defendant assumes the other half. Suit is dismissed and each party pay one of the costs.

MARY INGLE vs JOHN MARR - The jury returned to court and said that the defendant is guilty as charged and they assess the plaintiff's damages $275.00. The plaintiff to recover against the defendant his costs. Defendant prays for an appeal.

GEORGE W. HIGGINS, for the use &c vs WILLIAM B. HIGGINS - Debt - The parties by their attorneys came into court and a jury of men, to wit, JOHN HULSEY, ALEXANDER McCULLOUGH, JOHN HANBY, ARCHABALD McELROY, ARCHABALD D. GARVIN, LEMUEL BROADWAY, DANIEL BENSON, EDWARD SANDERSON, JOHN A. CHAPMAN, JOHN ORRICK, ANGUISH JOHNSON, and ALEXANDER ESLEMAN being elected and sworn and said that the defendant has not paid the debt of $125.00 and damages of $19.37½. The plaintiff to recover against the defendant his costs.

CHARLES McKINNEY vs ANTHONY HOGAN & PETER LUNA - Debt - This day came the parties by their attorneys and a jury of men, to wit, JOHN HULSEY, ALEXANDER McCULLOUGH, JOHN HANBY, ARCHABALD McELROY, ARCHABALD D. GARVIN, LEMUEL BROADWAY, DANIEL BENSON, EDWARD SANDERSON, JOHN A. CHAPMAN, JOHN ORRICK, ANGUISH JOHNSON, and ALEXANDER ESLEMAN being elected and sworn and said that the defendant has not paid the debt of $227.46 and damages of $11.35. The plaintiff to recover against the defendant his costs.

JESSEE GEORGE appeared in court and was appointed guardian for FRANCIS GEORGE, LUCRETIA GEORGE, HARDING GEORGE, JESSEE GEORGE, ELIJAH GEORGE and FRANCINE GEORGE, minor heirs of JOSEPH GEORGE, deceased, and gave bond with JOSEPH CAMPBELL and WILLIAM C. JACKSON his securities for $1600.00.

A Deed of Conveyance from JOHN CHILDRESS MARSHALL to EDWARD TEAL for 702 acres of land, proven by JOSEPH GREER and WILLIAM EDMISTON and ordered to be certified.

The Grand Jury returned into court with a Bill of Indictment, the State against BENJAMIN DORSEY, a true bill, the State against JOHN PARK, a true bill and the State against JOSEPH WHITAKER, a true bill and again returned to consider for further presentments.

WILLIAM DICKSON CASHIN vs BRICE M. GARNER - This day came the parties by their attorneys and a jury of men, to wit, ALEXANDER McCULLOUGH, JOHN BANBY, ARCHABALD McELROY, ARCHABALD GARVEN, LEMUEL BROADWAY, DANIEL BENSON, EDWARD SANDERSON, JOHN A. CHAPMAN, JOHN ORRICK, ANGUISH JOHNSON, and ALEXANDER ESLEMAN being elected and sworn and said that the defendant did not make a tender and assumed upon himself as charged and the damages of the plaintiff to $2197.92 3/4. Plaintiff to recover against the defendant his costs.

THURSDAY OCTOBER 19, 1820

Justices present were JAMES HOLEMAN, WILLIAM KENNON, SAMUEL BUCHANAN and PHILIP KOONCE, Esquires.

BAILEY & SHIRLY vs JOHN W. CRUNK - Case - The defendant confessed that he owes the plaintiff $70.41 and damages of $2.45. The plaintiff to recover against the defendant his costs.

The Grand Jury again returned into court with a Bill of Indictment, the State against HARDING FORRISTER, a true bill and again returned to consider for further presentments.

The State vs AUGUSTIN YEAGER - The defendant being charged pleads guilty and is fined $1.00 and pay costs. JOHN DAVIS security for defendant.

The State vs JOHN DUKE - Indictment - The defendant being charged pleads guilty and is fined $1.00 and pay costs of indictment.

The State vs JOHN PARKS - Indictment - The defendant being charged pleads guilty and is fined $1.00 and pay cost of this indictment.

JAMES GREER vs CALEB BLAGG - The plaintiff wishes to dismiss this suit and assumes the payment of all costs. This suit to be dismissed and the defendant recover against the plaintiff his costs.

It is ordered that the Clerk receive and place on the tax list 1630 acres of land in the name of DAVID MOORE and that he pay a single tax for the same.

BRICE M. GARNER vs URIAH BABBET - On motion by the court that HUGH McDOWELL the landlord of the tenant in possession be allowed a defendant in this case to confess lease entry and ouster and pleads not guilty and for his defence to rely upon the bill only.

The State vs BENJAMIN DORSEY - Indictment - The defendant appeared and being charged and pleads not guilty and a jury of men, to wit, ALEXANDER COWEN, HIRAM HOWELL, DAVID BYERS, EPHRAIM M. BUGG, PAYTON WELLS, ALDEN TUCKER, ARTHUR MARKHAM, CHARLES MAIZE, LEMUEL BROADWAY, CORNELIUS SLATER, JOHNSTON TURLEY, and AUGUSTIN YEAGER being elected and sworn and said that the defendant is guilty as charged and is fined $1.00 and pay costs.

The State vs JOSEPH WHITAKER - Indictment - The defendant being charged and pleads guilty and is fined $1.00 and pay costs.

The State vs JOHN HOLEMAN - Indictment - The defendant being charged and pleads guilty and is fined $1.00 and pay costs.

The State vs RICHARD PORTER - Indictment - The defendant being charged and pleads guilty and is fined $5.00 and pay costs. HIRAM HOWELL and JOHN DAVIS his securities.

The State vs WILLIAM A. TUCKER - The defendant acknowledged himself indebted to the State of Tennessee for $200.00 and ALDEN TUCKER for $200.00. The defendant is to appear at June next and answer the charge of an affray and not depart the same without leave first had and obtained of the court.

The State vs ALLEN TUCKER - Indictment - The defendant said that he was indebted to the State of Tennessee for $200.00 and ALDEN TUCKER for $200.00. The defendant is to appear in January next and answer the charge of an affray and not depart the same without leave first had and obtained by the court.

THOMAS W. HAMBLETON acknowledged himself indebted to the State of Tennessee for $100.00 and to appear in court in January next and give evidence in behalf of the State against WILLIAM A. TUCKER and not depart without leave first had and obtained of the court.

THOMAS W. HAMBLETON acknowledged himself indebted to the State of Tennessee for $100.00 and appear in court in January next and give evidence in behalf of the State against ALLEN TUCKER and not depart without leave first had and obtained of the court.

A Deed of COnveyance from JOHN NICHOLAS by his agent WILLIAM STREET to WILLIAM KENNON for 21 acres of land and ordered to be certified.

The transfer of a plat and certificate from JACOB LOCK to ABSOLUM LOCK for 25 acres of land, proven by NOAH LOCK and JAMES LOCK and ordered to be certified.

The transfer of a plat and certificate from JACOB LOCK to ABSOLUM LOCK for 10 acres of land, proven by NOAH LOCK and JAMES LOCK and ordered to be certified.

The transfer of a plat and certificate from JACOB LOCK to ABSOLUM LOCK for 6¼ acres of land, proven by NOAH LOCK and JAMES LOCK and ordered to be certified.

A transfer of a plat and certificate from ABSOLUM LOCK to NOAH LOCK for 25 acres of land and ordered to be certified.

A transfer of a plat and certificate from ABSOLUM LOCK to NOAH LOCK for 10 acres of land and ordered to be certified.

The transfer of a plat and certificate from ABSOLUM LOCK to NOAH LOCK for 6¼ acres of land and ordered to be certified.

The State vs WILLIAM ENGLAND - The defendant appeared in court and on motion of the Attorney General supported by the affidavit of EDWARD McBRIDE, the prosecutor for the defendant to enter into or cognizance to keep the peace to wards the citizens of Tennessee particular towards EDWARD McBRIDE. Court said the reasons were not sufficient to bind the defendant. It is ordered that the defendant be discharged.

The State vs MOSES SANDERS - The defendant being charged on this indictment pleads guilty and is fined $1.00 and pay the costs.

The State vs DAVID HOWELL - The defendant being charged on this indictment pleads guilty and fined $1.00 and pay the costs.

FRIDAY OCTOBER 20, 1820

Justices present were SAMUEL BUCHANAN, JAMES HOLEMAN and CHARLES BOYLES, Esquires.

The Grand Jury again returned into court with a Bill of Indictment, the State against SAMUEL PAINTER, a true bill and again returned to consider for further presentments.

A Deed of Conveyance from WILLIAM JOB to FREDERICK WAGGONER for 120 acres of land, proven by HARDY HOLEMAN and DAVID WAGGONER and ordered to be certified.

The Grand Jury again returned into court with a Bill of Indictment, the State against EDWARD McBRIDE, not a true bill and again returned to consider for further presentments.

The State vs HARDING FORRISTER - Indictment - The defendant being charged, pleads not guilty and a jury of men, to wit, ALEXANDER COWAN, HIRAM HOWELL, DAVID BYERS, EPHRAIM M. BUGG, PAYTON WELLS, GEORGE W. ESLEMAN, DANIEL TOUCHSTONE, WILLIAM PUGH, JAMES HAGUE, JOHN HULSEY, ABSOLUM COLLINS, and DANIEL YOUNG being elected and sworn and said that the defendant is not guilty. Court ordered the defendant be discharged and the county pay the costs.

WILLIAM TOWNSEND vs ELIJAH COPEL - The parties, by permission of the court, this cause is referred to the arbitration of BRICE M. GARNER, CORNELIUS SLATER and MICAJAH PARKER, arbitrators awarded to be returned to this court and make the judgement of this court.

The Grand Jury again returned to court with a Bill of Indictment, the State against PATRICK GILLASPIE, a true bill and again return to consider for further presentments.

ROBERT J. PAMPLIN acknowledged himself indebted to the State of Tennessee for $100.00 and to appear and prosecute and give evidence in behalf of the State against PATRICK GILLASPIE and not depart the same without leave first had and obtained of the court.

WILLIAM EDMISTON and others vs MICAJAH MUCKELROY - The defendant withdraws his plea and confessed that he owes the plaintiff $920.30¼. The plaintiff to recover against the defendant his costs.

The State vs SAMUEL PAINTER - The defendant being charged pleads not guilty and a jury of men, to wit, EDMOND CHITWOOD, LEMUEL BROADWAY, ALEXANDER COWEN, HIRAM HOWELL, DAVID BYERS, EPHRAIM M. BUGG, ALEXANDER ESLEMAN, JAMES BROADWAY, DANIEL WAGGONER, WILLIAM WHITE, and ANGUISH JOHNSTON being elected and sworn and said that the defendant is not guilty. Court orders that the defendant be discharged and the county pay the costs.

The State vs JOHN DYER - The defendant pleads guilty and is fined $1.00 and pay the costs.

WILLIAM JACKSON vs ELIJAH CAPEL - The plaintiff says he wishes to dismiss his suit and assumes the payment of all costs. Court dismisses the suit and the defendant recover against the plaintiff his costs.

The State vs DANIEL YOUNG - The court considered that the defendant be discharged and the county pay the costs.

The State vs CHRISTOPHER E. LOVE - The court considered that the defendant be discharged and the county pay the costs.

The State vs ABSOLUM COLLINS - The court considered that the defendant be discharged and the county pay the costs.

The State vs DANIEL YOUNG - On motion of WILLIAM B. MARTIN the Attorney General and by permission of the court, a noleprossque is entered in this cause.

The State vs C.E. LOVE - On motion of WILLIAM B. MARTIN the Attorney General and permission of the court, a poleprossque is entered in this cause.

SATURDAY OCTOBER 21, 1820

Justices present were PHILIP KOONCE, JAMES HOLEMAN and SAMUEL BUCHANAN, Esquires.

The State vs PATRICK GILLASPIE - Indictment - The defendant acknowledged himself indebted to the State of Tennessee for $200.00 and HENRY LAZENBY for $200.00 and PATRICK GILLASPIE to appear here and answer the State of Tennessee on a charge of an assault and battery and not depart the same without have first had and obtained of the court.

The Grand Jury again returned into court with a Bill of Indictment, the State against HIRAM WINTERS, a true bill and again returned to consider for further presentments.

Fayetteville Turnpike Bank vs JONATHAN ESTILL - Both parties came into court and a jury of men, to wit, ALEXANDER COWEN, HIRAM HOWELL, DAVID BYERS, EPHRAIM M. BUGG, PAYTON WELLS, WILLIAM PUGH, ARTHUR MARKHAM, ISAAC CONWELL, ALLEN TUCKER, GEORGE TITUS, and HARMON WALTON being elected and sworn and said that the defendant did assume upon himselv in manner and form as the plaintiff declared against him and the damages of the plaintiff is $5694.50. The plaintiff to recover against the defendant his costs.

PHILIP LITTIG vs JAMES COALTER - In Debt - Both parties by their attorneys came into court and a jury of men, to wit, ALEXANDER COWEN, HIRAM HOWELL, DAVID BYERS, EPHRAIM M. BUGG, PAYTON WELLS, WILLIAM PUGH, ARTHUR MARKHAM, ISAAC CONWELL, ALLEN TUCKER, GEORGE TITUS, FRANCIS SMITH, and HARMON WALTON being elected and sworn and said that the defendant has not paid the debt of $870.08 and damages of $65.80. The plaintiff to recover against the defendant his costs.

ANSLINE NOLEN vs WALTER KINNARD - The parties by their attorneys came into court and a jury of men, to wit, (same as above jurors) being elected and sworn and said that the defendant has not paid all the debt as charged for $260.00 and damages $25.75. The plaintiff to recover against the defendant his costs.

HUGH M. BLAKE vs MICAJAH MUCKELROY - In Debt - The parties by their attorneys came into court and a jury of men, to wit, (same as above jurors) being elected and sworn and said that the defendant has not paid the debt of $113.00 and damages of $6.36. The plaintiff to recover against the defendant his costs.

HUGH M. BLAKE vs MICAJAH MUCKELROY - In Debt - The parties by their attorneys came into court and a jury of men, to wit, (same as above jurors) being elected and sworn and said that the defendant has not paid his debt of $227.24 and damages of $10.97. Plaintiff to recover against the defendant his costs.

EDMOND FERRELL vs GEORGE W. DENNIS - In Debt - This day came the parties by their attorneys and a jury of men, to wit, (same as above jurors) being elected and sworn and said that the defendant has not paid the debt for $400.00 and damages of $18.00. The plaintiff to recover against the defendant his costs.

WILLIAM DYE vs WALTER KINNARD - In Debt - This day came the parties by their attorneys and a jury of men, to wit, ALEXANDER COWEN, HIRAM HOWELL, DAVID BYERS, EPHRAIM M. BUGG, PAYTON WELLS, WILLIAM PUGH, ARTHUR MARKHAM, ISAAC CONWELL, ALLEN TUCKER, GEORGE TITUS, FRANCIS SMITH and HARMON WALTON being elected and sworn and said that the defendant has not paid the debt of $350.62 and damages of $17.58. The plaintiff to recover against the defendant his costs.

JAMES COALTER vs ENOCK K. WEATHERS - In Debt - This day came the parties by their attorneys and a jury of men, to wit, (same as above jurors) being elected and sworn and said that the defendant has not paid the debt of $96.37½ and damages of $3.20. The plaintiff to recover against the defendant his costs.

ALLEN ELSTON vs MARTIN & LORANCE - In Debt - This day came the parties by their attorneys and a jury of men, to wit, (same as above jurors) being elected and sworn and said that the defendant has not paid the debt of $100.00 and damages of $3.50. The plaintiff to recover against the defendant his costs.

RICHARD COTTRELL vs WILLIAM McNEIL - The plaintiff says he wishes no further to prosecute this suit and assumes the payment of all costs. The case to be dismissed and the defendant recover against the plaintiff his costs.

JOHN BRYANT vs AMBROSE PEARCE - The plaintiff says he wishes to dismiss this suit and the defendant assumes the payment of costs. Court dismisses this suit and the plaintiff recover against the defendant his costs.

JOHN McCLARY vs JAMES ESLEMAN - The parties came by their attorneys and a jury of men, to wit, (same as above jurors) being elected and sworn and said that the defendant is guilty as charged and assess the damages of $8.54.

MONDAY OCTOBER 23, 1820

JOSEPH HINKLE is appointed overseer of the road in the room of JOHN DONELSON resigned and to call on the usual hands.

The due execution of an Indenture of Bargain and Sale from JOHN EDMISTON to JOHN M. ESTILL and BENJAMIN ESTILL for 1000 acres of land, proven by WILLIAM E. KENNEDY and WILLIAM EDMISTON and ordered to be certified.

LEWIS HOPPER is appointed overseer of the road in the room of WILLIAM HODGES resigned and call on the usual hands.

GIDEON PULLY is appointed overseer of the road in the room of JOHN HOLEMAN resigned and call on the usual hands.

It is ordered by the court that JAMES McCREE be allowed and receive from the County Trustee $20.00 for keeping and taking care of POLLY FRAME until 2nd Monday of next court.

It is ordered by the court that the Sheriff summon twelve freeholders of this county to inquire into the condition of POLLY FRAME now in the possession of JAMES McCREE of her lunacy and property and make return to next court.

JOHN STREET is appointed by the court overseer of the road in the room of JOSHUA WILLIAMS resigned and to call on the usual hands.

It is ordered by the court that WILLIAM HUSBANDS be allowed and to receive from the County Trustee $17.00 for removing of ERASMUS CHAPMAN from the jail of this county to Pulaski jail.

It is ordered by the court that PRESLEY S. GEORGE be allowed $3.50.

It is ordered by the court that JOHN CLIFTON overseer of a road, be authorized to purchase a stone hammer and crowbar for the use of the road and present his amount to the next court.

HUGH STEPHENS is appointed overseer of a road from JESSE GEORGE's cotton gin to ABRAHAM ISAACK's Spring Branch and ABRAHAM ISAACK is appointed to designate the hands to work on said road.

WILLIAM BAILY is appointed overseer of a road from ABRAHAM ISAACK's Spring

Branch to the county line and ABRAHAM ISAACKS is appointed to designate the hands to work on said road.

It is ordered by the court that JOHN P. McCONNELL, Jailer, be allowed and to receive from the County Trustee $273.25 out of the county monies in his hands not otherwise appropriated.

It is ordered by the court that JOHN P. McCONNELL be allowed $30.81¼ for articles furnished by him for repairing the courthouse and that the County Trustee pay the same out of any monies in his hands.

A Deed of Conveyance from ELIJAH CAPEL to MICHAEL ROBERTSON for 50 acres of land, proven by SMAUEL CAPEL and MICAJAH PARKER and ordered to be certified.

A Deed of Conveyance from CONSTANT SCALES and HUGH M. BLAKE to JOHN S. PRICE for 156 acres of land and ordered to be certified.

A Deed of Conveyance from JOHN W. SMITH to WILLIAM EDMISTON for 50 acres of land, proven by GENERAL W.C. EDMISTON and MOSES SMITH and ordered to be certified.

A transfer of a plat and certificate of survey from RANDOLPH QUARLES to WILLIAM EDMISTON for 3 acres of land and ordered to be certified.

The transfer of a plat and certificate from WILLIAM RAY to THOMAS BLYTH for 15 acres of land and ordered to be certified.

The transfer of a plat and certificate from WILLIAM RAY to JOSHUA W. MASSEY for 10 acres of land and ordered to be certified.

A transfer of a plat and certificate from JESSE BROWN to JOSHUA W. MASSEY for 20 acres of land and ordered to be certified.

HENRY KYMES is appointed overseer of the road from Cain Creek to MRS. WILEY's and call on the usual hands.

The court appointed EBENEZER McEWEN, ELI GARRETT, ROBERT M. WHITE, JOHN MARR, JOHN ENOCKS, JAMES HOLEMAN and JOHN GREER commissioners of the School Lands in this county.

It is ordered that WILLIAM KENNON, WILLIAM ROGERS, GEORGE RENEGER, SETH MEED and DANIEL WARREN be a Jury of View to view and turn the road leading from the big road below JOHN J. WHITAKER to DUKE's and ALEXANDER's Mill, the nearest and best way so as to leave DUKE's plantation to the left and make return to next court.

JOHN P. McCONNELL, FRANCIS PORTERFIELD and VANCE GREER is appointed Commissioners to let out the repairing of the Court House chimney to the lowest bidder.

ROBERT DICKSON, JOHN P. McCONNELL and ROBERT H. McEWEN is appointed Commissioners to get two stoves and put in the Court House.

It is ordered by the court that the county tax for this county be as high asthe law will allow.

WILLIAM G. WARREN is bound as an apprentice to JOHN DUSENBERRY until he is twenty one years of age to learn the Tanner's trade and is to give him a horse and bridle to be worth $75.00, a suit of trade cloths and to learn him to read, write and cypher through the rule of three. JOHN DUSENBERRY entered into bond and security.

It is ordered that JOAB BUCKLEY be overseer of the road leading from Fayetteville to Columbia by DOBBIN'S Mill from the county line to the top of the ridge between Richland and Swan Creek and that he call on all the hands on the north east side within two miles and a half of said road and all the hands within one mile on the south east side and that those hands be not compelled to work on any other road.

It is ordered that ROBERT EDMISTON be overseer of the new road from Sim's Ford on Elk River to where said road crosses Gray's Creek and to call on all the hands on the west side of the new road or now living on the waters of Elk River as far as the waters of Gray's Creek and all those on said road.

DOILY GRIFFIS is appointed overseer of the new road leading from Fayetteville to intersect the Fort Hampton Road near CAPTAIN DYER's to begin at Grays Creek to where said road intersects the Fort Hampton Road and to call on all the hands that south and east of the Fort Hampton Road that lived on the waters of McCullough Creek, also the hands that lives on the Barren cultivated by JOSHUA DALLAS and JOHN HENDERSON.

TUESDAY OCTOBER 24, 1820

Justices present were SAMUEL BUCHANAN, WILLIAM KENNON and JAMES HOLEMAN, Esquires.

JACOB WAGGONER vs VANCE GREER - The defendant by his attorney appeared in court and the plaintiff being called to come and prosecute this suit failed to do so but made default. The defendant to recover against the plaintiff his costs.

ROBERT H. McEWEN vs GEORGE E. SANDERSON - In Debt - The defendant confessed that he owes the plaintiff $106.25 and damages of $5.31¼. Plaintiff agrees to stay execution until next court. The plaintiff to recover against the defendant his costs.

ANDREW KILPATRICK for the use of WILLIAM TOWNZEND vs MARTHA BURTON - In Debt - Both parties by their attorneys came into court and a jury of men, to wit, RANDOLPH QUARLES, JONES BYERS, JOEL DODSON, ASA STREET, SAMUEL RAMSEY, DAVID COOPER, JOHN TOWERY, SAMUEL BUTLER, BENJAMIN PROCTOR, WILLIAM HORTON, JOSEPH DEAN, and JOHN MOREHEAD being elected and sworn and said that the defendant has not paid the debt of $105.00 and damages of $4.20. The plaintiff to recover against the defendant his costs.

MICAJAH McELROY vs SAMUEL H. SMITH - The plaintiff says he intends no further to prosecute this suit and assumes the payment of all costs. Court dismisses said suit and the defendant to recover against the plaintiff his costs.

JAMES BROADWAY vs THOMAS BUCHANAN - Both parties by their attorneys came into court and a jury of men, to wit, (same as above jurors) being elected and sworn and said that the defendant only paid $100.00 to HENRY FOSTER who assign the note to the plaintiff and the defendant has not paid all the debt but owes on account $400.00 and damages of $20.75. Plaintiff to recover against said defendant his costs. The defendant prays for an appeal on a Writ of Error to next court and gave bond and security.

WEDNESDAY OCTOBER 25, 1820

Justices present were WILLIAM KENNON, SAMUEL BUCHANAN and JAMES HOLEMAN, Esquires.

The State vs PATRICK GILLASPIE - The defendant being charged and pleads not guilty and a jury of men, to wit, PAYTON WELLS, DAVID BYERS, EPHRAIM M. BUGG, HIRAM HOWELL, ALEXANDER COWEN, THOMAS BUCHANAN, DAVID SMITH, ARCHABALD D. GARVEN, NATHANIEL B. BUCKINGHAM, JESSE LAMB, ELI MILSTEAD, and ARCHY BEASLY being elected and sworn and said that the defendant is guilty as charged and is fined 25¢ and pay the costs. WILLIAM C. JACKSON security for defendant.

BENJAMIN GEORGE vs ALDEN TUCKER and others - In Case - The plaintiff by his attorney says he wishes to dismiss this suit and assumes the payment of all costs except the attendance of the defendant's witnesses. Court dismisses this suit and the defendant recover against the plaintiff his costs.

JOEL PINSON, Exrs vs FRANCIS & JAMES WYATT - In Debt - The parties by their attorneys came into court and a jury of men, to wit, (same as above jurors) being elected and sworn and said that the defendant has not paid the debt of $150.00 and damages of $7.12½. The plaintiff to recover against said defendant his costs.

OBADIAH JONES and others vs JOHN P. McCONNELL and others - In Debt - This day came the parties by their attorneys and a jury of men, to wit, (same as above jurors) being elected and sworn and said that the defendant has not paid his debt of $110.00 and damages of $68.00. Plaintiff to recover against the defendant his costs.

OBADIAH JONES and others vs JOHN P. McCONNELL and others - In Debt - This day came the parties by their attorneys and a jury of men, to wit, (same as above jurors) being elected and sworn and said that the defendant has not paid his debt of $1100.00 and damages of $57.00. Plaintiff to recover against the defendant his costs.

GARNER & BEARD vs EDWARD TATUM, Exrs - In Debt - (same as above and jurors)

71

being elected and sworn and said that the defendant has not paid the debt of $79.00 and damages of $4.00. Plaintiff to recover against the defendant his costs.

JOHN YAUNT vs MICAJAH McELROY - In Debt - This day came the parties by their attorneys and a jury of men, to wit, PAYTON WELLS, DAVID BYERS, EPHRAIM M. BUGG, HIRAM HOWELL, ALEXANDER COWEN, THOMAS BUCHANAN, DAVID SMITH, ARCHABALD D. GARVEN, NATHANIEL B. BUCKINGHAM, JESSE LAMB, ELI MILSTEAD and ARCHY BEASLY being elected and sworn and said that the defendant has not paid the debt of $200.00 and damages of $13.66 2/3. Plaintiff to recover against the defendant his costs.

DRAKE RANDOLPH vs DANIEL COFFMAN - In Debt - This day came the parties by their attorneys and a jury of men, to wit, (same as above jurors) being elected and sworn and said that the defendant has not paid the debt of $200.00 and damages of $10.00. Plaintiff to recover against the defendant his costs.

HOLLET PEARCE vs JAMES MEEK & GEORGE CRAWFORD - In Debt - This day came the parties by their attorneys and a jury of men, to wit, (same as above jurors) being elected and sworn and said that the defendant has not paid the debt of $250.00 and damages of $11.50. Plaintiff to recover against the defendant his costs.

JOHN F. POOR vs SPENCER A. PUGH - In Debt - This day came the parties by their attorneys and a jury of men, to wit, (same as above jurors) being elected and sworn and said that the defendant has not paid the debt of $231.25 and damages of $9.24. Plaintiff to recover against the defendant his costs.

JOHN J. CARRINGTON vs JAMES MARTIN - This day came the parties by their attorneys and a jury of men, to wit, (same as above jurors) being elected and sworn and said that the defendant has not paid the debt of $2068.90 and damages of $99.93 1/3. Plaintiff to recover against the defendant his costs.

The State vs HIRAM WINTERS - Indictment - The defendant being charged and pleads not guilty and a jury of men, to wit, (same as above jurors) being elected and sworn and said that the defendant is guilty as charged and was fined $5.00 his costs.

THURSDAY OCTOBER 26, 1820

Justices present were CHARLES BOYLES, JAMES HOLEMAN and SAMUEL BUCHANAN, Esquires.

SAMUEL BRADLY vs THOMAS ALLSUP - This day came the parties by their attorneys and a jury of men, to wit, RANDOLPH QUARLES, JONES ROGERS, JOEL DODSON, BRITAIN PHELPS, DAVID COOPER, JOHN TOWERY, SAMUEL BUTLER, BENJAMIN PROCTOR, WILLIAM HORTON, JOSEPH DEAN, JOHN MOREHEAD and ALEXANDER CONWELL being elected and sworn and said that the defendant has not paid all the debt but owes $128.96¼ and damages of $9.31¼. Plaintiff to recover against the defendant his costs.

THOMAS BERRY vs JEREMIAH STUBBLEFIELD - The plaintiff says he wishes to dismiss this suit and assumes the payment of all costs. Suit to be dismissed and the defendant recover against the plaintiff his costs.

THOMAS JOINER vs JOHN D. SPAIN - Motion to Dismiss - On motion this case is to be dismissed and the plaintiff recover against the defendant and BRICE M. GARNER his security, the sum of $58.30 and interest.

WOODSON HALEY vs WILLIAM CUNNINGHAM - The defendant says he wishes to dismiss his ceriorari and says he owes the plaintiff $30.75 and the plaintiff agrees to stay execution ninety days. Plaintiff to recover against the defendant his costs.

THOMAS ALLISON vs THOMAS KELLY - Appeal - The parties by their attorneys came into court and a jury of men, to wit, ASA STREET, SAMUEL RAMSEY, HIRAM HOWELL, DAVID BYERS, PAYTON WELLS, EPHRAIM M. BUGG, JOHN McCLARY, SPENCER A. PUGH, ROBERT EDMISTON, ARCHABALD McELROY, JAMES COALTER, and THOMAS BOAZ being elected and sworn and said that the defendant is indebted to the plaintiff for $46.42¼. Plaintiff to recover against the defendant his costs.

JAMES BROADWAY vs THOMAS BUCHANAN - The defendant withdraws his appeal and the plaintiff dismisses his suit and the defendant assumes the payment of all costs. Suit be dismissed and the plaintiff recover against the defendant his costs.

72

ROBERT & WILLIAM DICKSON vs FRANCIS SMITH - The Sheriff is to expose to sale one town lot No. 90 in the town of Fayetteville levied on as the property of FRANCIS SMITH to satisfy a judgement that ROBERT & WILLIAM DICKSON recovered against SMITH for $31.20 3/4 and all legal costs before WILLIAM DICKSON on 5 April last.

BRICE M. GARNER vs RICHARD AUTON & FRANCIS SMITH - Motion - The Sheriff is to expose to sale one town lot No. 90 in the town of Fayetteville and known as the property of FRANCIS SMITH to satisfy a judgement that GARNER recovered against SMITH & RICHARD AUTON before CHARLES BOYLES on 1st day of May last for $11.o6 and all costs.

JOHN McCLARY vs JAMES ESLEMAN - Appeal - This day came the parties by their attorneys and a jury of men, to wit, RANDOLPH QUARLES, JONES ROGERS, JOEL DODSON, BRITON PHELPS, DAVID COOPER, JOHN TOWERY, SAMUEL BUTLER, BENJAMIN PROCTOR, WILLIAM HORTON, JOSEPH DEAN, JOHN MOREHEAD, and ALEXANDER COWEN being elected and sworn and said that the plaintiff is indebted to the defendant $4.21 3/4. Defendant to recover against the plaintiff his costs.

FRIDAY OCTOBER 27, 1820

Justices present were WILLIAM KENNON, SAMUEL BUCHANAN and PHILLIP KOONCE, Esquires.

PEABOY & CHAMBERLAIN vs JAMES COALTER - On petition of the plaintiff by their attorney, a Commission is awarded them to take the deposition of HOWARD HENDERSON in New Orleans by giving the defendant thirty days notice of time and place of taking the same and that the defendant be permitted to depositions generally in New Orleans by given the plaintiff's attorney thirty days notice and notice given to the plaintiffs five days notice of time and place of taking the same.

JAMES CARITHERS vs BRICE M. GARNER - The plaintiff by his attorney says he wishes to dismiss his suit and assumes the payment of all costs. Suit to be dismissed and the defendant recover against the plaintiff his costs.

The due execution of an Indenture of Bargain and Sale from JOHN BARNES to THOMAS SCURLOCK for 82 acres of land, proven by JOHN DAVIS and RICHARD FLYNT and ordered to be certified.

A Deed of Conveyance from RICHARD FOWLER to ANDREW CONNER for 152 acres of land, proven by JAMES McDAVID and THOMAS SHINAULT and ordered to be certified.

CLARIDGE B. ROBERTSON vs VANCE GREER - Both parties by their attorneys came into court and a jury of men, to wit, RANDOLPH QUARLES, JONES ROGERS, JOEL JOHNSON, ASA STREET, SAMUEL RAMSEY, DAVID COOPER, SAMUEL BUTLER, BENJAMIN PROCTOR, JOSEPH DEAN, JOHN MOREHEAD, PAYTON WELLS, and EPHRAIM M. BUGG being elected and sworn and said that the defendant is not indebted to the plaintiff anything. Defendant recover against the plaintiff his costs. Plaintiff prays for an appeal.

ROBERT & WILLIAM DICKSON vs JOHN TATUM - Appeal - Both parties by their attorneys came into court and a jury of men, to wit, (same as above jurors) being elected and sworn and said that the defendant doth owe the plaintiff $82.86 and damages of $4.51. Plaintiff to recover against the defendant his costs.

ROBERT & WILLIAM DICKSON vs WILLIAM CUNNINGHAM - Appeal - Both parties by their attorneys came into court and a jury of men, to wit, (same as above jurors) being elected and sworn and said that the defendant is indebted to the plaintiff for $76.36¼ and damages of $1.99 and $1.50 interest. Plaintiff recover against the defendant his costs.

ROBERT & WILLIAM DICKSON vs WILLIAM CUNNINGHAM - Appeal - Both parties by their attorneys came into court and a jury of men, to wit, (same as above jurors) being elected and sworn and said that the defendant is indebted to the plaintiff $73.52 1/3 and damages of $7.35. Plaintiff to recover against the defendant his costs.

ROBERT & WILLIAM DICKSON vs WILLIAM CUNNINGHAM - Appeal - Both parties by their attorneys came into court and a jury of men, to wit, (same as above jurors) being elected and sworn and said that the defendant is indebted to the plaintiff for $61.09 and damages of $3.81 and $1.22 interest. Plaintiff to recover against the defendant his costs.

SATURDAY OCTOBER 28, 1820

Justices present were JAMES HOLEMAN, CHARLES BOYLES and PHILIP KOONCE, Esquires.

The due execution of an Indenture of Bargain and Sale from JOHN TROY to NICHOLAS CARRIGER for 300 acres of land, proven by JOHN GREER and ordered to be certified.

MATHEW MYRICK vs HENRY DAWSON - The plaintiff says he wishes to dismiss his suit and assumes the payment of all costs. Suit to be dismissed and the defendant recover against the plaintiff his costs.

GUSTAVUS HENDRICK vs VANCE GREER - The defendant is awarded a Commission to take the deposition of JOHN BURK, THOMAS GOOD, LEWIS WAER, JONATHAN YORK, GABRIEL HANBY, JOHN GILBREATH, WILLIAM GILBREATH and POSEY (whose christian name is not known) of State of Alabama to be read as evidence on the trial of this cause by given the plaintiff counsel twenty days notice or five day is served on the plaintiff himself, for taking the same.

DANIEL HIGGINS vs THOMAS A. STRAIN - On motion of the defendant by his attorneys for a Writ of Certiorari, court overruled and that a proevidence be awarded to the magistrate to proceed to a judgement against the defendant and JAMES I(Q). STRAIN and DAVID EDMISTON who stayed the execution.

JOHN GIBSON, JAMES TOOL and HENRY CLIFT be appointed Commissioners to lay off one years provisions for the widow and children of ROBERT EDMISTON, deceased, and make return to next court.

It is ordered by the court that ANDREW HANNAH, WILLIAM CASHON, JOSEPH WHITAKER, JOHN WATKINS, MOSES STONE, JOHN NEECE, SAMUEL TOOD, JOHN LEE, AUGUST L. JONES, WILLIAM DOAK, WILLIAM PARKS, THOMAS PARKS, SOLOMON GULLETT, JORDAN REACE, JAMES LINGO, JOHN MOOR, BROWN PARKENSON, ELIJAH PHILIPS, TRYON GIBSON, SAMUEL M. CLAY, WILLIAM CRUNK, WILLIAM MUNROE, ALDEN TUCKER, JOB BELL, GEORGE W. DENNIS, ABNER WELLS, WILLIAM C. HODGES, FIELDING McDANIEL and JOSEPH JENKINS be summoned as Jurors to the next County Court held on 3rd Monday in January next and that WILLIAM P. PULLIAM be summoned to wiat of said Court and Jurors.

It is ordered by the court that JAMES FORSYTH, EDWARD OGLESVEY, JOHN WILLIAMS, JOHN SMITH, MARK WHITAKER, STEPHEN ALEXANDER, JOHN GEORGE, JONAS LEATHERMAN, AMBROSE BARKER, JAMES HOLEMAN, JOSEPH HINKLE, ANDREW McCARTNEY, CLIFFORD GRAY, JAMES BLAKEMORE, GEORGE BLAKEMORE, HUGH M. BLAKE, ISAAC BROYLES, WILLIAM MOORE, WILLIAM JENNINGS, THOMAS ROUNTREE, STEPHEN HIGHTOWER, ALEXANDER ESLEMAN, JOHN NORTON, ROBERT STEPHENS, WILLIAM SMITH, ROBERT DICKSON, WILLIAM YOUNG, SAMUEL BUCHANAN, JOHN CRAWFORD, and WILLIAM EDMISTON be summoned as Jurors to the next Circuit Court and that STERLING C. McLEMORE be summoned to wait of said Court and Jury.

JAMES A. McCLURE for the use of WILLIAM B. MARTIN vs SAMUEL H. SMITH - The plaintiff by his attorney came into court and the defendant being called to come and plea to this court failed to do so but made default. Plaintiff to recover against the defendant $113.52 and $3.50 interest his costs.

LEWIS GANT vs REECE PORTER - The plaintiff by his attorney came into court and says he wishes to dismiss his suit and assumes the payment of all costs. Suit to be dismissed and the defendant recover against the plaintiff his costs.

JOHN McCLARY vs JAMES ESLEMAN - Motion in Arrest of Judgement - The parties by their attorneys came into court and the court considered that the reason in Arrest of Judgement be overruled and the plaintiff recover against the defendant the sum of $18.54 and damages.

It is ordered by the court that REUBEN H. BOON be overseer to open a new road leaving the Shelbyville Road to where a small path leaves the ridge to MICAJAH STONE to ABNER STEED and NICHOLAS CARRIGER be appointed to assign the hands to work on said road.

JOHN REECE is appointed overseer of the new road from a small path that leaves the ridge to MICAJAH STONE to where the road leaves the top of the ridge.

JACK H. LEFTWICH is appointed overseer of the new road from where said road leaves the ridge to where is crosses a small branch near Mulberry and that ABNER STEED and NICHOLAS CARRIGER be appointed to lay off the hands to work on said road.

JAMES ELLIS is appointed overseer of the new road from a small branch near Mulberry to where it intersects the Lynchburgh Road and ABNER STEED and NICHOLAS CARRIGER be appointed to lay off the hands to work on said road.

MONDAY JANUARY 15, 1821

JOHN LEE is appointed overseer of the road in the room of ABRAHAM DUDNEY resigned and call on the usual hands.

JOHN REECE is appointed overseer to cut out a new road and to keep it in repair in the room of JACK H. LEFTWICH who was appointed at the last term of court and to have the hands allotted to said LEFTWICH.

Ordered by the court that the Sheriff let out POLLY FRAME, one of the poor of this county, to the lowest bidder, this day at the court house door.

Ordered by the court that JOHN PARK receive from the County Trustee $1.69 which he paid for taxes for the year 1819 more than he was entitled to pay.

CHAMPION BLYTH is appointed overseer of the road in the room of MARTIN L. PARKS resigned and call on the usual hands.

HARDY BROWN is appointed overseer of the road in the room of SAMUEL DAVIS resigned and to call on the usual hands.

CHARLES BOYLES and WILLIAM NEELD is appointed Commissioners to settle with the County Trustee and Sheriff of this County.

JOHN DOBBINS is appointed overseer of the road in the room of JOHN CLARK resigned and to call on the usual hands.

JOHN PRIOR is appointed overseer of the road in the room of MOSES SANDERS resigned and to call on the usual hands.

NICHOLAS WOODFIN is appointed overseer of the road in the room of WILLIAM HOWARD resigned and call on the usual hands.

JAMES CARTER is appointed overseer of the road in the room of ELIPHAS BOAZ resigned and call on the usual hands.

THOMAS WILLIAMS is appointed overseer of the road in the room of BOON WILSON resigned and call on the usual hands.

JESSE LEDBETTER is appointed overseer of the road in the room of JAMES LEDBETTER resigned and call on the usual hands.

Ordered by the court that the Sheriff let out ELIJAH CONWAY, one of the poor of this county, to the lowest bidder.

MANSFIELD HUSBANDS is appointed overseer of the road in the room of ROBERT PARKS resigned and call on the usual hands.

STERLING C. McLEMORE appointed Constable, took oath and gave bond.

Ordered by the court that FRANCIS WAID be allowed and to receive from the County Trustee for the use of SAMUEL DOBBINS $100.00 for keeping of ANN FARMER, one of the poor of this county, for the year 1817.

It is ordered by the court that the Sheriff bring RICHARD HALL, a natural born boy, before this court on the next day for doing of county business for this term in order that RICHARD HALL may be bound out to learn some useful trade and that a copy of this order be served on RICHARD HALL, SR., with whom he lives.

STERLING C. McLEMORE is appointed overseer of the road in the room of BENJAMIN DORSEY resigned and call on the usual hands.

REPS O. CHILDRESS, ROBERT CUNNINGHAM, JAMES WILSON, ALEXANDER

75

MORTON, STEPHEN CHITWOOD, THOMAS HENRY and JOHN PORTER is appointed a Jury of View to view and mark out a road, the nearest and best way from the mouth of Swan Creek to intersect the Nashville Road at the most convenient place near to JESSE RIGGS on Cain Creek and make return to next court.

ERWIN McADAMS, JOSEPH BIGGER, WILLIAM COOK, DAVID LORANCE, THOMAS SHORT, SAMUEL DAVIS, MOSES PARK, JOHN PARK be appointed a Jury of View to view and mark out a road the nearest and best way from Commin's Gap on Elk River Ridge through the north west corner of this county to Giles County line and make return to next court.

The Last Will and Testament of THOMAS EDWARDS, deceased, was exhibited in court to probate whereupon SAMUEL DAVIS, JOHN ROSSON and JAMES GARRETT, witnesses, and made oath that they heard the said THOMAS R. EDWARDS, deceased, acknowledge the same to be his Last Will and Testament and that he was at that time of sound mind and memory.

WILLIAM HUSBANDS, Deputy Sheriff, made return that he had let out ELIJAH CONWAY, one of the poor of this county, to FRANCIS WAID for $55.00 who gave bond with JOEL PINSON for security.

WILLIAM HUSBANDS, Deputy Sheriff, made return that he had let out POLLY FRAME, one of the poor of this county, to JAMES McCREE for $115.50.

GARLAND B. MILLER was appointed admr of all and singular the goods and chattels &c of JONATHAN ESTILL, deceased, who gave bond and security in sum of $5500.00.

STERLING C. McLEMORE is appointed a Constable who gave bond and security.

Ordered by the court that DAVID THWING be allowed and to receive from the County Trustee of the county out of the first county monies that comes to his hands, sum of $129.00 for enclosing of the Court House.

CHARLOTTE MAYFIELD was appointed admrx of all and singular goods and chattels rights and credits of JOHN MAYFIELD, deceased, who gave bond and security for $600.00.

JOSEPH PENN & DELILA PIGG was appointed admr and admrx of all and singular the right and credit of JOHN PIGG, deceased, who gave bond and security of $1200.00.

An inventory of the estate of JOHN PIGG, deceased, was returned to court and ordered to be certified.

ALEXANDER MORTON, SAMUEL CRAWFORD and HOWELL HARRIS is appointed Commissioners to lay off one years provision for the widow and children of JOHN PIGG, deceased.

WILLIAM SMITH, SR. was appointed admr of all and singular the rights and credits of WILLIAM SMITH, JR., deceased, who gave bond and security of $400.00.

DRURY BASSHAM was appointed guardian for D(illegible) W. WRIGHT, SHE(illegible) R. WRIGHT who gave bond and security of $250.00.

An inventory of the estate of JONATHAN ESTILL and was returned to court which was ordered to be certified.

Ordered by the court that GARLAND B. MILLER, admr of the estate of JONATHAN ESTILL, deceased, proceed to sell PARRIS, NANNY, DELILA, HENRY, MARIAH, PULINA, and MINERVA, slaves of the estate of JONATHAN ESTILL, deceased.

An inventory of the estate of WILLIAM SMITH and was returned to court which was ordered to be certified.

An inventory of the estate of JOHN WAKEFIELD, deceased, was returned to court which was ordered to be certified.

An amount of sale of the estate of JOHN WAKEFIELD, deceased, was returned to court which was ordered to be certified.

The Commissioners appointed at the last term of this court to lay off one years allowance for the widow and children of JOHN WAKEFIELD, deceased, made return to court the allowance by them laid off which was ordered to be certified.

JOHN DAVIS appointed a Constable who gave bond with DAVID SMITH and JOHN DOBBINS his security.

IRA CRUNK was appointed a Constable who gave bond with WILLIAM CRUNK and FRANCIS WYATT his securities.

ANTHONY HOGAN was appointed a Constable who gave bond with JAMES LUNA and PETER LUNA, his securities.

MATHEW MOSS was appointed a Constable who gave bond with DRURY BASSHAM and ABRAHAM SUMMERS, his securities.

JOHN ENOCKS & JONATHAN FLOYD, Esquires, is appointed Commissioners to settle with DANIEL ARCHER, exr of GEORGE ARCHER, deceased, and make return to next court.

ELI COLE produced in court one wolf scalp over six months old and made oath he killed the same within this county.

BENJAMIN HUDSON is appointed overseer of the road from Nix's Ford on Elk River past by SQUIRE McGEHEE to Franklin County line.

ROBERT S. JOHNSON produced in court one wolf scalp over six months old and made oath that he killed the same within the bounds of this county.

ALEXANDER McCORKE is appointed guardian of JOHN TOMLINSON, WILLIE TOMLINSON, SAMUEL O. TIMLINSON, JOSEPH TOMLINSON, HUGH TOMLINSON, and NANCY TOMLINSON who gave bond and security as such.

JOHN DEN, lessee of R. DAVIDSON vs JONATHAN ESTILL - Ejectment - It is ordered by the court that JOHN MILLER, the landlord of the tenant, in possession, be allowed a defendant in this cause upon the common rule to confess and pleads not guilty and for his trial to rely upon the title only.

The Justices proceeded to elect from their own body five persons to hold the Court of Pleas and Quarter Session for the county, and upon counting the ballots, it appeared that JAMES WILSON, WILLIAM DICKSON, PHILIP KOONCE, JAMES HOLEMAN and WILLIAM KENNON were elected to hold said court for one year.

A Deed of Conveyance from WILLIAM DICKSON to THOMAS HICKMAN for 408 acres of land and ordered to be certified.

A Deed of Conveyance from HENRY WEBB and FANNY WEBB to JAMES GARRETT for 40 acres of land, proven by RICHARD FLYNT and MARTIN HOLBERT and ordered to be certified.

A Deed of Conveyance from SAMUEL GARLAND to MOSES STONE for 45 acres of land and ordered to be certified.

A Deed of Conveyance from GEORGE W. DENNIS to JEREMIAH DENNIS for 25 acres of land and ordered to be certified.

A Deed of Conveyance from ISAIAH ALLY to THOMAS ÁLLY for 156½ acres of land, proven by ISAAC HOLEMAN and WRIGHT McLEMORE and ordered to be certified.

A Bill of Sale from ROBERT M. WHITE to PRESTON HAMPTON for one negro girl and ordered to be certified.

A Power of Attorney from STEPHEN & JOEL HOLBERT to AMOS DAVIS & DAVID SMITH, proven by JOHN GREER and ARGYLE CAMPBELL and ordered to be certified.

A Deed of COnveyance from ELINOR HAYS to THOMAS W. HAYS for 35 1/3 acres of land, proven by ABRAHAM SUMMERS and WILLIAM (blank) and ordered to be certified.

A deed of Conveyance from JOHN HENSON to JAMES BOREN for 19 acres of land, proven by BENJAMIN HARRIS and JOHN GEORGE and ordered to be certified.

A Deed of Conveyance from DRURY BASSHAM to MAJOR WALL for 34 acres of land and ordered to be certified.

A Deed of Gift from JOSHUA WALL to ELIZETTA WALL for 50 acres of land and ordered to be certified.

A Deed of Gift from JOSHUA HALL to LEROY WALL for 50 acres of land and ordered to be certified.

A Deed of Conveyance from ROBERT IRWIN to DAVID LORANCE for 100 acres of land, proven by JAMES RALSTON and SOLOMON MEADOWS and ordered to be certified.

EDWARD GORE was appointed guardian to VERLINA SMITH, 13 years old, WARREN SMITH, 11 years old, children of CHARLES and RACHEL SMITH, deceased.

TUESDAY JANUARY 16, 1821

Justices present were JAMES HOLEMAN, JAMES WILSON and JOHN ENOCKS, Esquires.

The Sheriff had summoned the following persons as Jurors to this term, to wit, ANDREW HANNAH, WILLIAM CASHON, JOSEPH WHITAKER, JOHN WATKINS, MOSES STONE, JOHN NEECE, JOHN LEE, AUGUST L. JONES, WILLIAM DOAK, WILLIAM PARKS, THOMAS PARKS, SOLOMON GULLETT, JORDAN REECE, JAMES LINGO, JOHN MOOR, BROWN PARKERSON, TRYON GIBSON, SAMUEL M. CLAY, WILLIAM CRUNK, WILLIAM MUNROE, ALDEN TUCKER, JOHN BELL, GEORGE W. DENNIS, ABNER WELLS, WILLIAM C. HODGES, FIELDING McDANIEL, and JOSEPH JENKINS being elected as Grand Jurors, to wit, WILLIAM DOAK, foreman, GEORGE W. DENNIS, JOHN WATKINS, TRYON GIBSON, JORDAN REECE, JAMES LINGO, JOSEPH WHITAKER, BROWN PARKERSON, FIELDING McDANIEL, WILLIAM MUNROE, WILLIAM C. HOFGES, THOMAS PARKS and SOLOMON GULLETT and after receiving the charge from the solicitor returned to consider for their presentments.

WILLIAM MUNROE, WILLIAM C. HODGES, THOMAS PARKS, and SOLOMON GULLETT and after receiving the charge from the solicitor returned to consider for their presentments.

WILLIAM P. PULLIAM, a Constable, sworn to wait on the Grand Jury this term.

WILLIAM CRUNK is released from serving as Juror this term.

ALDEN TUCKER is released from serving as a Juror this term.

JOHN NEW is released from serving as a Juror this term.

MARTIN HOLBERT vs BENJAMIN ANDERSON - The plaintiff says he wishes to dismiss this suit and assumes the payment of all costs. The defendant to recover against the plaintiff his costs.

ALEXANDER NEELD vs JOHN MURPHY - The plaintiff by his attorney wishes to dismiss this suit. It is considered to be dismissed and the plaintiff (defendant) recover against the plaintiff his costs.

BENJAMIN ANDREWS vs MARTIN HOLBERT - Appeal - The plaintiff wishes to dismiss this suit and assumes the payment of all costs. The suit to be dismisses and the defendant recover against the plaintiff his costs.

JOSEPH WHITAKER vs WILLIAM WALLACE - The plaintiff says he wishes to dismiss this suit and assumes the payment of all costs. The suit to be dismissed and the defendant recover against the plaintiff his costs.

A Deed of Conveyance from PETER ROSEL to JAMES D. EASTES for 83 acres of land, proven by DARRELL T. WILLIAMS and STEPHEN C. CHITWOOD and ordered to be certified.

On motion of PETER SHELTON and HAYMAN SHELTON, securities for LETTA DUNCAN, admrx of CHARLES DUNCAN, deceased, are released from their securityship and AMBROSE BARKER and BENJAMIN HUDSON enters into bond as securities for LETTA DUNCAN.

EDWARD GORE appointed guardian of VERLINA SMITH and WARREN SMITH, minor heirs of CHARLES SMITH, deceased, who gave bond and security.

The transfer of a plat and certificate of survey from JOHN R. ENOCKS to ENOCK

ENOCKS, proven by JOHN ENOCKS and JONATHAN FLOYD and ordered to be certified.

The transfer of a plat and certificate of survey from JAMES HILL to ALEXANDER FINNY, proven by EDWARD GORE and ordered to be certified.

The transfer of a plat and certificate of survey from WILLIAM ALEXANDER to ALEXANDER FINNY and ordered to be certified.

The transfer of a plat and certificate from ENOCK ENOCKS to ARON MOORE, proven by JOHN ENOCKS and JONATHAN FLOYD and ordered to be certified.

JOHNSTON WELLBORN vs KELLY STEGALL - Attachment - This day came the parties by their attorneys and a jury of men, to wit, JOBE BELL, JOHN LEE, WILLIAM PARKS, JOHN MOOR, JOHN McMILLIN, WYATT WOODRUFF, DANIEL HARKINS, HENRY MOORE, THOMAS ALLY, JOHN CAMPBELL, ZACHARIAH HARDAGE and JOSEPH MOONEY being elected and sworn and found the issue in favor of the plaintiff.

JAMES WYATT vs WILLIAM P. ANDERSON - Appeal - This day came the parties by their attorneys and a jury of men, to wit, (same as above jurors) being elected and sworn and said that the defendant is not indebted to the plaintiff anything. Defendant to recover against the plaintiff his costs.

MICHEL LUTTRELL vs WILSON FROST - Case - This day came the parties by their attorneys and a jury of men, to wit, (same as above jurors) being elected and sworn and said that the plaintiff to recover against the defendant and the damages of $83.60.

A Deed of Conveyance from PAULINE D. GRAY to REUBEN HARRIS for 35 acres of land, proven by JAMES CARITHERS and MEREDITH HARRIS and ordered to be certified.

A Deed of Conveyance from JAMES DOWNING to ABRAHAM SUMMERS for 85 acres of land and ordered to be certified.

A Deed of Conveyance from JONAS LEATHERMAN to BOON WILSON for 238 acres and 89 poles and ordered to be certified.

A Deed of Conveyance from JONAS LEATHERMAN to BOON WILSON for two negroes and ordered to be certified.

WEDNESDAY JANUARY 17, 1821

Justices present were JAMES WILSON, JAMES HOLEMAN and PHILIP KOONCE, Esquires.

BRICE M. GARNER vs JOHN HARDING - The plaintiff says he wishes to dismiss his suit and assumes the payment of all costs. Suit to be dismissed and the defendant recover against the plaintiff his costs.

PETER MOYERS vs DAVIS & NICHOLS - Debt - This day came the parties by their attorneys and a jury of men, to wit, JOB BELL, JOHN LEE, WILLIAM PARKS, JOHN MOORE, ROBERT ELLIS, ARCHABALD D. GARVEN, SPENCER A. PUGH, THOMAS WITT, DOILY GRIFFIS, ADLAI SHARP, FRANCIS PATTON, and WILLIAM PATTON being elected and sworn and said that the defendant has not paid the debt of $98.00 and damages of $5.62½. Plaintiff to recover against the defendant his costs.

McALISTER's Executors vs VANCE GREER - Debt - This day came the parties by their attorneys and a jury of men, to wit, (same as above jurors) being elected and sworn and said that the defendant has not paid the debt of $3150.00 and damages of $181.00. Plaintiff to recover against the defendant his costs.

JANE B. CAMPBELL vs MICHAEL OWEN - Debt - This day the parties by their attorneys and a jury of men, to wit, (same as above jurors) being elected and sworn and said that the defendant has not paid the debt of $139.00 and damages of $4.80. Plaintiff to recover against the defendant his costs.

JANE B. CAMPBELL vs WALTER KINNARD - Debt - This day the parties by their attorneys and a jury of men, to wit, (same as jurors above) being elected and sworn and said that the defendant did assumes upon himself and assess the plaintiff's damages of $113.56½. Plaintiff to recover against the defendant his costs.

JAMES WYATT vs ARCHABALD ESLEMAN - This day came the parties by their attorneys and a jury of men, to wit, JOB BELL, JOHN LEE, WILLIAM PARKS, JOHN MOORE, PETER MOYERS, ARCHABALD D. GARVIN, SPENCER A. PUGH, THOMAS WITT, DOILY GRIFFIS, ADLAI SHARP, FRANCIS PATTON and WILLIAM PATTON being elected and sworn and said that the defendant has not paid the debt of $350.00 and damages of $15.68 3/4. Plaintiff to recover against the defendant his costs.

WILLIAM McCLELLAN vs JOHN BOON - Debt - This day came the parties by their attorneys and a jury of men, to wit, (same as above jurors) being elected and sworn and said that the defendant has not paid the debt of $276.50 and damages of $13.00. Plaintiff to recover against the defendant his costs.

The Grand Jury again returned to court with a Bill of Indictment, the State against WILLIAM TOWNZEN, WILLIAM JACKSON and JOEL SMITH, a true bill and again returned to consider for further presentments.

ANDREW E. BEATY vs ROBERT BRADON - Debt - This day came the parties by their attorneys and a jury of men, to wit, (same as above jurors) being elected and sworn and said that the defendant has not paid the debt of $141.00 and damages of $8.81¼. Plaintiff to recover against the defendant his costs.

WILLIAM McCLELLAN vs MIXON & BUCHANAN - Debt - This day came the parties by their attorneys and a jury of men, to wit, (same as above jurors) being elected and sworn and said that the defendant has not paid the debt of $110.00 and damages of $6.87¼. Plaintiff to recover against the defendant his costs.

J.V. & C. McKINNEY vs BRICE M. GARNER - Debt - This day came the parties by their attorneys and a jury of men, to wit, (same as above jurors) being elected and swotn and said that the defendant has not paid the debt of $200.00 and damages of $9.50. Plaintiff to recover against the defendant his costs.

ALEXANDER DOBBINS vs WILLIAM DAVIS - Debt - This day came the parties by their attorneys and a jury of men, to wit, (same as above jurors) being elected and sworn and said that the defendant has not paid the debt of $175.00 and damages of $21.43 3/4. Plaintiff to recover against the defendant his costs.

PETER MOYERS vs MARTIN & McCONNELL - Debt - This day came the parties by their attorneys and a jury of men, to wit, (same as above jurors) being elected and sworn and said that the defendant has not paid the debt of $183.75 and damages of $8.73. Plaintiff to recover against the defendant his costs.

ISAAC ESTILL vs JOHN W. HILL - The plaintiff by his attorney says he wishes to dismiss his suit. Suit to be dismissed and the defendant recover against the plaintiff his costs.

JOHN OWSLY vs JAMES WYATT - This day came the parties by their attorneys and a jury of men, to wit, (same as above jurors) being elected and sworn and said that the defendant has not kept the covenant and assess the damages of $236.25. PLaintiff to recover against the defendant his costs.

GEORGE THORNBURGH vs JAMES COALTER - Debt - This day came the parties by their attorneys and a jury of men, to wit, (same as above jurors) being elected and sworn and said that the defendant has not paid the debt of $145.50 and damages of $21.62¼. Plaintiff to recover against the defendant his costs.

THURSDAY JANUARY 18, 1821

Justices present were PHILIP KOONCE, JAMES HOLEMAN and JAMES WILSON, Esquires.

The Grand Jury again returned into court with a Bill of Indictment, the State against RICHARD NALLY, a true bill and again return to consider for further presentments.

The State vs WILLIAM TUCKER - The defendant as well as WILLIAM B. MARTIN, the solicitor, and a jury of men, to wit, JOB BELL, JOHN LEE, JOHN MOORE, WILLIAM WHITE, JAMES BOON, RICHARD NALLY, DAVID JAMES, JAMES ISHAM, JOSEPH MOONEY, PETER MOYERS, WILLIAM FARRAR, and ADLAI SHARP being elected and sworn and said that the defendant is not guilty. Defendant be discharged and the county pay the costs.

The Grand Jury again returned to court with a Bill of Indictment, the State against DAVID JONES, a true bill and again return to conosider for further presentments.

The State vs ALLEN TUCKER - On motion of WILLIAM B. MARTIN, the Attorney General, a nolleprosequi (unwilling to persue) is entered. The defendant is discharged and the county pay the costs.

The State vs RICHARD NALLY - Indictment - The defendant came into court and being charged pleads guilty and is fined $10.00 and pay costs. WILLIAM HUSBANDS, ISAAC HOLEMAN and WILLIAM C. HODGES, securities.

The State vs DAVID JONES - The defendant came into court and pleads guilty and is fined $1.00 and pay the costs.

JANE B. CAMPBELL vs C. BOYLES & B.M. GARNER - On motion of the defendant by their attorneys, leave is given them to withdraw their plea.

The State vs WILLIAM JACKSON - Indictment - The defendant being charged pleads guilty and is fined $7.00 and costs. JOHN NORTON as security for the defendant.

The State vs JOEL SMITH, Indictment - The defendant being charged and pleads guilty and is fined $7.00 and costs. JOHN NORTON security for defendant.

A Deed of COnveyance from JOHN GREER, Sheriff, to WILLIAM TIMMONS for one town lot No. 90 in Fayetteville and ordered to be certified.

A Deed of Conveyance from GEORGE W. DENNIS to ROBERT H. McEWEN, proven by SPENCER A. PUGH and ELIJAH M. RINGO and ordered to be certified.

A Mortgage from FRANCIS SMITH to ROBERT H. McEWEN, proven by ELIJAH M. RINGO and THOMAS ALLY and ordered to be certified.

A Deed of Conveyance from BRICE M. GARNER to NATHANIEL PRATT for 160 acres of land, proven by JAMES COALTER and ROBERT H. McEWEN and ordered to be certified.

A Deed of Conveyance from PAYTON MADISON to SOLOMON BURFORD for 160 acres of land, proven by ROBERT H. McEWEN and SAMUEL E. GILLILAND and ordered to be certified.

A Deed of Conveyance from JOHN MADISON to SOLOMON BURFORD for 160 acres of land, proven by ROBERT H. McEWEN and SAMUEL E. GILLILAND and ordered to be certified.

An inventory of the estate of WILLIAM TATUM, deceased, was returned to court, ISAAC HOLEMAN, admr &c, which was ordered to be certified.

FRIDAY JANUARY 18, 1821

Justices present were PHILIP KOONCE, WILLIAM KENNON, JAMES HOLEMAN and JAMES WILSON, Esquires.

JOHN SMITH appeared in court and took the oath of a Justice of the Peace for Lincoln County.

ALLEN SCRUGGS vs JOHN TOMERSON - This day came the parties by their attorneys and on motion of the plaintiff and is awarded by the court that the plaintiff be non-suited and the defendant recover against defendant (plaintiff) his costs.

PETER MOYERS vs JOHN P. McCONNELL - Debt - Both parties by their attorneys came into court and a jury of men, to wit, WILLIAM DOAK, GEORGE W. DENNIS, JOHN WATKINS, TRYON GIBSON, JORDAN REECE, JAMES LINGO, JOSEPH WHITAKER, BROWN PARKERSON, FIELDING McDANIEL, WILLIAM MUNROE, WILLIAM B. HODGES, and THOMAS PARKS being elected and sworn and said that the defendant has not paid the debt of $351.25 and damages of $16.62½. Plaintiff to recover against the defendant his costs.

JOHN DAVIS vs SAMUEL BUCHANAN - Debt - Both parties by their attorneys came into court and a jury of men, to wit, (same as above jurors) being elected and sworn and said that the defendant has not paid the debt of $300.00 and damages of $12.50. Plaintiff to recover against the defendant his costs.

ALEXANDER McLIN vs ARCHABALD D. GARVIN - Debt - Both parties by their attorneys came into court and a jury of men, to wit, (same as above jurors) being elected and sworn and said that the defendant has not paid the debt of $195.14 and damages of $8.77½. Plaintiff to recover against the defendant his costs.

HENRY CRABB vs ROBERT HOGE - The plaintiff appeared in court and says he wishes to dismiss this his suit and the defendant assumes the payment of all costs. Ordered that this suit be dismissed and the plaintiff recover against the defendant his costs.

The transfer of a plat and certificate of survey from RANDOLPH QUARLES to JOHN GILLASPIE and ordered to be certified.

A Deed of Conveyance from WILLIAM EDMISTON to JOHN CRAWFORD for 11 acres of land, proven by WILLIAM CRAWFORD and HAY CRAWFORD and ordered to be certified.

SATURDAY JANUARY 20, 1821

Justices present were WILLIAM DICKSON, WILLIAM KENNON, JAMES WILSON and PHILIP KOONCE, Esquires.

JANE B. CAMPBELL vs C. BOYLES & B.M. GARNER - On motion of the plaintiff by his attorney, it is ordered by the court given the defendants to withdraw their (suit).

MANERING TOWERY vs DANIEL HASKINS, JR. - This day came the parties by their attorneys and a jury of men, to wit, WILLIAM DOAK, JOHN WATKINS, GEORGE W. DENNIS, TRYON GIBSON, JORDAN REECE, JAMES LINGO, JOSEPH WHITAKER, BROWN PARKERSON, FIELDING McDANIEL, WILLIAM MUNROE, WILLIAM C. HODGES and THOMAS PARKS being elected and sworn and said that the defendant is guilty and the damages of $225.00. Plaintiff to recover against the defendant his costs. Defendant prays for an appeal.

The transfer of a plat and certificate of survey from THOMAS BUCHANAN to SAMUEL BUCHANAN and ordered to be certified.

A Deed of Conveyance from DAVID Y. READ to WILLIAM NIXON for 160 acres of land, proven by SWAN THOMPSON and ABRAHAM ISAACS and ordered to be certified.

A Deed of Conveyance from JOHN GRAY to ALEXANDER GRAY for 20 acres of land, proven by WILLIAM H. McGINNIS and JAMES McFERRIN and ordered to be certified.

THOMPSON & WARDLOW vs JESSE LORANCE - Motion - JAMES MARTIN and ALEXANDER MOOR, his securities - The plaintiffs by their attorneys and it appearing to the court four executions were put into the hands of JESSE LORANCE as a Constable about the (blank) day of September 1820, issued by JAMES RALSTON, Esquire, a Justice of the Peace, in favor of the said plaintiffs one against HANCE CAUSBY for $9.52, one against BRADLY ACUFF for $3.43 3/4, one against JOHN HOWARD for $2.50, and against MAJOR WALL for $9.87½, amounting all to $25.33¼. Also it appearing to the court that JESSE LORANCE had received the aforesaid sum and failed to pay it over to THOMPSON & WARDLOW as required by law. Court ordered that the plaintiffs recover against JESSE LORANCE and JAMES MARTIN and ALEXANDER MOOR, his securities their costs and interest.

NATHAN GALSCO (GLASCO) vs JESSE LORANCE, JAMES MARTIN and ALEXANDER (MOOR) his securities - Motion - The plaintiff by his attorney came into court and that one execution was put into the hands of JESSE LORANCE as a Constable about 18 February 1820 issued by JAMES RALSTON, Esquire, a Justice of the Peace in favor of NATHAN GLASCO against WILLIAM LEONARD for $20.18 3/4 and said JESSE LORANCE has received said money and has failed to pay it over to NATHAN GLASCO. NATHAN GLASCO to recover against JESSE LORANCE and his securities, his costs.

TUESDAY JANUARY 23, 1821

Justices present were JAMES HOLEMAN and PHILIP KOONCE, Esquires, Justices.

Court adjourned until next day.

WEDNESDAY JANUARY 24, 1821

Justices present were JAMES HOLEMAN and PHILIP KOONCE, Esquires, Justices.

Court adjourned until next day.

Justices present were JAMES HOLEMAN, PHILIP KOONCE and WILLIAM KENNON, Esquires.

It appearing to the court that a competent court to do business did not set on Monday 22nd January 1821 and that the court now present that JOHN GREER, Sheriff, on that day opened and adjourned the court until the next day.

VANCE GREER vs HENRY MAYFIELD - On motion of the plaintiff by his attorney, a Commission is awarded him to take the deposition of BENJAMIN P. McLIN in Blount County, Tennessee, to be read as evidence on the trial of this cause and give the defendant ten days notice of time and place.

JANE B. CAMPBELL vs C. BOYLES and B.M. GARNER - On motion of the defendant by their attorneys, Commission is awarded them to take the deposition of SAMUEL CONWELL of Philadelphia and THOMAS TENNANT of Baltimore to be read as evidence on the trial of this cause and giving the plaintiff thirty days notice of time and place of taking the same.

THOMAS ALLY appeared in court and was appointed admr of all and singular the goods and chattels &c of CHARLES COPPAGE, deceased, who gave bond with JOHN P. McCONNELL and JAMES WYATT, securities, in sum of $500.00.

It is ordered that THOMAS ALLY proved to sell all personal estate of CHARLES COPPAGE, deceased.

A Deed of Conveyance from CHARLES BOYLES and JOHN MAZE to CONSTANT SCALES for 40 acres of land and ordered to be certified.

The transfer of a plat and certificate of survey from JAMES ROSEBOROUGH to JOHN YOUNG and ordered to be certified.

A Deed of Conveyance from JOHN GREER and VANCE GREER to EZEKIEL NORRIS for 121 3/4 acres and ordered to be certified.

It is ordered by the court that WILLIAM BONNER, DAVID JONES, HUGH PARKERSON, LEMUEL BROADWAY, RICHARD JONES, SAMUEL TODD, ROBERT PARKS, JAMES CRAWFORD, PETER LOONEY, SR., JACKSON BLAKEMORE, WILLIAM D. BLAKE, THOMAS WITT, ENOCH RUST, STEPHEN BEAVERS, JOHN TURLY, JAMES SMITH, EDWARD MOSS, CORNELIUS WEBB, ROBERT STEPHENS, WILLIAM CASHON, JOHN DUSENBERRY, SAMUEL HOWELL, JOSEPH COMMONS, WILLIAM TIMMONS, JAMES McFERRIN, PETER VAUGHN, ARCHABALD McELROY, and WILLIAM WALLACE be summoned as jurors for the next court of Pleas and Quarter Sessions to be held on 3rd Monday in April next and that WILLIAM P. PULLIAM, a Constable, be summoned to wait on said court and jury.

A Deed of Conveyance from WALTER KINNARD to SAMUEL H. SMITH for one town lot No. 19 in Fayetteville and ordered to be certified.

A Deed of Conveyance from GEORGE W. DENNIS to SAMUEL H. SMITH for one town lot No. 26 in Fayetteville and ordered to be certified.

The Grand Jury again returned into court with a Bill of Indictment, the State against WILLIAM BEARDEN, a true bill and again returned to consider for further presentments.

ARCHABALD McKEE, JOHN ALLBRIGHT, STEPHEN TOUCHSTON and ROBERT HAIRSTON appeared in court and acknowledged themselves indebted to the State of Tennessee each for $200.00 to be levied upon their respective goods and chattels &c but to be void on conditions that they appear in April court to give evidence in behalf of the State against WILLIAM BEARDEN and not depart the same without leave first had and obtained of the court.

GEORGE A. ALLEN appeared in court and acknowledged himself indebted to the State of Tennessee for $200.00 to be levied of his goods and chattels &c but to be void on conditions that he appear in April court and give evidence in behalf of the State against JOHN JOBE, JONATHAN WALCH, THOMAS LITTLE and SOLOMON JOBE and not depart the same without leave first had and obtained of the court.

The Grand Jury again returned into court with a Bill of Indictment, the State against HENDERSON WITT, not a true bill and again returned to consider for further presentments.

State of Tennessee and WILLIAM D. FERGUSON vs JOHN MAZE - It is considered by the court that the plaintiff recover against the defendant $100.00 and a cost of $11.62½ in original bill.

JAMES WYATT vs JOHN HAWKINS - The plaintiff appeared in court and says he intends no further to prosecute this suit and assumes the payment of all costs. Suit to be dismissed and the defendant recover against the plaintiff his costs.

ALLEN MOBLY vs CORNELIUS WEBB - On petition of the defendant that the papers relative to suit tried before STEPHEN ALEXANDER, Esquire, whereon ALLEN MOBLY was plaintiff and CORNELIUS WEBB was defendant.

On petition of CORNELIUS WEBB by his attorney, it is considered by the court that Writ of Certiorari &c to bring up to court the papers relative to a suit before JOHN JONES, Esquire, in January 1821.

THOMAS CHAPMAN vs ISAAC NORTHCUT - Motion - The Sheriff is ordered to expose to sale 40 acres of land, lying on Cane Creek including the plantation whereon CHRISTOPHER HOBBS now lives, levied on as the property of ISAAC NORTHCUT to satisfy a judgement for $20.50 and costs of suit.

DEMPSEY ALLEN vs ISAAC NORTHCUT - Motion - The Sheriff is ordered to expose to sale 40 acres of land lying on Cane Creek including the plantation whereon CHRISTOPHER HOBBS now lives to satisfy a judgement of $10.03 3/4 and costs of suit.

CHARLES BOYLES vs JOHN GREER - Motion - It appearing to the court that on execution at the suit of CHARLES BOYLES for $59.22½ debt and $11.65 costs against the body of WILLIAM Y. HIGGINS which said execution came to the hands of the Sheriff and was executed upon WILLIAM Y. HIGGINS who had voluntary and wished to go at large and it appearing that twenty days notice had been given about this motion. It is ordered that the plaintiff recover against JOHN GREER, Sheriff, and VANCE GREER, ROBERT DICKSON, JOSEPH HINKLE and ARGYLE CAMPBELL, securities, sum of $59.22½ and cost of $11.65.

FRIDAY JANUARY 26, 1821

Justices present were JAMES HOLEMAN, PHILIP KOONCE and WILLIAM KENNON, Esquires.

The State vs JONATHAN WALCH - JONATHAN WALCH acknowledged himself indebted to the State of Tennessee for $250.00 and HUGH M. BLAKE for $250.00 to be levied of their respective goods and chattels &c but to be void on conditions that said WALCH appear here in April next to answer a charge and not depart the same without first had and obtained of the court.

The State vs THOMAS LITTLE - THOMAS LITTLE acknowledged himself indebted to the State of Tennessee for $250.00 and HUGH M. BLAKE for $250.00 to be levied of their goods and chattels &c but to be void on conditions that THOMAS LITTLE appear here in April next and not depart without have first had and obtained of the court.

The State vs JOHN JOBE - JOHN JOBE acknowledged himself indebted to the State of Tennessee for $250.00 and WILLIAM SHAW for $250.00 to be levied of their respective goods and chattels &c but to be void on conditions that JOHN JOBE appear here in April next and not depart without first had and obtained of the court.

JOHN WITT & HENDERSON WITT appeared in court and acknowledged themselves indebted to the State of Tennessee for $200.00 to be levied of their goods and chattels &c but to be void on conditions that they appear here in April next and give evidence in behalf of the State against WILLIAM TOWNZEND and not depart without leave first had and obtained of the court.

JOHN DEN, lessee of ROBERT DICKSON vs JONATHAN ESTILL, WILLIAM WILLS and JOHN MILLER - The parties by their attorneys came into court, agreed that this cause be transferred for trial to next Circuit Court of Lincoln County to br held in Lincoln County at the Court House in Fayetteville on 3rd Monday in March next which is ordered by the court.

JESSE SMITH vs ARCHABALD McELROY - Debt - Both parties by their attorneys came into court and a jury of men, to wit, JOHN BELL, JOHN MOOR, WILLIAM PARKS, JOHN LEE, TRYON GIBSON, JORDAN REECE, JAMES LINGO, BROWN PARKERSON, FIELDING McDANIEL, WILLIAM MUNROE, WILLIAM C. HODGES and THOMAS PARKS being elected and sworn and said that the defendant has not paid the debt of $99.39 and damages of $5.39. Plaintiff to recover against the defendant his costs.

Fayetteville T. Bank vs WILLIAM KELLY and others - The plaintiffs by the attorney say they wish to dismiss this suit and assumes the payment of all costs. Suit dismissed and the plaintiffs pay the costs.

BRICE M. GARNER vs URIAH BOBBIT - Both parties by their attorneys came into court and agreed to have the court to transfer this cause for trial to next Circuit Court to be held in Fayetteville in April next which is ordered by the court.

REECE GULLETT vs JAMES HENDERSON - Appeal - The defendant by his attorney came into court and the plaintiff being called to come and prosecute his suit failed to do so. Defendant to recover against the plaintiff his costs.

JONATHAN BARKLEY vs HARDING FORRESTER - Appeal - The defendant by his attorney came into court and the plaintiff being called to prosecute failed to do so. Defendant to recover against the plaintiff his costs.

JOSEPH WILLIAMSON vs WILLIAM CUNNINGHAM - The defendant by his attorney came into court and the plaintiff being called failed to do so. Defendant to recover against the plaintiff his costs.

JOHN GREER, Commissioner vs JOHN SMITH & ROBERT STORY - Both parties said that they compromised this suit and the defendant assumes the payment of all costs. Plaintiff to recover against the defendant his costs.

JOHN DICKSON vs ENOCK K. WEATHERS - The plaintiff came into court and the defendant being called to come and defend this suit, failed to do so but made default. Plaintiff to recover against the defendant $94.95 and damages of $6.17.

THOMAS CHAMPLAIN vs Fayetteville T. Bank - The plaintiff by his attorney says he intends no further to prosecute this suit and assumes the payment of all costs. Court ordered suit to be dismissed and the defendant recover against the plaintiff his costs.

ARCHY BEASLY vs ISAAC WHITSON - The plaintiff said he intends no further to prosecute this suit and assumes the payment of all costs. Suit dismissed and the plaintiff pay the costs.

WILLIAM BAILY vs WILLIAM H. RAGSDALE - The plaintiff says he intends no further to prosecute this suit and assumes the payment of all costs. Suit to be dismissed and the plaintiff pay the costs.

JOSEPH BRADLEY vs ASA CROSTHWAIT - Attachment - The plaintiff by his attorney came into court and the defendant being called came not. It is ordered by the court that the plaintiff recover against the defendant in their Plea of Trespass the case but because it is not known in this court the amount of damages to which the plaintiff are entitled. It is considered by the court that a Writ of Inquiry issue to inquire of the damages at next term of court.

A Deed of Conveyance from SAMUEL PARKS and WILLIAM KERBY to JOHN PARKS for 133 3/4 acres of land, proven by JAMES TUCKER and BARTLEY WOOLAN and ordered to be certified.

A Deed of Conveyance from JOHN PARKS to HUGH M. BLAKE for 133 3/4 acres of land and ordered to be certified.

A Deed of Conveyance from JOEL REED to NATHANIEL REED for 95 acres of land and ordered to be certified.

A Deed of Conveyance from JOSHUA MOORE to DAVAULT BECK for 80 acres of land, proven by JOEL PINSON and DANIEL R. MOORE and ordered to be certified.

A Deed of Conveyance from ROBERT HERROLD and wife MARGARET HERROLD by their attorney JOHN HERROLD to WILLIAM EDMISTON, GENERAL WILLIAM CAMPBELL EDMISTON, VANCE GREER, and EBENEZER McEWEN and his wife MARY McEWEN for (blank) acres of land, proven by WILLIAM E. KENNEDY and THOMAS BUCHANAN and ordered to be certified.

The transfer of a plat and certificate of survey from JAMES GARRETT to WILLIAM

ROSSON and HENRY B. ROSSON, proven by JOEL PINSON and ordered to be certified.

The transfer of a play and certificate of survey from JAMES GARRETT to BENJAMIN SHORT, proven by JOEL PINSON and ordered to be certified.

JOHN LINDSEY is appointed overseer of the road in the room of JOHN LOYD resigned, CLIFFORD GRAY and JOHN JONES, Esquires, is appointed to lay off the hands to work on said road.

JAMES GRANT is released from the payment of the appraised value of two stray sheep which he posted.

An inventory of the estate of CHARLES COPPAGE, deceased, was returned into court by admrs which was ordered to be certified.

A Deed of Conveyance from PALAN D. GRAY to REUBEN HARRIS for 20 acres of land, proven by JAMES CARITHERS and MEREDITH HARRIS and ordered to be certified.

A Deed of Conveyance from JAMES ISBELL to WILLIAM MOREHEAD for 10 acres, proven by JOHN JONES and ordered to be certified.

A Deed of Conveyance from JAMES CARITHERS to MEREDITH HARRIS for 50 acres of land and ordered to be certified.

A Deed of Conveyance from JOHN HENSON to WINSTON HALL for 40 acres of land and ordered to be certified.

A Deed of Conveyance from MICHAEL LUTTRELL to WILLIAM MOREHEAD for 50 acres of land, proven by JOHN JONES and THOMAS W. HAMBLETON and ordered to be certified.

A Deed of Conveyance from JAMES DOWNING to WILLIAM SWAIN for 80 acres of land and ordered to be certified.

A Deed of Conveyance from SAMUEL BLAND to ALEXANDER GRAY for 20 acres of land, proven by JAMES McFERRIN and JOHN VANDERVILL and ordered to be certified.

A Deed of Conveyance from ISAAC ROGERS to ABSOLUM ROGERS for 115 acres of land and ordered to be certified.

A division of the land of ELIJAH HURLY, deceased, heirs, proven by BOON WILSON and ordered to be certified.

A Deed of Conveyance from ABISHA CAMP to JOSHUA WALL for 100 acres of land, proven by BENJAMIN SHORT and MERRITT H. SHORT and ordered to be certified.

A Deed of Conveyance from JOSEPH POOL to BENJAMIN ARRINGTON for 20 acres of·land, proven by JOHN GEORGE and ordered to be certified.

A Deed of Conveyance from GEORGE HOPPER to ALEXANDER GRAY for 8 acres of land, proven by JAMES McFERRIN and DAVID DODD and ordered to be certified.

A Deed of Conveyance from JESSE LORANCE to DAVID LORANCE and JOHN DAVIS for 444 acres, proven by JOHN PARK and C.M.D. GOURLY and ordered to be certified.

The transfer of a plat and certificate of survey from THOMAS EAST to WILLIAM MILNER, proven by MATHEW McGEHEE and ordered to be certified.

The transfer of a plat and certificate of survey from THOMAS EAST to WILLIAM MILNER, proven by MATHEW McGEHEE and ordered to be certified.

The transfer of a plat and certificate of survey from SAMUEL BYERS to EDWARD MOSS, proven by JAMES BYERS and ordered to be certified.

The transfer of a plat and certificate from ELIJAH LINCOLN to HENRY McKEE and ordered to be certified.

The Last Will and Testament of WILLIAM LEACH, deceased, was exhibited in court to probate, witnesses ANDREW W. WALKER and ABSOLUM DOWTHIT made oath that they heard WILLIAM LEACH acknowledge the same to be his Last Will and Testament and that he was at that time of sound mind and memory.

The Last Will and Testament of MALCOMB PATTERSON was exhibited on court to probate whereupon came ROBERT FLECHER and ALEXANDER KINNY and made oath that they saw MALCOMB PATTERSON sign, publish and declare this to be his Last Will and Testament and that he was at the time of sound mind and memory.

MONDAY APRIL 16, 1821

It is ordered by the court that THOMAS WITT and his hands ELI MILSTEAD, JAMES MILSTEAD and JOSEPH MILSTEAD work on the road from Fayetteville to Sims Ford on Elk River and they are released from working on any other road.

NATHANIEL REED produced two wolf scalps in court over four months old and made oath that he killed the same within this county.

JOSEPH McMILLIN is appointed by the court overseer of the road in the room of THOMAS BORDEN resigned and to call on the usual hands.

THOMAS GIBSON, Esquire, is appointed to take in lists of taxable property for the year 1821 in CAPTAIN HAMPTON's Company and make return in four weeks.

ABSOLUM BEARD is appointed overseer of the road in the room of JOHN DYER resigned and call on the usual hands.

JOHN DAVIS is appointed overseer of the road leading from JOHN PRYORS to the state line that intersects the Meridian Road near Estill gin and call on the usual hands.

LEVI ESLICK is appointed overseer of the road in the room of WILLIAM ESLICK resigned and call on the usual hands.

JAMES BLARE, SR. is appointed overseer of the road in the room of JOHN B. BUCHAN resigned and call on the usual hands.

WILLIAM FANNON is released from the payment of a stray mare which he posted and was valued at $30.00.

An additional inventory of the estate of J. BLACK, deceased, was returned to court by his admrs which was ordered to be certified.

The Commissioners appointed at the last term to settle with DANIEL ARCHER, exr of GEORGE ARCHER, deceased, made return of the settlement by them made which was ordered to be recorded.

On petition, JOHN CRAWFORD, JAMES CRAWFORD, SAMUEL S. BUCHANAN, JAMES TOOL, JOHN BEATIE, MOSES BUCHANAN, GENERAL W.C. EDMISTON, RANDOLPH QUARLES, and WILLIAM SMITH appointed a Jury of View to view and turn the Nashville around a large hill having the present road at the upper end of JOHN BUCHANAN's plantation and to intersect the road again at or near STEPHEN CLAYTON's and make return to next court.

Sn amount of sale of the property of WILLIAM SMITH, deceased, was returned to court by his admr which was ordered to be certified.

EBENEZER McEWEN and MARY GEORGE appeared in court and was appointed admr and admrx of the estate of PRESLEY GEORGE and who gave bond in sum of $805.00 with PHILIP KOONCE and WILLIAM C. HODGES their security.

ALEXANDER MEEK was appointed guardian for MILTON EDMISTON and ROBERT EDMISTON, infant heirs of ROBERT EDMISTON who gave bond as guardian as aforesaid.

An inventory of the property of PRESLEY GEORGE, deceased, was returned into court by his admr which was ordered to be certified.

JOHN WAGGONER is appointed overseer of the road in the room of JACOB WAGGONER resigned and call on the usual hands.

DANIEL WHITAKER is appointed overseer of the road in the room of JAMES McCORMACK resigned and call on the usual hands.

THOMAS GEORGE is appointed overseer of the road in the room of JAMES GEORGE resigned and call on the usual hands.

NEWBERRY JAMES, JAMES CRAIG, WILLIAM NIXON, WILEY GARRETT and ABRAHAM GOODWIN is appointed Jury of View to view and turn the Huntsville Road around ABRAHAM ISAAC's plantation and make return to next court.

ROBERT M. WHITE is appointed overseer of the road from Big Swan Creek to the Thirteen Mile Post and call on the usual hands.

AMOS DAVIS is appointed overseer of the road from the Thirteen Mile Post to Moores Gap and call on the usual hands.

On petition, JOHN GREER, Sheriff, is released from the payment of $33.63½ taxes for the year 1820 which could not be collected.

JOSHUA WILLIAMS is appointed overseer of the road leading from Fayetteville to Winchester from the Cross Roads to the Gum Spring and call on the hands within two miles of each side of said road.

JOHN GEORGE is appointed overseer of the road from the Gum Spring to the Franklin County line and call on the hands within two miles of each side of said road.

SAMUEL D. SANSON, JAMES RALSTON, Esquire, and DAVID LORANCE is appointed by the court to settle with JOAB BUCKLEY and JOSHUA NICHOLS, exrs of JOSEPH LOONEY, deceased, and make return to next court.

DAVID COWEN and ABSOLUM BOSTICK is appointed by the court Commissioners to settle with JAMES CARITHERS, admr of the estate of SAMUEL CARITHERS, deceased, also admr of the estate of JOHN CARITHERS, deceased, and make return to next court.

JOHN ENOCK and ANDREW W. WALKER, Esquires, are appointed Commissioners to settle with CHAMPION BLYTH, admr of the estate of JESSE B. CLARK, deceased, and make return to next court.

JOHN GREER, Sheriff, is allowed $50.00 for his exofficio services for the year 1820 and that the County Trustee pay the same out of any county monies in his hands not otherwise appropriated.

WILLIAM B. MARTIN, Solicitor General, is allowed $50.00 for his exofficio services for the year 1820 and that the County Trustee pay the same out of any county monies in his hands.

BRICE M. GARNER, Clerk, is allowed $50.00 for his exofficio services for the year 1820, also $25.00 for making out tax list for said year and the County Trustee pay the same out of any county monies in his hands.

A Deed of Conveyance from WILLIAM GRANT to THOMAS JONES for 10 acres of land, proven by WILLIAM ROWAN and DAVID JONES and ordered to be certified.

A Deed of Conveyance from WILLIAM GRANT to THOMAS JONES for 100 acres of land, proven by WILLIAM ROWAN and DAVID JONES and ordered to be certified.

A Deed of Conveyance from BENJAMIN GEORGE to JAMES GEORGE for 83 acres of land and ordered to be certified.

A Deed of Conveyance from MAJOR WALL to WILLIAM MONROE for 34 acres of land, proven by ALEXANDER MORTON and ANTHONY HOGAN and ordered to be certified.

A Power of Attorney from PETER WRIGHT to JAMES TITUS, proven by ROBERT H. McEWEN and SAMUEL E. GILLILAND and ordered to be certified.

A transfer of a plat and certificate of survey from RICHARD BASSHAM and ordered to be certified.

A transfer of a plat and certificate of survey from MAJOR WALL to WILLIAM MONROE and ordered to be certified.

A Deed of Conveyance from JOHN McKINNEY to JOHN PORTER and REPS O. CHILDRESS, proven by JOHN FRAZIER and HUGH BELL and ordered to be certified.

A Deed of Conveyance from JOHN WILSON to THOMAS GRAY and ordered to be certified.

A Deed of Conveyance from THOMAS FULLERTON to MARGARETT ADAMS for 100 acres of land, proven by JOHN MILLIKEN and JOHN J. TATE and ordered to be certified.

A Deed of Conveyance from THOMAS HOOPER to CORNELIUS SULLIVAN for 100 acres of land, proven by CRAVEN WEAVER and JOHN SULLIVAN and ordered to be certified.

A Deed of Conveyance from THOMAS KELLY to NOAH WARD for 10 acres of land and ordered to be certified.

A Deed of GEORGE PRICE and JOHN ENOCKS and ordered to be certified.

A Deed of Conveyance from BENJAMIN GEORGE to WILLIAM HOWARD for 333½ acres of land, proven by JOHN ENOCK and CHAMPION BLYTH and ordered to be certified.

A Deed of Conveyance from WILLIAM H. RAGSDALE to THOMAS & JESSE GIBSON for 340 acres of land, proven by WILLIAM GIBSON and JOEL FOSTER and ordered to be certified.

A Deed of Conveyance from JAMES BENNETT to JOHN STILES for 50 acres of land, proven by JOHN LANGSTON and JOHN LYNCH and ordered to be certified.

A Deed of Conveyance from JAMES KERR to JOHN W.A. LYNCH for 192 acres of land, proven by JOHN LANGSTON and SAMUEL YOUNG and ordered to be certified.

A Deed of Conveyance from JOHN W.A. LYNCH to JOHN LANGSTON for 80 acres of land and ordered to be certified.

A Bill of Sale from ELI GARRETT, AGATHA GARRETT, WILLIAM GARRETT, and POLLY GARRETT to ROBERT HAIRSTON for a negro girl named DELILA, proven by W.P. PULLIAM and ROBERT EDMISTON and ordered to be certified.

A Deed of Conveyance from EDWARAD CHITWOOD to HENRY LAZENBY for 58 acres of land, proven by E. McEWEN and WILLIAM P. PULLIAM and ordered to be certified.

A Power of Attorney from JOSEPH DILLENDER to JAMES NEAL and ordered to be certified.

WILLIAM GARRETT was appointed a Constable who gave bond and security.

ELI TAYLOR was appointed a Constable who gave bond and security.

WILLIAM SMITH was appointed a Constable who gave bond and security.

HENRY WARREN and WILLIS WARREN was appointed guardian for POLLY WARREN, otherwise POLLY LEWIS, JAMES WARREN, otherwise JAMES LEWIS, SELINIA LEWIS, BEDDA WARREN, otherwise BEDDA LEWIS, LUISA WARREN, otherwise LUISA LEWIS, JOHN WARREN, otherwise JOHN LEWIS.

It is ordered by the court that ABSOLUM BEARD, WALTER HARKINS, PHILIP KOONCE, ELI GARRETT, FRANCIS PORTERFIELD, ROBERT H. McEWEN, WILLIAM DICKSON, JOHN ENOCKS, JONATHAN FLOYD, THOMAS GIBSON, DAVID P. MUNROE, WILLIAM BEAVERS, WILLIAM DYE, ABRAHAM ISAACS, JAMES RALSTON, JOHN RHEA, JOHN WISEMAN, JOHN J. WHITAKER, WILLIAM KENNON, WILLIAM GIVENS, JOEL YOWEL, JOHN MOORE, REPS O. CHILDRESS, JOHN PORTER, JOHN WILSON and THOMAS CLARK be summoned as jurors to the next Circuit Court of this county held on 3rd September next and that REUBIN H. BOON be summoned to wait on court and jury.

It is ordered by the court that REECE HOWELL. PATON (PAYTON) WELLS, THOMAS McGAUGH, GILBERT KENNEDY, DOILY GRIFFIS, ARCHABALD CAMPBELL, WILLIAM WILLIAMS, JOHN ADKINS, WILLIAM WHITE, JOSEPH McMILLIN, ALLEN ELSTON, HENRY KYMES, JOSIAH SMITH, SAMUEL BUCHANAN, JR., JOHN BUCHANAN, JOHN B. TODD, CHARLES BRIGHT, THOMAS WHITAKER, BENJAMIN WHITAKER, WILLIAM C. HODGES, JAMES ESLEMAN, JAMES ISHAM, AUGUSTUS L. JONES, HENRY WARREN, CHARLES PORTER and ANDREW HANNAH, be summoned as to the next County Court held on 3rd Monday July next and that ROBERT BUCHANAN be summoned to wait on said court and jury.

Justices present were JAMES HOLEMAN, WILLIAM DICKSON and PHILIP KOONCE, Esquires.

The Sheriff made return that he had summoned the following venire to serve as Jurors to this term, to wit, WILLIAM BARROW, DAVID JONES, HUGH PARKERSON, LEMUEL BROADWAY, RICHARD JONES, SAMUEL TODD, ROBERT PARKS, JAMES CRAWFORD, PETER LUNA, SR., JACKSON BLAKEMORE, WILLIAM D. BLAKE, THOMAS WITT, ENOCH RUST, ·STEPHEN BEAVERS, JAMES SMITH, EDWARD MOSS, CORNELIUS WEBB, ROBERT STEPHENS, WILLIAM CASHON, JOHN DUSENBERRY, SAMUEL HOWELL, JOSEPH COMMONS, WILLIAM TIMMONS, JAMES McFERRIN, PETER VAUGHN, ARCHABALD McELROY and WILLIAM WALLACE.

WILLIAM P. PULLIAM, a Constable, summoned to wait on said court and jury.

A Deed of Conveyance from JOHN GREER, Sheriff, to DEMSEY ALLEN for 45 acres of land and ordered to be certified.

A Deed of Conveyance from LEMUEL BRANDON to JOSIAH K. BRANDON for 2 acres of land and ordered to be certified.

The transfer of a plat and certificate of survey from RICHARD McNATT to STORY GARRETT for 3 acres of land and ordered to be certified.

The transfer of a plat and certificate of survey from RICHARD McNATT to STORY GARRETT and ordered to be certified.

A Deed of Conveyance from JAMES McKISICK to RICHARD McNATT for 20 acres of land and ordered to be certified.

A Deed of Conveyance from SAMUEL GARLAND to CHARLES McNATT for 50 acres of land and ordered to be certified.

The State vs WILLIAM TOWNZEND - Assault and Battery - The defendant being charged on this Bill of Indictment pleads guilty and is fined $5.00 and pay the costs.

JOHN CLIFTON vs WILLIAM MOREHEAD - It is ordered that the clerk bring into court the papers on or in anywise relative to a suit tried before JOHN JONES, Esquire, on 19 January 1821.

JOHN CLIFTON vs WILLIAM MOREHEAD - (same as above).

The State vs GEORGE W. HUNT - The defendant acknowledged himself indebted to the State of Tennessee of $200.00 and PHILIP KOONCE his security of $250.00 to be levied on their goods and chattels &c but to be void on conditions that GEORGE W. HUNT appear here on 1st Thursday after 3rd Monday in July next and answer the State of Tennessee for an assault and battery and not depart the same without leave first had and obtained of the court.

The State vs GEORGE W. HUNT - JOHN CAMPBELL, BURWELL HORTON and ROBERT FLETCHER appeared in court and acknowledged to the use of the State indebted but to be void on condition that they appear in July next to prosecute and give evidence in behalf of the State against GEORGE W. HUNT and not depart the same without leave first had and obtained of the court.

The State vs GEORGE W. HUNT - Peace Warrant - The defendant acknowledged himself indebted to the State of Tennessee for $500.00 and PHILIP KOONCE and WILLIAM DICKSON his securities in sum of $250.00 each to be levied upon their goods and chattels &c but to be void on conditions that the said GEORGE W, HUNT will keep the peace towards the citizens of this State particular towards JOHN CAMPBELL for six months and appear in court in October next.

ROBERT & W. DICKSON vs PETER MOYERS - The plaintiffs appeared in court and dismisses their suit and the defendant assumes the payment of all costs. The suit be dismissed and the plaintiffs to recover against the defendant their costs.

JOHN J. WINSTON vs PETER VAUGHN & WILLIAM BRYAN - The plaintiff by attorney appeared in court and dismisses his suit and the defendants assumes the payment of the costs. The plaintiff recover against the defendants his costs.

PETER VAUGHN vs MAY BUCHANAN - The plaintiff says he wishes to dismiss this suit and assumes the payment of all costs. Suit dismissed and the defendant recover against the plaintiff his costs.

JOHN W. GORDON vs WILSON & JOHN DILLON - Motion - The Sheriff was ordered to expose to sale 30 acres of land lying on the road leading from Fayetteville to Huntsville, the place that JOHN DILLON now lives, levied on as the property of JOHN DILLON to satisfy a judgement that JOHN W. GORDON recovered against WILSON DILLON and that JOHN DILLON appear before CHARLES BOYLES, Esquire, in December next for $27.90 and all legal costs.

ROBERT CUNNINGHAM vs JOHN DILLON - Motion - The Sheriff was ordered to expose to sale 30 acres of land (same as above) to satisfy a judgement that ROBERT CUNNINGHAM recovered against JOHN DILLON before JOHN PORTER, Esquire, in January 1820 and for $12.16 3/4 and all costs.

WILLIAM C. KENNEDY vs WILLIAM WHITEHEAD - Motion - The Sheriff is ordered to expose to sale two tracts of land lying on Kelly Creek and containing 3½ acres, the other 4½ acres, levied on as the property of WILLIAM WHITEHEAD to satisfy a judgement held before WILLIAM DICKSON, Esquire, in September 1820 for $40.80 and all costs.

CHARLES BOYLES vs MARTIN HOLBERT & JOHN DILLON - Motion - The Sheriff is ordered to expose to sale 30 acres of land lying on the road leading from Fayetteville to Huntsville, the place that JOHN DILLON now lives on as the property of JOHN DILLON to satisfy a judgement against MARTIN HOLBERT and JOHN DILLON for $30.51 and all costs. Held in December 1820.

J.V. & C. McKINNEY vs JOHN DILLON & M. HOLBERT - Motion - The Sheriff is ordered to expose to sale 30 acres of land lying on the road leading from fayetteville to Huntsville, to satisfy a judgement against JOHN DILLON and MARTIN HOLBERT for $35.17 and costs, before CHARLES BOYLES, Esquire, in December 1820.

THOMAS ROUNTREE vs J.H. BELL - Motion - The Sheriff is ordered to expose to sale one town lot No. 9 in Lynchburgh, levied on as the property of J.H. BELL to satisfy a judgement that THOMAS ROUNTREE recovered, J.H. BELL for $78.26 3/4 and all costs, before ANDREW W. WALKER, Esquire, on 22 January 1821.

JOHNSTON WELLBORN vs KELLY STEGALL - Motion - Motion was overruled and the court says that the defendant by his attorney excepted and prays his Bill of Exception to be signed, sealed and made a part of this record which is done accordingly.

JOHNSTON WELLBORN vs KELLY STEGALL - Attachment - This day came the parties by their attorneys and a jury of men, to wit, WILLIAM TIMMONS, JOSEPH COMMONS, LEMUEL BROADWAY, THOMAS WITT, ROBERT PARKS, WILLIAM LEDFORD, RICHARD JONES, WILLIAM BOON, WILLIAM CASHON, SAMUEL HOWELL, JOHN McMILLIN and ARCHABALD McELROY being elected and sworn and said that they cannot agree upon their verdict in this cause. The jury to be discharged and the cause is continued until next court.

WEDNESDAY APRIL 18, 1821

Justices present were JAMES HOLMAN, WILLIAM DICKSON and PHILIP KOONCE, Esquires.

A Deed of Conveyance from GEORGE CUNNINGHAM to PETER MOYERS for 38 acres and 15 (poles) of land and ordered to be certified.

A Power of Attorney from WILLIAM ROBERT to JOSEPH GREER, proven by VANCE GREER and GEORGE ST. JOHN BASKINS and ordered to be certified.

A Deed of Conveyance from ANDREW ERWIN to RANDOLPH QUARLES for 200 acres of land, proven by JAMES BRIGHT and WILLIAM C. KENNEDY and ordered to be certified.

The order made appointing WILLIAM KENNON, STEPHEN ALEXANDER and ISAAC CONGER, Esquires, Commissioners to settle with SAMUEL ROSEBOROUGH, admr of the estate of JOSEPH WHITTENBURGH, deceased, is extended to next term of court.

WILLIAM McELROY vs MICAJAH McELROY - Motion - The Sheriff is ordered to expose to sale 600 acres of land lying on Cane Creek the (place) that MICAJAH McELROY's

McELROY's family did live, levied on as the property of MICAJAH McELROY to satisfy a judgement that WILLIAM B. MARTIN recovered against said McELROY for $15.62½ and costs, on 28 March 1821.

JANE B. CAMPBELL vs M. McELROY & C. BOYLES - Motion - The Sheriff is ordered to expose to sale 600 acres of land lying on Cane Creek, the (place) that MICAJAH McELROY formerly lived, levied on as the property of said McELROY to satisfy a judgement that JANE B. CAMPBELL recovered against McELROY for $95.25 debt and all costs on 19 May 1821.

JANE B. CAMPBELL vs MICAJAH McELROY - Motion - The Sheriff to expose to sale 600 acres of land on Cane Creek, the place that MICAJAH McELROY's family formerly lived, levied on as the property of said McELROY ro satisfy a judgement that JANE B. CAMPBELL recovered against MICAJAH McELROY for $11.25 debt and all costs on 11th May 1820.

JOHN A. CHAPMAN vs WILLIAM YOUNG - The plaintiff by his attorney appeared in court and the defendant being called to come and defend his in this behalf failed to do so but made default. Plaintiff to recover against the defendant $91.50 with interest.

CHARLES BOYLES vs ROBERT BRADON - Debt - The defendant confessed that he owed the plaintiff $98.10 balance of the debt and damages of $8.06. Plaintiff to recover against the defendant his costs.

WILLIAM C. KENNEDY vs WILIA GARRETT - The defendant confessed that he owes the plaintiff $120.00 debt and damages of $22.14. Plaintiff to recover against the defendant his costs.

JANE B. CAMPBELL vs C. BOYERS & B.M. GARNER - On motion of the defendant by his attorney, leave is given them to withdraw their plea filed.

THURSDAY APRIL 19, 1821

Justices present were WILLIAM KENNON, JAMES WILSON and JAMES HOLEMAN.

WILLIAM FLUTY, ARCHABALD McKEE, STEPHEN TOUCHSTON, JOHN ALLBRIGHT, and ROBERT HAIRSTON appeared in court and acknowledged themselves indebted to the State of Tennessee for $250.00 each to be levied of their respective goods and chattels &c but to be void on conditions that they appear here in July next to prosecute and give evidence in behalf of the State against WILLIAM BEARDEN and not depart the same without leave first had and obtained of the court.

JOHN C. McADA appeared in court and acknowledged himself indebted to the State of Tennessee for $250.00 and ROBERT DICKSON and JOHN A. McADA for $125.00 each to be levied of their goods and chattels &c but to be void on conditions that the said McADA appear here in July next to answer the State of Tennessee for a charge of an affray and not depart the same without leave first had and obtained of the court.

GEORGE A. ALLEN appeared in court and said that he was indebted to the State of Tennessee for $250.00 to be levied of his goods and chattels &c but to be void on conditions that he appear here in July next to prosecute and give evidence in behalf of the State against JOHN JOB, JONATHAN, WELCH, THOMAS LITTLE and SOLOMON JOBE and not depart the same without leave first had and obtained of the court.

GEORGE A. ALLEN (same as above).

JONATHAN WELCH appeared in court and said he is indebted to the State of Tennessee for $250.00 and LARY EPPS for $250.00 to be levied upon their goods and chattels &c but to be void on conditions that JONATHAN WELCH appear here in July next and answer the State for an affray and not depart the same without leave first had and obtained of the court.

JOHN JOBE (same as above) on conditions that JOHN JOBE appear here in July next to answer the State for an affray and not depart without leave had and obtained of the court.

PATSEY BLUBAKER appeared in court and acknowledged herself indebted to the State of Tennessee for $250.00 and HARDING FORRISTER and JORDAN SOLOMON for $120.00 each to be levied of their goods and chattels &c but to be void on conditions that PATSEY BLUBAKER appear here in July next to answer the State of Tennessee for a charge of a trespass and not depart without leave first had and obtained of the court.

NANCY STEGALL appeared in court and says she is indebted to the State of Tennessee for $250.00 to be levied of her goods and chattels &c but to be void on conditions that she appear here in July next to prosecute and give evidence in behalf of the State against JOSEPH C. McADA and not depart without leave first had and obtained of the court.

JOHN C. McADA appeared in court and says he is indebted to the State of Tennessee for $250.00 Tto be levied of his goods and chattels &c but to be void on conditions that he appear here in July next to prosecute and give evidence in behalf of the State against PATSEY BLUBAKER and not depart the same without leave first had and obtained of the court.

VANCE GREER vs HENRY MAXWELL- On motion of the plaintiff by his attorney, a Commission is awarded him to take the deposition of BENJAMIN P. McLIN tomorrow at WILLIAM E. KENNEDY's office in Fayetteville between the hours of 11:00 and 1:00 o'clock to be read as evidence in the trial of this case and that this order shall be sufficient notice for taking the same.

WILLIAM C. HODGE appeared and says he is indebted to the State of Tennessee for $250.00 and CONSTANT SCALES for $250.00 to be levied of their goods and chattels &c but to be void on conditions that said HODGE appear here in July next to answer the State for an assault and battery and not depart without leave first had and obtained of the court.

MARK STEED appeared here ans says he is indebted to the State of Tennessee for $250.00 to be levied of his goods and chattels &c but to be void on conditions that he appear here in July next to prosecute and give evidence in behalf of the State against WILLIAM C. HODGE and not depart the same without leave first had and obtained of the court.

JOHN LANE appeared here and says he is indebted to the State of Tennessee for $100.00 and MARK STEED for $100.00 to be levied of their goods and chattels but to be void on conditions that JOHN LANE will keep the peace towards the citizens of this State particular JAMES STRINGER for three months and appear here in July next to abide by the court.

ISAAC LAND and MARK STEED appeared and said they are indebted to the State of Tennessee for $100.00 each to be levied of their goods and chattels &c but to be void on conditions that the said ISAAC LANE will keep the peace towards the citizens of this State particular towards JAMES STRINGER for three months and appear here in July next and abide by the court.

JOHN LANE and MARK STEED (same as above) for $200.00 each (same as above) that JOHN LANE appear here in July next to answer the State of Tennessee for an assault and not depart without leave first had and obtained of the court.

JAMES STRINGER, THOMAS BARKER, SR., and THOMAS BARKER, JR., appeared and says they are indebted to the State of tennessee for $200.00 each (same as above) that they appear here in July next to give evidence in behalf of the State against JOHN LANE (same as above).

THOMAS LITTLE appeared and says he is indebted to the State of Tennessee for $250.00 and JACOB WRIGHT and ZACHARIAH GOLD for $125.00 each (same as above) that THOMAS LITTLE appear here in July next to answer the State of Tennessee for an affrat (same as above).

A Power of Attorney from JOHN C. SAWYERS to ROBERT DICKSON and ordered to be certified.

JOHN W. CRUNK vs ROBERT BRADON - Motion - On motion of the plaintiff by his attorney to set aside this case and on argument being heard, it is considered by the court that the motion be overruled.

JAMES HUNTER vs JESSE DODDS - Motion - The Sheriff to expose to sale 35 acres of land where JESSE DODD now lives, levied on as property of said DODD, a balance of a judgement that JAMES HUNTER recovered against JESSE DODD for $99.75 and costs before HENRY KELSO on 30th March 1821.

JOHN DAVIS vs ADLAI SHARP - Plaintiff appeared in court and dismiss his suit and assumes the payment of all costs. Plaintiff(defendant) to recover against the plaintiff his costs.

MALCOM GILCHRIST vs THOMAS HARPER - The plaintiff by his attorney came into court and the defendant being called to come and plea to this suit failed to do so but made a default. Plaintiff to recover against the defendant $160.00 and damages of $7.75.

JOHN MARR vs JOHN BERNARD, HICKS MILLSAP and WILLIAM MILLSAP - Plaintiff by his attorney came into court and the defendant being called to come and plead to this suit failed to do so but made default. Plaintiff to recover against the defendant $117.50 and damages of $1.95.

EDWARD ISHAM vs THOMAS L. TROTTER - On motion by both parties and their attorneys, a motion to dismiss this certiorari in this cause. Court dismissed this cause and on motion of the plaintiff, it is considered by the court that the plaintiff recover against the defendant and BRICE M. GARNER his security the sum of $90.50 and interest of $13.00.

DAVID JONES vs THOMAS L. TROTTER - On motion of both parties by their attorneys, a motion to dismiss this cause. Court overruled and that this cause be placed on the trial docket of next term of court.

FRIDAY APRIL 20, 1821

Justices present were WILLIAM KENNON, JAMES HOLEMAN and JAMES WILSON, Esquires.

NOTE: 4 pages missing.

GUSTAVUS HENDRICKS vs VANCE GREER - The order made at the last term to take the deposition in this cause, by consent of the parties by their attorneys, is renewed and extended to the next term of this court.

MALCOM GILCHRIST vs THOMAS HARPER - The defendant appeared in court and prays an appeal to the Circuit Court from a judgement rendered in this case heretofore at this term, having given bond and security the same is granted him.

MONDAY JULY 16, 1821

WILLIAM WILLIAMS is appointed overseer of the road in the room of MATHEW McGEHEE resigned and to call on the usual hands.

SION HOLLY is appointed overseer of the road in the room of WILLIAM HAYS resigned and SAMUEL GARLAND and ABNER STEED, Esquire, appointed the hands to work on said road.

CRAVEN WEAVER is appointed overseer of the road in the room of JOHN PRICE resigned and SAMUEL GARLAND and ABNER STEED, Esquires to appoint the hands to work on said road.

ZACHARIAH HARRISON is appointed overseer of the road in the room of JACK H. LEFTWICH and SAMUEL GARLAND and ABNER STEED to appoint the hands to work on said road.

DAVID HUNTER is appointed overseer of the road in the room of JOSHUA WILLIAMS and to call on the usual hands.

THOMAS KERCHEVALL is appointed overseer of the road in the room of ELIJAH DAVIS and call on the usual hands.

SAMUEL TODD is appointed overseer of the road in the room of DAVID RORAX resigned and to call on the usual hands.

STEPHEN CHITWOOD is appointed overseer of the road in the room of HOWELL HARRIS resigned and to call on the usual hands.

JONATHAN ANDERSON is appointed overseer of the road in the room of THOMAS CLARK resigned and to call on the usual hands.

JAMES CARTER is appointed overseer of the road from JOHN RHEA to Chinault Ford on Elk River and to call on the usual hands.

WILLIAM MOFFET is appointed overseer of the road in the room of JOSIAH SMITH and that ROBERT DICKSON hands work on said road in addition to the hands already allotted for said road.

JOHN DOUTHIT is appointed overseer of the road in the room of JOHN GAVIN resigned and to call on the usual hands.

WILLIAM DACUS is appointed overseer of the road in the room of JESSE ELLIS resigned and to call on the usual hands.

ABEL DUCKWORTH is appointed overseer of the road in the room of JOHN NICHOLS resigned and to call on the usual hands.

WALTER HAWKINS is appointed overseer of the road in the room of DAVID HOWELL resigned and to call on the usual hands.

SAMUEL S. BUCHANAN is appointed overseer of the road in the room of JOHN GIBSON resigned.

WILLIS WARREN is appointed overseer of the road from the lower ford on Mulberry Creek to Rountree Creek in the place of JAMES STEPHENS resigned.

Ordered by the court that ANN JOHNSON, one of the poor of this county, be let out to the lowest bidder this day at the court house door.

WILLIAM CRAWFORD is appointed overseer of the Nashville Road beginning at the mouth of JOHN BUCHANAN's lane to STEPHEN CLAYTON and that JAMES CRAWFORD hands, WILLIAM CRAWFORD, JR., JOHN CRAWFORD and his hands, STEPHEN CLAYTON, RANDOLPH QUARLES and his hands, JOHN MOORE, MOSES BUCHANAN, WILLIAM CRAWFORD's hands work on said road.

JEREMIAH HEDGEPETH is appointed overseer of the road in the room of GABRIEL SEAHORN resigned and call on the usual hands.

RIGDON BEAVERS is appointed overseer of the road from the Sulpher Spring to Morton Branch, in the room of LEWIS HOPER (HOPPER) resigned.

JAMES CHAPMAN is released from payment of two stray nags which he posted and was proven from him, valued to $90.00.

WILLIAM HUSBANDS return to court that he had let out ANN JOHNSON, one of the poor of this county, to THOMAS CHAPMAN for $48.00 who gave bond and security.

JOHN ENOCKS, JONATHAN FLOYD and ANDREW W. WALKER, Esquires is appointed by the Court Judges of the next election at Lynchburgh.

JOHN RHEA, ANDREW McCARTNEY and JOHN GIBSON is appointed Judges of the next election at Fayetteville.

THOMAS GIBSON, ELISHA BAGLEY and JAMES BLAKEMORE is appointed Judges of the next election at WILLIAM CRUNK's.

THOMAS CLARK, JOHN PORTER and JACOB WRIGHT is appointed Judges of the next election at Buckingham.

SAMUEL M. CLAY, MICHAEL ROBERTSON and JOHN PARR is appointed Judges of the next election at Hodges Old Place on Coldwater.

JOHN DONELSON, WILSON FROST, JOHN BOON, LARRY EPPS, JOSEPH HINKLE, COONROD KYMES, and ROBERT are appointed a Jury of View to view and turn the Nashville Road around a large (hill) north of JOHN BUCHANAN, the way that STEPHEN CLAYTON has cleared out and make return to next court.

It is ordered by the court that the road that crosses the river at Simm's Ford be discontinued and that the hands who worked on the Huntsville Road under JAMES CUNNINGHAM as overseer continue to work under him as before the opening of said first mentioned road.

DAVID THWING is allowed to receive from the County Trustee sum of $50.00 out of any county money in his hands not otherwise appropriated, for inclose the COurt House in addition to what he has already received.

VINCENT LUTTRELL is appointed overseer of the road leading from Fayetteville to Winchester, beginning at the place where JOHN GEORGE leaves off, to wit, three miles this side of the county line and work to the county line, and that AMBROSE BARKER and WILLIAM MILLNER, Esq., by appointed to lay off and divide the hands for JOHN GEORGE and said LUTTRELL.

Ordered by the court that THOMAS CLARK be released as the security of JAMES CARITHERS and HAMPTON BOSTICK, admrs on the estate of SAMUEL CARITHERS, deceased, upon the said admr given other bond and security which is done accordingly.

It is ordered by the court that WILLIAM EDMISTON, WILLIAM C. HODGE and JOHN McMILLIN be appointed to set apart so much of the crop and provisions on hand as may be necessary for the support of the widow and family of JOHN WARREN, deceased, one year and make return to next court.

HIRAM HOWELL is appointed overseer of the road from Shinnault Ford on Elk River to where it intersects the Mulberry Road and call on the usual hands.

JOHN STREET is appointed overseer of the road from the mouth of Mulberry to the Cross Roads on the south side of Elk River and call on the usual hands.

VANCE GREER is appointed admr of the estate of ALEXANDER BIRD, deceased, who gave bond in sum of $500.00 with JOHN DAVIS his security.

An nventory of the property of EZEKIEL NALE, deceased, was returned to court which was ordered to be certified.

The Commissioners heretofore appointed to settle with the admr of the estate of JOSEPH LOONEY, deceased, made return to court the settlement by them made which was ordered to be certified.

A Bill of Sale from MARK STEED to STERLING C. McLEMORE for a negro girl named PATSEY was proven in court by WILLIAM DICKSON and ordered to be certified.

A Deed of Conveyance from JOHN WILSON to JOHN MILLICAN for 15 acres of land and ordered to be certified.

A Deed of Conveyance from JOHN WILSON to JOHN PORTER for 44 acres of land and ordered to be certified.

A Deed of Conveyance from WILLIAM WILLIAMS to THOMAS BLYTHE for 65 acres of land, proven by ISAAC HOLEMAN and JONATHAN FLOYD and ordered to be certified.

A Deed of Conveyance from JESSE LUTTRELL to THOMAS LUTTRELL for 40 acres of land, proven by FRANCIS FINCHER and JOSEPH ELLISON and ordered to be certified.

A Deed of Conveyance from SOLOMON BURFORD to JOHN CLARK for 35 acres of land and ordered to be certified.

A Deed of Conveyance from SOLOMON BURFORD to WILLIAM BIRMINGHAM for 5 acres of land and ordered to be certified.

A Deed of Conveyance from WILLIAM EDMISTON, executor, to JAMES COWAN for 56 acres of land and ordered to be certified.

A Deed of Conveyance from WILLIAM MONTGOMERY to EDWARD MOSS for 160 acres of land and ordered to be certified.

A Deed of Conveyance from WILLIAM EDMISTON to THOMAS BLYTHE for 20 acres of land, proven by ISAAC HOLMAN and JONATHAN FLOYD and ordered to be certified.

A Deed of Conveyance from JOHN MURPHEY to JONATHAN ANDERSON for 8 acres of land and ordered to be certified.

A Deed of Conveyance from SAMUEL CAPLE to MOSES PARR for 139 acres of land, proven by JOHN PARR and BENJAMIN T. PARR and ordered to be certified.

A Deed of Conveyance from JESSE LUTTRELL to JOHN McFARLING for 100 acres of land, proven by FRANCIS FINCHER and ELI COUCH and ordered to be certified.

A Deed of Conveyance from JESSE LUTTRELL to JOSEPH ELLISON for 165 acres of land, proven by ELI COUCH and JOHN McFARLIN and ordered to be certified.

A Deed of Conveyance from MARY GRAY to HARLAND GRIFFIS for 163 acres of land, proven by DAVID COWAN and JAMES McFERRAN and ordered to be certified.

A Deed of Conveyance from TURNER WILLIAMS to JOSEPH GARNER for 215 acres of land, proven by DAVIDSON WATSON and JAMES D. ELLIS and ordered to be certified.

A Deed of Conveyance from JOSEPH HINKLE to JAMES SMITH for 183 acres of land and ordered to be certified.

A Deed of Conveyance from DAVID BUCHANAN, SR. to DAVID BUCHANAN, JR. for 200 acres, proven by JOHN GIBSON and PARK GIBSON and ordered to be certified.

A Deed of Conveyance from DANIEL BAKER to JOSIAH BRANDON for 375 acres of land, proven by B. BRANDON and JOSEPH UNDERWOOD and ordered to be certified.

A Deed of Conveyance from JOHN KINDRICK to BENJAMIN WALKER for 40 acres of land, proven by AESOP SHELTON and J. FORSYTH and ordered to be certified.

The transfer of a plat and certificate of survey from JOHN R. ENOCKS to ENOCK ENOCKS, proven by JOHN ENOCKS and A.W. WALKER and ordered to be certified.

A Deed of Conveyance from JOHN WILSON to RICHARD COMPTON for 49 acres of land and ordered to be certified.

A Deed of Conveyance from HENRY DAVIS to JOAB BAGLEY for 60 acres of land and ordered to be certified.

A Deed of Conveyance from JONATHAN GROSS to JACOB WRIGHT for 27 acres of land and ordered to be certified.

A Deed of Conveyance from BRICE M. GARNER to SHEROD HUNTER for 6 acres of land, proven by ADLAI SHARP and W. HIGGINS and ordered to be certified.

A Deed of Conveyance from JOHN WILSON to HENRY BECK for 100 acres of land and ordered to be certified.

It is ordered by the court that WILLIAM HOWARD, GEORGE PRICE, SHERROD HUNTER, WILLIAM DOAK, FRANCIS PATTON, JOHN DAVIS, PRESTON HAMPTON, JOHN DOWTHIT, GEORGE H. STOVALL, MOSES CHAMBERS, WILLIAM FRAME, RALPH ARNOLD, BENJAMIN HUDSON, THOMAS BRENTS, WILLIAM RUSSELL, JACOB GROSS, MARK STEED, THOMAS M. HARPER, WESLEY SMITH, SAMUEL CRAWFORD, ABNER WELLS, JOEL DODSON, JOHN KENNEDY, JOHN R. MOOR, JOHN DONELSON, STEPHEN CLAYTON, DAVID SMITH, WILLIAM SHAW, JOHN GAVIN and WILLIAM LANGSTON be summoned as jurors to next county court held on the 3rd Monday in October next and JAMES CURRY be summoned to wait on said court and jury.

A Deed of Conveyance from SAMUEL JAMES to JAMES GATLIN for 75 acres of land, proven by NEWBERY JAMES and JOHN GATLIN and ordered to be certified.

A Deed of Conveyance from JOHN WILSON to JOSHUA GUNTER for 73 acres of land and ordered to be certified.

A Deed of Conveyance from ANTHONY WELLS to PAYTON WELLS for 160 acres of land, proven by EDWARD MOSS and JAMES W. CUNNINGHAM and ordered to be certified.

A Deed of Conveyance from JONATHAN REYNOLDS to ALEXANDER DAVIS for 15 acres of land, proven by DANIEL SMITH and SION HOLLY and ordered to be certified.

A Deed of Conveyance from JAMES McCORMACK to JONATHAN ANDERSON for 60 acres of land, proven by JOHN PORTER and ELI TAYLOR and ordered to be certified.

A Deed of Conveyance from SAMUEL PAINTER and CHARLES BOYLES to JAMES ISHAM for 50 acres of land, proven by ANGUISH JOHNSON and YEWELL WILLIAMS and ordered to be certified.

A Deed of Conveyance from JACOB VANHOOSER to WILLIAM MAJORS for 40 acres of land, proven by A. ISAACK and WILLIAM BONNER and ordered to be certified.

A Deed of Conveyance from WILLIAM MAJORS to HUDSON ALLEN for 40 acres of land, proven by A. ISAACKS and WILLIAM BONNER and ordered to be certified.

A Deed of Conveyance from WILLIAM MAJORS to HUDSON ALLEN for 11 acres of land, proven by SOLOMON BURFORD and A. ISAACKS and ordered to be certified.

A Deed of Conveyance from SOLOMON BURFORD and JOSEPH ROPER for 50 acres of land and ordered to be certified.

A Deed of Conveyance from SOLOMON BURFORD to A. ISAACKS for 152¼ acres of land and ordered to be certified.

A Deed of Conveyance from SOLOMON BURFORD to WILLIAM MAJORS for 11 acres of land and ordered to be certified.

A Deed of Conveyance from DAVID BUCHANAN, SR. to SAMUEL S. BUCHANAN for 244 acres of land, proven by JOHN GIBSON, DAVID BUCHANAN, JR., and PARK GIBSON and ordered to be certified.

TUESDAY JULY 19, 1821

Justices present were PHILIP KOONCE, JAMES HOLMAN and WILLIAM KENNON, Esquires.

The Sheriff made return that he had summones the venire to serve as Grand Jurors and Petit Jurors this term, to wit, BENJAMIN DORSEY, REECE HOWELL, PAYTON WELLS, THOMAS McGAUGH, GILBERT KENNEDY, DOILY GRIFFIS, ARCHABALD ELSTON, HENRY KYMES, SAMUEL BUCHANAN, JOHN BUCHANAN, JOHN B. TODD, CHARLES BRIGHT, THOMAS WHITAKER, WILLIAM C. HODGES, JAMES ESLEMAN, JAMES ISHAM, AUGUSTUS L. JONES, HENRY WARREN, CHARLES PORTER, ANDREW HANNAH, and JOHN PARKS being elected to serve as Grand Jurors, to wit, CHARLES BRIGHT, foreman, WILLIAM C. HODGES, ANDREW HANNAH, HENRY WARREN, AUGUSTUS L. JONES, THOMAS McGAUGH, CHARLES PORTER, JOSEPH McMILLIN, JAMES ISHAM, JAMES ESLEMAN, JOHN PARKS, SAMUEL BUCHANAN and DOILY GRIFFIS who after receiving the charge from the solicitor returned to consider for their presentments.

STERLING C. McLEMORE, a Constable, sworn to wait on the Grand Jury.

A Deed of Conveyance from SAMUEL TODD and GEORGE W. HIGGINS to DANIEL EAVES and MATHEW L. DIXON for 3 acres of land in Franklin County and ordered to be certified.

A Deed of Conveyance from WILLIAM P. ANDERSON to NATHAN WOUSLEY for 111 acres of land, acknowledged by HARDY HOLEMAN, attorney and ordered to be certified.

A Deed of Conveyance from WILLIAM P. ANDERSON to NATHAN WOUSLEY for 21 acres of land, acknowledged by HARDY HOLEMAN, attorney, and ordered to be certified.

GILBERT KENNEDY is released from serving as a juror this term.

SIMION P. WILLETT vs THOMAS L. TROTTER - Appeal - The plaintiff says he wishes to dismiss his suit and the defendant assumes the payment of all costs. Court dismissed suit and the plaintiff recover against the defendant his costs.

SIMION P. WILLETT vs THOMAS L. TROTTER - Plaintiff says he wishes to dismiss his suit and the defendant assumes the payment of all costs. Court dismisses his suit and the plaintiff recover against the defendant his costs.

JOHN DURLY vs REUBEN HUNTER - Case - Plaintiff says he wishes to dismiss this suit and the defendant assumes the payment of all costs. Court dismissed this suit and the plaintiff recover against the defendant his costs.

WILLIAM P. ANDERSON vs FREDERICK HILL - The plaintiff says he wishes to dismiss his suit and assumes the payment of all costs. Court dismisses suit and defendant recover against the plaintiff his costs.

VANCE GREEN vs HENRY MAXWELL- Alexander Cowen the appearance bail of the defendant surrenders the defendant in discharge of himself whereupon he was ordered in custody of the Sheriff.

The Grand Jury returned into court with a Bill of Indictment, the State against GEORGE W. HUNT, a true bill and again returned to consider for further presentments.

JOHN P. McCONNELL vs NATHANIEL B. BUCHANAN   - Debt - This day came the parties by their attorneys and a jury of men, to wit, REECE HOWELL, PAYTON WELLS, WILLIAM WHITE, ALLEN ELSTON, HENRY KYMES, JOHN BUCHANAN, THOMAS WHITAKER, ROBERT TILFORD, PETER HOLLAND, JOHN LEE, SAMUEL CRAWFORD, and JAMES MAXWELL being elected and sworn and said that the defendant has not paid the debt $101.87½ and damages of $7.50. Plaintiff to recover against the defendant his costs.

GUSTAVUS HENDRICKS vs VANCE GREER - The plaintiff by his attorney says he intends no further to prosecute this suit. The court ordered the suit to be dismissed and the defendant recover against the plaintiff his costs.

HENRY CRABB vs VANCE GREER - Debt - This day came the parties by their attorneys and a jury of men, to wit, (same as above jurors) and being elected and sworn and said that the defendant has not paid the debt of $84827½ and damages of $89.10¼. The plaintiff to recover against the defendant his costs.

WILLIAM PILLOW and others vs ROBERT H. McEWEN and others - Debt - This day came the parties by their attorneys and a jury of men, to wit, (same as above jurors) and being elected and sworn and said that the plaintiff to recover against the defendant $1705.00 and damages of $127.87½.

WILLIAM PILLOW and others vs ROBERT McEWEN and others - Debt - This day came the parties by their attorneys and a jury of men, to wit, (same as above jurors) being elected and sworn and said that the plaintiff to recover against the defendant $1544.00 and damages of $138.96.

CLABORN WILLIAMS vs JAMES WILSON - Debt - This day came the parties by their attorneys and a jury of men, to wit, (same as above jurors) being elected and sworn and said that the plaintiff to recover against the defendant $127.62½ and damages of $9.62½.

VANCE GREER vs ARCHIBALD ESLLEMAN - Debt - This day came the parties by their attorneys and a jury of men, to wit, (same as above jurors) being elected and sworn and said that the plaintiff to recover against the defendant $350.00 and damages of $25.37½.

(out of order) On petition of SAMUEL CRAWFORD and CHARLOTT JOYCE, admr and admrx of THOMAS JOYCE, deceased, proceed to sell a negro girl named MARY ANN of the property of THOMAS JOYCE, deceased.

(out of order) THOMAS McGILL vs JESSE LORANCE - This day came the parties by their attorneys and plaintiff made motion to dismiss this cause. Court considered this cause to be dismissed. The court cannot give final judgement in this cause. This cause was sent to JAMES RALSTON, Esquire, for final decision.

(out of order) ROBERT BROOKS vs FRANCIS WYATT - (Same as above cause). This cause was sent to JAMES BLAKEMORE, Esquire, for final decision.

(out of order) WILLIAM W. TAYLOR vs NATHANIEL B. BUCKINGHAM - Appeal - The plaintiff came and the defendant called to come and prosecute the appeal brought up by him in cause failed to do so but made default. Plaintiff to recover against the defendant and VANCE GRIER (GREER) his security for $23.75 and interest.

(out of order) A Bill of Sale from ARCHABALD D. GARVEN to WILLIAM E. KENNEDY for two negroes, named ANN and CAROLINE and ordered to be certified.

(out of order) BUCHANAN & PORTERFIELD vs ENOCK K. WEATHERS - The plaintiff came by his attorney and the defendant was called to come and plead to the suit but failed to do so but made default. Plaintiff to recover against the defendant $106.47½ and 87½¢ damages.

(out of order) JOHN W. TILFORD vs NATHANIEL B. BUCKINGHAM - The plaintiff by his attorney and the defendant being called to come and prosecute the appeal but failed to do so, but made default. Plaintiff to recover against the defendant and VANCE GREER $35.42 and interest on 21 March last.

(out of order) HARDING FORRISTER vs MARY INGLE - Appeal - The defendant by his attorney and the defendant being called to come not but made (incomplete)...

THURSDAY JULY 19, 1821

Justices present were JAMES HOLEMAN, WILLIAM DICKSON and JAMES WILSON, Esquires.

A Deed of Conveyance from JAMES BRIGHT to FRANCIS PATTON for 50 acres of land and ordered to be certified.

A Deed of Conveyance from HENRY McKEE to ELIZABETH WHITEHEAD for 40 acres of land, proven by JOEL B. SANDERS and JOHN P. McCONNELL and ordered to be certified.

A Deed of Conveyance from BRICE M. GARNER to WILLIAM SNODDY for 426 2/3 acres of land and ordered to be certified.

A Deed of Conveyance from WILLIAM SNODDY to DAVID SNODDY for 276 acres of land and ordered to be certified.

The Grand Jury again returned into court with a Bill of Indictment, the State against JAMES WYATT, a true bill and again returned to consider for further presentments.

PETER MAYO vs JAMES LOCK - Debt - This day came the parties by their attorneys and a jury of men, to wit, REECE HOWELL, PAYTON WELLS, WILLIAM WHITE, ALLEN ELSTON, HENRY KYMES, THOMAS PARKS, THOMAS WHITAKER, PETER MOYERS, ELIJAH M. RINGO, ANGUISH JOHNSON, JAMES D. ALLFORD, and ALEXANDER BEARD being elected and sworn and said that the defendant has not paid the debt of $250.00 and damages of $25.00. Plaintiff to recover against the defendant his costs.

THOMAS MEEK vs JOHN BUCHANAN - The plaintiff says he wishes to dismiss this suit and the defendant assumes the payment of one half of the costs. The suit to be dismissed and each pay one (half) of the costs.

JAMES TILFORD and Co. vs THOMAS KERCHEVAL - The plaintiff appeared and says he intends no further to prosecute this suit. This suit to be dismissed and the defendant recover against the plaintiff his costs.

The State vs WILLIAM BEARDEN - It is considered by the court that the defendant be discharged and the county pay the costs.

The State vs JAMES WYATT - Assault - The defendant being charged on a Bill of Indictment for an assault and battery pleads guilty and is fined $15.00 and pay the costs.

The Grand Jury returned again into court with a Bill of Indictment, the State against JOHN LANE, a true bill and again returned to consider for further presentments.

The State vs WILLIAM C. HOGES (HODGES) - Assault and Battery - The defendant being charged for an assault and battery pleads guilty and is fined $5.00 and pay costs.

The State vs JOHN JOBE - The defendant being charged on a Bill of Indictment pleads not guilty and a jury of men, to wit, PAYTON WELLS, WILLLIAM WHITE, HENRY KYMES, ALLEN ALSTON, JOHN BUCHANAN, THOMAS WHITAKER, PETER LUNA, JOHN MARTIN, ANGUISH JOHNSON, DAVID FRANKLIN, ISAAC GATTIS, and JOHN WAGGONER being elected and sworn and said that the defendant is guilty as charged and fined $4.00 and pay the costs. DAVID COOPER as security for the defendant.

SAMUEL ALLEN vs CARTER WALKER - A Commission is awarded to the defendant to take the deposition of JOHN HODGE at Tuscaloosa, State of Alabama. If notice is served on the plaintiff's attorney twenty days notice and if served on the plaintiff ten days notice of time and place of taking the same.

FRIDAY JULY 20, 1821

Justices present were JAMES HOLEMAN, JAMES WILSON and WILLIAM DICKSON, Esquires.

JOEL JOHNSON for use &c vs J. WATKINS and G. MARTIN - The plaintiff by his attorney says he intends to dismiss this suit and assumes the payment of all costs. Suit dismissed and the defendant recover against the plaintiff his costs.

WALTER KINNARD vs FRANCIS WYATT and B.M. GARNER - The plaintiff by his attorney says he intends no further to prosecute this suit. The suit dismissed and the defendant recovers against the plaintiff his costs.

The State vs JOHN LANE - The defendant being charged of Indictment and pleads not guilty and a jury of men, to wit, PAYTON WELLS, ALLEN ELSTON, WILLIAM WHITE, HENRY KYMES, JOHN GIBSON, JOHN BUCHANAN, THOMAS WHITAKER, WILLIAM NEILD, NATHANIEL B. BUCKINGHAM, JOHN BRYANT, SAMUEL H. SMITH, and CORNELIUS WEBB being elected and sworn and said that the defendant is guilty and is charged 6¼ cents and pay costs.

The State vs PATSEY BLUBAKER - The defendant pleads not guilty and the cause was continued on affidavit of the defendant until next term of court.

PATSEY BLUBAKER appeared in court and acknowledged herself (indebted) in the sum of $200.00 and JORDAN SOLOMON for $200.00 to be levied of their goods and chattels &c but to be void on conditions that PATSEY BLUBAKER appear here in October and answer the State and not depart the same without leave first had and obtained of the court.

JOHN C. McADA appeared in court and acknowledged himself indebted to the State of Tennessee for $400.00 to be levied of his goods and chattels &c but to be void on conditions that he and his daughters, ISABELLA JANE and ELIZABETH McADA appear here in October next to prosecute and give evidence in behalf of the State against PATSEY BLUBAKER and not depart the same without leave first had and obtained of the court.

The Grand Jury again returned to court with a Bill of Indictment, the State against JOHN C. McADA, a true bill and again returned to consider for further presentments.

The Grand Jury again returned to court with a Bill of Indictment, the State against JOHN SMITH, a true bill and again returned to consider for further presentments.

A Deed of Conveyance from JOSEPH McWILLIAMS to JOHN V. McKINNEY for 100 acres of land and ordered to be certified.

A Deed of Conveyance from FRANCIS KERBY to HUGH M. BLAKE for 114½ acres of land, proven by WILLIAM D. BLAKE and WILLIAM C. KENNEDY and ordered to be certified.

The State vs JONATHAN WELCH - The defendant being charged and pleads not guilty and a jury of men, to wit, PAYTON WELLS, JOHN GIBSON, WILLIAM PARKS, WILLIAM NEILD, JOHN BRYANT, SAMUEL MIXON, SAMUEL H. SMITH, CORNELIUS WEBB, JAMES CARITHERS, ABSOLEM COLLINS, WILSON DAVIS, and RANDOLPH QUARLES being elected and sworn and said that the defendant is not guilty as charged.

The State vs JOHN C. McCIDDA - The defendant being charged, pleads not guilty and a jury of men, to wit, WILLIAM WHITE, JOHN BUCHANAN, ALLEN ALSTON, HENRY KYMES, ELIJAH WRIGHT, ANDREW A. KINCANNON, DAVIDSON McMILLIN, ALLEN H. JOHNSON, WILLIAM ESLICK, JAMES TOOL, RICHARD C. PREWITT, and EWELL WILLIAMS being elected and sworn and said that the defendant is guilty and is fined $5.00 and pay the costs and remain in custody of the Sheriff until the fine and costs are paid, ROBERT DICKSON being his security.

SATURDAY JULY 21, 1821

Justices present were JAMES HOLEMAN, JAMES WILSON and WILLIAM DICKSON, Esquires.

The State vs SOLOMON JOB - The fefendant being charged pleads guilty and is fined $1.00 and pay costs and remain in custody of the Sheriff until the costs and fine are paid, JOSEPH SHAW his security.

The State vs THOMAS LITTLE - The defendant being charged pleaded guilty and is fines $10.00 and pay the costs and remain in custody of the Sheriff until the costs and fine are paid, JOSEPH WRIGHT his security.

The State vs JOHN SMITH - The defendant being charged for an Assault and Battery pleads guilty and is fined 6¼ cents and pay costs of this indictment.

The Grand Jury returned again into court and brought with them a Bill of Indictment, the State against JACOB WRIGHT, THOMAS GOLD and JOHN H. BREWER, a true bill against JACOB WRIGHT and THOMAS GOLD and not a true bill against JOHN H.

BREWER, again returned to consider for further presentments.

GEORGE A. ALLEN acknowledged himself indebted to the State of Tennessee for $400.00 to be levied of his goods and chattels &c but to be void on conditions that he and his wife SARAH ALLEN appear here in October next to prosecute and give evidence in behalf of the State against JACOB WRIGHT and THOMAS GOLD for an affray and not depart the same without leave first had and obtained of the court.

JONATHAN WELCH and THOMAS LITTLE acknowledged themselves indebted to the State of Tennessee for $200.00, to be levied upon their goods and chattels &c but to be void on conditions that they appear here in October next and give evidence in behalf of the State against JACOB WRIGHT and THOMAS GOLD for an affray and not depart the same without leave first had and obtained of the court.

JAMES CARITHERS vs DANIEL YOUNG - Debt - This day came the parties by their attorneys and a jury of men, to wit, PAYTON WELLS, WILLIAM WHITE, ALLEN ALSTON, HENRY KYMES, JOHN BUCHANAN, THOMAS WHITAKER, DAVIDSON McMILLIN, ALLEN H. JOHNSON, WILLIAM ESLICK, JAMES TOOL, RICHARD C. PREWITT, and EWELL WILLIAMS being elected and sworn and said that the defendant has not paid the debt of $1127.48 and damages of $67.56. Plaintiff to recover against the defendant his costs.

ROBERT IRWIN vs JOHN EDMISTON - This day came the parties by their attorneys and a jury of men, to wit, (same as above jurors) being elected and sworn and said that the defendant has not paid the debt of $323.75 and damages of $10.50. Plaintiff to recover against the defendant his costs.

HENRY WARREN vs NOAH WARD - Debt - This day came the parties by their attorneys and a jury of men, to wit, (same as above jurors) being elected and sworn and said that the defendant has not paid the debt of $140.00 and damages of $5.62¼. Plaintiff to recover against the defendant his costs.

ANDREW McCLELLAN vs WILLIAM GIVENS - Debt - This day came the parties by their attorneys and a jury of men, to wit, (same as above jurors) being elected and sworn and said that the defendant has not paid the debt of $200.00 and damages of $9.50. Plaintiff to recover against the defendant his costs.

ANDREW McCLELLAN vs WILLIAM GIVENS - Debt - This day came the parties by their attorneys and a jury of men, to wit, (same as above jurors) being elected and sworn and said that the defendant has not paid the debt of $200.00 and damages of $21.50. Plaintiff to recover against the defendant his costs.

PETER MOYERS vs WILLIAM KERBY and F. WYATT - Debt - This day came the parties by their attorneys and a jury of men, to wit, (same as above jurors) being elected and sworn and said that the defendant has not paid the debt of $158.50 and damages of $12.25. Plaintiff to recover against the defendant his costs.

ROBERT H. McEWEN and Co. vs WALTER KINNARD - This day came the parties by their attorneys and a jury of men, to wit, (same as above jurors) being elected and sworn and said that the defendant assume in manner and form as the plaintiff declared against him and they assess the damages of $126.98. Plaintiff to recover against the defendant his costs.

SAMUEL CRAWFORD vs WILLIAM DRIVER - This day came the parties by their attorneys and a jury of men, to wit, (same as above jurors) being elected and sworn and said that the defendant has not paid the debt of $109.00 and damages of $4.36. Plaintiff to recover against the defendant his costs.

MONDAY JULY 23, 1821

Justices present were WILLIAM KENNON, JAMES HOLEMAN and PHILIP KOONCE, Esquires.

The State vs THOMAS GOLD - The defendant being charged for an affray pleads guilty and is fined $10.00 and costs and remain in custody of the Sheriff until the costs and fines are paid, PETER HOLLAND his security.

A Deed of Conveyance from JOSEPH McMILLIN to ANDREW E. BEATIE for 8 acres of land and ordered to be certified.

A Deed of Conveyance from ANDREW E. BEATIE to JOSEPH McMILLIN for 138 acres of land and ordered to be certified.

A Deed of Conveyance from ARGYLE CAMPBELL to SAMUEL BUCHANAN for 100 acres of land and ordered to be certified.

A Deed of Conveyance from ALEXANDER BOTELER to BENJAMIN CLEMENTS for 294 acres of land, proven by JOHN GREER and ELLIOTT HICKMAN and ordered to be certified.

A Transfer of a Plat and Certificate of Survey from GEORGE DAMAS to PRIOR STONE, proven by WILLIAM C. KENNEDY and B.W. SHIRLY and ordered to be certified.

The Transfer of a Plat and Certificate of Survey from JOAB BUCKLY to ROBERT BUCHANAN for 50 acres of land and ordered to be certified.

A Deed of Conveyance from JOAB (BUCKLY) to ROBERT BUCHANAN for 50 acres of land and ordered to be certified.

It is ordered by the court that DAVIS SMITH and ROBERT M. WHITE be appointed Commissioners to settle with JAMES DOWNING, admr of the estate of JOHN M. DOWNING, deceased, and make return to next court.

A Bill of Sale from ROBERT LACKY and POLLY LACKY to JOHN STREET for a negro girl named JANE, proven by oaths of TUNSTALL GREGORY and ordered to be certified.

REUBIN WOODWARD vs SPENCER A. PUGH - Debt - This day came the parties by their attorneys and a jury of men, to wit, WILLIAM C. HODGES, CHARLES BRIGHT, THOMAS McGAUGH, PAYTON WELLS, REECE HOWELL, JOHN BUCHANAN, WILLIAM WHITE, HENRY KYMES, THOMAS WHITAKER, DOILY GRIFFIS, SAMUEL BUCHANAN, and JAMES ISHAM being elected and sworn and said that the defendant has not paid his debt of $100.00 and damages of $11.00. Plaintiff to recover against the defendant his costs.

HENRY CRABB vs JAMES COALTER - This day came the parties by their attorneys and a jury of men, to wit, (same as above jurors) being elected and sworn and said that the defendant did assume do say the defendant and assumes upon himself in manner and form, the plaintiffin declaring against him has alledged and they assess the plaintiff's damages of $260.62¼. Plaintiff to recover against the defendant his costs.

The Transfer of a Plat and Certificate of Survey from JOHN MURPHY to MARTHA ADAMS and ordered to be certified.

A Deed of Conveyance from JOHN BROWN to WILLIAM STREET for 107 acres of land and ordered to be certified.

JOHN CLARK vs BEATY & EDMISTON - Debt - This day came the parties by their attorneys and a jury of men, to wit, (same as above jurors) being elected and sworn and said that the defendant has not paid all of the debt of $456.00 but owes a balance of $390.00 and damages of $26.65. Plaintiff to recover against the defendant his costs.

WILLIAM B. CARTER vs BUCKINGHAM & GREER - Debt - This day came the parties by their attorneys and a jury of men, to wit, ARCHABALD CAMPBELL, HENRY WARREN, JAMES ESLEMAN, JOHN PARKS, AUGUSTUS L. JONES, ANDREW HANNAH, JOSEPH McMILLIN, CHARLES PORTER, REECE HOWELL, JOHN GIBSON, ALEXANDER MORTON, and SAMUEL H. SMITH being elected and sworn and said that the defendant has not paid the debt of $523.54 and damages of $62.82. Plaintiff to recover against the defendant his costs.

ROBERT BUCHANAN vs PETER MOYERS - Debt - This day came the parties by their attorneys and a jury of men, to wit, WILLIAM C. HODGES, CHARLES BRIGHT, THOMAS McGAUGH, PAYTON WELLS, REECE HOWELL, JOHN BUCHANAN, WILLIAM WHITE, HENRY KYMES, THOMAS WHITAKER, DOILY GRIFFIS, SAMUEL BUCHANAN, and JAMES ISHAM being elected and sworn and said that the defendant has not paid the debt of $207.86¼ and damages of $6.21. Plaintiff to recover against the defendant his costs.

ROBERT & W. DICKSON vs SAMUEL S. HOLDING - This day came the parties by their attorneys and a jury of men, to wit, (same as above jurors) being elected and sworn and said that the defendant has not paid the debt of $111.60 and damages of $7.00. Plaintiff to recover against the defendant his costs.

ROBERT & WILLIAM DICKSON vsSAMUEL S. HOLDING -This day came the parties by their attorneys and a jury of men, to wit, (same as above jurors) being elected and sworn and said that the defendant has not paid the debt of $141.90½ and damages of $4.50. Plaintiff to recover against the defendant his costs.

BUCHANAN & PORTERFIELD vs JOHN L. PRICE - This day came the parties by their attorneys and a jury of men, to wit, WILLIAM C. HODGES, CHARLES BRIGHT, THOMAS McGAUGH, PAYTON WELLS, REECE HOWELL, JOHN BUCHANAN, WILLIAM WHITE, HENRY KYMES, THOMAS WHITAKER, DOILY GRIFFIS, SAMUEL BUCHANAN, and JAMES ISHAM being elected and sworn and said that the defendant has not paid the debt of $129.00 and damages of $11.63. Plaintiff to recover against the defendant his costs.

WILLIAM DAVIS vs JOHN L. PRICE - This day came the parties by their attorneys and a jury of men, to wit, (same as above jurors) being elected and sworn and said that the defendant has not paid the debt of $182.12½ and damages of $4.55. Plaintiff to recover against the defendant his costs.

THOMAS L. TROTTER vs DAVID JONES - The plaintiff says he intends no further to prosecute this suit and assumes the payment of all costs. Suit to be dismissed and the defendant recover against the plaintiff his costs.

DAVID JONES vs THOMAS L. TROTTER - (Same as above).

OLIVER B. HAYS vs Fayetteville T. Bank - This day came both parties by their attorneys and a jury of men, to wit, (same as above jurors) being elected and sworn and said that the damages sustained by the plaintiff of $238.40. Plaintiff to recover against the defendant his costs.

The Last Will and Testament of STEPHEN LOYD, deceased, was exhibited in court for probation whereupon came JOHN BALEY and JESSE PAYNE, witnesses, and made oath that they heard STEPHEN LOYD acknowledged the same to be his Last Will and Testament and was at that time of sound mind and memory and on motion of ERWIN LOYD, he was appointed admr of the estate of STEPHEN LOYD, deceased, who gave bond with STERLING C. McLEMORE and CHRISTOPHER SHOFNER his securities.

A Deed of Conveyance from JOHN AUSTIN to ROBERT MEEK for 140 acres of land, proven by JOHN H. McCURDY and ordered to be certified.

A Deed of Conveyance from WILIA GARRETT to JAMES G. FOGG for 120 acres of land, proven by WILLIAM STEPHENS and LEWIS BLEDSOE and ordered to be certified.

A Deed of Conveyance from BENJAMIN TALIAFERO to ELIZABETH PORTER for a negro girl named SOOKY and ordered to be certified.

TUESDAY JULY 24, 1821

Justices present were PHILIP KOONCE, JAMES HOLEMAN and JAMES WILSON, Esquires.

The Commissioners appointed to the last term of this court to settle with SAMUEL ROSEBOROUGH admr on the estate of JOSEPH WHITTENBURGH, deceased, made return of the settlement by them made and ordered to be certified.

WILLIAM McCLELLAN vs SPENCER A. PUGH - This day came the parties by their attorneys, to wit, ARCHABALD CAMPBELL, HENRY WARREN, JAMES ESLEMAN, JOHN PARKS, AUGUSTUS L. JONES, ANDREW HANNAH, JOSEPH McMILLIN, CHARLES PORTER, REECE HOWELL, JOHN GIBSON, ALEXANDER MORTON, and SAMUEL H. SMITH being elected and sworn and said that the defendant has not paid the debt of $100.25 and damages of $4.25. Plaintiff to recover against the defendant his costs.

THOMAS GREER vs RANDOLPH QUARLES and BRICE M. GARNER - This day came the parties by their attorneys and a jury of men, to wit, (same as above jurors) and being elected and sworn and said that the defendant has not paid the debt of $1000.00 and damages of $33.53. Plaintiff to recover against the defendant his costs.

A Deed of Conveyance from THOMAS HICKMAN to ELLIOTT HICKMAN for 408 acres of land, proven by HUGH M. BLAKE and OLIVER WILLIAMS and ordered to be certified.

CHARLES SCHROEDER vs JAMES COALTER - This day came the parties by their attorneys and a jury of men, to wit, WILLIAM C. HODGES, CHARLES BRIGHT, DOILY GRIFFIS, THOMAS McGAUGH, JAMES ISHAM, SAMUEL BUCHANAN, BENJAMIN DORSEY,

PAYTON WELLS, WILLIAM WHITE, JOHN BUCHANAN, HENRY KYMES, and THOMAS WHITAKER being elected and sworn and said that the defendant did assume upon himself in manner and form as charged and the plaintiff's damages of $350.00. Plaintiff to recover against the defendant his costs.

JOHN GREER, Chairman vs PETER HOLLAND - This day came the parties by their attorneys and a jury of men, to wit, ARCHABALD CAMPBELL, HENRY WARREN, JAMES ESLEMAN, JOHN PARKS, AUGUSTUS L. JONES, ANDREW HANNAH, JOSEPH McMILLIN, CHARLES PORTER, REECE HOWELL, JOHN GIBSON, ALEXANDER MORTON, and SAMUEL H. SMITH being elected and sworn and said that the defendant is not guilty. The defendant to recover against the plaintiff his costs.

ISAAC HOLEMAN vs WEBB K. JENNINGS - The plaintiff says he wishes to dismiss this suit and assumes the payment of all costs except defendant's witnesses. This suit to be dismissed and the defendant recover against the plaintiff his costs.

MOSES PARK vs BENJAMIN ARTHUR - The plaintiff by his attorney says he intends no further to prosecute this suit. This suit to be dismissed and the defendant recover against the plaintiff his costs.

HENRY & WILLIS WARREN, exrs vs VANCE GREER - This day came the parties by their attorneys and a jury of men, to wit, WILLIAM C. HODGES, CHARLES BRIGHT, DOILY GRIFFIS, ARCHABALD CAMPBELL, JAMES ISHAM, SAMUEL BUCHANAN, BENJAMIN DORSEY, PAYTON WELLS, WILLIAM WHITE, JOHN BUCHANAN, HENRY KYMES, and THOMAS WHITAKER being elected and sworn and said that the defendant has not paid the debt of $144.40 and damages of $4.30. Plaintiff to recover against the defendant his costs.

ROBERT Y. WELLFORD vs VANCE GREER - This day came the parties by their attorneys and a jury of men, to wit, (same as above jurors) being elected and sworn and said that the defendant has not paid the debt of $1261.10 and damages of $23.00. Plaintiff to recover against the defendant his costs.

RANDOLPH QUARLES vs ALEXANDER FURGUSON - This day came the parties by their attorneys and a jury of men, to wit, (same as above jurors) being elected and sworn and said that the defendant has not paid the debt of $98.00 and damages of 16.91. Plaintiff to recover against the defendant his costs.

WILLIAM HUDSON vs JONATHAN BARCKLY - This day came the parties by their attorneys and a jury of men, to wit, (same as above jurors) being elected and sworn and said that the defendant has not paid the debt of $400.00 and damages of $62.37½. Plaintiff to recover against the defendant his costs.

BARNES CLARK vs BENJAMIN GEORGE - Debt - This day came the parties by their attorneys and a jury of men, to wit, (same as above jurors) being elected and sworn and said that the defendant has not paid the debt of $110.00 and damages of $9.00. Plaintiff to recover against the defendant his costs.

WILLIAM W. TAYLOR vs HENRY ALLEN - Debt - This day came the parties by their attorneys and a jury of men, to wit, (same as above jurors) being elected and sworn and said that the defendant has not paid all the debt of $211.06½ and damages of $12.50. Plaintiff to recover against the defendant his costs.

DANIEL YOUNG vs JAMES CARITHERS - This day came the parties by their attorneys and a jury of men, to wit, (same as above jurors) being elected and sworn and said that they cannot agree on their verdict. They are to return next day.

WEDNESDAY JULY 25, 1821

Justices present were JAMES WILSON, PHILIP KOONCE and JAMES HOLEMAN, Esquires.

DANIEL YOUNG vs JAMES CARITHERS - The jury returned into court and say (incomplete)...

WILLIAM DOBBS vs VANCE GREER - The plaintiff recover against the defendant $136.50 and costs of $8.57½.

REPS O. CHILDRESS vs FRANCIS WYATT - Debt - This day came the parties by their attorneys and a jury of men, to wit, PAYTON WELLS, WILLIAM WHITE, JOHN BUCHANAN, HENRY KYMES, THOMAS WHITAKER, WILLIAM C. HODGES, DOILY

GRIFFIS, JAMES ISHAM, SAMUEL BUCHANAN, BENJAMIN DORSEY, ARCHABALD CAMPBELL, and ARCHABALD D. GARVEN being elected and sworn and said that the defendant has not paid the debt of $200.00 and damages of $27.00. Plaintiff to recover against the defendant his costs.

CHARLES McKINNEY vs GEORGE W. DENNIS & JAMES BROOKS - Motion - It is ordered that the Sheriff expose to sale 120 acres of land lying on the road from Fayetteville to Huntsville, levied on as the property of JAMES BROOKS to satisfy a judgement that CHARLES McKINNEY recovered against said BROOKS on 5 March 1821 for $28.04 and all costs.

CHARLES McKINNEY vs G.W. DENNIS & JAMES BROOKS - Motion - (same as above).

NICHOLAS CARRIGER vs ARCHABALD C. ESLEMAN - Appeal - This day came the parties by their attorneys and a jury of men, to wit, WILLIAM WHITE, PAYTON WELLS, JOHN BUCHANAN, HENRY KYMES, THOMAS WHITAKER, WILLIAM C. HODGES, DOILY GRIFFIS, JAMES ISHAM, SAMUEL BUCHANAN, BENJAMIN DORSEY, ARCHABALD CAMPBELL, and ARCHABALD D. GARVEN being elected and sworn and said that the defendant is indebted to the plaintiff for $56.50 and damages of 87½ cents. Plaintiff to recover against the defendant his costs.

SAMUEL H. SMITH vs THOMAS L. TROTTER - Appeal - This day came the parties by their attorneys and a jury of men, to wit, (same as above jurors) being elected and sworn and said that the defendant is indebted to the plaintiff for $7.50 and the plaintiff to recover against the defendant his costs.

VANCE GREER vs HENRY MAXFIELD - This day came the parties by their attorneys and a jury of men, to wit, REECE HOWELL, THOMAS McGAUGH, HENRY WARREN, JAMES ESLEMAN, JOHN PARKS, AUGUSTUS L. JONES, ANDREW HANNAH, JOSEPH McMILLIN, CHARLES PORTER, JOHN DOBBINS, JESSE B. CLEMENTS, and ALEXANDER MORTON being elected and sworn and said that they find in favor of the plaintiff and the defendant did assume upon himself of $81.02 3/4. Plaintiff to recover against the defendant his costs.

THURSDAY JULY 26, 1821

Justices present were WILLIAM KENNON, JAMES WILSON and JAMES HOLEMAN, Esquires.

JAMES D. EASTES vs SAMUEL DOBBINS - This day came the parties by their attorneys and a jury of men, to wit, PAYTON WELLS, WILLIAM WHITE, JOHN BUCHANAN, HENRY KYMES, THOMAS WHITAKER, WILLIAM C. HODGES, CHARLES BRIGHT, DOILY GRIFFIS, JAMES ISHAM, SAMUEL BUCHANAN, BENJAMIN DORSEY, and ARCHABALD CAMPBELL being elected and sworn and said that the defendant has not kept and performed the writing obligatory to the plaintiff and assess the damages of $328.40. Plaintiff to recover against the defendant his costs and the defendant prays for an appeal &c.

SAMUEL ROW vs ISAAC STREET - This day came the parties by their attorneys and a jury of men, to wit, REECE HOWELL, HENRY WARREN, JAMES ESLEMAN, JOHN PARK, AUGUSTUS L. JONES, ANDREW HANNAH, JOSEPH McMILLIN, CHARLES PORTER, THOMAS McGAUGH, CORNELIUS WEBB, JACK H. LEFTWICH and WILLIAM MEEK being elected and sworn and said that the defendant is guilty as charged and the damages of $12.00. The plaintiff to recover against the defendant his costs.

JOS. & W. PARK vs GARNER & BOYLES - This day came the parties by their attorneys and a jury of men, to wit, PAYTON WELLS, WILLIAM WHITE, JOHN BUCHANAN, HENRY KYMES, THOMAS WHITAKER, WILLIAM C. HODGES, CHARLES BRIGHT, DOILY GRIFFIS, JAMES ISHAM, SAMUEL BUCHANAN, BENJAMIN DORSEY, and ARCHABALD CAMPBELL being elected and sworn and said that they found in favor of the plaintiff and that THOMAS AUSTIN did assign the writing obligation in the plaintiff's declaration and that the defendants has not paid the debt of $1000.00 and damages of $34.25. The plaintiff to recover against the defendant his costs.

WILSON DAVIS vs THOMAS BRENTS - This day came the parties by their attorneys and a jury of men, to wit, (same as above jurors) being elected and sworn and said that the defendant has not paid the debt of $150.00 and damages of $5.25. Plaintiff to recover against the defendant his costs.

JANE B. CAMPBELL vs C. BOYLES & B.M. GARNER - The defendants by their

106

attorneys and in arrest of judgment and files the following reasons, to wit, first, because the jury which tried this cause were not legal jurors, second, that the court had not authority to appoint a jury at the last term on the day on which the jury was appointed, third, that this cause was tried by the jurors summoned under venire returned to this term, when this venire itself was not around and appointed by a court that had any authority to do so at the time it was done, fourth, that the issuance (illegible) issues, which motion being argued and the reason being fully understood and was overruled and the defendants prays for an appeal.

FRIDAY JULY 27, 1821

Justices present were JAMES WILSON, WILLIAM KENNON and JAMES HOLEMAN, Esquires.

A Deed of Conveyance from WILLIAM KERBY to GEORGE & JACKSON BLAKEMORE for 114½ acres of land, proven by MOSES HALL and THOMAS McFERRAN and ordered to be certified.

BRICE M. GARNER vs WILSON DAVIS - Debt - This day came the parties by their attorneys and a jury of men, to wit, WILLIAM WHITE, JOHN BUCHANAN, HENRY KYMES, THOMAS WHITAKER, WILLIAM C. HODGES, CHARLES BRIGHT, DOILY GRIFFIS, JAMES ISHAM, SAMUEL BUCHANAN, BENJAMIN DORSEY, ARCHABALD CAMPBELL, and REECE HOWELL being elected and sworn and said that the defendant has not paid all the debt of $246.91 and damages of $5.50. Plaintiff to recover against the defendant his costs.

JOHN MAZE vs BRICE M. GARNER - This day came the parties by their attorneys and a jury of men, to wit, (same as above jurors) being elected and sworn and said that the defendant did not assume upon himself in manner as charged. The defendant to recover against the plaintiff his costs. Plaintiff prays for an appeal.

JOHN R. MOORE vs GEORGE COALTER - This day came the partied by their attorneys and a jury of men, to wit, (same as above) being elected and sworn and said that the defendant has not paid the debt but owes a balance of $474.00 and damages of $9.48. Plaintiff to recover against the defendant his costs.

ABSALEM BOSTICK vs NATHANIEL B. BOSTICK - Appeal - This day came the parties and a jury of men, to wit, JAMES ESLEMAN, JOHN PARKS, AUGUSTUS L. JONES, ANDREW HANNAH, JOSEPH McMILLIN, THOMAS McGAUGH, ROBERT EDMISTON, SAMUEL S. HOLDING, SPENCER A. PUGH, SAMUEL RAMSEY, JOSEPH HINKLE, and JACKSON BLAKEMORE being elected and sworn and said that the defendant does owe the plaintiff $50.00 and damages of $1.62½. Plaintiff to recover against the defendant his costs.

W.D. MITCHELL vs BRICE M. GARNER - Appeal - This day came the parties and a jury of men, to wit, (same as above jurors) being elected and sworn and said that the defendant owes the plaintiff $73.00 and damages of $3.28. Plaintiff to recover against the defendant his costs.

PHAIN & CRAWFORD vs BRICE M. GARNER - A Commission is awarded the plaintiff to take the deposition of JOSEPH B. BACON in this State to be read as evidence in this cause by giving the defendant ten days notice of time and place of taking same.

THOMAS ALLY vs BENJAMIN W. SHIRLY - It is ordered by the court that a writ of certiorari &c issue to bring up to court the papers in the above cause. Tried before STEPHEN ALEXANDER, Esquire.

A Deed of Conveyance from OLIVER B. HAYS to JOEL EATON for 220 acres of land, proven by HARDY HOLEMAN, attorney, and ordered to be certified.

A Deed of Conveyance from OLIVER B. HAYS to SAMUEL HART for 60 acres of land, proven by HARDY HOLEMAN, attorney, and ordered to be certified.

THOMAS CHAMPLAIN vs Fayetteville T. Bank - Plaintiff by his attorney came into court and a jury of men, to wit, WILLIAM WHITE, JOHN BUCHANAN, HENRY KYMES, THOMAS WHITAKER, WILLIAM C. HODGES, CHARLES BRIGHT, DOILY GRIFFIS, JAMES ISHAM, SAMUEL BUCHANAN, BENJAMIN DORSEY, ARCHABALD CAMPBELL, and REECE HOWELL being elected and sworn and said that the damages of $550.73. Plaintiff to recover against the defendant his costs.

ALLEN MOBLEY vs CORNELIUS WEBB - Motion to Dismiss - This day the parties by their attorneys, a motion to dismiss this cause. Motion overruled and this cause be set for trial at next term of court.

ALLEN MOBLEY vs CORNELIUS WEBB - Motion to Dismiss - (same as above).

WILLIAM DOBBS vs VANCE GREER - It is considered by the court that this cause be sustained. The defendant prays for an appeal.

JAMES DENNIS vs M. McELROY & D.R. SUMNER - Motion - The Sheriff to expose for sale 600 acres of land lying on Cane Creek the place where MICAJAH McELROY formerly lived, levied on as property of MICAJAH McELROY to satisfy a judgment that JAMES DENNIS recovered against said McELROY and DANIEL R. SUMNER before CHARLES BOYLES, Esquire on 20 September last for $68.53 and all costs.

SATURDAY JULY 28, 1821

Justices present were WILLIAM KENNON, JAMES HOLEMAN and JAMES WILSON, Esquires.

JOHN CURRY vs JOHN COOK - Motion to set aside - Court ordered this cause to be set aside and this cause stand for trial at next term of court.

SAMUEL CRAWFORD vs JAMES COALTER - Defendant by his attorney was commissioned to take the deposition of WILLIAM WHITE, the Clerk & Master of the Chancery at Stanton in Virginia to be used as evidence on the trial of said cause by giving the plaintiff thirty days notice of time and place of taking the same.

It is ordered by the court that BRICE M. GARNER and CONSTANT SCALES be appointed Commissioners to settle with JOHN RHEA and ROBERT EDMISTON, executors of the Last Will and Testament of SAMUEL BARNES, deceased, and make return to next court.

WILLIAM C. KENNEDY vs SAMUEL LITTLEJOHN - Motion - On motion of the plaintiff by his attorney, it is ordered by the court that the Sheriff to expose to sale 10 acres of land lying on the waters of Coldwater Creek a south branch of Elk River, levied on as the property of SAMUEL LITTLEJOHN to satisfy a judgment of $4.00 before WILLIAM DICKSON, Esquire, on 30 June last.

JAMES STEWART vs BRICE M. GARNER - The court overruled and cannot determine the damage of the plaintiff.

ZACHARIAH ARNOLD vs JOHN D. SPAIN - Motion to dismiss cause. Motion overruled.

JOHN ALLBRIGHT vs JAMES FULGHAM - Motion to dismiss this cause. Motion was overruled.

SAMUEL H. SMITH vs JAMES WYATT - Motion to dismiss this cause. Motion carried. Plaintiff recover against the defendant his costs with damages of $44.49½ and interest.

WILLIAM W. TAYLOR vs JAS. & GEORGE COALTER - The defendant by his attorney was appointed a Commission to take the deposition of HUGH FINDLEY in Fayetteville to be read as evidence on the trial of said cause and five days notice of time and place of taking the same.

JAMES WYATT vs LUNTSFORD WYATT - The plaintiff appeared and said no further to prosecute this suit and assume the payment of the costs. Suit to be dismissed and the plaintiff pay the costs.

JAMES WYATT vs LUNTSFORD WYATT - (same as above).

LINSFIELD W. PARKS vs WILLIAM KERBY - The defendant agrees to pay one third of costs. Court dismisses the suit and plaintiff to pay two thirds part of costs.

JOHN CURRY vs JOSHUA W. MASSEY - Attachment - The plaintiff by his attorney came into court and the defendant being called to come and defend this suit failed to do so but made default. The plaintiff to recover against the defendant $150.00 and damages of $5.25. The Sheriff was ordered to expose to sale 150 acres of land levied on to satisfy said debt and damages and costs.

MONDAY OCTOBER 15, 1821

ALEXANDER COWEN is appointed overseer of the road to begin at the crossroads above JOHN D. SPAIN and work to the Old State line and call on the usual hands.

JAMES FORRISTER is appointed overseer of the road leading from Fayetteville to Shelbyville, beginning at the forks of the road on to NICHOLAS CARRIGER's Mill, and that EASON COALTER, ISAAC FORRISTER, MARK STEED, REUBEN LOGAN and JOHN SULLIVAN, JR. work on said road.

JAMES GRANT is appointed overseer of the road in the room of THOMAS SPENCER and call on the same hands.

ELIJAH BURCHFIELD is appointed overseer of the road in the room of WILLIS WARREN resigned, STEPHEN ALEXANDER and JOHN JONES, Esquires to lay off the hands to work on said road.

WILLIAM DICKSON is appointed overseer of the road in the room of PHILIP FOX and call in the same hands.

JAMES MILLS, HOWELL JOHNSON, TRAVIS ASHBY, WILLIAM DICKSON, PHILIP FOX, and THOMAS GROCE is appointed a Jury of View to view and turn the Shelbyville road on the land of JACOB GROCE and make return to next court.

JOSHUA CHURCH is appointed overseer of the road in the room of JOHN WISEMAN and call on the usual hands.

WILLIAM MARTIN is appointed overseer of the road in the room of SAMUEL HART and to call on the usual hands.

WILLIAM LANGSTON is appointed overseer of the road in the room of NICHOLAS WOODFIN and call on the same hands.

JAMES THARP is appointed overseer of the road in the room of LEWIS McCORKLE and to call on the same hands.

STEPHEN COLEMAN is appointed overseer of the road in the room of DAVID DODD and call on the usual hands.

WILLIAM LEDFORD is appointed overseer of the Mulberry Road in the room of FRANCIS WYATT resigned and call on the same hands.

RICHARD COMPTON is appointed overseer of the road in the room of JOSHUA GUNTER resigned and call on the usual hands.

THOMAS EVANS is appointed overseer of the road in the room of JAMES SIMONS (SIMMONS) and call on the usual hands.

THOMAS H. HAYS is appointed overseer of the road in the room of THOMAS SIMMONS resigned and to call on the usual hands.

WILSON FROST is appointed overseer of the road in the room of JOSEPH HINKLE resigned and call on the usual hands.

It is ordered by the court that WILLIAM GIVENS, Esquire, appoint the hands to work on the lower Pulaski Road in bounds of MORGAN CLAYTON part of said road and make return to next court.

It is ordered that JOHN PORTER, Esquire, appoint the hands to work on that part of the road that JAMES WILSON is overseer of and make return to next court.

CLIFFORD GRAY and JOHN JONES, Esquires, is appointed to lay off the hands to work on that part of the road that THOMAS GEORGE is overseer of.

WILLIAM EDMISTON, Esquire, SAMUEL BUCHANAN, Esquire, and JAMES BROADWAY are appointed to settle with EATON GRISSOM, admr on the estate of WILLIAM GRISSOM, deceased, and make return to next court.

MARTIN PUGH is appointed overseer of the road in the room of JOHN CAMPER and call on the usual hands.

The jury appointed at the last term to view and turn the road around a large hill between JOHN BUCHANAN and STEPHEN CLAYTON, return to court that they had viewed and marked out the road which was read by the court and the overseer of said road is ordered to open the same.

GEORGE CUNNINGHAM is appointed by the court guardian for ANISLEM (ANSYLUM) BARNES who gave bond for $2500.00 with JOSEPH HINKLE, WILLIAM EDMISTON and JOHN DAVIS his securities.

JOSEPH NICHOLS appeared in court and was appointed guardian for GEORGE, JOHN, STEPHEN, JOSEPH, and MARTIN LUNA, infant heirs of JOSEPH LUNA, deceased, who gave bond of $800.00 with JOHN PARK and MATHEW MOSS his secutiries.

JOHN BROADWAY appeared in court and was appointed guardian for ALTHANA HARRIS who gave bond of $400.00 with CORNELIUS DARNOL and JAMES BROADWAY, securities.

GEORGE PRICE is appointed guardian for MARY HEDGCOCK and ELIZABETH HEDGCOCK, heirs of THOMAS HEDGCOCK, who gave bond of $300.00 with JONATHAN FLOYD and WILLIAM HOWARD, his securities.

JOSEPH BELL and THOMAS BELL appointed admrs of the estate of WILLIAM BELL, deceased, who gave bond of $20,000.00 with DAVID SMITH, JOHN DURLEY and ABRAHAM SUMMERS, their securities and qualified.

MARY BRENT was appointed guardian for her children, JULIANN BRENT, MARY J. BRENT, ELIJAH H. BRENT, THOMAS C. BRENT, and JENNELL BRENT. JOHN GIBSON, her security.

LEONARD CARRIGER appointed a Constable who gave bond with NICHOLAS CARRIGER and SAMUEL GARLAND, his securities.

WILLIAM MOREHEAD appointed a Constable who gave bond with JAMES SMITH and JOHN MOREHEAD, his securities.

An inventory of the property of JOHN MAYFIELD was returned to court which was ordered to be certified.

An inventory of the property of WILLIAM BELL, deceased, was returned to court by his admrs and was ordered to be certified.

MESHACK BOYCE was appointed admr on the estate of ROBERT ABERNATHY, deceased, who gave bond of $500.00 with DANIEL R. MOORE and JOEL BUTLER, his securities.

The Last Will and Testament of JOHN HOLBERT, deceased, was exhibited in court for probate which was proven by HENRY BECK, RALLY BROWN and JOHN TATUM and ordered to be recorded whereupon came JAMES HOLBERT and PERRY FLYNT the executors named in said Will and Testament and gave bond of $3,000.00 with RICHARD FLYNT and PRESTON HAMPTON, their securities as executors aforesaid.

An inventory of the property of JOHN HOLBERT, deceased, was returned into court by his executors and ordered to be certified.

An inventory of the property of ROBERT ABERNATHY, deceased, was returned to court by his admr and ordered to be certified.

It is ordered by the court that MIRIAN WILLSON be allowed to receive from the County Trustee sum of $36.00 for taking care of her son JOSEPH EDINGTON one year, to be paid quarterly.

A Power of Attorney from PERRY FLYNT to THOMAS FLYNT, acknowledged, and ordered to be certified.

DANIEL R. MOORE and JOEL BUTLER is appointed to lay off one years support for the widow and children of ROBERT ABERNATHY, deceased, and make return to next court.

The Transfer of a Plat and Certificate of Survey from JAMES GARRETT to WILLIAM ROSSON and HENRY B. ROSSON and ordered to be certified.

The Transfer of a Plat and Certificate of Survey from JAMES GARRETT to

BENJAMIN SHORT and ordered to be certified.

A Deed of Conveyance from MOSES BARTON to MARTIN HOLBERT for 20 acres of land, proven by JOHN THOMPSON and RICHARD FLYNT and ordered to be certified.

A Deed of Conveyance from MARTIN HOLBERT to JOHN THOMPSON for 80 acres of land and ordered to be certified.

A Deed of Conveyance from JAMES SMITH to JOHN MOREHEAD for 309 acres of land and ordered to be certified.

A Deed of Conveyance from JOHN DURLEY to JOSEPH BELL for 150 acres of land and ordered to be certified.

A Bill of Sale from THOMAS H. BELL to the heirs of WILLIAM BELL, deceased, for five negroes and ordered to be certified.

A Deed of Conveyance from DAVID BUCHANAN, SR., SAMUEL S. BUCHANAN and DAVID BUCHANAN, JR. to JOHN GIBSON for 9¼ acres of land and ordered to be certified.

A Deed of Conveyance from WILLIAM FORD to JESSE ELLIS for 111¼ acres of land and ordered to be certified.

A Deed of Conveyance from ALEX. SMITH to ROBERT OZBURN for 125 acres of land and ordered to be certified.

A Deed of Conveyance from ROBERT OZBURN to EDWARD HARDING for 125 acres of land and ordered to be certified.

A Deed of Conveyance from RICHARD COTHAM to PETER FEREBAUGH for 50 acres of land and ordered to be certified.

A Deed of Conveyance from MICHAEL OWEN to THOMAS WHITE and SOLOMON OWEN for 56 acres of land, proven by R.H. McEWEN and SAMUEL E. GILLILAND and ordered to be certified.

A Deed of Conveyance from WILLIAM DAVIS to THOMAS BRENTS for 50 acres of land and ordered to be certified.

A Deed of Conveyance from DAVID McCRAKEN to JAMES McFERRAN for 50 acres of land, proven by CORDIAL SHUFFIELD and GEORGE GRAY and ordered to be certified.

A Deed of Conveyance from DAVID A. MOORE and WILLIAM MOORE to ELISHA, JOAB and HENRY BAGLEY for (blank), proven by JAMES F. DRIVER and JOSEPH McGAHEY and ordered to be certified.

A Deed of Conveyance from DAVID A. MOORE and WILLIAM MOORE to ELISHA, JOAB and HENRY BAGLEY, proven by JAMES F. DRIVER and JOSEPH McGAHEY and ordered to be certified.

A Deed of Conveyance from ISAAC TOWERY to JAMES CLARK for 20 acres of land and ordered to be certified.

A Deed of Gift from RACHEL BELL to WILLIAM CRAWFORD and GEORGE CRAWFORD was proven in court by JOHN CRAWFORD and ROBERT MELEAR and ordered to be certified.

A deed of Conveyance from JOHN SHUTTS, admr of JESSE ROBERTSON, deceased, to PARK GIBSON for 23 acres of land, proven by JOHN SMITH and JOHN GIBSON and ordered to be certified.

A Deed of Conveyance from TURNER WILLIAMS to DAVID WATSON for 215 acres of land, proven by JAMES D. EASTER and JOSEPH GARNER and ordered to be certified.

JOHN B. TODD is appointed overseer of the road in the room of JOHN DILLON and call on the usual hands.

TUESDAY OCTOBER 16, 1821

Justices present were PHILIP KOONCE, JAMES HOLEMAN and JAMES WILSON,

Esquires.

The Sheriff made return that he had summoned the following venire to serve as Grand Jurors and Petit Jurors to this term, to wit, WILLIAM HOWARD, GEORGE PRICE, SHERWOOD HUNTER, WILLIAM DOAK, FRANCIS PATTON, JOHN DAVIS, JOHN DOWTHIT, GEORGE H. STOVALL, MOSES CHAMBERS, WILLIAM FRAME, RALPH ARNOLD, BENJAMIN HUTSON, WILLIAM RUSSELL, JACOB GROSS, MARK STEED, THOMAS N. HARPER, WESLY SMITH, SAMUEL CRAWFORD, ABNER WELLS, JOEL DODSON, JOHN KENNEDY, JOHN R. MOORE, JOHN DONELSON, STEPHEN CLAYTON, DAVID SMITH, WILLIAM SHAW, and JOHN GAVEN of whom to serve as Grand Jurors, to wit, WILLIAM DOAK, foreman, SHERWOOD HUNTER, MOSES CHAMBERS, JOHN DONELSON, JOHN GAVEN, DAVID SMITH, JACOB GROSS, WILLIAM FRAME, JOHN W. SMITH, JOHN R. MOORE, JOHN DAVIS, JOHN DOWTHIT, and MARK STEED after receiving their charge returned to consider for their presentments.

STERLING C. McLEMORE, a Constable, sworn to wait on the Grand Jury this term.

A Transfer of a Plat and Certificate of Survey from JOSEPH RILEY to JOHN HAGGATT and ordered to be certified.

THOMAS ALLY vs ROBERT BUCHANAN - The plaintiff says he wishes to dismiss this suit and the defendant assumes the payment of all costs. Suit to be dismissed and the plaintiff to recover against the defendant his costs.

The Grand Jury returned into court and brought with a Bill of Indictment, the State against JOHN CLIFTON for an assault and battery, a true bill and again returned to consider for further presentments.

WILLIAM BONNER produced two old wolf scalps into court and made oath that he killed the same within the bounds of Lincoln County.

The Grand Jury again returned to court and brought with them, a Bill of Indictment, the State against WARNER CLIFTON for an assault, a true bill and again returned to consider for further presentments.

A Deed of Conveyance from DAVID CLARK to LEMUEL BROADWAY for 20 acres of land and ordered to be certified.

A Deed of Conveyance from DAVID CLARK to LEMUEL BROADWAY and ordered to be certified.

JOHN DAVIS vs THOMAS BUCHANAN - This day came the parties by their attorneys and a jury of men, to wit, STEPHEN CLAYTON, WILLIAM HOWARD, WILLIAM SHAW, GEORGE H. STOVALL, GEORGE PRICE, RALPH ARNOLD, SAMUEL DOBBINS, DAVIDSON McMILLIN, STERLING A. BRIANT, GENERAL W.C. EDMISTON, JOHN DAVIS, and NOAH WARD being elected and sworn and said that $29.50 part of the debt in the declaration of the plaintiff and damages of $7.50. Plaintiff to recover his costs.

WILSON & SHELTON vs NOAH WARD - Appeal - This day came the parties by their attorneys and a jury of men, to wit, RANDOLPH QUARLES, DAVID McCORMACK, JAMES HUNTER, JOHN CLIFTON, WILLIAM GRIFFIS, CORNELIUS WEBB, ROBERT PARKS, JOHN HULSEY, JOSEPH HINKLE, AUGUISH JOHNSON, ROBERT EDMISTON, and RALPH PHAGAN being elected and sworn and said that NOAH WARD paid the debt without costs the 13th January 1821 and that 50¢ costs had occured before debt was paid.

This day came JOHN DAVIS and SARAH, his wife, GEORGE CUNNINGHAM and MARY, his wife, THOMAS DOAK and ELIZABETH, his wife, JOHN WILSON and JANE, his wife, SAMUEL BELL and his wife MARGARET, JOHN EDMISTON and ROBERT EDMISTON by their attorney and their petition being heard and understood. This petition was granted and it is ordered and decreed, SHERWOOD HUNTER, ARCHABALD McELROY, WILLIAM McELROY, ANDREW HANNAH, and WILLIAM BOON be appointed Commissioners to lay off and divide the estate of ANDREW EDMISTON and make return to next court.

WEDNESDAY OCTOBER 17, 1821

Justices present were JAMES WILSON, PHILIP KOONCE, JAMES HOLEMAN and WILLIAM DICKSON, Esquires.

A Power of Attorney from MARY BRENT to JOHN N. BRIANT of Rockingham County, North Carolina and ordered to be certified.

JAMES STEWART vs BRICE M. GARNER - Case - This day came the parties by their attorneys and a jury of men, to wit, WILLIAM HOWARD, WILLIAM SHAW, GEORGE H. STOVALL, GEORGE PRICE, RALPH ARNOLD, THOMAS KERCHEVAL, DAVID McCORMACK, SAMUEL H. SMITH, JOSHUA DALLAS, EDWARD McBRIDE, and WILLIAM GEORGE being elected and sworn and said that the damages of the plaintiff of $2139.00. Plaintiff to recover against the defendant his costs.

(out of order) JOSIAH HACKETT vs JAMES WILSON - The defendant appeared in court and the plaintiff being called came not but made default. The defendant to recover against the plaintiff his costs.

(out of order) RALPH ARNOLD vs JAMES ?. STAIN - The defendant by his attorney appeared in court and the plaintiff being called came not but made default. The defendant to recover against the plaintiff his costs.

(out of order) ROBERT H. McEWEN and Co. vs NATHANIEL B. BUCKINGHAM - The plaintiffs by their attorney appeared in court and the defendant being called came and plead to the suit in this behalf failed to do so but made default. Plaintiffs to recover against the defendant $215.53 and damages of $16.16.

(out of order) THOMAS CHAMPLAIN vs Fayetteville Tennessee Bank - The plaintiff by his attorney came into court and the Fayetteville Tennessee Bank being called, came not but made default and JOHN GREER, JOHN P. McCONNELL, ROBERT DICKSON, ELIOTT HICKMAN, BRICE M. GARNER, NIMROD BAILY, CHARLES BOYLES, ARGYLE CAMPBELL, and HUGH M. BLAKE and WILLIAM DICKSON being called and defend this suit in this cause, failed to do so but made default. Plaintiff recover against Fayetteville Tennessee Bank, in their plea of trespass on this case but because it is not known to the court here, the amount of damages to which the plaintiff is entitled. It is considered by the court that a writ of inquiry be issued at next court.

(out of order) Fayetteville Tennessee Bank vs WILLIAM KELLY and others - This day came the defendant by his attorney and the plaintiff being called came not but made default, whereupon came CHARLES McKINNEY, one of the defendants, and assumes the payment of all costs. The plaintiff be non-suited and recover against CHARLES McKINNEY the costs.

(out of order) JOHN DAVIS vs THOMAS BUCHANAN - This day came the plaintiff by his attorney and the defendant plea filed in this case does not answer the whole of the plaintiff's charges but only as to $37.00, part of the debt. Plaintiff to recover against the defendant $54.00 that part of the debt and $3.11 damages.

SAMUEL CRAWFORD vs JAMES COALTER - This cause is continued until next term of court on affidavit of the defendant by his paying the cost of this term, and that order made at last term of court for the defendant to take deposition of WILLIAM WHITE and the Clerk and Master of the Court of Chancery at Stanton in State of Virginia be renewed.

DANIEL BACHMAN vs THOMAS BRENTS - The plaintiff says he wishes to dismiss this suit and assumes the payment of all costs. Suit to be dismissed and the defendant recover against the plaintiff his costs.

WILLIAM SMITH vs GEORGE R. MOSS - The defendant by his attorney says he wishes to dismiss his certiorari of this cause and assumes the payment of all costs. This cause to be dismissed and the plaintiff recover against the defendant his costs.

W. DAVID, Executor vs WILLIAM PUGH - The plaintiff is granted him to take the deposition of CHARLES QUILLEN also commission awarded the defendant to take the deposition of RICHARD AUTON to be taken this day at the house of RICHARD AUTON to be read as evidence on the trial of this cause and that this order be sufficient notice for taking the same.

WILLIAM P. ANDERSON vs GEORGE HUNT - The plaintiff by his attorney says he intends no further to prosecute this suit. This suit to be dismissed and the defendant recover against the plaintiff his costs.

WILLIAM P. ANDERSON vs WILLIAM TOWNZEND - Plaintiff by his attorney says he intends to dismiss this suit. This suit is dismissed and the defendant recover against the plaintiff his costs.

The Grand Jury returned to court and brought with them a Bill of Indictment for

Larceny against WILLIAM YOUNG, a true bill and again returned to consider for further presentments.

NANCY McDAVID and JAMES McDAVID, admrs vs WILLIAM PUGH - The defendant appeared in court and after the jury had been sworn in this cause and before the evidence was close and acknowledged himself indebted to the plaintiffs all the residue that is apecified in said note of $55.87½ which leaves a balance due of $24.00 together with $3.36 interest. This was not done at the request of the plaintiffs or their counsel nor their agent.

NANCY McDAVID and JAMES McDAVID, admrs vs WILLIAM PUGH - This day came the parties by their attorneys and a jury of men, to wit, STEPHEN CLAYTON, WILLIAM HOWARD, WILLIAM SHAW, GEORGE H. STOVALL, GEORGE PRICE, RALPH ARNOLD, DAVID McCORMACK, SAMUEL H. SMITH, JOSHUA DALLAS, WILLIAM GEORGE, JOHN CLIFTON, and WILLIAM LEDFORD being elected and sworn and said that the case is to be continued next day.

THURSDAY OCTOBER 18, 1821

Justices present were JAMES WILSON, PHILIP KOONCE and JAMES HOLMAN, Esquires.

The State vs WILLIAM YOUNG - Indictment for Larceny - The defendant being charged on this bill and pleads not guilty and for his trial puts himself upon the county and WILLIAM B. MARTIN, the Attorney General does the like.

The State vs JACOB WRIGHT - Indictment for an Affray - The defendant being charged and pleads guilty and fined $2.00, JONATHAN WELCH, his security.

The State vs JOHN CLIFTON - Assault and Battery - The defendant being charged pleads not guilty and for his trial puts himself upon the county and WILLIAM B. MARTIN, the Attorney General, does the like.

The State vs WARNER CLIFTON - Assault and Battery - The defendant being charged pleads not guilty and for his trial puts himself upon the county and WILLIAM B. MARTIN, the Attorney General, does the like.

JAMES and NANCY McDAVID, admrs vs WILLIAM PUGH - The jury found the defendant indebted to the plaintiff $26.11½.

OLIVER B. HAYS vs Fayetteville Tennessee Bank - The execution was issued against the defendant which was returned by the coronor of this county, that no property of the said Bank could be found in this county out of which said execution or any part could be made and it appearing that the coronor on the 18th August 1821 served a written notice upon WILLIAM DICKSON to appear at this term and answer as garnishee in the above case. WILLIAM DICKSON being called to court and answer as garnishee as aforesaid came not but made default. Plaintiff to recover against WILLIAM DICKSON $238.40 and damages of $10.99 and costs. DICKSON to make return at next court.

OLIVER B. HAYS vs Fayetteville Tennessee Bank - Plaintiff by his attorney came into court and the court issued an execution in this cause since last term of court against the defendant which was returned by the Coronor (same as above) on the 21 August 1821 served a written notice upon ROBERT DICKSON (same as above), plaintiff to recover against ROBERT DICKSON $238.40 (same as above only it is ROBERT DICKSON instead of WILLIAM DICKSON).

OLIVER B. HAYS vs Fayetteville Tennessee Bank - (same as above) on the 15 August 1821 served a written notice upon JOHN GREER to appear at this court and answer as garnishee in the above cause. JOHN GREER being called came not but made default. Plaintiff to recover against JOHN GREER $238.40 and damages of $10.99.

OLIVER B. HAYS vs Fayetteville Tennessee Bank - (same as above) 15 day of August 1821 served a written notice upon ELLIOTT HICKMAN (same as above). Plaintiff to recover against ELLIOTT HICKMAN $238.40 and damages of $10.99.

OLIVER B. HAYS vs Fayetteville Tennessee Bank - (same as above) 19 August 1821 served a written notice upon JOSEPH HINKLE (same as above). Plaintiff to recover against JOSEPH HINKLE $238.40 and damages of $10.99.

THOMAS CHAMPLAIN vs Fayetteville Tennessee Bank - (same as above) 18 Aug 1821 served a written notice upon WILLIAM DICKSON (same as above). Plaintiff to recover against WILLIAM DICKSON $550.73 and damages of $13.32½.

THOMAS CHAMPLAIN vs Fayetteville Tennessee Bank - (same as above) 21 August 1821 served as written notice upon ROBERT DICKSON (same as above). Plaintiff to recover against ROBERT DICKSON $550.73 and damages of $13.32½.

THOMAS CHAMPLAIN vs Fayetteville Tennessee Bank - (same as above) 15 August 1821 served a written notice upon JOHN GREER (same as above). Plaintiff to recover against JOHN GREER $550.73 and damages of $13.32½.

THOMAS CHAMPLAIN vs Fayetteville Tennessee Bank - (same as above) 15 August 1821 served a written notice upon ELLIOTT HICKMAN (same as above). Plaintiff to recover against ELLIOTT HICKMAN $550.73 and damages of $13.32½.

THOMAS CHAMPLAIN vs Fayetteville Tennessee Bank - (same as above) 19 August 1821 served a written notice upon JOSEPH HINKLE (same as above). Plaintiff to recover against JOSEPH HINKLE $550.73 and damages of $13.32½.

FRIDAY OCTOBER 19, 1821

Justices present were PHILIP KOONCE, JAMES WILSON and JAMES HOLEMAN, Esquires.

JOHN J. CARRINGTON vs JAMES MARTIN - The plaintiff by his attorney says he wishes to dismiss this suit and the defendant came and assumes the payment of all costs. Suit to be dismissed and the plaintiff recover against the defendant his costs.

The Grand Jury again returned to court and brought with them a Bill of Indictment against HENRY CLIFT for an assault and battery, a true bill and again returned to consider for further presentments.

STERLING TALLEY appeared in court and acknowledged himself indebted to the State of Tennessee for $150.00 to be levied of his goods and chattels &c but to be void on conditions that he appear here and prosecute and give evidence in behalf of the State against HENRY CLIFT for an assault and battery and not depart the same without leave first had and obtained of the court.

SOLOMON REECE vs JOHN McKINLY - EZEKIEL GILLUM the appearance bail of JOHN McKINLY, summons him in open court whereupon EZEKIEL GILLUM is released as appearance bail for the defendant and DAVID HUDDLESTON appeared in court and entered into bond with said JOHN McKINLY as appearance bail.

The State vs WILLIAM YOUNG - Indictment for Larceny - This day came the defendant also WILLIAM B. MARTIN, the Attorney General, and came a jury of men, to wit, STEPHEN CLAYTON, WILLIAM SHAW, WILLIAM HOWARD, RALPH ARNOLD, JOHN CLIFTON, NATHANIEL B. BUCKINGHAM, HAMBLETON MOFFET, ELIAS SCOTT, WILLIAM DAVIS, ROBERT NIX, RICHARD C. PREWETT, and WILLIAM GEORGE being elected and sworn and said that the defendant as well as the State, the jury was under the care of an officer until next day.

SATURDAY OCTOBER 20, 1821

Justices present were PHILIP KOONCE, JAMES WILSON, and JAMES HOLEMAN, Esquires.

PHAIN & CRAWFORD vs BRICE M. GARNER - A Commission be awarded to the plaintiff to take the deposition of JOSEPH B. BACON in Washington County in this State, to be read as evidence on the trial of the above cause and it appearing to the satisfaction of the court that the defendant is at this time out of this State a considerable distance from this place and will not return for two months. Sufficient notice be given if the plaintiffs give ARGYLE CAMPBELL the defendant's attorney twenty days notice and if notice be served on the defendant ten days notice of time and place of taking the same.

The State vs WILLIAM YOUNG - The jury elected and sworn said that the defendant is guilty as charged in the Bill of Indictment.

MONDAY OCTOBER 22, 1821

It is ordered that JAMES McDAVID be allowed to receive from the County Trustee $16.12½ out of the county monies for apprehending and bring to justice JOEL SIMMS.

115

ROBERT TEDFORD is appointed overseer of the road leading up the middle fork of Norris Creek to Shelbyville, beginning at the branch below the five mile tree on to the top of the hill above WILLIAM C. HOGES, in the room of PRESLEY GEORGE and call on all the usual hands.

An additional inventory of the estate of THOMAS JOYCE, deceased, was returned into court and ordered to be certified.

On petition of JOHN BUCHANAN it is ordered by the court that HUGH M. BLAKE, DAVID P. MUNROE, JOHN MARR, JAMES BLAKEMORE, GEORGE BLAKEMORE, WILLIAM HODGES, JAMES BROADWAY, JAMES HIGGINS, WILLIAM BEAVER, PETER LOONEY, SR., WILLIAM DRIVER and JOHN S. PRICE being appointed a Jury of View to view and assess the damages that JOHN BUCHANAN may sustain in consequence of a new road lately laid off to run west of a large hill between said BUCHANAN and STEPHEN CLAYTON through said BUCHANAN's land, or turn said road to the most convenient plan taking into view the public good, as well as the injury which JOHN BUCHANAN may sustain and make return to next court.

An amount of sale of the property of ROBERT ADAMS, deceased, was returned by his admr and ordered to be certified.

Ordered by the court that JAMES CARITHERS, KINCHEON HOLCOM, ROBERT CUNNINGHAM, JOB H. BELL, JOHN WATSON, JAMES WILSON, JAMES McCORMACK, and MATHEW WILSON be a Jury of View to view and mark out a road leading the nearest and best way from MICAJAH McELROY's plantation and to intersect the Columbia Road at or near KINCHEON HOLCOM and make return to next court.

SAMUEL M. CLAY, WILLIAM BARROW, WILLIAM STEPHENS, MICHAEL ROBERTSON, WILLIAM SHIP, and WILLIAM TOWNZEND is appointed a Jury of View to view and mark out a road the nearest and best from the mouth of Swan Creek to intersect a road opened in Madison County to the State line and make return to next court. NOTE: Madison County is in Alabama.

An additional inventory of the estate of DAVID SAWYERS, deceased, was returned to court by his admr and ordered to be certified.

JOHN C. SAWYERS appeared in court and was appointed admr on the estate of ELIZABETH SAWYERS, deceased, who gave (bond) of $1000.00 with JOHN BEATY and SAMUEL CRAWFORD his securities.

An inventory of the property of MARGARET RORAX, deceased, was returned to court by her admr and ordered to be certified.

FRANCES TEAL appeared in court and was appointed admrx on the estate of EDWARD TEAL, deceased, who gave bond of $6000.00 with JESSE DANIEL, JOHN D. SPAIN and HENRY WARREN her securities.

An inventory of the property of EDWARD TEAL, deceased, was returned to court by his admrx and ordered to be certified.

JOHN D. SPAIN appeared in court and was appointed admr on the estate of LEWIS DUVALL, deceased, who gave bond of $1500.00 with JESSE DANIEL and PHILIP KOONCE his securities.

An inventory of the estate of LEWIS DUVALL was returned to court by his admr and ordered to be certified.

It is ordered by the court that JOHN RHEA be allowed $50.00 for attending the estate of SAMUEL BARNES, deceased, as executor to the Last Will and Testament of said BARNES.

GEORGE CUNNINGHAM appeared in court and was appointed guardian for WILLIAM BARNES and SAMUEL R. BARNES, infant heirs of SAMUEL BARNES, deceased, who gave bond of $5000.00 with JOSEPH HINKLE, JOHN P. McCONNELL, GENERAL W.C. EDMISTON, and CHARLES BOYLES his securities.

It is ordered by the court that JACOB WAGGONER, FRANCIS PORTERFIELD, ARCHABALD D. GARVEN, VANCE GREER, REECE HOWELL, WILLIAM DOAK, and RANDOLPH MAYFIELD be allowed to receive from the County Trustee $6.00 for serving as jurors six days on the trial of WILIA GARRETT at last Circuit Court.

The Commissioners appointed at this term to settle with JOHN RHEA, executor of SAMUEL BARNES, deceased, made return to court the settlement and ordered to be certified.

A Deed of Gift from RICHARD COMPTON, SR. to RICHARD COMPTON, JR. was proven in court by the witnesses and ordered to be certified.

The Commissioners appointed at this term to settle with JOHN RHEA, executor of SAMUEL BARNES, deceased, made return to court the settlement and ordered to be certified.

A Deed of Gift from RICHARD COMPTON, SR. to RICHARD COMPTON, JR. was proven and ordered to be certified.

A Deed of Conveyance from ABRAHAM HOGLAND to WILLIAM PARADICE for 98 acres of land, proven by WILLIAM GIVENS and JOHN BOYLES and ordered to be certified.

The Transfer of a Plat and Certificate of Survey from THOMAS MAYFIELD to REUBEN WASHBURN, proven by NICHOLAS JONES and JAMES BLACKLEDGE and ordered to be certified.

It is ordered by the court that TUNSTAL GREGORY, ABRAHAM FITCH and JAMES MARTIN be appointed Commissioners to lay off one years support out of the estate of EDWARD TEAL, deceased, for the widow of said deceased.

It is ordered by the court that JOHN MARR, ROBERT BUCHANAN and GENERAL W.C. EDMISTON be appointed Commissioners to settle with JOHN BEATY and WILLIAM B. BENGE, admrs on the estate of ROBERT C. EDMISTON and make report to next court.

It is ordered that JOHN PORTER, WILLIAM BEAVERS and THOMAS CLARK be appointed Commissioners to settle with GILBERT KENNEDY and JAMES McCORKLE, admrs on the estate of ROBERT ADAMS, deceased, and make return to next court.

It is ordered that ISHAM PARR, WILLIAM BOON, WILLIAM MARTIN, WILLIAM MARR, ZACHARIAH HARRISON, ISAAC BROYLES, DAVID McCLAMROCK, DANIEL WARREN, MATHEW PRICE, JOHN ATKINS, SR., WILLIAM FORD, JOEL DODSON, JAMES PHILLIPS, TRYON GIBSON, ELIJAH DILLENDER, WILLIAM C. KENNEDY, JOSEPH SHAW, HOWEL JOHNSON, STERLING BRYANT, JAMES MARTIN, JOHN WILSON, JR., HUGH C. GAULT, KINCHEON HALCOM, WILLIAM ANDERSON, WILLIAM BONNER, JOEL BRUCE, JOSEPH WHITAKER, JAMES GRANT, BRITON PHELPS, WILLIAM HODGES, KINCHEON HALCOM*, WILLIAM ANDERSON*, WILLIAM BONNER*, JOEL BRUCE* and ALEXANDER McCORKLE be summoned as jurors to next county court in January next. * repeated.

It is ordered by the court that ISAAC HOLEMAN, JOHN WATKINS, JACOB WAGGONER, JOHN R. JOHNSON, ELIJAH YATES, BENJAMIN THURSTON, NICHOLAS CARRIGER, ANTHONY CRAWFORD, JORDAN REECE, JOSEPH GREER, JOHN WISEMAN, JOHN FORSYTHE, JOHN T. KING, SAMUEL McCORMACK, ROBERT CUNNINGHAM, WILLIAM SMITH (Mulberry), JAMES HOLEMAN, CORNELIUS DARNELL, HUGH M. BLAKE, WILLIAM OLD, GEORGE BLAKEMORE, RICHARD FLINT, JOHN CAMPBELL, HARRISON JOHNSON, ELI GARRETT, THOMAS ROUNTREE, CLIFFORD GRAY, JACOB WRIGHT (Swan), and DAVID SMITH be summoned as jurors to the next Circuit Court in April next.

TUESDAY OCTOBER 23, 1821

Justices present were JAMES WILSON, WILLIAM KENNON and JAMES HOLEMAN, Esquires.

The State vs WARNER CLIFTON - Assault and Battery - The defendant came as well as WILLIAM B. MARTIN, Attorney General, and a jury of men, to wit, STEPHEN CLAYTON, WILLIAM SHAW, WILLIAM HOWARD, GEORGE H. STOVALL, ISAAC HOLEMAN, WILLIAM NORRIS, GEORGE PRICE, RALPH ARNOLD, THOMAS KERCHEVAL, HENRY WARREN, SAMUEL MIXON, and ROBERT NIX being elected and sworn and said that the defendant is not guilty. Defendant to be discharged and that JOHN JONES, the prosecutor, pay the costs.

The State vs HENRY CLIFT - Assault and Battery - The defendant pleads guilty and is fined $5.00 and pay the costs.

The Grand Jury again returned into court and brought with them a Bill of Indictment against HARDING FORRISTER and WILLIAM FORRISTER for assault and battery, a true bill, again returned to consider for further presentments.

The State vs JOHN CLIFTON - Assault and Battery - The defendant came as well as WILLIAM B. MARTIN, the Attorney General, and a jury of men, to wit, HENRY CLIFT, THOMAS W. HAMBLETON, JOHN DAVIS, JACOB ALLBRIGHT, BERRY BRITTON, JOHN D. NIX, JOHN ALLBRIGHT, SOLOMON SMITH, STEPHEN CLAYTON, SAMUEL E. GILLILAND, JOHN D. SPAIN, and DAVIDSON McMILLIN being elected and sworn and said that the defendant is guilty and is fined $5.00 and pay the costs, whereupon came ISAAC HOLEMAN as security.

The State vs WILLIAM YOUNG - Indictment for Larceny - The defendant being found guilty of larceny appeared this day in court. It is considered by the court that the defendant receive on his back ten lashes well laid on by the Sheriff of this county at the public whipping post this day between the hours of eleven and twelve o'clock and that he pay the costs of this indictment.

WEDNESDAY OCTOBER 24, 1821

Justices present were JAMES HOLEMAN, JAMES WILSON and PHILIP KOONCE, Esquires.

The State vs HARDING FORRISTER - Indictment for Assault and Battery - This day came the defendant and being charged and pleads not guilty and a jury of men, to wit, WILLIAM SHAW, WILLIAM HOWARD, GEORGE H. STOVALL, GEORGE PRICE, STEPHEN CLAYTON, RALPH ARNOLD, WILLIAM ESLICK, WILLIAM A. TUCKER, JOHN DAVIS, LINSFIELD W. PARKS, JOHN ALLBRIGHT, and JACOB ALLBRIGHT being elected and sworn and said that the defendant is guilty and is fined $2.00 and pay the costs of this indictment and remain in prison until the fine and costs are paid or give security, whereupon came JORDAN SOLOMON as security.

The State vs WILLIAM FORRISTER - Assault and Battery - The defendant came into court and pleads not guilty and a jury of men, to wit, (same as above jurors) being elected and sworn and said that the defendant is guilty of an assault as charged but not guilty of an affray as charged. Defendant is fined $1.00 and pay the costs and remain in custody of the Sheriff until the costs and fine are paid or give security, whereupon came NATHANIEL BLACKMORE as security.

A Deed of Conveyance from JOHN EDMISTON, heir and executor of the Last Will and Testament of SAMUEL EDMISTON, deceased, to WILLIAM EDMISTON, GENERAL WILLIAM CAMPBELL EDMISTON, VANCE GREER, EBENEZER McEWEN and his wife MARY McEWEN, JAMES GILLESPIE and his wife PATSEY GILLESPIE, ROBERT HERROLD and his wife MARGARET HERROLD, JOHN BEATY and his wife SALLY BEATY for 500 acres of land in this county, proven by ROBERT EDMISTON and WILLIAM E. KENNEDY and ordered to be certified.

A Deed of Conveyance from JOHN BASINGER and his wife EADY BASINGER to JACOB & JOHN WAGGONER for (blank), proven by JOHN BASINGER and his wife EADY BASINGER and ordered to be certified.

The State vs PATSEY BLUBAKER - PATSEY BLUBAKER was bound and to appear at the court house in Fayetteville on 1st Thursday after the 3rd Monday in October instant and answer the State of Tennessee for an affray and not depart the same without leave first had and obtained of the court, was this day called, came not but made default. Judgment was entered against her for $200.00.

JORDAN SOLOMON who was bound in a recognizance for the appearance of PATSEY BLUBAKER at this term was called to bring the body of said PATSEY BLUBAKER as he was found, failed to do so but made default. The recognizance is forfeited and judgment against him for $200.00.

ROBERT IRWIN vs GARNER & MARTIN - Case - This day came the parties by their attorneys and a jury of men, to wit, SHERWOOD HUNTER, MOSES CHAMBERS, WILLIAM DOAK, JOHN DONELSON, JOHN GAVIN, DAVID SMITH, JACOB GROSS, WILLIAM FRAME, JOHN D. SMITH, JOHN R. MOOR, JOHN DAVIS, and JOHN DOWTHIT being elected and sworn and said that the plaintiff's damages were $262.00. Plaintiff to recover against the defendant his costs.

WILLIAM W. TAYLOR vs GEORGE & JAMES COALTER - Debt - This day came the parties by their attorneys and a jury of men, to wit, (same as above jurors) being elected and sworn and said that the defendant has not paid all of the debt of $1000.00 but owes a balance of $856.00 and damages of $59.92. PLaintiff to recover against the defendant his costs.

THURSDAY OCTOBER 25, 1821

Justices present were PHILIP KOONCE, WILLIAM KENNON and JAMES WILSON, Esquires.

ELIJAH MAYFIELD vs WILLIAM McWHIRTER and GEORGE WEBB - The plaintiff be non-suited and the defendant go home without day and recover against the plaintiff their costs.

JOHN SAWYERS vs JOHN MURPHY - The plaintiff to recover amount of a judgment which said JOHN SAWYERS had paid for said JOHN MURPHY as admr of DAVID SAWYERS, deceased, to EZEKIEL GILLUM and it appearing from the records of this office that said DAVID SAWYERS was security for JOHN MURPHY. Plaintiff to recover against the defendant $29.86.

JOHN CLIFTON vs WILLIAM MOREHEAD - This day came the parties by their attorneys and a jury of men, to wit, SHERWOOD HUNTER, MOSES CHAMBERS, WILLIAM DOAK, JOHN DONELSON, DAVID SMITH, WILLIAM FRAME, JOHN W. SMITH, JOHN DAVIS, JOHN R. MOORE, JOHN DOWTHIT, JOHN GAVIN and MARK STEED being elected and sworn and said that the defendant is not indebted to the plaintiff anything. Defendant recover against the plaintiff his costs. Plaintiff prays for an appeal to next Circuit Court and gave bond &c.

JOHN CLIFTON vs WILLIAM MOREHEAD - (same as above) says the defendant is not indebted to the plaintiff anything. The defendant recover against the plaintiff his costs. The plaintiff again appeals to the Circuit Court next and is granted.

FRIDAY OCTOBER 26, 1821

Justices present were JAMES WILSON, WILLIAM DICKSON and PHILIP KOONCE, Esquires.

MILES MURY (MURRY) vs JOHN H. MOORE - Debt - (same as above) says the defendant has not paid all of the debt of $100.00 but owes a balance of $91.50 and damages of $10.00. Plaintiff to recover against the defendant his costs.

PILLOW & BRADSHAW vs BRICE M. GARNER - Covenant - (same as above) says the defendant has not kept and performed the covenant. The plaintiff's damages are $7404.50. Plaintiff to recover against the defendant his costs.

GARNER & MARTIN for the use of &c vs DAVID LORANCE - Debt - (same as above) says that the defendant has not paid the debt of $600.00 and damages of $62.50. Plaintiff to recover against the defendant his costs.

ROBERT H. McEWEN vs SOLOMON GULLETT - The defendant appeared in court and acknowledged that he owes the plaintiff $99.00 and damages of $20.79. The plaintiff to recover against the defendant his costs.

JOSIAH F. DANFORTH vs STEPHEN MARLOW - Debt - This day came the parties by their attorneys and a jury of men, to wit, SHERWOOD HUNTER, MOSES CHAMBERS, WILLIAM DOAK, JOHN DONELSON, DAVID SMITH, WILLIAM FRAME, JOHN W. SMITH, JOHN DAVIS, JOHN R. MOORE, JOHN DOWTHITT, JOHN GAVIN, and MARK STEED being elected and sqorn and said that the defendant has not paid the debt of $100.00 and damages of $5.00. The plaintiff to recover against the defendant his costs.

EZEKIEL PHILLIPS vs JOSEPH HINKLE - Debt - (same as above) says that the defendant has not paid the debt of $450.00 and damages of $22.50. Plaintiff to recover against the defendant his costs. Defendant prays for an appeal to next court and granted.

EZEKIEL PHILLIPS vs HAMBLETON MOFFIT - Case - This day came the parties by their attorneys and a jury of men, to wit, WILLIAM SHAW, WILLIAM HOWARD, GEORGE PRICE, STEPHEN CLAYTON, RALPH ARNOLD, JACOB GROSS, FRANCIS WYATT, KEYS MEEK, THOMAS W. HAMBLETON, JOHN CLIFTON, HENRY KYMES, and JOHN ALLBRIGHT being elected and sworn and said that the defendant did assume upon himself as charged and that they assess the damages to be $472.50. Plaintiff to recover against the defendant his costs. Defendant prays for an appeal to the Circuit Court and was granted.

119

ROBERT H. McEWEN vs ROBERT CUNNINGHAM - (same as above) said that the defendant has not paid the debt of $130.00 and damages of $3.56 3/4. Plaintiff to recover against the defendant his costs.

JOHN DAVIS vs GEORGE TITUS - (same as above) says that the defendant has not paid the debt of $101.41 and damages of $8.87½. Plaintiff to recover against the defendant his costs.

JOSEPH BRITTON vs BRICE M. GARNER - (same as above) find in favor of the plaintiff and that the defendant has not paid the debt of $3000.00 and damages of $90.00. The plaintiff to recover against the defendant his costs.

JOSEPH BRITTON vs BRICE M. GARNER - (same as above) finds in favor of the plaintiff and that the defendant has not paid the debt of $78.75 and damages of $2.75. The plaintiff to recover against the defendant his costs.

JOHN ALLBRIGHT vs JAMES FULGHAM - The plaintiff was commissioned to take the deposition of FREDERICK BOWLEN to be read as evidence on the trial of the above cause, if taken in the State of Alabama ten days notice, if taken in this county four days notice of time and place of taking the same. Also to take the deposition of ARCHABALD McKEE and MANERING TOWER by giving five days notice and a commission also awarded the defendant to take the deposition of ROBERT EDMISTON in this county by giving the plaintiff five days notice of tie and place of taking the same.

SOLOMON REECE vs JOHN McKINLEY - The plaintiff was commissioned to take the deposition of WILLIAM KYMES at the house of WILLIAM GIVENS, Esquire, on tomorrow the 27th instant.

SATURDAY OCTOBER 27, 1821

Justices present were JAMES HOLEMAN, WILLIAM KENNON, PHILIP KOONCE and WILLIAM DICKSON, Esquires.

BERWELL HORTON vs JOEL DODSON - The plaintiff by his attorney was commissioned to take the deposition of JOHN SHORT and THOMAS HORTON of Madison County, in Alabama, to be given in evidence of the trial of the above cause by giving the defendant ten days notice of time and place of taking the same.

JOEL R. FIELDES by his next friend NIMROD FIELDES vs STERLING C. McLEMORE - The plaintiff was commissioned to take the deposition of ADAM HALL of Madison County to be read as evidence on the trial of the above cause by giving the defendant ten days notice of time and place of taking the same.

CHARLES H. EDMISTON vs RICHARD PRYOR - The plaintiff was commissioned to take the evidence of WILLIAM PATTON in Huntsville to be read as evidence on the trial of said cause by giving the defendant's attorney ten days notice and if served on the defendant five days notice of time and place of taking the same.

JOHN LANDIS, admr vs ROBERT FLETCHER - The plaintiff by his attorney was commissioned to take the deposition of EBENEZER TITUS of Huntsville to be read as evidence on the trial of the above cause by giving the defendant ten days notice of time and place of taking the same.

WATKINS & WHORTON vs THOMAS L. TROTTER - The plaintiff by his attorney was commissioned to take the deposition of GEORGE R. WHORTON of Huntsville to be read as evidence on the trial of the above cause by giving the defendant ten days notice of time and place of taking the same.

It is ordered by the court that GENERAL W.C. EDMISTON be overseer of the road in the room of JOHN PARKS resigned and call on the usual hands.

On motion of THOMAS W. HAMBLETON, it is ordered by the court that Writs of Certiorari issue to bring up to the court the papers in a suit tried before CLIFFORD GRAY on the (blank) day of August last wherein ASA PENNINGTON was plaintiff and THOMAS W. HAMBLETON was defendant.

JOHN MILROY vs WILLIAM DAVIS - The defendant appeared in court and said he owes the plaintiff $110.00 and damages of $5.50. The plaintiff to recover against the defendant his costs.

THOMAS ALLEY vs JAMES WYATT - The plaintiff says he intends to dismiss this suit and assumes the payment of all costs. Suit to be dismissed and the defendant recover against the plaintiff his costs.

A Letter of Attorney from GREEN B. HENDRIX to DANIEL WARREN was acknowledged in court by said HENDRIX and ordered to be certified.

AUGUSTIN YEAGER vs JAMES MOORE - The plaintiff came into court and the defendant being called to come and defend this suit failed to do so but made default. Plaintiff to recover against the defendant $97.68 3/4 and damages of $10.22½.

JOHN MAZE vs BRICE M. GARNER - The court gave the defendant until the 3rd Monday in September last past to plead and it appearing to the court that the defendant failed to plead within the time prescribed and also he failed as yet to plead to the said suit of the plaintiff. The plaintiff to recover against the defendant his costs. A jury of men, to wit, SHERWOOD HUNTER, WILLIAM DOAK, WILLIAM SHAW, JOHN DONELSON, DAVID McCLAMROCK, SPENCER A. PUGH, URIAH BOBBITT, ABRAHAM DEPOSITER, OLIVER WILLIAMS, REUBEN HUNTER, WILLIAM LEDFORD, and THOMAS DOAK being elected and sworn and said plaintiff recover $1212.50 against the defendant. Defendant prays for an appeal at next Circuit Court and was granted him.

ELIJAH MAYFIELD vs McWHERTER & WEBB - The court ordered that the plaintiff give security for the prosecution of his suit on or before the next term of court or suit will be dismissed.

It is ordered by the court that the following Justices of the Peace take in lists of the taxable property in Lincoln County for the year 1822 and make return to next court.
STEPHEN ALEXANDER in CAPTAIN McCLAMROCK Company
ABNER STEED in CAPTAIN MORGAN's Company
JONATHAN FLOYD in CAPTAIN DOWTHIT's Company
JOHN MARR in CAPTAIN CHITWOOD's Company
JOHN PORTER in CAPTAIN GAULT's Company
WILLIAM SMITH in CAPTAIN BAUCHMAN's Company
THOMAS GAITHER in CAPTAIN BEATY's Company
JOEL PINSON in CAPTAIN ROBERTSON's Company
DAVID COWAN in CAPTAIN McCORKLE's Company
CHARLES BOYLES in CAPTAIN TODD's Company
RICHARD FLYNT in CAPTAIN DAVIS' Company
HUGH M. BLAKE in CAPTAIN BLAKEMORE's Company
DAVID P. MUNROE in CAPTAIN BROOK's Company
JOHN H. MOORE in CAPTAIN MILLER's Company
AMBROSE BARKER in CAPTAIN RUTHERFORD's Company
CLIFFORD GRAY in CAPTAIN EASLICK's Company
WILLIAM MILLNER in CAPTAIN BRYANT's Company
JOHN SMITH in CAPTAIN SPENCER's Company
ELI GARRETT Iin CAPTAIN DYER's Company
ABRAHAM ISAACK in CAPTAIN NORTON's Company
JAMES RALSTON in CAPTAIN LORANCE's Company
WILLIAM C. ABELS in CAPTAIN LOVELADY's Company
ELISHA BAGLEY in CAPTAIN HAMPTON's Company
PHILIP KOONCE in CAPTAIN WELL's Company

A Deed of Conveyance from GEORGE CARROLL to JOSEPH ROPER was proven by NEWBERRY JAMES and MALACHI REAVES and ordered to be certified.

A Deed of Conveyance from JAMES RUTHERFORD to JOSEPH VINES for 15 acres of land and ordered to be certified.

A Deed of COnveyance from SAMUEL GARLAND and MOSES STONE to JOSHUA HOLT, THOMAS JONES and others for 2 acres of land and ordered to be certified.

A Deed of Conveyance from the heirs of DANIEL SHIPP, deceased, to POLLY SHIPP for 50 acres of land and ordered to be certified.

A Deed of Conveyance from the heirs of DANIEL SHIPP, deceased, to JOHN BOLIN for 52 acres of land and ordered to be certified.

A Deed of Conveyance from the heirs of DANIEL SHIPP, deceased, to SARAH SHIPP for 50 acres of land and ordered to be certified.

A Deed of Conveyance from the heirs of DANIEL SHIPP, deceased, to BENJAMIN NEILD for 50 acres of land and ordered to be certified.

A Deed of Conveyance from the heirs of DANIEL SHIPP, deceased, to LEWIS SHIPP for 175 acres of land and ordered to be certified.

A Deed of Conveyance from the heirs of DANIEL SHIPP, deceased, to WILLIAM SHIPP for 155 acres of land and ordered to be certified.

It is ordered by the court that the County of Lincoln pay the costs in three cases, the State of Tennessee against ARCHELUS WILSON, three cases, the State of Tennessee against JAMES WILSON, in four cases, the State of Tennessee against GEORGE WILSON and one against JOHN PARKERSON and one against THOMAS GROOMS in which the foregoing cases executions had issued and returned by the Sheriff that there could be no property found in this county to satisfy said costs or any part thereof. Court ordered that the County Trustee of Lincoln County pay the costs.

The State vs WILLIAM WOODS - It is ordered by the court that Lincoln County pay the costs of this cause.

The State vs JAMES NELSON - It is ordered by the court that Lincoln County pay the costs of this case.

MONDAY JANUARY 21, 1822

Justices present. (Justices not named)

ASARIAH McAFEE is appointed overseer of the road in the room of PHILIP KOONCE resigned and call on the usual hands.

JOHN PARKISON is appointed overseer of the road in the room of JOSEPH DEAN and to call on the same hands.

ABSOLUM BLYTH is appointed overseer of the road in the room of THOMAS WASHBURN and call on the usual hands.

GEORGE HORNING is appointed overseer of the road in the room of JOHN MARSH and call on the same hands.

JAMES ISHAM is appointed overseer of the road in the room of MANSFIELD HUSBANDS and to call on the usual hands.

PRESTON HAMPTON is appointed overseer of the road in the room of RIGDON BEAVERS and to call on the usual hands.

JACOB HAMBLETON is appointed overseer of the road in the room of CHAMPION BLYTH resigned and call on the same hands.

JOHN BALEY is appointed overseer of the road in the room of GIDEON PULLY and to call on the usual hands.

It is ordered by the court that ALEXANDER McCORKLE, JR., LEWIS McCORKLE, JOHN McCRACKEN, SOLOMON BENNETT, STEPHEN HIGHTOWER, KINCHEN HOLCOM, and MR. THORP be a Jury of View to view and mark out a road the nearest and best way from Giles County line by LEATHERMAN's mill to intersect the Huntsville Road crossing at CHICK's Ford on Elk River.

It is ordered that JOHN MARR and WILLIAM BEAVERS, Esquires, be appointed Commissioners to settle with JENNET FARIS and JOHN BRACKENRIDGE, admrs on the estate of SAMUEL FARIS, deceased, and make return to next court.

It is ordered that MIRIAM WILLSON be allowed to receive from the County Trustee $6.00 for the time she kept JOSEPH EDINGTON, a pauper of this county.

An inventory of the property of JOHN HALBERT, deceased, was returned to court by his admr and ordered to be certified.

An inventory of the property of ROBERT ABERNATHY, deceased, was returned to court by his admr and ordered to be certified.

It is ordered that the Sheriff let out ELIJAH CONWAY, one of the poor of this county, at courthouse door this day.

An inventory of the property of EDWARD TEAL, deceased, was returned into court by his admrx and ordered to be certified.

It is ordered that JOHN P. McCONNELL be allowed $195.20½ for keeping the State prisoners &c and that the County Trustee pay the same out of the first county monies.

The Commissioners appointed at the last term of court to settle with SARAH FOWLER, admrx of the estate of JOHN FOWLER, deceased, made return of the settlement and ordered to be certified.

EASTHER CUMMINS and HUGH M. BLAKE appeared in court and was appointed admrx and admr on the estate of THOMAS CUMMINS, deceased, who gave bond for $500.00 with JOHN MARR their security.

JACOB GILLUM appeared in court and was apointed guardian for SALLY ALEXANDER, CAROLINE ALEXANDER and RACHEL ALEXANDER who gave bond for $250.00 with EZEKIEL GILLUM his security.

On petition, it is ordered by the court that URIAH BOBBIT established a ferry across Elk River at the mouth of Mulberry Creek who gave bond with J. WATKINS his security.

WILLIAM ANDERSON and HUGH PARKERSON appeared in court and sworn in as Justices of the Peace for Lincoln County.

JOHN MARR, Esquire, ROBERT BUCHANAN and JOHN GIBSON are appointed by the court Commissioners to settle with the admrs of the estate of ROBERT BUCHANAN, deceased, and make return to next court.

It is ordered by the court that ROBERT CUNNINGHAM, HUGH C. GAULT, JAMES McCORMACK, RICHARD WYATT, ELI TAYLOR, REPS O. CHILDRESS, THOMAS CLARK, JOHN DAVIS, WILLIAM BEAVERS, JOHN PORTER, JAMES WILSON, or any five of them be a Jury of View to mark and alter the road leading from CUNNINGHAM's mill and intersecting the road leading to Elkton and so to alter it as they may seem right and make return to next court.

WILLIAM HUSBANDS, Deputy Sheriff, made return to court that he had let out ELIJAH CONWAY, one of the poor of this county, to JOHN BROADWAY for $85.00 who gave bond and security. Issued 22 February 1822. J. BROADWAY.

JOHN H. TAYLOR was appointed a Constable who gave bond with JOSEPH ADKINS and WOODY TAYLOR his securities.

HUGH C. GAULT was appointed a Constable who gave bond with ELI TAYLOR and JOHN WILSON his securities.

JOSEPH ALLSUP was appointed a Constable who gave bond with JOHN DUNLEY and WILLIAM COLLINS his securities,

JAMES McDAVID was appointed a Constable who gave bond with WILLIAM P. PULLIAM and RICHARD FLYNT his securities.

TUNSTALL GREGORY was appointed a Constable who gave bond with JESSE DANIEL and JOHN H. WILLIAMS his securities.

WILLIAM STEPHENS was appointed a Constable who gave bond with SAMUEL M. CLAY and ABRAHAM ISAACKS his securities.

CHARLES BARKER was appointed guardian for McKENONE (McKENDRE) W. WHITENBURGH, ELEN H. WHITENBURGH, NORMAN H. WHITENBURGH, and JOSEPH WHITENBURGH,infant heirs of JOSEPH WHITENBURGH, deceased, who gave bond of $1000.00 with AMBROSE BARKER and WILLIAM KENNON his securities.

MOSES HALL was appointed a Constable who gave bond with security.

GEORGE BLAKEMORE, Esquire, JOHN W. BLAKE and BENJAMIN WOODRUFF are appointed Commissioners to lay off one years provision for the widow of THOMAS

CUMMINS, deceased, and make return to next court.

ABSOLUM BOSTICK and JONAS LEATHERMAN appointed to settle with the admrs of the estate of ELIJAH HURLEY, deceased, and make return to next court.

GIDEON PILLOW appeared in open court and renounced the executorship on the estate of ARTHUR BROOKS, deceased, OLIVER WILLIAMS the other executor renounced his executorship in writing and the widow of the said ARTHUR BROOKS, deceased declined administering on said deceased estate whereupon came JAMES BROOKS and was appointed admr on said estate and gave bond and security.

ELISHA BAGLEY, Esquire, and WILLIAM CRUNK are appointed to lay off one years provision for the widow of ARTHUR BROOKS, deceased, and make return to next court.

The due execution of an Indenture of Bargain and Sale from THOMAS BRIGHT to THOMAS JONES for 106 acres of land, by JAMES BRIGHT, attorney, and ordered to be certified.

The due execution of an Indenture of Bargain and Sale from WILLIAM VINES to PETER FINEBAUGH for 20 acres of land, proven by WILLIAM EDMISTON and JOHN ELLIS and ordered to be certified.

The due execution of an Indenture and Bargain and Sale from JAMES ISBELL to EDMOND TAYLOR for 60 acres of land, proven by SHEPARD SHELTON and ENOCK SHELTON and ordered to be certified.

The due execution of an Indenture of Bargain and Sale from GEORGE COBLE to JOHN KENNEDY for 104 acres of land, proven by EDWARD GARRETT and THOMAS KENNEDY and ordered to be certified.

The due execution of an Indenture of Bargain and Sale from ROBERT FINLEY to JOHN B. ABEL for 50 acres of land, proven by SAMUEL BROWN and WILLIAM C. ABEL and ordered to be certified.

The due execution of an Indenture of Bargain and Sale from ISAAC ROGERS to JONES ROGERS for 160 acres of land and ordered to be certified.

The due execution of an Indentureof Bargain and Sale from WALTER BOWEN to JOSEPH A. DILLENDER for 50 acres of land and ordered to be certified.

CHARLES BOYLES, VANCE GREER, BENJAMIN CLEMENTS, CHARLES McKINNEY, JAMES FULTON, WILLIAM E. KENNEDY, THOMAS H. FLETCHER, and ARGYLE CAMPBELL are appointed by the court Trustees of the Fayetteville Academy to fill the vacancy of some of the former Trustees.

The due execution of an Indenture of Bargain and Sale from WILLIAM SHAW to JOHN DOWNING for 13 acres of land and ordered to be certified.

The due execution of an Indenture of Bargain and Sale from JOHN ROSSON to JOAB BAGLEY, proven by THOMAS D. PETTY and ordered to be certified.

The due execution of an Indenture of Bargain and Sale from ROBERT FINDLEY to EDMOND D. PARKER for 64 acres of land, proven by WILLIAM C. ABELS and SAMUEL BROWN and ordered to be certified.

The execution of an Indenture of Bargain and Sale from JOSEPH BYERS to WILLIAM WOOSLEY for 85 acres of land, proven by JOHN PINKERTON and ordered to be certified.

The due execution of an Indenture of Bargain and Sale from THOMAS McALPIN to WILLIAM ARMSTRONG for 50 acres of land, proven by THOMAS McFERRAN and MOSES HALL and ordered to be certified.

The due execution of an Indenture of Bargain and Sale from WILLIAM DOWNING to JOHN DOWNING for 50 acres of land and ordered to be certified.

The due execution of an Indenture of Bargain and Sale from MIDDLETON FANNON to YOUNG TAYLOR for 25 acres of land, proven by CLIFFORD GRAY and SHEPHARD SHELTON and ordered to be certified.

The due execution of an Indenture of Bargain and Sale from JOHN COPELAND to JOHN LYNCH for 24 acres of land and ordered to be certified.

The due execution of an Indenture of Bargain and Sale from WILLIAM GUNTER to JOSHUA GUNTER for 29 3/4 acres of land and ordered to be certified.

The due execution of an Indenture of Bargain and Sale from WILLIAM SHAW to WILLIAM H. GOWAN for 70 acres of land and ordered to be certified.

The due execution of an Indenture of Bargain and Sale from JOHN HAZEL to the heirs of MARTIN FLYNT, deceased, for 25 acres of land, proven by JAMES GARRETT and RICHARD FLYNT and ordered to be certified.

The due execution of an Indenture of Bargain and Sale from JAMES HUMPHREYS to ROBERT TEDFORD for 5 acres of land, proven by WILLIAM EDMISTON and JOHN McMILLIN and ordered to be certified.

The due execution of an Indenture of Bargain and Sale from JOHN KENDRICK to JOHN COPELAND for 25 acres of land, proven by ELI COUCH and MILLINGTON COUCH and ordered to be certified.

The due execution of an Indenture of Bargain and Sale from JOHN CALVERT to ANDREW MERRELL for 12 acres of land, proven by JOSEPH CALVERT, attorney in fact, and ordered to be certified.

The due execution of an Indenture of Bargain and Sale from JOHN HAZEL to the heirs of MARTIN FLYNT, deceased, for 50 acres of land, proven by JAMES GARRETT and RICHARD FLYNT and ordered to be certified.

The due execution of an Indenture of Bargain and Sale from WILLIAM ROBERTSON to ELISHA ROBERTSON for 66 2/3 acres of land and ordered to be certified.

The due execution of an Indenture of Bargain and Sale from WILLIAM FARRAR to WILLIAM ROBERTSON for 125 acres of land and ordered to be certifed.

The Transfer of a Plat and Certificate of Survey from EDWARD WILLETT to DOAK NIX and ordered to be certified.

The Transfer of a Plat and Certificate of Survey from JOSHUA SIMMONS to JOHN PARR, proven by MARCUS WHITLEY and ordered to be certified.

Agreeable to an Act of Assembly, the Justices proceed to class themselves in the following manner, to wit, JAMES WILSON, SAMUEL BUCHANAN, ISAAC CONGO (CONGER), GEORGE BLAKEMORE, ELISHA BAGLEY, WILLIAM DICKSON, WILLIAM KENNON, TALEFERO DOLLINS, JAMES RALSTON, WILLIAM GIVENS, PHILIP KOONCE, JAMES BLAKEMORE, and SAMUEL GARLAND were put on the first class to hold the January Term 1822, and ELI GARRETT, CORNELIUS DARNELL, EBENEZER McEWEN, THOMAS GAITHER, JONATHAN FLOYD, JOEL PINSON, JOHN H. MOORE, HENRY KELSO, JAMES HOLEMAN, AMBROSE BARKER, JOHN PINKERTON, and WILLIAM ANDERSON were clssed in the second class and to hold the April Term 1822. HUGH PARKERSON, HUGH M. BLAKE, WILLIAM SMITH, WILLIAM MILLNER, JOHN JONES, CLIFFORD GRAY, JOHN SMITH, STEPHEN ALEXANDER, JACOB WAGGONER, DAVID P. MUNROE, RICHARD FLYNT, WILLIAM BEAVERS, and CHARLES BOYLES were classed in the third class and to hold the July Term 1822. And ABNER STEED, JOHN ENOCKS, ABRAHAM ISAACKS, ANDREW W. WALKER, JOHN WISEMAN, WILLIAM C. ABELS, WILLIAM EDMISTON, ABRAHAM SUMMERS, JOHN PORTER, JAMES MARTIN, ROBERT DICKSON, and DAVID COWEN were classed in the fourth class and are to hold the October Term 1822 of said court.

TUESDAY JANUARY 22, 1822

Justices present were JAMES HOLEMAN, JOHN ENOCKS and JONATHAN FLOYD, Esquires.

The Sheriff made return that he had summoned the following venire to serve as Grand Jurors and Petit Jurors to this term, to wit, ISHAM PARR, WILLIAM BOON, WILLIAM MARTIN, WILLIAM MOORE, ISAAC BROYLES, WILLIAM FORD, JOEL DODSON, TRYON GIBSON, DAVID McCLAMROCK, MARTIN PRICE, JOHN ADKINS, ELIJAH DILLENDER, WILLIAM C. KENNEDY, JOSEPH SHAW, HOWELL JOHNSON, STERLING BRYANT, JAMES MARTIN, JOHN WILSON, JR., JOSEPH WHITAKER, JAMES GRANT,

BRITON PHELPS, WILLIAM HODGES, ALEXANDER McCORKLE, KINCHEN HALCOM, WILLIAM BONNER, and JOEL BRUCE of whom were elected as Grand Jurors, to wit, WILLIAM C. KENNEDY, foreman, JOEL BRUCE, JOEL DODSON, DAVID McCLAMROCK, JOSEPH SHAW, WILLIAM FORD, STERLING BRYANT, WILLIAM HODGES, JAMES GRANT, JOSEPH WHITAKER, JOHN ADKINS, HOWELL JOHNSON, and ELIJAH DILLENDER.

BENJAMIN GIBSON sworn to wait on the Grant Jury this term.

TRYON GIBSON released from serving as a juror this term.

GEORGE CONWAY appointed a Constable, gave bond with ELISHA BAGLEY and ANTHONY HOGAN his securities.

A Deed of Trust from JAMES COALTER and Co. to GEORGE ST. JOHN BASKINS for sundry goods, wares and merchandise, proven by JAMES RALSTON and JAMES MARTIN and ordered to be certified.

Proclamation being made for the election of Coroner whereupon came ELIJAH M. RINGO and declared himself as a candidate and on counting the votes he was declared duly elected Coroner for Lincoln County for two years and gave bond and security.

Proclamation being made for the election of Sheriff whereupon came JOHN GREER and FRANCIS PORTERFIELD and declared themselves candidates and on counting the votes FRANCIS PORTERFIELD was declared to be duly elected Sheriff for Lincoln County for two years and gave bond and security.

Proclamation being made for the election of County Trustee whereupon came EBENEZER McEWEN and JOHN RHEA and declared themselves as candidates and on counting the votes EBENEZER McEWEN was declared to be duly elected for two years and gave bond and security.

THOMAS H. FLETCHER, Esquire, produced a license and was sworn as a practising attorney in this court.

DAVID P. MUNROE, Esquire, resigned his appointment as a Justice of the Peace for Lincoln County.

The due execution of an Indenture of bargain and Sale from JOHN WHITAKER to JAMES WEST for 97½ acres of land and ordered to be certified.

The due execution of an Indenture of Bargain and Sale from WILLIS L. CALVERT to WILLIAM TOWNSEND for 67 acres of land and ordered to be certified.

MOSES PARK vs WILLIAM & WILSON DAVIS - The plaintiff says he intends to dismiss this suit and assumes the payment of all costs. Suit to be dismissed and plaintiff to pay the costs.

WEDNESDAY JANUARY 23, 1822

Justices present were JOEL PINSON, JAMES WILSON and ISAAC CONGO (CONGER), Esquires.

BRITON PHELPS is released from serving as a juror.

BERWELL HORTON vs JOSHUA DODSON - This cause is continued as an affidavit of the plaintiff and a Commission is awarded him to take the deposition of JOHN SHORT, JOHN GIBSON, JOHN HORTON, THOMAS HORTON, and PATRICK McDAVID in Madison County, Alabama, to be read as evidence on the trial of taking the same.

The due execution of an Indenture of Bargain and Sale from JOHN MOORE to EDWARD ICUM (ISOM) for 40 acres of land and ordered to be certified.

The due execution of an Indenture of Bargain and Sale from WILLIAM MOORE to ROBERT TEDFORD for 30 acres of land, proven by ROBERT H. McEWEN and SAMUEL E. GILLILAND and ordered to be certifed.

SAMUEL B. MARSHALL & E. CHILDRESS, admr &c vs JOHN PARK - The plaintiffs by their attorney says they intend no further to prosecute their suit and the defendant assumes the payment of all costs. Suit to be dismissed and the plaintiffs recover against the defendant their costs.

The due execution of a Bill of Sale from RICHARD R. ROYALL to BENJAMIN CLEMENTS for a negro boy named HENRY, proven by HARDY CLEMENTS and ENOCK K. WEATHERS and ordered to be certified.

SAMUEL CRAWFORD vs JAMES COALTER - This day came the parties by their attorneys and a jury of men, to wit, WILLIAM MOORE, ISHAM PARR, ISAAC BROYLES, ALEXANDER McCORKLE, JAMES MARTIN, ISAAC HOLEMAN, CORNELIUS WEBB, MARTIN PUGH, JOHN ALLBRIGHT, WILLIAM MUNROE, WILLIAM PARKS, and JAMES MOOR being elected and sworn and said that the defendant did assume upon himself in manner and form as the plaintiff is declaring against hath alleged and they assess the plaintiff's damages of $208.49. Plaintiff recover against the defendant his costs.

JAMES BRADLEY, admr vs ASA CROSTHWAIT - The plaintiff by his attorney and a jury of men, to wit, WILLIAM MOORE, ISHAM PARR, ISAAC BROYLES, ALEXANDER McCORKLE, JAMES MARTIN, WILLIAM BOON, JOHN WILSON, JOHN DAVIS, ISAAC BRIDGEWATERS, OBADIAH PINSON, PETER VAUGHN and NATHAN G. PINSON being elected and sworn and said that the damages were $95.97½. Plaintiff to recover against the defendant his costs.

MARY INGLE vs WILLIAM HUSBANDS - The plaintiff by her attorney says she wishes no further to prosecute this suit and the defendant assumes the payment of all costs. Suit to be dismissed and the plaintiff recover against the defendant her costs.

A Commission at the last term of the court to settle with EATON GRISHAM execution of the Last Will and Testament of WILLIAM B. GRISHAM, deceased, made return to court and ordered to be certified.

On petition of EATON GRISHAM it is ordered by the court that he be allowed and to receive from the estate of WILLIAM B. GRISHAM, deceased, for $100.00 for his services as executor of the Last Will and testament of WILLIAM B. GRISHAM, deceased.

WILLIAM GIVENS, Esquires, resignes his appointment as a Justice of the Peace for Lincoln County.

JOHN CURY vs JOHN COOK - On motion by the plaintiff by his attorney that he be non-suited and the defendant recover against the plaintiff his costs.

THURSDAY JANUARY 24, 1822

Justices present were WILLIAM DICKSON, JAMES WILSON and CHARLES BOYLES, Esquires.

The due execution of an Indenture and Bargain and Sale from JOHN GREER, Sheriff &c, to WILLIAM KELLY for 313½ acres of land and ordered to be certified.

The due execution of an Indenture of Bargain and Sale from WILLIAM KELLY to WILLIAM BONNER for 313½ acres of land and ordered to be certified.

SPENCER A. PUGH vs ROBERT BRADON & MOSES HARDEN - The plaintiff says he intends no further to prosecute this suit and assumes the payment of all costs. Suit to be dismissed and the defendants recover against the plaintiff their costs.

WILLIAM WILLIAMS, assignee &c vs SOLOMON GULLETT - Debt - This day came the parties by their attorneys and a jury of men, to wit, WILLIAM MOORE, ISHAM PARR, ISAAC BROYLES, ALEXANDER McCORKLE, JAMES MARTIN, JOHN WILSON, THOMAS WITT, SPENCER A. PUGH, WILLIAM HOLEMAN, SAMUEL H. SMITH, DAVID FRANKLIN, and THOMAS TEDFORD being elected and sworn and said that the defendant has not paid the debt of $161.05 and damages of $9.50. Plaintiff to recover against the defendant his costs.

The due execution of an Indenture of Bargain and Sale from GIDEON PILLOW to ALEXANDER SMITH for 357 acres of land and ordered to be certified.

It is ordered by the court that CHARLES BOYLES and WILLIAM NEELD be allowed $20.00 each for settling with the Sheriff and County Trustee for the years 1820-1821. Also that CHARLES BOYLES be allowed $1.37½ for furnishing a book that contains said settlement and that the County Trustee pay this order immediately and that the receipt for the same shall be sufficient voucher for him in his settlement.

WILLIAM DICKSON resigned his appointment as a Trustee of Fayetteville Academy.

JOHN MAZE vs CORNELIUS SCALES - Debt - This day came the parties by their attorneys and a jury of men, to wit, WILLIAM MOORE, ISHAM PARR, ISAAC BROYLES, ALEXANDER McCORKLE, JAMES MARTIN, JOHN WILSON, THOMAS WITT, SPENCER A. PUGH, WILLIAM HOLEMAN, SAMIEL H. SMITH, DAVID FRANKLIN, and THOMAS TEDFORD being elected and sworn and said that the defendant has not paid all the debt of $500.00 but owed a balance of $135.41 and damages of $23.39. Plaintiff to recover against the defendant his costs.

THOMAS SHORT vs ROBERT BRADON - Debt - This day came the parties by their attorneys and a jury of 'men, to wit, (same as above jurors) being elected and sworn and said that the defendant has not paid the debt of $206.40 and damages of $10.66. Plaintiff to recover against the defendant his costs.

THOMAS JOINER vs BRICE M. GARNER - (same as above) and said that the defendant did assume upon himself the charges and damages of $525.00. Plaintiff to recover against the defendant his costs.

GEORGE & JAMES BAILY vs JAMES COALTER - (same as above) said that the defendant has not paid the debt of $883.74 and damages of $167.77. Plaintiff to recover against the defendant his costs.

RICHARD ASHURST vs MICHAEL OWEN - (same as above) said that the defendant has not paid the debt of $298.73 and damages of $8.96. Plaintiff to recover against the defendant his costs.

EICHELBERGER & CLINE vs RICHARD C. PREWITT - (same as above) said that the defendant has not paid the debt of $111.80 and damages of $16.21. Plaintiff to recover against the defendant his costs.

A. & J. CONWELL vs STERLING C. McLEMORE - (same as above) the jury was permitted to disperse until tomorrow.

FRIDAY JANUARY 25, 1822

Justices present were WILLIAM DICKSON, ISAAC CONGO (CONGER) and ROBERT DICKSON.

The due execution of an Indenture of Bargain and Sale from JOHN GREER, Sheriff, to CHARLES McKINNEY for 112 acres of land and ordered to be certified.

The due execution of an Indenture of Bargain and Sale from JOHN FARRAR to RICHARD MITCHELL for 400 acres of land in Madison County, Kentucky, proven by JAMES WILSON and WILLIAM WILSON and ordered to be certified.

The Major and Alderman of the town of Fayetteville vs S.A. PUGH & JOHN P. McCONNELL - Motion - Motion against the defendants for judgment against them for the penalty of their bond with the condition for the faithful discharge of the duties of the Office of Town Constable on the part of SPENCER A. PUGH, Town Constable.

A Bill of Sale from JEREMIAH HAISLIP to WESLY SANDERS and ordered to be certified.

NOTE: Part of page missing.

The Grand Jury returned into court and brought with them a Bill of Indictment, the State against PLEASANT RHEA, PATTON ANDERSON, WILLIAM MASON, DAVIDSON McWILLIS and JOHN MORGAN for an affray, not a true bill against WILLIAM MASON and PLEASANT RHEA, a true bill against all others charged and returned to consider for further presentments.

The due execution of a Play and Certificate of Survey from JOSEPH HENDERSON to WESLEY ALLSBROOK for 5 acres of land and ordered to be certified.

The due execution of the Transfer of a Plat and Certificate of Survey from JOSEPH HENDERSON to WESLEY ALLSBROOK for 5 acres of land and ordered to be certified.

The due execution of the Transfer of a Plat and Certificate of Survey from JOSEPH GREER to JOHN GREER for 18 acres of land and ordered to be certified.

The due execution of an Indenture of Bargain and Sale from THOMAS ROUNTREE to JAMES P. BAXTER for one town lot in the town of Lynchburg, proven by THOMAS H. SHAW and JOHN GUTHERIE and ordered to be certified.

An inventory pf the property of the estate of ARTHUR BROOKS, deceased, was returned to court by his admr and ordered to be certified.

NOTE: Some items missing.

JOSEPH WHITAKER vs VANCE & JOHN GREER - This day came the parties by their attorneys and a jury of men, to wit, WILLIAM MOORE, ISHAM PARR, ISAAC BROYLES, ALEXANDER McCORKLE, JAMES MARTIN, JOHN WILSON, THOMAS WITT, SPENCER A. PUGH, WILLIAM HOLEMAN, SAMUEL H. SMITH, DAVID FRANKLIN and THOMAS TEDFORD being elected and sworn and said that the defendant has not paid all of the debt and a balance of $376.13 and damages of $18.33. Plaintiff to recover against the defendant his costs.

WILLIAM W. TAYLOR vs THOMAS GAITHER - (same as above) said that the defendant has not paid the debt of $227.00 and damages of $14.18. Plaintiff to recover against the defendant his costs.

SATURDAY JANUARY 26, 1822

Justices present were ROBERT DICKSON, CLIFORD GRAY and WILLIAM SMITH, Esquires.

A. & J. CONWELL vs STERLING C. McLEMORE - The jury elected came into court and said that they cannot agree upon their verdict and by consent of the parties and permission of the court, WILLIAM MOORE, one of the jurors, was withdrawn and the rest are discharged from rendering a verdict in this cause and is to be continued until next term of court.

SAMUEL CRAWFORD vs JAMES COALTER - Motion for new trial - This day came the parties by their attorneys and upon argument of the defendant motion to show cause why a new trial should be granted. Court ordered that the defendant have a new trial. A Commission is also awarded the defendant to take the deposition of WILLIAM ESKRIDGE of Stantown in Virginia by giving the plaintiff thirty days notice of time and place of taking the same.

JOEL DODSON vs BERWELL HORTON & RICHARD FLYNT - Debt - This day came the parties by their attorneys and a jury of men, to wit, WILLIAM MOORE, ISHAM PARR, ISAAC BROYLES, ALEXANDER McCORKLE, JAMES MARTIN, JOHN WILSON, THOMAS WITT, SPENCER A. PUGH, WILLIAM HOLEMAN, SAMUEL H. SMITH and THOMAS TEDFORD being elected and sworn and said that the defendant has not paid the debt of $150.00 and damages of $6.00. Plaintiff to recover against the defendant his costs.

R.H McEWEN vs PETER MOYERS - Debt - (same as above) said that the defendant has (not) paid the debt of $183.51 and damages of $24.86. Plaintiff to recover against defendant his costs.

JOHN WILSON vs THOMAS KERCHEVAL & WILLIAM E. KENNEDY - Debt - (same as above) said that the defendant has not paid the debt of $228.34 and damages of $7.22½. Plaintiff to recover against the defendant his costs.

WILLIAM C. KENNEDY vs ANDREW E. BEATY - Debt - (same as above) said that the defendant has not paid the debt of $187.34¼ and damages of $5.61. Plaintiff to recover against the defendant his costs.

SAMUEL H. SMITH vs ANDREW HANNAH - The plaintiff by hs attorney says he intends no further to prosecute this suit and assumes the payment of all costs. Suit to be dismissed and the defendant recover his costs.

ELIJAH McLAUGHLIN vs ELI TOWNZEND - The plaintiff says he intends no further to prosecute this suit and assumes the payment of all costs. Suit to be dismissed and the defendant recover his costs.

MONDAY JANUARY 28, 1822

EASTHER MONTGOMERY appeared in court and was appointed admrx of the estate of WILLIAM MONTGOMERY, deceased, gave bond of $1000.00 with HENRY KELSO and FRANCIS PATTON her securities.

It is ordered by the court that SHERWOOD HUNTER be appointed overseer of the road in the room of JAMES HIGGINS resigned and call on the usual hands.

ELISHA THOMASON, JAMES LINGO and WILLIAM WALLACE are appointed Commissioners to lay off one years support for the widow of WILLIAM MONTGOMERY, deceased, and make return to next court.

The Commissioners appointed at the last term of this court to settle with the admrs on the estate of ROBERT C. EDMISTON, deceased, made return of the settlement and ordered to be certified.·

REUBEN H. BOON was appointed a Constable, took oath and gave bond with DANIEL BOON and WILLIAM HUSBANDS his securities.

WILLIAM HUSBANDS was appointed a Constable who took oath and gave bond with THOMAS H. SHAW and REUBEN H. BOON his securities.

It is ordered by the court that HENRY WARREN, WILLIS WARREN, STEPHEN BEAVERS, TUNSTALL GREGORY and JESSE DANIEL be a Jury of View to lay off and mark out a road to cross Elk River at the mouth of Mulberry Creek and to intersect the public road crossing above the mouth of Mulberry on both sides in the nearest and best way possible and make return to next court.

JAMES HOLEMAN, Esquire, resignes his appointment as a Justice of the Peace for Lincoln County.

It is ordered by the court that the clerk make settlement with the County Trustee and make return to next court and that his claim against the county shall be set off against the claim that the county has against him.

A Deed of Conveyance from PARK GIBSON to WILLIAM HODGES for 34 acres of land and ordered to be certified.

An inventory of the estate of WILLIAM MONTGOMERY, deceased, was returned to court by his admr and ordered to be certified.

BENJAMIN BOON, JOHN MARSH, WILLIAM GROCE, WILLIAM BOON and THOMAS MARSH is appointed a Jury of View to turn the road that runs through SAMUEL ROE's land and make return to next court.

It is ordered by the court that JOSEPH PENN, MICHAEL BEAVERS, WILLIAM CUNNINGHAM, SAMUEL BUCHANAN, JOSEPH PIGG, THOMAS PIGG, HOWELL HARRIS and hands, JAMES BROADWAY, HARRIS MOULDEN, LEMUEL BROADWAY, JAMES MORTON, JOHN BRACKENRIDGE, JOHN PAUL and THOMAS MORTON work that part of the road that ALEXANDER MORTON is overseer of.

The Jury of View appointed to assess the damages that JOHN BUCHANAN may have sustained in consequence of a new road lately laid off to runwest of a large hill between BUCHANAN's and STEPHEN CLAYTON's or to turn said road to the most convinent plan, made return to this court and do say that the said BUCHANAN has sustained no damages inconsequence of the road running west of said hill nor do they assess him any and said that the road run west of CLAYTON's spring and stables. The overseer appointed to keep in repair and proceed to open the same and THOMAS GAITHER and SAMUEL BUCHANAN, Esquires, shall call on the usual hands.

The amount of sale of the property of WILLIAM BELL, deceased, was returned to court by his admrs and ordered to be certified.

MILES MURRY is appointed by the court overseer of the road in the room of JAMES D. COLE resigned and call on the usual hands.

It is ordered by the court that the admrs on the estate of ROBERT C. EDMISTON, deceased, be allowed 5% on the amount of sale of the said deceased estate.

It is ordered by the court that the road leading from Lynchburg by SAMUEL HART's to intersect the road near FREDERICK WAGGONER be discontinued.

The due execution of an Indenture of Bargain and Sale from SPENCER A. PUGH to WILLIAM E. KENNEDY for one town lot No. 24 in Fayettevile, proven by GEORGE ST. JOHN BASKINS and E.M. RINGO and ordered to be certified.

THOMAS H. SHAW was appointed admr on the estate of WILLIAM BROWN, deceased, who gave bond of $2000.00 with JAMES CURRY and WILLIAM PARKS securities.

JOHN ENOCKS, JONATHAN FLOYD and ANDREW W. WALKER, Esquires, are appointed Commissioners to lay off one years support for the widow of WILLIAM BROWN, deceased, and make return to next court.

It is ordered by the court that the prison bounds for Lincoln County be extended to the limits of the town of Fayetteville.

It is ordered by the court that SAMUEL HALL be overseer of the road from this place to Dobbins Mill, from Dobbins Branch to the top of the Richland Ridge and that JOHN DOBBINS be overseer of the remainder of his former bounds and that JOHN PORTER and WILLIAM BEAVERS, Esquires, apportion and divide the hands between said overseer and make return to next court.

THOMAS GAITHER and SAMUEL BUCHANAN, Esquires, are appointed to lay off the hands to work on that part of the Nashville Road that WILSON FROST is overseer of.

It is ordered by the court that the county tax for the year 1822 be as high as the law will allow.

It is ordered by the court that the clerk be allowed $50.00 for his services for the year 1821, also $25.00 for making out the tax list for said year and that the County Trustee pay the sum out of amy county monies in his hands not otherwise appropriated.

It is ordered that JOHN GREER be allowed $50.00 for his services for the year 1821 and that the County Trustee pay the same.

It is ordered that WILLIAM B. MARTIN, the Attorney General, be allowed $50.00 for his services for the year 1821 and that the County Trustee pay the same.

It is ordered that MATHEW PRICE, THOMAS BLYTH, EDWARD EAVANS, JOSHUA SMITH, SAMUEL CRAWFORD, DAVID P. MUNROE, ANDREW KING, WILLIAM JENNINGS, WILLIAM GRIFFIS, THOMAS H. SHAW, JACOB SILVERTOOTH, HENRY WARREN, JAMES COWLY, JAMES HIGGINS, ADLAI SHARP, JAMES LINGO, JOSIAH SMITH, WILLIAM DYE, SAMUEL M. CLAY, WALTER HARKINS, ANDREW HANNAH, ANTHONY B. CLENDENING, JAMES COALTER, JOHN RHEA, JOHN BUCHANAN and WILLIAM NORRIS be summoned as Jurors to the next Court of Pleas and Quarter Sessions for Lincoln County on 3rd Monday in April next.

TUESDAY JANUARY 29, 1822

Justices present were ISAAC CONGO (CONGER), JAMES WILSON and WILLIAM DICKSON, Esquires.

PHAIN & CRAWFORD vs BRICE M. GARNER - This day came the parties by their attorneys and a jury of men, to wit, WILLIAM FORD, JOSEPH SHAW, DAVID McCLAMROCK, JOEL BRUCE, STERLING A. BRYANT, WILLIAM HODGES, JOSEPH WHITAKER, JAMES GRANT, HOWELL JOHNSON, ELIJAH DILLENDER, WILLIAM MOORE, and ISAAC BROYLES being elected and sworn and said that the writing obligatory was not the defendant act and deed as the plaintiffs declaring against him hath alledged. The defendant to recover against the plaintiffs his costs. Plaintiff prayed for an appeal was granted same.

ZACHARIAH ARNOLD vs JOHN D. SPAIN - (same as above) said that the defendant is indebted to the plaintiff for $27.00. Plaintiff to recover against the defendant and JESSE CRAWSLEY and JOHN COOK his securities.

JOHN ALLBRIGHT vs JAMES FULGHAM - Cause is continued on affidavit of the plaintiff and a Commission is awarded him to take the deposition of ARCHABALD McKEE of Laurence County, Alabama, by giving the adverse party ten days notice also to take the deposition of FREDERICK BROWHER of Roan County, North Carolina by giving the defendant thirty days notice and if taken in Morgan County, Alabama, ten days notice of time and place of taking the same.

The due execution of an Indenture of Bargain and Sale from PETER WRIGHT to SAMUEL BUCHANAN for (blank) acres of land, proven by ROBERT BUCHANAN and ELIJAH DAVIS and ordered to be certified.

131

ANDREW A. KINCANNON appeared in court and was appointed Deputy Sheriff for Lincoln County and took oath.

JOSIAH HACKET vs JAMES WILSON - Appeal - This day came the parties by their attorneys and a jury of men, to wit, ISHAM PARR, ALEXANDER McCORKLE, WILLIAM BOON, JAMES MARTIN, JOHN WILSON, THOMAS WITT, SOLOMON GULLETT, JOHN WATKINS, JAMES MOORE, WILLIAM C. KENNEDY, HENRY KYMES, and GEORGE CUNNINGHAM being elected and sworn and said that the defendant is indebted to the plaintiff 37½ cents. Plaintiff to recover his costs. Defendant prays for an appeal and is granted same.

JACOB and JOHN WAGGONER vs RICHARD HALL - Debt - (same as above) said that the defendant has not paid the debt of $164.25 and damages of $19.71. Plaintiff to recover his costs.

The Commissioners appointed at the last term to divide the lands of ANDREW EDMISTON, deceased, made return to court and ordered to be certified.

The Commissioners appointed at the last term of court to divide the lands of JOHN EDMISTON, deceased, made return and ordered to be certified.

WEDNESDAY JANUARY 30, 1822

Justices present were JAMES WILSON, AMBROSE BARKER and ELISHA BAGLEY, Esquires.

WILSON F. DILLON vs DAVID REED - It is ordered by the court that the plaintiff give better security or his suit will be dismissed.

THOMAS HILL vs CHARLES GOODE - The defendant confessed that he owes the plaintiff $280.19 and damages of $43.40. Plaintiff to recover his costs.

PERRY FLYNT vs A. YEAGER & M. PUGH - Plaintiff says he intends no further to prosecute this suit and assumes the payment of all costs. Suit to be dismissed and the defendant recover his costs.

JAMES WYATT vs SAMUEL H. SMITH - This day came the parties by their attorneys and a jury of men, to wit, ALEXANDER McCORKLE, ISAAC BROYLES, JOHN WILSON, JAMES MARTIN, WILLIAM C. KENNEDY, JOEL BRUCE, WILLIAM HODGES, JAMES GRANT, WILLIAM FORD, ELIJAH DILLENDER, JOSEPH SHAW, and VANCE GREER being elected and sworn and said that the defendant is indebted for $20.85. Plaintiff to recover his costs.

ALEXANDER DOBBINS vs GEORGE R. MOSS - Plaintiff by his attorney says he intends no further to prosecute this suit and assumes the payment of all costs. Suit to be dismissed and defendant to recover his costs.

WILLIAM RICE VS THOMAS TEDFORD - Appeal - This day came the parties by their attorneys and a jury of men, to wit, WILLIAM BOON, ISHAM PARR, DAVID McCLAMROCK, STERLING A. BRYANT, HOWELL JOHNSON, JOHN DONELSON, THOMAS WILLIAMS, GABRIEL SEAHORN, ALEXANDER McLIN, REUBIN WOODWARD, ELI TAYLOR, and JAMES McFERRAN being elected and sworn and said that the defendant is indebted for $40.00 and damages of $20.12½. Plaintiff to recover his costs.

JOHN LANDIS, admr vs ROBERT FLETCHER - This cause is continued until next term of court. The plaintiff is to take the deposition of E. TITUS of Huntsville, to be read as evidence and the defendant be given ten days notice of time and place of taking the same.

HENRY & WILLIS WARREN vs ELI ETHERIDGE - Motion - The Sheriff is to expose to sale 24 acres of land in three different tracts, all lying on Stephens Creek, a north branch of Elk River, property of ELI ETHERIDGE, to satisfy a judgment that HENRY & WILLIS WARREN, executors of JOHN WARREN, deceased, recovered against him for $91.62½ and all legal costs before CHARLES BOYLES, Esquire, on 14 January 1822.

ALEXANDER & KEYS MEEK vs HUGH RANDOLPH - This day came the parties by their attorneys and a jury of men, to wit, WILLIAM MOORE, ALEXANDER McCORKLE, ISAAC BROYLES, JAMES MARTIN, WILLIAM C. KENNEDY, JOEL BRUCE, WILLIAM HODGES, JAMES GRANT, WILLIAM FORD, ELIJAH DILLENDER, JOSEPH SHAW, and JOHN WILSON being elected and sworn and said that the jury was permitted to disperse

132

until tomorrow.

THURSDAY JANUARY 31, 1822

Justices present were JAMES WILSON, AMBROSE BARKER, ROBERT DICKSON and ELISHA BAGLEY, Esquires.

The due execution of an Indenture of Bargain and Sale from JOHN CLIFTON to AMBROSE BARKER for a tract of land and ordered to be certified.

An inventory of the property of WILLIAM BROWN, deceased, was returned to court by his admr and ordered to be certified.

ALEXANDER & KEYS MEEK vs HUGH RANDOLPH - This suit is returned to court and jury finds in favor of the plaintiff and find his damages to be $85.00. Plaintiff to recover his costs. Defendant prays for an appeal and is granted the same.

NIMROD FIELDER vs STERLING C. McLEMORE - Case - This day came the parties by their attorneys and a jury of men, to wit, ALEXANDER McCORKLE, ISAAC BROYLES, JOHN WILSON, JAMES MARTIN, ISHAM PARR, JOSEPH SHAW, WILLIAM C. KENNEDY, JOEL BRUCE, WILLIAM HODGES, JAMES GRANT, ELIJAH DILLENDER, and HOWEL JOHNSON being elected and sworn and said that the defendant is guilty and the plaintiff's damages are $51.12½. Plaintiff to recover his costs.

CHARLES H. EDMISTON vs RICHARD PRYOR - The plaintiff is to take the deposition of WILLIAM PATTON in Huntsville to be read as evidence in this trial.

The State vs PATTON ANDERSON, DAVIDSON McMILLIN and JOHN MORGAN - The defendants by their attorneys be charged and the County of Lincoln pay the costs of this indictment.

FRIDAY FEBRUARY 1, 1822

Justices present were JAMES RALSTON, WILLIAM SMITH and JAMES WILSON, Esquires.

JAMES COALTER & Co. vs NATHANIEL BLACKMORE - Appeal - This day came the parties by their attorneys and a jury of men, to wit, WILLIAM BOON, ISHAM PARR, ISAAC BROYLES, ALEXANDER McCORKLE, JAMES MARTIN, JOHN WILSON, JOEL BRUCE, DAVID McCLAMROCK, JOSEPH SHAW, WILLIAM FORD, JAMES GRANT, and HOWELL JOHNSON being elected and sworn and said that the defendant is indebted to the plaintiff for $35.00 and damages of 35 cents. Plaintiff to recover against the defendant and VANCE GREER his security.

ARTHUR ALBERTSON vs NATHANIEL B. BUCKINGHAM - Appeal - (same as above) The plaintiff's damages are $45.86¼. Plaintiff to recover his costs.

PETER SHELTON vs BENJAMIN WILSON & ELIAS SCOTT - Appeal (same as above) and said that the defendant is indebted to the plaintiff for $40.00 and damages of 40 cents. Plaintiff to recover his costs and JONATHAN COUCH their security.

RICHARD PRYOR vs FRANCIS HAYNES - The court said that the plaintiff be non-suited and the defendant go hence with day and recover against the plaintiff his costs.

ALLEN MOBLY vs CORNELIUS WEBB - The plaintiff is to give security for the prosecution of the above cause at next term or cause be dismissed. The defendant is to take the deposition of MORDICAI MOBLEY in Giles County to be read as evidence in above cause by giving ten days notice of time and place of taking same.

ALLEN MOBLEY vs CORNELIUS WEBB - The plaintiff to give security for the prosecution of the above cause or cause will be dismissed.

SAMUEL ALLEN vs CARTER WALKER - This cause is continued on affidavit of the defendant and returned to next court.

BUCHANAN & PORTERFIELD vs SAMUEL H. SMITH - Debt - The plaintiff by his attorney came into court and the defendant being called to come and plead to this suit failed to do so but made default. Plaintiff to recover $131.00 and damages of $7.00 his costs.

ROBERT H. McEWEN & Co, vs SPENCER A. PUGH - Debt - The plaintiff by his attorney came into court and the defendant being called to defend this suit failed to do so but made default. Plaintiff to recover against the defendant $135.15 and damages of 67½ cents, his costs.

JAMES WYATT vs JACOB WRIGHT - Attachment - (same as above). Plaintiff to recover against the defendant in this said Plea of Transpass but because it is not known to the court what the amount of damages. A Writ of Inquiry be awarded the plaintiff at next term of court.

JAMES WYATT vs J. & D. WRIGHT - Case - The plaintiff says he intends no further to prosecute this suit and assumes the payment of all costs. Suit to be dismissed and the defendant recover against the plaintiff their costs.

ELIJAH MAYFIELD vs McWHERTER & WEBB - On order by the court that this suit be dismissed and the defendant recover against the plaintiff his costs.

J. & A. WHITENBURGH vs HUGHSTON & WATKINS - This cause be sustained and the plaintiff recover against the defendants $942.16 balance of the debt and $13.61 damages. Defendant prays for an appeal to next court.

WILLIAM SIMMONS vs THOMAS W. HAMILTON - Motion - It appearing to the court that executions were put into the hands of THOMAS W. HAMILTON as a Constable about the __ day of ____ 1821, issued by CLIFFORD GRAY, Esquire, in favor of WILLIAM SIMMONS for $69.97 and that THOMAS W. HAMILTON failed to return said executions within the time required by law and also that THOMAS W. HAMILTON, JOHN JONES and JOHN CLIFTON his securities had received written notice of the motion. Plaintiff to recover against said HAMILTON his costs.

RICHARD C. PREWITT vs THOMAS W. HAMILTON - Motion - (same as before) WILLIAM PREWITT for $98.00 (same as above)

REBECCAH TOMLINSON vs ALEXANDER McCORKLE - Petition - It appearing to the court that ten days notice had been served on the admr of HUGH TOMLINSON, deceased, and his heirs and the guardian of those who are minors and her statements in the petition being admitted to be true. Petition to be granted. The Sheriff is to proceed to lay off to REBECCAH her dower out of the estate of HUGH TOMLINSON, deceased, both real and personal and make return to next court.

JOEL FIELDER by his next friend NIMROD FIELDER vs STERLING C. McLEMORE - By consent of both parties that both of them is granted to take the deposition of any witnesses they may want by giving ten days notice and if said witnesses are not more than fifty miles from Fayetteville and twenty days notice for all over fifty miles and notice served on plaintiff or NIMROD FIELDER should be good and notice served on defendant or ISAAC HOLEMAN shall be good and sufficient notice of place of taking the same.

B. & C. HOWELL - Petition for Dower - The petition of BENNETT B. HOWELL and CHARLOTTE his wife being read and heard and it appearing to the court that ten days notice had been served on the admr of THOMAS JOYCE, deceased, and his heirs and the guardian of those who are minors, being admitted to be true. Petition granted and it is ordered that the Sheriff proceed to lay off to BENNETT B. and CHARLOTTE his wife out of the estate of THOMAS JOYCE, deceased, both real and personal and make return to next court.

ALEXANDER & BENJAMIN BOTELER vs HENRY ALLEN - Petition - On petition of A. & B. BOTELER by their attorney, it is ordered that HENRY ALLEN, admr of ARCHABALD ALLEN, deceased, appear here in court in April next and give good security.

The State vs WARNER CLIFTON - On petition of JOHN JONES, it is ordered that Lincoln County pay the cost in the above cause instead of JOHN JONES, the prosecutor.

MONDAY APRIL 15, 1822

It is ordered that WILLIAM SOLOMON be overseer of that part of the road that WILLIAM LEDFORD was overseer of and call on the usual hands.

It is ordered by the court that WESLEY ALLBROOK be released from the payment of the appraised value of a stray horse posted by him, appraised to $20.00 and proven.

It is ordered that ROBERT ALLSUP be overseer of the road in the room of

STEPHEN HIGHTOWER resigned and call on the usual hands.

It is ordered that FRANCIS PATTON, JR. be overseer of the road in the room of JAMES CARTER resigned and call on the usual hands.

It is ordered that BENJAMIN ARRINGTON be overseer of the road in the room of JOHN GEORGE resigned and call on the usual hands.

It is ordered that THOMAS J. HAYS be overseer of the road in the room of THOMAS SIMMONS resigned and call on the usual hands.

It is ordered that JOHN DOWTHIT be overseer of the road leading from the Franklin County line near JOHN CURRY'S on by JOHN ENOCKS and JOHN GAVIN's to the Shelbyville Road near WILLIAM BATEMAN's and call on the usuual hands.

It is ordered that WILLIAM LANGSTON be overseer of the road leading up East Mulberry from Gibson's Old Shop to the county line and call on the usual hands.

It is ordered that JAMES CUNNINGHAM be released from the payment of the appraised value of a stray mare posted by him and valued at $40.00 and was proven from him.

It is ordered that JOHN DAVIS be overseer of a road in the room of ROBERT FLETCHER resigned and call on the usual hands.

It is ordered that THOMAS CHAPMAN be overseer of the road in the room of DEMPSEY ALLEN resigned and call on the usual hands.

It is ordered that HENRY TALLEY be overseer of the road in the room of JAMES BROOKS resigned and call on the usual hands.

WILLIAM BEAVERS and JOHN PORTER, Esquires, appointed to designate the hands to work on the Pulaski Road between JONATHAN ANDERSON and JAMES BLAIR and make return to next court.

It is ordered that WILLIAM FORD be overseer of the road from CAPTAIN DORSEY's by said FORDS to the Bedford COunty line and call on the usual hands.

It is ordered that JAMES WILSON be overseer of that part of the road leading from Cunningham Mill to Elkton which he was formerly overseer of and call on the usual hands.

MORGAN CLAYTON is appointed overseer of the road leading from Cunningham Mill and intersecting the road leading to Elkton on that part which he was formerly overseer of and call on the usual hands.

JOHN STILES, SR., ISHAM BURNETT, JOHN COPLIN (COPELAND), JOHN LYNCH, BENJAMIN WALKER, SAMUEL YOUNG and JOHN LANGSTON be a Jury of View to mark and lay off a road beginning at the Shelbyville Road at or near the south east corner of ZACHARIAH ARNOLD's plantation whereon MOSES ARNOLD now lives on by JOHN STILES'Ford on Elk River so as to leave the field whereon JOHN STILES' dwelling house is entirely to the left hand on up Robins Creek so as to intersect the Pharis Creek road near BUCK SMITH and make return to next court.

ROBERT BEARD appeared in court and made oath that he killed one wolf within Lincoln County over four months old.

A Bill of Sale from BRICE M. GARNER to THOMAS ALLSUP and ordered to be certified.

On petition, it is ordered that JOHN CLIFTON be allowed $1.50 per day for nine days for apprehending and bringing to justice ERASMUS CHAPMAN and that the County Trustee of Lincoln County pay the same.

On petition, JAMES SMITH is allowed $1.50 per day for following of ERASMUS CHAPMAN.

ANDREW W. WALKER resigns his appointment as Justice of the Peace for Lincoln County.

JAMES GIBSON, JOSEPH PORTER and COLLIN CAMPBELL are appointed

Commissioners to settle with SALLY LOYD, admrx of EPHRAIM LOYD, deceased, and make return to next court.

CHARLES H. EDMISTON is appointed overseer of the road in the place of ABSALUM BEARD resigned and to call on the usual hands.

ANDREW HANNAH is permitted to establish a ferry across Elk River between three or four hndred yards below what is now called Hannah Ford on Elk River.

CHARLES BOYLES, ROBERT DICKSON and PHILIP KOONCE, Esquires, appointed Commissioners to settle with Commissioners of Lincoln County and make return on Monday next.

DOAK NIX is appointed overseer of the road in the room of ROBERT TEDFORD and call on the usual hands.

THOMAS CLARK is appointed a Commissioner of the school lands in this county in the place of ROBERT M. WHITE removed.

On petition, it is ordered a separate election be held at the Gun Spring on the Winchester Road in this county.

JAMES HUNTER is appointed overseer of the road in the room of SAMUEL THOMPSON and call on the usual hands.

JAMES CURRY is appointed a Constable for this county who gave bond with JOHN ENOCHS and JONATHAN FLOYD his securities and took oath.

PRESLEY S. GEORGE appointed a Constable who gave bond with JESSE GEORGE and WILLIAM MOOR his securities and took the oath.

AMOS SMALL appointed a Constable who gave bond with JOEL DODSON and PHILIP KOONCE his securities and took oath.

Amount of Sale of the property of EZEKIEL NALL, deceased, was returned to court by his admr and ordered to be certified.

The Commissioners appointed at the last term of court to lay off one years support for the widow of THOMAS CUMMINS and made return of the allowance by them made and ordered to be certified.

The Commissioners appointed at last term to lay off one years support for the widow of ARTHUR BROOKS, deceased, and ordered to be certified.

The Commissioners appointed at last term to lay off one years support for the widow of WILLIAM BROWN, deceased, and ordered to be certified.

The Last Will and Testament of WILLIAM RUDD, deceased, was exhibited in court for probation whereupon came BENJAMIN RUDD and LEMUEL RUDD, witnesses, said they heard WILLIAM RUDD acknowledge the same to be his Last Will and testament and that at that time he was of sound mind and memory, whereupon came NATHANIEL RUDD and WILLIAM FORD, executors gave bond and security.

MOSES CHAMBERS appeared in court and was appointed guardian for SARAH J. COOK, MOSES COOK and JOHN M. COOK, infant heirs of DANIEL COOK, deceased, who gave bond and security.

JOHN ENOCKS, Esquire, appeared in court and was appointed admr on the estate of JONATHAN LUNA, deceased, who gave bond and security.

BENNETT BLACKMAN appeared in court and was appointed guardian for SARAH C. JOYCE, BENNETT A. JOYCE and JOSEPH T. JOYCE, infant heirs of THOMAS JOYCE, deceased, who gave bond and security.

The Last Will and Testament of JESSE HAYS, deceased, was exhibited in court for probate whereupon came JOSEPH GREER and JOHN H. MOOR, witnesses and made oath that they saw JESSE HAYS sign, seal and publish and declare the same to be his Last Will and Testament and that at that time was of sound mind and memory.

A Deed of Conveyance from BRICE M. GARNER to MARY GLENN for 80 acres of land and ordered to be certified.

A Deed of Conveyance from BRICE M. GARNER and JACOB SCOTT to SILAS McCLELLAND for 263 acres of land and ordered to be certified.

A Deed of Conveyance from JOSHUA GIBSON to MARTHA HAMILTON for 125 acres of land and ordered to be certified.

A Deed of Conveyance from JOHN GIBSON to PARK GIBSON for 113 acres of land and ordered to be certified.

A Deed of Conveyance from HENRY J. HAYS to THOMAS H. HAYS for 190 acres of land and ordered to be certified.

A Deed of Conveyance from BRICE M. GARNER and JACOB SCOTT to JOHN COWDEN for 263 acres of land and ordered to be certified.

A Deed of Conveyance from SAMUEL DAVIS to J.J. CARRINGTON for 100 acres of land and ordered to be certified.

A Deed of Conveyance from JEREMIAH SULLIVAN to THOMAS PARKER for 100 acres of land and ordered to be certified.

A Deed of Conveyance from GENERAL W.C. EDMISTON to COONRAD KYMES for 22 acres of land and ordered to be certified.

A Deed of Conveyance from SAMUEL E. WATSON to CHARLES H. EDMISTON for 320 acres of land, proven by WILLIAM EDMISTON, attorney in fact, and ordered to be certified.

A Deed of Conveyance from SAMUEL MIXON to JAMES BLAIR for 108 acres of land and ordered to be certified.

A Deed of Conveyance from WILLIAM P. ANDERSON to JOHN ZIVELY for 166 acres of land, proven by WILLIAM E. KENNEDY and DANIEL ZIVELY and ordered to be certified.

A Deed of Conveyance from JOHN GILLASPIE to GEORGE CRAWFORD for 14 acres of land and ordered to be certified.

A Deed of Conveyance from JOHN B. BUCHANAN to JAMES HOLBERT for 52 acres of land and ordered to be certified.

A Deed of Conveyance from MARTIN PUGH to JAMES McDAVID for 260 acres of land and ordered to be certified.

A Deed of COnveyance from JOHN WAGGONER to DANIEL WAGGONER for 177 acres of land and ordered to be certified.

A Deed of Conveyance from JOHN WAGGONER to DANIEL WAGGONER for 2½ acres of land and ordered to be certified.

TUESDAY APRIL 16, 1822

Justices present were EBENEZER McEWEN, JOHN PINKERTON and HENRY KELSO, Esquires.

SAMUEL CRAWFORD vs JAMES COALTER - The plaintiff by his attorney says he intends no further to prosecute this suit and assumes the payment of all costs. Suit to be dismissed and the defendant recover his costs.

ALLEN MOBLEY vs CORNELIUS WEBB - The plaintiff says he intends no further to prosecute his suit and the defendant appeared in court and assumes the payment of all costs. Suit to be dismissed and the plaintiff recover against the defendant his costs.

ALLEN MOBLEY vs CORNELIUS WEBB - Plaintiff says he intends no further to prosecute his suit and the defendant assumes the payment of all costs. Suit to be dismissed and the plaintiff recover his costs.

The Sheriff made return and that he had summoned the venire to serve as Petit

Jurors and Grand Jurors this term, to wit, MATHEW PRICE, THOMAS BLYTH, EDWARD EVANS, JOSHUA SMITH, SAMUEL CRAWFORD, DAVID P. MUNROE, ANDREW KING, WILLIAM JENNINGS, WILLIAM GRIFFIS, THOMAS H. SHAW, JOHN SILVERTOOTH, HENRY WARREN, JAMES COWLEY, JAMES HIGGINS, ADLAI SHARP, JAMES LINGO, JOSIAH SMITH, WILLIAM DYE, SAMUEL M. CLAY, WALTER HARKINS, ANDREW HANCOCK, ANTHONY B. CLENDENING, JAMES COALTER, JOHN RHEA, JOHN BUCHANAN and WILLIAM NORRIS who were elected to serve as Grand Jurors, to wit, ADLAI SHARP, foreman, EDWARD EVANS, HENRY WARREN, THOMAS H. SHAW, JOSHUA SMITH, JAMES COWLEY, WILLIAM GRIFFIS, ANDREW KING, MATHEW PRICE, JAMES LINGO, JOHN RHEA, JOHN BUCHANAN and JACOB SILVERTOOTH.

MOSES HALL a Constable sworn to wait on the Grand Jury this term.

WILLIAM JENNINGS, JAMES COALTER, WALTER HARKINS, ANDREW HANNAH, and WILLIAM NORRIS is released from serving as Jurors this term.

It is ordered that DAVID P. MUNROE, SAMUEL CRAWFORD and THOMAS BLYTH and JAMES HIGGINS be fined $10.00 each for not attending as Jurors.

The Grand Jury returned to court and brought a Bill of Indictment, the State against FRANCIS SMITH for an assault and battery, a true bill, and again returned to consider for further presentments.

The State vs FRANCIS SMITH - Indictment for an Assault and battery - The defendant appeared in court and being charged pleads guilty and is fined $1.00 and pay costs, whereupon came CLIFFORD GRAY as security, confessed judgment with defendant.

The Grand Jury returned to court and brought with them a Bill of Indictment, the State against GEORGE W. GREEN for an assault and battery, a true bill, and again returned to consider for further presentments.

WATKINS & WHORTON vs THOMAS L. TROTTER - A Commission is awarded the plaintiff to take the deposition of GEORGE R. WHORTON at WILLIAM E. KENNEDY's office in Fayetteville between the hours of one and four o'clock this evening to be read as evidence on the above trial and that this order shall be sufficient notice.

A. & J. CONWELL vs STERLING C. McLEMORE - This cause is continued until next term of court.

RICHARD GEORGE vs JOHN CLIFTON - The defendant confess that he owes the plaintiff $34.82¼. Plaintiff to recover his costs.

SAMUEL ALLEN vs CARTER WALKER - Debt - This day came the parties by their attorneys and a jury of men, to wit, FRANCIS WYATT, JOEL ORRICK, HAMILTON MOFFIT, SAMUEL ROSEBOROUGH, JOHN McMILLIN, JOEL DODSON, THOMAS ALLY, JESSE B. CLEMENTS, WILLIAM DYE, SAMUEL M. CLAY, ANTHONY B. CLENDENING, and REECE HOWELL being elected and sworn and said that the defendant has not paid the debt of $350.00 and damages of $72.75. Plaintiff to recover his costs.

SAMUEL H. SMITH vs JAMES WYATT - This day came the parties by their attorneys and a jury of men, to wit, THOMAS ALLY, JOEL ORRICK, HAMILTON MOFFIT, SAMUEL ROSEBOROUGH, ROBERT FLETCHER, JOHN McMILLIN, JOEL DODSON, REECE HOWELL, JESSE B. CLEMENTS, ANTHONY B. CLENDENING, SAMUEL M. CLAY, and WILLIAM DYE being elected and sworn and said that the defendant is not guilty. Defendant to recover his costs.

The Grand Jury again returned to court and brought with them a Bill of Indictment, the State against GEORGE W. HUNT for an assault and battery, a true bill, and again returned to consider for further presentments.

The Grand Jury again returned to court and brought with them a Bill of Indictment, the State against WILLIAM BEARDEN, not a true bill, and again returned to consider for further presentments.

The State vs GEORGE W. HUNT - JOHN DAVIS and JOHN CAMPBELL appeared in court and acknowledged themselves indebted to the State of Tennessee for $125.00 each to be levied of their goods and chattels &c but to be void on condition that they appear here in July next to prosecute and give evidence in behalf of the State against GEORGE W. HUNT for an assault and battery.

RICHARD C. PREWETT vs THOMAS W. HAMILTON & others - AMBROSE BARKER, a garnishee being sworn answers but .....
Question - Are you indebted to either of the defendants, THOMAS W. HAMILTON, JOHN CLIFTON or JOHN JONES and if so how much and to which of them?
Answer - I am not indebted to either of them.
Question - Do you know of any person or persons who have any effects or debts of either of the defendants to your knowledge and belief and if so who?
Answer - I know of no effects of either HAMILTON, CLIFTON or JONES in their own hands, in the hands of any person or persons, perhaps WILLIAM MOOREHEAD may owe CLIFTON something but if he does I don't know how much.
Question - Have you any effects or debts of either of the said defendants in your hands?
Answer - I have not.

NATHANIEL BLAKEMORE vs FRANCIS SMITH - The plaintiff says he wishes no further to prosecute this suit and the defendant assumes the payment of all costs. The suit to be dismissed. Plaintiff to recover his costs.

BALDWIN & IVES vs LEWIS & IVES - The plaintiff says he intends no further to prosecute this suit and assumes the payment of all costs. This suit to be dismissed and the defendant recover his costs.

JAMES COALTER & Co. vs THOMAS L. TROTTER - Debt - The defendant acknowledged that he owes the plaintiff $66.41. The plaintiff to recover his costs.

WEDNESDAY APRIL 17, 1822

Justices present were HENRY KELSO, JOHN PINKERTON and ROBERT DICKSON, Esquires.

The due execution of an Indenture of Bargain and Sale from WALTER HARKINS to ANDREW McCARTNEY for 144½ acres of land and ordered to be certified.

The State vs GEORGE W. SHAW - Assault and Battery - The defendant being charged pleads guilty and is fined $1.00 and pay cost of this indictment.

BURWELL HORTON vs JOEL DODSON - This day came the parties by their attorneys and a jury of men, to wit, JOHN ALLBRIGHT, STEPHEN TOUCHSTONE, WILLIAM McELROY, RANDOLPH MAYFIELD, RANDOLPH QUARLES, SPENCER A. PUGH, ANGUISH JOHNSON, JACOB ALLBRIGHT, JAMES MAXFIELD, ABRAHAM DEPOSITER, FRANCIS PATTON, and WILLIAM SOLOMON being elected and sworn and said that the defendant is not guilty. Defendant to recover his costs.

The due execution of a Bill of Sale from WILLIAM GRIFFIS to WILLIAM E. KENNEDY for a negro man named ALLEN and ordered to be certified.

The due execution of an Indenture of Bargain and Sale from ROBERT BRADON to JOHN BEATIE for 48 acres of land and ordered to be certified.

The due execution of an Indenture of Bargain and Sale from ROBERT BRADON to JOSHUA GIBSON for 160 acres of land and ordered to be certified.

JOHN ALLBRIGHT vs JAMES FULGHAM - This cause is continued until next term of this court on affidavit of the plaintiff by his paying the cost of this term.

The due execution of an Indenture of Bargain and Sale from JOHN GREER, Sheriff &c to JOHN P. McCONNELL for 150 acres of land, proven by ARGYLE CAMPBELL and CONSTANT SCALES and ordered to be certified.

The due execution of an Indenture of Bargain and Sale from WILLIAM P. ANDERSON to WILLIAM LINTICUM and AUSTIN COOK for 229 acres of land, proven by JAMES BRIGHT, Attorney in fact, and ordered to be certified.

RANDOLPH MAYFIELD vs RICHARD REYNOLDS - This day came the parties by their attorneys and a jury of men, to wit, WILLIAM DYE, ANTHONY B. CLENDENING, SAMUEL M. CLAY, JOEL DODSON, JOHN DAVIS, NATHAN G. PINSON, JORDAN SOLOMON, WILLIAM PARKS, JOSHUA DODSON, JOEL ORRICK, JOSHUA DALLAS, and NOTLEY HARRIS being elected and sworn and said that the defendant is guilty and the plaintiff's damages of $110.77. Plaintiff to recover his costs.

139

THURSDAY APRIL 18, 1822

Justices present were HENRY KELSO, ELI GARRETT and JOHN PINKERTON, Esquires.

The due execution of a Power of Attorney from ROBERT H. McEWEN to WILLIAM TODD was proven by RICHMOND P. DOBBINS and WILLIAM F. MASON and ordered to be certified.

JOEL R. FIELDEN by his next friend vs STERLING C. McLEMORE - This cause is continued the next term of this court on affidavit of ISAAC HOLEMAN, agent for the defendant and a commission is warded him to take the deposition of RICHARD RANKIN and ALEXANDER RANKIN of Bedford County, Tennessee, JOHN K. DUNN of Huntsville, SAMUEL WILLIAMS, JOHN SULLIVAN on the road, THOMAS McGEE and ROBERT IRWIN of Madison County, Alabama by giving the advance party ten days notice of time and place and if taken over one hundred miles twenty days notice.

NATHANIEL B. BUCKINGHAM vs THOMAS H. MAY - A commission is awarded to both parties to take the deposition of GEORGE LYONS of Huntsville to be read as evidence on the trial of this cause by giving the advance party ten days notice of time and place of taking the same.

JOHN P. McCONNELL vs JOS. HAGUE & E. McEWEN - This day came the parties by their attorneys and a jury of men, to wit, ADLAI SHARP, HENRY WARREN, THOMAS H. SHAW, JACOB SILVERTOOTH, JAMES LINGO, EDWARD EVANS, ANTHONY B. CLENDENING, SAMUEL M. CLAY, ROBERT H. McEWEN, SOLOMON GULLETT, JOSEPH McMILLIN, and MATHEW PRICE being elected and sworn and said that the defendant has not paid the debt of $200.00 and damages of $14.50. Plaintiff to recover his costs.

MOSES BUCHANAN vs JOHN MOOR & JOHN BUCHANAN - Debt - This day came the parties by their attorneys and a jury of men, to wit, (same as above jurors) and said that the defendant has not paid the debt of $252.00 and damages of $37.35. Plaintiff to recover his costs.

WILLIAM POLK vs JOHN TATUM - Debt - (same as above) and said that the defendant has not paid the debt of $162.00 and damages of $6.88. Plaintiff to recover his costs.

JOHN P. McCONNELL vs JAMES WYATT - (same as above) and said that the defendant has not paid the debt of $100.00 and damages of $7.75. Plaintiff to recover his costs.

JABE B. CAMPBELL vs HENRY ALLEN - (same as above) and said that the defendant has not paid the debt of $228.00 and damages of $15.00. Plaintiff to recover his costs.

CHARLES H. EDMISTON vs RICHARD PRYOR - (same as above) and said that the defendant did assume upon himself to pay the damages of the plaintiff of $193.50. Plaintiff to recover his costs.

JANE B. CAMPBELL vs JAMES WYATT - (same. as above) and said that the defendant has not paid the debt of $100.00 and damages of $9.18. Plaintiff to recover his costs.

WILLIAM MOFFIT vs ADLAI SHARP - Debt - This day came the parties by their attorneys and a jury of men, to wit, SAMUEL M. CLAY, WILLIAM DOAK, JOEL ORRICK, WILLIS WARREN, JAMES H. NELSON, ARCHABALD CAMPBELL, DOILY GRIFFIS, PETER KENT, JOHN REECE, ISAAC HOLEMAN, JORDAN SOLOMON and ANTHONY B. CLENDENING being elected and sworn and said that the defendant has not paid the debt of $125.18 3/4 and damages of $5.31¼. Plaintiff to recover his costs. Defendant prays for an appeal and is granted same.

THOMAS EDMISTON vs SAMUEL BUCHANAN - (same as above) and said that the defendant has not paid the debt of $151.50 and damages of $23.37½. Plaintiff to recover his costs.

BENJAMIN W. SHIRLY for use vs JAMES WYATT - This day came the parties by their attorneys and a jury of men, to wit, EDWARD EAVANS, JACOB SILVERTOOTH, JOHN BUCHANAN, JOHN RHEA, JAMES LINGO, MATHEW PRICE, ANDREW KING, WILLIAM GRIFFIS, THOMAS H. SHAW, ADLAI SHARP, HENRY WARREN and JAMES

COWLEY and being elected and sworn and said that the defendant is indebted to the plaintiff for $20.00 and damages of $1.12½. Plaintiff to recover his costs. Defendant prays for an appeal and is granted the same.

WATKINS & WHORTON vs THOMAS L. TROTTER - This cause is continued on affidavit of the defendant by his paying the cost of this term and a commission is awarded him to take the deposition of LEGRAND W. WILSON of Huntsville, Alabama, and DENNIS MURPHY of Franklin County, Tennessee to be as evidence in this cause and by giving the plaintiff's attorney ten days notice of time and place of taking the same. The plaintiffs by their attorney contends that the defendant may take the deposition of any person else he may want wheresoever he may live and wheresoever he may be found without notice or commission.

WILLIAM SHIPMAN vs JOHN GREER - Motion - Plaintiff by his attorney move the court to enter a motion against the defendant and his securities for a judgement against them which was granted.

THOMAS KERCHEVAL vs JOEL ORRICK - This cause is continued on an affidavit of the plaintiff and a commission awarded him to take the deposition of HIRAM H. HIGGINS of Limestone County, Alabama, to be read as evidence on the trial of this cause by the defendant ten days notice of time and place of taking the same.

The State vs WILLIAM TOWNZEND - WILLIAM TOWNZEND was bound to appear at last January term of court and answer the State of Tennessee into matter alledged against him and not depart without leave first had and obtained of the court, was this day called but came not. The recognizance is forfeited and that judgment (illegible) be entered against him for $100.00.

ROBERT STUBBLEFIELD who was bound in recognizance for the appearance of WILLIAM TOWNZEND at the last term of court, was this day called to bring with him the body of WILLIAM TOWNZEND, failed to do so but made default. Recognizance is forfeited and fined $50.00.

WILLIAM PITCOCK (same as above) and is fined $50.00.

PRISSILLA HUNTER vs JAMES GREEN (GREER?) - This day came the parties by their attorneys and a jury of men, to wit, JOHN BUCHANAN, EDWARD EAVANS, JACOB SILVERTOOTH, JAMES LINGO, MATHEW PRICE, ANDREW KING, JAMES COWLY, HENRY WARREN, THOMAS H. SHAW, ADLAI SHARP, FRANCIS WYATT, and JOHN ST. JOHN BASKINS being elected and sworn and said that the defendant has not paid the debt of $112.00 and damages of $7.25. Plaintiff to recover his costs.

FRIDAY APRIL 19, 1822

Justices present were EBENEZER McEWEN, AMBROSE BARKER and THOMAS GAITHER, Esquires.

The due execution of an Indenture of Bargain and Sale from WILLIAM JENNINGS to THOMAS M. HARPER for 60 acres of land in this county, proven by HARDY HOLMAN and ANDREW KING and ordered to be certified.

The due execution of an Indenture of Bargain and Sale from WILLIAM P. ANDERSON to WILLIAM MARTIN for 100 acres of land, proven by HARDY HOLMAN, Attorney in fact and ordered to be certified.

JOHN BECKTELL vs HENRY MORGAN and others - The defendants acknowledged themselves to be indebted to the plaintiff for $66.12½. Plaintiff to recover his costs.

WILLIAM COATS vs HENRY MORGAN and others - The defendants acknowledged themselves to owe the plaintiff $57.09½. Plaintiff to recover his costs.

EUNICE HUNTER vs JAMES GREEN (GREER ?) - THIS DAY CAME THE PARTIES BY THEIR ATTORNEYS AND A JURY OF MEN, TO WIT, EDWARD EAVANS, JACOB SILVERTOOTH, JOHN BUCHANAN, JAMES LINGO, MATHEW PRICE, ANDREW KING, JAMES COWLY, HENRY WARREN, THOMAS H. SHAW, ADLAI SHARP, SAMUEL M. CLAY, and WILLIAM DYE being elected and sworn and said that the defendant has not paid the debt of $112.00 and damages of $7.75. Plaintiff to recover his costs.

WILLIAM HUSBANDS vs JAMES WYATT - (same as above) and said that the defendant has not paid the debt of $200.00 and damages of $15.50. Plaintiff to recover his costs.

OLIVER B. HAYS vs WILLIAM DICKSON - The plaintiff says he wishes to dismiss this his suit and the Fayetteville Tennessee Bank, by attorney, assumes the payment of all costs. Suit to be dismisses and the plaintiff to recover against the Fayetteville Tennessee Bank his costs.

OLIVER B. HAYS vs ELLIOTT HICKMAN - The plaintiff says he wishes to dismiss this his suit and the Fayetteville Tennessee Bank assumes the payment of all costs. Suit to be dismissed and plaintiff to recover his costs.

OLIVER B. HAYS vs ROBERT DICKSON - (Same as above).

THOMAS CHAMPLAIN vs ROBERT DICKSON - (same as above).

THOMAS CHAMPLAIN vs JOSEPH HINKLE - (same as above).

THOMAS CHAMPLAIN vs WILLIAM DICKSON - (same as above).

THOMAS CHAMPLAIN vs JOHN GREER - (same as above).

WILSON F. DILLON vs DAVID READ - The defendant by his attorney and moves to dismiss this suit. This suit to be dismissed and defendant recover against the plaintiff his costs.

ROBERT BUCHANAN vs Fayetteville Tennessee Bank - The plaintiff by his attorney, says he wishes to dismiss his suit and the defendant by his attorney assumes the payment of all costs. Suit to be dismissed and plaintiff to recover his costs.

SAMUEL GREENWELL vs Fayetteville Tennessee Bank - The plaintiff by his attorney says he wishes to dismiss this suit and the defendant by his attorney assumes the payment of all costs. Suit to be dismissed and plaintiff to recover his costs.

JANE B. CAMPBELL vs HENRY ALLEN - The defendant prays for an appeal in the nature of a Writ of Error to next Circuit and was granted same.

HENRY BADLENS vs Fayetteville Tennessee Bank - The plaintiff says he wishes to dismiss this his suit and the defendant by his attorney comes and assumes the payment of all costs. Suit to be dismissed and plaintiff to recover his costs.

JACOB BECK vs Fayetteville Tennessee Bank - The plaintiff by his attorney and says he wishes to dismiss this his suit and the defendant by his attorney comes and assumes the payment. This suit to be dismissed and plaintiff recover his costs.

JAMES & WILLIAM PARK vs Fayetteville Tennessee Bank - (same as above).

JOHN MAZE vs CONSTANT SCALES - This day came the parties by their attorneys and a jury of men, to wit, EDWARD EAVANS, JACOB SILVERTOOTH, JOHN BUCHANAN, JAMES LINGO, MATHEW PRICE, ANDREW KING, JAMES COWLY, HENRY WARREN, THOMAS H. SHAW, ADLAI SHARP, SAMUEL M. CLAY, and WILLIAM DYE being elected and sworn and said that the defendant has not paid the debt of $250.00 and damages of $4.00. Plaintiff to recover his costs. Defendant prays for an appeal and is granted same.

WILLIAM W. TAYLOR vs SPENCER A. PUGH & JOHN R. JOHNSON - (same as above) and said that they find in favor of the plaintiff.

PHILIP ANDERSON vs LEVI M. TODD - Appeal - The defendant by his attorney and moved the court to squash the proceedings below. This suit to be squashed and the defendant recover against the plaintiff his costs.

JAMES WYATT vs JACOB WRIGHT - This day came the plaintiff by his attorney and a jury of men, to wit, EDWARD EAVANS, JACOB SILVERTOOTH, JOHN BUCHANAN, JAMES LINGO, MATHEW PRICE, ANDREW KING, JAMES COWLY, HENRY WARREN, THOMAS H. SHAW, ADLAI SHARP, SAMUEL M. CLAY, and WILLIAM DYE being elected and sworn and said that they assess the damages of the plaintiff to $434.37+ damages of $134.37. Plaintiff to recover his costs. The Sheriff was ordered to expose to sale a negro woman levied by an attachment to satisfy the aforesaid judgment and costs.

JANE B. CAMPBELL vs C. BOYLES & JAS. WYATT - Upon argument by the defendant and their attorneys, they file exceptions to the aforesaid case.

SATURDAY APRIL 20, 1822

Justices present were SAMUEL BUCHANAN, EBENEZER McEWEN and ELI GARRETT, Esquires.

JAMES WRIGHT vs DENNIS WRIGHT - The plaintiff says he wishes to dismiss this suit and assumes the payment of all costs. Suit to be dismissed and the defendant recover his costs.

JOEL & NATHAN G. PINSON vs JAMES CHAPMAN - The plaintiffs by their attorney and says he wishes to dismiss this suit and assumes the payment of all costs. Suit to be dismissed and the defendant recover his costs.

BENJAMIN CLEMENTS vs SAMUEL RAGSDALE - The plaintiff says he wishes to dismiss this suit and assumes the payment of all costs. Suit to be dismissed and defendant recover his costs.

MONDAY APRIL 22, 1822

It is ordered that ELLIOTT HICKMAN, ROBERT H. McEWEN and VANCE GREER are appointed by the court, Commissioners, to settle with JAMES BRIGHT and FRANCIS PORTERFIELD, executors of the Last Will and Testament of GEORGE C. WITT, deceased, and make return to this court.

A. & B. BOTELER vs HENRY ALLEN - The court said that HENRY ALLEN give security for his administration with VANCE GREER as security as admr on said estate. It is considered by the court that bond and security be received and made of record and bond be given by HENRY ALLEN and ALEXANDER & BENJAMIN BOTELER securities, thereto be given up by the Clerk of the COurt and that ALEXANDER & BENJAMIN BOTELER be released from liability as security for administration.

It is ordered that BRICE M. GARNER, CHARLES BOYLES and FRANCIS PORTERFIELD be appointed Commissioners to settle with HENRY ALLEN, administrator on the estate of ARCHABALD ALLEN, deceased, and make return to next court.

It is ordered that WILLIAM INGLE be appointed guardian for PALSER INGLE, a minor under fourteen years of age, and REBECCAH BERRY and FANNY INGLE, minirs over fourteen years of age, appeared in court and made choice of the said WILLIAM INGLE as guardian. WILLIAM INGLE gave bond and security for $4000.00 and tendered bond with THOMAS MARSH and NICHOLAS CARRIGER his securities as guardian and ordered to be recorded.

JOHN JONES, Esquire, resigns his appointment as a Justice of the Peace for Lincoln County.

It is ordered by the court that THOMAS BLYTH be released from the fine entered against him at this term.

SAMUEL D. MILLIKIN is appointed overseer of the road in the room of ROBERT M. WHITE and to call on the usual hands.

YOUNG TAYLOR is appointed overseer of the road from Rountrees Creek to JOHN GREY's spring and call on the usual hands.

CORNELIUS SLATER is appointed overseer of the road in the room of JOSEPH McMILLIN and call on the usual hands.

KENNETH McKINSEY is appointed overseer of the road in the room of DANIEL W. HARRISON and call on the usual hands.

JOHN McCLURE is appointed overseer of the road in the room of THOMAS GEORGE resigned and call on the usual hands.

ALEXANDER McCORKLE is appointed overseer of a new road from the county line below Leatherman's Mill to where it intersects the Huntsville Road and call on the usual hands.

WILLIAM NORRIS is appointed overseer of the Huntsville Road from Fayetteville to the ford on Elk River and ROBERT DICKSON, Esquire, to designate the hands to work on said road.

JOSHUA GIBSON is appointed overseer of the Nashville Road from MAJOR WILLIAM SMITH to JOHN WATT's old place, in the room of ROBERT BRADON and call on all the hands.

ABSALEM BOSTICK, BOON WILSON, JONAS LEATHERMAN, ARON WELLS, THOMAS WILLIAMS, JOHN DIVEN, and WILLIAM DIVEN are appointed a Jury of View to view and turn the road leading from Cunningham Mill to leave the old at or near the corner of THOMAS H. BELL's field leaving his lots on the right on to intersect the old road at or near ABSALEM BOSTICK's and make return to next court.

HUGH M. BLAKE, Esquire, is appointed Commissioner of the School Lands in this county in the place of JOHN MARR, resigned.

An account of sale of property of WILLIAM BROWN, deceased, was returned to court by his admr and ordered to be certified.

An amount of sales of the property of JOHN WARREN was returned to court and ordered to be certified.

An inventory of the estate of THOMAS CUMMINS, deceased, was returned to court by his admr and ordered to be certified.

An amount of sale of the estate of THOMAS CUMMINS, deceased, was returned to court and ordered to be certified.

An amount of sale of the estate of ARTHUR BROOKS was returned to court and ordered to be certified.

The Commissioners appointed to settle with JAMES BRIGHT and FRANCIS PORTERFIELD, executors of GEORGE C. WITT and made return to court and ordered to be certified.

The Last Will and testament of CHRISTOPHER MILLER was exhibited in court for probate whereupon came JACOB GROSS and THOMAS MARSH, witnesses, and made oath that they heard the said CHRISTOPHER MILLER acknowledge the same and that he was at that time of sound mind and memory. NICHOLAS CARRIGER, executor, gave bond and security.

An inventory of the property of CHRISTOPHER MILLER was returned to court by his executor and ordered to be certified.

It is ordered that ROBERT DICKSON, VANCE GREER and FRANCIS PORTERFIELD be appointed Commissioners to contract for and superintend the repairing of the Court House, and that an order from said Commissioners to the County Trustee for such sum or sums of money for carrying the foregoing in effect such order or a receipt thereon shall be a sufficient vouchers for the Trustee in the settlements of his amounts.

CHARLES BOYLES, WILLIAM KENNON and STEPHEN ALEXANDER are appointed to settle with HENRY & WILLIS WARREN, executors of JOHN WARREN, deceased, and make return to next court.

JOHN PORTER, THOMAS CLARK and REPS O. CHILDRESS are appointed to settle with JOHN C. SAWYERS, admr of DAVID SAWYERS and also admr of ELIZABETH SAWYERS, deceased, amd make return to next court.

The Commissioners appointed at this term to settle with the Commissioners of the County of Lincoln made return to court, also returned a note on GEORGE COALTER and JOHN GREER for $97.75 dated 4 September 1810 and payable twelve months after date which note was deposited with the County Trustee for collection.

It is ordered that the County Trustee of this county pay the Sheriff $284.72½, the balance of the judgment that EZEKIEL NORRIS recovered against the Commissioners of Lincoln County and that said Trustee pay the same out of the first county monies that comes to his hands.

A Deed of Conveyance from JOHN TERRY to JAMES SCOTT for 44 acres of land and ordered to be certified.

A Deed of Conveyance from JOHN TERRY to JAMES SCOTT for 50 acres of land and ordered to be certified.

A Deed of Conveyance from ALEXANDER McDANIEL to JESSE JENNINGS for 60 acres of land and ordered to be certified.

A Deed of Conveyance from ABRAHAM HOGLAND to DAVID DODD, proven and ordered to be certified.

A Deed of Conveyance from JESSE JENNINGS to ROBERT R. ALLSUP for 60 acres of land, proven by JAMES CARITHERS and DANIEL LEE and ordered to be certified.

A Deed of Conveyance from ALEXANDER McDANIEL to RANDOLPH ALLSUP for 22½ acres of land, proven by JAMES ALLSUP and ROBERT R. ALLSUP and ordered to be certified.

A Deed of Conveyance from BRICE M. GARNER to WILLIAM LOCK for 50 acres of land and ordered to be certified.

A Deed of Conveyance from JOSEPH GREER to GEORGE TINKLE for 250 acres of land and ordered to be certified.

A Deed of Conveyance from GEORGE TINKLE to JOHN MARR for 260 acres of land and ordered to be certified.

It is ordered that JOHN LEE, DAVID SNODDY, BENJAMIN HUDSON, JAMES RUTHERFORD, JAMES GOWEN, ALEXANDER FINNEY, JOHN BROADWAY, HOWELL HARRIS, PRESTON HAMPTON, CONROD KIMES, HENRY CLIFT, JAMES CRAWFORD, JAMES TOOL, WILLIAM TIMMONS, ALEXANDER McLIN, ABNER WELLS, GEORGE W. DENNIS, ABSOLEM BOWEN, BENJAMIN PROCTOR, JOHN G. PRICE, JOHN WAGGONER and WILLIAM BROWN be summoned as Jurors to the County Court of Pleas and Quarter Sessions for this county on 3rd Monday in July next.

It is ordered that WILLIAM MILLNER, ASA STREET, AMBROSE BARKER, ANDREW HANNAH, Shelton Creek; HUGH M. BLAKE, GENERAL W.C. EDMISTON, WILLIAM EDMISTON, WILLIAM BEAVERS, THOMAS H. BELL, JOHN ENOCHS, HENRY KELSO, PHILIP KOONCE, JOHN PORTER, DAVID COWEN, DOILY GRIFFIS, RICHARD FLYNT, JONATHAN FLOYD, SAMUEL D. MILLIKIN, SAMUEL DOBBINS, OLIVER WILLIAMS, JOHN A. MOORE, THOMAS CLARK, REPS O. CHILDRESS, DAVID P. MUNROE, ANDREW W. WALKER and WILLIAM KENNON be summoned as Jurors to next Circuit Court of this county held on the 3rd Monday September next.

TUESDAY APRIL 23, 1822

Justices present were JOHN H. MOORE, WILLIAM ANDERSON and WILLIAM DICKSON, Esquires.

WILLIAM W. TAYLOR vs SPENCER A PUGH and JOHN R. JOHNSON - Case - It is considered by the court that the plaintiff recover against the defendants $915.92.

The due execution of an Indenture of Bargain and Sale from WALTER B. OWEN to ARTHUR N. DAVIS for 17½ acres of land and ordered to be certified.

FRANCIS MAYS, executor vs BRICE M. GARNER - The plaintiff by hs attorney says he wishes to dismiss this suit and assumes the payment of all costs. Suit to be dismissed and defendant recover his costs.

JAMES STEWART vs CHARLES BOYLES - The plaintiff (defendant) acknowledged that he owes the plaintiff $2203.00. Plaintiff to recover against the defendant his costs.

MONDAY JULY 15, 1822

ABEL HOLLEWAY is appointed overseer of the road in the room of WILLIAM WILLIAMS resigned and to call on the usual hands.

ANDREW McCARTNEY is appointed overseer of the road in the room of WALTER HARKINS resigned and to call on the usual hands.

It is ordered that JOHN PORTER, Esquire, give up the sledge hammer and crow bar to JONATHAN ANDERSON and RICHARD CRUMPTON for the use of that part of the Pulaski Road which they are overseer of.

JOHN DAVIS is appointed overseer of the road in the room of JOHN STREET resigned and to call on the usual hands.

PETER FIREBAUGH is appointed overseer of the road in the room of JOSEPH HARKINS resigned and call on the usual hands.

DAVID P. MUNROE is appointed overseer of the road in the room of STEPHEN C. CHITWOOD resigned and call on the usual hand.

BENJAMIN WHITAKER, SR. is appointed overseer of the road in the room of JACOB WAGGONER resigned and call on the usual hands.

JOHN WILSON, ROBERT CUNNINGHAM, GABRIEL SEAHORN, NATHAN COLLINS, SOLOMON REECE, and SAMUEL HAMPTON is appointed a Jury of View to view and mark out a road the nearest and best way from Cunningham Mill to the mouth of Swan and make return to next court.

MAY BUCHANAN is appointed overseer of the road from the mouth of Swan to SAMUEL M. CLAY and call on the usual hands.

WILLIAM TOWNZEND is appointed overseer of the road from SAMUEL M. CLAY to Robertson's Mill and call on the usual hands.

MICHAEL ROBERTSON is appointed overseer of the road from Robertson Mill to the State line and call on the usual hands.

JERY WALKER is appointed overseer of the road in the room of WILLIAM BONNER resigned and call on the usual hands.

DANIEL HALBERT is apointed overseer of the road from near JOHN WILSON on Swan Creek to Morton Creek and call on REPS O. CHILDRESS' hands, DANIEL HOLBERT's hands, CHARLES GOODE, HOLBERT GOODE, CLAYTON DEVER, ROBERT RAGSDALE, and WILLIAM SAUNDERS to work on said road.

THOMAS CAMPBELL is appointed overseer of the road from DAVID P. MUNROE to the top of the ridge near said THOMAS CAMPBELL in the room of ABEL DUCKWORTH and call on the usual hands.

JAMES LINGO is appointed overseer of the road of WILLIAM MOFFIT resigned and call on JAMES LINGO, LEA SMITH, KENNEDY MOFFIT, HAMBLETON MOFFIT, and GEORGE CASE in addition to the former hands that work on said road.

STEPHEN CLAYTON is appointed overseer of the road in the room of WILLIAM CRAWFORD resigned and call on the usual hands.

JOSEPH STEPHENS is appointed overseer of the road in the room of ELIJAH BURCHFIELD resigned and call on the usual hands.

JAMES WILSON is appointed overseer of the road from Cunningham Mill to MRS. WILIAS (?) and call on the usual hands.

DAVID COOPER is appointed overseer of the road in the room of THOMAS ALLEY resigned and call on the usual hands.

It is ordered that the road leading up the middle fork of Norris Creek be discontinued from the forks of the road at JOHN McMILLINS and on above to the county line, but that the same be kept open as near its present route as convenient to the neighborhood, sufficient for mill road and that the same may be attended at any time and place previous that is not move more than one hundred yards and or passable around.

MORGAN CLAYTON is appointed overseer of the road from MRS. WILIAS to Hannah's Road near Cane Creek and call on the usual hands.

ISHAM BURNETT is appointed overseer of a new road from the Shelby Road near the south east corner of ZACHARIAL ARNOLD's field up Robins Creek to the Pharis Creek Road near BUCK SMITH and call on the usual hands.

An amount of sale of the estate of JONATHAN LOONEY and was returned to court by JOHN ENOCK, the admr which was ordered to be certified.

HOWELL HARRIS, JOHN BEATY and WILLIAM B. BENGE are appointed

Commissioners to settle with SAMUEL CRAWFORD, admr, and CHARLOTTE HOWELL, admrx of THOMAS JOYCE, deceased, and make return to next court.

JOHN DOBBINS is released from the payment of the appraised value of a stray mare which he posted and ran away from him.

JOHN W. SMITH, WILLIAM B. BENGE and SAMUEL CRAWFORD are appointed Commissioners to settle with HOWELL HARRIS, executor of WILLIAM HARRIS, deceased, and make return to next court.

The Commissioners appointed at the last term of this court to settle with JOHN C. SAWYERS, admr on the estate of DAVID SAWYERS, deceased, make return to court for the settlement by them and was ordered to be certified.

An additional inventory of the estate of GEORGE WAGGONER, deceased, was returned to court by his admr and ordered to be certified.

The Commissioners appointed at the last term of court to settle with HENRY & WILLIS WARREN, executors of JOHN WARREN, deceased, made return to court of the settlement by them made and ordered to be certified.

On motion of HENRY KELSO and it appearing to the court that ARCHABALD MAYFIELD, late of this county, died intestate. Administration is granted to HENRY KELSO on the estate of said ARCHABALD MAYFIELD, deceased, who took oath and entered into bond for $400.00 with WILLIAM C. KENNEDY and GEORGE CUNNINGHAM, securities.

An inventory of the estate of ARCHABALD MAYFIELD, deceased, was returned to court by his admr and ordered to be certified.

The Last Will and Testament of ROBERT NIX, deceased, was exhibited in court for probate whereupon came JOEL HOWELL and JOHN LINDSEY, witnesses, made oath that they saw the said ROBERT NIX sign, seal and declare the same to be his Last Will and testament and that he was at that time of sound mind and memory, whereupon came SUSANNAH NIX, one of the executors, qualified as executrix and entered into bond with JOEL HOWELL and JOHN LINDSEY, securities for $1600.00.

The Last Will and Testament of JOHN BEARD, deceasedd, was exhibited in court for probate, whereupon came WILLIAM DICKSON, witness, and made oath that he saw JOHN BEARD sign, seal and declare the same to be his Last Will and Testament and that he was at the time of sound mind and memory and EZEKIEL CLOYD, executor, therein named renounced his executorship in writing and on motion of ALEXANDER MOORE, he is appointed admr of said deceased with the Will annexed, who took oath and gave bond of $6000.00 with CONSTANT SCALES, JOSEPH HINKLE and ARGYLE CAMPBELL his securities.

A Power of Attorney from THOMAS GAULT, HUGH C. GAULT, JOHN WILSON, JOHN C. TAYLOR and JAMES McCORMACK to JAMES GAULT was this day acknowledged and ordered to be certified.

The due execution of an Indenture of Bargain and Sale from JAMES BRIGHT to ISAAC JAMES for 100 acres of land and ordered to be certified.

The due execution of an Indenture of Bargain and Sale from EDWARD GORE to JAMES ELLIS for 40 acres of land, proven by JOHN ENOCKS and JONATHAN FLOYD and orderd to be certified.

The due execution of an Indenture of Bargain and Sale from WILLIAM CARITHERS to JAMES BELL for 31 acres of land, proven by ENOCK RUST and JAMES BROOKS and ordered to be certified.

The due execution of an Indenture of Bargain and Sale from FRANCIS WYATT, JAMES WYATT and BRICE M. GARNER to HENRY ROBERTSON for 160 acres of land, proven by JAMES COALTER and GEORGE T. LASLEY and ordered to be certified.

The due execution of an Indenture of Bargain and Sale from JAMES BROOKS to JAMES BRYANS for part of town lot No. 71 in Fayetteville and ordered to be certified.

The due execution of an Indenture of Bargain and Sale from ARON WELLS to NATHAN COLLINS for 50 acres of land and ordered to be certified.

The due execution of an Indenture of Bargain and Sale from NATHAN N.G. ALLEN to JOHN HARRISON for 63 acres of land, proven by DAVID COWAN and JOSEPH ALLSUP and ordered to be certified.

The due execution of an Indenture of Bargain and Sale from JAMES HUDDLESTON to ELISHA & ELIJAH BENNETT for 10 acres of land and ordered to be certified.

The due execution of an Indenture of Bargain and Sale from THOMAS MIDDLETON and JOHN HARRISON to JAMES McGOWAN for 185½ acres of land, proven by STEPHEN HIGHTOWER and WILLIAM B. BAUGH and ordered to be certified.

The due execution of an Indenture of bargain and Sale from JAMES MACGOWAN to JOHN HARRISON for 12 acres of land, proven by STEPHEN HIGHTOWER and WILLIAM B. BAUGH and ordered to be certified.

The due execution of an Indenture of bargain and Sale from SAMUEL WAKEFIELD to CHARLES WAKEFIELD for 96 acres of land and ordered to be certified.

The due execution of an Indenture of Bargain and Sale from ROBERT HODGE to WILLIAM FINDLEY for 24 acre of land, proven by ELSTON & FRANCIS FINDLEY and ordered to be certified.

The due execution of an Indenture of Bargain and Sale from JOHN HOLCUM to JOSEPH McCRACKEN for 12 acres of land, proven by SOLOMON BENNETT and THOMAS C. McCRACKEN and ordered to be certified.

The due execution of an Indenture of bargain and Sale from SAMUEL WAKEFIELD to ROBERT YARBROUGH for 100 acres of land, proven by CHARLES WAKEFIELD and JOSEPH GARNER and ordered to be certified.

A Deed of Conveyance from THOMAS PULLY to HENRY RENNERGER for 28 acres of land and orderd to be certified.

A Deed of Conveyance from ROBERT TEDFORD to DOAK NIX for 5 acres of land, proven by JOHN McMILLIN and WILSON A. MOOR and ordered to be certified.

A Deed of Conveyance from ROBERT TEDFORD to DOAK NIX for 30 acres of land, proven by JOHN McMILLIN and WILSON A. MOOR and ordered to be certified.

A Deed of Conveyance from WILLIAM LINTICUM to JOHN DAVIS for 114¼ acres of land, proven by WILLIAM SANSON and THOMAS SCURLOCK and ordered to be certified.

A Deed of Conveyance from ROBERT YARBROUGH to JOSEPH GARNER for 100 acres of land, proven by CHARLES WAKEFIELD and SAMUEL WAKEFIELD and ordered to be certified.

A Deed of Conveyance from DAVID HUDDLESTON to MORGAN HOLBERT for 100 acres of land and ordered to be certified.

A Deed of Conveyance from NATHAN G. PINSON to JAMES CHEATHAM for 153 acres of land and ordered to be certified.

A Deed of Conveyance from JAMES HUDDLESTON to BARNEY LIVINGSTON for 56 acres of land and ordered to be certified.

A Deed of Conveyance from JAMES GARRETT to RICHARD FLYNT for 40 acres of land and orderd to be certified.

A Deed of Conveyance from JOHN HENDERSON to ARON BOYD for 75 acres of land, proven by JOHN T. CUNNINGHAM and MARCUS WHITNEY and ordered to be certified.

The Transfer of a Plat and Certificate from JAMES WILKINS to THOMAS H. SHAW, proven by JAMES & JOHN COATS and ordered to be certified.

The Transfer of a Plat and Certificate from JESSE HADEN to MARTIN JONES, proven by JASPER SMITH and ordered to be certified.

A Transfer of a Plat and Certificate from MARTIN JONES to JOHN WILKINS and ordered to be certified.

A Transfer of a Plat and Certificate of Survey from JOHN WILKINS to THOMAS H. SHAW, proven by MARTIN JONES and JOHN COATS and ordered to be certified.

It is ordered that JONATHAN MERRELL, THOMAS WASHBURN, ISAAC BROYLES, JOHN MOOR, JOHN DAVIS (Norris Creek), SAMUEL TODD, ZACHARIAH HARRISON, ISHAM PARR, JOEL JOHNSON, JOHN BOON, JOSEPH HINKLE, WILLIAM SHIPP, DAVID HOWELL, JOEL DODSON, ROBERT MOOR, ARON WELLS, JOHN DAVIS (Swan Creek), DANIEL WAGGONER, THOMAS WITT, JOHN R. JOHNSON, DAVID JONES (Coldwater, block head DAVEY), THOMAS BRENTS, JESSEY McCLAIN, SAMUEL CRAWFORD, and CHARLES BRIGHT be summoned as Jurors to next Court of Pleas and Quarter Sessions held on the 3rd Monday in October next.

On petition, it is ordered by the court that the clerk receive and plan on the Tax List 374½ acres of land and six black poles, the property of MRS. DRIVER's and that she pay a single tax only.

TUESDAY JULY 16, 1822

Justices present were CHARLES BOYLES, HUGH M. BLAKE, WILLIAM BEAVER and RICHARD FLYNT, Esquires.

The Sheriff made return that he had summoned the following venire to serve as Grand Jurors and Petit Jurors, to wit, JOHN LEE, DAVID SNODDY, JAMES RUTHERFORD, JAMES GOWEN, ALEXANDER FINNEY, HOWELL HARRIS, JOHN BROADWAY, PRESTON HAMPTON, CONROD KYMES, HENRY CLIFT, JAMES CRAWFORD, JAMES TOOL, WILLIAM TIMMONS, ALEXANDER McLIN, ABNER WELLS, GEORGE W. DENNIS, ABSOLEM BOWEN, WILLIAM McCLELLAND, WILLIAM DOAK, SAMUEL BUTLER, JOHN DOBBINS, BENJAMIN PROCTOR, JOHN S. PRICE, JOHN WAGGONER and WILLIAM BROWN of whom were elected as Grand Jurors, to wit, GEORGE W. DENNIS, foreman, WILLIAM TIMMONS, ABSOLEM BOWEN, ABNER WELLS, JOHN BROADWAY, JAMES TOOL, HENRY CLIFT, BENJAMIN PROCTOR, JAMES GOWEN, ALEXANDER FINNEY, SAMUEL BUTLER, WILLIAM DOAK and JAMES RUTHERFORD, and after receiving this their charge from the solicitor, returned to consider for their presentments.

WILLIAM P. PULLIAM, a Constable, sworn to wait on the Grand Jury this term.

WILLIAM BROWN is released from any further attendance as a Juror this term.

The Grand Jury returned into court and brought with them a Bill of Indictment, the State against JOSEPH ELISON for an assault and battery, a true bill and again returned to consider for further presentments.

The due execution of an Indenture of Bargain and Sale from JOHN GREER to JAMES BRYANS for one town lot No. 44 in the town of Fayetteville and ordered to be certified.

The due execution of an Indenture of Bargain and Sale from WALTER BELL & THOMAS BELL to GIDEON PILLOW for 230 acres of land, proven by JOSEPH McMILLEN and JACOB WRIGHT and ordered to be certified.

The Grand Jury again returned into court and brought with him a Bill of Indictment for Petit Larceny, the State against GABRIEL SEAHORN, a true bill and again returned to consider for further presentments.

The Grand Jury again returned into court and brought with them a Bill of Indictment for an Assault and Battery, the State against WILLIAM LITTLE, a true bill and again returned to consider for further presentments.

The due execution of an Indenture of Bargain and Sale from JACOB V. HOOZER to HUDSON ALLEN for 20 acres of land, proven by WILLIAM BONNER and ROBERT McGUIRE and ordered to be certified.

The Grand Jury again returned into court brought with them a Bill of Indictment for an Assault and Battery, the State against JOHN COATS, a true bill and again returned to consider for further presentments.

The Grand Jury again returned into court and brought with them a Bill of

Indictment for an Assault and Battery against JOHN GAVIN and again returned to consider for further presentments.

The due execution of an Indenture of Bargain and Sale from JOHN OWEN to DAVID OWEN for 8 acres of land and ordered to be certified.

The due execution of an Indenture of Bargain and Sale from JOHN OWEN to JOHN OWEN, JR. for 50 acres of land and ordered to be certified.

The Grand Jury again returned into court and brought with them a Bill of Indictment for an Assault and Battery against JOHN D. McCONNELL, a true bill and again returned to consider for further presentments.

The Grand Jury again returned into court and brought with them a Bill of Indictment for an Assault and Battery against MAY BUCHANAN, a true bill and again returned to consider for further presentments.

The Grand Jury again returned into court and brought with them a Bill of Indictment for Petit Larceny against FRANCIS BRADLEY,a true bill and again returned to consider for further presentments.

The State vs JOSEPH ELISON - Assault and Battery - The defendant being charged pleads guilty and fined to the State for $1.00 and pay the costs, whereupon came ELIJAH McLAUGHLIN as security.

The State vs JOHN COATS - Assault and Battery - The defendant being charged, pleads guilty and is fined $1.00 and pay the costs.

The State vs JOHN GAVIN - Assault and Battery - The defendant being charged, pleads guilty and is fined $1.00 and pay the costs.

The Grand Jury again returned into court and brought with them a Bill of Indictment for an Assault and Battery against JOHN W. ISAACKS, a true bill and again returned to consider for further presentments.

The due execution of an Indenture of Bargain and Sale from ENOCK ENOCKS to EDWARD GORE for 150 acres of land, proven by JOHN ENOCKS and ALEXANDER FINNEY and ordered to be certified.

The due execution of an Indenture of Bargain and Sale from WILLIAM EDMISTON to CATHARINE JOHNSON for 140 acres of land and ordered to be certified.

The Grand Jury again returned into court and brought with them a Bill of Indictment for an Affray, the State against HENRY, JOSHUA and ADAM LAZENBY, a true bill and again returned to consider for further presentments.

The due execution of an Indenture of Bargain and Sale from JEREMIAH HARBISON to THEODRICK F. BRADFORD for 160 acres of land, it being the north west quarter of Section 24 of Township 56 north, in Range 21 west in the tract of land appropriated by an Act of Congress for Miitary Bounties in Territory of Missouri north, acknowledged in court by JEREMIAH HARBISON and ordered to be certified.

The Grand Jury again returned into court and brought with them a Bill of Indictment, the State against JEREMIAH HARBISON, a true bill and again return to consider for further presentments.

The State vs JEREMIAH HARBISON - The defendant being charged and pleads guilty and is fined $1.00 and pay the costs.

HENRY CRABB vs McGOWN & BAUGH - The plaintiff by his attorney says he wishes no further to prosecute this suit and the defendant assumes the payment of all costs. Suit to be dismissed. Plaintiff to recover his costs.

WILLIAM E. KENNEDY vs WILLIAM EDMISTON - The plaintiff says he wishes no further to prosecute this suit and assumes the payment of all costs. Suit to be dismissed and defendant recover his costs.

ENOS IVES vs ELISHA LOYD - The plaintiff says he wishes no further to prosecute this suit and the defendant assumes the payment of all costs. Suit to be dismissed and the plaintiff recover his costs.

THOMAS ALLEY vs MARIBLE & HARTSFIELD - The plaintiff by his attorney says he wishes to dismiss this suit and the defendant assumes the payment of all costs. Suit to be dismissed and the plaintiff recover his costs.

THOMAS ALLEY vs MARIBLE & HARTSFIELD - (same as above).

FRANCIS PORTERFIELD vs WILLIAM MOREHEAD - The plaintiff says he wishes to dismiss this suit and the defendant assumes the payment of all costs. Suit to be dismissed and the plaintiff recover his costs.

A Deed of Conveyance from ABNER PILLOW & GIDEON PILLOW to ELIJAH WRIGHT & GEORGE L. LENARD for 230 acres of land and ordered to be certified.

JOHN ROBB vs JOHN OWENS - The defendant confessed that he owes the plaintiff $688.00 Plaintiff to recover his costs.

WEDNESDAY JULY 17, 1822

Justices present were CHARLES BOYLES, RICHARD FLYNT and WILLIAM SMITH, Esquires.

The State vs FRANCIS A. BRADLEY - Indictment for Petit Larceny - The defendant being charged pleads not guilty. THOMAS H. FLETCHER, Attorney General. This cause is continued on affidavit of EVEN B. BRADLEY until next term of court. FRANCIS A. BRADLEY appeared in court and acknowledged himself indebted to the State of tennessee for $200.00 and EVEN B. BRADLEY acknowledged himself indebted to the State of tennessee for $500.00 to be levied on their goods and chattels &c but to be void on condition that FRANCIS A. BRADLEY appear in court in October next and answer the charge for Petit Larceny and not depart the same without have (leave) first had and obtained of the court.

SAMUEL BRADLEY vs ELI GARRETT - This day came the parties by their attorneys and a jury of men, to wit, CONRAD KYMES, DAVID SNODDY, JAMES F. DRIVER, JOHN NICHOLS, AMOS DEAVERS, JOSHUA DALLAS, DANIEL WAGGONER, SAMUEL WILSON, JOHN B. BUCHANAN, SOLOMON REECE, AUGUSTUS L. JONES, and THOMAS ALLEY being elected and sworn and said that JOHN KELLY, in his life time did assume and undertake in manner and form as charged, and they assess the plaintiff's damages of $300.00. Plaintiff to recover his costs.

JACOB STONEBRAKER appeared in court and acknowledged himself indebted to the State of Tennessee $100.00 to be levied of his goods and chattels &c but to be void on condition that he appear in court in October next to prosecute and give evidence in behalf of the State against FRANCIS A. BRADLEY upon a Bill of Indictment for Petit Larceny and not depart the same without leave first had and obtained of the court.

A Power of Attorney from ROBERT SMITH and MILDRED SMITH to AMOS HURLEY was acknowledged. MILDRED SMITH being first examined by the court separate and apart from her husband and ordered to be certified.

NATHANIEL B. BUCKINGHAM vs THOMAS H. MAY - This cause in continued and on order at last term to take the deposition is renewed.

THOMAS CHAPMAN vs JAMES D. EASTIS - The plaintiff says he wishes to dismiss this suit and the defendant assumes the payment of all costs. Suit to be dismissed and the plaintiff recover his costs.

JOSHUA GRAHAM vs JAMES WYATT - The plaintiff by his attorney says he intends no further to prosecute this suit and assumes the payment of all costs. Suit to be dismissed and the defendant recover his costs.

JOHN P. McCONNELL vs JAMES P. BAXTER - The plaintiff says he wishes to dismiss this suit and assumes payment of half of the costs and the defendant assumes payment of the other half. Suit to be dismissed and each party pay half the costs.

JOHN ALLBRIGHT vs JAMES FULGHAM - This day came the parties by their attorneys and a jury of men, to wit, ABSOLEM BEARD, THOMAS McGAUGH, BENJAMIN NEELD, CHARLES TULY, THOMAS KERCHEVAL, WILLIAM CONWAY, CLABORN WHITWORTH, ELIHU ROE, JOHN WITT, ALEXANDER BEARD, JOEL ORRICK, and URIAH BABBIT being elected and sworn and said that the plaintiff is indebted to the defendant for $8.50. Defendant to recover his costs.

SOLOMON REECE vs JOHN McKINLY - This day came the parties by their attorneys and a jury of men, to wit, DAVID SNODDY, JOSHUA DALLAS, JOHN DEVIN, PATRICK O'CALAGHAN, SAMUEL BUCHANAN, SAMUEL BRADLEY, FRANCIS PATTON, RANDOLPH QUARLES, JORDAN SOLOMON, DANIEL WHITAKER, THOMAS TOWERY, and ABRAHAM DEPOSITER being elected and sworn and said that they found in favor of the plaintiff and the jury was permitted to disperse until next day.

THURSDAY JULY 18, 1822

Justices present were CHARLES BOYLES, WILLIAM BEAVERS and HUGH M. BLAKE, Esquires.

A Power of Attorney from CASSANDER McLIN to THOMAS BOTELER of Washington County, Maryland, acknowledged and CASSANDER McLIN first being examined in court separate and apart from her husband and was ordered to be certified.

The State vs HENRY LITTLE - Indictment for an Assault and Battery - The defendant being charged and pleads guilty and is fined $5.00 and pay cost of this indictment. HENRY KYMES his security.

The State vs JOHN W. ISAACKS - The defendant being charged and pleads guilty and is fined $1.50 and pay the cost of this indictment whereupon came JACOB WAGGONER and HUGH M. BLAKE as securities.

The Grand Jury again returned into court and brought with them a Bill of Indictment against DRURY K. SMITH for Petit Larceny, a true bill and again returned to consider for further presentments.

The Grand Jury again returned into court abd brought with them a Bill of Indictment against DAVID H. MARKHAM for an Assault, a true bill and again returned to consider for further presentments.

The execution of an Indenture of Bargain and Sale from MAY BUCHANAN to JACOB WRIGHT for 38 3/4 acres of land and ordered to be certified.

The Grand Jury again returned into court and brought with them a Bill of Indictment against JOHN BERRY and JOHN FORD, a true bill and again returned to consider for further presentments.

The due execution of an Indenture of Bargain and Sale from JOHN OWEN, JR. to AMOS DAVIS for 110 acres of land and ordered to be certified.

The due execution of an Indenture of Bargain and Sale from BENJAMIN WHITAKER to JOHN DUSENBURG for 10 acres of land and ordered to be certified.

An inventory of the estate of ROBERT NIX, deceased, was returned to court by his admrx which was ordered to be certified.

A Power of Attorney from JOSEPH MOORE to JAMES TUCKER, proven by WILLIAM CRUNK and THOMAS S. MILAM and ordered to be certified.

The State vs JOHN P. McCONNELL - Assault and Battery - The defendant being charged pleads guilty and is fined $5.00 and pay costs.

The State vs JOHN FORD - An Affray - The defendant being charged pleads guilty and is fined $5.00 and pay costs.

The State vs DAVID A. MARKHAM - DAVID A. MARKHAM to appear at this term for an assault upon WILLIAM MOREHEAD and not depart the same without leave first had and obtained of the court, was this day called, came not but made default and judgment be entered against DAVID A. MARKHAM for $250.00.

ERROM LOYD was bound for the appearance of DAVID A. MARKHAM at this court, was called to bring the body of said MARKHAM, failed to do so but made default. Said recognizance be forfeited and judgment be entered against ERROM LOYD for $125.00.

JOHN SMITH was bound for the appearance of DAVID A. MARKHAM at this court this day, was called to bring with him the body of said MARKHAM but failed to do so but made default. The court ordered that said recognizance is forfeited and that judgment be entered against JOHN SMITH for $125.00.

The State vs CARTER WEBB & JOHN WEBB - This day CARTER WEBB, JOHN WEBB, GEORGE WEBB, ROBERT LACKEY, JAMES TAYLOR and RICHARD WEBB appeared in court and acknowledged themselves indebted to the State of tennessee for $250.00 each to be levied of their goods and chattels &c to the use of the State rendered but to be void on conditions that CARTER WEBB and JOHN WEBB appear at next Circuit Court in September next to answer the State of Tennessee for Grand Larceny.

ABRAHAM FITCH & JOHN H. WILLIAMS appeared in court and acknowledged themselves indebted to the State of Tennessee for $250.00 to be levied upon their respective goods and chattels &c to the use of the State rendered but to be void on conditions that ABRAHAM FITCH appear here at next Circuit Court in September next for Grand Larceny.

SOLOMON REECE vs JOHN McKINLEY - The jury empaneled at last court, returned to consider their verdict and said that the defendant is guilty and the damages were $163.68. Plaintiff recover against the defendant his costs.

The State vs DRURY K. SMITH - Petit Larceny - The defendant being charged, pleads not guilty and a jury of men, to wit, CONRAD KYMES, JOHN DAVIS, ABSOLEM DAVIS, MANSFIELD HUSBANDS, PRESTON HAMPTON, JOHN CAMPBELL, JORDAN REECE, JACOB WRIGHT, MATHEW WILSON, WILLIAM SOLOMON, JOSEPH HENDERSON, and ELIJAH DILLENDER being elected and sworn and said that the jury was put under the care of WILLIAM P. PULLIAM, a Constable, until next day.

RUBEN H. BOON is appointed by the court overseer of the road in the room of DANIEL W. HARRISON and call on the usual hands.

JOHN WHITAKER and others, Commissioners vs JOHN GREER - About 4 o'clock in the evening of 4th day of this term, being Thursday, DRURY K. SMITH who was indicted for larceny and has laid in jail for some time was brought into court and charged and plead to the indictment, the Sheriff had summoned the jury and delivered a copy to the defendant's council and the jury called, and about to be put to the defendant, for election, but had not been so put to him and at this time in the case of JOHN WHITAKER and others against JOHN GREER on the appearance docket, the defendant himself entered his appearance in person, moved the court to dismiss the said case because no declaration had been filed, which motion was objected to by the plaintiff's attorney. The court decided that it was not the proper time to take up said motion but might be made next day.

FRIDAY JULY 19, 1822

Justices present were JACOB WAGGONER, WILLIAM SMITH and CHARLES BOYLES, Esquires.

The Commissioners appointed at the last term to settle with SARAH LOYD, admrx on the estate of EPHRAIM LOYD, deceased, made return to court the settlement by them made and was ordered to be certified.

The due execution of an Indenture of Bargain and Sale from WILLIAM BOON to WILLIAM SANDERS for 7 acres of land and ordered to be certified.

JOHN LANDRES, admr vs ROBERT FLETCHER - This cause is continued and a Commission is awarded the plaintiff to take the deposition of EBENEZER TITUS of Huntsville to be read as evidence on the trial of the above cause by giving the defendant ten days notice of time and place of taking the same.

The Grand Jury again returned into court and brought with them a Bill of Indictment against JOHN FORD for an Assault and Battery, a true bill and again returned to consider for further presentments.

DRURY K, SMITH, PHILIP KOONCE, EDWARD MOSS, THOMAS WHITWORTH and HAMILTON MOFFIT appeared in court and acknowledged themselves indebted to the State of Tennessee for $250.00 to be levied of their respective goods and chattels &c but to be void on conditions that DRURY K. SMITH appear here on next day to answer the State of Tennessee for Petit Larceny.

SATURDAY JULY 20, 1822

Justices present were HUGH M. BLAKE, AMBROSE BARKER and WILLIAM SMITH, Esquires.

SATURDAY JULY 20, 1822

Justices present were HUGH M. BLAKE, AMBROS BARKER and WILLIAM SMITH, Esquires.

The due execution of an Indenture of bargain and Sale from JESSE W. COCK to THOMAS JACKSON for 40 acres of land and ordered to be certified.

It is ordered by the court that the clerk receive and place on the Tax List 4 town lots in the town of Fayetteville, the property of MATHEW GIBSON and that he pay a single tax for the same.

KENNEDY MOFFIT vs WILLIAM CRABTREE - The plaintiff says he intends no further to prosecute this suit and assumes the payment of all costs. Suit to be dismissed and the defendant recover his costs.

The State vs DRURY K. SMITH - Petit Larceny - The jury returned into court and say that the defendant is not guilty as charged and on order of the court the defendant be discharged.

An Indenture of bargain and Sale from BRICE M. GARNER to STEPHEN ALEXANDER and JOHN DUKE for 126 acres of land, proven by A. CAMPBELL and JOSEPH HINKLE and ordered to be certified.

The State vs GEORGE W. HUNT - JOHN DAVIS & JOHN CRAWFORD appeared in court and acknowledged themselves indebted to the State of Tennessee for $1000.00 each to be levied of their respective goods and chattels &c but to be void on conditions that they appear here in October next to prosecute and give evidence in behalf of the State against GEORGE W. HUNT for an assault and battery.

The State vs WILLIAM WHAM - This day came THOMAS H. FLETCHER, Attorney General, and says he wishes to dismiss this suit and the defendant assumes the payment of all costs. Suit to be dismissed and defendant pay the costs.

MONDAY JULY 22, 1822

Justices present were HUGH M. BLAKE, WILLIAM BEAVER and CHARLES BOYLES, Esquires.

The due execution of an Indenture of Bargain and Sale from BRICE M. GARNER to BENJAMIN PORTER for 4 acres of land and ordered to be certified.

The due execution of an Indenture of Bargain and Sale from THOMAS BUCHANAN to SAMUEL BUCHANAN for 55 acres of land, proven by GEORGE MITCHELL and JOSEPH COMMONS and ordered to be certified.

The due execution of an Indenture of Bargain and Sale from DAVID LAWRANCE to WILLIAM COOK for 100 acres of land and ordered to be certified.

The due execution of an Indenture of Bargain and Sale from ALEXANDER DACUS to WILLIAM DACUS for 52 acres of land and ordered to be certified.

The due execution of an Indenture of bargain and Sale from ROBERT M. WHITE to JOHN KENNEDY for 200 acres of land and ordered to be certified.

The due execution of an Indenture of Bargain and Sale from JOHN DAWDY to JAMES C. SMITH for 18 acres of land and ordered to be certified.

An amount of sale of the estate of CHRISTOPHER MILLER, deceased, was returned to court by his executor and ordered to be certified.

The due execution of an Indenture of Bargain and Sale from BRICE M. GARNER to LUCY WHITE for 20 acres of land, proven by E. COBB and BENJAMIN FA(illegible) and ordered to be certified.

The Transfer of a Plat and Certificate from SAMUEL RAGSDALE to JOHN HOLCOM, proven by ROBERT HOLCOM and HARDY HIGHTOWER and ordered to be certified.

The Transfer of a PLat and Certificate from SAMUEL RAGSDALE to KINCHEN

HOLCOME, proven by ROBERT HOLCOME and HARDY HIGHTOWER and ordered to be certified.

A Power of Attorney from SAMUEL CRAWFORD to JOHN CRAWFORD of Virginia and ordered to be certified.

EPHRAIM KING is appointed by the court overseer of the road leading from Looneys Settlement to the Pond Spring in the room of DAVID ARMSTRONG and call on the same hands that worked under said ARMSTRONG.

SAMUEL CUNNINGHAM is appointed overseer of that part of the road leading from Fayetteville to Shelbyville which RICHARD COTHAM was overseer of and call on the same hands that worked under said COTHAM.

CLEMENT HILL vs JOHN GIBSON - Appeal - The defendant acknowledged that he owes the plaintiff $1.50. Plaintiff to recover his costs.

ANDREW KING is appointed by the court overseer of the road in the room of STERLING C. McLEMORE resigned and call on the usual hands.

The due execution of an Indenture of Bargain and Sale from RICHARD COTHAM to PETER FIREBAUGH for 20 acres of land and ordered to be certified.

The due execution of an Indenture of Bargain and Sale from RICHARD COTHAM to FIREBAUGH for 40 acres of land and ordered to be certified.

The due execution of an Indenture of bargain and Sale from WILLIAM RICHARDSON to DANIEL WARREN for 15 acres of land and orderd to be certified.

The due execution of an Indenture of Bargain and Sale from KINCHEN HOLCOM to JAMES CARITHERS for 43 acres of land and ordered to be certified.

The due execution of an Indenture and Bargain and Sale from WILLIAM H. RAGSDALE to JAMES CARITHERS, MATHEW CARITHERS, FANNEY R. CARITHERS, and SAMUEL CARITHERS, heirs of SAMUEL CARITHERS for 185 acres of land, proven by THOMAS H. WILLIAMS and HARDY HIGHTOWER and ordered to be certified.

The due execution of an Indenture of bargain and Sale from FREDERICK A. BURNES to JAMES DANIEL for 45 acres of land, proven by ELNATHAN DAVIS and P. GILLASPIE and ordered to be certified.

The due execution of an Indenture of Bargain and Sale from FREDERICK A. BURNES to JAMES DANIEL and ordered to be certified.

The State vs GABRIEL SEAHORN - Indictment for Larceny - The defendant being charged pleads not guilty and a jury of men, to wit, CONRAD KYMES, DAVID SNODDY, BENJAMIN CLEMENTS, JOHN McMILLIN, JOHN LEE, JOHN GIBSON, JAMES BROWN, WILLIS WARREN, JACKSON BLAKEMORE, BENJAMIN WHITAKER, and ALEXANDER DACUS being elected and sworn and said that the defendant is not guilty. The defendant be discharged and that EZEKIEL GILLIUM , the prosecutor pay the costs of this indictment.

The State vs DANIEL WHITAKER - Indictment for an Assault and Battery - The defendant being charged pleads guilty and is fined $3.00 and pay the costs.

WATKINS & WHORTON vs THOMAS L. TROTTER - This day came the parties by their attorneys and a jury of men, to wit, SAMUEL BUTLER, BENJAMIN PROCTOR, JOHN· LEE, JAMES D. ALLFORD, WILLIAM DOAK, WILLIAM TIMMONS, JAMES TOOL, JAMES RUTHERFORD, REECE HOWELL, SAMUEL WILSON, STEPHEN PHILLIPS, and JOEL ORRICK being elected and sworn and said that the defendant did assume upon himself and assess the damages of the plaintiff $98.58. Plaintiff to recover his costs.

ROBERT BOYD for the use &c vs M. & J. WILSON - This day came the parties by their attorneys and a jury of men, to wit, (R(illegible) LEWIS, JESSE B. CLEMENTS, JAMES H. PULLIAM, SAMUEL BAKER, VANCE GREER, PATRICK O'CALAGHAN, JOHN R. MOORE, ABSOLEM BEARD, DAVID SNODDY, ROBERT S. HULME, JOHN BREWER, and WILLIAM MOFFIT being elected and sworn and said that the defendant has not paid the debt of $184.30 and damages of $10.75. Plaintiff to recover his costs.

THOMAS CHAMPLAIN vs HENRY ALLEN - (same as above) said that the defendant has not paid the debt of $157.67 and damages of $23.66. Plaintiff to recover his costs.

THOMAS CHAMPLAIN vs VANCE GREER - Debt - This day came the parties by their attorneys and a jury of men, to wit, R(illegible) LEWIS, JESSE B. CLEMENTS, JAMES H. PULLIAM, SAMUEL BAKER, VANCE GREER, PATRICK O'CALAGHAN, JOHN R. MOORE, ABSOLEM BEARD, DAVID SNODDY, ROBERT S. HULME, JOHN BREWER, and WILLIAM MOFFIT being elected and sworn and said that the defendant has not paid the debt to the plaintiff of $200.00 and damages of $6.50. Plaintiff to recover his costs.

PETER VAUGHN vs MAY BUCHANAN - Debt - (same as above) and said that the defendant has not paid the debt of $102.87½ and damages of $2.80. Plaintiff to recover his costs.

ROBERT & M. HARROLD vs EBENEZER McEWEN - (same as above) and said that the defendant has not paid the debt of $100.00 and damages of $12.75. Plaintiff to recover his costs.

TUESDAY JULY 23, 1822

Justiced present were HUGH M. BLAKE, WILLIAM BEAVERS and JAMES RALSTON, Esquires.

A Bill of Sale from THOMAS ALLEY and ISAIAH ALLEY to JAMES HOLMAN for a negro girl named MOURNING and ordered to be certified.

A Grand Jury returned into court and brought a Bill of Indictment against WILLIAM SMITH, JAMES HOBBS and GEORGE ST. JOHN, JOHN BASKINS for an affray, a true bill, and again returned to consider for further presentments.

N. PINDLAND vs LIVINGSTON J. BROWN - Debt Appeal - This day came the parties by their attorneys and a jury of men, to wit, SAMUEL WILSON, ASBURY CHAMNESS, CLABOURN WHITWORTH, JORDAN SOLOMON, DAVID SNODDY, JOHN LEE, SAMUEL BAKER, CONRAD KYMES, JOHN WATKINS, ELIJAH YATES, THOMAS ALLEY, and JOHN SHOEMAKER being elected and sworn and said that the defendant has not paid the debt of $1272.00 and damages of $57.00. Plaintiff to recover his costs.   Defendant prays for an appeal to the next Circuit Court and granted same.

EDMOND WILLIAMSON vs BRICE M. GARNER - (same as above) and said that the defendant did assume upon himself the charge against him and assessed the damages of $141.50. Plaintiff to recover his costs.

JOSEPH MOONEY vs JOHN P. McCONNELL - (same as above) and said that the defendant has not paid the debt of $225.66 2/3 and damages of $11.25. Plaintiff to recover his costs. Defendant prays for an appeal and is granted same.

ABRAHAM HOGLAND vs JOHN BOYLES - (same as above) and said that the defendant has not paid the debt of $137.00 and damages of $3.00. Plaintiff to recover his costs.

JOHN H. SMITH vs JAS. COALTER & B.M. GARNER - (same as above) and said that the defendant has not paid the debt of $4108.22 and damages of $82.00. Plaintiff to recover his costs. Defendant prays for an appeal and granted same.

ROBERT & M. HARROLD vs VANCE GREER - (same as above) and said that the defendant has not paid the debt of $100.00 and damages of $12.33 1/3. Plaintiff recover his costs.

JOSHUA GRAHAM vs PETER MOYERS - (same as above) and said that the defendant has not paid the debt of $187.50 and damages of $5.15½. Plaintiff recover his costs.

WILLIAM DYE vs JOHN P. McCONNELL - (same as above) and said that the defendant has not paid all the debt and left a balance of $432.83 and damages of $12.25. Plaintiff to recover his costs. Defendant prays for an appeal and is granted same.

JAMES GILLASPIE vs VANCE GREER - (same as above) and said that the defendant has not paid the debt of $200.00 and damages of $6.62½. Plaintiff recover his costs.

GEORGE PEARCE vs NATHANIEL B. BUCKINGHAM - (same as above) and said that the defendant has not paid the debt of $178.75 and damages of $10.72. Plaintiff recover his costs.

BENJAMIN PATTERSON, assignee vs HENRY ALLEN - This day came the partied by their attorneys and a jury of men, to wit, SAMUEL WILSON, ASBERRY CHAMNESS, CLABOURN WHITWORTH, JORDAN SOLOMON, DAVID SNODDY, JOHN LEE, SAMUEL BAKER, CONRAD KYMES, JOHN WATKINS, ELIJAH YATES, THOMAS ALLEY, and JOHN SHOEMAKER being elected and sworn and said that the defendant has not paid the debt of $361.01 and damages of $29.25. Plaintiff recover his costs.

BENJAMIN PATTERSON, assignee vs HENRY ALLEN - (same as above) and said that the defendant has not paid the debt of $156.37 and damages of $3.00. Plaintiff recover his costs.

THOMAS MILTON vs THOMAS ALLEY and JNO. WATKINS - (same as above) and said that the defendant has not paid the debt of $105.00 and damages of $3.50. Plaintiff recover his costs.

SAMUEL HART vs BENJAMIN GEORGE - (same as above) and said that they find in favor of the plaintiff and that the defendant has not paid all of the debt and owes a balance of $143.28 and damages of $11.06¼. Plaintiff recover his costs.

WILLIAM H. MURPHEY for the use of vs JAS. & WILLIAM BROWN - (same as above) and said that the defendant has not paid the debt of $400.00 and damages of $182.00. Plaintiff recover his costs.

JOHN P. McCONNELL vs THOMAS ALLEY - This day came the parties by their attorneys and a jury of men, to wit, SAMUEL BUTLER, BENJAMIN PROCTOR, JOHN LEE, JAMES D. ALLFORD, WILLIAM DOAK, WILLIAM TIMMONS, JAMES TOOL, JAMES RUTHERFORD, REECE HOWELL, SAMUEL WILSON, STEPHEN PHILIPS, and JOEL ORRICK being elected and sworn and said that the defendant has not paid the debt of $147.72½ and damages of $8.00. Plaintiff recover his costs.

JOHN P. McCONNELL vs THOMAS ALLEY - This day came the parties by their attorneys and a jury of men, to wit, SAMUEL WILSON, ASBERRY CHAMNESS, CLABORN WHITWORTH, JORDAN SOLOMON, DAVID SNODDY, JOHN LEE, SAMUEL BAKER, CONRAD KYMES, JOHN WATKINS, ELIJAH YATES, SAMUEL BUTLER, and BENJAMIN PROCTOR being elected and sworn and said that the defendant has not paid the debt of $99.68 3/4 and damages of $1.25. Plaintiff recover his costs. Defendant prays for an appeal and granted same.

The State vs SAMUEL WILSON - THOMAS H. FLETCHER, Attorney &c, says he wishes no further to prosecute this suit and the defendant assumes the payment of all costs. Suit to be dismissed and HENRY LAZENBY security for the defendant who bore the above costs.

The due execution of an Indenture of Bargain and Sale from WILLIAM EDMISTON to CATHARINE JOHNSON for 140 acres of land and ordered to be certified.

The Grand Jury again returned into court and brought with them a Bill of Indictment for an affray, the State against HENRY, JOSHUA and ADAM LAZENBY, a true bill and again returned to consider for further presentments.

The due execution of an Indenture of Bargain and Sale from JEREMIAH HARBISON to THEODRICK F. BRADFORD for 160 acres of land, it being the north west quarter of Section 24 of Township 56 north, in Range 21 west in the tract of land appropriated by Act of Congress for Military Bounties in Territory of Missouri north, acknowledged and ordered to be certified.

The Grand Jury again returned into court and brought with them a Bill of Indictment, the State against JEREMIAH HARBISON, a true bill and again returned to consider for further presentments.

The State vs JEREMIAH HARBISON - The defendant being charged pleads guilty and is fined $1.00 and pay cost of this indictment.

HENRY CRABB vs McGOWEN & BAUGH - The plaintiff by his attorney says he wishes no further to prosecute this suit and the defendant assumes the payment of all costs. This suit to be dismissed and the plaintiff recover his costs.

WILLIAM E. KENNEDY vs WILLIAM EDMISTON - The plaintiff says he intends no further to prosecute this suit and assumes the payment of all costs. This suit to be dismissed and the defendant recover his costs.

ENOS IVES vs ELIJAH LOYD - The plaintiff says he wishes no further to prosecute this suit and the defendant assumes the payment of all costs. Suit to be dismissed and the plaintiff recover his costs.

THOMAS ALLEY vs MARIBLE & HARTSFIELD - The plaintiff by his attorney and says that he wishes to dismiss this suit and the defendant assumes the payment of all costs. This suit to be dismissed and the plaintiff recover his costs.

THOMAS ALLEY vs MARIBLE & HARTSFIELD - The plaintiff by his attorney and says he wishes to dismiss this suit and the defendant assumes the payment of all costs. Suit to be dismissed and the plaintiff recover his costs.

FRANCIS PORTERFIELD vs WILLIAM MOREHEAD - The plaintiff says he wishes to dismiss this suit and the defendant assumes the payment of all costs. This suit be dismissed and the plaintiff recover his costs.

A Deed of Conveyance from ABNER PILLOW & GIDEON PILLOW to ELIJAH WRIGHT & GEORGE L. LENARD for 230 acres of land and ordered to be certified.

JOHN ROBB vs JOHN OWENS - The defendant confessed that he owes the plaintiff $688.00. Plaintiff to recover against the defendant his costs.

WEDNESDAY JULY 17, 1822

Justices present were CHARLES BOYLES, RICHARD FLYNT and WILLIAM SMITH, Esquires.

The State vs FRANCIS A. BRADLEY - Indictment of Petit Larceny - The defendant being charged and pleads not guilty. This cause is continued on affidavit of EVEN B. BRADLEY until next term of this court.

FRANCIS A. BRADLEY appeared in court and acknowledged himself indebted to the State of Tennessee for $200.00 and EVEN A. BRADLEY appeared into court and acknowledged himself indebted to the State of Tennessee for $500.00 to be levied of their goods and chattels &c but to be void on conditions that said FRANCIS A. BRADLEY appear here in October and answer upon a charge of Petit Larceny.

SAMUEL BRADLEY, admr vs ELI GARRETT, admr - This day came the parties by their attorneys and a jury of men, to wit, CONRAD KYMES, DAVID SNODDY, JAMES F. DRIVER, JOHN NICHOLS, AMOS DEAVERS, JOSHUA DALLAS, DANIEL WAGGONER, SAMUEL WILSON, JOHN B. BUCHANAN, SOLOMON REECE, AUGUSTUS L. JONES, and THOMAS ALLEY being elected and sworn and said that JOHN KELLY in his lifetime did assume and undertake in manner and form as charged and they assess the plaintiff's damages of $300.00. Plaintiff recover his costs.

JACOB STONEBRAKER acknowledged himself indebted to the State of Tennessee for $100.00 to be levied upon his goods and chattels &c but to be void on conditions that he appear here in October to prosecute and give evidence in behalf of the State against FRANCIS A. BRADLEY upon a Bill of Indictment for Petit Larceny.

A Power of Attorney from ROBERT SMITH and MILDRED SMITH to AMOS HURLEY. MILDRED SMITH being examined apart fron her husband and ordered to be certified.

NATHANIEL B. BUCKINGHAM vs THOMAS H. MAY - This cause is continued and an order to take depositions.

THOMAS CHAPMAN vs JAMES D. EASTIS - The plaintiff says he wishes to dismiss this suit and the defendant assumes the payment of all costs. Suit to be dismissed and plaintiff recover his costs.

JOSHUA GRAHAM vs JAMES WYATT - The plaintiff by his attorney says he intends no further to prosecute this suit and assumes the payment of all costs. Suit to be dismissed and defendant recover his costs.

JOHN P. McCONNELL vs JAMES P. BAXTER - The plaintiff says he wishes to dismiss this suit and assumes the payment of half and the defendant assumes the other half. Suit to be dismissed and each party pay half of the costs.

JOHN ALLBRIGHT vs JAMES FULGHAM - This day came the parties by their attorneys and a jury of men, to wit, ABSOLEM BEARD, THOMAS McGAUGH, BENJAMIN NEELD, CHARLES TULY, THOMAS KERCHEVAL, WILLIAM CONWAY, CLABORN WHITWORTH, ELIHU ROE, JOHN WITT, ALEXANDER BEARD, JOEL ORRICK, and URIAH BABBIT being elected and sworn and said that the plaintiff is indebted to the defendant for $8.50. Defendant recover his costs.

SOLOMON REECE vs JOHN McKINLEY - This day came the parties by their attorneys and a jury of men, to wit, DAVID SNODDY, JOSHUA DALLAS, JOHN DEVIN, PATRICKO'CALAGHAN, SAMUEL BUCHANAN, SAMUEL BRADLEY, FRANCIS PATTON, RANDOLPH QUARLES, JORDAN SOLOMON, DANIEL WHITAKER, THOMAS TOWERY, and ABRAHAM DEPOSITER being elected and sworn and said that they found in favor of the plaintiff.

THURSDAY JULY 18, 1822

Justices present were CHARLES BOYLES, WILLIAM BEAVERS and HUGH M. BLAKE, Esquires.

A Power of Attorney from CASSANDRA McLIN to THOMAS BOTELER of Washington, Maryland, acknowledged, she first being examined separate and apart from her husband and ordered to be certified.

The State vs HENRY LITTLE - Assault & Battery - The defendant being charged pleads guilty and is fined $5.00 and pay costs of this indictment. HENRY KYMES as security.

The State vs JOHN W. ISAACKS - Assault & Battery - The defendant being charged pleads guilty and is fined $7.50 and pay the cost of this indictment. JACOB WAGGONER and HUGH M. BLAKE his securities

The Grand Jury again returned to court and brought with them a Bill of Indictment against DRURY K. SMITH for Petit Larceny, a true bill and again returned to consider for further presentments.

The Grand Jury again returned into court and brought with them a Bill of Indictment against DAVID A. MARKHAM for an assault, a true bill and again returned to consider for further presentments.

The due execution of an Indenture of Bargain and Sale from MAY BUCHANAN to JACOB WRIGHT for 38 3/4 acres of land and ordered to be certified.

The Grand Jury again returned into court and brought with them a Bill of Indictment against JOHN BERRY and JOHN FORD, a true bill and again returned to consider for further presentments.

The due execution of an Indenture of Bargain and Sale from JOHN OWENS, JR. to AMOS DAVIS for 110 acres of land and ordered to be certified.

The due execution of an Indenture of Bargain and Sale from BENJAMIN WHITAKER to JOHN DUSENBURY for 10 acres of land and ordered to be certified.

An inventory of the estate of ROBERT NIX, deceased, was returned to court by his admrx and ordered to be certified.

A Power of Attorney from JOSEPH MOORE to JAMES TUCKER was proven by WILLIAM CRUNK and THOMAS S. MILAM and ordered to be certified.

The State vs JOHN P. McCONNELL - An Assault and Battery - The defendant being charged and pleads guilty and is fined $5.00 and pay the costs of this indictment.

The State vs JOHN FORD An Affray - The defendant being charged pleads guilty and is fined $5.00 and pay the costs of this indictment.

The State vs DAVID A. MARKHAM - The defendant being charged for an assault upon WILLIAM MOREHEAD failed to appear into court but made default and that the said recognizance is forfeited and DANIEL A. MARKHAM to pay $250.00.

ERRON LOYD who was bound in a recognizance for the appearance of DAVID A. MARKHAM at this term of court, was called to bring in DAVID A. MARKHAM, failed to do so but made default. ERRON LOYD to pay $100.25.

JOHN SMITH who was bound in a recognizance for the appearance of DAVID A. MARKHAM at this term of court, was called to bring in DAVID A. MARKHAM, failed to do so but made default. JOHN SMITH to pay $100.25.

The State vs CARTER WEBB & JOHN WEBB - CARTER WEBB & JOHN WEBB, GEORGE WEBB, ROBERT LACKEY, JAMES TAYLOR and RICHARD WEBB appeared into court and acknowledged themselves indebted to the State of Tennessee for $250.00 each and to be levied of their respective goods and chattels &c but to be void on conditions that CARTER WEBB and JOHN WEBB appear in next court in September to answer the State of Tennessee for Grand Larceny.

ABRAHAM FITCH & JOHN H. WILLIAMS appeared in court and acknowledged themselves indebted to the State of Tennessee for $250.00 to be levied of their respective goods and chattels &c but to be void on conditions that ABRAHAM FITCH appear here at next Circuit Court in September to prosecute and give evidence in behalf of the State against CARTER WEBB & JOHN WEBB for Grand Larceny.

SOLOMON REECE vs JOHN McKINLEY - The jury elected returned into court and said that the defendant is guilty as charged and assess the plaintiff's damages of $163.68. Plaintiff recover his costs.

The State vs DRURY K. SMITH - Indictment for Petit Larceny - The defendant being charged pleads not guilty and a jury of men, to wit, CONRAD KYMES, JOHN DAVIS, ABSOLEM DAVIS, MANSFIELD HUSBANDS, PRESTON HAMPTON, JOHN CAMPBELL, JORDAN REECE, JACOB WRIGHT, MATHEW WILSON, WILLIAM SOLOMON, JOSEPH HENDERSON, and ELIJAH DILLENDER being elected and sworn and said that the jury was put under the care of WILLIAM P. PULLIAM, a Constable, until next day.

RUBEN H. BOON is appointed overseer of the road in the room of DANIEL W. HARRISON and call on the usual hands.

JOHN WHITAKER & others, Commissioners vs JOHN GREER - About 4 o'clock in the evening of this day, Thursday, DRURY K. SMITH who was indicted for larceny and had laid in jail for some time was brought into court and was charged and plead to the indictment, a jury was summoned and was to deliver a copy to the defendant's council and about to be put to the defendant for election but had not been put to him and at this time in the case of JOHN WHITAKER and others against JOHN GREER on the appearance docket. A motion wa made to dismiss said case. Motion was objected. To be taken up next day at court.

FRIDAY JULY 19, 1822

Justices present were JACOB WAGGONER, WILLIAM SMITH and CHARLES BOYLES, Esquires.

The Commissioners appointed by the court at last term to settle with SARAH LOYD, admrx on the estate of EPHRAIM LOYD, deceased, made return to court the settlement by them made and ordered to be certified.

The due execution of an Indenture of Bargain and Sale from WILLIAM BOON to WILLLIAM SANDERS for 7 acres of land and ordered to be certified.

JOHN LANDRESS, admr vs ROBERT FLETCHER - This cause is continued and a Commission is awarded the plaintiff to take the deposition of EBENEZER TITUS of Huntsville to be read as evidence on the trial of the above cause by giving the defendant ten days notice of time and place of taking same.

The Grand Jury again returned into court and brought with them a Bill of Indictment against JOHN FORD for an assault and battery, a true bill and again returned to consider for further presentments.

DRURY K. SMITH, PHILIP KOONCE, EDWARD MOSS, THOMAS WHITWORTH and HAMILTON MOFFIT appeared in court and acknowledged themselves indebted to the State of Tennessee for $250.00 to be levied of their respective goods and chattels &c but to be void on condition that DRURY K. SMITH appear here tomorrow and answer the State of Tennessee for Petit Larceny.

SATURDAY JULY 20, 1822

Justices present were HUGH M. BLAKE, AMBROSE BARKER and WILLIAM SMITH, Esquires.

The due execution of an Indenture of Bargain and Sale from JESSE W. COCK to THOMAS JACKSON for 40 acres of land and ordered to be certified.

On petition, it is ordered by the court that the clerk receive and place on the Tax List four town lots in the town of Fayetteville, the property of MATHEW GIBSON and that he pay a single tax for the same.

KENNEDY MOFFIT vs WILLIAM CRABTREE - The plaintiff says he intends no further to prosecute this suit and assumes the payment of all costs. Suit to be dismissed and defendant recover his costs.

The State vs DRURY K. SMITH - Indictment for Petit Larceny - The jury elected and says the defendant is not guilty as charged. Defendant be dismissed.

An Indentire of Bargain and Sale from BRICE M. GARNER to STEPHEN ALEXANDER and JOHN DUKE for 126 acres of land, proven by A. CAMPBELL & JOSEPH HINKLE and ordered to be certified.

The State vs GEORGE W. HUNT - JOHN DAVIS and JOHN CRAWFORD appeared in court and acknowledged themselves indebted to the State of Tennessee for $100.00 each to be levied of their respective goods and chattels &c but to be void on condition that they appear here in October next to prosecute and give evidence in behalf of the State against GEORGE W. HUNT for an assault and battery.

The State vs WILLIAM WHAM - THOMAS H. FLETCHER, the Attorney General, came into court and says he wishes to dismiss this suit and the defendant assumes the payment of all costs. Suit to be dismissed and the defendant pay the costs.

MONDAY JULY 22, 1822

Justices present were HUGH M. BLAKE, WILLIAM BEAVER and CHARLES BOYLES, Esquires.

The due execution of an Indenture of Bargain and Sale from BRICE M. GARNER to BENJAMIN PORTER for 4 acres of land and ordered to be certified.

The due execution of an Indenture of bargain and Sale from THOMAS BUCHANAN to SAMUEL BUCHANAN for 55 acres of land, proven by GEORGE MITCHEL and JOSEPH COMMONS and ordered to be certified.

The due execution of an Indenture of bargain and Sale from DAVID LAWRANCE to WILLIAM COOK for 100 acres of land and ordered to be certified.

The due execution of an Indenture of Bargain and Sale from ALEXANDER DACUS to WILLIAM DACUS for 52 acres of land and ordered to be certified.

The due execution of an Indenture of Bargain and Sale from ROBERT M. WHITE to JOHN KENNEDY for 200 acres of land and orderd to be certified.

The due execution of an Indenture of Bargain and Sale from JOHN DAWDY to JOHN C. SMITH for 146 acres of land and ordered to be certified.

The due execution of an Indenture of Bargain and Sale from JOHN DAWDY to JAMES C. SMITH for 18 acres of land and ordered to be certified.

An amount of sale of the estate of CHRISTOPHER MILLER, deceased, was returned to court by his executor and ordered to be certified.

The due execution of an Indenture of Bargain and Sale from BRICE M. GARNER to LUCY WHITE for 20 acres of land, proven by E. COBB and BENJAMIN FARREL and ordered to be certified.

The Transfer of a PLat and Certificate from SAMUEL RAGSDALE to JOHN HOLCOM, proven by ROBERT HOLCOM and HARDY HIGHTOWER and ordered to be certified.

The Transfer of a Plat and Certificate from SAMUEL RAGSDALE to KINCHEN HOLCOM, proven by ROBERT HOLCOM and HARDY HIGHTOWER and ordered to be certified.

A Power of Attorney from SAMUEL CRAWFORD TO JOHN CRAWFORD of Virginia and ordered to be certified.

EPHRAIM KING is appointed overseer of the road leading from Looney's settlement to the Pond Spring in the room of DAVID ARMSTRONG and call on the same hands that worked under ARMSTRONG.

SAMUEL CUNNINGHAM is appointed overseer of that part of the road leading from Fayetteville to Shelbyville which RICHARD COTHAM was overseer of and call on the same hands that worked under COTHAM.

CLEMENT HILL vs JOHN GIBSON - Appeal - The defendant acknowledged that he owes the plaintiff $1.50. Plaintiff to recover his costs.

ANDREW KING is appointed overseer of the road in the room of STERLING C. McLEMORE resigned and call on the usual hands.

The due execution of an Indenture of Bargain and Sale from RICHARD COTHAM to PETER FIREBAUGH for 20 acres of land and ordered to be certified.

The due execution of an Indenture of Bargain and Sale from RICHARD COTHAM to PETER FIREBAUGH for 40 acres of land and ordered to be certified.

The due execution of an Indenture of Bargain and Sale from WILLIAM RITCHARDSON to DANIEL WARREN for 15 acres of land and ordered to be certified.

The due execution of an Indenture of Bargain and Sale from KINCHEN HOLCOM to JAMES CARITHERS for 43 acres of land and orderd to be certified.

The due execution of an Indenture of Bargain and Sale from WILLIAM H. RAGSDALE to JAMES CARITHERS , MATHEW CARITHERS, FANNEY R. CARITHERS, and SAMUEL CARITHERS, heirs of SAMUEL CARITHERS, for 185 acres of land, proven by THOMAS H. WILLIAMS and HARDY HIGHTOWER and ordered to be certified.

The due execution of an Indenture of Bargain and Sale from FREDERICK A. BURNES to JAMES DANIEL for 45 acres of land, proven by ELNATHAN DAVIS and P. GILLASPIE and ordered to be certified.

The State vs GABRIEL SEAHORN - Indictment for Larceny - The defendant being charged and pleads not guilty and a jury of men, to wit, CONRAD KYMES, DAVID SNODDY, BENJAMIN CLEMENTS, JOHN McMILLIN, JOHN LEE, JOHN GIBSON, JAMES BROWN, WILLIS WARREN, JACKSON BLAKEMORE, BENJAMIN WHITAKER, and ALEXANDER DACUS being elected and sworn and said that the defendant is not guilty. Defendant be discharged and that EZEKIEL GILLIUM, the prosecutor, pay the costs.

The State vs DANIEL WHITAKER - Indictment for an Assault and Battery - The defendant being charged pleads guilty and is fined $3.00 and pay the cost.

WATKINS & WHORTON vs THOMAS L. TROTTER - This day came the parties by their attorneys and a jury of men, to wit, SAMUEL BUTLER, BENJAMIN PROCTOR, JOHN LEE, JAMES D. ALLFORD, WILLIAM DOAK, WILLIAM TIMMONS, JAMES TOOL, JAMES RUTHERFORD, REECE HOWELL, SAMUEL WILSON, STEPHEN PHILLIPS, and JOEL ORRICK being elected and sworn and said that they assess the plaintiff's damages of $98.58. Plaintiff to recover his costs.

ROBERT BOYD for the use of vs M. & J. WILSON - This day came the parties by their attorneys and a jury of men, to wit, ROMEO LEWIS, JESSE B. CLEMENTS, JAMES H. PULLIAM, SAMUEL BAKER, VANCE GREER, PATRICK O'CALAGHAN, JOHN R. MOORE, ABSOLEM BEARD, DAVID SNODDY, ROBERT S. HULME, JOHN BREWER, and WILLIAM MOFFIT being elected and sworn and said that the defendant has not paid the debt of $184.50 and damages of $10.75. Plaintiff to recover his costs.

THOMAS CHAMPLAIN vs HENRY ALLEN - (same as above) and said that the defendant has not paid the debt of $157.67 and damages of $23.66. Plaintiff to recover his costs.

THOMAS CHAMPLAIN vs VANCE GREER - This day came the parties by their attorneys and a jury of men, to wit, ROMEO LEWIS, JESSE B. CLEMENTS, JAMES H. PULLIAM, SAMUEL BAKER, VANCE GREER, PATRICK O'CALAGHAN, JOHN R. MOORE, ABSOLEM BEARD, DAVID SNODDY, ROBERT S. HULME, JOHN BREWER, and WILLIAM MOFFIT being elected and sworn and said that the defendant has not paid the debt of $200.00 and damages of $6.50. Plaintiff to recover his costs.

PETER VAUGHN vs MAY BUCHANAN - Debt - (same as above) and said that the defendant has not paid the debt of $102.87½ and damages of $2.80. Plaintiff to recover his costs.

ROBERT & M. HERROLD vs EBENEZER McEWEN - (same as above) and said that the defendant has not paid the debt of $100.00 and damages of $12.75. Plaintiff to recover his costs.

TUESDAY JULY 23, 1822

Justices present were HUGH M. BLAKE, WILLIAM BEAVERS and JAMES RALSTON, Esquires.

A Bill of Sale from THOMAS ALLY and ISAIAH ALLEY to JAMES HOLMAN for a negro girl named MOURNING and ordered to be certified.

The Grand Jury returned into court and brought with them a Bill of Indictment against WILLIAM SMITH, JAMES HOBBS and GEORGE ST. JOHN BASKINS for an affray, a true bill and again returned to consider for further presentments.

N. PINDLAND vs LIVINGSTON J. BROWN - Debt Appeal - This day came the parties by their attorneys and a jury of men, to wit, SAMUEL WILSON, ASBURY CHAMNESS, CLABOURN WHITWORTH, JORDAN SOLOMON, DAVID SNODDY, JOHN LEE, SAMUEL BAKER, CONRAD KYMES, JOHN WATKINS, ELIJAH YATES, THOMAS ALLEY, and JOHN SHOEMAKER being elected and sworn and said that the defendant owes the plaintiff $19.25. Plaintiff to recover his costs and NANCY BROWN his security.

JAMES McLAUGHLIN for the use vs GARNER & BOYLES - (same as above) and said that the defendant has not paid the debt of $1272.00 and damages of $57.00. Plaintiff to recover his costs.

EDMOND WILLIAMSON vs BRICE M. GARNER - (same as above) and said that the defendant did assume upon himself as charged and the damages assessed to $141.50. Plaintiff to recover his costs.

JOSEPH MOONEY vs JOHN P. McCONNELL - (same as above) and said that the defendant has not paid all of the debt but owes a balance of $225.66 2/3 and damages of $7.25. Plaintiff to recover his costs. Defendant prays for an appeal and is granted same.

ABRAHAM HOGLAND vs JOHN BOYERS - (same as above) and said that the defendant has not paid all the debt but owes a balance of $137.00 and damages of $3.00. Plaintiff to recover his costs.

JOHN H. SMITH vs JAS. COALTER & B.M. GARNER - (same as above) and said that the defendant has not paid the debt of $4108.22 and damages of $82.00. Plaintiff recover his costs. Defendant prays for an appeal and is granted same.

ROBERT & M. HERROLD vs VANCE GREER - Debt - (same as above) and said that the defendant has not paid the debt of $100.00 and damages of $12.33½. Plaintiff to recover his costs.

JOSHUA GRAHAM vs PETER MOYERS - (same as above) and said that the defendant has not paid the debt of $187.50 and damages of $5.15½. Plaintiff to recover his costs.

WILLIAM DYE vs JOHN P. McCONNELL - (same as above) and said .that the defendant has not paid all the debt but leaves a balance of $432.83 and damages of $12.25. Plaintiff recover his costs. Defemdamt prays for an appeal and is granted same.

JAMES GILLASPIE vs VANCE GREER - (same as above) and said that the defendant has not paid the debt of $200.00 and damages of $6.62½. Plaintiff recover his costs.

GEORGE PEARCE vs NATHANIEL B. BUCKINGHAM - Debt Appeal - This day came the parties by their attorneys and a jury of men, to wit, SAMUEL WILSON, ASBURY CHAMNESS, CLABORN WHITWORTH, JORDAN SOLOMON, DAVID SNODDY, JOHN LEE, SAMUEL BAKER, CONRAD KYMES, JOHN WATKINS, ELIJAH YATES, THOMAS ALLEY, and JOHN SHOEMAKER being elected and said that the defendant has not paid the debt of $178.75 and damages of $10.72. Plaintiff recover his costs.

BENJAMIN PATTERSON vs HENRY ALLEN - (same as above) and said that the defendant has not paid the debt of $361.01 and damages of $29.25. Plaintiff recover his costs.

BENJAMIN PATTERSON vs HENRY ALLEN - (same as above) and said that the defendant has not paid the debt of $156.87 and damages of $3.00. Plaintiff recover his costs.

THOMAS MILTON vs THOMAS ALLEY & JNO. WATKINS - (same as above) and said that the defendant has not paid the debt of $105.00 and damages of $3/50. Plaintiff to recover his costs. Defendant prays for an appeal and is granted same.

SAMUEL HART vs BENJAMIN GEORGE - (same as above) and said that the defendant has not paid all the debt, but a balance of $143.28 and damages of $11.06¼. Plaintiff to recover his costs.

WILLIAM H. MURPHEY for the use vs JAS. & WILLIAM BROWN - (same as above) and said that the defendant has not paid the debt of $400.00 and damages of $182.00. Plaintiff recover his costs.

JOHN P. McCONNELL vs THOMAS ALLEY - (same as above) and said that the defendant has not paid the debt of $147.72½ and damages of $8.00. Plaintiff recover his costs.

JOHN P. McCONNELL vs THOMAS ALLEY - (same as above) and said that the defendant has not paid the debt of $99.68 3/4 and damages of $1.25. Plaintiff to recover his costs. Defendant prays for an appeal and is granted same.

The State vs SAMUEL WILSON - THOMAS H. FLETCHER, Attorney, says he wishes no further to prosecute this suit and the defendant assumes the payment of all costs. Suit to be dismissed and defendant pay costs and HENRY LAZENBY his security.

JACOB HAMILTON vs BENJAMIN GEORGE - This day came the parties by their attorneys and a jury of men, to wit, (same as above jurors) being elected and sworn and said that the defendant has not paid all the debt but owes a balance of $239.30 and damages of $23.81¼. Plaintiff recover his costs.

A. CRAWFORD vs BENJAMIN GEORGE - (same as above) and said that the defendant has not paid the debt of $122.38 and damages of $3.00. Plaintiff recover his costs.

The State vs MAY BUCHANAN - Indictment A & B (Assault & Battery) - The defendant being charged pleads guilty and is fined $5.00 and pay costs. ROBERT CUNNINGHAM and CHARLES T. REECE, securities.

The State vs ROBERT STUBBLEFIELD - The defendant, on motion, it is considered by the court that this case be set aside and defendant paying the costs.

The State vs HENRY LAZENBY and others - The defendant being charged pleads guilty and is fined $5.00 and pay costs. MORGAN CLAYTON, security.

A. & J. CONWELL vs STERLING C. McLEMORE - The plaintiff says he wishes to dismiss this suit and assumes the payment of one half of the costs and the defendant assumes payment of the other half. Suit to be dismissed and each pay one half of the costs.

GEORGE W. HIGGINS for use of vs SAMUEL BUCHANAN - The plaintiff recover against defendant $144.37½ and $15.12½ damages besides the further sum of $9.14 costs of the original suit. Defendant prayed for an appeal and granted same.

JAMES D. ALLFORD vs JAMES WYATT - This cause is continued on affidavit of the defendant and a Commission is awarded to take the deposition of JOHN WYATT or any other person wheresoever they may be, to be read on evidence on above by giving the

the plaintiff twenty days notice of time and place of taking same.

GEORGE W. HOPKINS vs Y.H. MERRELL - The defendant by his attorney moved the court to dismiss this suit because the plaintiff did not appear to prosecute. Suit to be dismissed and defendant recover his costs.

WILLIAM SHIPMAN vs JOHN GREER - The plaintiff by his attorney says he wishes no further to prosecute this suit and assumes payment of all costs. Suit to be dismissed and defendant recover his costs.

CHARLES BOYLES vs JOHN GREER - (same as above).

LENNAN WATSON vs JOHN DILLON - Motion - The Sheriff was directed to expose to sale 14½ acres of land lying on the waters of Flint River adjoining the trial that said DILLON now lives on to satisfy a judgment that LENNAN WATSON recovered against DILLON before ROBERT DICKSON, Esquire, on 3rd April 1822 for $16.75 and all costs.

MALCOM GILCHRIST vs ISAAC GATTIS - The defendant acknowledged that he owes the plaintiff $62.25. Plaintiff to recover his costs.

ALEXANDER McLIN vs NIMROD BAILEY - The defendant acknowledged that he owes the plaintiff $165.00 and damages of $10.31¼. Plaintiff to recover his costs.

STEPHEN PHILLIPS vs JOSEPH HINKLE - The plaintiff by his attorney, says he intends no further to prosecute this suit and assumes the payment of all costs. Suit to be dismissed and defendant recover against WILLIAM E. McKINNEY the costs.

On petition of JOEL PINSON, security for JOHN W. SMITH and JESSE HOLBERT, admrs of JOEL HOLBERT, deceased. Court ordered that JOHN W. SMITH appear here at next term of court to give security or surrender the effects in his hands of the deceased.

A Deed of Conveyance from THOMAS BUCHANAN to SAMUEL BUCHANAN for 100 acres of land, proven by HENRY CLIFT and ordered to be certified.

A Deed of Conveyance from CHARLES SPRINKLE to JAMES BRYANS for one town lot, proven by F. PORTERFIELD and ordered to be certified.

A Deed of Conveyance from JAMES DANIEL to ELNATHAN DAVIS and ordered to be certified.

STEWART & HARGRAVE vs R.C. & J. PREWITT - The defendant confessed judgment to the plaintiff for $83.00. Plaintiffs to recover their costs.

MONDAY OVTOBER 21, 1822

JESSE LEDBETTER is appointed overseer of the road in the room of DANIEL COBLE resigned and call on the usual hands.

PETER COTTON is appointed overseer of the road from the east corner of DAVID ARMSTRONG's field to JOSEPH GREER's mill and that he call on JOHN H. MOORE for five hands.

JAMES PITTS is appointed overseer of the road in the room of ALEXANDER COWEN and call on the usual hands.

DOAK NICKS is appointed (overseer) of the road leading up Norris Creek from the fork of the road above JOHN McMILLIN to the top of the ridge above WILLIAM C. HODGES and call on the ususal hands.

JAMES FORISTER is appointed overseer of the road from the top of the ridge above WILLIAM H. HODGE to NICHOLAS CARRIGER's meadow and call on the usual hands.

JOHN MARR, CORNELIUS DARNELL, JOSEPH HINKLE and JOHN BEATY are appointed to lay off the hands to work on the road leading from Fayetteville by DAVID P. MUNROE to the Fishingford to the county line.

WILLIAM EDMISTON, CHARLES BOYLES, SAMUEL BUCHANAN and EBENEZER McEWEN, Esquires, are appointed to lay off the hands to work on the road leading from Fayetteville to Shelbyville as far as the county line.

WILLIAM FROST, JOSEPH HINKLE, JOHN CRAWFORD, WILLIAM CRAWFORD, SR., JAMES BLAIR, WILLIAM C. KENNEDY, and JOSHUA GIBSON are appointed a Jury of View to view and mark out a road the nearest and best way from Fayetteville to JAMES CRAWFORD's mill and make return to next court.

SAMUEL CRAWFORD is appointed overseer of the road in the place of DAVID P. MUNROE and call on the usual hands.

GABRIEL SEAHORN is appointed overseer of theroad leading from CUNNINGHAM's mill to the mouth of Swan Creek and JOHN PORTER, Esquire, is appointed to lay off the hands to work on said road.

DAVID SMITH, AMOS DAVIS, JESSE DAVIS, ABNER COLLINS, WILLIAM HUCABY, RANDOLPH ALLSUP and JOHN TRIMBLE are appointed a Jury of View to view and mark out a road beginning at DAVID SMITH to the county line and in a direction to EDMUND WILLIAMSON in Giles County and make return to next court.

ALEXANDER HEWEY is appointed overseer of the new road from CUNNINGHAM's mill to ABSALUM BOSTICK and call on the usual hands.

NIMROD BAILY is appointed overseer of the road in the place of JAMES LINGO resigned and call on the usual hands.

ANTHONY B. CLENDENING is appointed overseer of the road in the room of JESSE BONNER resigned and call on the usual hands.

WILLIAM R. WOODRUFF is appointed overseer of the road in the room of a LARY EPPS and call on the usual hands.

WILLIAM SOLOMON is allowed a sledge hammer for use of that part of the road which he is overseer of.

JOHN PINKERTON, Esquire, is appointed to lay off the hands to work on that part of the road which JOHN PARKERSON is overseer of from EDWARD MOSS to JOSEPH DEAN.

It is ordered by the court that JOHN GREER be allowed and to receive from the County Trustee of this county the sum of $15,73 the amount of taxes which he could not collect for the year 1814.

ANDREW McCARTNEY, CHARLES H. EDMISTON, REECE HOWELL, HENRY KELSO, PHILIP KOONCE, JOSHUA DODSON, and ELISHA THOMASON are appointed a Jury of View to turn the road leading up Stewarts Creek so as to injure the lands of WILLIAM EDMISTON and make return to next county day.

It is ordered by the court that the road leading from Fayetteville to Shelbyville by WILLIAM EDMISTON and the road leading from Fayetteville to Huntsville and the road leading from Fayetteville to and by DAVID P. MUNROE to the Fishingford be on the first class. The road leaving from Fayetteville up Mulberry Creek by JOHN RHEA, from Fayetteville to Winchester crossing Elk River at Dennis Ferry from Fayetteville to Pulaski the road leading up Stewarts Creek. The road on to Athens, the road that passes by HUGH M. BLAKE's are in the second class and all other roads that are not mentioned above in this county are considered in the third class.

It is ordered that JOSEPH McMILLIN, JOHN CRAWFORD, JOSEPH JENKINS, STEPHEN COLE, JOHN GRIFFIS, HUGH PARKERSON, ELI GARRETT, SAMUEL BUCHANAN, Esquire, WILLIAM DICKSON, JAMES FORSYTH, ISAAC HOLMAN, JACOB WAGGONER, HENRY KELSO, BENJAMIN HUDSON, DAVID SMITH, JOSEPH COMMONS, ABRAHAM SUMNERS, JOHN PINKERTON, FRANCIS PATTON, JESSE DANIEL, WILLIAM ABELS, WILLIAM ANDERSON, WILLIAM SMITH, ALEXANDER MEEK, WILLIAM PATTERSON, and SILAS McCLELLAN be appointed as Jurors to the next Circuit Court in March next.

It is ordered that JAMES HIGGINS, HAY CRAWFORD, JAMES HAGUE, ABRAHAM DUDNEY, RANDOLPH QUARLES, RANDOLPH BRYANT, ZACHARIAH ARNOLD, JOSEPH PENN, ALEXANDER MORTON, JAMES PHILLIPS, SHEPPARD SHELTON, JOSEPH DEAN, HIGDON HARPER, SAMUEL BUCHANAN, HOWEL HARRIS, ISAAC SEBASTIAN, JOHN J. WHITAKER, DANIEL READ, WILLIAM SPENCER, WILLIAM WOODRUFF, SOLOMON GULLETT, JAMES BRYANT, WILLIAM McELROY, JOHN WITT, DAVID TWING, BENJAMIN PORTER, and JOHN R. JOHNSON be summoned as Jurors to the next County Court in

January next.

DAVID ARMSTRONG is appointed overseer of the road from AMOS SMALL to the east corner of said ARMSTRONG's field and WILLIAM EDMISTON give a list of hands.

JONATHAN FLOYD, Esquire, resigns his appointment as a Justice of the Peace for Lincoln County.

JOEL DODD is appointed overseer of the road in the room of DAVID DODD resigned and call on the usual hands.

ANDREW W. WALKER is released from paying a double tax for the year 1822 and that he pay a single tax only.

JOSEPH SEBASTIAN is released from paying a double tax for the year 1822 and that he pay a single tax only.

CHRISTOPHER SHOFNER is released from paying a double tax for the year 1822 and that he pay a single tax only.

JOHN PARKS is appointed overseer of a road in the room of JOSEPH NICHOLS and call on the usual hands.

SHEPPARD SHELTON is released from paying a tax on 252 acres of land.

ENOCH SHELTON is released from paying a tax on 119 acres of land.

The Sheriff made return that he had let out MRS. JOHNSON, one of the poor of this county, to THOMAS CHAPMAN for $47.00 to maintain one year from last court who gave bond and security.

It is ordered by the court that WILLIAM E. KENNEDY and ARGYLE CAMPBELL procure two stones for the use of the courthouse and that the COunty Trustee pay for the same out of the county monies that comes to his hands.

DANIEL LOONEY, ENOCK K. RUST, WILLIAM DYE, JESSE DANIEL and JOSEPH McCRACKEN appeared in court and took the oath of Justice of the Peace for Lincoln County.

OBIA HOLLAWAY is appointed overseer of the road from Teal's mill to the Gum Spring and call on the usual hands.

JOHN ENOCKS and JAMES CURRY are appointed Commissioners to settle with JONATHAN FLOYD, executor of WILLIAM N. PATTERSON, deceased, and make return to next court.

JOEL JOHNSON is released from paying a double tax for the year 1822 and that he pay a single tax only.

The due execution of an Indenture of Bargain and Sale from SOLOMON BURFORD to JAMES PHILLIPS for 71½ acres of land and ordered to be certified.

A Deed of Conveyance from JOHN CLARK to SOLOMON BURFORD for 105 acres of land and ordered to be certified.

A Deed of Conveyance from MARGARET ROSEBOROUGH, executrix of WILLIAM ROSEBOROUGH, deceased, to JAMES ROSEBOROUGH for 120 acres of land and ordered to be certified.

A Deed of Conveyance from MARGARET ROSEBOROUGH, exrx of WILLIAM ROSEBOROUGH, deceased, to JAMES ROSEBOROUGH for 14¼ acres of land and ordered to be certified.

A Deed of Conveyance from SAMUEL S. BUCHANAN to WILLIAM C. KENNEDY for 100 acres of land and ordered to be certified.

A Deed of Conveyance from ISAAC JAMES to ISAAC SMITH for 225 acres of land and ordered to be certified.

A Deed of Conveyance from JOSEPH UNDERWOOD to JOHN SIVILLY for 20 acres of land, proven and ordered to be certified.

A Deed of Conveyance from JOSEPH PENN to WILLIAM BEAVERS for 100 acres of land and ordered to be certified.

A Deed of Conveyance from ROBERT BIGGERS to FRANCIS HODGES for 60 acres of land, proven by JAMES & WILLIAM NIXON and ordered to be certified.

A Deed of Conveyance from JOHN MURDOCK to DEMPSAY ALLEN for 52 acres of land and ordered to be certified.

A Deed of Conveyance from HENRY M. RUTLEDGE to SAMUEL BUCHANAN, JR. for 50 acres of land and ordered to be certified.

A Deed of Conveyance from HENRY M. RUTLEDGE to JOHN R. MOORE for 200 acres of land and ordered to be certified.

A Deed of Conveyance from EZEKIEL NORRIS to WILLIAM TIMMINS for 75½ acres of land and ordered to be certified.

A Deed of Conveyance from MICAJAH McELROY to WILLIAM EDMONDSON for 30 acres of land and ordered to be certified.

A Deed of Conveyance from WILLIAM MOORE to the heirs of PRESLEY GEORGE for 185 acres of land and ordered to be certified.

A Deed of Conveyance from JOHN WAGGONER to PHILIP FOX for 400 acres of land and ordered to be certified.

A Deed of Conveyance from JAMES ROSEBOROUGH to JOSEPH PETTY for 26 acres of land and ordered to be certified.

A Deed of Conveyance from JONATHAN HAYS to THOMAS W. HAYS for 70 acres of land and ordered to be certified.

A Deed of Conveyance from JOHN OWEN to WILLIAM HOLBERT for 50 acres of land and ordered to be certified.

A Deed of Conveyance from WILLIAM SMITH to JOSEPH UNDERWOOD for 20 acres of land and ordered to be certified.

A Deed of Conveyance from ROBERT BIGGERS to DAVID REID for 160 acres of land, proven by JAMES BROWN and JAMES REID and ordered to be certified.

A Deed of Conveyance from JAMES BROWN to JESSE LOVELESS for 60 acres of land and ordered to be certified.

A mortgage from CHARLES BOYLES to ROBERT DICKSON, HUGH M. BLAKE and CONSTANT SCALES for 26 negroes, proven by J.W. GORDON and C. GILLILAND and ordered to be certified.

A Deed of Conveyance from ROBERT MOORE to JOHN DEVIN for 50 acres of land and ordered to be certified.

A Power of Attorney from JAMES L. GRAY to REPS O. CHILDRESS, proven and ordered to be certified.

A Deed of Conveyance from WILLIAM P. ANDERSON to JACOB PREWITT for 50 acres of land, proven by HARDY HOLMAN, Attorney in Fact, and ordered to be certified.

A Deed of Gift from ESTHER KENNEDY to WILLIAM E. KENNEDY was proven and ordered to be certified.

WILLIAM BATES and FRANCIS GRIFFIN came into court and makes oath that they were present at the dwelling house of MAJOR GORDON's more than fourteen days previous to this day and within six months when they heard said GORDON who is now dead, make his Last Will and Testament verbally, that he the said GORDON was in his last sickness, and that he declared his intentions with regard to the deposition of his property to be as follows, to wit, He wish all his just debt be paid, after that was done, all the property then left be bequeathed to his wife PATSEY GORDON and after he had thus declared his

168

intentions, he called on said BATES to bear witness hereto, whereupon came PATSEY GORDON and was appointed by said court admrx of the said MAJOR GORDON, deceased, and gave bond with HUGH M. BLAKE her security for $700.00 and took the oath &c.

The Last Will and Testament of WILLIAM AMONS was proven in court by witnesses, whereupon came JOHN PRYOR, SR., one of the executors and gave bond with JOHN EDMISTON his security for $1000.00 and took oath &c.

It is ordered by the court that the following Justices take in list of taxable property in this county for the year 1823 and make return to next court, to wit:
JOHN ENOCKS in CAPTAIN SMITH's Company
JACOB WAGGONER in CAPTAIN SHAW's Company
WILLIAM KENNON in CAPTAIN McCLAMOURS (McCLURES) Company
JOHN WISEMAN in CAPTAIN SPENCER's Company
AMBROSE BARKER in CAPTAIN RUTHERFORD's Company
WILLIAM MILLNER in CAPTAIN BRYANT's Company
HENRY KELSO in CAPTAIN WELL's Company
RICHARD FLYNT in CAPTAIN DAVIS' Company
CHARLES BOYLES in CAPTAIN RINGO's Company
SAMUEL GARLAND in CAPTAIN HARRISON's Company
WILLIAM DYE in CAPTAIN GARRETT's Company
ABRAHAM ISAACKS in CAPTAIN NORTON's Company
GEORGE BLAKEMORE in CAPTAIN BLAKEMORE's Company
HUGH PARKERSON in CAPTAIN POOL's Company
CLIFFORD GRAY in CAPTAIN ESLICK's Company
CORNELIUS DARNELL in CAPTAIN CHITWOOD's Company
ENOCK RUST in CAPTAIN BROOKS' Company
ELISHA BAGLEY in CAPTAIN HAMPTON's Company
WILLIAM BEAVERS in CAPTAIN GANT's Company
WILLIAM SMITH in CAPTAIN BAUCHMAN's Company
JOEL PINSON in CAPTAIN ROBINSON's Company
DAVID COWEN in CAPTAIN McCORKLE's Company
SAMUEL BUCHANAN in CAPTAIN CRAWFORD's Company
JAMES RALSTON in CAPTAIN McCLELLAN's Company
JOHN H. MOORE in CAPTAIN MEEK's Company

TUESDAY OCTOBER 1822

The Sheriff made return that he had summoned the following venire, to wit, JONATHAN MURRELL, THOMAS WASHBURN, ISAAC BROYLES, JOHN MOOR, JOHN DAVIS, SAMUEL TODD, ISHAM PARR, JOEL JOHNSON, JOHN BOONE, JOSEPH HINKLE, WILLIAM SHIPP, DAVID HOWELL, JOEL DODSON, ROBERT MOORE, ARON WELLS, DANIEL WAGGONER, THOMAS WITT, JOHN R. JOHNSON, DAVID JONES, THOMAS BRENTS, JESSE McCLAIN, SAMUEL CRAWFORD, CHARLES BRIGHT, JOHN DAVIS and DANIEL HARRISON of whom were elected as Grand Jurors, to wit, JOSEPH HINKLE, foreman, JOHN DAVIS, WILLIAM SHIPP, ARON WELLS, JOEL JOHNSON, JOHN BOON, JONATHAN MURRELL, THOMAS WITT, DANIEL WAGGONER, CHARLES BRIGHT, ROBERT MOORE, JOEL DODSON, and SAMUEL TODD, after receiving a charge returned to consider of their presentments.

STEPHEN C. CHITWOOD, a Constable, sworn to wait on the Grand Jury this term.

JOHN R. JOHNSON, THOMAS WASHBURN, DANIEL HARRISON, JOHN DAVIS and SAMUEL CRAWFORD released from serving on the (blank) jury this term.

It is ordered that ISHAM PARR, DAVID JONES and THOMAS BRENTS be fined $5.00 each for not attending as Jurors this term.

JOEL R. FIELDER by his next friend vs STERLING C. McLEMORE - A Commission is awarded the defendant to take the deposition of WILLIAM ALLEN at his house in this county on this day between the hours of 12 A.M. and 3 P.M. to be read in evidence on the above cause.

JOHN LANDRES, admr vs ROBERT FLETCHER - This cause is continued on affidavit of defendant and he is to take the deposition of PITTMAN PITTS and HALY ANDREWS of Madison County, Alabama, to be read in evidence on the above trial by giving ten days notice of time and place of taking the same.

The State vs GEORGE W, HUNT - Indictment for an Assault and Battery - The defendant being charged pleads guilty and is fined 25 cents and pay costs.   JOHN P.

McCONNELL security for the defendant.

ELIJAH MAYFIELD vs WILLIAM McWHERTER - The plaintiff says he intends no further to prosecute this suit and assumes the payment of all costs. Suit to be dismissed and defendant recover his costs.

ELIJAH MAYFIELD vs GEORGE WEBB - The plantiff by his attorney says he intends no further to prosecute this suit and assumes the payment of all costs. Suit to be dismissed and defendant recover his costs.

OBADIAH PINSON vs Fayetteville Bank - The plaintiff by his attorney says he intends no further to prosecute this suit and assumes the payment of all costs. Suit to be dismissed and defendant recover his costs.

GEORGE THALL vs F.T. Bank - The plaintiff by his attorney says he wishes to dismiss this suit and assumes the payment of all costs. This suit to be dismissed and defendant recover his costs.

DAVID McGAVOCK vs ERNEST BENOIT - The plaintiff by his attorney says he wishes to dismiss this suit and the defendant assumes the payment of all costs. Suit to be dismissed and plaintiff recover his costs.

On petition, it is ordered that ALEXANDER FULTON be released from paying a double tax for year 1822 and that he pay a single tax only.

JAMES B. CAMPBELL vs CHARLES BOYLES & JAS. WYATT - This day came the parties by their attorneys and a jury of men, to wit, JOHN MOORE, JESSE McCLAIN, DAVID HOWELL, OLLIVER WILLIAMS, JOHN R. JOHNSON, SAMUEL BRADLEY, JOHN W. SMITH, JOHN BUCHANAN, YEWELL WILLIAMS, JACOB HOOSER, WALTER B. OWENS and HENRY ROBERTSON being elected and sworn and said that the defendant has not paid the debt of $6164.39 and damages of $1048.00. Plaintiff to recover his costs.

THOMAS ALLY vs ROBERT BUCHANAN - This day came the parties by their attorneys and a jury of men, to wit, JESSE McCLAIN, DAVID HOWELL, OLIVER WILLIAMS, JOHN R. JOHNSON, SAMUEL BRADLY, PHILIP FOX, JOHN W. SMITH, YEWELL WILLIAMS, JOHN BOYLES, JACOB HOOSER, WALTER B. OWENS, and HENRY ROBERTSON being elected and sworn and said that they cannot agree upon a verdict. OLIVER WILLIAMS was withdrawn and the rest are discharged and this trial is transferred for trial to next Circuit Court in March next.

A Bill of Sale from JOHN GREER to ROBERT DICKSON for a negro woman named HANNAH, proven by CONSTANT SCALES and ordered to be certified.

A Bill of Sale from JAMES KING, JR. to ROBERT DICKSON for a negro boy named HENRY, proven by GEORGE T. LASLEY and ordered to be certified.

A Deed of Conveyance from BRICE M. GARNER to ROBERT & WILLIAM DICKSON for two town lots in Fayetteville and ordered to be certified.

A Deed of Conveyance from DANIEL WARREN to JOSEPH SEBASTIAN for 259 acres of land and ordered to be certified.

ABNER STEED resigned his appointment as a Justice of the Peace for Lincoln County.

WEDNESDAY OCTOBER 23, 1822

Justices present were ROBERT DICKSON, WILLIAM ANDERSON and WILLIAM EDMISTON, Esquires.

THOMAS ALLY vs ROBERT BUCHANAN - The defendant to recover against the plaintiff his costs.

THOMAS KERCHEVAL vs JOEL ORRICK - This cause is continued on affidavit of the plaintiff and was ordered to take the deposition of HIRAM H. HIGGINS of Limestone County, Alabama, to be read in evidence on the trial of the above cause, is renewed.

JOEL FIELDER by his next friend vs STERLING C. McLEMORE - This cause is continued on affidavit of the plaintiff on his paying the costs of this term. A Commission is awarded each party to take depositions taken in this county or Madison County, five days notice or if taken in West Tennessee ten days notice of time and place of taking the same.

JAMES FORSYTH appeared in court and was sworn in as a Justice of the Peace for Lincoln County.

NATHANIEL B. BUCKINGHAM vs THOMAS H. MAY - This cause is continued on affidavit of the plaintiff and a commission is awarded the defendant to take the deposition of WILLIAM WILLBORN of Huntsville, to be read as evidence on the trial of the above cause by giving the defendant ten days notice of time and place of taking the same.

JAMES BROOK, admr vs JAMES L. DRIVER- This cause, by consent of the parties, is referred to the arbitrament of JOHN MARR and DAVID P. MUNROE and if they cannot agree they are to choose a third person and they return the award in writing to next term of court.

WILLIAM A. TUCKER vs AMBROSE BARKER - It is ordered that the plaintiff give other or better security for the prosecution of this suit at anytime before this cause is called for trial or his suit will be dismissed.

JAMES D. ALLFORD vs JAMES WYATT - This day came the parties by their attorneys and a jury of men, to wit, FRANCIS PATTON, JOHN W. SMITH, HENRY CLIFT, JAMES L. DRIVER, PHILIP FOX, JOHN MOORE, ROBERT BROOKS, CHARLES ABELS, JESSE McCLAIN, DAVID HOWELL, SAMUEL WILSON, and HAMBLETON MOFFIT being elected and sworn and said that the plaintiff's damages of $92.85. Plaintiff recover his costs.

ROBERT HERROLD vs WILLIAM EDMISTON - The plaintiff by his attorney, says he wishes to dismiss this suit and the defendant assumes the payment of all costs. Suit to be dismissed and the plaintiff recover his costs.

The Grand Jury again returned to court and brought with them a Bill of Indictment against SAMUEL H. SMITH for an assault and battery, a true bill and again returned to consider for further presentments.

A Bill of Sale from JOHN GREER to ROBERT DICKSON for a negro woman was acknowledged and ordered to be certified.

A Bill of Sale from GARLAND B. MILLER, admr of JONATHAN ESTILL, deceased, to ROBERT DICKSON for seven negroes, proven by JOHN GREER and ordered to be certified.

A Bill of Sale from GARLAND B. MILLER, admr of JONATHAN ESTILL, deceased, to ROBERT DICKSON for six negroes, proven by JOHN GREER and ordered to be certified.

A Deed of Conveyance from JOSEPH MORGAN to HIRAM S. MORGAN for 100 acres of land and ordered to be certified.

JOHN WAGGONER vs VANCE GREER & WILLIAM EDMISTON - This day came the parties by their attorneys and a jury of men, to wit, (same as above jurors) and said that the defendant has not paid the debt of $628.93 and damages of $9.42. Plaintiff to recover his costs.

DOILY GRIFFIS vs C. SLATER & A. CAMPBELL - (same as above) and said that the defendants has not kept and performed the covenant and assessed the damages to the plaintiff of $104.93 3/4. Plaintiff to recover his costs.

DOILY GRIFFIS vs C. SLATER & A. CAMPBELL - (same as above) and said that the defendants has not paid the debt of $100.00 and damages of $4.62½. Plaintiff to recover his costs.

JONATHAN BARKLEY vs PETER MOYERS - (same as above) and said that the defendant has not paid the debt of $135.50 and damages of $2.50. Plaintiff recover his costs.

Fayetteville T. Bank vs B.M. GARNER & C. BOYLES - This day came the parties by their attorneys and with their consent this cause is transferred to the next Circuit Court with leave to the defendant to file any plea at next Circuit Court.

R. & M. HERROLD vs G.W.C. EDMISTON - (same as above with jurors) and said that the defendant has not paid the debt of $300.00 and damages of $23.50. Plaintiff to recover his costs.

PETER MOYERS vs THOMAS ALLY - (same as the prevoius jurors) and said that the defendant has not paid the debt of $104.96 and damages of $4.68 3/4. Plaintiff recover his costs.

JAMES WYATT vs JACOB WRIGHT - This day came the parties by their attorneys and a jury of men, to wit, JOHN MOOR, JESSE McCLAIN, DAVID HOWELL, ELI MILSTEAD, JOSHUA DALLAS, GRIFFITH CUNNINGHAM, YEWELL WILLIAMS, EDWARD MOSS, RANDOLPH QUARLES, JORDAN SOLOMON, THOMAS HENRY and FRANCIS FINCHER being elected and sworn and said that they cannot agree on their verdict, the jury was permitted to disperse until next day.

THURSDAY OCTOBER 24, 1822

Justices present were ROBERT DICKSON, WILLIAM EDMISTON and WILLIAM C. ABELS, Esquires.

The State vs WILLIAM SMITH - Assault and Battery - The defendant being charged pleads guilty and is fined $1.00 and pay cost of this indictment. WILLIAM HUSBANDS, security.

The State vs JAMES HOBBS - Indictment for an Assault and Battery - The defendant being charged pleads guilty and fined $1.00 and pay cost of indictment. WILLIAM SMITH, security.

The Grand Jury again returned to court abd brought with them a Bill of Indictment against REUBEN HUNTER and ELIJAH DAVIS for an assault and battery, a true bill and again returned to consider for further presentments.

JAMES WYATT vs JACOB WRIGHT - The jury said that they cannot agree upon their verdict. JOHN MOORE, one of the jurors, is withdrawn and the rest are discharged from rendering a verdict in this cause. Cause is continued until next court.

GENERAL W.C. EDMISTON vs VANCE GREER - Debt - (same as above jurors) and said that the defendant has not paid the debt of $529.75 and damages of $25.80. Plaintiff recover his costs.

POLLY BROWN vs JOEL JOHNSON - The plaintiff by her attorney says he wishes to dismiss this suit and JAMES HAGUE appeared in court and confess judgment for the costs. Suit to be dismissed and the defendant recover against JAMES HAGUE his costs.

JOEL JOHNSON vs JAMES WYATT - The plaintiff by his attorney says he intends no further to prosecute this suit and assumes the payment of all costs. Suit to be dismissed and the defendant recover his costs.

DANIEL HARKINS vs WILLIAM McELROY & JOHN GREER - (same as above jurors) and said that the defendant has not paid the debt of $400.00 and damages of $18.62½.

The State vs GEORGE BIRDWELL - Indictment for an Assault and Battery - The defendant being charged pleads guilty and is fined $5.00 and pay costs of this indictment. JOEL B. SANDERS, security.

The Grand Jury again returned into court and brought with them a Bill of Indictment against OBADIAH ECOLS for malicious mischief, a true bill and again returned to consider for further presentments.

The Grand Jury again returned into court and brought with them a Bill of Indictment against JOHN H. ROGERS for retailing a spirits without a license, a true bill and again returned to consider for further presentments.

The Grand Jury again returned into court and brought with them a Bill of Indictment against WILLIAM COX for retailing of spirits without a license, a true bill and again returned for further presentments.

WILLIAM PARKS vs JAS. SMITH & WILLIAM MOREHEAD - (same as above jurors)and said that the defendant has not paid the debt of $400.00 and damages of $11.50. Plaintiff to recover his costs.

172

The Grand Jury again returned into court and brought with them a Bill of Indictment against PHILIP FIELD for an assault and battery, a true bill and again returned to consider for further presentments.

The Grand Jury again returned into court and brought with them a Bill of Indictment against CHARLES EDMISTON, a true bill and again returned to consider for further presentments.

The Grand Jury again returned into court and brought with them a Bill of Indictment against JAMES LINGO, a true bill and again returned to consider for further presentments.

The State vs JOHN H. ROGERS - Indictment - The defendant being charged pleads guilty and is fined $5.00 and pay the costs of this indictment. WILLIAM HUSBANDS, security.

The State vs WILLIAM COX - Indictment - The defendant being charged and pleads guilty and is fined $1.00 and pay the costs of this indictment. JOSEPH HINKLE, security.

The State vs JOHN FORD - Indictment - The defendant being charged and pleads guilty and is fined 25 cents and pay the cost of this indictment.

The State vs ERROM LOYD - The defendant came into court and confesses and made motion that this suit be dismissed and the State recover against the defendant the costs whereupon came WILLIAM ESLICK as security.

The State vs WILLIAM A. TUCKER - The defendant confessed judgment for the costs. A motion considered that this suit be dismissed and the State recover against the defendant the costs whereupon came JOHN LINDSEY and ALLEN TUCKER as securities.

The State vs DAVID A. MARKHAM - The costs of this suit is to be paid by Lincoln County.

The State vs WYATT TUCKER - The defendant was called to come to court and failed to do so but made default. Judgment of $100.00 be filed against him.

JOSIAH DARK who was bound for the appearance of WYATT TUCKER was called to bring with him the body of WYATT TUCKER, failed to do so but made default. Fines $50.00.

WILLIAM LACKEY who was bound for the appearance of WYATT TUCKER was called to bring with him the body of WYATT TUCKER, failed to do so but made default, Fined $50.00.

J. PENDERGRASS vs FRANCIS FINCHER - On motion of the defendant by his attorney, it is ordered by the court that the issue in this cause is to bring up to court the papers in this case.

The State vs ELIJAH DAVIS - Indictment - This day came the defendant as well as the solicitor and the defendant being charged pleads not guilty and a jury of men, to wit, ARCHABALD D. GARREN, JOHN EDMISTON, GEORGE BIRDWELL, JESSE BIRDWELL, JOHN MOORE, JESSE McCLAIN, DAVID HOWELL, SAMUEL H. SMITH, JOHN DAVIS, LEVI TODD, ISAAC HOBBS, and WILLIAM A. TUCKER being elected and sworn and said that the defendant is guilty and is fined $35.00 and pay the costs of this indictment.

FRIDAY OCTOBER 25, 1822

Justices present were WILLIAM EDMISTON, WILLIAM C. ABLES and WILLIAM ANDERSON, Esquires.

A Mortgage from BRICE M. GARNER to EZRA STILES ELY for two lots and ordered to be certified.

The State vs REUBIN HUNTER - Indictment for an Assault and Battery - The defendant being charged pleads guilty and is fined $20.00 and pay the costs of this indictment.

The State vs GEORGE ST. JOHN BASKINS - The defendant came into court and being charged and pleads guilty and is fined $1.00 and pay cost of this indictment.

The State vs SAMUEL H. SMITH - The defendant being charged pleads guilty and is fined $25.00 and pay the cost of this indictment.

SMITH JONES vs REUBEN HUNTER and others - The plaintiff says he wishes to dismiss this suit and the defendant assumes the payment of all costs. Suit to be dismissed and the plaintiff recover his costs.

A Deed of Conveyance from JAMES MOORE to DOAK NICKS for 30 acres of land, proven by WILLIAM MOORE and JOEL B. SANDERS and ordered to be certified.

A Power of Attorney from BENJAMIN MARSHALL, POLLY   MARSHALL   and PETER KENT to WILIE DANIEL. POLLY MARSHALL being first examined by the court apart from her husband. It was ordered to be certified.

MARNOCK GLAZIER appeared in court and sworn in as a Justice of the Peace for Lincoln County.

PETER HOLLAND vs JOHN EAST - On petition of the defendant, court orders that the papers in this case be brought into court.

The State vs FRANCIS BRADLEY - The defendant is ordered to appear to answer the State of Tennessee upon a charge of Petit Larceny, was called, came not but made default. Judgment against him for $200.00.

EVEND B. BRADLEY was bound for the appearance of FRANCIS BRADLEY, was called to bring with him the body of FRANCIS BRADLEY, failed to do so but made default. Judgment against him for $500.00.

The State vs OBADIAH C. ECOLS - Indictment for Malicious Mischief - The defendant being charged pleads not guilty and a jury of men, to wit, JOHN MOORE, DAVID HOWELL, JESSE McCLAIN, JOHN KENT, HENRY ROBERTSON, WILLIAM HORTON, SAMUEL WILSON, JOHN W. SMITH, WILLIAM CRAWFORD, JOHN NEECE, HIRAM S. MORGAN, and DAVID JONES being elected and sworn and said that the defendant is guilty as charged and is fines $25.00 and pay cost of this indictment and that the defendant remain in custody of the Sheriff until the fine and cost are paid and give security.

SATURDAY OCT 26, 1822

Justices present were ROBERT DICKSON, WILLIAM ANDERSON and WILLIAM C. ABELS, Esquires.

The due execution of a Bill of Sale from HENRY SCALES, admr of JOHN WATT, deceased, to ROBERT DICKSON for a negro man named JACOB, proven by JOHN W. GORDON and ordered to be certified.

JANE B. CAMPBELLvs CHARLES BOYLES & JAS. WYATT -   The plaintiff came into court and releases the sum of $4868.83½ part of the judgment heretofore at this term entered against the said defendants.

ANDREW DALTON vs WILLIAM WHAM - The plaintiff by his attorney and moves the court for a non-suit in this cause. It is ordered that the plaintiff nonsuited and the defendant recover against the plaintiff his costs.

WILLIAM BROWN vs BENJAMIN NOLES - This came the parties by their attorneys and a jury of men, to wit, JOSEPH HINKLE, JOHN DAVIS, WILLIAM SHIPP, ARON WELLS, JOHN BOON, JOEL JOHNSON, JONATHAN MURRELL, THOMAS WITT, DANIEL WAGGONER, CHARLES BRIGHT, JOEL DODSON, and SAMUEL TODD being elected and sworn and said that the defendant has not paid the debt of $150.00 and damages of $7.50. Plaintiff recover his costs.

The Grand Jury again returned into court and brought with then a Bill of Indictment against WILLIAM TOWNZEND and WILLIAM JACKSON for an affray, a true bill and again returned to consider for further presentments.

ALEXANDER HUGHY, assignee vs BENNETT B. HOWELL - On motion, the Sheriff to expose to sale all the right title and interest that BENNETT B. HOWELL has in and the tract of land he now lives on, levied on to satisfy a judgment that ALEXANDER HUGHY and for the use of ARON WELLS against said BENNETT B. HOWELL before JOHN MARR, Esquire, on 17 October 1822 and all legal costs.

JOHN McANALLY vs WILLIAM WHAM - The defendant by his attorney and the plaintiff being called to come and prosecute his suit, came not. Court ordered that the defendant recover his costs.

ALEXANDER MOORE vs JOHN A. CHAPMAN - The defendant being called to come and plead this case, came not but made default. Plaintiff recover $105.06 the debt and $10.35 cost of original suit and also $8.90 damages.

WILLIAM WHITE vs WILLIS L. CALVERT& SPENCER LEATHERWOOD - The plaintiff says he intends no further to prosecute the suit and assumes payment of all costs. Suit to be dismissed and defendant recover his costs.

ANDREW BUCHANAN vs JOSEPH PENN - The defendant says he owes the plaintiff $122.62 and damages of 61 cents. Plaintiff to recover his costs.

WILLIAM H. MURFREY vs DAVID LORANCE & JOHN DAVIS - The plaintiff by his attorney, and the defendant being called to come and plead this suit failed to do so but made default. The plaintiff to recover against the defendant $286.50 and damages of $11.24.

DAVID McCLAMOR(K) vs JOHN A. CHAPMAN - The plaintiff by his attorney and the defendant being called to come and plead to this suit, failed to do so but made default. Plaintiff to recover $120.14¼ and damages of $4.44.

A Mortgage or Sale of goods, wares and merchandise &c from BRICE M. GARNER and THOMAS W. BOOTH to ROBERT & WILLIAM DICKSON, acknowledged.

FIELDLAND LUCAS vs CONSTANT SCALES - This day came the parties by their attorneys and a jury of men, to wit, JOSEPH HINKLE, JOHN DAVIS, WILLIAM SHIPP, ARON WELLS, JOHN BOON, JOEL JOHNSON, JONATHAN MURRELL, THOMAS WITT, DANIEL WAGGONER, CHARLES BRIGHT, JOEL DODSON, and SAMUEL TODD being elected and sworn and said that the defendant has not paid the debt of $500.00 and damages of $54.50. Plaintiff to recover his costs. Defendant prays for an appeal and is granted same.

JAMES BRIGHT vs C. SCALES and others - (same as above) and said that the defendants has not paid the debt of $1016.50 and damages of $74.20¼. Plaintiff to recover his costs.

CHARLES H. EDMISTON vs JOHN P. McCONNELL - The court says that there is such a record in this cause. The plaintiff to recover against the defendant $193.50 and damages of $6.14.

WILLIAM EDMISTON, CHARLES BOYLES, EBENEZER McEWEN, SAMUEL BUCHANAN, HUGH M. BLAKE, ROBERT DICKSON, WILLIAM C. ABELS, WILLIAM ANDERSON, HUGH PARKERSON, Magistrates and Justices of the Peace for this county being present and holding court.

WILLIAM E. KENNEDY appeared in court and petitioning the court to grant him leave to emancipate his negro man slave named ALLEN. Petition granted and permitted the said ALLEN to be emancipated and WILLIAM C. KENNEDY giving bond and security.

PATRICK GILLASPIE vs OBADIAH PINKNEY - The plaintiff by his attorney says he intends no further to prosecute this suit and assumes the payment of all costs. Suit to be dismissed and defendant recover his costs.

The due execution of an Indenture of Bargain and Sale from ANDREW E. BEATIE to WILLIAM McCLELLAN for 195 acres of land, proven by WILLIAM B. BENGE and JOEL PIGG and ordered to be certified.

ABSALUM B. BAILY vs ROBERT ROSS - The court ordered that the papers in this cause be brought into court.

ROBERT SEABURY vs HOLMAN & POOL, admr of J.H. ZIVELY, deceased - The plaintiff by his attorney and the defendants being called, came not but made default and the plaintiff recover against the defendant $84.27 and damages of $3.50. The debt to be levied upon the goods and chattels &c of the said JOHN H. ZIVELY, deceased, if any be in the hands of the admr, if any exists.

JOHN D. SPAIN vs STRAIN & GILBREATH - This case being called and neither of the parties appearing. Suit to be stricken from the docket.

DOILY GRIFFIS vs C. SLATER & A. CAMPBELL - The defendant prays for an appeal in this cause to next Circuit Court and ten days are allowed them. They gave bond and security.

DOILY GRIFFIS, admr vs C. SLATER & A. CAMPBELL - (same as above).

WILLIAM W. THOMPSON vs JOS. GEORGE TAYLOR - This day came the parties by their attorneys and a jury of men, to wit, JOSEPH HINKLE, JOHN DAVIS, WILLIAM SHIPP, ARON WELLS, JOHN BOON, JOEL JOHNSON, JONATHAN MERRELL, THOMAS WITT, DANIEL WAGONER, CHARLES BRIGHT, JOEL DODSON, and SAMUEL TODD being elected and sworn and said that the defendant has not paid the debt of $120.00 and damages of $26.75. Plaintiff to recover his costs.

THOMAS STANFIELD vs THOMAS W. HAMILTON and others - One execution was put into the hands of THOMAS W. HAMILTON as Constable about 16 July 1821 and found in favor of the plaintiff for $1.96¼. THOMAS W., JOHN JONES and JOHN CLIFTON, his securities.

THOMAS STANFIELD vs THOMAS W. HAMILTON and others - It appearing to the court that one execution had been put into the hands of THOMAS W. HAMILTON as a Constable about 6th May 1821 issued by ANDREW W. WALKER, a Justice of the Peace, found in favor of said THOMAS STANFIELD for $9.59¼. THOMAS W., JOHN JONES and JOHN CLIFTON, his securities.

THOMAS HARPER vs THOMAS W. HAMILTON - Motion - Two executions were put into the hands of THOMAS W. HAMILTON, as Sheriff, issued by ANDREW W. WALKER, a Justice of the Peace, in favor of THOMAS HARPER for $37.50 and that said THOMAS W. HAMILTON failed to return within the time required by law and that THOMAS W. HAMILTON, JOHN JONES and JOHN CLIFTON, his securities had received written notice of this motion. Plaintiff to recover against THOMAS W. HAMILTON, as Constable and his securities his costs.

A Deed from JOHN PR--- to JOHN COFFIN for 25 acres of land and ordered to be certified.

A release from JOHN CRAWFORD to WILLIAM EDMISTON was proven in court and ordered to be certified.

A Deed of Conveyance from WINSTON HALL to GEORGE PETTY for 40 acres of land and ordered to be certified.

A Deed of Conveyance from ALEXANDER MORTON to JOSEPH PENN andordered to be certified.

A Deed of Conveyance from SOLOMON BENNETT to RANDOLPH ALLSUP for 65 acres of land and ordered to be certified.

A Deed of Conveyance from ALEXANDER McDONALD to JOHN, ELIJAH and ELISHA BENNETT for 50 acres of land and ordered to be certified.

A Deed of Conveyance from JOHN COFFMAN to ALEXANDER MEEK for 70 acres of land and ordered to be certified.

The Transfer of a Plat and Certificate from WILLIAM BAILY to MIDDLETON BEDINGFIELD and ordered to be certified.

A Transfer of a Plat and Certificate from LARKIN MAJORS to BARSHABA HOPPER and ordered to be certified.

The Transfer of a Plat and Certificate from WILLIAM BAILY to MIDDLETON BEDINGFIELD and ordered to be certified.

STERLING C. McLEMORE was appointed a Constable and took oath with WILLIAM DICKSON, his security.

ELIJAH McLAUGHLIN was appointed a Constable and took oath with AMBROSE BARKER, his security.

JOHN WARDEN was appointed a Constable and took oath with DANIEL LOONEY and JAMES WARREN, his securities.

STEPHEN C. CHITWOOD was appointed a Constable and took oath with JOSEPH PENN, his security.

ROBERT BUCHANAN was appointed a Constable and took oath with RANDOLPH QUARLES and WILLIAM C. KENNEDY, his securities.

LEMUEL BAGGETT is bound to ROBERT DICKSON to learn the saddler trade until he is twenty one years of age.

The Commissioners appointed to settle (with) the executors of WILLIAM HARRIS, deceased, and make return and ordered to be certified.

AN Inventory of the estate of JOHN C. BEARD, deceased, was returned to court by his admr and ordered to be certified.

JOHN H. ROGERS is permitted to keep a tavern at his house one year from this time who gave bond.

JAMES HARPER is permitted to keep a tavern at his house in Fayetteville one year from this time who gave bond.

PEYTON WELLS is permitted to keep a tavern at his house one year from this time who gave bond.

MONDAY JANUARY 1823

WILLIAM MARSH is appointed overseer of the road in the room of GEORGE HARMING resigned and call on the usual hands.

JOSEPH JENKINS is appointed overseer of the road in the room of SAMUEL TODD resigned and EBENEZER McEWEN, Esquire, to appoint the hands to work on said road.

DAVID JONES is appointed overseer of the road in the room of JAMES ISHAM resigned and call on the usual hands.

THOMAS ALLY, JOHN DUKE, JOHN DAVIS, HENRY WARREN and JOHN STREET are appointed a Jury of View to view and turn the road through the lands of STEPHEN ALEXANDER, JOHN DUKE and STEPHEN BEAVERS and make return to next court.

JOHN BOON is appointed overseer of the road in the room of WILSON FROST resigned and to call on the usual hands.

JOHN WILLIAMSON is appointed overseer of the road in the room of DANIEL BACHMAN and to call on the usual hands.

JOHN CUNNINGHAM is appointed overseer of the road in the room of WILLIAM VANCE and to call on the usual hands.

THOMAS BLYTH is appointed overseer of the road in the room of ABSOLEM BLYTH resigned and call on the usual hands.

ALEXANDER McLIN is allowed $25.25 for repairing of the courthouse and that the County Trustee of this county pay the same out of any county monies his hands not otherwise appropriated.

THOMAS H. SHAW is appointed overseer of the road in the room of JACOB HAMBLETON resigned and call on the usual hands.

HOWELL HARRIS, WILLIAM B. BENGE and JOHN BEATIE are appointed Commissioners to settle with SAMUEL CRAWFORD, admr, CHARLOTTE HOWELL, admrx of THOMAS JOYCE, deceased, and to make return to next court.

SAMUEL HOWELL is appointed overseer of the road in place of HIRAM HARRIS resigned and to call on the usual hands.

It is ordered that the Sheriff be released from the payment of $28.24¼ the amount of taxes which he returned that he could not collect for the year 1822.

177

OWEN W. HIGGINS is appointed overseer of the road in the room of SHERWOOD HUNTER resigned and to call on the usual hands.

DANIEL JONES is appointed overseer of the road in the room of THOMAS KERCHEVAL resigned and call on the usual hands.

JOEL EATON is appointed overseer of the road in the room of WILLIAM DAVIS resigned and call on the usual hands.

WILLIAM CASHION is appointed overseer of the road from Finchers Mill to where it intersects the Mulberry Road, in the room of JAMES HUNTER and call on the usual hands.

SOLOMON BURFORD appeared in court and was appointed admr on the estate of JONAS OAKS, deceased, who gave bond of $300.00 with JESSE GEORGE and ALEXANDER MEEK, securities.

LEWIS HOPPER and JOSEPH BROADWAY was appointed admrs of the estate of GEORGE HOPPER and gave bond of $500.00 with SAMUEL BUCHANAN and JOHN GIBSON, securities.

MARY WALLIS appeared in court and was appointed admrx on the estate of WILLIAM WALLACE, deceased, who gave bond of $500.00 with MATHIAS TURNER and ELISHA LAWRANCE, securities.

An inventory of the estate of ISAAC OAKS was returned by his admr and ordered to be certified.

An additional inventory of the estate of EDWARD TEAL, deceased, was returned to court by his admrx and ordered to be certified.

An inventory of the estate of WILLIAM WALLACE, deceased, was returned to court by his admrx which was ordered to be certified.

An amount of sale of the property of ARCHABALD MAYFIELD was returned to court and ordered to be certified.

MIKE McCOWEN, THOMAS McFERREN, MARTIN McFERREN, JAMES BYERS, SAMUEL JONES and WILLIAM ROWAN are appointed a Jury of View to view and turn the road from the forks of the road at EDWARD MOSS' to Athens and make return to next court.

WILLIAM BROWN, THOMAS H. SHAW, ANTHONY CRAWFORD, JOHN SILVERTOOTH, JAMES C. SMITH, HENRY LANDRESS, PETER TIPPS, JACOB SILVERTOOTH, SAMUEL HART and FREDERICK WAGGONER are appointed a Jury of View to view and mark out a road from the end of WILLIAM BROWN's lane on by Blyth Mill, the nearest and best way to Carrigers Mill and make return to court.

RYLY YATES is appointed overseer of the road in the room of BENJAMIN RUDD resigned and call on the usual hands.

WILLIAM TOWNZEN is released from paying a double tax for the year 1822 and to pay a single tax only.

JOHN MAZE is released from paying a double tax for the year 1822 and to pay a single tax only.

MICHAEL ROBINSON is released from paying a double tax for the year 1822 and to pay a single tax only.

JANE BRADLEY is released from paying a double tax for the year 1822 and to pay a single tax only.

ISAAC HOLMAN, THOMAS H. SHAW and ANDREW W. WALKER are appointed Commissioners to settle with the admr and admrx on the estate of JOHN WAKEFIELD, deceased, and make return to court.

WILLIAM BEAVERS, Esquire, WILLIAM CRAWFORD and WILLIAM HODGES are appointed Commissioners to lay off one years support for the widow of GEORGE HOPPER, deceased, and make return to court.

178

HARDY HOLMAN is appointed a Commissioner from this county to run the line between this county and Bedford County.

JOHN DURLEY appeared in court and was appointed guardian for MALVENEY M. OLIVER and GEORGE G. OLIVER, minor heirs of ZEBULON OLIVER, deceased, who gave bond of $1500.00 with JAMES THORP and ARON WELLS, his securities.

HENRY LITTLE is appointed overseer of the road from Hancocks Ford on Elk River to the top of the ridge west of WILLIAM DYE. Esquire and call on the usual hands.

The Commissioners appointed at the last term of court to settle with JONATHAN FLOYD, executor of WILLIAM N. PATTERSON, deceased, made return and ordered to be certified.

DAVID BECK is appointed overseer of the road from Swan Creek to Shilo Meeting House and call on the usual hands.

An inventory of the estate of GEORGE HOPPER was returned to court by his admrs and ordered to be certified.

It is ordered by the court that JOHN H. ROGERS, ELIJAH DAVIS, WILLIAM P. PULLIAM, SAMUEL S. BUCHANAN, LEMUEL BROADWAY, JOSIAH SMITH, CHARLES H. EDMISTON, PETER SHELTON, ELI COUCH, JOHN STREET, JOSEPH PEDDY (PETTY), WILLIAM LANGSTON, JOHN DOWTHIT, ELISHA TOMERSON, JAMES MAXFIELD, BENJAMIN CLEMENTS, JOHN M. BLAKE, GENERAL W.C. EDMISTON, HENRY ROBINSON, WILLIAM PATTERSON, WILLIAM CRAWFORD, MATHEW WILSON, MORGAN CLAYTON, JONATHAN FROST and JAMES MILSTEAD be summoned as jurors to the next County Court of this county held in April next.

The Justices proceeded to class themselves in the following manner, to wit, HUGH PARKERSON, JESSE DANIEL, WILLIAM ANDERSON, JOHN H. MOORE, JAMES FORSYTH, ABRAHAM SUMNERS, RICHARD FLYNT, WILLIAM KENNON, PHILIP KOONCE, JOHN SMITH, WILLIAM BEAVERS, ROBERT DICKSON and ELI GARRETT were classed in the first class to hold the January Term 1823. JOHN PINKERTON, JOHN ENOCHS, WILLIAM DYE, MARNOCK GLAZIER, JOEL PINSON, CLIFFORD GRAY, CHARLES BOYLES, HUGH M. BLAKE, JOSEPH McCRACKEN, GEORGE BLAKEMORE, WILLIAM C. ABELS, and WILLIAM DICKSON were classed in the second class to hold the April Term 1823. DAVID COWN, SAMUEL GARLAND, ENOCK RUST, WILLIAM SMITH, CORNELIUS DARNELL, ABRAHAM ISAACKS, JOHN PORTER, JACOB WAGGONER, WILLIAM MILNER, WILLIAM EDMISTON, DANIEL LOONEY and EBENEZER McEWEN were classed in the third class to hold the July Term 1823. HENRY KELSO, AMBROSE BARKER, JOHN MARR, JAMES RALSTON, JAMES WILSON, JOHN WISEMAN, STEPHEN ALEXANDER, TALIFERO DOLLARS, THOMAS GAITHER, SAMUEL BUCHANAN, ISAAC CONGO (CONGER), JAMES BLAKEMORE and ELISHA BAGLEY were classed in the fourth class to hold the October Term 1823.

It is ordered by the court that JAMES FORSYTH, AMBROSE BARKER and JAMES SMITH be appointed Commissioners of the school tract of land on Sheltons Creek.

JOHN ENOCK, JESSE ELLICE (ELLIS) and SAMUEL HART is appointed Commissioners of the school tract of land on the middle fork of Mulberry Creek.

JOHN KING, CLIFFORD GRAY and JAMES GEORGE is appointed Commissioners of the school tract of land lying on Tuckers Creek.

ISHAM PARR, NICHOLAS CARRIGER and ZACHARIAH HARRISON is appointed Commissioners of the school tract of land lying on the west fork of Mulberry Creek.

EBENEZER McEWEN, ABNER STEED and WILLIAM DICKSON is appointed Commissioners of the school tract of land lying on little west fork of Mulberry.

WILLIAM CRUNK, JNO. CRUNK and F. LUNA is appointed Commissioners of the school tract of land on Cane Creek near CRUNK's.

HUGH M. BLAKE, G.W.C. EDMISTON and GEORGE BLAKEMORE are appointed Commissioners of the school tract of land near BLAKE's.

THOMAS CLARK, REPS O. CHILDRESS and JOHN PARKER are appointed Commissioners of the school tract of land on Swan Creek.

ELI GARRETT, WILLIAM BRIGHT and JOEL JOHNSON are appointed Commissioners of the school tract of land on McCullock Creek.

JOHN GREER, F. KOONCE and ANDREW McCARTNEY are appointed Commissioners of the school tract of land on Stewarts Creek.

JOEL PINSON, JAMES WILSON and DAVID COWEN are appointed Commissioners of the school tract of land on Carrs Creek.

JAMES HOLMAN, JOHN J. WHITAKER and WILLIAM KENNON are appointed Commissioners of the school tract of land on east fork of Norris Creek.

It appearing to the court that the defendant in the following cases, to wit, The State against WILLIAM TOWNZEN, The State against WILLIAM PITCOCK, The State against DAVID A. MARKHAM, The State against the same, The State against OBADIAH C. ECHOLS, The State against WYATT TUCKER, The State against FRANCIS BRADLEY lave no estate either real or personal out of which the costs in cases can be made. It is ordered that the clerk issue certificates to the lawful claimants for all costs, which certificates the County Trustee is ordered to pay.

It is ordered that THOMAS H. FLETCHER be allowed $50.00 for his exofficia services for the year 1822.

It is ordered that BRICE M. GARNER be allowed $50.00 for his services for the year 1822, also $25.00 for making out the tax list for year 1822.

TUESDAY JANUARY 21, 1823

Justices present were ROBERT DICKSON, WILLIAM DICKSON and JAMES FORSYTH, Esquires.

The Sheriff made return that he had summoned the following venire, to wit, JAMES HIGGINS, HAY CRAWFORD, JAMES HAGUE, ABRAHAM DUDNEY, RANDOLPH QUARLES, RANDOLPH BRYANT, ZACHARIAH ARNOLD, JOSEPH PENN, ALEXANDER MORTON, JAMES PHILLIPS, SHEPARD SHELTON, JOSEPH DEAN, HIGDON HARPER, SAMUEL BUCHANAN, HOWELL HARRIS, ISAAC SEBASTIAN, JOHN J. WHITAKER, WILLIAM SPENCER, WILLIAM R. WOODRUFF, SOLOMON GULLETT, JAMES BRYANS, WILLIAM McELROY, JOHN WITT, DAVID THWING, BENJAMIN PORTER, and JOHN R. JOHNSON were elected as Grand Jurors, to wit, HOWELL HARRIS, foreman, JOSEPH DEAN, JOHN WITT, JOHN R. JOHNSON, BENJAMIN PORTER, JOHN J. WHITAKER, ABRAHAM DUDNEY, HIGDON HARPER, HAY CRAWFORD, JAMES BRYANS, WILLIAM SPENCER, SOLOMON GULLETT, SHEPARD SHELTON who after receiving the charge returned to consider of their presentments.

WILLIAM HUSBANDS, Constable, sworn to wait on the Grand Jury, this term.

JAMES HAGUE, ZACHARIAH ARNOLD, ALEXANDER MORTON and WILLIAM R. WOODRUFF is released from serving as jurors this term.

It is ordered that WILLIAM SMITH be released from the payment of the appraised value of two stray nags which he posted.

The due execution of an Indenture of Bargain and Sale from ALISHA CAMP to HARDIN TAYLOR for 50 acres of land, proven by JAMES RUST and ALLEN ELSTON and ordered to be certified.

The due execution of an Indenture of Bargain ans Sale from HARDIN TAYLOR to DEMPSEY ALLEN for 50 acres of land and ordered to be certified.

The due execution of an Indenture of Bargain and Sale from ISAAC BROYLES to ANDREW WHITENBURGH for 21 acres of land and ordered to be certified.

JOHN LAN----, ADMR vs ROBERT FLETCHER - This day came the parties by their attorneys and a jury of men, to wit, RANDOLPH QUARLES, SAMUEL BUCHANAN, JAMES HIGGINS, ISAAC SEBASTIAN, JOSEPH PENN, JAMES PHILLIPS, DAVID THWING, JAMES BROOKS, WILLIAM CUNNINGHAM, JOEL ORRICK, JOHN NEECE, and WILLIAM MUNROE being elected and sworn and said the jury was permitted to disperse until next day.

WEDNESDAY JANUARY 22, 1823

Justices present were ROBERT DICKSON, WILLIAM ANDERSON and RICHARD FLYNT, Esquires.

DAVID COWEN appeared in court and was appointed admr on the estate of JAMES CAMPBELL, JR., deceased, who gave bond of $100.00 with STEPHEN HIGHTOWER and JOSEPH McCRACKEN, his securities.

The due execution of an Indenture of Bargain and Sale from DANIEL GILLASPIE by his attorney in fact JOHN GILLASPIE to PATRICK GILLASPIE for 481 3/4 acres of land, proven by WILLIAM BOON and JAMES PITTS and ordered to be certified.

The due execution of an Indenture of Bargain and Sale from GABRIEL BUFORD to JAMES FLEMMING for 279 acres of land and ordered to be certified.

A Deed of Conveyance from ANTHONY B. CLENDENING and JAMES H. PATTERSON to ALEXANDER McCORKLE for 164 acres of land, proven by JOSEPH CAMPBELL and ALEXANDER McCORKLE, JR. and ordered to be certified.

A Power of Attorney from ALEXANDER FULTON to HARDY HOLMAN, proven by JOHN COCHRAN and DANIEL HOLMAN and ordered to be certified.

A Deed of Conveyance from PATRICK GILLASPIE to WILLIAM & ISAAC YOUNG for 311 acres of land, proven by JAMES McDAVID and JAMES PITTS and ordered to be certified.

A Deed of Conveyance from MIDDLETON BEDINGFIELD to JAMES BAUGH for 60 acres of land, proven by ASA T. STONE and MARTIN BAUGH and ordered to be certified.

A Deed of Conveyance from BEN W. SHIRLY to NIMROD BAILY for 89 acres of land, proven by JAMES McKINNEY and GEORGE W. DENNIS and ordered to be certified.

A Deed of Trust from BENNETT B. HOWELL to BENNETT BLACKMAN, acknowledged and ordered to be certified.

WILLIAM BROOKS appeared in court and was appointed guardian of JOSIAH BROOKS, REBECCAH BROOKS, LOUISA BROOKS and THOMAS BROOKS, minor heirs of ARTHUR BROOKS, deceased, who gave bond of $12000.00 with ROBERT BROOKS and ANTHONY HOGAN, his securities.

WILLIAM A. TUCKER vs AMBROSE BARKER - The plaintiff says he intends np further to prosecute this suit and assumes the payment of all costs. Suit to be dismissed and defendant recover his costs.

The State vs WILLIAM TOWNZEN - The defendant being charged pleads guilty and is fined 25 cents and pay costs of this indictment.

DRURY K. SMITH vs JOHN R. JOHNSON - The plaintiff by his attorney says he intends no further to prosecute this suit and assumes the payment of all costs. This suit to be dismissed and the defendant recover his costs.

The Grand Jury returned into court and brought with them a Bill of Indictment for an Assault and Battery against JAMES BLAIR, a true bill and again returned to consider for further presentments.

JOSEPH McBRIDE vs BENJAMIN PHIPPS - The plaintiff says he intends no further to prosecute this suit and assumes the payment of all costs. Suit to be dismissed and the defendant recover his costs.

THOMAS CHAPMAN vs CHARLES WAKEFIELD - The plaintiff by his attorney and says he intends no further to prosecute this suit and assumes the payment of all costs. Suit to be dismissed and the defendant recover his costs.

The Grand Jury again returned into court and brought with them a. Bill of Indictment for an Assault and Battery, The State against NIMROD FIELDER, a true bill and again returned to consider for further presentments.

The due execution of an Indenture of Bargain and Sale from RANDOLPH QUARLES to WILLIAM YOUNG for 40 acres of land and ordered to be certified.

JOHN LANDRES vs ROBERT FLETCHER - The jury said they cannot agree upon their verdict. The jury was permitted to disperse until next day.

The State vs PHILLIP FIELD - Indictment for Assault and Battery - The defendant being charged pleads guilty and is fined 25 cents and pay the cost of this indictment and remain in custody of the Sheriff until the cost and fine are paid.

It is ordered that the clerk issue orders to bring to court the papers relative to a suit tried before PHILIP KOONCE, Esquire, wherein HENRY KELSO, admr of ARCHABALD MAYFIELD, deceased, was plaintiff and ELIJAH MAYFIELD was defendant.

AMOS LILES and wife vs JOSEPH ELLISON and wife - This cause is referred by the consent of the parties to the arbitrament of WILLIAM MILNER, Esquire, who is to choose five men and their award to be returned in writing to the next term of court.

J. & J.W. SITLER vs PATER MOYERS - The defendant confessed judgment to the plaintiff for $238.00. Plaintiff to recover his costs.

J. & J.W. SITLER vs PETER MOYERS - The defendant confessed that he owes the plaintiff $575.60. PLaintiff to recover his costs.

THOMPSON BROWN vs MOSES CAWOOD - The plaintiff by his attorney says he intends no further to prosecute this suit and assumes the payment of all costs. Suit to be dismissed and the defendant recover his costs.

A Deed of Conveyance from STEPHEN PHILLIPS to ELIAS PATRICK for 25 acres of land and ordered to be certified.

A Deed of Conveyance from STEPHEN PHILLIPS to ELIAS PATRICK for 10 acres of land and orderedto be certified.

A Bill of Sale from WILLIAM HUSBANDS to REECE HOWELL for three negroes, proven and ordered to be certified.

JOEL R. FIELDER by his next friend vs STERLING C. LEMORE - This day came the parties by their attorneys and a jury of men, to wit, WILLIAM McELROY, THOMAS KERCHEVAL, JOHN ORRICK, WILLIAM SMITH, HIRAM BUCHANAN, MATHIAS NICHOLS, PETER HOLLAND, AMOS LILES, PETER VAUGHN, SAMUEL BUCHANAN, SAMUEL HOWELL, and EWEL WILLIAMS being elected and sworn and said that after going through the testimony in behalf of the plaintiff by consent of the parties of their attorneys, the jury was permitted to disperse until next day court.

THURSDAY JANUARY 23, 1823

Justices present were RICHARD FLYNT, PHILIP KOONCE and JAMES WILSON, Esquires.

A Deed of Conveyance from JAMES CARITHERS to JAMES HARRIS for 50 acres of. land, proven by ARGYLE CAMPBELL and F. PORTERFIELD and ordered to be certified.

A Power of Attorney from ETHELARED COBB to JOHN RHEA and ordered to be certified.

On motion, it is ordered that JAMES BROOKS, admr of ARTHUR BROOKS, deceased, proceeds to sell a negro boy BEN, the property of said ARTHUR BROOKS, deceased.

The State vs JAMES ISHAM - The defendant being charged pleads guilty and is fined $1.00 and pay the cost of this presentment.

The State vs NIMROD FIELDER - Indictment for Assault and Battery - The defendant being charged pleads guilty and is fined 25 cents and pay the cost of this presentments and remain in custody of the Sheriff until the fine and costs are paid or give security.

It is ordered that JAMES MAYFIELD be released from the payment of the appraised value of two stray sheep which he posted.

A Deed of Conveyance from STERLING C. McLEMORE to JOHN WHITE for 29 acres of land and ordered to be certified.

A Bill of Sale from THOMAS KERCHEVAL to EASTHER KENNEDY, proven by VANCE GREER and ordered to be certified.

A Deed of Gift from ESTHER KENNEDY to ROBERT K(E). KERCHEVAL, WILLIAM R. KERCHEVAL and JULIET E. KERCHEVAL for seven head of sheep and one cow, proven by VANCE GREER and ordered to be certified.

A Deed of Gift from ESTHER KENNEDY to WILLIAM E. KENNEDY, proven by VANCE GREER and ordered to be certified.

The State vs WILLIAM SOLOMON - The defendant pleads guilty and is fined $1.00 and pay the costs of this presentments.

The State vs JAMES LINGO - The defendant being charged pleads guilty and is fined $1.00 and pay the costs of this presentments.

A Mortgage from JOHN JONES to ROBERT & WILLIAM DICKSON and ordered to be certified.

The State vs CHARLES E. EDMISTON - The defendant being charged pleads guilty and is fined one cent and pay the costs of this prosecution.

The due execution of an Indenture of Bargain and Sale from the heirs of ANDREW GREER to JOHN MOOR for 60 acres of land, proven by VANCE GREER, attorney in fact for the said heirs and ordered to be certified.

It is ordered that JACK H. LEFTWICH be released from paying a double tax for the year 1822.

The State vs PHILIP FIELD - JACOB SUMMERS appeared in court and confessed judgment jointly with the defendant for the fine and cost entered against him.

FRIDAY JANUARY 24, 1823

Justices present were ROBERT DICKSON, WILLIAM ANDERSON and CHARLES BOYLES, Esquires.

J. & J.W. SITLER vs PETER MOYERS - The plaintiff by his attorney releases ALEXANDER McLIN the appearance bail for the said defendant from any further liability appearance bail for said defendant.

J. & J.W. SITLER vs PETER MOYER - (same as above).

The due execution of an Indenture of Bargain and Sale from JAMES TOOL to SAMUEL S. BUCHANAN for one half acre of land, proven by DAVID BUCHANAN, JR. and WILLIAM BEVELL and ordered to be certified.

A Deed of Conveyance from WILLIAM EDMISTON to SAMUEL S. BUCHANAN for 16 acres of land, proven by DAVID BUCHANAN and WILLIAM BEVELL and ordered to be certified.

A Deed of Conveyance from GEORGE TITUS to DAVID BUCHANAN for part of town lot No. 74 in town of Fayetteville, proven by A. CAMPBELL and THOMAS H. FLETCHER and ordered to be certified.

EBENEZER ALEXANDER vs HENRY McKINNEY - It is ordered that a Commission be awarded the defendant to take the deposition of JOHN CARTER living on the Obion River, WILLIAM McKINNEY of Caldwekk County, Kentucky, JOSEPH DARNELL of Logan County, Kentucky, to be read in evidence on the trial of the above cause be giving the defendant attorney WILLIAM E. McKENNEDY twenty days notice of time and place of taking the same.

On motion of JAMES FULTON, Esquire, and it appearing to the court here that RUFUS K. ANDERSON is a man of good and moral character and that he has attained the age of twenty one years and upwards. It is ordered by the court that the clerk grant him a copy hereof as a preparatory step for his obtaining license to practice law in this state.

On motion of ARGYLE CAMPBELL, Esquire, and it appearing to the court that CHARLES BOYLES is a man of good and moral character and that he has attained the age of twenty one years and upwards. It is ordered that the clerk grant him a copy hereof as a preparatory step for his obtaining license to practice law in this state.

On motion of ARGYLE CAMPBELL, Esquire, (same as above) that JAMES F. TROTTER is a man of good and moral character (same as above).

JOEL R. FIELDER by his next friend NIMROD FIELDER vs STERLING C. McLEMORE - The jury returned to consider of their verdict and again returned to court and said that the defendant is guilty and is assessed damages of the plaintiff of $286.19. Plaintiff to recover his costs.

JOHN LANDRES vs ROBERT FLETCHER - The jury returned and said that they cannot agree upon their verdict in this cause. Whereupon by consent of the parties by their attorneys and by permission of the court RANDOLPH QUARLES, one of the jurors is withdrawn and the rest are discharged from rendering a verdict and this cause is continued until next term of this court.

PETER MAYO vs JAMES LOCK - MICAJAH PARKER, a garnishee in the above cause being sworn -
Question - Are you indebted to JAMES LOCK?
Answer - I gave a note to JAMES LOCK for $50.00 due on first November last which note has not been issued to any person, the amount thereof I yet owe to LOCK.
THOMAS BROWN, a garnishee of the said cause being sworn -
Question - Are you indebted to JAMES LOCK and if so how much?
Answer - I gave said LOCK my note which he yet holds for $50.00 due the first of December last on which there is a credit of $15.00, I owe him nothing else.

THOMAS KERCHEVAL vs JOEL ORRICK - This day came tha parties by their attorneys and a jury of men, to wit, JOSEPH DEAN, JOHN WITT, JOHN R. JOHNSON, BENJAMIN PORTER, JOHN J. WHITAKER, ABRAHAM DUDNEY, HIGDON HARPER, HOWELL HARRIS, HAY CRAWFORD, JAMES BRYANS, WILLIAM SPENCER, and SOLOMON GULLETT being elected and sworn and said that the jury was permitted to disperse until next day.

SATURDAY JANUARY 25, 1823

Justices present were ROBERT DICKSON, JESSE DANIEL and JOHN PORTER, Esquires.

The State vs THOMAS H. FLETCHER - Indictment for an Assault and Battery - The defendant being charged pleads guilty and fined $2.00 and pay the cost of this prosecution.

The State vs WILLIAM JACKSON - The court ordered the county to pay the costs of this cause.

SAMUEL BUCHANAN is released from serving as a juror any further this term.

The due execution of an Indenture of Bargain and Sale from GEORGE HARDING to JOHN WHITAKER for one town lot No. 23 in Fayetteville, proven by JOHN P. McCONNELL and JOSEPH WHITAKER and ordered to be certified.

STEPHEN PHILLIPS vs JOSEPH HINKLE - The plaintiff by his attorney says he wishes to dismiss this suit and RANDOLPH QUARLES assumes the payment of all costs. Suit to be dismissed and the defendant recover against RANDOLPH QUARLES his costs.

CHARLES BOYLES vs JEREMIAH SULLIVAN - Motion - On motion of the plaintiff by his attorney, the clerk issued an order to the Sheriff to expose to sale 120 acres of land on the waters of the west fork of Mulberry Creek, levied on as the property of JEREMIAH SULLIVAN, it being the place whereon he now lives to satisfy a judgment that CHARLES BOYLES recovered against him before WILLIAM EDMISTON, Esquire, on 4 day of October 1821 for $22.84 and legal costs &c.

A.B. SHELBY vs A.B. CLENDENING - Debt - The defendant confessed that he owes the plaintiff $106.00. Plaintiff to recover his costs.

PETER MAYO vs JAMES LOCK - SAMUEL BLAIR, a garnishee in this cause asked the plaintiff he was indebted to the defendant and if so how much. Plaintiff says he gave JAMES LOCK a note for $28.00 with interest on 1 November 1821 which is now due. I owe him nothing else. Plaintiff to recover against SAMUEL BLAIR $28.00 and interest of $2.00.

THOMAS KERCHEVAL vs JOEL ORRICK - The jury returned to court and find in favor of the plaintiff and assess the damages of $152.09. Plaintiff to recover his costs.

A Deed of Conveyance from PETER MOYERS to ROBERT DICKSON for one town lot No. 2 in the town of Fayetteville and ordered to be certified.

A Deed of Conveyance from JOHN JONES to JOEL HOWELL for 90 acres of land and ordered to be certified.

A Deed of Conveyance from EDWARD POWER to JARRY COONRAD for 2 acres of land and ordered to be certified.

A Deed of Conveyance from JAMES MAYS to THOMAS CAPMAN (CASSMAN ?) for 80 acres of land and ordered to be certified.

FRANCIS PORTERFIELD, Sheriff and Collector of Public Taxes for Lincoln County, made the following report on tract of land as having been admitted to be given for the taxes for year 1822. That the same is liable to double tax and that double tax remain due and unpaid. There being no goods or chattels within this county on which the Sheriff can distrain for said double taxes, to wit, heirs of DAVID GUNN one tract of land claimed by Entry No. 11733 made by virtue of a Military Warrant No. 1902, dated December 6, 1820, lying adjoining a tract of land of 640 acres granted to JOHN BRAHAN including what is called the Rock Spring, beginning on his line at or near the place where the southern boundary line of the State of Tennessee as lately run intersects the same and running west 320 poles, north 160 poles, east to the boundary line, thence south to beginning. Containing 320 acres. Heirs of DAVID GUNN, one tract of land claimed by Entry No. 11754 made by virtue of a Military Warrant No. 1902, dated December 6, 1820, lying on the waters of Flint River, beginning at the northwest corner of JOHN GORDON's 640 acre tract, with his line east, then north, then west, then south and east according to the lines marked by LEROY MAY containing 200 acres. Heirs of DAVID GUNN, one tract of land claimed by Entry No 11930 made by virtue of a Military Warrant No. 1902, dated 9 October 1821, lying on waters of Hesters Creek of Flint River, beginning at a small gum and dogwood in west boundary line of JOHN BRAHAN 640 acre tract which includes the Rock Spring, running north and west containing 120 acres. Court ordered the tracts to be sold to pay double taxes.

MONDAY JANUARY 27, 1823

Justices present were ABRAHAM SUMMERS, SAMUEL BUCHANAN and WILLIAM MILNER, Esquires.

WILLIAM SPENCER is released from serving as a juror this term.

The Transfer of a PLat and Certificate from JOHN STROUD to JOHN KELLER and ordered to be certified.

A Deed of Conveyance from DAVID A. MOORE to ELISHA JOAB and HENRY BAGLEY for 10 acres of land, proven by JOHN R. BAGLEY and R.H.C. BAGLEY and ordered to be certified.

A Deed of Conveyance from THOMAS LENARD to COLLIN CAMPBELL for 135 acres of land and ordered to be certified.

A Deed of Conveyance from THOMAS LENARD to COLLIN CAMPBELL for 20 acres of land and ordered to be certified.

A Deed of Conveyance from SMITH JONES to REUBEN HUNTER for 30 acres of land and ordered to be certified.

A Deed of Conveyance from JAMES ALEXANDER to ANTHONY BLEDSOE for 705 acres of land, proven by THOMAS H. HAYS and H.J. HAYS and ordered to be certified.

A Deed of Conveyance from JOHN COFFEE to WILLIAM SMITH for 190 acres of land and ordered to be certified.

A Deed of Conveyance from FRANCIS HODGE to JAMES HODGE for 62 acres of land and ordered to be certified.

A Deed of Conveyance from WILLIAM NICHOLSON to JOHN DAVIS for 100 acres of landand ordered to be certified.

A Deed of Conveyance from BENJAMIN BOON to JOHN KELLER for 28 acres of land and ordered to be certified.

AN inventory of the estate of WILLIAM AMMONDS, deceased, was returned to court by his executor and ordered to be certified.

It is ordered that the Sheriff purchase three or four loads of wood and have the same cut and stored away in one of the rooms above stairs in the courthouse for the use of the court and church and that the Sheriff be paid out of any monies in the hands of County Trustee.

NATHANIEL B. BUCKINGHAM vs THOMAS H. MAY - This day came the parties by their attorneys and a jury of men, to wit, RANDOLPH QUARLES, JAMES HIGGINS, ISAAC SEBASTIAN, JOSEPH PENN, DAVID THWING, JAMES HIGGINS, HOWELL HARRIS, JOSEPH DEAN, HAY CRAWFORD, SHEPARD SHELTON, ABRAHAM DUDNEY and JOHN J. WHITAKER being elected and sworn and that on motion of the plaintiff by his attorney, the jury to be discharged. The defendant recover his costs.

HENRY ROBERTSON is appointed overseer of the road in the room of WILLIAM SOLOMON resigned and call on the usual hands.

JAMES WYATT vs JACOB WRIGHT - Appeal - This day came the parties by their attorneys and a jury of men, to wit, SOLOMON GULLETT, JOHN R. JOHNSON, JOHN WITT, BENJAMIN PORTER, WILLIAM McELROY, HIGDON HARPER, JAMES HIGGINS, ISAAC SEBASTIAN, JOSEPH PENN, DAVID THWING, JAMES PHILLIPS, and HOWELL HARRIS being elected and sworn and tryed the matter in dispute between the parties and said the defendant is not indebted to the plaintiff anything. Defendant recover his costs.

DAVID McGAVOCK vs ISAIAH ALLY - (same as above) and say that the defendant has not paid the debt of $250.00 and damages of $15.81¼. Plaintiff to recover his costs.

JOHN B. ALEXANDER vs SAMUEL TODD & EBENEZER McEWEN - Debt - (same as above) and say that the defendant has not paid all of the debt but owes a balance of $1226.00 and damages of $83.62½. Plaintiff to recover his costs.

WILLIAM SNODDY vs GEORGE W. DENNIS - Debt - (same as above) and said that the defendant has not paid the debt of $209.10 and damages of $33.63. Plaintiff to recover his costs.

SAMUEL RAMSEY vs RANDOLPH QUARLES - Debt - (same as above) and say that the defendant has not paid the debt of $132.00 and damages of $9.50. Plaintiff to recover his costs.

JESSE B. CLEMENTS vs BENNETT B. HOWELL - Debt - (same as above) and say that the defendant has not paid the debt of $100.00 and damages of $1.83. PLaintiff to recover against the defendant his costs.

WILLIAM McELROY vs ARCHABALD McELROY - Debt - (same as above) and say that the defendant has not paid the debt of $550.00 and damages of $31.62½. Plaintiff to recover his costs.

JAMES GREER vs WILLIAM McELROY - Debt - (same as above) and say that the defendant has not paid the debt of $199.18 and damages of $14.25. Plaintiff recover his costs.

JAMES WYATT vs DENNIS WRIGHT - The plaintiff by his attorney says he wishes to dismiss this suit and the defendant assumes the payment of all costs. Suit to be dismissed and plaintiff recover his costs.

TUESDAY JANUARY 28, 1823
Justices present were WILLIAM ANDERSON, CHARLES BOYLES and ROBERT DICKSON, Esquires.

It is ordered that JAMES WYATT be released from paying a double tax for the year 1822.

It is ordered that JOHN GREER be released from paying a double tax for the year 1822.

It is ordered that BRICE M. GARNER be released from the payment of a double tax for the year 1822.

A Deed of Conveyance from WILLIAM CUNNINGHAM to RICHARD WYATT for 95 acres of land and ordered to be certified.

JANE B. CAMPBELL vs NIMROD BAILY - The plaintiff by his attorney and moves the court for a non-suit in this cause. The plaintiff be non-suited and the defendant recover against the plaintiff his costs.

R. & W. DICKSON vs BENNETT B. HOWELL - This day came the parties by their attorneys and a jury of men, to wit, JOHN WITT, SOLOMON GULLETT, DAVID THWING, JOSEPH DEAN, JAMES BRYANS, HOWELL HARRIS, SHEPARD SHELTON, JOHN R. JOHNSON, JOHN J. WHITAKER, HAY CRAWFORD, JAMES PHILLIPS, and RANDOLPH QUARLES being elected and sworn and say that the defendant did assume upon himself in manner and form as the plaintiff's in declaring against him had alleged and they assess the plaintiff's damages by reason of $87.92½. Plaintiff to recover his costs.

WILLIAM GIVENS vs JOHN P. McCONNELL - Debt - (same as above) and said that the defendant has not paid all of the debt but owes a balance of $120.68 and damages of $2.41. Plaintiff recover his costs.

JOHN P. McCONNELL vs RICHARD PRYOR - Motion - The plaintiff by his attorney was security for the defendant in the case of CHARLES H. EDMISTON against RICHARD PRYOR and that JOHN P. McCONNELL had paid the sum of $236.19¼ as security for PRYOR. Plaintiff to recover his costs.

A Bill of Sale from JAMES WYATT to EZEKIEL NORRIS for a negro man named PHILLIP was proven by FRANCIS PORTERFIELD and RICHARD P. DOBBINS and ordered to be certified.

A Bill of Sale from PETER MOYERS to WILLIAM NORRIS for a negro man named GEORGE, proven by EZEKIEL NORRIS and WRIGHT McLEMORE and ordered to be certified.

It is ordered by the court that JOHN P. McCONNELL recover against RICHARD PRYOR $406.40. Together with $3.19 interest from 24 August 1822.

A. & J. WHITENBURGH vs G. MARTIN & WILLIAM KENNON - This day came the parties by their attorneys and a jury of men, to wit, JOHN WITT, SOLOMON GULLETT, DAVID THWING, JOSEPH DEAN, JAMES BRYANT, HOWELL HARRIS, SHEPARD SHELTON, JOHN R. JOHNSON, JOHN J. WHITAKER, HAY CRAWFORD, JAMES PHILLIPS and RANDOLPH QUARLES being elected and sworn that the defendant has not paid all of the debt but owes a balance of $1200.50 and damages of $69.00. Plaintiff to recover his costs.

WILLIAM McELROY is released from serving as a juror any further this term.

A Deed of COnveyance from WILLIAM DOAK to HENRY ROBERTSON for 148 acres of land, proven by JAMES FULTON and A. CAMPBELL and ordered to be certified.

A Bill of Sale from WILLIAM EDMISTON to ROBERT DICKSON for a negro man named CHARLES and ordered to be certified.

JOHN W. SMITH vs PRESLEY S. GEORGE - This day came the parties by their attorneys and a jury of men, to wit, SOLOMON GULLETT, DAVID THWING, JOSEPH DEAN, JAMES BRYANS, HOWELL HARRIS, SHEPARD SHELTON, JOHN R. JOHNSON, JOHN J. WHITAKER, HAY CRAWFORD, RANDOLPH QUARLES, HIGDON HARPER, and JOHN WITT being elected and sworn and said that by consent of the court that the jury be dispersed until next day.

WEDNESDAY JANUARY 29, 1823

Justices present were DAVID COWEN, ROBERT DICKSON and WILLIAM BEAVERS, Esquires.

BAILY & SHIRLY vs NATHANIEL B. BUCKINGHAM - This day came the parties by their attorneys and a jury of men, to wit, JAMES HIGGINS, ISAAC SEBASTIAN, JOSEPH PENN, ABRAHAM DUDNEY, BENJAMIN PORTER, SAMUEL BRADLEY, JOHN W. SMITH, WILLIS L. CALVERT, JOHN ROADS, ENOCK K. WEATHERS, JOHN NEECE and JACOB GODWIN being elected and sworn and said that the defendant recover his costs. Plaintiff asked for an appeal and was granted same.

SAMUEL THOMPSON vs SAMUEL H. SMITH - This day came the parties by their attorneys and a jury of men, to wit, JAMES HIGGINS, ISAAC SEBASTIAN, JOSEPH PENN, ABRAHAM DUDNEY, BENJAMIN PORTER, SAMUEL BRADLEY, JOHN W. SMITH, WILLIS L. CALVERT, JOHN ROADS, ENOCK K. WEATHERS, JOHN NEECE, and JACOB GODWIN being elected and sworn and said that the defendant has not paid the debt of $300.00 and damages of $9.95. Plaintiff to recover his costs. Defendant prays for an appeal and is granted same.

BENJAMIN JOHNSON vs JAMES R. BROWN - Appeal - The plaintiff by his attorney and the defendant being called to prosecute his appeal failed to do so but made default. Plaintiff to recover his costs and JOEL McLEMORE, security.

JOHN W. SMITH vs PRESLEY S. GEORGE - The jury returned to court and said that they cannot agree upon their verdict and by consent of both parties by their attorneys that SOLOMON GULLETT, one of the jurors be withdrawn and the rest discharged from rendering a verdict in this cause. This cause is transferred to the next Circuit Court for trial.

DAVID THWING vs JOHN McFARLAND - Appeal - This day came the parties by their attorneys and a jury of men, to wit, JOSEPH PENN, ISAAC SEBASTIAN, JAMES HIGGINS, BENJAMIN PORTER, ABRAHAM DUDNEY, ENOCK K. WEATHERS, JACOB GODWIN, BENJAMIN CLEMENTS, SAMUEL BOON, JOSIAH SMITH, URIAH BOBBIT and JOSEPH HALL being elected and sworn and said that the defendant is indebted to the plaintiff for $2.00. Plaintiff to recover his costs and ZACHARIAH ARNOLD, security.

JOHN RHEA & R. EDMISTON for the use of &c vs ROBERT DICKSON and others - (same as above jurors) and said that the defendants has not paid the debt of $610.31¼ and damages of $88.62½. Plaintiff to recover his costs.

JOEL JOHNSON vs JAMES WYATT - The defendant being called to come and defend this suit failed to do so but made default. Plaintiff to recover his costs. A jury of men, to wit, HOWELL HARRIS, HIGDON HARPER, RANDOLPH QUARLES, JOSEPH DEAN, SHEPARD SHELTON, JAMES BRYANS, HAY CRAWFORD, BENJAMIN CLEMENTS, DAVID THWING, BENJAMIN PORTER, ROMEO LEWIS and DAVIDSON McMILLIN said that the plaintiff's damages of $16.00. Plaintiff to recover his costs.

WILLIAM FRAME vs THOMAS KERCHEVAL - The plaintiff made a motion to dismiss this cause. Court ordered the cause to be dismissed and the plaintiff recover against the defendant $84.60 and interest of $4.65.

The Transfer of a Plat and Certificate of Survey from ABNER FREEMAN to SAMUEL CUNNINGHAM and ordered to be certified.

A Deed of Conveyance from HUGH McADAMS to JOSEPH BIGGER for 20 acres of land and ordered to be certified.

A Deed of Conveyance from EDWARD POWERS to BENJAMIN BLAKE for 20 acres of land and ordered to be certified.

A Deed of Conveyance from EDWARD POWERS to JERY COONRAD WINKLER for 10 acres of land and ordered to be certified.

A Deed of Conveyance from MICHAEL ROBINSON to WILLIAM PAUL for 50 acres of land and ordered to be certified.

A Deed of Conveyance from SAMUEL DOBBINS to JAMES GARRETT for 22½ acres of land and ordered to be certified.

A Deed of Conveyance from WILLIAM WOOSLEY to EDWARD MOSS for 85 acres of land and ordered to be certified.

The Transfer of a Plat and Certificate from JAMES ALEXANDER to SAMUEL CUNNINGHAM and ordered to be certified.

SOLOMON REECE vs JOHN GREER - By permission of both the parties and the court, this cause is transferred for trial to next Circuit Court.

THURSDAT JANUARY 30, 1823

Justices present were ROBERT DICKSON, EBENEZER McEWEN and CHARLES BOYLES, Esquires.

BRICE M. GARNER vs JOHN BROWN - This cause is continued on affidavit of the defendant and a commission is awarded him to take the deposition of SAMUEL McGEHEE of Jackson County, Alabama, to be read in evidence on the trial of said cause be giving the plaintiff ten days notice of time and place of taking same.

JOHN LANDRES vs ROBERT FLETCHER - The plaintiff is awarded a commission to take the deposition of EBENEZER TITUS of Huntsville to be read in evidence on the trial of this cause by giving the defendant ten days notice of time and place of taking same.

A Bill of Sale from HENRY McKINNEY to JOHN MILLIKEN and ordered to be certified.

J. & J. SPENCE vs WILLIAM B. & Y. HIGGINS - On motion of the plaintiff by his attorney have given him to amend the alias writ by stricking out the letter R at the end of the plaintiff name so as to read SPENCE instead of SPENCER.

R.H. McEWEN vs JOHN VIGERS - The defendant being called to come and defend this suit failed to do so but made default. A judgment was filed against him and that a writ of inquiry be awarded the plaintiff at the next term of court.

J. PENDERGRASS vs FRANCIS FINCHER - Upon motion by both parties, this case being heard and understood, the court overruled the motion to dismiss said suit. Plaintiff prays for an appeal to next Circuit Court and was granted same.

A.B. BAILEY vs ROBERT ROSS - The plaintiff being called to come and prosecute this cause failed to do so but made default. The defendant to recover against the plaintiff his costs.

PHILLIP BROWN vs WALTER KINNARD - The plaintiff being called to come and prosecute his suit failed to do so but made default. Defendant to recover his costs.

JOHN McCARTY vs PHILIP FIELD - The defendant being called to come and defend this suit failed to do so but made default. Judgment entered against the defendant and that a writ of inquiry be awarded the plaintiff at next court.

MONDAY APRIL 21, 1823

CLABOURN WHITWORTH is appointed overseer of the road from Dennis Ferry on Elk River to the Five Mile Post on the Winchester Road.

MATHIAS TURNER is appointed overseer of the road from the Five Mile Post to the crossroads at WILLIAM PATTERSON.

WILLIAM McCLELLAN is appointed overseer of the road in the room of JOSHUA GIBSON resigned and call on the usual hands.

JAMES BLACKLEDGE is appointed overseer of the road in the room of ASARIAH McAFEE and call on the usual hands.

ARCHABALD McELROY is appointed overseer of the road from Hannah Ford to the top of the ridge near CAPTAIN DYE's and call on the usual hands.

JAMES BROWN is appointed overseer of the road from the top of the ridge near CAPTAIN DYE's to the Privy Ridge on the other side of COldwater Creek and call on the usual hands.

It is ordered that WILLIAM McELROY & (blank) BLANE work on that part of the road which JOHN CRAWFORD is overseer of.

JOHN HEATH is appointed overseer of the road in place of JOHN PARKERSON resigned and call on the usual hands.

ALLEN ELSTON is appointed overseer of the road in place of THOMAS CAMPBELL resigned and call on the usual hands.

189

ANTHONY HOGAN is appointed overseer of the road in place of HENRY TALLEY resigned and call on the usual hands.

SAMUEL BOON is appointed overseer of the road in place of WILLIAM MARSH and call on the usual hands.

JOHN SAWYERS is appointed ovewrseer of the road in place of JONATHAN ANDERSON and call on the usual hands.

JOHN ARMSTRONG is appointed overseer of the road in place of JOHN LEE and call on the usual hands.

CHARLES BRIGHT is appointed overseer of the road in place of ISAAC BROYLES resigned and call on the usual hands.

BAILY RAINS is appointed overseer of the road in place of WILLIAM LANGSTON resigned and call on the usual hands.

JOSHUA KELLY is appointed overseer of the road in place of RICHARD WELCH resigned and call on the usual hands.

JOHN EATON is appointed overseer of that part of the road from JASPER SMITH's to the ford of Mulberry at JAMES BROWN's and JACOB WAGGONER, Esquire, to appoint the hands to work on said road.

JOHN H. BELL is appointed overseer of the road in place of AMOS HURLEY resigned and call on the usual hands.

WILLIAM HORD is appointed overseer of the road from Nixon's Ford on Elk River up Tuckers Creek to the top of the ridge between Mulberry and said creek and call on the usual hands.

JAMES PARR is appointed overseer of the road from Chicks Ford on Elk River to the State line and call on the same hands that worked under WILLIAM BONNER as overseer.

PHILIP FOX is appointed overseer of that part of the road which JOHN WAGGONER was formerly overseer of.

JOHN TEAL is appointed overseer of the road from the gap of the ridge near WIDOW TEAL's on to WILLIAM PATTERSON and JESSE DANIEL, Esquire, to appoint the hands to work on said road.

JAMES CURRY, JOHN GAVIN, EDWARD GORE, WILLIAM MEADOW, BAILEY RAINS, JOHN F. CAWSET, JOSHUA W. MASSEY and WILLIAM WILLIS are appointed a Jury of View to view and turn that part of the Mulberry road that ran through the lands of JOHN ENOCK and make return to next court.

COLEMAN McDANIEL is appointed overseer of the Winchester road from PATTERSON's to the Gum Spring and AMBROSE BARKER to appoint the hands.

JOHN McGEE is appointed overseer of the road beginning at the end of that part which ARRINGTON is overseer of the Franklin County line and AMBROSE BARKER to appoint the hands.

JOHN SMITH, WILLIAM CHAPMAN, WILLIAM SMITH, LEMUEL BRANDON, SPENCER ROGERS, JOSIAH BRANDON, MOSES CHAMBERS and BENJAMIN BAKER are appointed a Jury of View to view and mark out a road the nearest and best way from Blyths Mill to the head of Coffees Creek to intersect the road leading from Fayetteville to Winchester down Coffee Creek and make return to next court.

It is ordered that ELIJAH M. RINGO be allowed $5.00 for holding an inquest over the body of JOSEPH SHAW and that the County Trustee pay the same.

It is ordered that WILLIAM C. ABELS, JOHN ENOCKS, WILLIAM EDMISTON, WILLIAM BEAVERS, SAMUEL GARLAND, CLIFFORD GRAY, RICHARD FLYNT, JOHN H. MOORE, JAMES FORSYTH, JOHN SMITH, JOSEPH McCRACKEN, ENOCK RUST, DANIEL LOONEY, JAMES RALSTON, THOMAS GAITHER, CORNELIUS DARNELL, WILLIAM MILLNER, WILLIAM SMITH, Esquire, JOHN WISEMAN, JOHN PORTER, JAMES WILSON, GEORGE BLAKEMORE, JACOB WAGGONER, FRANCIS PATTON, JOHN KING, and

190

NATHANIEL REED be and are hereby appointed jurors to the next Circuit Court in September.

It is ordered that ABNER STEED, REUBEN LOGAN, THOMAS GEORGE, ARON STYLES, MARTIN L. PARKS, JACOB HAMBLETON, JOEL COMMONS, THOMAS FLACK, JAMES GRANT, JAMES BROOKS, JOHN MURDOCK, JAMES BRYANS, HARRISON JOHNSON, HERBERT GRIFFIS, JOHN LATHAM, JOSEPH CAMBELL, STEPHEN BEAVERS, JAMES COOLY, DAVID HOWELL, JOSIAH MOORS, JOHN CRAWFORD, PARK GIBSON, WILLIAM McCLELLAN, JOHN STILES, SR., and HENRY WARREN be summoned as jurors to next County Court in July next.

An inventory of the estate of GEORGE HOPPER, deceased, was returned to court by his admr and ordered to be certified.

The Commissioners appointed to lay off one years provisions for the support of the widow of GEORGE HOPPER, deceased, made return and ordered to be certified.

An amount of sale of the estate of WILLIAM WALLACE, deceased, was returned to court and ordered to be certified.

An additional inventory of the estate of ARCHABALD MAYFIELD, deceased, was returned by his admr and ordered to be certified.

Amount of sale of the property of ISAAC OAKS, deceased, was returned by his admr and ordered to be certified.

THOMAS H. SHAW appeared in court and was appointed guardian for LEROY SHELTON, SUSIANA SHELTON, JAMES SHELTON and MARY SHELTON, heirs of DAVID SHELTON, deceased, who gave bond of $1000.00 and JACOB WAGGONER and JAMES CURY, his securities.

JANE BRADLEY the admrx of ARON BRADLEY, deceased, and the guardian for RACHEL BRADLEY, formerly RACHEL CHILDRESS, one of the orphan children of ARON BRADLEY, deceased, the said JANE is allowed by the court $150.00 out of said RACHEL portion of the estate of said ARON, for raising and supporting the said RACHEL from the deceased of said ARON up to this time and that she retain so much of the said RACHEL distributive share in her hands.

JOHN ENOCK & ANDREW W. WALKER are apppointed commissioners to settle with EDWARD GORE, admr of CHARLES SMITH, deceased, and make return to next court.

THOMAS CLARK & JOHN PORTER are appointed commissioners to settle with JAMES DOWNING, admr of JOHN DOWNING, deceased, and make return to next court.

HARMAN SHELTON & CATHARINE RUTHERFORD are appointed admr and admrx of DUDLEY RUTHERFORD, who gave bond of $1800.00 with AMBROSE BARKER and BENJAMIN HUDSON, their securities.

On petition of WILLIAM FROST and ROBERT BUCHANAN, it is ordered that the Sheriff summons a jury to ascertain the damage that WILSON FROST and ROBERT BUCHANAN may have sustained by the new road running through their land and make return to next court.

It is ordered by the court that ISAAC LAYMAN be allowed and to receive from the County Trustee $40.00 out of any county monies in his hands &c.

AMBROSE BARKER, ELIJAH McLAUGHLIN and BENJAMIN HUDSON are appointed commissioners to lay off one years support for the widow of DUDLEY RUTHERFORD, deceased, and make return to next court.

PHILIP FAGAN produced one wolf scalp over six months old and made oath that he killed the same within the county.

The Commissioners appointed to settle with the admr of the estate of JOHN WAKEFIELD and make return and ordered to be certified.

The Last Will and Testament of MOSES SATERFIELD, deceased, was proven in court for probate whereupon came JOHN COCK and JOHN MARTIN, witnesses, made oath that they saw him sign, seal and deliver his Last Will and Testament and that he was at that time of sound mind and memory whereupon came JAMES CHILDRESS, one of the executors and renounces his executorship to said will.

A Deed of Conveyance from SAMUEL DAVIS to JOSEPH NICHOLS for 80 acres of land, proven by MOSES PARK and JOHN COWDEN and ordered to be certified.

A Deed of Conveyance from ZACHARIAH HARRISON to REUBEN LOGAN for 25 acres of land and ordered to be certified.

A Transfer of a Plat and Certificate from JAMES STANDREDIG to HOWELL SIKES for 10 acres of land and ordered to be certified.

A Deed of Conveyance from JOHN OWENS, SR. to VARNER D. COWN for 160 acres of land and ordered to be certified.

The Transfer of a Play and Certificate of Survey from JOHN SULLIVAN to NICHOLAS CARRIGER for 15 acres of land and ordered to be certified.

The Transfer of a Play and Certificate from WILLIAM RAY to JACOB ADAMS, proven by JOSEPH HARKINS and ordered to be certified.

A Deed of Conveyance from HENRY GAINES to JOSEPH HARKINS for 60 acres of land and ordered to be certified.

A Deed of Conveyance from PETER FIREBAUGH to JOSEPH HARKINS for 20 acres of land and orderd to be certified.

A Deed of Conveyance from HENRY GAINS to EPHRAIM KING for 76 acres of land and ordered to be certified.

A Deed of Conveyance from ISAAC MILLER to JOSEPH HARKINS for 50 acres of land and ordered to be certified.

A Deed of Conveyance from PETER FIREBAUGH to JOSEPH HARKINS for 40 acres of land and ordered to be certified.

A Bill of Sale from THOMAS ALLEY to ISAIAH ALLEY for a negro woman named MARY and her child named MELVINA, proven by JAMES HOLMAN and ordered to be certified.

A Deed of Conveyance from WILLIAM DYE to EDWARD ISHAM for 144½ acres of land and ordered to be certified.

A Deed of Conveyance from HAMILTON MOFFIT to WILLIAM MOFFIT for 20 acres of land and ordered to be certified.

A Deed of Conveyance from WILLIAM SHAW to JAMES LEDBETTER for 20 acres of land and ordered to be certified.

A Deed of Conveyance from JOHN McMULLIN to MARTHA McMULLIN for 6 acres of land and ordered to be certified.

A Bill of Sale from JOSHUA NICHOLS to JOSEPH NICHOLS for one negro man named JACK and ordered to be certified.

A Deed of Conveyance from MOSES SATERFIELD to BENJAMIN BUTLER for 130 acres of land, proven by JOHN CHILDRESS and SAMUEL WALLACE and ordered to be certified.

A Deed of Conveyance from WILLIAM MURRY to LITTLEBURY L. STONE for 60 acres of land and ordered to be certified.

A Deed of Conveyance from MARY YOUNGand DANIEL YOUNG to WILLIAM ROBINSON, proven and ordered to be certified.

A Deed of Conveyance from JOHN COFFEY to JOHN DOWTHIT for 25 acres of land and ordered to be certified.

A Deed of Conveyance from JOHN COFFEE to JOHN DOWTHIT for 51 acres of land and ordered to be certified.

A Transfer of a Plat and Certificate from WILLIAM BARNETT to ELIAS HULSON (HUDSON, HUTSON) and ordered to be certified.

ARCHABALD CAMPBELL was appointed a Constable and took oath.

TUESDAY APRIL 22, 1823

Justices present were CHARLES BOYLES, WILLIAM DICKSON and JOHN PINKERTON, Esquires.

The Sheriff made a return that he had summoned the following venire, to wit, JOHN H. ROGERS, ELIJAH DAVIS, WILLIAM P. PULLIAM, SAMUEL S. BUCHANAN, LEMUEL BROADWAY, JOSIAH SMITH, CHARLES H. EDMISTON, PETER SHELTON, ELI COUCH, JOHN STREET, JOSEPH PETTY, JOHN DOWTHIT, ELISHA THOMASON, JAMES MAXFIELD, BENJAMIN CLEMENTS, JOHN W. BLAKE, GENERAL W.C. EDMISTON, HENRY ROBERTSON, WILLIAM PATTERSON, WILLIAM CRAWFORD, MATHEW WILSON, MORGAN CLAYTON, JONATHAN FROST, and JAMES MILSTEAD of whom were elected Grand Jurors, to wit, BENJAMIN CLEMENTS, foreman, JOHN STREET, JOHN W. BLAKE, PETER SHELTON, JONATHAN FROST, ELI COUCH, LEMUEL BROADWAY, JAMES MILSTEAD, JAMES MAXFIELD, SAMUEL S. BUCHANAN, WILLIAM CRAWFORD, WILLIAM P. PULLIAM, and JOSEPH PETTY who after receiving the charge returned to consider for their presentments.

WILLIAM HUSBANDS a Constable sworn to wait on the Grand Jury.

CHARLES BOYLES produced a license and was permitted to be qualified as a practicing attorney.

The due execution of an Indenture of Bargain and Sale from PETER MOYERS to ISAAC SITLER and JAMES W. SITLER for the half of town lot No. 59 in the town of Nashville and ordered to be certified.

The due execution of an Indenture of Bargain and Sale from PETER MOYERS to ISAAC SITLER and JAMES SITLER for two town lots in town of Fayetteville, Nos. 20 and 25 and ordered to be certified.

The due execution of an Indenture of Bargain and Sale from PETER MOYERS to ISAAC SITLER and JAMES SITLER for 38 acres and 15 poles of land and ordered to be certified.

The due execution of an Indenture of Bargain and Sale from PETER MOYERS to ISAAC SITLER and JAMES W. SITLER for a negro girl named MATILDA and ordered to be certified.

The Grand Jury returned to court and brought with them a Bill of Indictment, the State against DANIEL S. AYERS for an assault and battery, a true bill and again returned to consider for further presentments.

The Grand Jury again returned and brought with them a Bill of Indictment, the State against TRYON GIBSON for an assault and battery and again returned to consider for further presentments.

The State vs JAMES BLAIR - Assault and Battery - The defendant being charged pleads guilty and fines 6¼ cents and pay the costs of this indictment.

The State vs TRYON GIBSON - Assault and Battery - The defendant being charged pleads guilty and is fined 50 cents and pay the costs of this indictment.

The State vs DANIEL L. AYERS - Assault and Battery - The defendant being charged pleads guilty and is fined 50 cents and pay the costs of this indictment.

The due execution of a Bill of Sale from JOSEPH HINKLE to MALCOM McCOWEN for a negro woman named CATY, proven by ROBERT H. McEWEN and ordered to be certified.

NASH GLIDEWELL vs JOHN CLIFTON - It is ordered that the clerk issue an order to bring to court the papers in the above cause.

CLABORN W. HUGHES vs JAMES BLAIR - The plaintiff says he intends no further to prosecute this suit and assumes the payment of all costs. Suit to be dismissed and the defendant recover his costs.

BENJAMIN CLEMENTS vs GEORGE W. DENNIS - The plaintiff says he wishes to dismiss this suit and the defendant assumes the payment of all costs. Suit to be dismissed and plaintiff recover his costs.

BENJAMIN DUNCAN vs HENRY McKINNEY - The plaintiff by his attorney says he intends no further to prosecute this suit. Suit to be dismissed and the defendant recover his costs.

BALDWIN & IVES vs ROMEO LEWIS - In debt - This day came the parties by their attorneys and a jury of men, to wit, BENJAMIN CLEMENTS, JOHN STREET, JOHN W. BLAKE, PETER SHELTON, JONATHAN FROST, ELI COUCH, LEMUEL BROADWAY, JAMES MILSTEAD, JAMES MAXFIELD, SAMUEL S. BUCHANAN, WILLIAM CRAWFORD, and JOSEPH PETTY being elected and sworn and said that the defendant has not paid the debt of $498.49 and damages of $100.00. Plaintiff to recover his costs.

JOHN GILLASPIE vs THOMAS KERCHEVAL - In debt - (same as above) and said that the defendant has not paid the debt of $100.00 and damages of $21.50. Plaintiff recover his costs.

WILLIAM GIVENS vs MORGAN CLAYTON - In debt - (same as above) and says that the defendant has not paid all the debt but owes a balance of $265.00 and damages of $4.85. Plaintiff to recover his costs.

THOMAS GREER vs HUGH M. BLAKE - In debt - (same as above) and says that the defendant has not paid the debt of $450.00 and damages of $16.87½. Plaintiff to recover his costs.

HUGH PINKERTON vs ALEXANDER McLIN - In debt - (same as above) and says that the defendant has not paid the debt of $100.10 and damages of $13.75. Plaintiff to recover his costs.

JASON HOPKINS vs BRICE M. GARNER - In debt - (same as above) and said that the defendant has not paid the debt of $146.00 and damages of $3.62½. Plaintiff to recover his costs.

JOHN WAGGONER vs MOSES HARDEN - In debt - (same as above) and said that the defendant has not paid the debt of $186.50 and damages of $23.00. Plaintiff to recover his costs.

JOHN WAGGONER vs NOAH WARD - In debt - (same as above) and said that the defendant has not paid the debt of $100.00 and damages of $6.25. Plaintiff to recover his costs.

JOHN WAGGONER vs NOAH WARD - In debt - (same as above) and said that the defendant has not paid the debt of $100.00 and damages of $3.25. Plaintiff to recover his costs.

JOHN WAGGONER vs JOHN SMITH - Debt - (same as above) and says that the defendant has not paid the debt of $175.00 and damages of $12.81¼. Plaintiff to recover his costs.

WEDNESDAY APRIL 23, 1823

Justices present were JOHN PINKERTON, ROBERT DICKSON and ENOCK RUST, Esquires.

The due execution of an Indenture of Bargain and Sale from WILLIAM LEA to GABRIEL BUFORD for 279 acres of land, proven by JOHN DABNEY and JOHN PARK and ordered to be certified.

The Grand Jury again returned to court and brought with them a Bill of Indictment against THOMAS H. WILLIAMS foran assault and battery, a true bill and again returned to consider for further presentments.

RUBEN WOODWARD vs JOSEPH JENKINS - Debt - (same as above jurors)and said that the defendant has not paid the debt of $221.55 and damages of $3.68 3/4. Plaintiff to recover his costs.

JAMES COWEN vs WILLIAM McCLELLAN - Indebt - This day came the parties by their attorneys and a jury of men, to wit, BENJAMIN CLEMENTS, JOHN STREET, JOHN W. BLAKE, PETER SHELTON, JONATHAN FROST, ELI COUCH, LEMUEL BROADWAY, JAMES MILSTEAD, JAMES MAXFIELD, SAMUEL S. BUCHANAN, WILLIAM CRAWFORD, and JOSEPH PETTY being elected and sworn and said that the defendant has not paid the debt of $281.10 and damages of $36.00. Plaintiff to recover his costs.

RICHARD ROBERTSON vs NOAH WARD - Indebt - (same as above) and said that the defendant has not paid the debt of $100.00 and damages of $3.25. Plaintiff to recover his costs.

WILLIAM GIVENS vs RUBEN WOODWARD and ROBERT BUCHANAN - Indebt - (same as above) and said that the defendant has not paid the debt of $300.00 and damages of $5.80. Plaintiff to recover his cocts.

JAMES HOPPER vs SMITH & McCLELLAN - Indebt - (same as above) and said that the defendant has not paid the debt of $93.87½ and damages of $1.68 3/4. Plaintiff to recover his costs.

ROBERT M. CLARK vs AMBROSE BARKER - Indebt - (same as above) and said that the defendant has not paid the debt of $75.00 and damages of $1.25. Plaintiff to recover his costs.

ROBERT H. McEWEN vs JOHN LEE - Indebt - (same as above) and said that the defendant has not paid the debt of $96.00 and damages of $2.25. Plaintiff to recover his costs.

BUCHANAN & PORTERFIELD vs EPHRAIM M. BUGG - Indebt - (same as above) and said that the defendant has not paid the debt of $100.60 and damages of $3.25. Plaintiff to recover his costs.

PETER HOLLAND vs JOHN EAST - The plaintiff says he wishes to dismiss this suit and assumes the payment of half of the costs and the defendant assumes the payment of the other half. Suit to be dismissed and each party one half of the costs.

JOHN SIVELY vs PATRICK GILLASPIE - The plaintiff says he wishes to dismiss this suit and assumes the payment of all costs. Suit to be dismissed and the defendant recover his costs.

The due execution of an Indenture of Bargain and Sale from FRANCIS PORTERFIELD, Sheriff, to ROBERT DICKSON for 50 acres of land and ordered to be certified.

An inventory of the property of DUDLEY RUTHERFORD was returned to court by his admrs and ordered to be certified.

The Last Will and Testament of JAMES CLARK was proven in court by CORDALL SHUFFIELD and NANCY FULLER and ordered to be certified. Whereupon came JOSEPH CLARK, the executor, gave bond with JOHN PINKERTON and CORDALL SHUFFIELD his securities.

GABRIEL SEAHORN vs FRANCIS SMITH - Motion, the Sheriff was ordered to expose to sale two town lots in the town of Fayetteville, Nos. 90 and 94, levied as the property of FRANCIS SMITH to satisfy a judgment and that GABRIEL SEAHORN recovered against him before WILLIAM EDMISTON, Esquire, in March 1823 for $21.72 and all legal costs.

HENRY KELSO vs ELIJAH MAYFIELD - It is ordered that the defendant give other and better security for the prosecution of this suit on or before next court or suit will be dismissed.

JOHN J. CARRINGTON vs JAMES MARTIN - The plaintiff by his attorney says he intends no further to prosecute this suit. Suit to be dismissed and the defendant recover his costs.

FULTON & KENNEDY vs HINKLE & GREER - The defendants confessed that they owe the plaintiffs $1166.69 debt and damages of $17.50. Plaintiffs to recover their costs.

JOHN LANDRES vs ROBERT FLETCHER - This day came the parties by their attorneys and a jury of men, to wit, ELIJAH DAVIS, CHARLES H. EDMISTON, ELISHA

TOMERSON, JOHN H. ROGERS, JOHN DOWTHIT, MATHEW WILSON, JORDAN SOLOMON, SHEPARD SHELTON, PERU PATENN, JACOB GODWIN, PETER LUNA, and HENRY DACUS being elected and sworn and said that they cannot agree upon their verdict and by consent of the parties by their attorneys the jury was permitted to disperse until next day.

Justices present were ROBERT DICKSON, JOSEPH McCRACKEN and ENOCK RUST, Esquires.

ROBERT H. McEWEN vs JABEZ VIGUS - This day came the parties by their attorneys and a jury of men, to wit, PATRICK O'CALLIGHAN, GEORGE ST. JOHN BASKINS, ENOS IVES, WILLIAM F. MASON, JOHN NEECE, BENJAMIN CLEMENTS, JOHN STREET, JOHN W. BLAKE, PETER SHELTON, ELI COUCH, JAMES MILSTEAD, and WILLIAM P. PULLIAM being elected and sworn and said that the damages sustained by the plaintiff of $97.94. Plaintiff to recover his costs.

THOMAS H. FLETCHER, ARGYLE CAMPBELL and NATHAN GREEN are appointed Commissioners to settle with GARLAND B. MILLER, admr of JONATHAN ESTILL, deceased, and make return to nect court.

The Grand Jury again returned to court and brought with them a Bill of Indictment against THOMAS LINGO for an assault and battery, a true bill and again return to consider for further presentments.

JAMES CAMPBELL vs BOYLES & GARNER - The plaintiff says he wishes to dismiss this suit. The suit to be dismissed and the defendants recover their costs.

The Grand Jury again returned into court and brought with them a Bill of Indictment against GIDEON AUSTIN and GREEN AUSTIN for an assault and battery, a true bill and again return to consider for further presentments.

WILLIAM NEILD vs MARY INGLE - Motion - It is ordered by the court that the Sheriff expose to sale one town lot in the town of Fayetteville No. 44 to satisfy a judgment that the plaintiff recovered against the defendant before ROBERT DICKSON, Esquire, on April 1823 for $45.18 and all legal costs.

The due execution of an Indenture of Bargain and Sale from JAMES LOCKART surviving executor of JOHN STROTHER, deceased, and JAMES BRIGHT to JAMES NEELD for 50 acres of land in Giles County, proven by JOHN GREEN and WILLIAM EDMISTON and ordered to be certified.

JOHN LANDRIS vs ROBERT FLETCHER - The jury returned to court and said that they cannot agree upon their verdict in this cause and by consent of the parties by their attorneys and by permission of the court ELIJAH DAVIS one of the Jurors is withdrawn and the rest are discharged and this cause is continued until the next term of court.

JOHN LANDRIS vs ROBERT FLETCHER - A Commission is awarded the plaintiff to take the deposition of EBENEZER TITUS of Huntsville, Alabama, to be read in evidence on the trial of the above cause by giving the defendant ten days notice of time and place of taking the same.

The State vs GREEN AUSTIN - Assault and Battery - The defendant being charged pleads guilty and is fined 50 cents. JACK H. LEFTWICH as his security.

The State vs THOMAS LINGO - Indictment for an Assault and Battery - The defendant being charged pleads not guilty and a jury of men, to wit, ISHAM PARR, PETER HOLLAND, JAMES BROKS, HENRY TALLEY, VEZY HUSBANDS, WILSON FROST, RANDOLPH QUARLES, DANIEL MALLARD, DAVIDSON McMILLEN, ROBERT BROOKS, RUFUS K. ANDERSON, and JAMES SANDERS being elected and sworn and said that the defendant is guilty and is fined 6¼ cents and pay cost of the indictment. The defendant prays for an appeal to next Circuit Court in September next.

THOMAS LINGO is charged for an assault and battery from BENJAMIN NEELD, acknowledged himself indebted to the State of Tennessee for $100.00 and MAY BUCHANAN for $50.00, to be levied upon their goods and chattels &c but to be void on condition that THOMAS LINGO appear at next court in September next and answer the charge.

BENJAMIN NEELD & BENJAMIN GIBSON appeared in court and acknowledged themselves indebted to the State of Tennessee for $50.00 to be levied upon their goods and chattels &c to be void on conditions that they appear at the next Circuit Court in September next and give evidence in behalf of the State against THOMAS LINGO.

JAMES BROOKS vs JAMES F. DRIVER - This day came the parties by their attorneys and a jury of men, to wit, BENJAMIN NEELD, JOHN NEECE, JOSEPH ELLISON, JESSE LEDBETTER, CHAMPION BLYTH, ABSOLUM GOFORTH, SAMUEL BOON, HIRAM S. MORGAN, CLEMENT HILL, NICHOLAS CARRIGER, THOMAS JAMES, and ROBERT NEECE being elected and sworn and found in favor of the plaintiff and assess the damages of $145.93 3/4. Plaintiff to recover his costs. Defendant prays for an appeal and is granted same.

A Bill of Sale from WILLIE JONES to JAMES McWHIRTER for two negroes was proven by GEORGE McWHIRTER and ordered to be certified.

An amount of sale of the property of ARTHUR BROOKS, deceased, was returned to court by his admr and ordered to be certified.

FRIDAY APRIL 25, 1823

Justices present were ROBERT DICKSON, JAMES WILSON and ENOCK RUST, Esquires.

The due execution of an Indenture of Bargain and Sale from BRICE M. GARNER and BENJAMIN HARRIS to WILLIAM LOCK for 50 acres of land and ordered to be certified.

On motion of JAMES FULTON, Esquire, and it appearing the the court that DAVIDSON McMILLEN is a man of good and moral character and that he has attained the age of twenty one years and upwards. The clerk is to grant him a copy hereof as a preparitory step for his obtaining license to practive law.

JAMES H. MALLARD vs JOHN NEECE - This day came the parties by their attorneys and a jury of men, to wit, ELIJAH DAVIS, CHARLES H. EDMISTON, ELISHA TOMERSON, JOHN H. ROGERS, JOHN DOWTHIT, MATHEW WILSON, BENJAMIN CLEMENT, JOHN STREET, JOHN W. BLAKE, PETER SHELTON, ELI COUCH, and JAMES MILSTEAD being elected and sworn and found in favor of the plaintiff and assess the damages of $117.59¼. Plaintiff to recover his costs.

EBENEZER ALEXANDER vs HENRY McKINNEY - This day came the parties by their attorneys and a jury of men, to wit, JONATHAN FROST, LEMUEL BROADWAY, JAMES MILSTEAD, SAMUEL S. BUCHANAN, WILLIAM · CRAWFORD, WILLIAM P. PULLIAM, JOSEPH PETTY, JOHN NEECE, REUBEN WOODWARD, DAVIDSON McMILLIN, JAMES H. MALLARD, and DANIEL MALLARD being elected and sworn and said that the defendant has not paid all the debt but owes a balance of $40.00 and damages of $8.79. Plaintiff to recover his costs.

JOHN McCARTY vs PHILIP FIELD - This day came the parties by their attorneys and a jury of men, to wit, ELIJAH DAVIS, CHARLES H. EDMISTON, ELISHA THOMASON, JOHN H. ROGERS, JOHN DOWTHIT, MATHEW WILSON, BENJAMIN CLEMENTS, JOHN STREET, JOHN W. BLAKE, PETER SHELTON, ELI COUCH, and JAMES MILSTEAD being elected and sworn and said that the damages are $150.00. Plaintiff to recover his costs.

BRICE M. GARNER vs JOHN BROWN - This cause is continued on affidavit of the defnedant by his paying the cost of this term.

THOMAS HOPKINS vs BRICE M. GARNER - This cause is continued on affidavit of the defendant and a commission is awarded him to take the deposition of NATHAN GREEN of Winchester, Tennessee, by giving the plaintiff ten days notice also the deposition of BENJAMIN HARRIS of Russellville, Alabama, by giving the plaintiff fifteen days notice of time and place of taking the same, to be read in evidence on the trial of this cause.

HENRY LEDBETTER vs RODERICK OLIVER - Appeal - This day came the parties by their attorneys and a jury of men, to wit, JONATHAN FROST, LEMUEL BROADWAY, JAMES MAXFIELD, SAMUEL S. BUCHANAN, WILLIAM CRAWFORD, JOSEPH PETTY, DAVID THWING, ELIAS SCOTT, JOHN GREER, WILLIAM MOORE, WILSON FROST, and HENRY McKENNY being elected and sworn and said that the defendant owes the plaintiff $30.00 and damages of $2.40. Plaintiff to recover his costs.

CHAMPION BLYTH vs JAMES WALKER - This cause is referred to the arbitration of WILLIAM DICKSON, JOSEPH WHITAKER, ABNER STEED, WILEA JONES, and THOMAS

H. SHAW or any three of them whose award shall be returned in writing to next term and make judgment.

DAVID THWING vs NOAH WARD - (same jurors as above) and said that the defendant is indebted to the plaintiff for $2.00. Plaintiff to recover his costs. Defendant prays for an appeal and is granted same.

The due execution of an Indenture of Bargain and Sale from DAVID BUCHANAN and MARGARET BUCHANAN to ROBERT JONES for 25 acres of land in Washington County, Virginia, acknowledged by said MARGARET, she first being examined separate and apart from her husband and WILLIAM CRAWFORD and SAMUEL S. BUCHANAN as witnesses and ordered to be certified.

ALEXANDER FINDLEY vs ARGYLE CAMPBELL - The defendant confessed that he owes the plaintiff $397.25. Plaintiff agrees to stay execution until next Christmas. Plaintiff to recover his costs.

SATURDAY APRIL 26, 1823

Justices present were WILLIAM DICKSON, AMBROSE BARKER and JESSE DANIEL, Esquires.

JOEL B. SANDERS vs FRANCIS SMITH - Motion - It is ordered that the Sheriff expose to sale two town lots in town of Fayetteville, No. 90 and No. 94 to satisfy judgment that the JOEL B. SANDERS recovered against before ROBERT DICKSON, Esquire, in April 1823 for $28.60 and all legal costs.

WILLIAM GIVENS vs RUBEN WOODWARD and ROBERT BUCHANAN - The defendant prays an appeal to next Circuit Court and is granted.

JAMES READ vs HENRY ROBERTSON - The Commissioners is granted each of them to take depositions generally by giving the adverse party twenty five days notice of time and place of taking the same.

AMOS LILES and wife vs JOSEPH ELLISON and wife - On motion of the defendants by their attorneys, this suit be dismissed and the defendant recover against the plaintiff their costs.

ROBERT H. McEWEN vs JOHN LEA - The defendant prays an appeal to the next Circuit Court from a judgment rendered against him heretofore at this time, he giving bond and security.

JOEL PINSON vs JOHN W. SMITH - Motion - It is ordered by the court that the letters of administration be granted to the defendant upon the estate of JOEL HOLBERT, deceased, be repealed and letters be granted to JOEL PINSON who gave bond and security. It is ordered that the defendant deliver to JOEL PINSON all the goods and chattels &c of the said intestate. JOEL PINSON gave bond of $6000.00 with ROBERT H. McEWEN and FRANCIS PORTERFIELD his securities.

NATHANIEL B. BUCKINGHAM vs NIMROD FIELDER - The plaintiff says he wishes to dismiss this suit and assumes the payment of the costs. Suit to be dismissed and the defendant recover his costs.

WILSON & SHELTON vs NOAH WARD - This cause is transferred to the next Circuit Court.

CARNEY MEIRS vs JAMES LEDBETTER - A Commission is granted the defendant and is awarded him to take the deposition of THOMAS MEIRS, JR. of Alabama by giving the adverse party ten days notice of time and place of taking the same.

HUGH PINKTON vs ALEXANDER McLIN - The defendant prays an appeal to next Circuit Court from a judgment entered against him at this term. He gave bond and security.

JOHN H. LEWIS vs JOHN P. McCONNELL, admr - A Commission is awarded each of the parties to take the deposition by giving advance party ten days notice of time and place of taking the same.

F.T. Bank vs JAMES MARTIN - The plaintiff says he wishes to dismiss this suit and assumes the payment of all costs. Suit to be dismissed and the defendant recover his costs.

ABRAHAM LUMBRICK vs JOHN OWEN - The plaintiff by his attorney and says he wishes to dismiss this suit and assumes the payment of all costs. Suit to be dismissed and the defendant recover his costs.

JAMES COWEN vs WILLIAM McCLELLAN - The defendant prays for an appeal to the next Circuit Court for a judgment entered against him before at this term. He giving bond and security and is granted him.

JAMES HOPPER vs SMITH & McCLELLAN - The defendant prays for an appeal to the next Circuit Court. He giving bond and security and is granted same.

SAMUEL KELLY vs JOSEPH HINKLE - The plaintiff by his attorney, on motion to dismiss this suit. Suit to be dismissed and the plaintiff recover against the defendant and CONSTANT SCALES his security of $27.12½ and 56¼ cents interest.

MONDAY JULY 21, 1823

ROBERT MOORE is appointed overseer of the road in the room of JOHN BOYLES resigned and call on the usual hands.

WILLIAM STEVENSON is appointed overseer of the road from JESSE GEORGE on by ABRAHAM ISAAC's plantation on to the Huntsville Road and call on the usual hands.

ISAAC SMITH is appointed overseer of the road from the Huntsville Road to the Giles County line and call on the usual hands.

JOHN COCK is appointed overseer of the road from JESSE GEORGE to the Frozen Grove and call on the usual hands.

JOEL DODSON is appointed overseer of the road in the place of ANDREW McCARTNEY resigned and call on the usual hands.

ISAAC McCOLLOM is appointed overseer of the road in the place of THOMAS CHAPMAN resigned and call on the usual hands.

MONDAY JULY 21, 1823

JOHN DOBBINS is appointed overseer of the road from Mortons Creek to SAMUEL DOBBINS' mill and call on the usual hands.

SAMUEL HALL is appointed overseer of the road from Dobbins Mill to the top of the ridge between Swan and Richland Creek and call on the usual hands.

MATHEW MOSS is appointed overseer of the road from the top of the ridge between Richland and Swan Creek to the Huntsville road at NICHOLS and call on the usual hands.

JAMES SHORTER is appointed overseer of the road in the place of MAY BUCHANAN and call on the usual hands.

JOHN W. BLAKE is appointed overseer of the road in place of JOHN S. PRICE resigned and call on the usual hands.

ISHAM PARR is appointed overseer of the road in place of SION HOLLY resigned and call on the usual hands.

NATHAN COLLINS is appointed overseer of the road in place of LEWIS HOPPER resigned and call on the usual hands.

HENRY RENEGER is appointed overseer of the road in place of DAVID COOPER resigned and call on the usual hands.

BROWN PARKERSON is appointed overseer of the road in place of DAVID BYERS resigned and JOHN PINKERTON and HUGH PARKERSON, Esquires, to appoint hands to work on said road.

On petition, it is ordered by the court that the said road leading from HENRY WARREN to ALDEN TUCKER be opened as was formerly laid out and that said road be on the third class and STEPHEN ALEXANDER and CLIFFORD GRAY, Esquires, are appointed to lay off the hands.

HENRY BECK is appointed overseer of the road in place of RICHARD COMPTON and call on the usual hands.

SAMUEL BUCHANAN, THOMAS GAITHER and WILLIAM BEAVERS are appointed to designate the hands to work on the road under JOHN BOON, JOHN QUARLES and STEPHEN CLAYTON, overseers of the Nashville Road, also to appoint the hands to work under JOHN CRAWFORD, overseer of the road from Fayetteville to Crawford's Mill.

THOMAAS LUTTRELL is appointed overseer of the road in place of BENJAMIN HUDSON and that AMBROSE BARKER and WILLIAM MILLNER, Esquires, appoint the hands to work under said overseer.

WILLIAM A. TUCKER is appointed overseer of the road on Tuckers Creek which lies between the fork of said creek at JAMES GEORGE's to the top of the ridge between Mulberry and Tuckers Creek and JACOB WAGGONER and CLIFFORD GRAY, Esquires, to appoint the hands &c.

JASPER SMITH, ROBERT MOORE, BENJAMIN WHITAKER, SR., MARK WHITAKER, PHILIP FOX, PETER WHITESELL, LEWIS WAGGONER, and JOHN BALEY are appointed a Jury of View to view and turn the road which runs through the hands of JACOB WAGGONER, Esquire, and make return to next court.

THOMAS BLAIR, JOHN LOCK, SAMUEL M. CLAY, JOHN THERMAN, WILLIAM PAUL, and JOHN SCOTT are appointed a Jury of View to view and mark out a road the nearest and best way from SAMUEL M. CLAY's on Coldwater up the west fork of said creek to the State line in a direction to Huntsville and make return to next court.

WILLIAM DICKSON, ISAAC CONGO (CONGER) and EBENEZER McEWEN, Esquires, are appointed to lay off six hands more to work on the road leading up middle fork of Norris Creek to the west fork of Mulberry on by WILLIAM DICKSON to Moores Gap on Duck River Ridge and make return to next court.

JOHN MOORE, JOSEPH JENKINS, FRANCIS PATTON, JOHN RHEA, HENRY ROBERTSON, JAMES ELLIS, and JOHN GUYDER are appointed a Jury of View to view and turn the road leading up Stewarts Creek on direction to Deposit leaving the Winchester Road at or near where it originally left said road as to discontinue said road and make return to next court.

CHAMPION BLYTH is appointed overseer to open and keep in repair a new road from his mill to the top of the ridge and JOHN SMITH and JOHN ENOCK to appoint the hands to open said road.

WILLIAM SMITH is appointed overseer of a new road from the top of the ridge to the Winchester Road on Coffees Creek and JOHN SMITH and JOHN ENOCK to appoint hands to open said road.

JOSEPH JENKINS, JOHN P. McCONNELL, GEORGE CUNNINGHAM, JOHN RHEA, WILLIAM HUSBANDS, HENRY KYMES, and JOHN H. ROGERS are appointed a Jury of View to view and turn the Shelbyville Road on by JOSEPH JENKINS leaving the old road at the southeast corner of BOYLES' land to the northwest corner of HENRY ROBERTSON's land thence intersecting the old road near the mouth of JOSEPH JENKINS' lane and make return to next court.

GEORGE SMALL, AMOS SMALL, WILLIAM DOLLINS, JOHN TATE, HENRY MOORE, JAMES COLE and JORDAN REECE are appointed a Jury of View to view and turn the Shelbyville Road at or near WILLIAM McKENZIE's plantation and intersect the old road again at or near JAMES PYBAS and make return to next court.

It is ordered that CHARLES BRIGHT, THOMAS WHITAKER, JOHN DONELSON, WILSON FROST, SOLOMON GULLETT, WILLIAM TIMMONS, SHERWOOD HUNTER, ADLAI SHARP, JAMES BROADWAY, WILLIAM CUNNINGHAM, REECE HOWELL, JAMES LINGO, ISAAC REED, JONATHAN MERRELL, SR., THOMAS W. HAYS, WILLIAM JONES, JACK H. LEFTWICK, JOHN S. JOHNSON, JAMES PIGG, ANDREW W. WALKER, THOMAS CRAWFORD, JOHN SIVELLY, JOSHUA SMITH, WILLIAM LANGSTON, and JOHN ROBERTSON be summoned as Jurors to the next County Court in October next.

JOHN PINKERTON & HUGH PARKERSON, Esquires, appointed by the court to divide the road between JOEL DODD and BROWN PARKERSON as overseer, also to appoint the hands to work under said overseer.

The Sheriff made return to court that he had let out NANCY JOHNSON, one of the poor of this county, to CHARLES WAKEFIELD for $46.00 to maintain one year from this time who gave bond with THOMAS CHAPMAN and SAMUEL WAKEFIELD his securities.

WILLIAM MILLNER, ZACHARIAH ARNOLD, JOHN ROBINSON and JAMES SMITH are appointed judges of the next election at the Gum Spring and STERLING C. McLEMORE, Sheriff.

THOMAS CRAWFORD, JOHN ENOCKS and ANDREW W. WALKER are appointed judges of the next election at Lynchburgh and JAMES HOLMAN, Sheriff.

DAVID P. MUNROE, JOEL YOWELL and ENOCK K. RUST are appointed judges of the next election at WILLIAM CRUNK's and ELISHA BAGLEY, Sheriff.

ABRAHAM SUMMERS, JACOB WRIGHT and THOMAS CLARK are appointed judges of the next election held at the Big Spring and RICHMOND P. DOBBINS, Sheriff.

SAMUEL M. CLAY, WILLIAM BARROW and ABRAHAM ISAACS are appointed judges of the next election held on Coldwater and WILLIAM STEPHENS, Sheriff.

JOHN RHEA, THOMAS GAITHER and PAYTON WELLS are appointed judges of the next election held in Fayetteville and ANDREW A. KINNANON, Sheriff.

On motion of SAMUEL WALLACE, one of the heirs of MOSES SATERFIELD, deceased, it is ordered that a subpoena issue against MICHAEL ROBERTSON to appear in court on the first day of next term and bring with him the Last Will and Testament of said MOSES SATERFIELD, deceased, and prove the same and take out letters and renounce his right of proving and executing said will as executor therein named.

JAMES McCORMACK appeared in court and was appointed guardian for REBECCAH & POLLY JOHNSON, heirs of JAMES JOHNSON, deceased, who gave bond of $500.00 with JAMES WEST and WILLIAM COLLINS his securities.

CHARLES BOYLES appeared in court and resigned his appointment as a Justice of the Peace for this county.

JOHN LANE appeared in court and was appointed admr on the estate of JAMES M. WARD, deceased, took oath and gave bond of $60.00 with THOMAS ORRICK and CORNELIUS SULLIVAN, securities.

AN inventory of the property of JAMES M. WARD was returned to court by his admr and ordered to be certified.

An amount of sale of the property of JAMES PYBUS, deceased, was returned to court by his executor and ordered to be certified.

The Commissioners appointed at last term to settle with the admr of CHARLES SMITH, deceased, made return of the settlement and ordered to be certified.

The due execution of an Indenture of Bargain and Sale from JAMES ELLIOTT to JOHN CURRY for 20 acres of land and ordered to be certified.

The due execution of an Indenture of Bargain and Sale from JOHN WILSON to ARTHUR ALBERTSON for 61 acres of land and ordered to be certified.

The due execution of an Indenture of Bargain and Sale from ALLEN YOWELL to JAMES HEMPHILL for 90 acres of land, proven by ALLEN ELSTON and JAMES RUST and ordered to be certified.

The due execution of an Indenture of Bargain and Sale from WILLIAM LEONARD to SQUIRE WILLIAMS for 50 acres of land, proven by SHADRACK W. REED and WILLIAM B. REID and ordered to be certified.

The due execution of an Indenture of Bargain and Sale from JOHN WILSON to JOHN K. TAYLOR for 62½ acres of land and ordered to be certified.

The due execution of an Indenture of Bargain and Sale from JOHN DEVEN to THOMAS WILLIAMS for 50 acres of land, proven by SQUIRE McMULLEN and ELIJAH WILLIAMS and ordered to be certified.

The due execution of an Indenture of Bargain and Sale from EDWARD GORE to BAILY ROGERS for 110 acres of land, proven by JOHN ENOCKS and ARON MOORE and ordered to be certified.

The due execution of an Indenture of Bargain and Sale from JAMES McADAMS to JESSE McADAMS for 66½ acres of land, proven by LEWIS SHAW and REBECCAH BLAND and ordered to be certified.

The due execution of an Indenture of bargain and Sale from JACOB V. HOOSER to JEREMIAH WALKER for 40 acres of land, proven by JOHN T. CUNNINGHAM and ordered to be certified.

The due execution of an Indenture of Bargain and Sale from THOMAS ROUNTREE to THOMAS LANDISS for 2 acres of land, proven by WILLIAM BOON and ISAAC HOLMAN and ordered to be certified.

The due execution of an Indenture of Bargain and Sale from FRANCIS PORTERFIELD, Sheriff of Lincoln County, to DAVID BURFORD for seven town lots in the town of Fayetteville, Nos. 10, 39, 41, 105, 117, 123, and 124 and ordered to be certified.

The due execution of an Indenture of Bargain and Sale from ROBERT ELLIOTT to HENRY BAGLEY for 168 acres of land, proven by JOAB BAGLEY, JESSE McCLAIN and ordered to be certified.

The due execution of an Indenture of bargain and Sale from NATHAN COLLINS to PRESTON HAMPTON for a negro boy named JACOB and ordered to be certified.

The Transfer of a Plat and Certificate of Survey from JAMES ELLIOTT to GEORGE CURRY for 5 acres of land, proven by JOHN ENOCKS and JOHN CURRY and ordered to be certified.

The Transfer of a Plat and Certificate of Survey from JOHN McNATT to MAJOR BIDWELL for 11 acres of land, proven by SAMUEL GARLAND and ordered to be certified.

The due execution of an Indenture of Bargain and Sale from SAMUEL MOORE to JOHN CLARK and others for 3 acres of land, proven by WILLIAM COLLINS and JOHN DOBBINS and ordered to be certified.

The due execution of an Indenture of Bargain and Sale from JOHN DOWTHIT to WILLIAM ELLIS for 25½ acres of land and ordered to be certified.

The due execution of an Indenture of Bargain and Sale from SAMUEL WALLACE to WILLIAM DYE for 160 acres of land and ordered to be certified. No tax on this, the land in Illinois.

The due execution of an Indenture of bargain and Sale from ROBERT BUCHANAN to SOLOMON H. OWEN for 24 acres of land, proven by VANCE GREER and EDWARD MOSS and ordered to be certified.

The due execution of an Indenture of Bargain and Sale from NATHAN COLLINS to JEREMIAH HEDGEPETH and ordered to be certified.

The Transfer of a Plat and Certificate of Survey from PATIENCE JONES to JAMES ELLIOTT and from JAMES ELLIOTT to GEORGE CURRY and ordered to be certified.

The due execution of an Indenture of Bargain and Sale from ARCHABALD BASSHAM to WILLIAM ROSSON and HENRY B. ROSSON for 75 acres of land and ordered to be certified.

The due execution of an Indenture of bargain and Sale from JAMES GARRETT to HENRY B. ROSSON for 65 acres of land and ordered to be certified.

A Deed of Gift from HENRY BAGLEY to JOSIAH BAGLEY for 100 acres of land and ordered to be certified.

The due execution of an Indenture of Bargain and Sale from PATRICK GILLASPIE to JOHN HURLEY for 175 acres of land and ordered to be certified.

The due execution of an Indenture of Bargain and Sale from NATHAN COLLINS to JEREMIAG HEDGEPETH for 13 acres of land and ordered to be certified.

The due execution of an Indenture of Bargain and Sale from ROGER B. SAPPINGTON to OLIVER WILLIAMS for 49 acres of land and ordered to be certified.

The due execution of an Indenture of Bargain and Sale from EASON COALTER to ABRAHAM CUNNINGHAM for 70 acres of land and ordered to be certified.

The due execution of an Indenture of Bargain and Sale from JAMES GARRETT to JOHN SHORT and ordered to be certified.

The due execution of an Indenture of Bargain and Sale from JAMES GARRETT to MERRIT H. SHORT for 35 acres of land and ordered to be certified.

The due execution of an Indenture of Bargain and Sale from JAMES BOREN to THOMAS H. SHAW for three negroes, proven by CHAMPION BLYTH and ordered to be certified.

The due execution of an Indenture of Bargain and Sale from TRACIS CARTER to JAMES THORP for 215 acres of land and ordered to be certified.

The due execution of an Indenture of Bargain and Sale from WILLIAM EDMISTON to BARNABASS BOYLES for 85 acres of land and ordered to be certified.

The due execution of an Indenture of Bargain and Sale from THOMAS WHITE to SOLOMON OWEN for 56 acres of land and ordered to be certified.

The due execution of an Indenture of Bargain and Sale from MARGARETT ROSEBOROUGH to WILLIAM CRAWFORD for 6 3/4 acres of land and ordered to be certified.

The due execution of an Indenture of Bargain and Sale from NATHAN COLLINS to JEREMIAH HEDGEPETH for 20 acres of land and ordered to be certified.

The due execution of an Indenture of Bargain and Sale from PETER FIREBAUGH to SAMUEL CUNNINGHAM for 50 acres of land, proven by JOHN BEDWELL and DANIEL WARREN and ordered to be certified.

The due execution of an Indenture of Bargain and Sale from RUBEN H. BOON to CORNELIUS SULLIVAN for 90 acres of land and ordered to be certified.

The due execution of an Indenture of Bargain and Sale from DAVID LORANCE to JOSEPH & GEORGE W. McBRIDE for 60 acres of land and ordered to be certified.

The due execution of an Indenture of Bargain and Sale from DAVID LORANCE to GEORGE W. McBRIDE for 90 acres of land and ordered to be certified.

The due execution of an Indenture of Bargain and Sale from ELIJAH YATES to GRIFFITH CUNNINGHAM for 40 acres of land and ordered to be certified.

The due execution of an Indenture of Bargain and Sale from SPENCER LEATHERWOOD to BERRY T. PARR for a negro boy, proven by JOHN H. NORTON and JESSE GEORGE and ordered to be certified.

The due execution of an Indenture of Bargain and Sale from MEREDITH HARRIS to REUBEN HARRIS for 50 acres of land and ordered to be certified.

The due execution of an Indenture of Bargain and Sale from WILLIAM WISEMAN & JOHN CHURCH to JOSHUA CHURCH for 75 acres of land and ordered to be certified.

The due execution of an Indenture of Bargain and Sale from JOHN McBRIDE to IRWIN McADAMS for 61½ acres of land and ordered to be certified.

The due execution of an Indenture of Bargain and Sale from RICHARD McNATT to DANIEL WARREN for 20 acres of land, proven by LEVY CHANEY and JOHN BEDWELL and ordered to be certified.

The due execution of an Indenture of Bargain and Sale from JOHN HILL to WILLIAM C. DRINKARD, proven and ordered to be certified.

The Last Will and Testament of JOSEPH McADAMS, deceased, was exhibited in open court for probate, JAMES RALSTON and JESSE McCLAIN, witnesses, made oath that they heard the said JOSEPH McADAMS, deceased, to be his Last Will and testament and that he was at that time of sound mind and memory, whereupon came MARGARETT McADAMS.

ONE BOOK MISSING - (July 1823 - January 1826)

MONDAY JANUARY 2, 1826

Justices present were JOEL PINSON, CORNELIUS DARNEL, JESSE DANIEL, WILLIAM MILNER, WILLIAM EDMISTON, THOMAS CLARKE, ABRAM SUMMERS, HUGH PARKERSON, JOSEPH McBRIDE, STEPHEN SHELTON, JAMES SMITH, CHARLES BRIGHT, ASA HOLLAND, HUGH M. BLAKE, ENOCH RUST, ALLEN ELSTON, JAMES RALSTON, B. BOYERS, JOHN ENOCHS, WILLIAM ANDERSON, ABRAM ISAAC, ROBERT DICKSON, JAMES McDAVID, and JOHN PINKERTON, who proceeded to lay the tax for the year 1826 on each 100 acres of land.

ANDREW HANNAH is released from further attendance as a juror at this term.

THOMAS GLIDEWELL is permitted to keep a tavern in this county at his own house for twelve months, who entered into bond and security.

Ordered by the court that HENRY KIMES and WILLY WINGO met as overseer of the public road and that HARMON B. WALTON be overseer of the balance of said road.

Ordered by the court that JOEL PINSON and JAMES WILSON be appointed to settle with MOSES CLARK, admr of the estate of JAMES WOODWARD, deceased, and make return to next term of this court.

Ordered that STEPHEN JONES be overseer of the public road to Williamsons Gap on the road leading to Shelbyville and that A. SUMNERS and WILLIAM SMITH designate the hands to work under him.

Ordered by the court that JOHN P. McCONNELL be allowed to receive of the Trustee of thie county sum of $99.50 for prison fees for keeping JACOB KITCHEN and LEWIS JONES, State prisoners.

Ordered by the court that WILLIAM McCLELLAND, G.W.C. EDMISTON, OWEN CARPENTER, MOSES HALL, JOHN BEATY, JACKSON BLAKEMORE, and GEORGE BLAKEMORE be appointed a Jury of View to view a road from the mouth of JOHN McKINNEY's lane running on the east side of the old road and intersect it again at or near the creek.

Ordered by the court that ZADOCK MOTLOE, JOSEPH ADKINS, JAMES CURRY, WALTER B. OWENS, JOSEPH HINKLE, JOHN DONALDSON, DOILY GRIFFIS, ROBERT MEEK, OBADIAH PINSON, WILLIAM SMITH, MALCOM McCOWN, ANDREW W. WALKER, WILLIAM ROSSON, JOHN McMILLEN, JOHN RHEA, ABNER STEED, JESSE ELLIS, JAMES PHILIPS, CHARLES H. EDMISTON, JEREMIAH HUDSPETH, MOSES MIRICK, JAMES HURLY, JOHN BOONE, and JAMES CALHOUN be jurors to the April Term 1826 of this court.

WILLIAM WHITE is released from attendance as a juror at this term.

JAMES K. BLAIR was appointed a Constable who took oath and gave bond.

Ordered by the court that OBADIAH PINSON be released from the payment of the fine imposed on him at the last term of this court.

Ordered that BURGESS GAITHER be overseer of the public road in the room of SAMUEL HINKLE and call on the usual hands.

GEORGE CUNNINGHAM presented his amount in court against the heirs of SAMUEL BARNES, deceased, for whom he is guardian which was admitted by the court.

Ordered of the Trustee of the county to pay to JOSEPH COMMONS $4.00 and to JAMES BRYANS $4.00 for work and labor done to the jail and to R. & W. DICKSON $10.17½ for iron furnished for repairing said jail.

JOHN C. TAYLOR was appointed Constable who gave bond and security.

It appearing to the court that JOHN BOYLES departed this life without making his

Last Will and Testament in writing, whereupon came BARNABAS BOYLES and he was appointed admr of the estate of JOHN BOYLES, deceased, and gave bond and security.

It appearing to the court that THOMAS LEMONS, late of this county, departed this life without making his Last Will and testament in writing, whereupon appeared JOEL PINSON and was appointed admr of the estate of THOMAS LEMON, deceased, and entered into bond and gave security.

Ordered by the court that THOMAS WHITAKER be appointed overseer of the public road in the room of ANDREW KING and call on the usual hands.

The Commissioners heretofore appointed to settle with AGATHA and GREENBERRY GARRETT, admrs of the estate of ELI GARRETT, deceased, made return which was received and ordered by the court to be recorded.

ELIZABETH McCURDY appeared in court and was appointed guardian to her infant children, that is, LAURY ANN, ELIJAH ROWAN, NANCY WARREN and SAMUEL WASHINGTON McCURDY and entered into bond and gave security.

The Commissioners heretofore appointed to settle with the admrs and admrx of PRESLEY GEORGE, deceased, now make return of that settlement which is received and ordered to be recorded.

Ordered that JOHN WATKINS be overseer of the public road in the room of WILLIAM MOORE and call on the usual hands.

Ordered by the court that GEORGE McWHERTER & SAMUEL D. MULIKIN be appointed Commissioners to lay off out of the estate of THOMAS LEMONS one years support for the widow and children and make return at next court.

NICHOLAS R. SMITH was appointed a Constable and gave bond.

TUNSTALL GREGORY was appointed a Constable and gave bond and security.

Ordered that JESSE DAVIS be overseer of the road in the room of JESSE DAVIS and call on the usual hands.

Ordered that JOSEPH McMILLEN be overseer of the public road in the room of WILLIAM C. BLAKE and call on the usual hands.

An Amount of the sales of the estate of THOMAS SUMMERS, deceased, was returned by SOLOMON SUMMERS, the admr, and ordered to be recorded.

SAMUEL ROWAN was appointed a Constable and gave bond and security.

Ordered by the court that JOSEPH PEN be overseer of the public road in the room of BENNET B. HOWELL and call on the usual hands.

A Power of Attorney from JESSE & ASA LOVE to THOMAS W. HAYS was acknowledged in court and ordered to be certified.

Ordered by the court that THOMAS KERCHEVAL, JOHN MOORE (N.C.), JAMES HIGGINS, JOHN RHEA, WILLIAM EDMISTON, ISAAC CONGER, DANIEL JONES, JOHN LEA, ELLIJAH DAVIS, JOHN GIBSON, and STEPHEN CLAYTON be a Jury of View to view and see if the road leading to Crawford's mill ought not to be ommitted entirely and if in their opinion it should not be ommitted &c made void then to view and mark out another, the same so as not to interfere with the improvement or clearing of WILSON FROST, and that said jury if in their opinion said road is necessary at all, lave liberty to mark the same and take it out of the Nashville Road at any point north of where it now leaves said road, and make return to next court.

Ordered by the court that all allowances heretofore made to the clerk of this court for exoficia services &c be retained by clerk out of any monies belonging to the county.

Ordered that WILLIAM EDMISTON, JOHN P. McCONNELL, ELIJAH DAVIS, THOMAS KERCHEVAL, ROBERT H. McEWEN, and RUBEN HUNTER be a Jury of View to view and turn the public road leading from Fayetteville to Shelbyville along the line of JOHN P. McCONNELL and BARNABAS BOYLES and make return at next court.

Ordered by the court that MOSES HARDEN be allowed to turn the   road at the eastern end of his land.

JOHN DALTON appointed overseer of the public road in the room of THOMAS RICHARDSON and call on the usual hands.

Ordered that the public road leading up the middle fork of Norris Creek be put in the second class of public roads and kept in repair.

Ordered by the court that JAMES SANDERS be overseer of the public road in the room of JOHN SMITH and call on the usual hands.

A Power of Attorney from SAMUEL BUCHANAN to JOHN BUCHANAN was acknowledged and ordered to be certified.

A Deed of Conveyance from JOHN GREER to SHACKLEFORD & ARNOLD for 200 acres of land in the western district and ordered to be certified.

GEORGE COUNTS, JOHN McGEHEE and JAMES SMITH who were appointed at the last term of court to view and mark a road from the mouth of Beans Creek to the State line now make return that they have marked a road beginning above the mouth of Beans Creek at the County line where a new road in Franklin County strikes the line of this county, thence to the State line between Alabama and Tennessee near where the old Mulberry Road crosses the same. Ordered by the court that said road be established as one of the third class.

Ordered by the court that the public road leading down Elk River from near the mouth of Beans Creek by ISHAM BURNET's and JAMES FORSYTHE's to STILES' as laid off and marked be discontinued.

Ordered that WILLIAM SHAW, SR., WILLIAM SHAW, JR., THOMAS SHAW, WILLIAM SOLOMON and (BLANK) ROBINSON be a Jury of View and turn the public road leading through JOHN RAY's land and make return to next court.

Ordered that STEPHEN JONES be overseer of the public road in the room of WILLIAM DAVIS and call on the usual hands.

ANDREW W. WALKER appeared in court and entered into bond and security and was duly qualified as executor of the Last Will and testament of AGNESS MOTLOW, deceased,

Ordered by the court that the Clerk, Sheriff and Attorney General be each allowed $45.00 for their exoficio services for the year 1825.

The Justices of this county proceeded to class themselves to hold the different terms of the County Court for the year 1826 and was ordered that the first class consist of ALLEN ELSTON, JOHN PINKERTON, ROBERT DICKSON, JACOB WAGGONER, JESSE DANIEL, SHEPHERD SHELTON, ISAAC CONGER, JOHN SMITH, JOSEPH McCRACKEN, ZACHARIAH HARRISON, B. BOYLES, SAMUEL BUCHANAN and ALEXANDER McLIN. The second class consist of PHILIP KOONCE, JOHN H. MOORE, ENOCH RUST, WILLIAM DYE, JAMES WILSON, JAMES FORSYTHE, HUGH PARKESON, JOSEPH McBRIDE, JOEL PINSON, H.M. BLAKE, ELISHA BAGLEY, CHARLES BRIGHT, and HENRY KELSO. The third class consist of CLIFFORD GRAY, T. DOLLINS, WILLIAM SMITH, ABRAM ISAACKS, JAMES RALSTON, WILLIAM MILNER, M.L. PARKS, WILLIAM ANDERSON, CORNELIUS DARNELL, JOHN ENOCKS, ABRAM SUMMERS, JAMES SMITH, and WILLIAM EDMISTON. And the fourth class consist of JOHN WISEMAN, GEORGE BLAKEMORE, DAVID COWAN, THOMAS H. SHAW, THOMAS GAITHER, JOHN MARR, SAMUEL GARLAND, JOHN PORTER, ASA HOLLAND, JAMES BLAKEMORE, JAMES McDAVID, THOMAS CLARK, EBENEZER McEWEN, and STEPHEN ALEXANDER.

Ordered by the court that JAMES THORP be released as one of the securities of JOHN P. DURLEY for his guardianship of ZEBULON OLIVER, and that NICHOLAS R. SMITH be taken in his stead who made bond and security.

WILLIAM D. BLAKE was appointed a Constable who gave bond and security.

Ordered that MATHEW HUGHS, a pauper of this county, be immediately let by the Sheriff to the lowest bidder for keeping him the present year. RUBEN WASHBURN became the lowest bidder at $79.00 and gave bond and security.

Ordered that the certificate issue to THOMAS HUGHS instead of GEORGE

McWHERTER for keeping MATHEW HUGHS, a pauper, for the last nine months.

Ordered that the Trustee of this county pay immediately to CORNELIUS SLATER the sum of $33.00 for his expenses and trouble in taking MRS. BROYLES to Columbia and back.

The Clerk of this court produced Commissioners from the Governor of this state to JAMES SMITH, CHARLES BRIGHT and ASA HOLLAND as Justices of the Peace for this county who made bond and security.

Ordered that HUGH PARKESON (PARKERSON) and WILLIAM SMITH be Commissioners to settle with SAMUEL M. CLAY and WILLIAM STEPHENS, executors of LUCINDA STREET and make report to next court.

AGATHA & GREENBERRY GARRETT, executors of ELI GARRETT, deceased, be allowed for their trouble with said estate 5% on $1283.00.

RUBEN HUNTER takes SELMA WARREN, an orphan girl, until she arrives at the age of eighteen years and to give her comfortable clothing, diet &c and six months schooling.

JOHN H. SMOOT takes JENSEY WARREN, an orphan girl aged about (blank) years, until she arrives at the age of eighteen years and to give her (blank).
ELIZABETH & MARGARET PATTERSON are allowed by the court $200.00 for taking care of ALEXANDER PATTERSON, CATHERINE PATTERSON and NANCY PATTERSON and to find them comfortable lodging, clothing, died &c.

On motion of ROBERT DICKSON and it appearing to the court that JEREMIAH BROYLES, late of this county, departed this life without making his Last Will and testament in writing, whereupon administrator on the estate is granted to said DICKSON who gave bond and security.

Ordered by the court that MARY BOWERS be allowed $40.00 for keeping her insane child for the present year.

JOSEPH GREER, TUNSTALL GREGORY and DAVID SNODDY are appointed to settle with FRANCIS TEAL, admr of the estate of EDWARD TEAL, deceased, and make return to next court.

SUSANNAH PITTS is allowed out of the county treasury $40.00 for keeping and taking care of JAMES E. PITTS one year from this day.

Ordered that WILLIAM CRUNK be permitted to keep a house of ordinary at his own in this county for one year who gave bond and security.

Ordered that POLLY COUCH be allowed $30.00 for keeping REBECAH COUCH one year out of the public money in the hands of the Trustee of this county.

Ordered that JONATHAN COUCH be allowed $30.00 for keeping POLLY COUCH one year.

Ordered that ISAAC LAYMAN be allowed $30.00 out of the public taxes in the hands of the Trustee for this year.

Ordered that RICHARD ROBERTSON be allowed $60.00 for keeping JOHN ESTERS for one year whereupon came WILLIAM MOORE and entered as security for RICHARD ROBERTSON.

TUESDAY JANUARY 3, 1826

Justices present were THOMAS H. SHAW, ROBERT DICKSON and WILLIAM EDMISTON, Esquires.

WILLIAM HUSBANDS, High Sheriff of Lincoln County, made return into court of the states writ of venire facias to him directed executed on REECE HOWELL, ABSALOM BEARD, JEREMIAH HUDSPETH, JEREMIAH GANT, EDMOND TAYLOR, ANDREW HAMILTON, MURIEL NIXON, ISHAM BURNET, WILLIAM BRIGHT, JAMES RANDOLPH, WILLIAM SMITH, SR., WILLIAM HAMILTON, JAMES SANDERS, WILLIAM WOODWARD, GRIFFITH LEONARD, ANTHONY CRAWFORD, JAMES WILSON, JAMES McCORMACK, BARNES CLARK, WILLIAM WHITE, WILLIAM McELROY, JESSE B. CLEMENTS, DAVID

BARCLAY and SAMUEL BUCHANAN, JR. out of whom are selected as the statue in such cases provides, the following persons a grand inquest and jury, that is to say, WILLIAM BRIGHT, foreman, ABSALOM, BEARD, BARNS CLARK, ANDREW HAMILTON, SAMUEL BUCHANAN, JR., JAMES WILSON, JEREMIAH GANT, JAMES SANDERS, DAVID BARCLAY, EDMOND TAYLOR, WILLIAM McELROY, JEREMIAH HUDSPETH, and JAMES McCORMACK are to inquire for the state and for the body of the county then recover their charge from the Solicitor General.

Proclamation being made that the court was about to proceed to the election of a Coroner for this county for the ensuing two years. Whereupon came ELIJAH M. RINGO and declared himself a candidate for that appointment and no other candidate appearing, he declared duly elected.

Proclamation being made that the court to proceed to the election of a Sheriff for the ensuing two years. Whereupon came WILLIAM HUSBANDS and ANDREW A. KINCANNON and each declared themselves candidates for that appointment whereupon a balloting took place. Twenty six votes for WILLIAM HUSBANDS and twenty three votes for ANDREW A. KINCANNON. WILLIAM HUSBANDS was declared duly elected and gave bond and security.

Proclamation being made that the court was about to proceed to the election of a Trustee for the ensuing two years. EBENEZER McEWEN and WILLIAM NEILD appeared as candidates. Whereupon a balloting took place and twenty three votes for WILLIAM NEILD and twenty two votes for EBENEZER McEWEN. WILLIAM NEILD was declared duly elected and gave bond and security.

Ordered by the court that WILLIAM NEILD and CHARLES BOYLES be each allowed $20.00 for their trouble in settling with the Trustee for the years 1824 and 1825 and the Trustee pay the same immediately.

Ordered by the court that FRANCIS PORTERFIELD and WILLIAM F. MASON be appointed Commissioners to settle with the Clerks of this county and Circuit Courts.

POWER &HAUGHTON vs DANIEL COFFMAN - This cause is continued on affidavit of the defendant and leave is granted the defendant to take the deposition of BENJAMIN FRANKS, JUDITH DAMRON and JAMES HODGES of Madison County, Alabama, by giving ten days notice of time and place of taking the same.

JAMES RANDOLPH is released from further attendance as a juror at this term.

HENRY MOORES and JAMES D. COLE, DAVID COWAN, HARBERT GRIFFIS and JAMES FRAME each appeared in court and was permitted to give bond and security as inspectors, packers and markers of cotton and took oath &c.

The due execution of a Deed of Conveyance from JOHN BUCHANAN and ROBERT BUCHANAN for 1 acre of land to DANIEL JONES and others and ordered to be certified.

The due execution of a Deed of Trust from URIAH BOBBET to WILLIAM F. MASON for sundry personal property and land and ordered to be certified.

The due execution of a Deed of Conveyance from GEORGE CUNNINGHAM and MARY CUNNINGHAM, his wife, to JAMES MAXWELL for 28 acres of land, acknowledged by GEORGE and the acknowledgment of said MARY as the due execution of the same on her part was taken by WILLIAM DYE and ALEXANDER McLINN and ordered to be certified.

The due execution of a Deed of Conveyance from WILLIAM KERBY to WILLIAM R. WOODRUFF for 38 acres of land and ordered to be certified.

The due execution of an agreement between HENRY LAZENBY and ELIAS LAZENBY was acknowledged and ordered to be certified.

The due execution of a Deed of Conveyance from WILLIAM C. HODGE to THOMAS GROCE and ordered to be certified.

The due execution of a Deed of Conveyance from JOHN YOUNG to JOHN EMMERSON for 100 acres of land and ordered to be certified.

The due execution of a Deed of Conveyance from JOHN YOUNG to JOHN EMMERSON for 49 acres of land and ordered to be certified.

The due execution of a Deed of Conveyance from JOHN DEVIN to JOHN FARRAR for 60 acres of land, proven by oaths of JOEL PINSON and BENJAMIN GIBSON and ordered to be certified.

The due execution of a Bill of Sale from WILLIAM HUSBANDS, Sheriff, to WILLIAM H. MURPHREE for sundry property and ordered to be certified.

JOSEPH WHITAKER appeared in court and on motion was permitted to keep an ordinary at his own house in this county for the ensuing twelve months and gave bond and security.

WEDNESDAY JANUARY 4, 1826

Justices present were HUGH M. BLAKE, SAMUEL GARLAND and SHEPHERD SHELTON, Esquires.

JOHN McCALISTER for the use &c vs GEORGE McWHERTER - This case to be continued and that each party be at liberty to take the depositions they think proper in Madison County, Alabama, by giving the opposite party ten days notice of time and place of taking the same.

JOHN P. McCONNELL vs THOMAS LINTHCOMB - The defendant was called but came not but made default. The plaintiff to recover $15.02 damages.

LUCY SULIVAN vs WILLIAM OAKS - The parties came into court and the plaintiff by her attorney says she wishes no further to prosecute her suit but wishes the same to be dismissed and the defendant assumes the payment of one half of the cost of this suit. Suit was dismissed and each parties pay their half of costs of case.

ALFRED SMITH was appointed a Deputy Sheriff by WILLIAM HUSBANDS, High Sheriff and took oath.

JOHN WAGGONER vs WILLIAM EDMISTON and JOS. & THOMAS GREER, Executors of V. GREER - This day came the parties by their attorneys and a jury of men, to wit, EDWARD MOSS, HENRY DAVIS, JOHN PORCH, JOHN CLAYTON, WILLIAM CRAWFORD, SR., WILLIAM CRAWFORD, JR., RANSOM FLUTA, THOMAS MOORE, DANIEL T. WILLIAMS, A.J. BLAKEMORE, WILLIAM H. TALBOT and JOHN R. JOHNSON being elected and sworn to speak, and said that the defendant has not paid the debt of $264.41 and damages of $18.50. Plaintiff to recover his costs.

JAMES HOLLIS for the use &c vs J. & T. GREER, executors - (same as above) said that the defendants have not paid the debt of $114.00 and damages of $13.68. Plaintiff to recover his costs.

WILLIAM STREET vs RANDOLPH QUARLES - (same as above) and said that the defendant has not kept his covenant and has broken the same and assess damages of $212.80. Plaintiff to recover his costs.

THOMAS BOAZ for the use vs JOHNSTON TURLEY and others - (same as above) and said that the defendant has not kept his covenant and assess the damages of $265.12½. Plaintiff to recover his costs.

DANIEL MORPHIS vs FIRMAN GILLAM - (same as above) and said that the defendant has not kept his covenant and assess damages of $141.75. Plaintiff to recover his costs.

DOILY GRIFFIS vs JOEL COMMONS - (same as above) and said that the defendant has not kept his covenant and assess damages of $265.12. Plaintiff to recover his costs.

MOSES HALL vs CONSTANT SCALES - (same as above) and said that the defendant has not paid the debt of $102.12½ and damages of $16.93 3/4. Plaintiff recover his costs.

THOMAS SPENCER vs JOHN WISEMAN - The plaintiff says he wishes no further to prosecute his suit but wishes the same to be dismissed. Case dismissed and the defendant recover his costs.

The due execution of a Mortgage Deed from JOHN BROYLES to ROBERT & WILLIAM DICKSON for sundry personal property, proven and ordered to be certified.

Ordered that WILLIAM EDMISTON and FRANCIS PORTERFIELD be Commissioners to settle with JOEL B. SANDERS, admr of the estate of ESTHER KENNEDY, deceased, and make return to next court.

RANSOM FLUTA vs JOHN PORCH - This day came the parties by their attorneys and a jury of men, to wit, HENRY DAVIS, WILLIAM CRAWFORD, SR., WILLIAM CRAWFORD, JR., WILLIAM H. TALBOT, JOHN R. JOHNSON, GEORGE ST. JOHN BASKINS, WILLIAM SMITH, WILLIAM THOMAS, JOSEPH COMMONS, JOHN D. NICKS, and WILLIAM GRIFFIS being elected and sworn and said that the defendant did not assume the manner and form as stated by the plaintiff. The defendant go hence without day and recover against the plaintiff his costs.

THOMAS HUGHS vs BENJAMIN HINKLE - (same as above) and said that they find in favor of the defendant. Defendant to recover his costs.

The due execution of a Deed of Mortgage from JOHN ANDERSON to ROBERT & WILLIAM DICKSON for sundry articles of personal property, proven and ordered to be certified.

The due execution of a Deed of Mortgage from REDICK PRICE to ROBERT DICKSON for sundry articles of personal property, proven and ordered to be certified.

EDWARD TATUM vs STEPHEN BEAVERS - Plaintiff says he wishes no further to prosecute his suit but wishes the same to be dismissed, Suit dismissed and the defendant recover his costs.

HENRY TALLY appeared in court, entered into bond and security as a Gin Holder, inspector and marker of cotton.

The execution of a Deed of Conveyance from WILLIAM ROBERTSON to JOEL DOLLINS for 115 acres of land, proven by JOSEPH GREER, attorney, and ordered to be certified.

Ordered by the court that a fine of $5.00 be entered against WILLIAM HAMILTON, ISHAM BURNET and GRIFFITH LEONARD for not attendance as jurors at this term.

A Grand Jury returned to court and brought with them two Bills of Indictment, true bills, against ABRAHAM LUMBRIC for assault and battery, committed on WILLIAM B. HAMPTON and JOS. M. HAMPTON and then retired to consider for further presentments.

The due execution of a Deed of Conveyance from JANE WILIE to JOHN WILIE for 51½ acres of land and ordered to be certified.

The due execution of a Deed of Conveyance from ANDREW CANNON to VALLENTINE ALLEN for 152½ acres of land and ordered to be certified.

The due execution of a Deed of Conveyance from VALLENTINE ALLEN to ROBERT TRAVIS for 152½ acres and proven to be certified.

The Grand Jury again returned to court and brought with them two Bills of Indictment, true bills, one against SAMUEL BECKET and the other against STERLING A. BRYANT and returned to consider for further presentments.

The due execution of a Deed of Conveyance from JOHN ASTON to EDMOND PARKER for 40 acres of land and ordered to be certified.

The due execution of a Deed of Conveyance from EDMOND D. PARKER to JOHN WALKER for 40 acres of land and ordered to be certified.

The due execution of a Deed of Conveyance from ENOCH DOWTHIT to JOHN ALBRIGHT for 55 acres of land and ordered to be certified.

The due execution of a Bill of Sale from ALLEN YOWELL to WILLIAM MONROE for one negro girl, proven by JAMES MONROE and ordered to be certified.

The due execution of a Deed of Conveyance from JOHN P. McCONNELL to ROBERT PARKS for 32 acres of land and ordered to be certified.

The due execution of a Deed of Conveyance from JOSEPH McBRIDE to DAVID & JAMES McGAHEY for 47 3/4 acres of land and ordered to be certified.

The due execution of a Deed of Conveyance from BARNEY L. McELROY to JOHN YOUNT for 55 acres of land and ordered to be certified.

The due execution of a Deed of Conveyance from RANDOLPH QUARLES to JOHN C. PATTON for 120 acres of land and ordered to be certified.

The due execution of a Deed of Conveyance from JOEL HOWELL to HARRY RENEGER for 90 acres of land and ordered to be certified.

THURSDAY JANUARY 5, 1826

Justices present were ALLEN ELSTON, WILLIAM EDMISTON and ?. BOYLES.

JACOB WAGGONER vs WILLIAM MOORE and ISAAC HOLMAN, executors of S.C. McLEMORE - It is ordered that the plaintiff be at liberty to take the deposition of ARGYLE CAMPBELL by giving the defendants five days notice of time and place of taking same.

JOHN & JACOB WAGGONER vs ISAAC HOLMAN & WILLIAM MOORE, executors ordered by the court that the plaintiff be at liberty to take the deposition of ARGYLE CAMPBELL by giving the defendant five days notice of time and place of taking the same.

JOHN WISEMAN vs WILLIAM C. KENNEDY - Ordered by the court that the defendant be at liberty to take the deposition of BENJAMIN HARRIS, a citizen of Franklin County, Alabama, and give the plaintiff ten days notice of time and place of taking the same.

LEVI M. TODD vs SAMUEL TODD - The defendant by his attorney moved the court that several cases returned to this term against him in favor of the plaintiff may be consolidated and the same of the actions of defendant.

JOHN P. McCONNELL vs WILLIAM SMALL - The plaintiff by his attorney came into court and a jury of men, to wit, WILLIAM BRIGHT, BARNS CLARK, ANDREW HAMILTON, SAMUEL BUCHANAN, JAMES WILSON, JEREMIAH GANT, JAMES SANDERS, DAVID BARCLAY, EDMOND TAYLOR, WILLIAM McELROY, JEREMIAH HUDSPETH, WILLIAM SMITH and GEORGE ST. JOHN BASKINS being elected and sworn and said that the damages in favor of the plaintiff to be $107.00. Plaintiff to recover his costs.

JAMES REED vs HENRY ROBERTSON - Ordered by the court that the former order of this court be renewed as to taking depositions &c.

ROBERT ELAM vs JOHN BROYLES - This day the defendant came by his attorney and the plaintiff being called came not but made default. Defendant recover his costs.

WILLIAM C. GIBSON vs THOMAS HODGE - This day came the plaintiff by his attorney and the defendant being called came not but made default. On motion of the plaintiff that judgment be entered against THOMAS HODGE, JOHN SMITH, SHEROD PARRISH and JAMES D. ALFORD his securities for $24.00 and the plaintiff recover his costs.

NATHAN COLLINS vs MICAJAH McELROY - This day came the plaintiff by his attorney and the defendant being called came not but made default. Plaintiff to recover his costs. Sustained.

WILLIAM HUSBANDS, High Sheriff, reports to the court that the jail of this county is insecure and not sufficient for the safe keeping of such prisoners as may be committed to his charges and prays that the same be rendered secure &c.

State of Tennessee vs JOHN T. SMITH - The defendant says he is indebted to the State of Tennessee for $250.00 to be void on condition that he make his personal appearance here in April next and be ready to answer on a charge for malicious mischief &c.

The State vs HARDY HOLCOMB - This day came the Attorney General, prosecutor for the State and the defendant who pleads guilty. Defendant is fined $1.00 and pay cost of said indictment.

The State vs DANIEL BENSON - This day came the Attorney General, prosecutor for the State and the defendant who pleads guilty. Defendant is fined $1.00 and pay cost of this indictment.

The State vs JOHN HIAT - Bastardy - (same as above) The defendant is fined $90.00 and pay costs of this prosecution. Whereupon came DANIEL BENSON and confessed judgment jointly with the defendant for the cost only.

The State vs ABRAHAM LUMBRIC - (same as above) Defendant be fined $15.00 and pay costs.

The State vs ABRAM LUMBRIC - (same as above) The defendant be fined $5.00 and pay costs.

The State vs STERLING A. BRYANT - (same as above) The defendant be fined $1.00 and pay costs.

The State vs JOHN BRYANT - (same as above) The defendant is fined 6¼ cents and pay costs. Whereupon came STERLING A. BRYANT and confessed judgment jointly with the defendant for the above fine and costs.

The State vs SAMUEL LEE - (same as above) The defendant is fined $5.00 and pay costs. Whereupon came H. HOLCOM and confessed judgment jointly with defendant for the above fine and costs.

The State vs ISREAL HILL - This day the defendant appeared in court and the prosecutor not appearing or requiring the defendant to be further bound for his good behavior. The defendant to be released from his undertaking in his recognizance and that he pay cost of this suit.

The State vs HENRY J. HAYES - The defendant called but came not into court but made default. It is considered that he and his securities, JAMES H. HAYES and EPHRAIM KING be forfeited and State recover against each.

The State vs GREEN W. LANE - Bastardy - The defendant being called but came not but made default. it is considered that the recognizance and his securities be forfeited and State recover against them.

WILLIAM MADDOX vs CLAIBORN WILLIAMS - This day came the defendant by his attorney and it appearing to the court that the plaintiff gave no security for the prosecution of this suit. Suit to be dismissed and the defendant recover his costs.

The due execution of a Deed of Conveyance from EZEKIEL NORRIS to JOHN CRAWFORD for 50 acres of land and ordered to be certified.

The due execution of a Deed of Conveyance from BENJAMIN BUTLER to MOSES CLARK for 50 acres of land and ordered to be certified.

Ordered by the court that ALEXANDER McLIN and B. BOYLES, Esquires, be appointed to take the examination of POLLY BLACKAMORE, wife of NATHANIEL BLACKAMORE, as to her consent and whether she executed the deed to WILLIAM EDMISTON's heirs dated 15 Oct 1821.

The due execution of a Deed of Conveyance from JOHN McCOWAN, admr of FRANCIS McCOWAN, deceased, to JOHN FRANK for 30 acres of land and ordered to be certified.

FRIDAY JANUARY 6, 1826

Justices present were SAMUEL BUCHANAN, B. BOYLES and WILLIAM EDMISTON, Esquires.

The due execution of a Deed of Conveyance from JOHN GREER, VANCE GREER, NATHANIEL BLACKAMORE and POLLY BLACKAMORE to the heirs of WILLIAM EDMISTON, deceased, for two tracts of land containing in the whole of 138 acres as to the due execution of the same by JOHN GREER and VANCE GREER by oaths of WILLIAM NEILD and NICHOLAS CARRIGER and execution of said deed by NATHANIEL BLACKAMORE by oaths of ALEXANDER McLIN and B. BOYLES, witnesses. The due execution being proven by ALEXANDER McLIN and B. BOYLES, Commissioners appointed to take such examination and ordered to be certified.

NATHANIEL BLACKAMORE by oaths of ALEXANDER McLIN and B. BOYLES, witnesses, the due execution being proven and they appointed to take such examination and ordered to be certified.

WILLIAM HUSBANDS, executor &c of JAMES C. SMITH, returned an account of the sale of the property of said estate and also an inventory of the property of estate and ordered to be certified.

A settlement with CHARLES McKINNEY, admr of ROBERT LITTLE, deceased, was returned to court by the Commissioners and ordered to be certified.

The due execution of a Deed of Conveyance from CORNELIUS SULIVAN to WILLIAM BOONE for 80 acres of land, proven by R.H. McEWEN and JOSHUA B. SMITH and ordered to be certified.

The due execution of a Power of Attorney from PETER KENT to JAMES K. POLK was acknowledged and ordered to be certified.

The due execution of a Bill of Sale from HENRY ROBERTSON to WILLIAM TODD for a negro girl named PHILIS, acknowledged and ordered to be certified.

The due execution of a Deed of Conveyance from ELIZABETH E. GREER to JOEL B. SANDERS for (blank) acres of land and ordered to be certified.

MONDAY APRIL 3, 1826

Justices present were ROBERT DICKSON, JOEL PINSON, JOHN H. MOORE, CHARLES BRIGHT, PHILIP KOONCE, JOSEPH McBRIDE, SAMUEL BUCHANAN, THOMAS H. SHAW, JAMES WILSON, SHEPHERD SHELTON, ELISHA BAGLEY, JOHN SMITH, WILLIAM SMITH, JOHN PORTER, ABRAHAM ISAACS, HUGH PARKINSON and JESSE DANIEL.

Ordered that WILLIAM BROOKS be appointed overseer of the public road in the place of BRICE W. BROOKS and call on the usual hands.

Ordered that WILLIAM DYE, ABRAHAM ISAACS, WILLIAM ANDERSON, HUGH PARKINSON, DAVID COWAN, WILLIAM MILLNER, SHEPHERD SHELTON, JAMES SMITH, JAMES FORSYTHE, JOHN WISEMAN, JOHN ENOCKS, THOMAS H. SHAW, JAMES BLAKEMORE, HUGH M. BLAKE, ASA HOLLAND, ELISHA BAGLEY, JOSEPH McBRIDE, ALLEN ELSTON, ENOCK RUST, ALEXANDER McLIN, FRANCIS PORTERFIELD, JESSE B. CLEMENTS, JACK H. LEFTWICK, THOMAS CLARK, SAMUEL ROSEBOROUGH and ABNER STEED to be serve the September term of the Circuit Court for year 1826.

Ordered that NATHANIEL HOPPER be appointed overseer of the public road in the place of NATHAN COLLINS and call on the usual hands.

Ordered that SAMUEL DUCKWORTH be appointed overseer of the public road in the place of SQUIRE WILLIAMS and call on the usual hands.

Ordered that THOMAS WILLIAMS be released from working on the road leading from the Giles County line to Cunningham's mill as overseer.

Ordered that ABNER HOLLANDSWORTH be bound as an apprentice to WILLIAM ROSEBOROUGH until he arrives at the age of twenty one years to learn the blacksmith trade, entered into bond and security.

Ordered that BARISTER COUCH be allowed $30.00 for keeping and providing for SEWELL COUCH, a pauper of this county, up to first of January next.

Ordered that WILLIAM REEVES, DAVID BECK, THOMAS H. HAYS, WILLIAM WILLIAMS, NEILSON YARBERRY, ARCHIBALD RAY, EDMOND TAYLOR, WILLIAM KENNON, DAVID FRANKLIN, CARTER ROBINSON, JAMES McCOLLUM, JOHN H. RODGERS, PATON WELLS, WILLIAM CASSIN, VINCENT LITRELL, WILLIAM D. BLAKE, WILLIAM BARROW, JASPER SMITH, JAMES BROWN, KINCHEN HOLCOMB, THOMAS W. HAYS, KEYS MEEK, RICHARD P. DOBBINS, DANIEL T. WILLIAMS, JAMES D. ALFORD, and PETER VAUGHN summoned to serve next July of this court.

The Sheriff reports the jail here insufficient which report is ordered to be entered on the minutes.

Ordered that JAMES HAMILTON be allowed $10.00 for one year from this time.

On the petition of sundry persons ordered that the road leading from Campbells Ferry on Elk River towards HUntsville be entirely discontinued.

Ordered that PAXTON SAWYERS be appointed overseer of the public road in the place of JNO. CRAWFORD.

Ordered that JAMES TUCKER be appointed overseer of the public road in the place of HENRY TALLY resigned and call on the usual hands.

Ordered that HENRY KYMES, HARMON B. WALTON, JOHN WANSLOW, JONATHAN HAYS, JOHN WAGGONER and ELI MILSTEAD be appointed to view and mark and lay off a road to start one quarter of a mile below MICAJAH McELROY's field and run so as to intersect the road leading from Fayetteville to Cunningham's mill at the mouth of HENRY KYMES' lane and report to the next term of court.

Ordered that JOHN BIGGER be appointed overseer of the new road leading from Cunningham's Gap to Cook's mill on Richland Creek and that the hands layed off by JAMES RALSTON and ELISHA BAGLEY keep road in repair.

Ordered that JAMES CALHOON be overseer of the road leading to Pulaski from Fayetteville to Cane Creek.

Ordered that the overseers appointed to work on a road opened persuant to an order of last court leaving the Elkton Road near JOSHUA OWENS and intersecting another road near KINCHEN HOLCOMB's be discharged and released.

Ordered that JOHN T. KING be appointed overseer of the road from the forks at the south west corner of ISAAC HOLMAN's pasture to the forks of the road at JOHN J. WHITAKER's in the room of ISAAC HOLMAN and that CHARLES BRIGHT, Esquire, be appointed to allott the hands to work on road between said KING and THOMAS WHITAKER overseer of a road in same neighborhood.

Ordered that PARK GIBSON be appointed overseer of the road in place of CHAMBRISS(?) BUCHANAN resigned.

Ordered that JOHN PARKS call upon the following hands to keep the road in repair of which he is overseer, viz, ROBERT PARKS, ISAAC PARKS, JAMES FLEMING, JESSE LAWRENCE, JOHN HARRIS, JAMES COOPER, G.W. HUNTER, HIRAM DEMPSEY, GEORGE GLEN, GEORGE ROBERTSON and his own hands.

Ordered that JOHNSON TURLEY, ISAAC BROYLES, WRIGHT McLEMORE, JAMES RAMSEY, and LAWSON TURLEY be appointed a Jury of View to view and mark and lay off and turn the road leading from Shelbyville to Huntsville crossing Elk River at the mouth of Mulberry to leave the road as it now runs at the north end of THOMAS ALLEY's plantation running north so as to intersect the old road near the upper end of JOHNSON TURLEY's field the plantation of JNO. MORGAN and report to next court.

Ordered that JAMES MAXWELL, ANDREW HANNAH, ARCHABALD McELROY, B. McELROY, DOILY GRIFFIS, B. FRANKLIN, and WILLIAM MORTON be appointed a jury to view, lay off and mark a road beginning on the road that leads from Fayetteville to ESQUIRE WILLIAM DYE's on the east side of Dry Creek at the forks of the road where JAMES LAWSON has cut a new road leading along the ridge that divides the waters of Dry Creek from the waters of Albrights Spring Branch passing by L(illegible)'s house and intersecting the old road again near JNO. ALBRIGHT's and that said jury report to next court.

Ordered that ARCHIBALD YOUNG be overseer in the room of PARKS and call on the usual hands.

Ordered that GRIFFITH CUNNINGHAM be overseer in the room of THOMAS SHAW.

On motion of PEYTON WELLS by his attorney and it appearing to the court here that ABNER WELLS, late of this county, departed this life without making his Last Will and Testament in writing, administration on the estate of ABNER WELLS, deceased, is granted him. PEYTON WELLS entered into bond and security.

WILLIAMD. BLAKE who was appointed a Constable in CAPTAIN BLAKEMORE's

Company now resigns that appointment.

The Last Will and Testament of JAMES DOWNING was produced in court for probate, witnesses, JAMES CLARK and ABRAM SUMMERS said that they saw JAMES DOWNING sign, seal and publish and declare the same to be his Last Will and Testament and that he was of sound mind and memory.

Ordered that GEORGE D. PETTY be appointed overseer of the road leading from Fayetteville to Nashville in the room of ASA HOLLAND.

Ordered that RICHMOND WALL be allowed $40.00 for the maintenance of NATHANIEL GADBERRY for one year from this date.

Ordered that NATHANIEL HOPPER be appointed overseer in the room of NATHANIEL COLLINS resigned and call on the usual hands.

Ordered that MARMADUKE D. MIRES and WILLIAM H. GOWAN be appointed overseer of the public road in the room of ABSALOM COLLINS removed and call on the usual hands to work to the ridge above MARMADUKE D. MIRES near JAMES FLEMIN's.

Ordered that the road leading from Huntsville to intersect the Nashville Road at JESSE RIGGS be discontinued.

Ordered by the court that ANTHONY WELLS be released from paying anything for a mare by him posted sometime since as said mare has been taken out of his possession.

Ordered that JOSEPH McCRACKEN, Esquire, be appointed to lay off of the hands to work on the road of which JAMES THORP and SAMUEL LEE are overseers and give to each a proper number.

Ordered that JOHN LEE be appointed overseer of the public road leading from Fayetteville to Shelbyville in place of ELIJAH DAVIS resigned.

Ordered that JAMES CALHOON, A. DEPOYSTER, JNO. BOON, THOMAS FORSYTHE, MILTON CALHOON, and WILLIAM McELROY be appointed a jury to view, mark and turn the road for some distance by WILLIAM GARRETT's on the Pulaski Road and report to next court.

Ordered that WILLIAM ROSEBOROUGH be appointed guardian to McKINLEY W. WHITENBURG in the place of CHARLES BARKER resigned and that JOHN J. WHITAKER, WILLIAM KENNON and JOHN DUKE be appointed to settle with C. BARKER and make return to next court.

Ordered that BEDA WARREN be bound to WILLIAM GINNINGS (JENNINGS) until she arrives at the age of eighteen whereupon said GINNINGS (JENNINGS) entered into bond and security.

Ordered that SALINA WARREN be bound as an apprentice to PINKNEY PILANT until she arrives at the age of eighteen and PILANT entered into bond with security.

On motion of WILLIAM CRAWFORD and WILLIAM B. BENGE by their attorneys and it appearing to the vourt that JOHN WHAM, late of this county, departed this life intestate, administration on the estate of said JOHN WHAM is granted them. CRAWFORD and BENGE entered into bond with security.

On motion of JOHN P. McCONNELL by his attorney and it appearing to the court that STEPHEN BOLEN, late of this county, departed this life intestate, administration on the estate of STEPHEN BOLEN, deceased, is granted him and he entered into bond with security.

On motion of WILLIAM FITCH by his attorney and it appearing to the court that JOHN C. GILLILAND, late of this county, departed this life intestate, adminstration on the estate of JOHN C. GILLILAND, deceased, is granted him and he entered into bond with security.

The court proceeded to the election of Constable, whereupon it was ordered by the court that JOHN ASHLEY, AMOS SMALL, ROBERT BUCHANAN and REECE HOWELL be duly elected Constables for this county which they entered into bond with security.

An inventory of the personal estate of ABNER WELLS, deceased, was exhibited in by the admr and received and ordered to be recorded.

SAMUEL BUTLER appeared in court and was appointed guardian of his children, CONSTANT, THOMAS, WILLIAM, TERESA P., SAMUEL HENDERSON, NANCY CAROLINE and JOHN BUTLER, who entered into bond and security.

An Account of Sale of the personal property of the estate of REPS O. CHILDRESS, deceased, was returned to court by the executors of the estate and ordered to be recorded.

An Account of Sale of the personal property belonging to the estate of JOHN BOYLES, deceased, was returned by the admr and ordered to be recorded.

WILLIAM SMITH allowed $35.00 for keeping JANE WOODWARD for twelve months, a pauper of this county, to be paid quarterly.

WILLIAM SMITH, Esquire, offers his resignation to the court as a Justice of the Peace, which is received.

Ordered that the clerk be allowed $25.00 for making out the tax list for 1826.

Ordered that JOHN PORTER, THOMAS CLARK and REPS O. CHILDRESS be appointed Commissioners to settle with JOHN C. SAWYERS, admr of DAVID SAWYERS, deceased, and report to next court.

Ordered that CAPTAIN LEE SMITH be released from the payment of the State and County Tax on his stud horse as given in for the year 1826.

Ordered that ABNER HOLLANDSWORTH be bound as an apprentice til the age of twenty one years to WILLIAM ROSEBOROUGH to learn the blacksmith trade and he gave bond.

JAMES WILSON, WILLIAM MILNER, JOHN H. MOORE, SAMUEL BUCHANAN, HENRY KELSO, CHARLES BRIGHT, THOMAS H. SHAW, JOEL PINSON, and JOSEPH McBRIDE being present holding court. ROBERT DICKSON appeared in court and presented his petition setting forth his reasons and requiring said court to grant him leave to emancipate his negro man slave named JIM, and it appearing to the court that said JIM be emancipated and ROBERT DICKSON gave bond and security and the said JIM be from henceforth know and designated by the name of JAMES GOODLOE.

STEPHEN CLAYTON and PATON (PEYTON) WELLS each paid $5.00 to the State and the clerk's fee for a tavern license who entered bond and security.

Ordered that WILLIAM B. BENGE be appointed guardian to HUGH McCLUNG EDMONDSON and OBADIAH EDMONDSON, minors, who entered into bond.

Ordered by the court that JOSEPH COMMONS be appointed guardian to WILLIAM COMMONS, a minor, and entered into bond.

RICHMOND WALL entered into bond with security for maintainance of NATHANIEL GADBERRY, a pauper of this county, and is allowed $40.00.

FRIDAY APRIL 4, 1826

Justices present were SAMUEL GARLAND, JOHN H. MOORE, JAMES WILSON and CHARLES BRIGHT, Esquires.

WILLIAM HUSBANDS, High Sheriff, made return into court and called the following out of which a Grand Jury should be selected, to wit, ZADOCK MOTLOW, JOSEPH ADKINS, JAMES CURRY, WALTER B. OWEN, JOSEPH HINKLE, JOHN DONALDSON, DOILY GRIFFIS, ROBERT MEEK, OBADIAH PINSON, WILLIAM SMITH, MALCOLM McCOWN, ANDREW W. WALKER, JOHN McMILLEN, JOHN RHEA, ABNER STEED, JESSE ELLIS, JAMES PHILIPS, CHARLES H. EDMISTON, BENJAMIN THURSTON, MOSES MYRIC, JAMES HURLEY, JOHN BOONE, and JAMES CALHOON out of whom was selected the following persons a Grand Inquest and Jury, that is to say, ABNER STEED, foreman, JAMES PHILIPS, MALCOMB McCOWN, JOHN BOONE, WILLIAM SMITH, JOHN DONALDSON, WALTER B. OWEN, OBADIAH PINSON, JOHN McMILLEN, CHARLES H. EDMISTON, ZADOCK MOTLOW, JAMES HURLEY, and JESSE ELLIS being elected and sworn.

Ordered that BENJAMIN THURSTON be released from further attendance as a juror at this time.

The Grand Jury returned into court, an indictment against JACOB TOWRY for an assault and battery committed on the body of ISAAC ROBERTS, a true bill and withdrew to consider for further presentments.

AARON WELLS vs JOHN PORTER - The plaintiff is commissioned to take the deposition of REPS O. CHILDRESS by giving the party five days notice of time and place of taking the same.

JAMES D. EASTES vs ALLEN YOWELL - The parties are commissioned to take the deposition of their witnesses by giving the party five days notice in the county and twenty days for out of state notice of time and place of taking the same.

ALEXANDER DOBBINS vs A.J. BLACKBURN, admr - This day came the parties by their attorneys and a jury of men, to wit, JAMES CURRY, JAMES CALHOON, DOILY GRIFFIS, ROBERT MEEK, JAMES W. BARNES, JOHN LANE, JR., HENRY DAVIS, JOHN BURNS, REUBEN LOGAN, DANIEL T. WILLIAMS, VIZY HUSBANDS, and WILLIAM H. TALBOT being elected and sworn and said that the defendant did assume upon himself in manner and form as declared against him. They assess plaintiff's damages to $92.09 besides his costs. Plaintiff to recover his costs. A suit to be levied upon the goods and chattels &c of HAMPTON BOSTIC, deceased, in the hands of BLACKBURN to administer.

LAWSON H. ALEXANDER vs MARTIN L. & T.L.D. PARKS - This day came the parties by their attorneys and a jury of men, to wit, (same as above jurors) and said that the defendants have not paid a balance of the debt of $432.37½ and damages of $25.94. Plaintiff to recover his costs.

LAWSON H. ALEXANDER, assignee &c vs JOHN T. SMITH and others - (same as above) and said that the defendants have not paid the debt of $235.50 and damages of $14.12½. Plaintiff to recover his costs.

GEORGE W. CAMPBELL vs ANDREW J. BLAKEMORE and others - (same as above) and said that the defendants have not kept their covenant and the plaintiff to recover damages of $331.18 3/4. Plaintiff to recover his costs.

GEORGE W. CAMPBELL vs ANDREW J. BLAKEMORE and others - (same as above) and said that the defendants have not kept their covenant and the plaintiff to recover damages of $337.37½.

OLIVER B. HAYES vs ANTHONY & W. STREET - (same as above) and said that the defendants have not paid the debt of $226.66 and damages of $16.37. Plaintiff to recover his costs.

ANDREW CAMPBELL vs NIMROD BAILEY - (same as above) and said that the defendant has not paid the debt of $245.00 and damages of $35.50. Plaintiff to recover his costs.

SAMUEL TODD vs THOMAS & ISAIAH ALLY - (same as above) and said that the defendant has not paid the balance of the debt of $260.37½ and $8.00 besides his costs. Plaintiff to recover his costs.

E. & J. ADKISON vs JOBE G. SELPH - (same as above) and said that the defendant has not paid the debt of $98.00 and damages of $5.88. Plaintiff to recover his costs.

E. & J. ADKISON vs JOBE G. SETH - (same as above) and said that the defendant has not paid the debt of $95.00 and damages of $5.37½. Plaintiff to recover his costs.

E. & J. ADKISON vs JOBE G. SETH - (same as above) and said that the defendant has not paid the debt of $97.45 and damages of $5.84. Plaintiff to recover his costs.

SAMUEL WILSON, assignee &c vs EASON COALTER - (same as above) and said that the defendant hath not kept his covenant ans assess damages of $107.50 besides his costs. Plaintiff to recover his costs.

REUBEN LOGAN vs SAMUEL GARLAND and NICHOLAS CARRIGER - This day came the parties by their attorneys and the defendants say they cannot deny the plaintiff's action for $80.00 and damages of $1.20. Plaintiff recover his costs.

LESLEY GILHAM vs WILLIAM STEPHENS - This case is continued on affidavit of the defendant and commissions are awarded him to take the depositions of BASALOM YANCY and NATHANIEL ROBERTS in Granville County, North Carolina by giving forty days notice of time and place of taking the same.

JOEL B. SANDERS vs THOMAS ALLEY - The plaintiff by his attorney says he wishes no further to prosecute his suit against the defendant. Suit to be dismissed and the defendant recover his costs.

POWER & HAUGHTON vs DANIEL COFFMAN - Case is continued on affidavit of the defendant and he is to take the deposition of THOMAS CRUTCHER by giving twenty days notice of time and place of taking same.

AARON WELLS vs JOHN PORTER - Trespass - Entered elsewhere.

DAVID KELLER for the use of JAMES RORAX vs ARGYLE CAMPBELL - The plaintiff says he intends no further to prosecute his suit. Case dismissed. Defendant recover his costs.

ELIZABETH SHAW vs ROLAND TANKESLEY - The plaintiff by his attorney ans says she intends no further to prosecute her suit. Case to be dismissed and the defendant recover his costs.

WEDNESDAY APRIL 5, 1826

Justices present were SAMUEL GARLAND, ENOCK RUST and THOMAS GAITHER, Esquires.

SAMUEL HAMPTON vs A.J. BLACKBURN, admr - Case continued.

J. & J. WAGGONER vs J. HOLMAN and W. MOORE AND JACOB WAGGONER vs J. HOLMAN and WILLIAM MOORE - Case continued and the parties are allowed commissions to take the depositions of their witnesses by giving them five days notice of time and place in this county and twenty days notice if taken out of the county.

The State vs HENRY J. HAYS - Case to be continued.

ISAIAH ALLY vs URIAH BABBETT - This day came the parties by their attorneys and a jury of men, to wit, JAMES CURRY, JAMES CALHOON, DOILY GRIFFIS, ROBERT MEEK, JOHN LANE, JR., BARTLETT WOOLUN, EDWARD HARDIN, HENRY DAVIS, BRITTON PHELPS, DRURY CONLY, HENRY ROBERTSON, and THOMAS WITT being elected and sworn and said that they found in favor of the plaintiff and assess damages of $386.00 besides his costs. Plaintiff to recover his costs.

The Grand (Jury) again returned to court an indictment against GIDEON AUSTON for an assault and battery committed on the body of RACHEL FLEMMING, a true bill, and withdrew to consider for further presentments.

The Grand Jury again returned to court an indictment against TODD ADAMS, JAMES GREEN and JACOB PITCOCK for an assault and battery committed on the body of JOHN W. CRUNK, a true bill, and withdrew to consider for further presentments.

JAMES D. ALFORD vs PATTON ANDERSON - The plaintiff by his attorney is allowed to amend his declaration on the payment of the costs of this term.

The Grand Jury again returned to court an indictment against RACHEL FLEMMING for illtreating GIDEON AUSTON, not a true bill, also an indictment against TODD ADAMS for an assault and battery on JAMES W. MYRICK, a true bill, and also an indictment against PLEASANT FLEMMING for an assault and battery committed on the body of GIDEON AUSTON, a true bill, and withdrew to consider for further presentments.

JAMES CRAWFORD vs JOSEPH HINKLE - This day came the parties by their attorneys and a jury of men, to wit, JAMES CURRY, JAMES CALHOON, DOILY GRIFFIS, ROBERT MEEK, JOHN LANE, JR., BARTLETT WOOLEM, EDWARD HARDIN, HENRY DAVIS, BRITTON PHELPS, DRURY CONLEY, THOMAS WITT and SAMUEL TODD being elected and sworn and said that the plaintiff neither in proper person nor by attorney further prosecutes his suit. Defendant to recover his costs.

BARTLETT WOOLEM vs JOHN S. PRICE - This case is continued on affidavit of the plaintiff.

ELIJAH M. RINGO and wife vs SAMUEL TODD - This cause is referred to WILLIAM GILCHRIST, ARCHABALD YELL and WILLIAM P. MARTIN, Esquires, whose verdict shall be the verdict of this case and the court to give judgment accordingly.

JAMES COALTER vs JORDAN SOLOMON - This day came the parties by their attorneys and a jury of men, to wit, JAMES CURRY, JAMES CALHOON, DOILY GRIFFIS, ROBERT MEEK, JOHN LANE, JR., BARTLETT WOOLEM, EDWARD HARDIN, HENRY DAVIS, BRITTON PHELPS, DRURY CONLEY, THOMAS WITT, and SAMUEL TODD being elected and sworn and said that they find in favor of the plaintiff and assess the damages of $155.37½ besides his costs. Plaintiff to recover his costs.

E.A. COCHRAN vs JOHN GREER - (same as above) and said that the defendant did assume upon himself in manner and form as alleged and assess damages of $35.00 besides his costs. Plaintiff to recover his costs.

EDWARD HARDIN vs WILLIAM JACKSON (same as above) and assess the damages of $64.80 besides his costs. Plaintiff to recover his costs.

LEVI M. TODD vs WILLIAM A. PAMPLIN - This day came the parties by their attorneys and a jury of men, to wit, JAMES CURRY, JAMES CALHOON, DOILY GRIFFIS, ROBERT MEEK, JOHN LANE, JR., BARTLET WOOLEM, EDWARD HARDIN, HENRY DAVIS, BRITTON PHELPS, DRURY CONLEY, THOMAS WITT and VEZY HUSBANDS being elected and sworn and said that the defendant does owes the plaintiff $7.75. Plaintiff to recover his costs.

MICAJAH McELROY vs HENRY DAVIS - This day came the parties by their attorneys and a jury of men, to wit, JAMES CURRY, JAMES CALHOON, DOILY GRIFFIS, ROBERT MEEK, JOHN LANE, JR., BARTLET WOOLEM, BRITTON PHELPS, DRURY CONLEY, THOMAS WITT, JOHN BURUS, WILSON FROST and WILLIAM PARKER being elected and sworn and find the issues in favor of the defendant. Defendant to recover his costs.

WILLIAM LACKAY vs JOHN W. CRUNK - The plaintiff says he intends no further to prosecute his suit. Suit to be dismissed and the defendant recover his costs.

JAMES REED vs HENRY ROBERTSON - The defendant came by his attorney and the plaintiff being called came not nor is his suit prosecuted. The defendant recover his costs.

THOMAS GAITHER vs ALFRED J. MOORE - The plaintiff is awarded commission to take the deposition of UNICE BESHULL in Madison County, Alabama, by giving thirty days notice.

ALPHANSO WHITING vs JOB G. SELPH - This day came the parties by their attorneys and a jury of men, to wit, JAMES CURRY, JAMES CALHOON, DOILY GRIFFIS, ROBERT MEEK, JOHN LANE, JR., BARTLET WOOLEM, HENRY DAVIS, BRITTON PHELPS, DRURY CONLEY, THOMAS WITT, JAMES W. BURUS and JOHN BURUS being elected and sworn and said that the defendant has not paid the debt or #132.02 and damages of $5.98 besides his costs. Plaintiff to recover his costs.

ROLEN BURKS vs JAMES GRINDLE - Plaintiff says he intends no further to prosecute his suit. Case to be dismissed and the defendant recover his costs.

A receipt from WILLIAM & ELIZABETH BEAVERLY to JOSEPH COMMONS was proven and ordered to be certified.

The due execution of a Deed of Conveyance for 100 acres of land from BRICE M. GARNER to JNO. W.P. McGIMPSAY was proven and ordered to be certified.

Ordered that CORNELIUS SLATER be allowed $3.00 for summoning a Jury of Inquist over the body of STEPHEN BOLEN.

The due execution of a Deed of Conveyance from EDWARD TOWREY to ROBERT MEEK for 80 acres of land and ordered to be certified.

The due execution of a Bill of Sale from ROBERT DICKSON to ROBERT HAIRSTON for a negro boy named AMOS and ordered to be certified.

The due execution of a Deed of Conveyance from JOHN T. CUNNINGHAM to JOHN H. NORTON for 65 acres of land and ordered to be certified.

Justices present were THOMAS GAITHER, ENOCK RUST and SAMUEL GARLAND, Esquires.

The State vs GIDEON AUSTON - The parties came by their attorneys and the said defendant being arraigned and pleaded not guilty and a jury of men, to wit, JAMES CURRY, JAMES CALHOON, DOILY GRIFFIS, ROBERT MEEK, JAMES D. ALFORD, VEZT HUSBANDS, JACOB MOYERS, HIRAM DAVIS, DAVID A. GREER, ISAAC HOLMAN, WILLIAM P. PULLIAM and DRURY CONLEY being elected and sworn and said that the defendant is not guilty and it is ordered that the prosecutor PLEASANT FLEMMING be taxed with the costs of the prosecution of this suit.

The State vs LAWSON B. HUGHS - This day came the Attorney General who prosecutes for the State and therefore came the defendant who pleads guilty and submits to the mercy of the court. The defendant to be fined $2.50 and pay the costs, whereupon DAVISON McMILLEN and HUGH A. KINCANNON confessed judgment jointly with the defendant for the above fine and costs.

JAMES COOPER vs ALEXANDER MILLER - The parties are allowed Commissioners to take the deposition of their witnesses by giving twenty days notice of the time and place of taking the same.

The State vs JACOB TOWRY - The defendant pleads guilty and is fined $2.50 and pay costs of this suit.

GIDEON AUSTON, WILLI JONES and MOSES STONE said that they are indebted to the State of Tennessee for $300.00. To be void on condition that GIDEON AUSTON keep the State's peace for six months from this date.

JOSEPH WHITAKER vs HENRY BASINGER - The plaintiff says he intends no further to prosecute his suit. Suit to be dismissed and the plaintiff and defendant to pay the costs.

GREEN W. LANE and JOHN LANE, JR., acknowledged themselves indebted to the Justices of the County of Lincoln for $500.00. To be void on condition that GREEN W. LANE keep from the charge of the county, WINNIE SULLIVAN, a bastard child, sworn to him.

The State vs GIDEON AUSTON - The Attorney General says he intends no further to prosecute his suit against said defendant and PLEASANT FLEMMING, the prosecutor in person, assumes the payment of the costs.

The State vs GRAY BRYANT - The Attorney General said the defendant came into court and pleaded guilty and is fined $10.00 and pay the cost of suit.

The State vs JAMES LAWSON - The defendant pleads guilty and is fined $5.00 and pay the cost of this indictment.

The State vs PLEASANT FLEMMING - The defendant pleads not guilty and a jury of men, to wit, JAMES CURRY, JAMES CALHOON, DOILY GRIFFIS, ROBERT MEEK, JAMES D. ALFORD, VEZY HUSBANDS, JACOB MOYERS, HIRAM DAVIS, DAVID A. GREER, ISAAC HOLMAN, WILLIAM P. PULLIAM and DRURY CONLEY being elected and sworn and said that the defendant is not guilty. It is ordered that GIDEON AUSTON be taxed with the costs of this suit.

The State vs GREEN W. LANE - SCI FA (You should cause to know and review a judgment)
    and

The State vs JOHN LANE - The defendant appeared in court and assumes the payment of all costs.
    and
The State vs LEWIS LANE

JOHN T. SMITH said he was indebted to the State for $250.00 to be levied on his own goods and chattels &c. To be void on condition that he appear in person at next July Term on charge of malicious mischief.

JOHN SMITH and JOHN T. SMITH acknowledged themselves indebted to the State for $250.00 each, to be levied upon his goods and chattels &c to be void on condition that JOHN SMITH appear in July Term of court to answer charge of malicious mischief.

JESSE OVERTON acknowledged himself indebted to the State for $250.00 to be levied upon his goods and chattels &c, to be void on condition that OVERTON appear in July next court to answer to charge of malicious mischief.

Ordered that JAMES D. ALFORD be fined $5.00 for his non-attendance as a juror when called this day, also pay costs.

The State vs PHILIP FIELDS and JACOB SUMMERS - The defendant, PHILIP FIELDS who had entered into bond and gave JACOB SUMMNERS as his security. Now at this day the said PHILIP FIELDS having failed to come forward and take oath required by law or pay the debt due to said State. The State to recover against said PHILIP FIELDS and JACOB SUMMERS his security for $21.48½ and costs.

The fine entered against JAMES D. ALFORD is remitted and ordered that ALFORD pay the costs &c.

FRIDAY APRIL 7, 1826

Justices present were CHARLES BRIGHT, ROBERT DICKSON and ENOCK RUST.

The Transfer of a Plat and Certificate from WILLIAM HUSBANDS to JAMES P. BAXTER for 50 acres of land and ordered to be certified.

The State vs JOHN McCONNELL - The defendant has assumed the payment of all costs that has occurred in the prosecution of different suits &c against DAVID J. HOLT who was security for the defendant. State to recover all costs.

WILLIAM McELROY vs ROBERT DICKSON - This day came the parties by their attorneys and a jury of men, to wit, JAMES CALHOON, JAMES CURRY, DOILY GRIFFIS, ROBERT MEEK, JOHN McMILLEN, SAMUEL S. HOLDING, DAVID A. GREER, WILLIAM P. PULLIAM, JAMES W. MYRICK, CHRISTOPHER R. WITT, JOSEPH B. HILL, and WARREN CALHOON being elected and sworn and said that JAMES CALHOON, one of the jurors is withdrawn and rest of said jurors from rendering their verdict are discharged.

ANDREW HUNT vs WILLIAM McCLELLAN - (same as above) and said that they find the issue in favor of the defendant. Defendant to recover his costs. Plaintiff prays for an appeal and is granted and entered into bond with CHARLES BOYLES as security.

JOHN LANE vs ISAAC CONGER - This day came the parties by their attorneys and a jury of men, to wit, ABNER STEED, JAMES PHILIPS, MALCOMB McCOWN, JOHN BOONE, WILLIAM SMITH, JOHN DONALDSON, WALTER B. OWEN, OBADIAH PINSON, CHARLES H. EDMISTON, ZADOCK MOTLOW, JAMES HURLEY, and JESSE ELLIS being elected and sworn and said that ABNER STEED, one of the jury is withdrawn, and the rest of said jurors from rendering their verdict, are discharged.

The State vs TODD ADAMS - The defendant pleads guilty of assault and is fined $5.00 and pay the costs whereupon SAMUEL BOLES acknowledged judgment jointly with defendant for the above fine and costs.

S. BUCHANAN & J. McWHERTER vs PETER ADAMS - (same as JOHN LANE vs ISAAC CONGER) and said that they find in favor of the plaintiff and assess damages of $30.00 besides their costs. Plaintiff to recover his costs. Defendant prays for an appeal and is granted and having given bond with BARNABAS L. McELROY and MICAJAH McELROY, JR.

JOHN W. CRUNK acknowledged himself indebted to the State of Tennessee for $250.00 to be levied upon his goods and chattels &c, to be void on condition that JOHN W. appear at next July court to give evidence for the State against TODD ADAMS. ADAMS on an Indictment for a Riot.

JOHN W. CRUNK (same as above) against TODD ADAMS for an Assault and Battery.

TODD ADAMS & DELILA ADAMS - (same as above) on condition that TODD ADAMS appear in next July court to answer the State on an Indictment of Assault and Battery.

TODD ADAMS & DELILA ADAMS - Acknowledged themselves indebted to the State of Tennessee for $250.00 to be levied upon their goods and chattels &c, to be void on condition that TODD ADAMS appear in next July Court to answer the State on an indictment of assault and battery.

JOHN LANE vs ISAAC CONGER - A Commission is awarded the defendant to take the deposition of MALINDA MARTIN by giving the plaintiff ten days notice of time and place of taking the same.

SAMUEL WILSON vs T. GROCE & A. CUNNINGHAM - The plaintiff said he intends no further to prosecute his suit and the said defendant THOMAS GROCE in person assumes the payment of all costs. Suit to be dismissed.

JOSEPH HINKLE vs GREEN B. SAVORY - The plaintiff says he intends no further to prosecute his suit and the defendant assumes the payment of all costs and JOSEPH B. EDWARDS here confesses judgment jointly with the defendant for above costs. Suit to be dismissed.

The State vs DAVID J. HOLT - The defendant being called came not and the Attorney General moved for judgment final against defendant. Final judgment for $400.00.

FRIDAY APRIL 7, 1826

State of Tennessee, County of Lincoln
"This is to testify that I have made a settlement with GREEN W. LANE concerning a female bastard child, I swore to him some time ago, for which he is bound to appear and answer for to the next court of Pleas and Quarter Sessions for the county foresaid provided said LANE pays all fines and costs for the same. 24 November 1825. Attest - ABNER STEED. Signed: NANCY SULIVAN."

It is considered that the property mentioned in the schedule of property belonging to SAMUEL REEVES is worth fourteen and a half dollars and not more.

WILLIAM M. QUESENBURY vs NATHANIEL ALEXANDER, JOHN INMAN and DANIEL WRIGHT - The defendants confessed that they jointly and severally owe to said plaintiff for $183.81 debt and damages. Plaintiff to recover his costs.

HIRAM H. HIGGINS vs SAMUEL DURHAM - The defendant is permitted now to take the benefit of the different Acts of Assembly made for the benefit of insolvent debtors and DURHAM took oath. Plaintiff pay the costs of this motion.

ZACHARIAH ARNOLD vs EBENEZER PICKETT - It is considered by the court that this case be dismissed and that the plaintiff recover against the defendant and his security GRAHAM SNODDY his debt and damages of $101.73 at 12½%.

JAMES BRYANS vs JOHN BROWN & JOHN LUSK - Plaintiff to recover against the defendant his debt of $30.50 damages.

GEORGE W. CAMPBELL vs A.J. BLAKEMORE - The defendant prays for an appeal to next court and is granted and entered into bond with G.W.C. EDMISTON and WILLIAM CRUNK securities.

O.B. HAYS vs ANTHONY & WILLIAM STREET, admrs &c - (same as above) and granted and entered into bond with JOHN DAVIS, security.

GEORGE W. CAMPBELL vs A.J. BLAKEMORE and others - The defendants prays for an appeal to next Circuit COurt and granted and entered into bond with WILLIAM CRUNK and G.W.C. EDMISTON as securities.

MICAJAH McELROY vs HENRY DAVIS - The plaintiff prays for an appeal to next Circuit COurt and granted and entered into bond with MICAJAH McELROY, JR. and BARNABAS L. McELROY his securities.

SAMUEL WILSON vs EASON COALTER - The defendant prays for an appeal to next Circuit Court and is granted and entered into bond with THOMAS ORRICK his security.

ABNER G. SAWYERS takes PAYTON SAWYERS, an apprentice to the blacksmith trade, tillhe arrives at the age of twenty years and entered into bond.

222

JOHN P. McCONNELL, admr of the estate of STEPHEN BOLEN exhibited in court an inventory of the personal estate of said BOLEN, received by court and ordered to be recorded.

The due execution of a Bill of Sale from OBADIAH PINSON to WILLIAM SMITH for a negro girl named VINY, proven and ordered to be certified.

Ordered that FRANCIS PORTERFIELD and A.A. KINCANNON be Commissioners to settle with R. DICKSON, admr of the estate of PATRICK O'CALAHAN and make return to next court.

The due execution of a Transfer of a Plat and Certificate from MARIA WILLIAMS to JOEL PINSON, proven by SAMUEL W. CARMACK and THOMAS H. WILLIAMS and ordered to be certified.

The due execution of a Plat and Certificate from WILLIAM McKINSEY to KENNETH McKINSEY and ordered to be certified.

The due execution of a Deed of Conveyance from JOSEPH CARROLL to WILLIAM SWAIN for 60 acres of land and ordered to be certified.

The due execution of a Deed of Conveyance from JOHN PINKERTON to WILLIAM PUGH for 100 acres of land and ordered to be certified.

The due execution of an indenture between AUSTON NOLIN and DAVID P. MONROE and ordered to be certified.

The due execution of a Bill of Sale from ISAIAH & THOMAS ALLY to SAMUEL TODD for a negro boy named SAM and ordered to be certified.

The due execution of a Deed of Conveyance from S. MARSH to JEREMIAH GANT and ordered to be certified.

The due execution of a Deed of Conveyance from REECE HOWELL to SAMUEL HOWELL for 19 acres of land and ordered to be certified.

The due execution of a Deed of Conveyance from SAMUEL (WELLS) to ABNER WELLS for 20 acres of land and ordered to be certified.

The due execution of a Deed of Conveyance from JOHN SANDERS to MATTHEW COLE for 82½ acres of land and ordered to be certified.

The due execution of a Deed of Conveyance from BRICE M. GARNER to JAMES W. CUNNINGHAM for 65 acres of land and ordered to be certified.

The due execution of a Title Bond from THOMAS (ALLSUP) to ROBERT R. ALLSUP, proven by A.B. CLENDENING and LEVI SHERRILL and ordered to be certified.

The due execution of a Deed of Conveyance from JAMES SMITH to JOHN T. CUNNINGHAM for one acre of land and ordered to be certified.

The due execution of a Bill of Sale from SAMUEL ROSEBOROUGH to STEPHEN CLAYTON for five negroes and ordered to be certified.

The due execution of a Deed of Conveyance from JAMES COWLEY to JOHN WATKINS for 15 3/4 and 8 poles of land and ordered to be certified.

The due execution of a Bill of Sale from JOHN A. ALLEN to GEORGE W. DENNIS for a negro man named SAMUEL and ordered to be certified.

The due execution of a Deed of Conveyance from DAVID MOORE to PRESTON HAMPTON for 50 acres of land, proven by WILLIAM BEAVERS and ordered to be certified.

The due execution of a Deed of Conveyance from THOMAS HENRY to ISAAC McCOLLUM for 96 acres of land and ordered to be certified.

The due execution of a Deed of Conveyance from PAYTON (WELLS) to ABNER WELLS for 100 acres of land and ordered to be certified.

LAWSON H. ALEXANDER vs M.L. & T.L.D. PARKS - The defendants prays for an appeal to next Circuit Court and is granted and entered into bond with ANDREW A. KINCANNON, HENRY ROBERTSON and CHAMPION BLYTH his securities.

The court ordered several routes examined. They found that the route running through WILSON FROST's land to be annulled and to take off at the gap of the ridge at a large oak root between JOHN DONALDSON's and the widow BUCHANAN's, thence running eastwardly and with DONALDSON's line and HINKLE's into the Nashville Road, THOMAS KERCHEVAL, WILLIAM EDMISTON, JOHN GIBSON, JOHN LEE, ELIJAH DAVIS and JAMES HIGGINS.

CHILDRESS & PATTERSON vs ANDREW A. KINCANNON & R. DICKSON - The defendant confessed that they owe the plaintiff $5050.00 and damages of $32.00. Plaintiff to recover his costs.

The due execution of an Indenture of Bargain and Sale from ANTHONY WELLS, HAIRSTON WELLS, WILLIAM ALLEN and FRANKEY ALLEN for 285 acres of land, proven by JAMES W. CUNNINGHAM & R.H. CUNNINGHAM as to the execution thereof by ANTHONY WELLS, HAIRSTON WELLS and WILLIAM ALLEN and as to the execution of the same on the part of FRANKEY ALLEN, wife of WILLIAM ALLEN. She was examined privately and apart from her husband. The same ordered to be certified.

The due execution of a Deed of Conveyance for a lot in Nashville from DAVID THOMPSON and his wife LORRETTA C. THOMPSON to WILLIAM M. BERYHILL, acknowledged and LORRETTA C. THOMPSON was examined apart from her husband by JOEL PINSON and JOHN PORTER, Esquires, Justices and ordered to be certified.

WILLIAM PARKER vs ROBERT DICKSON - The plaintiff by his attorney made motion to dismiss this cause. Ordered that the plaintiff take nothing but that the same stand for trial at next term.

SATURDAY APRIL 8, 1826

Justices present were JOHN PARKER, SAMUEL BUCHANAN and ROBERT DICKSON, Esquires.

The due execution of a Bill of Sale from WILLIAM TIMMINS to ROBERT DICKSON was duly proven and ordered to be certified.

The due execution of a Bill of Sale from JOHN LINVILLE to ROBERT DICKSON was duly proven and ordered to be certified.

The due execution of an Indenture between ROBERT ROSS and ROBERT DICKSON was duly proven and ordered to be certified.

"Nashville, November 17th, 1825 - Received of BRICE M. GARNER, Clerk of Lincoln County $552.54. The amount of State Tax by him collected for the year ending 1st day October 1825. THOMAS CRUTCHER, Treasurer of West Tennessee." The above receipt was ordered to be spread on the minutes."

JAMES COOPER vs ALEXANDER MILLER - The defendant being called to court came not but made default. It is ordered that judgment interlocutory be entered against the defendant and a Writ of Inquiry to be executed at the next term of court to inquire of damages.

The due execution of a Deed of Conveyance from MARY INGLE to ROBERT DICKSON for a town lot in Fayetteville, proven by JOHN MORGAN and ordered to be certified.

EWELL SHIPP vs THOMAS D. CLARK - The defendant being called to court came not but made default. The plaintiff to recover his costs of $500.00 and damages of $7.50 and cost of suit.

EWELL SHIPP vs THOMAS D. CLARK - (same as above). Plaintiff to recover his debt and interest amounting to $408.20 and his costs.

Ordered that the clerk be allowed to retain $84.22, the amount of fees due to him from 1 January 1825 to 1 January 1826 on cause where the State either failed in its prosecution where the debts were unable to pay the costs.

224

The administrator of the estate of JOHN C. GILLILAND returned to court an inventory of thereof and was ordered to be recorded.

A Bill od Sale from THOMAS R. GARNER to ROBERT DICKSON was acknowledged and ordered to be certified.

ANDREW HUNT vs JAMES CLIFT - A Commission is awarded the plaintiff to take the deposition of PARLIMUS(?) HUNT in the State of Kentucky and giving the defendant twenty days notice of the time and place of taking the same.

Received of BRICE M. GARNER by CHARLES BOYLES $5.57, the amount due from him to the Trustee of Lincoln County as Clerk of the Court of Pleas and Quarter Sessions of said county. The County Court having made a special order to pay the clerk aforesaid $84.22 for fees due him as stated. 8 April 1826. WILLIAM NEELD, Trustee of Lincoln County. Above ordered to be spread on the minutes.

WILLIAM M. QUESENBURY vs SAMUEL ROSEBOROUGH - The defendant being called came not but made default. The plaintiff to recover his costs and damages of $142.45.

MONDAY JULY 3, 1826

Justices present were ROBERT DICKSON, chairman, JAMES BLAKEMORE, JAMES SMITH, ALEXANDER McLINN, WILLIAM MILNER, WILLIAM EDMISTON, JOHN ENOCKS, SAMUEL BUCHANAN, PHILIP KOONCE, CHARLES BRIGHT, WILLIAM DYE, THOMAS H. SHAW and JESSE DANIEL.

JOHN GARDNER, Esquire, appeared in court and on motion was admitted to take the oath.

On motion of HANNAH COWLEY and JOHN WATSON, administration is granted them on the estate of JAMES COWLEY, deceased, and entered into bond and gave security.

Ordered that the Coroner of this county be allowed $5.00 for his fees in holding an inquest on the body of STEPHEN BOLEN, deceased.

Ordered that the following persons be released from the payment of double tax for the present year: RANDOLPH QUARLES, FRANCIS FINCHER, JOHN EDMISTON, three white poles, JAMES LEWIS 1049 acres in different tracts, DAVID THWING 170 acres land and two black poles, JAMES FORSYTHE 340 acres and one white and four black poles, ANCIL RICHARDSON 228 acres, JAMES SCOTT 200 acres and one white pole and three black poles, ARCHIBALD BOYD 120 acres of land, McEWEN & GILLILAND one store, WILLIAM DYE one store, and JOHN HIGGINS one town lot.

Ordered that WILLIAM S. SMITH be appointed guardian to WESTLY R. GREEN, TOWNZEN P. GREEN and STAUNTON I. GREEN and entered into bond and gave security.

Ordered by the court at last term appointing JOSEPH GREER, DAVID SNODDY and TUNSTALL GREGORY Commissioners to settle with the admr of EDWARD TEAL, deceased, and report to next court.

On motion of the admrs of STERLING C. McLEMORE, deceased, and it appearing that it was necessary for the payment of the debts of said estate that some of the negroes properly belonging thereto be sold. It is ordered that the said admrs sell a negro woman named CHLOE belonging to said estate.

Ordered that WILLIAM LACKEY be allowed $25.00 for keeping and supporting BETSEY RASBERRY for twelve months from this day. Whereupon came EZEKIEL GILLAM as security.

Ordered that HUGH PARKESON, WILLIAM SMITH and MICHAEL ROBERTSON be Commissioners to settle with SAMUEL M. CLAY and WILLIAM STEPHENS, executors of LUCINDA STREET, deceased, and make return.

Ordered that JAMES FORSYTHE, CLIFFORD GRAY and BENJAMIN PROCTOR be Commissioners to settle with E.C. McLAUGHLIN, admr of AMBROSE BARKER, SR., deceased, and also to settle with E.C. McLAUGHLIN, executor of JANE BARKER, executrix of AMBROSE BARKER, JR., deceased.

225

ANDREW HAMILTON vs JAMES D. ESTES - The defendant's bail surrenders him in discharge of themselves whereupon the defendant was prayed in custody of the Sheriff.

Ordered that RICHARD ROBERTSON be allowed $26.00 as full pay and compensation for keeping JOHN ESTERS from January term last until he died and that a certificate issue to the said ROBERTSON for that sum forthwith and that the order of January term allowing him $60.00 for keeping ESTERS one year be totally void and of no effect.

Ordered that ZADOCK MOTLOW, ISHAM PARR, ROBERT FROST, CLAYBORN WHITWORTH, ALEXANDER BEARD, JACOB CASTLEMAN, HENRY ROBERTSON, JONATHAN MUSE, SR., JOHN MORRIS, JOHN DOWTHIT, BENJAMIN ARRINGTON, THOMAS EAST, THOMAS KERCHEVAL, JORDAN REESE, JOHN GIBSON, WILLIAM SMITH, C. CRUNK, WILLIAM D. BLAKE, JOHN CRAWFORD, JOHN CAMPBELL, JOHN C. FLYNT, JOHN BEATY, DAVID SMITH, HENRY CLIFT, WILLIAM CRAWFORD and NICHOLAS CARRIGER be jurors to next county court.

Ordered that JAMES C. TEAL be overseer of the public road in the room of ANTHONY STREET and call on the usual hands.

Ordered that JOSEPH YEAGER be overseer of the public road in the room of BENJAMIN HOPKINS and call on the usual hands.

Ordered that WILLIAM BRIGHT, ALEXANDER MEEK, KEYS MEEK, HERBERT GRIFFIS, WILLIAM BARROW, PETER VAUGHN, and JOHN MARTIN be a jury to view and turn the public road leading down the river crossing Hannahs Ford leaving the old road near JOHN ALBRIGHT and leaving his peach orchard on the left and coming in to the old road again at or near the foot of the first small hill below ALBRIGHT's and make return to next court.

Ordered that ROBERT MOORE be appointed overseer of the public road in the room of JASPER SMITH and call on the usual hands.

On motion of WILLIAM MOORE & ISAAC HOLMAN the executors named in the Last Will and Testament of BENJAMIN DORSEY the same was submitted to probate whereupon came CHRISTOPHER SHOFNER as witness and proved the due execution thereof on the part of the testator and the signature of DRURY M. CONNALLY other witness and court ordered the same to be certified and recorded.

The Last Will and Testament of HARDY HOLMAN, deceased, was presented in court for probate whereupon came FRANCIS PORTERFIELD, JESSE B. CLEMENTS and CHARLES BOYLES, witnesses, proved the execution of the testator. And JOHN WILLIAMSON, a witness to the codicil annexed to said Last Will, appeared in court at the same time and proved the due execution by the testator. It was ordered to be certified and recorded. And therefore came ABNER STEED, CHARLES BRIGHT and JACK H. LEFTWICH, the executors named in said Last Will entered into bond and gave security.

The Last Will and Testament of THOMPSON A. GREER was presented for probate whereupon came WILLIAM McELROY and BAILY RAINS, witnesses, proved the execution of the testator and was ordered to be certified and recorded.

REUBIN H. BOONE appeared in open court and proven guardian to BENJAMIN PYBUS and WILLIAM PYBUS, minor orphans of JAS. PYBUS, deceased, took oath and gave security.

It appearing to the court that JACOB WAGGONER has purchased by EDY SUSAND and JANE their part of shares of 244 acres of land lying on the East Fork of Mulberry Creek formerly the property of GEORGE WAGGONER, deceased, and the other representatives of said GEORGE WAGGONER had notice of this motion, viz, MATHIAS, CATHARINE and STOKELY. It is ordered that JASPER SMITH, JOHN DUSENBERRY and ISAAC HOLMAN be appointed Commissioners to make partition of said tract of land.

Ordered that GENERAL W.C. EDMISTON and WILLIAM B. BENGE be appointed to settle with the admrs of THOMAS CUMMINS, deceased.

An Indenture of Bargain and Sale from LIVINGTON J. BROWN to JAMES BROWN for 220 acres, proven by ARCHIBALD FERGUSON and ALEXANDER R. KERR and ordered to be certified.

JOSEPH CLARK produced one wolf scalp in court over four months old and four under four months old.

The Last Will and Testament of JEREMIAH DENNIS was exhibited in court for probation, whereupon came AMOS SMALL, witness, made oath that he saw JEREMIAH DENNIS sign, seal and publish and declare this to be his Last Will and Testament and that he was at the time of signing the same of sound mind and memory and that PETER J. COTTON was a witness to the same and on motion of JAMES DENNIS, the executor, took oath and gave security.

The Executors of HARDY HOLMAN's estate returned the inventory to court.

Ordered that GEORGE WEBB be overseer of the road in the room of JOHN TINDLE or JOSEPH STEPHENS and call on the usual hands.

Ordered that THOMAS SPENCER be appointed overseer of the road in the room of WILSON BRYANT and call on the usual hands.

Ordered that SAMUEL BUCHANAN, Esquire, FRANCIS PORTERFIELD and WILLIAM EDMISTON be appointed Commissioners to settle with the executors of the estate of JAMES PYBAS, deceased.

Ordered that PAYTON WELLS be appointed overseer of the road in the room of JESSE B. CLEMENTS and call on the usual hands.

Ordered that PLEASANT McGEEHEE be appointed overseer of the road from the house of WILLIAM PATTERSON to the Gum Spring and call on the usual hands.

Ordered that JOSEPH SEBASTIAN be overseer of the road in the room of ELIFUS BOAZ and call on the usual hands.
NOTE: This article was marked "ERROR".

Ordered that THOMAS PARKER be appointed overseer of the road in the room of JOSEPH SEBASTIAN and call on the usual hands.

Ordered that JESSE DAVIS be appointed overseer of the road in the room of JOHN CLAYTON and call on the usual hands.

Ordered that JOHN WALKER, SR. be appointed overseer of the road in the room of JAMES PARR from Clicks Ford on Elk River to Walkers Mill Branch and call on the hands that was allotted to work on said road by ABRAM ISAACS and WILLIAM ANDERSON, Esquires.

Ordered that JOHN H. NORTON be overseer of the road from Walkers Mill Branch to the county line and the hands to be laid off by ANDERSON & ISAACS.

Ordered that WILLIAM DAVIS be appointed overseer of the road in the room of NATHANIEL REED and call on the usual hands.

Ordered that PETER NIPP be appointed overseer of the road in the room of ALEXANDER HUGHY and call on the usual hands.

Ordered that MILES HUSBANDS be appointed overseer of the road in the room of WOODROOFF PARKS and call on the usual hands.

Ordered that HIRAM GUNTER be overseer of the road in the room of HENRY BECK and call on the usual hands.

On petition of JOHN SAWYERS, WILLIAM P. SAWYERS, ABNER G. SAWYERS, ETHAN G. SAWYERS, ALLEN SAWYERS, and WASHINGTON SAWYERS, being heirs of DAVID SAWYERS, deceased, and it appearing to the court here, they together with MADISON SAWYERS, JAMES PAYTON, ELLINOR ELIZABETH and ELISHA SAWYERS are entitled to and are the owners of 470 acres of land on the waters of Swan Creek, it is ordered that NATHAN G. PINSON, THOMAS H. WILLIAMS and THOMAS CLARK be appointed Commissioners to make partition agreeable and proved.

Ordered that NATHAN SMITH be overseer of the road from Nicks Ford on Elk River up to Tuckers Creek to the ford of said creek at OBADIAH BENNETT's and that WILLIAM McCLURE be overseer of the road from OBADIAH BENNETT's to the top of the ridge and that CLIFFORD GRAY, Esquire, divide the hands between them.

227

Ordered that THOMAS H. BELL be overseer of the public road from near his house on Swan Creek to WILLIAM ROBERTSON in the room of THOMAS WILLIAMS and call on the usual hands.

Ordered that the road leading from near THOMAS H. BELL's toward Giles County which was annulled at the last court be now established as one of the public roads of this county of third class.

Ordered that SAMUEL LEA be overseer of the public road from where THOMAS H. BELL quits working on it to the Giles County line and call on the usual hands.

Ordered that AMOS REED, an orphan boy fourteen or fifteen years old, be bound to MICAJAH McELROY, JR. until he arrives at the age of twenty one years to learn the art of farming. McELROY entered into bond with security to treat him well, school and give him a horse &c.

BENNET BLACKMAN guardian of the minor heirs of THOMAS JOICE (JOYCE), deceased, presented in court his account against said heirs and also two receipts of SAMUEL CRAWFORD, admr of the estate of said JOICE and was ordered to be certified.

The jury appointed at the last court to view and turn the public road running by JAMES LAMBS, now return that they have performed that duty and said that the new road is to leave the old one east of Dry Creek at the top of the ridge where said LAMB has cut a new road running along the ridge dividing the waters of Albrights Spring Branch from Dry Creek by said LAMB's gin intersecting the old road near ALBRIGHT's house. But the court refused to establish said road as marked out as the public road at this time.

Ordered by the court that REPS O. CHILDRESS, JONAS LEATHERMAN, HENRY SWINEBROAD, DAVID SMITH, JESSE DAVIS and JOHN DAVIS be a Jury of View to view and see if the public road leading from Fayetteville to Pulaski cannot be with advantage to the public so laid out as to leave the present road on the east side of Swan Creek running up a small branch to the line between POLK and CHILDRESS, and thence with that line so as to intersect the old road at or near Little Swan Creek and report to next court.

Ordered that JOHN McGEHEE, GEORGE COUNTS, FRANCIS FINCHER, JAMES SMITH, WILLIAM & ISAAC PARKER be a jury to view and mark a road beginning about two miles below the mouth of Beans Creek running the nearest and best way to Hazelgreen and make return to next court.

An Indenture of Bargain and Sale from JAMES D. ALFORD to HENRY ROBERTSON for 12 3/4 acres of land and ordered to be certified.

The due execution of a Deed of Bargain and Sale from ALEXANDER GRAY to SAMUEL YEAGER for 20 acres of land and ordered to be certified.

The due execution of a Deed of Bargain and Sale from JOHN H. ROGERS to JAMES D. ALFORD for 12 3/4 acres of land and ordered to be certified.

The due execution of a Deed of Bargain and Sale from NANCY BROWN to JACOB HAMILTON for 18 acres of land, proven by THOMAS H. SHAW and THOMAS H. CATLIN and ordered to be certified.

The due execution of a Deed of Bargain and Sale from WILLIAM McCLELLAND to ALFORD SMITH for 64 acres of land, proven by JOSEPH C. BUCHANAN and LEANDER BUCHANAN and ordered to be certified.

The Transfer of a Plat and Certificate of Survey from EDWARD TATUM to WILLIAM JAMES for 10 acres of land, proven by WILLIAM SANSOM and ordered to be certified.

The due execution of a Deed of Bargain and Sale from THOMAS ROUNDTREE to THOMAS H. CATLIN for a lot, proven by JACOB HAMILTON and JAMES CURRY and ordered to be certified.

The due execution of a Deed of Bargain and Sale from ISAAC COLLINS and SION DAMRON to E. & T. OGLETREE for 50 acres of land and ordered to be certified.

The due execution of a Bargain and Sale from DANIEL COFFMAN to STEPHEN WILLIAMSON for 50 acres of land and ordered to be certified.

The due execution of a Deed of Bargain and Sale from JOHN H. ROGERS to SOLOMON GULLET for a lot and ordered to be certified.

The due execution of a Deed of Bargain and Sale from MICHAEL BEAVERS to JOHN BROADWAY for 94 acres of land, proven by HOWELL HARRIS and JOHN SMITH and ordered to be certified.

Ordered that DANIEL JONES, ELIJAH DAVIS, JOHN McMILLEN, RANDOLPH QUARLES, HENRY CLIFT and (blank) be a jury of view to lay off a private way through the land of OWEN HIGGINS, principally for the benefit of the persons living above him on the branch and the Commissioners make report to next court.

TUESDAY JULY 4, 1826

Justices present were WILLIAM EDMISTON, SAMUEL GARLAND and JOHN WISEMAN, Esquires.

WILLIAM HUSBANDS, High Sheriff, made return into court of the States Writ of Venire facias to him directed executed on DAVID BECK, THOMAS H. HAYS, WILLIAM WILLIAMS, NELSON YARBOROUGH, MOSES BUCHANAN, EDMOND TAYLOR, WILLIAM CANNON, DAVID FRANKLIN, CARTER ROBERTSON, JAMES McCOLLUM, JAMES CUNNINGHAM, PAYTON WELLS, ANDREW W. WALKER, VINCENT LUTTRELL, WILLIAM D. BLAKE, WILLIAM BARROW, KINCHEN HOLCOMB, JASPER SMITH, THOMAS W. HAYS, JAMES D. ALFORD, and PETER VAUGHN, out of whom were selected as the statute in such cases provides the following persons a Grand Inquest and Jury that is to say JASPER SMITH, foreman, THOMAS H. HAYS, MOSES BUCHANAN, WILLIAM WILLIAMS, JAMES CUNNINGHAM, PETER VAUGHN, KINCHEN HOLCOMB, JAMES BROWN, EDMOND TAYLOR, JAMES McCOLLUM, NELSON YARBOROUGH, WILLIAM BARROW, and JAMES D. ALFORD impaneled and sworn.

Ordered that CARTER ROBERSON, WILLIAM D. BLAKE and VINCENT LUTTRELL be released from serving on the jury at this time.

WILLIAM CROCKET produced eight wolf scalps under four months old and proved he killed them in the bounds of Lincoln County.

The due execution of an obligation from JAMES W. and ISAAC SITLER to DAVID THWING for 140 acres of land, proven by JAMES BRIGHT and ordered to be certified.

POWER & HAUGHTON vs DANIEL COFFMAN - This cause was continued on affidavit of the defendant and former order is renewed and ordered that the deposition of THOMAS FLETCHER be taken and that defendant pay the costs of this term.

THOMAS ROUNDTREE vs ISAAC HOLMAN - This day came the parties by their attorneys and a jury of men, to wit, DAVID BECK, THOMAS H. HAYS, WILLIAM WILLIAMS, NELSON YARBOROUGH, MOSES BUCHANAN, EDMOND TAYLOR, WILLIAM CANNON, DAVID FRANKLIN, CARTER ROBERTSON, JAMES McCOLLUM, JAMES CUNNINGHAM, ...(incomplete)...

THOMAS ROUNDTREE vs ISAAC HOLMAN - This day came the parties by their attorneys and a jury of men, to wit, RICHMOND P. DOBBINS, DANIEL T. WILLIAMS, ANDREW W. WALKER, DAVID BECK, WILLIAM CANNON, VIZY HUSBANDS, DAVID RORAX, BENJAMIN GIBSON, BARKLEY WOOLAM, GRASHAM LEE, DAVID BARKLY, and DANIEL R. MOORE being elected and sworn and says that the defendant hath not paid the debt but owes a balance of $95.00 and damages of $24.00 besides his costs. Plaintiff to recover his costs.

SAMUEL WILSON vs EASON COALTER - (same as above) and said that the defendant hath not kept his covenant to the plaintiff and they assess damages of $103.00. Plaintiff to recover his costs.

ROBERT DICKSON vs E.C. McLAUGHLIN - The plaintiff by his attorney says he wishes no further to prosecute his suit and the defendant assumes the payment of all costs. Plaintiff to recover his costs.

R. & WILLIAM DICKSON vs JOHNSTON TURLEY - (same as above jurors) and said that the defendant has not paid the debt of $103.26 and damages of $7.50. Plaintiff to recover his costs.

ROBERT DICKSON vs WILLIAM CASHION - The plaintiff appeared in court and

229

says he intends no further to prosecute his suit and the defendant assumes the payment of all costs. Plaintiff to recover his costs.

AUGUSTINE KERNEY vs ENOCH RUST - This day came the parties by their attorneys and a jury of men, to wit, RICHMOND P. DOBBINS, DANIEL T. WILLIAMS, ANDREW W. WALKER, DAVID BECK, WILLIAM CANNON, VIZY HUSBANDS, DAVID RORAX, BENJAMIN GIBSON, BERKLY WOOLAM, GASHAM LEE, DAVID BARKLEY and DANIEL R. MOORE being elected and worn and said that the defendant has not kept his covenant and they assess damages of $107.16. Plaintiff to recover his costs.

JOSEPH GREER vs WILLIAM R. and W.W. WOODROFF - (same as above) and said that the defendant has not paid the debt of $100.00 and damages of $9.00. Plaintiff to recover his costs.

THOMAS THOMPSON vs JOHN MEEKS - (same as above) and said that the defendant has not kept his covenant and damages of $108.00. Plaintiff to recover his costs.

BENJAMIN WALKER vs JOB G. SELPH - The plaintiff by his attorney said he wishes no further to prosecute his suit and assumes the payment of all costs. Defendant to recover his costs.

E.N. ROBERTSON vs H.M. BLAKE & G. BLAKEMORE - This day came the parties by their attorneys and a jury of men, to wit, RICHMOND P. DOBBINS, DANIEL T. WILLIAMS, ANDREW W. WALKER, DAVID BECK, WILLIAM CANNON, VIZY HUSBANDS, DAVID RORAX, BENJAMIN GIBSON, BARKLY WOOLAM, GERSHAM LEE, DAVID BARKLY and DAVID R. MOORE being elected and sworn and said that the defendant has not kept the covenant and they assess damages of $380.25. Plaintiff to recover his costs.

WILLIAM McCLELLAND vs RANDOLPH QUARLES - (same as above) and said that the defendant has not paid the balance of the debt of $345.25 and damages of $10.25. Plaintiff to recover his costs.

A.G. MORGAN vs JOHN COX - This cause is continued by consent.

JOHN P. COLE vs JAMES D. ALFORD - (same as above and jurors) and said that the defendant has not paid the debt of $89.00 and assess damages of $3.07. Plaintiff to recover his costs.

JOHN MAZE vs ROBERT S. HULME - (same as above) and said that the defendant has not paid the debt of $123.12½ and assess damages of $3.69. Plaintiff to recover his costs.

JOHN McCALESTER vs GEORGE McWHERTER - (same as above) and said that the defendant has not paid the debt of $127.69 and assess damages of $58.00. Plaintiff to recover his costs.

JACOB WAGGONER vs WILLIAM MOORE and ISAAC HOLMAN, admr of S.C. McLEMORE, deceased - (same as above) and said that they find in favor of the plaintiff and assess his damages of $127.21. Plaintiff to recover his costs.

HYNES, NOLES & WOOD vs JOB G. SELPH - The plaintiff by his attorney desires the court to dismiss their suit and assumes the payment of one half the costs and the defendant assumes the other half of the costs. Suit dismissed.

ANDREW HYNES vs JOB G. SELPH - The plaintiff by his attorney says he wishes no further to prosecute his suit but wishes the same to be dismissed and assumes the payment of one half the costs and the defendant assumes the payment of the other half of payment. Suit dismissed.

ROBERT DICKSON vs JOB G. SELPH - (same as above).

SAMUEL B. MARSHALL vs JOB G. SELPH - (same as above).

SAMUEL E. GILLILAND vs JAMES D. ESTES - The plaintiff says he wishes no further to prosecute his suit and desires the suit to be dismissed. Suit to be dismissed and plaintiff pay the costs.

JAMES D. ALFORD vs JAMES D. ESTES - (same as above).

EBENEZER McEWEN, a Justice of the Peace, appeared in court and resigns the appointment of Justice of the Peace as aforesaid.

JACOB WAGGONER vs WILLIAM MOORE & ISAAC HOLMAN, admrs of S.C. McLEMORE, deceased - This day came the parties by their attorneys and a jury of men, to wit, RICHMOND P. DOBBINS, D.T. WILLIAMS, A.W. WALKER, DAVID BECK, WILLIAM KENNON, VIZY HUSBANDS, DAVID RORAX, BENJAMIN GIBSON, B. WOOLAM, G. LEE, DAVID BARCLAY, and DANIEL R. MOORE being elected and sworn and said that they find in favor of the plaintiff and assess damages of $177.21. Plaintiff to recover his costs.

WEDNESDAY JULY 5, 1826

Justices present were WILLIAM EDMISTON, JOHN WISEMAN and SAMUEL BUCHANAN, Esquires.

JACOB WAGGONER & JOHN WAGGONER vs WILLIAM MOORE & I. HOLMAN, admrs of S.C. McLEMORE, deceased - This day came the parties by their attorneys and a jury of men, to wit, DAVID FRANKLIN, R.P. DOBBINS, A.W. WALKER, DAVID BECK, WILLIAM KENNON, JOS. COMONS, JOHN LANE, ANTHONY WELLS, OWEN W. HIGGINS, JOS. McMILLEN, and WILLIAM B. BENGE being elected and sworn and said that they find in favor of the defendants. Defendants to recover their costs.

THURSDAY JULY 6, 1826

Justices present were WILLIAM EDMISTON, ALEXANDER McLIN and JAMES SMITH.

JAMES RALSTON, Esquire, appeared in court and resigns his appointment as a Justice of the Peace.

JAMES D. ESTES vs ALLEN YOWELL - The order of last term as to the taking depositions in this cause is renewed at this term by order of court on application of the defendant.

JAMES GARRET vs JESSE MOORE - The defendant says he cannot deny but that he owes to the plaintiff the debt of $100.00 and damages of $3.10. Plaintiff to recover his costs.

Ordered that a fine of $4.00 be entered against THOMAS W. HAYES for neglecting to attend this term as a joror, subject to be set aside at next term by said HAYES applying and showing good cause for so doing.

A.G. MORGAN vs JOHN COXE - On motion by the court that each party be at liberty to take depositions of this cause by giving the party twenty days notice of time and place of taking the same.

The due execution of a Transfer of a Plat and Certificate from JOHN GREER to WILLIAM CROCKET for 10 acres of land and ordered to be certified.

Ordered that the former order of this court appointed Commissioners to settle with JOEL B. SANDERS, admr of ESTHER KENNEDY, deceased, be received and to extend to the next term of court.

FRIDAY JULY 7, 1826

Justices present were WILLIAM EDMISTON, JOHN ENOCKS and SAMUEL BUCHANAN, Esquires.

The due execution of two Plats and Certificates from WILLIAM HUSBANDS, Sheriff, to B. BOYLES, one for 50 and the other for 28 3/4 acres of land and ordered to be certified.

JAMES D. ESTES vs ALLEN YOWELL - On motion of the defendant this cause is continued to next term of court and it is ordered that the defendant pay the costs of this term.

State of Tennessee vs JOHN SMITH - Malicious Mischief - The defendant being called but came not but made default. JOHN SMITH's security JOHN T. SMITH be forfeited. State of Tennessee to recover against them accordingly and JOHN T. SMITH security was called to come and bring JOHN SMITH but came not and made default.

231

The State vs HENRY SAUNDERS - Bastardy - The defendant came and made bond and security to keep the child becoming chargeable to the county and gave bond and security to pay for its support $40.00 for first year, $30.00 for the second and $20.00 for the third and GEORGE W. HUNT appeared in court and confessed jointly with the defendant for his costs.

The State vs DAVID HOWELL - Peace Warrant - The defendant and prosecutor being called but came not. It is ordered that the defendant be no further bound and that he pay the costs of this prosecution.

The State vs CLISBY RIGGS - Peace Warrant - Both Attorney General and the defendant came into court and it is considered that the defendant be further bound to keep the peace towards JOHN GOLIHER for the next six months and find security whereupon came JESSE RIGGS and entered security of $1000.00 and costs.

The State vs JAMES HARDEN - The defendant being charged pleads guilty and pay costs of this indictment and further he be imprisoned until the 9th instant at 5 o'clock and that he remain in custody until he gives security for fine &c. Whereupon on motion ELIAS PHILIIPS entered security of the above fine and costs.

BARTLET WOOLEM vs JOHN S. PRICE - On motion ordered by the court that the plaintiff give security for the costs of this suit before the trial.

The State vs JOHN T. SMITH - The defendant acknowledged himself indebted to the State of Tennessee to be levied upon his goods and chattels &c to be void in condition that he made his personal appearance in October next to answer the State on a charge of Malicious Mischief.

The State vs THOMAS T. SMITH - JESSE OVERTON, JAMES W. COOK, JOHN FULGUM and SALLY FULGUM, his wife, acknowledged themselves indebted to the State of Tennessee, that is the said JESSE OVERTON sum of two $500.00 and the others each in sum of $250.00, to be void on condition that they make their appearance here in October next.

The State vs DAVID BECK - SOLOMON REESE acknowledged himself to owe to the State of Tennessee for $250.00, to be void on condition that he appear here in October next. And JOHN F. HUSBANDS, GABRIEL SEAHORN, JAMES WARFORD and WILY MINGO and WILLIAM CUNNINGHAM each acknowledged themselves to owe to the State $125.00 to be void on condition that they appear in October next.

The State vs TODD ADAMS - JOHN W. CRUNK acknowledged himself indebted to the State of Tennessee for $250.00, to be void on condition that he appear here in October next, also ALEXANDER YOUNG, WILLIAM DYER and WRIGHT BRYANT each is indebted to the State for $125.00, to be void on condition they appear here in October next.

JAMES COWLEY vs WRIGHT McLEMORE - On motion of HANNAH COOLEY and JOHN WATSON and it appearing to the court that JAMES COOLEY died intestate and that administration on his estate was granted to HANNAH and JOHN.

SATURDAY JULY 8, 1826

Justices present were WILLIAM EDMISTON, ALEXANDER McLINN and WILLIAM DYE, Esquires.

JAMES COOPER vs ALEXANDER MILLER - The plaintiff by his attorney says he wishes no further to prosecute his suit and wishes to dismiss this suit. Suit dismissed and the plaintiff pay the costs of the same.

MATHEW WATSON vs JOB G. SELPH - (same as above).

HINCHMAN & STARR vs JOB G. SELPH - (same as above).

SAMUEL M. CLAY who was summoned to appear here as a witness for WILLIAM WYATT in the case of the said WYATT against WILLIAM TOWNZEN was called but came not. Whereupon on motion of WILLIAM WYATT by his attorney, it is ordered that he be fined $125.00 to the use of said WILLIAM WYATT unless sufficient cause for his non-attendance.

MATHEW WATSON vs JOB G. SELPH - The following persons returned, summoned by the Sheriff, as garnishees, to wit, STEPHEN C. CHITWOOD, ROBERT S. HULME,

HOLMES H. HOPKINS, PETER ROSS, ALEXANDER McLINN, SOLOMON GULLETT, JOHN DAVIS, JOHN BOONE, SPENCER A. PUGH, JOHN P. McCONNELL, JOHN MEEK, EDWARD McBRIDE, JOHN MARR, THOMAS H. WILLIAMS, JAMES SMITH, WILLIAM SANSOM, REESE HOWELL, A.J. BLAKEMORE, ZACHARIAH ARNOLD, JAMES D. ALFORD, E.M. RINGO, JOHN GREER, ELLIOTT HICKMAN, THOMAS H. BELL, R.P. DOBBINS, ROBERT DICKSON, H. ROBERTSON, ISAAC HOLMAN, THOMAS SHAW, D. McMILLEN, WILLIAM NORRIS, DAVID BARCLAY, JESSE B. CLEMENTS, JOEL PINSON, and THOMAS GAITHER whereupon came the plaintiff by his attorney and says he does not wish said garnishees to be examined in this cause but wishes them to be discharged from further attendance &c. They are discharged and the plaintiff pay the costs.

The due execution of a Power of Attorney from JOHN KENT and LYDIA KENT, his wife, to (blank), acknowledged and ordered to be certified.

The due execution of a Power of Attorney from PETER KENT to (blank) and ordered to be certified.

HENCHMAN & STARR vs JOB G. SELPH - The following persons were returned by the Sheriff summoned as garnishees in this cause, to wit, ALEXANDER McLINN, GEORGE STONEBRAKER, THOMAS SHAW, HENRY ROBERTSON, D. THOMPSON, STEPHEN C. CHITWOOD, JAMES SMITH, WILLIAM SANSOM, A.J. BLAKEMORE, REESE HOWELL, ZACHARIAH ARNOLD, JOHN ASHLY, ROBERT DICKSON, R.P. DOBBINS, E.M. RINGO, DAVIDSON McMILLEN, EDWARD McBRIDE, ROBERT S. HULME, MICAJAH McELROY, JR., H.H. HOPKINS, FELIX CRUNK, NIMROD BAILY, GEORGE MOYERS, SOLOMON GULLETT, ISAAC HOLMAN, THOMAS R, GARNER, and JACOB MOYERS whereupon came the plaintiffs by their attorney and said they wish those here attending and summoned as garnishees in this cause to be discharged without examination. Court dismissed cause and plaintiff pay all costs.

MONDAY JULY 10, 1826

Justices present were WILLIAM EDMISTON, WILLIAM MILLNER and JOHN WISEMAN.

The due execution of a Deed of Bargain and Sale from JOHN COFFEE to JOHN MOTLOW for 130 acres of land, proven by JAMES BRIGHT and ANDREW A. KINCANNON and ordered to be certified.

The due execution of a Deed of Bargain and Sale from JOHN COFFEE to JOHN GUTTERY for 150 acres of land, proven by JAMES BRIGHT and ANDREW A, KINCANNON and ordered to be certified.

The due execution of a Deed of Bargain and Sale from JOHN COFFEE to JAMES CLARK for 334 acres, proven by JAMES BRIGHT and ANDREW A. KINCANNON and ordered to be certified.

The due execution of a Deed of Bargain and Sale from JOHN COFFEE to ZADOC MOTLOW for 204 acres of land, proven by JAMES BRIGHT and ANDREW A. KINCANNON and ordered to be certified.

The due execution of a Plat and Certificate from WILLIAM EDMISTON to JAMES HIGGINS and ordered to be certified.

SAMUEL HAMPTON vs A.J. BLAKEBURN and wife, admrs &c - This day came the parties by their attorneys and a jury of men, to wit, RICHMOND P. DOBBINS, A.W. WALKER, DAVID BECK, WILLIAM KENNON, WASH. SMITH, HENRY WARREN, HIRAM E. DAVIS, WILLIAM B. BENGE, WILLIAM McELROY, JORDAN SOLOMON, and RICHARD HALL being elected and sworn and said that they found in favor of the defendants. And on motion of the plaintiff by his attorney that this suit be set aside and the above to stand for trial on its merit at next term of court. And on motion, it is ordered that each party have liberty to take depositions by giving the adverse party twenty days notice of the time and place of taking the same, if taken out of this State and if in this State ten days notice.

THOMAS W, HAYES appeared in court and on motion, ordered by the court that the judgment entered at this term against him for a fine of $4.00 be set aside and he pay the costs.

State of Tennessee vs TODD ADAMS - Riot - TODD ADAMS and JAMES SMITH each appeared in court and acknowledged themselves to be indebted to the State for

$250.00 to be levied upon their goods and chattels &c to be void on condition that the said TODD ADAMS appear here in October next to answer the charge of having committed a riot.

State of Tennessee vs TODD ADAMS - (same as above) on charge of committing an assault and battery.

WARNER & FISHER, executors &c vs NIMROD BAILEY - This cause is continued until January term and leave is granted each party to take depositions by giving ten days notice in State and thirty days if taken out of State.

JAMES SMITH appeared in court and it appearing to the court that THOMAS LUSK, late of this county, departed this life without making his Last Will and Testament in writing. JAMES SMITH was appointed admr of the estate who took bond and gave security.

DAVID BARCLAY vs JOHN BROYLES - The defendant came into court and moved for liberty to take the benefit of the several Acts of the General Assembly made for the relief of insolvent debtors as to the imprisonment of their persons, whereupon he was permitted to take the oath for insolvent debtors and was discharged. Court orders that the plaintiff pay the costs of this cause.

JAMES SMITH, the admr of the estate returns an inventory of said estate and ordered to be recorded.

GEORGE STONEBRAKER being called as a talisman juror and called by the Sheriff, failed to appear and it is ordered that he be fined $2.00.

JOHN A. ALLEN and HENRY WINFREY appeared in court and it appearing to the court that THOMAS SLAUGHTER, late of this county, died intestate. ALLEN & WINFREY were appointed to administer upon the estate of SLAUGHTER and they gave bond and security.

JOHN LANE vs ISAAC CONGER - This day came the parties by their attorneys and a jury of men, to wit, DANIEL T. WILLIAMS, JOHN WATSON, THOMAS ORRICK, OWEN W. HIGGINS, JOB G. SELPH, EDWARD MOSS, M. McELROY, SR., WILLIAM LEDFORD, HENRY CLIFT, LEWIS HOPPER, JOHN DALTON, and JOHN SIMPSON being elected and sworn and said found in favor of the plaintiff and assess damages to $10.00. Plaintiff to recover his costs. Defendant prays for an appeal and is granted same.

The State vs SAMUEL PURTLE - The defendant being called came not but made default. Defendant is to pay the costs of this prosecution.

The State vs WILLIAM B. BENGE - This cause is continued on the affidavit of RICHARD HALL to next term of this court.

TUESDAY JULY 11, 1826

Justices present were WILLIAM MILLNER, WILLIAM EDMISTON and JOHN PORTER.

The due execution of an Indenture of Bargain and Sale from ROBERT S. HOLME to SAMUEL S. HOLDING for part of a lot and ordered to be certified.

AARON WELLS vs JOHN PORTER - This day came the parties by their attorneys and a jury of men, to wit, DAVID FRANKLIN, DANIEL T. WILLIAMS, ANDREW W. WALKER, JAMES HAGUE, RICHARD HALL, PETER KENT, JOHN SMITH, OWEN W. HIGGINS, DAVID BECK, JOSEPH COMMONS, MAXFIELD McCANT, and JOHN SIMPSON being elected and sworn and said that the defendant is guilty of trespass. They assess damages to $5.00. Plaintiff to recover his costs.

JOHN WISEMAN vs WILLIAM C. KENNEDY - (same as above) and says that the defendant has not kept his covenant with the plaintiff and assess damages of $32.40 and pay costs. PLaintiff to recover his costs.

The due execution of an Indenture of Bargain and Sale from FRANCIS PORTERFIELD, Sheriff, to WILLIAM SOLOMON for two town lots and ordered to be certified.

JAMES B. CABINESS vs JOHN A. ALLEN - This day came the parties by their

234

attorneys and a jury of men, to wit, DAVID FRANKLIN, RICHMOND P. DOBBINS, DANIEL T. WILLIAMS, DAVID BECK, ANDREW W. WALKER, WILLIAM CANNON, JAMES HAGUE, RICHARD HALL, KELEN FELPS, PETER KENT, and JOHN SMITH and OWEN W. HIGGINS being elected and sworn and said that the defendant has not paid the debt of $82.00 and damages of $4.56. Plaintiff to recover his costs.

JAMES B. CABINESS vs JOHN A. ALLEN - (same as above) and said the defendant has not paid the debt of $62.00 and damages. PLaintiff to recover his costs.

HANNAH COWLEY and JOHN WATSON, admrs of JAMES COWLEY vs WRIGHT McLEMORE - (same as above) and said that the plaintiff has sustained damages to amount of $96.38 and costs. Plaintiff's to recover his costs.

JASON THOMPSON vs WELLS & DOBBINS - Ordered that each party be at liberty to take depositions by giving ten days notice in the State and twenty days out of State of the time and place of taking the same.

RUBEN WASHBURN vs JOHN SIMPSON - (same as above with same jurors) and says that the defendant did assume and take upon himself in manner and form as declaring hath alleged and assess damages of $5.00. Plaintiff to recover his costs.

LESLIE GILLIAM vs WILLIAM STEPHENS, admr &c - The order of last term of court authorizing the parties to take depositions is renewed.

E.M. RINGO and wife vs SAMUEL TODD - The court set aside this suit and the cause to stand for trial next term of court.

WEDNESDAY JULY 12, 1826

Justices present were JOHN PORTER, WILLIAM MILLNER and WILLIAM EDMISTON, Esquires.

DAVID BARKLEY vs PETER ROSS - The plaintiff says he wishes no further to prosecute his suit and assumes the payment of all costs. Defendant to recover his costs.

The due execution of an Indenture of Bargain and Sale from BRICE M. GARNER to ROBERT SHANNON for 5 acres of land and ordered to be certified.

WILLIAM B. MARTIN vs JOHN C. McADY - This day came the parties by their attorneys and a jury of men, to wit, DAVID FRANKLIN, RICHMOND P. DOBBINS, DANIEL T. WILLIAMS, ANDREW W. WALKER, DAVID BECK, WILLIAM CANNON, JAMES W. BURNS, HOSA GREGORY, JOURDON SOLOMON, WILLIAM CUNNINGHAM, WILLIAM CUNNINGHAM, and DAVID BARKLEY being elected and sworn and said that the defendant has not paid the plaintiff and assess damages of $13.67½. Plaintiff to recover his costs.

HOSIA GREGORY vs THOMAS H. BELL - (same as above) and says they find in favor of the plaintiff of $30.00.

On motion ordered by the court that FRANCIS PORTERFIELD and A.A. KINCANNON be appointed to settle with ROBERT DICKSON, admr of PATRICK O'CALAGHAN, deceased, and make return to next court.

On motion ordered that FRANCIS PORTERFIELD and ALEXANDER McLINN be appointed to settle with ROBERT DICKSON, admr of JAMES H. NELSON, deceased, and make return to next court.

On motion of JACOB STONEBRAKER and for reasons satisfactory, he is released from the fine imposed on him for not attendance as a talesman juror at this time and he pay the costs.

WILLIAM B. MARTIN vs JOHN C. McADA - It is ordered that JOHN S. McADA be released as security for the appeal in this case and ALFRED SMITH by permission of the court, enters as the security of the defendant for his appeal.

HENRY M. RUTLEDGE vs JOSEPH HINKLE - (same as above) and says that the defendant has not paid the debt of $249.00 and assess damages of $12.00. Plaintiff to recover his costs.

HENRY M. RUTLEDGE vs JOSEPH HINKLE - (same as above) and says that the defendant has not paid the debt of $249.00 and assess damages of $5.50. Plaintiff to recover his costs.

Fayetteville, Tennessee Bank vs GEORGE SHULL - The plaintiff by his attorney came into court and the defendant being called but came not but made default. The plaintiff to recover the debt of $9.32½ and costs of case.

MOSES HALL vs CONSTANT SCALES and others - The plaintiff came by his attorney and the defendant being called but came not but made default. Plaintiff to recover against the defendant and A.A. KINCANNON, F. PORTERFIELD, C. BOYLES, WILLIAM HUSBANDS, WILLIAM FITCH, H.T. JOHNSTON, and D. McMILLEN his security for $$122.64 along with $9.14 the costs.

On motion ordered that the parties, plaintiff and defendant in the suit of WILLIAM WYATT vs WILLIAM TOWNZEN be at liberty to take depositions in this cause by giving the other ten days notice.

The due execution of an Indenture of Bargain and Sale from ELLIOTT HICKMAN to BENJAMIN BOONE for 230 acres of land and ordered to be certified.

ANDREW HUNT vs JAMES CLIFT - This day came the parties by their attorneys and a jury of men, to wit, DAVID FRANKLIN, R.P. DOBBINS, D.T. WILLIAMS, A.W. WALKER, DAVID BECK, WILLIAM KENNON, JAMES W. BURNS, HOSEA GREGORY, M. McELROY, JORDAN SOLOMON, WILLIAM CUNNINGHAM, WILLIAM CUNNINGHAM, DAVID BARCLAY and JAMES D. ALFORD being elected and sworn and said that they find in favor of the defendant. Defendant recover his costs.

DANIEL WRIGHT vs JOHN INMAN - This day came the parties by their attorneys and upon argument by the attorneys and it fully understood by the court that this cause be dismissed and the plaintiff recover his costs of $4.25 and cost of this cause.

JORDAN SOLOMON vs REDDICK PRICE - The defendant being ordered to give other and better security before the trial of this cause or the same would be dismissed and the defendant having failed to give other or better security as was ordered, the same is now dismissed. Plaintiff to recover and TIMOTHY MERSHON and CHARLES A. GILLIAM his security for $10.22 debt and 50 cents costs.

WILLIAM McELROY vs ROBERT DICKSON - The plaintiff by his attorney says he wishes no further to prosecute his suit but wishes the same to be dismissed and assumes the payment of all costs. Suit to be dismissed and the defendant recover his costs.

BARTLET WOOLLAM vs JOHN S. PRICE - The plaintiff was ordered to give security before the trial and the same being now ready for trial and no security given. It is ordered to be dismissed and the plaintiff pay the costs.

HINCHEY PETWAY vs JOHN BOYLES - The plaintiff by his attorney and it appearing to the court that the defendant departed this life intestate and that administration on his estate was granted to BARNABAS BOYLES. It is ordered that this suit stand revived against the administrator.

ANDREW HAMILTON vs JAMES D. ESTES - The plaintiff by his attorney says he wishes no further to prosecute his suit but wishes the same to be dismissed. Suit to be dismissed and the defendant recover his costs.

E. & J. FRANKLIN, admr vs JAMES SMITH, MARGARET STILES and AARON STILES - The plaintiff came into court by his attorney and the defendants being called came not but made default. Plaintiff to recover the costs to be set at next court.

WILLIAM M. QUESENBURY vs JOHN BOONE - (same as above). Plaintiff to recover his costs of $123.50 and damages.

WILLIAM M. QUESENBURY vs JOHNSTON TURLEY - This day came the plaintiff by his attorney and the defendant being called came not but made default. Plaintiff to recover his costs of $60.00 and $3.00 damages.

JOHN BAILEY vs JAMES SMITH and SAMUEL ROSEBOROUGH - (same as above). Plaintiff to recover his costs which is to be set at next court.

The due execution of an Indenture of Bargain and Sale from REPS O. CHILDRESS and SALLY his wife to THOMAS R. MOORE for 605 acres of land in Davidson County, was

236

acknowledged and SALLY was examined apart from her husband and ordered to be certified.

The due execution of a Bill of Sale from FLOYD BOSTICK to WILLIAM BOSTICK for one sorrel mare was acknowledged and ordered to be certified.

The due execution of a Deed of Conveyance for 113 3/4 acres from GEORGE M. MARTIN, MARGARET M. MARTIN, JOEL B. SANDERS, MERIAM L. SANDERS, WILLIAM E. KENNEDY and MARY M. KERCHEVAL to JAMES HAGUE was as to the execution thereof by WILLIAM E. KENNEDY, acknowledged, and as to the execution of the same by MARY M. KERCHEVAL wife of THOMAS KERCHEVAL. She was examined by the court apart from her husband and the same was ordered to be certified.

The Last Will and Testament of ADLAI SHARP was presented in court for probate whereupon came JOHN DAVIS and ELIJAH DAVIS as witnesses and proved the execution and publishing thereof by said testator and the same ordered to be certified. Whereupon came WILLIAM EDMISTON and ALICE SHARP, executor and executrix of said will and took upon them the execution thereof and gave bond and security.

The due execution of an Indenture of Bargain and Sale from MALCOM GILCHRIST and ISAAC GATTIS for 54 acres of land, proven by WILLIAM GILCHRIST, the attorney for MALCOM GILCHRIST and ordered to be certified.

The due execution of a Deed of Conveyance from EWELL SHIPP to THOMAS D. CLARK for 160 acres of land and ordered to be certified.

The due execution of a Deed of Conveyance from BRICE M. GARNER and ROBERT DICKSON to EDMOND RUSSELL for part of a town lot in Fayetteville and ordered to be certified.

The due execution of a Deed of Conveyance from DANIEL WAGGONER to MOSES BUCHANAN for 100 acres of land and ordered to be certified.

The due execution of a Deed of Conveyance from ALEXANDER McCORKLE to RICHARD SMITH for 208 acres of land and ordered to be certified.

The due execution of a Deed of Conveyance from THOMAS ROUNTREE to RICHARD FERRELL for one town lot in Lynchburg and ordered to be certified.

The due execution of a Deed of Conveyance from JOHN OLIVER to JOHN LANDESS for 50 acres of land and ordered to be certified.

"I, BRICE M. GARNER, Clerk of the Court of Pleas and Quarter Sessions for Lincoln County, do certify that the aggregate number of free male inhabitants within the bounds of the said county on the first day of January last, was two thousand eight hundred and twenty five according to the returns made by the different Justices of the Peace who took the list thereof and which has been by them returned to my office.
Signed this 19th day August A.D. 1826
BRICE M. GARNER."

The following are persons who have failed to give in their taxable property but who may give in by paying the Clerk's fee:
WILSON DAVIS, 110 acres
JAMES BROWN, 393 acres of land and two black poles.
JOSEPH KERR, 709 acres
KERR & GRAHAM, 250 acres
FRANCIS PATTON, 246 acres of land, 1 black pole and 1 white pole
G.W. CAMPBELL, 3220 acres in different tracts
SAMUEL PAXTON, 1381¼ acres of land
THOMAS GRAY and heirs, 600 acres of land

OCTOBER 2, 1826

The court met on first Monday in October 1826, those present were JOHN ENOCKS, THOMAS H. SHAW, WILLIAM DYE, HUGH PARKESON, WILLIAM ANDERSON, JOHN PINKERTON, B. BOYLES, SAMUEL GARLAND, ZACHARIAH HARRISON, SHEPHERD SHELTON, JAMES SMITH, ALLEN ELSTON, THOMAS CLARK, JOHN PORTER, CORNELIUS DARNELL, JOHN MARR, HUGH M. BLAKE, PHILIP KOONCE, and JACOB WAGGONER, Justices of the Court of Pleas and Quarter Sessions for County of Lincoln in the State of Tennessee.

WILLIAM TALL, Esquire, was permitted to take the oaths prescribed by law for practicing attorneys and was qualified as an attorney.

Ordered that TRAVIS ASHBY be released entirely from the payment of the tax upon a stud horse by him given in for tax for this year.

WILLIAM SAUNDERS produced a wolf scalp in court and proved that it was over six months old and killed by him in this county.

Ordered that the order of the last term of court be received appointing WILLIAM B. BENGE and HUGH M. BLAKE to settle with JOHN S. PRICE, admr of JOHN S. HUGHS, deceased, and make report to next court.

The Last Will and testament of JOHN BLAKE, deceased, was produced in court for probate, whereupon came JOHN C. GARNER, a witness, proved the due execution of the testator. And ELIZABETH BLAKE the executrix named in the will came forward in court and refused to take upon herself the execution thereof. When WILLIAM D. BLAKE, the executor, appeared in court and took upon himself the execution thereof. They were qualified. Inventory of the property of said JOHN BLAKE, deceased, and ordered to be recorded.

Ordered that JOSEPH McMILLEN, JAMES BLAKEMORE and ROBERT WILSON be appointed to lay off out of the property of JOHN BLAKE, deceased, one years support for his widow and children and make return to next court.

SHEPHERD SHELTON, Esquire, a Justice of the Peace, offers his resignation of that appointment which is accepted.

EDWARD ISHAM is allowed $1.00 per week until the next January Term of Court for keeping and supporting JACOB NELMS, a pauper of this county.

Ordered that MICAJAH STONE be overseer of the public road from the mouth of JAMES HIGGIN's lane to the end of AMOS SMALL's lane in the room of JACOB CASTLEMAN.

The State vs DEMSEY BROWN - WILLIAM ROWELL who was the defendant's appearance bail, now surrenders him in court in discharge of himself, and thereupon came JAMES R. ONEAL and entered as the appearance bail of the said defendant for the sum of $125.00.

An Inventory of the estate of THOMPSON A. GREEN, deceased, was returned to court by JOHN ENOCHS the executor and also an account of the sale of the property belonging to the estate which was ordered to be recorded.

Ordered that the last term of court appointed SAMUEL BUCHANAN, WILLIAM EDMISTON and FRANCIS PORTERFIELD Commissioners to settle with ISAAC CONGER executor of the estate of JAMES PYBUS be renewed and they made said settlement and report to the next court.

Ordered that RHODY WEST be overseer of part of the public road from Lumbric's Mill to Fayetteville beginning at RICHARD WYATT's east line and ending at HENRY KYMES east line.

Ordered that JOHN K. TAYLOR be a overseer of the public road from beginning at A. LUMBRIC's Mill and from there to the east boundary line of RICHARD WYATT's land in the room of WILEY WINGO.

Ordered that CHRISTOPHER E. LOVE be overseer of the public road from SAMUEL DOBBINS to Mortons Creek in the place of CHARLES WAKEFIELD.

Ordered that BARNABAS L. McELROY be overseer of the public road from Hannah's Ford on Elk River to the top of the hill below WILLIAM DYE's in the room of JACOB ALBRIGHT.

Ordered that JOSEPH McCRACKEN, Esquire, lay off and designate the hands to work on the road under JOHN TRIMBLE, AARON WELLS, THOMAS BELL, JAMES THORP and SAMUEL LEA and make return to next court.

Ordered that CONSTANT SCALES be overseer of the public road leading to Nashville from old Mr. BUCHES to D.P. MONROE.

Ordered that the Trustee pay to JAMES BRIGHT, Clerk of the Circuit Court of $22.45 the fees due to him as Clerk in sundry state cases.

Ordered that the road as heretofore laid out and cut from CAPTAIN CARRIGER's to Linchburgh be reviewed and established, and that SAMUEL HART be overseer thereof and that THOMAS H. SHAW lay off the hands to work under him on said road.

Ordered that a public road heretofore ordered to be opened from BASINGER's Mill to the head of Coffee Creek be annuled and made void.

A settlement of HUGH PARKISON, WILLIAM SMITH and MICHAEL ROBERTSON, Commissioners appointed to settle with the executors of LUCINDA STREET, deceased, was returned into open court and ordered to be recorded and that executors be allowed 5% on the amount of said estate as pay and compensation for their trouble in settling the same.

Ordered that RICHMOND PACE, ZENAS READ, ISAAC ENOCHS, JOHN FULGHAM, JOHN DOWTHIT, NATHAN CURRY, and LABAN CURRY be a jury to view and lay off a road so as to alter the present road near to AMBROSE McCULLOUGH's so as not to injure his farm and make return to next court.

Ordered that FREDERICK WAGGONER, CHARLES WESTERMAN, N. CARRIGER, RUBEN LOGAN, JONATHAN EATON and JOHN MASH and JESSE ELLIS be a jury to view and alter the public road leading through the lands of BRITTAIN PHELPS above CAPTAIN CARRIGER's if they should think proper and make return to next court.

It appearing to the court that CHRISTOPHER SHOFNER, late of this county, had departed this life without making his Last Will and testament in writing, whereupon came ELIZABETH SHOFNER, the widow of the deceased, and WEBB K. JENNINGS and took upon themselves to the administration of the estate of the deceased, who entered into bond and security.

Ordered that the Trustee of the county pay to the Clerk of this court $38.50 for blank books &c furnished for the use of his office. Received November 1826.

An amount of the sale of the property belonging to the estate of JEREMIAH DENNIS, deceased, was returned to court by JAMES DENNIS, the executor, and ordered to be recorded.

ABNER STEED and G.W.C. EDMISTON is appointed Commissioners to settle with the admr of THOMAS CUMMINS, deceased, and report to this court.

Ordered that the Trustee of this County pay to JOHN WARDEN $2.25, his fee in the case of the State vs THOMAS S. MILAM.

Ordered that JOHN DALTON be permitted to keep the public road as he has turned it near to his plantation and that it be there established, the road leading from Winchester to the mouth of Farris Creek.

Ordered that JAMES ELLIS be overseer of the public road in the room of AARON MOORE.

Ordered that MARY DODD, an orphan seven years old, be bound to JAMES BYERS until she arrives to the age of eighteen years. He is to give her reasonable schooling, diet, washing and lodging &c, a good bed and furniture, horse and saddle to be worth $70.00 and a good suit of cloths at her freedom.

An account of the sale of part of the estate of HARDY HOLMAN, deceased, was exhibited in court by the executors and ordered to be recorded.

Ordered that the road leading down Elk River crossing at Hannahs Ford be established as viewed and marked by the Commissioners and returned to this court. That is beginning at the first branch east of ALBRIGHT's farm at a red oak and running southwardly so as to leave said ALBRIGHT's peach orchard on the east and with the mark so as to intersect the old road at or near the foot of a small hill below ALBRIGHT's, and that the overseer hereafter work on the same as the public road.

A settlement of the estate of DAVID SAWYERS between the admr and the guardian for the heirs of said estate was returned to court and ordered to be recorded.

Ordered that the Trustee of this county pay to WILLIAM HUSBANDS, Sheriff, the sum of $22.12½ for his expenses incurred in removing state prisoners from Pulaski.

An account of the sale of the estate of THOMAS LEMONS was returned to court by JOEL PINSON the admr and ordered to be recorded.

An account of the sale of the personal property belonging to the estate of THOMAS SLAUGHTER, deceased, was returned to court by admr and was ordered to be recorded.

Ordered that EDMOND RORAX be overseer in the room of HIRAM BUCHANAN.

Ordered that JOHN C. CRAIG be released from the payment of the appraised value of a stray mare by him taken up and that the suit which the trustee has instituted against him for the recovery thereof be dismissed and that the said CRAIG pay the costs and cost of this motion.

CORDELL SHUFFIELD, STEPHEN C. CHITWOOD, ELIJAH A. LOYD, and JOHN H. NORTON were each appointed Constable for this county for the ensuing two years who entered into bond and security.

The due execution of a Bill of Sale from JOHN COX to JOHN FORSYTHE for various personal property and ordered to be certified.

Ordered that ABRAM FITCH, BENJAMIN FANNIN, JAMES BROWN, EDWIN McADAMS, JOHN S. PRICE, PETER COLE, JONATHAN MERRELL, SR., JOHN B. TODD, MOSES STONE, JOHN REESE, DAVID HOWELL, JAMES W. CUNNINGHAM, ROBERT CUNNINGHAM, RICHARD WYATT, WILLIAM BLAIZE, JAMES HIGGINS, ELIJAH DAVIS, WILLIAM McCLELLAND, PLEASANT PRICE, ANDREW JOURDON, UTY SHERRELL, JOHN McMILLEN, ROBERT ALSUP, DOILY GRIFFIS, and WILLIAM SHIPP be jurors to the next term of this court.

Agreeable to an order of the last term of court, we, CORNELIUS DARNELL and THOMAS CLARK have proceeded to designate the hands to work under JOSEPH PENN overseer of the public road, in addition to the former hands. We say that the following shall work under him, that is MAJOR BEVIL, WILLIAM LEA, JOHN ORICK and JAMES PIGG and the hands where EDMOND CHITWOOD and WILLIAM HOPPER lives.

JOHN MARR, Esquire, a Justice of the Peace, appeared in court and resigns his appointment as a Justice of the Peace which was accepted and ordered to be recorded.

The due execution of a Power of Attorney from LEVI ESLICK to JAMES PORTER, proven by ROBERT STONE and JOHN C. TATUM and ordered to be certified.

Ordered that JAMES WARREN, a minor orphan, be bound to SAMUEL S. HOLDING until he arrives to the age of twenty one years, said HOLDING to learn him the trade and mystery of a cabinet maker, give him decent and comfortable clothing during the time of his apprenticeship, find him in boarding, washing and lodging, and to send him to school during the said term until he learns arithmetic through the double rule of three, when he is free, give him a good suit of cloths and a horse, saddle and bridle worth $75.00 and HOLDING gave bond and security.

TUESDAY OCTOBER 3, 1826

Justices present were THOMAS CLARK, THOMAS GAITHER and THOMAS H. SHAW, Esquires.

WILLIAM HUSBANDS, High Sheriff, made return to court and he was directed to bring into court the State's Writ of Venire facias, to wit, ZADOK MOTLOW, ISHAM PARR, ROBERT FROST, CLAIBORN WHITWORTH, ALEXANDER BEARD, JACOB CASTLEMAN, JONATHAN MERRELL, SR., JOHN NORRIS, JOHN DOWTHIT, BENJAMIN ARRINGTON, THOMAS EAST, THOMAS KERCHEVAL, JORDON REESE, MICAJAH STONE, SR., WILLIAM SMITH, WILLIAM D. BLAKE, JOHN CRAWFORD, JOHN CAMPBELL, JOHN C. FLYNT, JOHN BEATY, DAVIS SMITH, HENRY CLIFT, WILLIAM CRAWFORD, SR., NICHOLAS CARIGER and WILLIAM CRUNK out of whom selected provides the following persons a Grand Inquest and Jury, to wit, THOMAS KERCHEVAL, foreman, ISHAM PARR, ROBERT FROST, JOHN DOWTHIT, NICHOLAS CARIGER, CLAIBORN WHITWORTH, JOHN NORRIS, JACOB CASTLEMAN, WILLIAM CRAWFORD, JORDAN REESE, JOHN CRAWFORD, DAVIS SMITH, and ALEXANDER BEARD being impaneled and sworn to inquire for the State aforesaid and for the body of the county, then received from WILLIAM H. FIELD, Esquire, who acted as Solicitor General pro-tem, a charge after which they returned under the charge of a Constable sworn for that purpose to consider for presentments.

THOMAS EAST and WILLIAM D. BLAKE excused the court from attendance as jurors until Thursday morning next.

ROBERT DICKSON vs WYATT W. WOODRUFF - This day came the parties by their attorneys and a jury of men, to wit, ZADOK MOTLOW, JOHN BEATY, HENRY CLIFT, WALTER KINNARD, D.B. WALTON, WILLIAM C. BLAKE, BENJAMIN WOODRUFF, JOHN DOBBINS, JOSEPH FROST, M. McELROY, SR., JOHN WAGGONER, and THOMAS BOAZ being elected and sworn do say that the defendant had not paid the debt of $53.81¼ and assess damages of $2.37½. Plaintiff to recover his costs.

DAVID McREA vs JOHN GREER - (same as above) do say that the defendant hath not paid all the debt but find a balance of $266.20 and damages of $13.30. Plaintiff to recover his costs.

DAVID McREA vs WILLIAM C. KENNEDY - (same as above) do say 'that the defendant hath not paid the debt a balance of $41.46 and damages of $4.00 besides the costs. Plaintiff to recover his costs.

ROBERT DICKSON vs P.S. & J.H. GEORGE - (same as above) do say that they find in favor of the plaintiff and assess damages of $88.25. Plaintiff to recover his costs.

HINCHMAN & STARR vs BOOKER FOSTER - (same as above) do say that the defendant has not paid the debt of $73.57 and assess damages of $1.75 besides their costs. Plaintiff to recover his costs.

DAVID McREA vs JAMES D. ALFORD - (same as above) do say that the defendant hath not paid the debt of $50.00 and damages of 75 cents. Plaintiff to recover his costs.

PETER ADAMS for use of vs HARMAN B. WALTON & SAMUEL BARCLAY - (same as above) do say that the defendant hath not paid the whole debt and find a balance of $159.50 and assess damages of $3.56 besides his costs. Plaintiff to recover his costs.

JOHN BAILY for use of vs JAMES SMITH & S. ROSEBOROUGH - (same as above) find that the damages sustained by reason of the defendants breach of their covenant of $156.25 besides his costs. Plaintiff to recover his costs.

JAMES DOZWELL vs ANTHONY HAMPTON - (same as above) do say that the defendant hath not paid the debt of $350.00 and assess damages of $50.75 besides his costs. Plaintiff to recover his costs.

JOSHUA KELLY vs WILLIAM McCLELLAND - (same as above) do say that the defendant hath not paid the debt of $270.00 and assess damages of $14.85 besides his costs. Plaintiff to recover his costs.

MATHEW WATSON vs JOB G. SELPH (same as above) do say that the defendant hath not paid the balance of the debt of $1294.81 and damages of $22.64 besides his costs. Plaintiff to recover his costs.

ALEXANDER KERR vs JOSEPH ALSUP - The defendant came into court and confesses that he owes to the plaintiff the sum of $27.25. Plaintiff to recover his costs.

WEDNESDAY OCTOBER 4, 1826

Justices present were THOMAS CLARK, JOHN PORTER, THOMAS GAITHER and THOMAS H. SHAW, Esquires.

PEYTON WELLS, admr of the estate of ABNER WELLS, deceased, returned into court an account of the sales of the personal property belonging to the estate and was ordered to be recorded.

JASPER SMITH, JOHN DUSENBERRY and ISAAC HOLMAN, Commissioners appointed at the last term to divide the land belonging to the heirs of GEORGE WAGGONER and returned to court an exhibit of said division.

The Clerk and others vs THOMAS STUBBLEFIELD - This day came the plaintiff by his attorney and the defendant being called but came not but made default. Plaintiff to recover his costs amounting to $9.35½.

JAMES ELLISON vs AMOS LILES - This day came the plaintiff by his attorney and a judgment against AMOS LILES and JAMES SMITH his security for $7.12½. Plaintiff to recover his costs.

GEORGE W. CAMPBELL vs SAMUEL & P.P. DAVIS - Whereas on 26 July 1826, there did issue from the office of the Clerk of the Court, which came to the hands of the Sheriff on the day it was issued against the defendant for $2.20 debt and $7.20 costs. Cause was executed on 12 September 1826. The defendant was called but came not but made default. Plaintiff to recover his costs.

GEORGE W. CAMPBELL vs SAMUEL & P.P. DAVIS - On 22 July 1826, did issue from the office of the clerk (same as above) for $40.39 debt and $7.20 costs. Cause was executed 12 September 1826 who gave bond and security. The defendant being called but came not but made default. Plaintiff to recover his costs.

LEEMAN WATSON vs JOHN DILLON - Whereas on 26 July 1826 (same as above) for $16.25 and $5.25 costs. Defendant being called but came not but made default. Plaintiff to recover his costs.

JOHN LANIER vs WILLIAM COLE - It is ordered that the clerk issue a venditioni exponas directed to the Sheriff commanding him to expose to sale a tract of land in Lincoln County containing 100 acres, lying on Elk River, bounded by lands of STEPHEN COLE and JOSEPH CAMPBELL, to satisfy a judgment that the plaintiff recovered before HUGH PARKESON, a J.P., on 2 October 1826 for $26.16 debt and costs also costs of this motion.

JAMES BLAIR, SR. vs CLAIBORN W. HUGHS - Whereas on 25 July 1826, the clerk of this court issued a Writ of Capias from JAMES BLAIR, SR. to the defendant. The defendant was arrested on 26 September 1826. The defendant being called came not but made default. Plaintiff to recover $9.37½ and costs of this motion.

Ordered that the clerk issue to PETER LENEHAN(?) a license as a tavern keeper in this town for one year from this day and gave bond and security.

The due execution of an Indenture of Bargain and Sale from JAMES STEPHENSON to ZADOCK WALKER for 44 acres of land and ordered to be certified.

The due execution of a Deed of Conveyance from JOHN BROWN to JAMES SMITH for 107 acres of land and ordered to be certified.

The due execution of a Deed of Conveyance from JAMES ARMSTRONG and WILLIAM ARMSTRONG to JAMES WARREN for 180 acres of land, proven by JOHN WARDEN and THOMAS HALL and ordered to be certified.

The due execution of a Deed of Conveyance from BAILEY RAINS to JAMES ELLIS for 110 acres of land, proven by JOHN ENOCHS and JOHN G. BERRY and ordered to be certified.

The due execution of a Deed of Conveyance from WILLIAM WHITE to DANIEL JONES for 50 acres of land and ordered to be certified.

The due execution of a Deed of Conveyance from HARDY HOLMAN to ISAAC RUTLEDGE for 365 acres of land, proven by DANIEL HOLMAN and DANIEL W. HARRISON and ordered to be certified.

The due execution of a Deed of Conveyance from NEWTON WILKERSON to SAMUEL CUNNINGHAM for 10 acres of land and ordered to be certified.

THURSDAY OCTOBER 5, 1826

Justices present were THOMAS CLARK, HUGH PARKESON and THOMAS H. SHAW, Esquires.

Upon the application of WILLIAM D. BLAKE, one of the jurors summoned to the present term of court and for reasons appearing to the court, he is released from further attendance as a juror.

JOHN SHORT vs WILLIAM P. PULLIAM - On motion of the plaintiff by his attorney, it is ordered that the defendant give better security for his appeal. Whereupon came STEPHEN ALEXANDER and entered as security.

The State vs WRIGHT McLEMORE - DANIEL WARREN who was the defendant's appearance bail now surrenders him in court in discharge of himself. Court ordered the defendant into the custody of the Sheriff.

The State vs L.T(?). BROWN - WILLIAM F. LONG who was the appearance bail of the defendant now surrenders him to court in dischagre of himself. On motion, the defendant is ordered into custody of the Sheriff. JOHN BROWN entered as the appearance bail of said defendant.

BENJAMIN WOODRUFF vs JOHN YOUNG - Upon motion of the plaintiff by his attorney supported by affidavit, it is ordered that the defendant give other and better sexurity in this cause. (blank) BELLER entered as defendant's security.

The State vs DEMSEY BROWN - JAMES R, ONEAL, the defendant's appearance bail, surrenders him in court in discharge of himself. On motion, the defendant is ordered into the custody of the Sheriff.

THOMAS EAST is discharged from further attendance as a juror until next Tuesday.

PARKES & LONG appeared in court, gave bond and security as gin holders and inspectors of cotton and took oath.

The State vs JOHN JONES - Bastardy - The defendant by his attorney moved to be discharged from his recognizance in this cause and the court decided that the defendant take nothing by his motion. The defendant filed his affidavit requiring an issue to be made up to try the truth of the charge whereof he stands recognized to appear here and answer, to wit, his having begotten a bastard on the body of SARAH HUGHS. Court ordered the following jury, to wit, JOHN BEATY, ZADOK MOTLOW, E. PARHAM, PETER NIPP, SOLOMON REESE, ANTHONY STREET, and THOMAS HOLLAND being elected and sworn and said that the defendant is the father of a illegitimate child of which SARAH HUGHS was delivered. Court ordered that he give bond and security to keep child from becoming chargeable to the county and that he pay the mother SARAH HUGHS for three years the following, for this year $30.00, next year $25.00 third year $15.00 and he pay cost of this prosecution and that he be in custody of the Sheriff until he pay and give security. SAMUEL JONES came and confessed judgment for the same.

The State vs THOMAS HOLLAND - Affray - The defendant being charged and pleads guilty and is fined $1.00 and pay costs of this indictment and remain in custody until the fine and costs are paid and security is given whereupon came JAMES SIMMONS and confessed judgement with said defendant.

The State vs WILLIAM BRYANT - (same as above) and is fined $1.00 and pay costs.

The State vs GIDEON AUSTIN - The defendant came and no person appearing to urge anything against said defendant. It is considered by the court that the defendant be no further bound and he pay the costs of this prosecution. Whereupon came WILEY JONES and confessed judgment jointly with said defendant for the costs.

The due execution of a Deed of Conveyance from NEWTON WILKERSON to SAMUEL CUNNINGHAM for 30 acres of land and ordered to be certified.

ENOCH DOWTHIT appeared in court and was appointed an inspector of cotton, being the owner of a cotton gin in this county, gave bond and security.

The State vs JOHN T. SMITH - Malicious Mischief - The defendant appeared in court and being charged and pleads not guilty and a jury of men, to wit, JOHN BEATY, ZADOK MOTLOW, H. CLIFT, JOHN B. ABELS, GERSHAM LEA, M. McELROY, JR., D. BECK, E. PARHAM, P. NIPP, SOLOMON REESE, ANTHONY STREET, and HENRY WARREN being elected and sworn and after hearing part of the testimony on the part of the State, the court adjourned until next day.

FRIDAY OCTOBER 6, 1826

Justices present were THOMAS H. SHAW, HUGH PARKESON and JACOB WAGGONER, Esquires.

The State vs DEMSEY BROWN - It is ordered that the Attorney General prefer an indictment against the defendant.

Ordered that ROBERT H. McEWEN be appointed guardian to HETTY E.K. GREER, one of the minor orphans of VANCE GREER, deceased, and he entered bond and security with the clerk of the court in January next in the penalty of $1000.00 for performance of his dais guardianship.

Ordered that WILLIAM EDMISTON be appointed guardian to ANDREW J. GREER, and that WILLIAM P. MARTIN be appointed giardian to WILLIAM K. GREER and that each entered bond and security for $1000.00.

Ordered that FRANCIS PORTERFIELD and ANDREW A. KINCANNON be appointed Commissioners to settle with JOSEPH & THOMAS GREER, executors of VANCE GREER, deceased, and make return to court.

THOMAS GAITHER vs ALFRED J. MOORE - The defendant be allowed to take the deposition of JOSEPH HINKLE at Hinkle's own house tomorrow between 12 and 6 o'clock to be read in evidence in this cause and be given sufficient time and place of taking same.

The State vs JOHN T. SMITH - The jury impaneled in this cause appeared in court and said that the defendant is not guilty as charged. Trustee of this county to pay the costs of this indictment.

The State vs JOHN SMITH - Malicious Mischief - The court decided to dismiss this indictment. The Trustee of this county pay the costs of its prosecution.

The State vs WILLIAM T. HALL - Affray - The defendant being charged pleads not guilty and a jury of men, to wit, ZACOK MOTLOW, HENRY CLIFT, ABRAM BARNS, H.B. WALTON, A. LUMBRIC, JOHN S. McADA, EDWARD MOSS, ANTHONY WELLS, S.S. HOLDING, JAMES RANDOLPH, DAVID BARCLAY, and A. DEPOYSTER being elected and sworn and said that the defendant is guilty as charged. Ordered that the defendant be fined $10.00 and pay costs of this prosecution and on motion he is ordered into the custody of the Sheriff until the fine and costs are paid or security given. RICHARD HALL came confessed judgment jountly with the defendant for fine and costs.

The State vs DEMSEY BROWN - Assault and Battery - The defendant being charged pleads guilty and is fined $10.00 and pay the costs of this prosecution and whereupon came JAMES BROWN and confessed judgment jointly with the defendant for said fine and costs.

The State vs FRANCIS COFFMAN - Assault and Battery - The defendant being charged pleads guilty and is fined 50 cents and pay costs of this prosecution and whereupon came JOHN COFFMAN and confessed judgment for the above fine and costs.

The State vs JOHN SMITH and JOHN T. SMITH - The defendant by his attorney moved the court to dismiss said cause and assumes payment of the costs. Cause dismissed and the defendants pay the costs.

ALEXANDER R. KERR vs JOHN PORTER - The defendant confesses that he owes to the plaintiff $176.75. Plaintiff to recover against the defendant his costs.

SATURDAY OCTOBER 7, 1826

Justices present were THOMAS H. SHAW, THOMAS CLARKE and HUGH PARKESON, Esquires.

The State vs LIVINGSTON J. BROWN - The defendant being charged upon this Bill of Indictment pleads guilty and is fined $1.00 and pay the cost of this prosecution. Whereupon came JOHN BROWN and confessed judgment jointly with the defendant for the above fine and costs.

The State vs DEVAULT BECK - The defendant being charged and pleads not guilty and a jury of men, to wit, JOHN BEATY, JAMES McWHERTER, J.C. BROWN, JOHN R. JOHNSTON, ABSALOM BEARD, JAMES W. BURNS, HENRY DAVIS, GEORGE T. HIGGINS, WILLIAM BRYANT, OVERTON WOODALL, RICHARD HALL and DAVID BIGGS being elected and sworn to speak upon the issue joined, with the assent of the court and with the consent of the defendant in person. JOHN BEATY, one of the jurors are with drawn and the other eleven jurors from rendering a verdict in this cause are excused.

The State vs JABE DABNEY - The defendant pleads that his name is JABEY DABNEY and not JABE DABNEY to which the Attorney General replies that he is as well known by the name of JABE DABNEY which he prays may be required of by the country and the defendant doth the like, whereupon came a jury of men, to wit, HENRY CLIFT, Z. MOTLOW, WILLIAM P. PILLIAM, ROBERT CUNNINGHAM, H.E. DAVIS, JOHN ROBERTSON, D.A. GREER, A. PARKS, A.J. BLAKEMORE, ELLIOTT H. FLETCHER, JAMES RANDOLPH, and D.B. WALTON being elected and sworn to speak on the issue, but with the assent of the court and the consent of the defendant, HENRY CLIFT, one of the jurors is withdrawn and the rest from rendering a verdict in this cause are excused.

The State vs WILLIAM B. BENGE - Affray - The defendant being charged pleads not guilty and a jury of men, (same as above) and said that the defendant is guilty as charged and is fined $20.00 and pay cost of this prosecution. Whereupon on motion came ANDREW A. KINCANNON and confessed judgment jointly with the defendant for the above fine and costs.

The State vs JOBE DABNEY - JABE DABNEY (alias JABEZ DABNEY) and WILLIAM TAUL acknowledged themselves to owe and be indebted to the State of Tennessee, DABNEY for $250.00 and TAUL for $125.00 to be levied upon their respective goods and chattels &c, to be void in condition that DABNEY make his personal appearance in court in January next to answer the State for an assault and battery by him committed on WILEY JONES.

The State vs JABE DABNEY - (same as above) JABE DABNEY (alias JABEZ DABNEY) and WILLIAM TAUL acknowledge themselves to owe the State of Tennessee, DABNEY for $250.00 and TAUL for $125.00 to be leviedupon their respective goods and chattels &c to be void on condition that DABNEY make his personal appearance in court in January next to answer the State for an assault and battery by him committed on WILEY JONES.

The State vs DWAULD BECK - SOLOMON REESE acknowledged himself to owe to the State of Tennessee $250.00, to be levied upon his goods and chattels &c, to be void on condition that he appear here in court next January and give testimony on behalf of the State against DWAULD BECK upon a charge of maiming.

The State vs WILLIAM B. BENGE - In this cause, JOHN R. JOHNSTON, JAMES D. ALFORD, JOHN INMAN and WILLIAM BONNER, witnesses, subpoened on behalf of the State to appear here and being called came not but made default and is fined $125.00 each to be set aside for cause shown.

The Commissioners, FRANCIS PORTERFIELD and ANDREW A. KINCANNON, appointed to settle with JOSEPH and THOMAS GREER, executors of VANCE GREER, deceased, now make return to court and ordered to be recorded.

The due execution of a Deed of Conveyance from ALEXANDER MORE to PETER COLE for (blank) acres of land on Flint River and ordered to be certified.

The due execution of a Deed of Conveyance from JAMES GREER to WALTER KINNAIRD for one town lot in Fayetteville and ordered to be certified.

The due execution of a Mortgage Deed upon one lot in Fayetteville from WALTER KINNAIRD to PHILIP KINNAIRD and ordered to be certified.

The due execution of a Deed of Conveyance from JAMES LEWIS to CHARLES WESTERMAN for 153 acres of land and ordered to be certified.

The State vs PHILIP FIELDS and JACOB SUMMERS - On 25 July 1826, there did issue an order of the court that the Sheriff to execute on 30 August 1826 by arresting the bodies of PHILIP FIELDS and JACOB SUMMERS who themselves entered into bond and security and issued a fine and cost due the State. The defendants being called came not into court. It was ordered that the State recover against the defendants and JAMES McWHERTER their security in said bond of $25.03½ the fine and costs.

Upon motion of JOHN R. JOHNSTON, JAMES D. ALFORD, JOHN INMAN and WILLIAM BONNER against whom forfeitures were entered and it appearing to the court the said forfeitures are set aside upon the payment of the costs and costs of motion.

Ordered that JEFFREY, a black boy, be bound to DAVID THOMPSON to learn the shoemaking business and to serve him until he arrives to the age of twenty one years and THOMPSON is to treat him well as an apprentice and at his freedom give him a suit of cloths worth $40.00.

The due execution of a Deed of Conveyance from JACOB WHITTENBURGH to

WILLIAM KENNON for 37 acres of land, proven by DANIEL WHITTENBURGH, attorney and agent for JACOB WHITTENBURGH and ordered to be certified.

The due execution of a Deed of Bargain and Sale from JAMES LEWIS to THOMAS BLYTHE for 183 acres of land and ordered to be certified.

The due execution of a Deed of Conveyance from NATHAN PINSON & JOEL PINSON to DEMSEY ALLEN for 175 acres of land in Obion County and ordered to be certified.

The due execution of a Deed of Conveyance from ALEXANDER SMITH to WILLIAM WILSON for 115 acres of land, proven by WILLIAM HUSBANDS and D. McMILLEN and ordered to be certified.

MONDAY OCTOBER 9, 1826

Justices present were THOMAS CLARKE, JOHN PORTER, CORNELIUS DARNEL, ALLEN ELSTON, HUGH M. BLAKE, ROBERT DICKSON, THOMAS H. SHAW, JOHN ENOCHS, JESSE DANIEL, WILLIAM MILNER, JAMES SMITH, JOEL PINSON, WILLIAM DYE, JACOB WAGGONER, HUGH PARKESON and SAMUEL BUCHANAN, Esquires.

ANDREW A. KINCANNON and ELLIOTT H. FLETCHER is appointed Commissioners to settle with BENJAMIN PROCTOR, admr of the estate of JAMES PROCTOR, deceased, and make return to present court.

Ordered that ANDREW CUMMINS, a minor orphan of THOMAS CUMMINS, deceased, be bound an apprentice to SPENCER A. PUGH to learn the saddling business and entered into bond and security.

JOHN MIMMS, Esquire, appeared in court and took an oath to support the Constitution of the United States also the Constitution of the State of Tennessee and the oath of an attorney of this court.

Ordered that ANDREW A. KINCANNON be appointed an additional commissioner to settle with the admrx of EDWARD TEAL, deceased.

The Commissioners heretofore appointed to settle with BENJAMIN PROCTOR, admr of JAMES PROCTOR, deceased, now make return of that settlement into court and ordered to be recorded.

Ordered that MARY ANN PARRISH, an orphan about thirteen years of age, be bound to MOSES BUCHANAN until she arrives to the age of eighteen years and that he give her ten months schooling and give a good bed and furniture at her freedom and decent clothing, diet and lodging during said term of service.

It appearing to the court that ALEXANDER McLIN, late of this county, departed this lide intestate without making his Last Will and Testament in writing, and on motion of CHARLES McKINNEY and JOHN P. McCONNELL, admrs on estate of ALEXANDER McLIN is granted them and entered into bond and security. Issued 9 October 1826.

Ordered that BENJAMIN CLEMENTS, PEYTON WELLS and JAMES W. CUNNINGHAM be Commissioners to lay off out of the property of ALEXANDER McLIN, deceased, one years support for his widow and children.

Ordered that WILLIS WARREN be released from his undertaking as guardian of the orphan children of JOHN WARREN, deceased. And that HENRY WARREN remain their guardian and he entered into bond and security.

It appearing to the court that REPS O. CHILDRESS, late of this county, departed this life without making his Last Will and Testament in writing whereupon came THOMAS CLARK and RUFUS M. CHILDRESS and they are granted administration on said estate of REPS O. CHILDRESS, deceased, and they gave bond and security.

SAMUEL D. MILIKIN, BOONE WILSON and JONAS LEATHERMAN are appointed to lay off out of the property of REPS O. CHILDRESS, deceased, one years support for his widow and children.

Ordered that the Trustee of this county pay to JOHN P. McCONNELL $19.87½ for taking State prisoners to Pulaski jail.

The administrators of the estate of CHRISTOPHER SHOFNER returned into court the inventory of said estate and ordered to be recorded.

WILLIAM HUSBANDS, High Sheriff, now reports that the jail is sufficient to keep any person committed to his charge either on criminal or civil process.

Ordered that JOHN GRIFFIS be overseer of the public road in the room of WILLIAM BRYANT from the mouth of Swan Creek to SAMUEL M. CLAY's old place.

G.W.C. EDMISTON and ABNER STEED, Commissioners appointed to settle with the admr and admrx of THOMAS CUMMINS, deceased, now return to court that settlement and ordered to be recorded.

The Last Will and Testament of JAMES RANDALL was produced in court for probate whereupon came WILLIAM P. MARTIN and JOHN MORGAN, witnesses, proved the due execution. Whereupon came ROBERT DICKSON and JOHN P. McCONNELL, executors, entered into bond and security.

Ordered that SAMUEL GARLAND, JESSE DANIEL, DANIEL T. WILLIAMS, DAVID H. EDMISTON, JACOB WAGGONER, HARIEL NIXON, HERBERT GRIFFIS, JOEL PINSON, WILLIAM SMITH (Coldwater), BOONE WILSON, ELI COUCH, JOHN CRAWFORD, JOHN BUCHANAN, WILLIAM WILLIAMS, JAMES BOREN, JOHN GRAY, DAVID JONES, JOHN SIVELY, ISAAC CONGER, JOSEPH JENKINS, BERRY T. PARR, JESSE GEORGE, JACOB WRIGHT, JAMES WILSON, WILLIAM CARITHERS, and HENRY TALLY be jurors to the March Term 1827 Circuit Court.

Majistrates to take tax list for the year 1827.
JOSEPH McBRIDE in CAPTAIN COOPER's Company
WILLIAM DYE in CAPTAIN MEEK's Company
ABRAM SUMMERS in CAPTAIN HAYES' Company
CORNELIUS DARNELL in CAPTAIN WILLIAMS' Company
THOMAS H. SHAW in CAPTAIN CLARKE's Company
THOMAS CLARKE in CAPTAIN TAYLOR's Company
JAMES McDAVID in CAPTAIN GARRET's Company
JOSEPH McCRACKEN in CAPTAIN McCRACKEN's Company
WILLIAM ANDERSON in CAPTAIN ANDERSON's Company
ZACHARIAH HARRISON in CAPTAIN MORGAN's Company
HUGH PARKESON in CAPTAIN POOL's Company
JAMES SMITH in CAPTAIN ARNOLD's Company
ELISHA BAGLEY in CAPTAIN MOORE's Company
ALLEN ELSTON in CAPTAIN BROOK's Company
JOEL PINSON in CAPTAIN DILLENDER's Company
WILLIAM EDMISTON in CAPTAIN RINGO's Company
CHARLES BRIGHT in CAPTAIN SHOFNER's Company
CLIFFORD GREY in CAPTAIN ESLICK's Company
JESSE DANIEL in CAPTAIN PICKETT's Company
SAMUEL BUCHANAN in CAPTAIN CRAWFORD's Company
PHILIP KOONCE in CAPTAIN SMITH's Company (Stewarts Creek)
JOHN H. MOORE in CAPTAIN OLDS' Company
JAMES BLAKEMORE in CAPTAIN BLAKEMORE's Company
JOHN ENOCHS in CAPTAIN SMITH's Company (Mulberry)
JOHN WISEMAN in CAPTAIN SPENCER's Company

Ordered that ROBERT BROOKS be allowed to file with the Tristee of this county his claim for attendance as a witness in the case of the State against THOMAS S. MILAM amounting to $5.50 and that he receive pay for same and that JOSIAH BLACKWELL do the same with his claim for similar services in same case amounting to $5.50, and that JOHN LUNA be permitted to do the same with his claim for like services amounting to $3.50 and also that DUE BOND file his claim for $5.00 and that GEORGE CRAWFORD file his claim for $5.50 and that LAURENCE (X) BOND file his claim for $5.50 and receive pay as above.

The due execution of a Bill of Sale for a negro boy PETER from JOHN OWEN to GARLAND HILL and ordered to be certified.

TUESDAY OCTOBER 10, 1826

Justices present were THOMAS CLARKE, JOHN PORTER and HUGH PARKESON, Esquires.

The State vs WRIGHT McLEMORE - The defendant being charged pleads not guilty and a jury of men, to wit, JOHN BEATY, HENRY CLIFT, ZADOK MOTLOW, KEYS MEEK, STEPHEN LOYD, SAMUEL HAMPTON, JOHN ROBERTSON, JOHN HUSBANDS, EDWARD MOSS, WILEY JONES, WILLIAM C. BLAKE, and THOMAS EAST being elected and sworn do say that the defendant is guilty as charged. Defendant be fined $5.00 and pay the costs of this prosecution and on motion ordered that he be in the custody until said fine and costs be paid or security given for the payment. WYLIE M. JONES appeared and confessed judgment jointly with the defendant for said fine and costs.

It appearing to the court that JAMES VINES, late of this county, departed this life without making his Last Will and Testament in writing. And on motion of BETSEY VINES, his widow, administration is granted her on the estate of said JAMES VINES, deceased, and entered into bond and security.

Ordered that JESSE DANIEL, JAMES SMITH and ZACHARIAH ARNOLD lay off one years support for the widow and children of JAMES VINES, out of his estate.

THOMAS GAITHER vs ALFRED J. MOORE - This cause by consent of the plaintiff and defendant is referred to the award and arbitration of JOHN MARR, HUGH M. BLAKE, JOHN DONELSON and JOHN PORTER or two of them and if they cannot agree to choose as umpire who are to report to court. It is also ordered that the defendant be permitted to take the deposition of JOSEPH HINKLE on tomorrow at court.

The State vs WRIGHT McLEMORE - This day the Attorney General who prosecutes on behalf of the State and the defendant being called came not but made default. He is to pay the costs.

The State vs WILLIAM SOLOMON - The defendant being charged pleads guilty and is fined $5.00 and pay costs of this indictment, whereupon came ANDREW A. KINCANNON and confessed judgment jointly with the defendant for the above fine and costs.

The State vs ALEXANDER ABELS & JOHN WALLIS - Riot - The defendants and WILLIAM SHIPP acknowledged themselves indebted to the State of Tennessee for $250.00 to be levied of their goods and chattels &c but to be void on condition that they appear in court in January next to answer the State.

The State vs JOHN ABELS & JOHN HUNT - Riot - The defendants and JOHN DEVIN came into court and acknowledged that they are indebted to the State of Tennessee for $250.00 to be levied upon their goods and chattels &c to be void on condition that they appear in court in January next and to answer the State upon a charge for having committed a riot.

HINCHEY PETWAY vs BARNABAS BOYLES, admr - This day came the parties by their attorneys and a jury of men, to wit, THOMAS KERCHEVAL, ISHAM PARR, ROBERT FROST, JOHN DOWTHIT, NICHOLAS CARIGER, CLAIBORN WHITWORTH, JOHN MORRIS, JACOB CASTLEMAN, WILLIAM CRAWFORD, JOHN CRAWFORD, JORDAN REESE, and DAVIS SMITH being elected and sworn and said that they find in favor of the defendant and he recover his costs.

BENJAMON WOODRUFF vs JOHN YOUNG - (same as above) and said they find in favor of the defendant and he recover his costs.

ROBERT DICKSON vs DAVID BARCLAY - (same as above) and said that the defendant has not kept his covenant and they assess the damages of $104.50 and costs.

The State vs WILLIAM BIRD - The defendant being called came not but made default. State to recover against the defendant $100.00.

The State vs WILLIAM BIRD - The defendant being called came not but made default and JOSEPH BROOKS, security for the defendant, was called to come and bring with him the defendant as he was bound to do who therein failed and made default. State to recover $50.00.

The State vs WILLIAM BIRD - GEORGE TEDFORD who was recognized to appear here and prosecute and give testimony against the defendant for $50.00. TEDFORD being called came not but made default. State to recover its costs.

PHILEMON HIGGINS vs ANTHONY B. CLENDENING - A motion to dismiss this cause. Cause to be dismissed and the plaintiff recover against the defendant and JOHN

W. SMITH his security for $310.77½ for five judgments ordered by DAVID COWAN, a Justice of the Peace, along with 427.40 for interest.

SAMUEL HAMPTON vs A.J. BLACKBURN and wife - This cause is continued on the affidavit of the plaintiff and it is ordered that he pay the costs.

LARRY EPPS vs CHARLES THOMPSON - On motion in this cause to dismiss this case. It is ordered that this cause be dismissed and the plaintiff recover his debt of $2.50 and JOHN GARDNER his security.

A Jury of View appointed at the last court to mark a road from near the mouth of Beans Creek towards Hazelgreen, now make return that they begin at the new road at the line of Franklin COunty two miles above the mouth of Beans Creek and running from thence as it is marked to the line of the State of Alabama and that JOSEPH ELLISON be overseer from the Franklin County line to JAMES SMITH's and FRANCIS FINCHER to Big Creek. JOSHUA SCURLOCK to the road leading from Pryor's Mill to Concord Meeting House, and then RICHARD FLYNT to the State line and each to call on the hands that are covenant.

WEDNESDAY OCTOBER 11, 1826

Justices present were THOMAS CLARKE, JOHN PORTER and THOMAS GAITHER, Esquires.

Ordered that FRANCIS PORTERFIELD and ELLIOTT H. FLETCHER be appointed Commissioners to settle with ROBERT DICKSON, admr de bonis now of the estate of PATRICK O. CALAGHAN, deceased, makes return of their settlement to this court.

JAMES ESTLEMAN vs DAVID BARCLAY - This day came the parties by their attorneys and a jury of men, to wit, JOHN BEATY, HENRY CLIFT, ZADOK MOTLOW, JOHN HEATH, DANIEL JONES, S. CLYNE, EDWARD MOSS, WILLIAM P. PULLIAM, JOHN C. BROWN, WILLIAM PARKER, DAVID RORAX, and JOSEPH COMMONS being elected and sworn and said that they find for the defendant and he recover his costs.

LESLIE GILLIAM vs WILLIAM STEPHENS - Both plaintiff and defendant are allowed to take depositions by giving the party thirty days notice if taken in North Carolina and fifteen days if taken anywhere else notice.

DANIEL JONES vs JOHN WHITE - Appeal from a Justice of the Peace - This day came the parties by their attorneys and a jury of men, to wit, THOMAS KERCHEVAL, ISHAM PARR, ROBERT FROST, JOHN DOWTHIT, N. CARIGER, CLAIBORN WHITWORTH, JOHN MORRIS, J. CASTLEMAN, WILLIAM CRAWFORD, JORDAN REESE, DAVIS SMITH and A. BEARD being elected and sworn and say they find in favor of the defendant and he recover his costs.

WILLIAM PATTON vs GEORGE W. SMITH - The plaintiff being called came not but made default and the defendant recover his costs.

WILLIS AUSTIN vs SOLOMON WOODWARD - The plaintiff being called came not but made default. The defendant recover his costs against the plaintiff.

JAMES FULTON vs LAWSON B. HUGHS - The plaintiff says he wishes no further to prosecute this case and wishes to dismiss the same and the defendant by his attorney assumes the payment of all costs. Suit to be dismissed. Plaintiff to recover his costs.

A.G. MORGAN vs JOHN COX - On motion supported by the affidavit of the plaintiff's attorney, this cause is continued and the plaintiff pay the cost of this term.

POWER & HAUGHTON, admrs vs DANIEL COFFMAN - This day came the parties by their attorneys and a jury of men, to wit, JOHN BEATY, H. CLIFT, ZADOK MOTLOW, THOMAS KERCHEVAL, I. PARR, J. DOWTHIT, JACOB CASTLEMAN, WILLIAM CRAWFORD, JOHN CRAWFORD, DAVIS SMITH, ALEXANDER BEARD and ROBERT FROST being elected and sworn and say that they find in favor of the defendant. Defendant recover his costs.

WILLIAM PARKER vs ROBERT DICKSON - This day came the parties by their attorneys and a jury of men, to wit, JOHN MORRIS, N. CARIGER, E.A. FLETCHER, ELIHU ROBERTSON, JERE. WALKER, ANTHONY WELLS, SAMUEL INMAN, JOHN HEATH, WILLIAM CONAWAY, JOHN ROBERTSON, JAMES MILSTEAD, and EDWARD MOSS being elected and sworn and say that they find in favor of the plaintiff and assess

249

his damages to $16.76 and his costs. Plaintiff to recover his costs.

JAMES S. ESTES vs ALLEN YOWELL - The plaintiff and the defendant may take depositions by giving the party thirty days notice in Georgia or fifteen days if taken in Tennessee.

RANSOM HUNT vs ROBERT DICKSON, admr of P.O. CALAGHAN & V. GREER, executors - The plaintiff says he wishes no further to prosecute his suit but wishes it to be dismissed, Case dismissed. Defendant to recover his costs.

THOMAS GEORGE, guardian vs ROBERT DICKSON, admr of P.O. CALAGHAN & V. GREER executors. The plaintiff by his attorney says he wishes no further to prosecute his suit and wishes to dismiss same. Suit dismissed and the defendant recover against the plaintiff their costs.

E. & J. FRANKLIN, admr vs JAMES SMITH and others - This day came the parties by their attorneys and a jury of men, to wit, THOMAS KERCHEVAL, JAMES PARR, ROBERT FROST, JOHN DOWTHIT, N. CARIGER, CLABORN WHITWORTH, JOHN MORRIS, J. CASTLEMAN, WILLIAM CRAWFORD, JOHN CRAWFORD, JORDAN REESE, and DAVIS SMITH being elected and sworn to inquire of damages in this cause and they say that the plaintiff has sustaines damages of $272.62. Plaintiff to recover his costs.

SAMUEL M. CLAY vs JESSE GEORGE - The defendant confessed that he owes the plaintiff $104.35 besides his costs. Plaintiff to recover his debt and costs.

BUCHANAN & PORTERFIELD vs SAMUEL HAMPTON - The defendant confesses that he owes the plaintiff $104.75 besides the costs. Plaintiff to recover his debt and costs.

RICHARD PRYOR vs ELIJAH SPARKS - The defendant being called to court but came not and made default. Plaintiff to recover his debt and costs.

DANIEL JONES vs JOHN WHITE - By order of the court WILLIAM WHITE is released as the security of the defendant for the prosecution and AARON WELLS is taken as security in his place.

DAVID ELLMAKER vs HIRAM E. DAVIS - The defendant confesses that he owes to the plaintiff $102.12½ besides his costs. Plaintiff to recover against the defendant his debt and costs.

A.R. KERR & Co. vs JAMES ESTLEMAN - The defendant confesses that he owes to the plaintiff $96.43 3/4 besides his costs. Plaintiff to recover his debt and costs.

THURSDAY OCTOBER 12, 1826

Justices present were HUGH M. BLAKE, CORNELIUS DARNELL and JAMES BLAKEMORE.

The Commissioners FRANCIS PORTERFIELD and ELLIOTT H. FLETCHER appointed to settle with ROBERT DICKSON, admr of the estate of PATRICK O. CALAGHAN, deceased, now make return to court and order to be recorded.

D.I. & A.J. TURRENTINE vs HENRY HUNT - The defendant may take ABSALOM HUNT's deposition by giving the plaintiff's attorney thirty days notice of the time and place of taking the same.

JASON THOMPSON vs JOHN DOBBINS & AARON WELLS - Leave is granted the defendants to take the deposition of HIRAM BYLER by giving the plaintiff fifteen days notice of time and place of taking the same.

A.G. MORGAN vs JOHN COX - Each party in this cause is permitted to take depositions generally by giving the adverse party twenty days notice of time and place of taking the same.

JOHN SHORT vs WILLIAM P. PULLIAM - Appeal from Justice of the Peace - The parties by their attorneys came and a jury of men, to wit, THOMAS KERCHEVAL, ISHAM PARR, ROBERT FROST, JOHN DOWTHIT, N. CARIGER, JOHN MORRIS, JACOB CASTLEMAN, WILLIAM CRAWFORD, DAVIS SMITH, A. BEARD, JOHN BEATY, and ZADOK MOTLOW being elected and sworn and say that they find for the plaintiff and assess his damages to $5.00 besides his costs. Plaintiff to recover his debt and STEPHEN

ALEXANDER his security.

LEVI M. TODD vs SAMUEL TODD - The plaintiff says he wishes no further to prosecute his suit and wishes the same to be dismissed. Suit to be dismissed and the defendant recover his costs.

LEVI M. TODD vs SAMUEL TODD - (same as above).

LEVI M. TODD vs SAMUEL TODD - (same as above).

LEVI M. TODD vs SAMUEL TODD - (same as above).

LEVI M. TODD vs SAMUEL TODD - (same as above).

DANIEL WRIGHT vs SAMUEL INMAN - The defendant confesses that he owes the plaintiff $47.00. Plaintiff to recover his costs.

JOHN W. CRUNK vs TODD ADAMS - Trespass - The parties came by their attorneys and a jury of men, to wit, HENRY CLIFT, ISHAM PARR, R. FROST, JOHN DOWTHIT, N. CARIGER, JOHN MORRIS, JACOB CASTLEMAN, WILLIAM CRAWFORD, DAVIS SMITH, A. BEARD, JOHN BEATY, and ZADOK MOTLOW being elected and sworn and said that they find in favor of the plaintiff ans assess his damages of $300.00. Plaintiff to recover his costs.

JOB G. SELPH vs GEORGE McWHERTER - The parties came by their attorneys and a jury of men, to wit, THOMAS KERCHEVAL, I. PARR, R. FROST, J. DOWTHIT, N. CARIGER, J. MORRIS, J. CASTLEMAN, WILLIAM CRAWFORD, J. CRAWFORD, ALEXANDER BEARD, J. BEATY, and ZADOK MOTLOW being elected and sworn and said they find in favor of the plaintiff and assess his damages to $60.52¼ besides his costs. Plaintiff to recover his costs.

ALEXANDER R. KERR &c vs JOSEPH & THOMAS GREER, executors of VANCE GREER, deceased - (same as above) and say that they find in favor of the plaintiff and they find a balance of $162.42 and assess damages of $17.64. Plaintiff to recover his costs.

JOHN GREER vs R. DICKSON, admr of PATRICK O. CALAGHAN, deceased - (same as above) and say that they find in favor of the plaintiff and that the debt had not fully administered the estate of said PATRICK O. CALAGHAN and find that the deceased nor the defendant had paid the debt of $74.10 and assess damages of $12.21. Plaintiff to recover his costs.

JOHN NEWMAN vs SWITT & DAVIS - Both parties may take the depositions by giving the adverse party ten days notice of time and place. if taken in Tennessee.

ROBERT DICKSON, admr vs JOSEPH & THOMAS GREER, executor - This day came the parties by their attorneys and a jury of men, (same as above jurors) and said that they find in favor of the plaintiff and that the defendants had not fully administered the estate of the said VANCE GREER and that a balance unpaid is $337.41 and assess damages of $50.00 besides his costs. Plaintiff to recover his costs.

THOMAS ROBERTSON and wife vs JAMES BROWN - The plaintiffs says that they wish no further to prosecute this suit but wish the same to be dismissed. Court ordered this suit to be dismissed and the defendant recover his costs.

HENRY COOK vs JOSEPH & THOMAS GREER, executors of VANCE GREER, deceased - (same as above jurors) and said that they find in favor of the defendant and they have fully administered the goods and chattels of the said testator in his lifetime or the said defendants since his death hath not kept the covenant made by the testator with the plaintiff, and they assess the damages of $405.49. Plaintiff to recover his costs.

The State vs TODD ADAMS - Riot - The defendant being charged pleads guilty and is fined 6¼ cents and pay the cost of this indictment and be in custody until the same is paid or security given, whereupon came JAMES ROSEBOROUGH and confessed judgment jointly with the defendant for the fine and costs.

The State vs TODD ADAMS - The defendant being charged pleads guilty and is fined 6¼ cents and to remain in custody until the fine and costs are paid or security given, whereupon came ROSEBOROUGH and confessed judgment jointly with the defendant for the fine and costs.

WILLIAM WYATT vs WILLIAM TOWNZEN - Both parties are permitted to take depositions generally by giving adverse party thirty days notice of time and place of taking the same.

E.M. RINGO and wife vs SAMUEL TODD - The plaintiff is permitted to take the deposition of LEVI M. TODD by giving the adverse party five days notice of the time and place of taking the same.

JEREMIAH WALKER vs JOHN DEVIN - Both parties are permitted to take depositions generally in this case by giving the adverse party fifteen days notice of the time and place of taking the same.

The due execution of a Deed of Bargain and Sale from ROBERT BUCHANAN to DANIEL JONES and H. CUMMINS for one town lot in Fayetteville and was ordered to be certified.

The due execution of a Deed of Conveyance from DEMSEY ALLEN to ISAAC HOBBS for 180 acres of land and ordered to be certified.

The due execution of a Deed of Conveyance from SAMUEL BUCHANAN to JOHN LEA for 55 acres of land and ordered to be certified.

The due execution of a Deed of Conveyance from BENJAMIN GIBSON to OBADIAH PINSON for 50 acres of land and ordered to be certified.

The due execution of a Bill of Sale from R.S. JOHNSTON to MOSES STONE for sundry articles of personal property, proven by WILIE JONES and LEONARD CARIGER and ordered to be certified.

The due execution of a Deed of Conveyance from DEMSEY ALLEN to MAJOR SANDERS for 137½ acres of land and ordered to be certified.

The due execution of a Deed of Conveyance from STEPHEN PORTER to THOMAS & JOSEPH HALL for 101 acres of land and ordered to be certified.

The due execution of a Deed of Bargain and Sale from SAMUEL BRYANT to WILLIAM WILSON for 125 acres of land, proven by WALTER B. OWEN and JAMES WILSON and ordered to be certified.

The due execution of a Deed of Conveyance from ADAM HOUSE to JOHN S. PRICE for 115 acres of land and ordered to be certified.

The due execution of a Deed of Conveyance from JOHN P. THOMAS to EZEKIEL HUGHEY for 50 acres of land and ordered to be certified.

FRIDAY OCTOBER 13, 1826

Justices present were ROBERT DICKSON, THOMAS GAITHER and JOHN PORTER, Esquires.

The due executors of BENJAMIN DORSEY, deceased, returned into court an inventory and amount of the sales of the personal property of said estate.

The due execution of a Bill of Sale from WILLIAM H. DOUGLASS to BENJAMIN CLEMENTS for one negro and ordered to be certified.

The administrators of JOHN WHAM, deceased, returned into court an account of the sales of the estate and ordered to be recorded.

The due execution of a Deed of Trust from WALTER W. KEY to CHARLES BOYLES and ordered to be certified.

The Commissioners appointed to settle with the admr of EDWARD TEAL, deceased, now made return and ordered to be recorded.

The due execution of a Bill of Sale from JAMES COALTER, admr &c to WILLIAM DYE for three negroes, proven by SAMUEL M. CLAY and ordered to be certified.

JOHN SHORT vs WILLIAM P. PULLIAM - Motion for new trial - It is ordered that the judgment entered in this cause on yesterday be set aside and a new trial granted him. Defendant pay the costs of this term.

JACOB SILVERTOOTH vs ISAAC HOLMAN - This day came the parties by their attorneys and a jury of men, to wit, THOMAS KERCHEVAL, N. CARIGER, JOHN MORRIS, ISHAM PARR, A. BEARD, R. FROST, Z. MOTLOW, JOHN DOWTHIT, JACOB CASTLEMAN, H. CLIFT, WILLIAM CRAWFORD, and JOHN CRAWFORD being elected and sworn and said that they find in favor of the plaintiff and assess his damages of $197.19 besides his costs. Plaintiff to recover his costs.

The due execution of a Deed of Conveyance from JOHN P. McCONNELL to BARNABAS BOYLES and ordered to be certified.

JOHN P. McCONNELL vs ROBERT DICKSON, admr of P.O. CALAGHAN, deceased - (same as above jurors) and said that they found in favor of the defendant and that he has fully administered the estate of said PATRICK O. CALAGHAN, deceased. Also found that ROBERT DICKSON since his death has not paid the debt of $171.62½ and assess damages for the non-payment of $133.38. Plaintiff to recover his costs.

WILLIAM HINKLE vs MICAJAH McELROY, JR. - (same as above jurors) and said that they find in favor of the defendant. Plaintiff to recover his costs.

JOB G. SELPH vs DAVID A. GREER - This cause was put into the hands of REESE HOWELL on the same day and who then executed it by arresting the defendant thereon and gave bond and security. Plaintiff to recover against the defendant and JOHN GREER his security. Bond of $48.50 with interest.

Ordered that the Sheriff summon twelve freeholders as a jury &c to try the lunacy or idiocy of JAMES L. TODD and make return to next term of court also report what funds or chattels he has or is possessed of at the time of taking such inquisition.

STEPHEN LOYD vs WILLIAM C. THOMPSON - On order of the court, the proceedings in this cause is ordered to be quashed and that the defendant recover his costs.

JAMES GREER vs ARCHIBALD McELROY - (same as above jurors) and they find in favor of the plaintiff and that there is a balance of $214.73 and damages of $63.00 besides his costs. Plaintiff to recover his costs.

JOHN P. McCONNELL vs C.R. WITT and JACOB REESE - This day came the parties by their attorneys and a jury of men, to wit, JOHN BEATY, JOHN HEATH, A. McELROY, P.S. GEORGE, JOHN W. SMITH, J.M. BELL, JACOB MOYERS, JOHN TEAL, JOHN HUNT, ALEXANDER EDMISTON, JOSEPH PEN, and HENRY SMITH being elected and sworn and said that they find in favor of the defendants. Defendants to recover their costs.

SAMUEL WILLIAMS vs WHITE & TRENTHAN - The defendant being called came not but made default. Plaintiff to recover his damages and a jury to come to next court to inquire of damages.

ROBERT BUCHANAN vs DANIEL T. WILLIAMS - (same as above). Plaintiff to recover his debt of $100.00 and $1.80 interests and his costs.

The State vs LEWIS JENO(?) - The court dismisses this prosecution and the Trustee pay the costs of this suit.

The State vs WILLIAM BEARDEN - (same as above).

The State vs ALEXANDER YOUNG - (same as above).

The State vs JOHN LINVILLE - (same as above).

Ordered by the court that JOEL PINSON, JOSEPH McCRACKEN and JOEL BRICE lay off one years support for the widow and children of DAVID COWAN and JOSEPH CAMPBELL out of each of their personal property.

It appearing to the court that DAVID COWAN, late of this county, departed this life without making his Last Will and Testament in writing, whereupon motion of JAMES C. COWAN and STEPHEN HIGHTOWER, administration on the estate of DAVID COWAN is granted them and they gave bond and security.

GEORGE ELGIN vs JOHN HODGES - Plaintiff by his attorney says he wishes no further to prosecute this suit and wishes this suit to be dismissed, therefore came the defendant and RUBEN H. BOONE and assumes the payment of all costs. Suit to be dismissed and the plaintiff recover his costs.

It appearing to the court that JOSEPH CAMPBELL, late of this county, departed this life without making his Last Will and testament in writing. Therefore on motion of JAMES CAMPBELL and STEPHEN HIGHTOWER, administration on the estate of the said JOSEPH CAMPBELL is granted them who entered into bond and security.

259

263

www.ingramcontent.com/pod-product-compliance
Lightning Source LLC
Chambersburg PA
CBHW021033210326
41598CB00016B/1004